Business and Industry

EDITORS

William R. Childs
Scott B. Martin
Wanda Stitt-Gohdes

VOLUME 11

RESOURCES, GLOSSARY, STATISTICS,
LEGAL DOCUMENTS, and INDEXES

MARSHALL CAVENDISH
NEW YORK · TORONTO · LONDON · SYDNEY

Marshall Cavendish
99 White Plains Road
Tarrytown, New York 10591-9001

www.marshallcavendish.com

© 2004 Marshall Cavendish Corporation

Library of Congress Cataloging-in-Publication Data

Business and industry / editors, William R. Childs, Scott B. Martin, Wanda Stitt-Gohdes.
    p. cm.
  Includes bibliographical reference and index.
  Contents: v. 1. Accounting and Bookkeeping to Burnett, Leo--v. 2. Business Cycles to Copyright--v. 3. Corporate Governance to Entrepreneurship--v. 4. Environmentalism to Graham, Katharine--v. 5. Great Depression to Internship--v. 6. Inventory to Merrill Lynch--v. 7. Microeconomics to Philip Morris Companies--v. 8. Price Controls to Sarnoff, David--v. 9. Savings and Investment Options to Telecommuting--v. 10. Temporary Workers to Yamaha--v. 11. Index volume
    ISBN 0-7614-7430-7 (set)--ISBN 0-7614-7441-2 (v. 11)
      1. Business--Encyclopedias. 2. Industries--Encyclopedias. I. Childs, William R., 1951-II. Martin, Scott B., 1961-III. Stitt-Gohdes, Wanda.

HF1001 .B796 2003
338'.003--dc21   2002035156

Printed in Italy

06 05 04 03 5 4 3 2 1

MARSHALL CAVENDISH
Editorial Director   Paul Bernabeo
Production Manager   Alan Tsai

Produced by The Moschovitis Group, Inc.

THE MOSCHOVITIS GROUP
President, Publishing Division   Valerie Tomaselli
Executive Editor   Hilary W. Poole
Associate Editor   Sonja Matanovic
Design and Layout   Annemarie Redmond
Illustrator   Richard Garratt
Assistant Illustrator   Zahiyya Abdul-Karim
Photo Research   Gillian Speeth
Production Associates   K. Nura Abdul-Karim, Rashida Allen
Editorial Assistants   Christina Campbell, Nicole Cohen, Jessica Rosin
Copyediting   Carole Campbell
Proofreading   Paul Scaramazza
Indexing   AEIOU, Inc.

Table of Contents

Bibliography

Reference Works

Anthony, Robert, and Leslie Pearlman. *Essentials of Accounting.* 7th ed. Upper Saddle River, N.J.: Prentice Hall, 2000.

Applegate, Jane. *The Entrepreneur's Desk Reference: Authoritative Information, Ideas, and Solutions for Your Business.* Princeton, N.J.: Bloomberg Press, 2003.

Argenti, Paul A. *Corporate Communication.* 2nd ed. New York: McGraw-Hill Higher Education, 1997.

Bodie, Zvi, Alex Kane, and Alan J. Marcus. *Essentials of Investments.* New York: McGraw-Hill, 2001.

Bowie, Norman E. *The Blackwell Guide to Business Ethics.* Malden, Mass.: Blackwell, 2002.

Bryer, Lanning G., and Reese Taylor, eds. *2000 Trademark Handbook US and International.* Vol. 2. New York: International Trademark Association, 2000.

Business Organizations, Agencies, and Publications Directory. Farmington Hills, Mich.: Gale Group, 2002.

Campbell, R. McConnell, and Stanley L. Brue. *Economics: Principles, Problems, and Policies.* Boston: Irwin/McGraw-Hill, 1999.

Carbaugh, Robert J. *International Economics.* 8th ed. Cincinnati, Ohio: South-Western, 2002.

Covello, Joseph A., and Brian J. Hazelgren. *The Complete Book of Business Plans.* Naperville, Ill.: Sourcebooks, 1995.

Craft, Donna, and Sheila M. Dow, eds. *Brands and Their Companies.* 24th ed. Farmington Hills, Mich.: Gale Group, 2002.

Cross, Wilbur L. *The Prentice Hall Encyclopedia of Model Business Plans.* Paramus, N.J.: Prentice Hall Press, 1998.

Downs, Buck, ed. *National Trade and Professional Associations of the United States, 2001.* Washington, D.C.: Columbia Books, 2001.

Encyclopedia of American Business History and Biography. New York: Facts On File, 2002.

Evans, Rupert N., and Edwin L. Herr. *Foundations of Vocational Education.* 2nd ed. Columbus, Ohio: Charles E. Merrill Publishing, 1978.

Folsom, W. Davis. *Understanding American Business Jargon.* Westport, Conn.: Greenwood Press, 1997.

Fortune Directories. *Directory of U.S. Corporations: The Fortune 500.* New York: Fortune Publishing, 2001.

Friedman, Jack P. *Dictionary of Business Terms.* Hauppauge, N.Y.: Barron's Educational Series, 2000.

Frumkin, Norman. *Guide to Economic Indicators.* 3rd ed. Armonk, N.Y.: M. E. Sharpe, 2000.

Glasner, David. *Business Cycles and Depressions: An Encyclopedia.* New York: Garland Publishing, 1997.

Goleman, Daniel. *Business: The Ultimate Resource.* Cambridge, Mass.: Perseus Publishing, 2002.

Heilbroner, Robert, and Lester Thurow. *Economics Explained: Everything You Need to Know about How the Economy Works and Where It Is Going.* New York: Simon & Schuster, 1998.

Karp, Rashelle S. *The Basic Business Library: Core Resources.* 4th ed. Westport, Conn.: Greenwood Press, 2002.

Landsburg, Steven E. *The Armchair Economist.* New York: Free Press, 1993.

Mansfield, Edwin, and Nariman Behravesh. *Economics U$A.* 6th ed. New York: Norton, 2001.

Mattera, Philip. *Inside U.S. Business: A Concise Encyclopedia of Leading Industries.* Burr Ridge, Ill.: Irwin Professional Publishing, 1994.

McCormick, John. *Understanding the European Union: A Concise Introduction.* 2nd ed. New York: Palgrave, 2002.

Miller, Roger LeRoy, and David D. VanHoose. *Money, Banking, and Financial Markets.* Mason, Ohio: South-Western, 2003.

Mokyr, Joel. *The Oxford Encyclopedia of Economic History.* New York: Oxford University Press, 2003.

Morkes, Andrew, ed. *Encyclopedia of Careers and Vocational Guidance.* Chicago: Ferguson Publishing, 2003.

Nohria, Nitin. *The Portable MBA Desk Reference: An Essential Business Companion.* Hoboken, N.J.: John Wiley & Sons, 1998.

O'Sullivan, Arthur, and Steven M. Sheffrin. *Microeconomics: Principles and Tools.* 2nd ed. Upper Saddle River, N.J.: Prentice Hall, 2001.

Pallister, John, and Allan Isaacs. *A Dictionary of Business.* 3rd ed. New York: Oxford University Press, 2002.

Peterson's/Thomson Learning Internships, 2002. 22nd ed. Princeton, N.J.: Peterson's/Thomson Learning, 2001.

Presner, Louis A. *The International Business Directory and Reference.* Hoboken, N.J.: John Wiley & Sons, 1991.

Robinson, Richard. *U.S. Business History, 1602–1988: A Chronology.* Westport, Conn.: Greenwood Press, 1990.

Scaletta, Phillip, and George Cameron. *Foundations of Business Law and Regulation.* 5th ed. Cincinnati, Ohio: West Publishing, 2002.

Sheets, Tara, ed. *Encyclopedia of Associations.* Detroit, Mich.: Gale Group, 2001.

Sherrow, Victoria. *A to Z of American Women Business Leaders and Entrepreneurs.* New York: Facts On File, 2002.

Slavin, Stephen L. *Macroeconomics.* 6th ed. Boston: McGraw-Hill, 2002.

Sowell, Thomas. *Basic Economics: A Citizen's Guide to the Economy.* New York: Basic Books, 2000.

Steingold, Fred S. *The Employers Legal Handbook.* 4th ed. Berkeley, Calif.: Nolo, 2000.

Sweeny, Simon. *English for Business Communication.* New York: Cambridge University Press, 2003.

Tucker, Irvin B. *Economics for Today.* Mason, Ohio: South-Western, 2003.

The Ultimate Business Dictionary: Defining the World of Work. Cambridge, Mass.: Perseus Publishing, 2003.

Walker, Juliet E. K. *Encyclopedia of African American Business History.* Westport, Conn.: Greenwood Press, 1999.

Walsh, E. T. *The Corporate Directory to U.S. Public Companies, 2003 Edition.* San Mateo, Calif.: Walker's Research, 2003.

Zikmund, William G. *Business Research Methods.* Mason, Ohio: South-Western, 2003.

Biographies

Alberts, Robert C. *The Good Provider: H. J. Heinz and His 57 Varieties.* London: Barker, 1974.

Altman, Diana. *Hollywood East: Louis B. Mayer and the Origins of the Studio System.* New York: Carol Publishing, 1992.

Anders, George. *Perfect Enough: Carly Fiorina and the Reinvention of Hewlett Packard.* New York: Portfolio, 2003.

Anderson, Jervis. *A. Philip Randolph: A Biographical Portrait.* Berkeley: University of California Press, 1987.

Ash, Mary Kay. *Mary Kay.* New York: HarperTrade, 1994.

Baldwin, Neil. *Edison: Inventing the Century.* Chicago: University of Chicago Press, 2001.

Batchelor, Ray. *Henry Ford, Mass Production, Modernism and Design.* Manchester, U.K.: Manchester University Press, 1994.

Beatty, Jack. *The World According to Peter Drucker.* New York: Broadway Books, 1999.

Berlin, Isaiah. *Karl Marx: His Life and Environment.* 1939. Reprint, New York: Oxford University Press, 1996.

Bibb, Porter. *Ted Turner: It Ain't as Easy as It Looks.* New York: Johnson Books, 1997.

Bilby, Kenneth. *The General: David Sarnoff and the Rise of the Communications Industry.* New York: HarperTrade, 1986.

Blair, Gwenda. *The Trumps: Three Generations That Built an Empire.* New York: Simon & Schuster, 2000.

Blashfield, Jean F. *Women Inventors: Catherine Green, Harriet Hosmer, Madame C. J. Walker, Yvonne Brill, Nancy Perkins.* Minneapolis, Minn.: Capstone Press, 1996.

Bowden, Mary Ellen. *Chemical Achievers.* Philadelphia: Chemical Heritage Foundation, 1997.

Bowden, Mary Ellen, Amy Beth Crow, and Tracy Sullivan. *Pharmaceutical Achievers.* Philadelphia: Chemical Heritage Foundation, 2002.

Boyle, T. Coraghessan. *The Road to Wellville.* New York: Penguin, 1993.

Broadbent, Simon, ed. *The Leo Burnett Book of Advertising.* London: Business Books, 1984.

Brookhiser, Richard. *Alexander Hamilton, American.* New York: Free Press, 1999.

Brown, E. Cary, and Robert M. Solow, eds. *Paul Samuelson and Modern Economic Theory.* Boston: McGraw-Hill, 1983.

Buckhorn, Robert F. *Nader: The People's Lawyer.* Englewood Cliffs, N.J.: Prentice-Hall, 1972.

Bundles, A'Leila. *On Her Own Ground: The Life and Times of Madame C. J. Walker.* Waterville, Maine: Thorndike Press, 2001.

Burnett, Leo. *A Tribute to Leo Burnett: Through a Selection of the Inspiring Words that He Wrote or Spoke.* Chicago: Leo Burnett Co., 1971.

Byman, Jeremy. *Andrew Grove and the Intel Corporation.* Greensboro, N.C.: Morgan Reynolds, 1999.

Byron, Christopher. *Martha Inc.: The Incredible Story of Martha Stewart Living Omnimedia.* Hoboken, N.J.: John Wiley & Sons, 2003.

Carey, Charles W. *American Inventors, Entrepreneurs, and Business Visionaries.* New York: Facts On File, 2002.

Carnegie, Andrew. *The Empire of Business.* New York: Harper & Brothers, 1903.

Chernow, Ron. *The House of Morgan: An American Banking Dynasty and the Rise of Modern Finance*. New York: Simon & Schuster, 1991.

———. *Titan: The Life of John D. Rockefeller*. New York: Alfred A. Knopf, 1999.

Clutterbuck, David, and Stuart Crainer. *Makers of Management: Men and Women Who Changed the Business World*. London: Macmillan, 1990.

Cohen, Ben, and Jerry Greenfield. *Ben & Jerry's Double Dip: Lead with Your Values and Make Money, Too*. New York: Simon & Schuster, 1997.

Colman, Penny. *Madame C. J. Walker: Building a Business Empire*. Brookfield, Conn.: Millbrook Press, 1994.

Daley, Robert. *An American Saga: Juan Trippe and His Pan Am Empire*. New York: Random House, 1980.

Davis, Daniel S. *Mr. Black Labor: The Story of A. Philip Randolph, Father of the Civil Rights Movement*. New York: E. P. Dutton, 1972.

Davis, Deborah. *Katharine the Great: Katharine Graham and Her Washington Post Empire*. New York: Institute for Media Analysis, 1991.

Delear, Frank J. *Igor Sikorsky: His Three Careers in Aviation*. New York: Bantam Books, 1992.

Denis, Brian. *Pulitzer: A Life*. Hoboken, N.J.: John Wiley & Sons, 2001.

Diggins, John Patrick. *Bard of Savagery: Thorstein Veblen, Theorist of the Leisure Class*. Princeton, N.J.: Princeton University Press, 1999.

Drucker, Peter F. *Adventures of a Bystander*. New York: John Wiley & Sons, 1998.

Ebling, Richard M. *The Age of Economists: From Adam Smith to Milton Friedman*. Hillsdale, Mich.: Hillsdale College Press, 1999.

Falkof, Lucille. *John H. Johnson: The Man from Ebony*. Ada, Okla.: Garrett Educational Corp., 1992.

Farber, David R. *Sloan Rules: Alfred P. Sloan and the Triumph of General Motors*. Chicago: University of Chicago Press, 2002.

Felix, David. *Keynes: A Critical Life*. Westport, Conn.: Greenwood Press, 1999.

Felsenthal, Carol. *Power, Privilege, and the Post: The Katharine Graham Story*. New York: Putnam's, 1993.

Finch, Christopher. *Jim Henson: The Works: The Art, the Magic, the Imagination*. New York: Random House, 1993.

Ford, Henry. *Today and Tomorrow*. 1926. Reprint, Cambridge, Mass.: Productivity Press, 1988.

Friedman, Milton, and Rose D. Friedman. *Free to Choose: A Personal Statement*. San Diego, Calif.: Harcourt Brace Jovanovich, 1990.

———. *Two Lucky People: Memoirs*. Chicago: University of Chicago Press, 1998.

Gorey, Hays. *Nader and the Power of Everyman*. New York: Grosset & Dunlap, 1975.

Graham, Katharine. *Personal History*. New York: Knopf, 1997.

Green, Constance McLaughlin. *Eli Whitney and the Birth of American Technology*. Boston: Little, Brown, 1956.

Greising, David. *I'd Like the World to Buy a Coke: The Life and Leadership of Roberto Goizueta*. New York: John Wiley & Sons, 1999.

Griswold del Castillo, Richard, and Richard Garcia. *Cesar Chavez: A Triumph of Spirit*. Norman: University of Oklahoma Press, 1995.

Heilbroner, Robert L. *The Worldly Philosophers: The Lives, Times, and Ideas of the Great Economic Thinkers*. Rev. 7th ed. New York: Simon & Schuster, 1999.

Hirahara, Naomi. *Distinguished Asian American Business Leaders*. Westport, Conn.: Greenwood Press, 2003.

Israel, Lee. *Estée Lauder: Beyond the Magic*. New York: Macmillan, 1985.

Johnson, John H., and Lerone Bennett, Jr. *Succeeding against the Odds*. New York: HarperTrade, 1993.

Jorgensen, Elizabeth Watkins. *Thorstein Veblen: Victorian Firebrand*. Armonk, N.Y.: M. E. Sharpe, 1999.

Lager, Fred. *Ben & Jerry's, The Inside Scoop: How Two Real Guys Built a Business with Social Conscience and a Sense of Humor*. New York: Crown Publishing, 1994.

Lauder, Estée. *Estée: A Success Story*. New York: Random House, 1985.

Lear, Linda. *Rachel Carson: Witness for Nature*. New York: Henry Holt, 1997.

Lewis, Reginald F., and Hugh B. Price. *"Why Should White Guys Have All the Fun?": How Reginald Lewis Built a Billion-Dollar Business Empire*. Hoboken, N.J.: John Wiley & Sons, 1996.

Livesay, Harold C. *Andrew Carnegie and the Rise of Big Business*. White Plains, N.Y.: Longman, 1999.

Lommel, Cookie. *Madame C. J. Walker*. Los Angeles: Melrose Square Publishing, 1993.

Lowe, Janet. *Oprah Winfrey Speaks: Insights from the World's Most Influential Voice*. Hoboken, N.J.: John Wiley & Sons, 2001.

———. *Welch: An American Icon*. Hoboken, N.J.: John Wiley & Sons, 2002.

Lyons, Eugene. *David Sarnoff: A Biography*. New York: Harper & Row, 1966.

Mabee, Carleton. *The American Leonardo: A Life of Samuel F. B. Morse*. 1943. Reprint, New York: Octagon Books, 1969.

Meltzer, Milton. *The Many Lives of Andrew Carnegie*. Danbury, Conn.: Scholastic Library, 1997.

Mirsky, Jeanette, and Allan Nevins. *The World of Eli Whitney*. New York: Macmillan, 1952.

Moggridge, D. E. *Keynes*. 3rd ed. Toronto: University of Toronto Press, 1993.

Morita, Akio, Edwin M. Reingold, and Mitsuko Shimomura. *Made in Japan: Akio Morita and Sony*. New York: NAL, 1989.

Moss, Laurence S., ed. *Joseph A. Schumpeter, Historian of Economic Thought*. London: Routledge, 1996.

Nasaw, David. *The Chief: The Life of William Randolph Hearst*. Boston: Houghton Mifflin, 2001.

Packard, David. *The HP Way: How Bill Hewlett and I Built Our Company*. Collingdale, Penn.: DIANE Publishing, 1995.

Pasachoff, Naomi. *Frances Perkins: Champion of the New Deal*. New York: Oxford University Press, 2000.

Petersen, William. *Malthus*. New Brunswick, N.J.: Transaction Publishers, 1999.

Posner, Gerald L. *Citizen Perot: His Life and Times*. New York: Random House, 1996.

Procter, Ben. *William Randolph Hearst: The Early Years, 1863–1910*. New York: Oxford University Press, 1998.

Raphael, D. D., Donald Winch, and Robert Skidelsky. *Three Great Economists: Smith, Malthus, Keynes*. New York: Oxford University Press, 1997.

Reef, Catherine. *A. Philip Randolph: Union Leader and Civil Rights Crusader*. Berkeley Heights, N.J.: Enslow Publishers, 2001.

Robinson. Judith. *The Hearsts: An American Dynasty*. Newark: University of Delaware Press. 1991.

Rockefeller, John D. *Dear Father/Dear Son: Correspondence of John D. Rockefeller and John D. Rockefeller, Jr*. Edited by Joseph W. Ernst. New York: Fordham University Press, 1994.

Rodengen, J. *Legend of Cornelius Vanderbilt*. New York: Write Stuff Syndicate, 2000.

Rosenberg, John. *Alexander Hamilton: America's Bold Lion*. Brookfield, Conn.: Twenty-First Century Books, 2000.

Samuelson, Paul. *Paul Samuelson and the Foundations of Modern Economics*. Somerset, N.J.: Transaction Publishers, 2001.

Silk, Leonard. *The Economists*. New York: Avon Books, 1978.

Slater, Robert. *Jack Welch and the G.E. Way: Management Insights and Leadership Secrets of the Legendary CEO*. New York: McGraw Hill, 1998.

Smith, George David, and Frederick Dalzell. *Wisdom from the Robber Barons: Enduring Business Lessons from Rockefeller, Morgan, and the First Industrialists*. Cambridge, Mass.: Perseus Publishing, 2000.

Staiti, Paul J. *Samuel F. B. Morse*. Cambridge and New York: Cambridge University Press, 1989.

Stanfield, J. Ron. *John Kenneth Galbraith*. New York: St. Martin's Press, 1996.

Strouse, Jean. *Morgan: American Financier*. New York: Random House, 1999.

Swanberg, W. A. *Citizen Hearst: A Biography of William Randolph Hearst*. New York: Galahad Books, 1996.

Swedberg, Richard. *Schumpeter: A Biography*. Princeton, N.J.: Princeton University Press, 1991.

Taylor, William C., and Alan M. Webber. *Going Global: Four Entrepreneurs Map the New World Marketplace*. New York: Viking, 1996.

Trimble, Vance H. *The Empire Undone: The Wild Rise and Hard Fall of Chris Whittle*. Secaucus, N.J.: Carol Publishing Group, 1995.

Trump, Donald J., with Tony Schwartz. *Trump: The Art of the Deal*. New York: Random House, 1988.

Tuccille, Jerome. *Alan Shrugged: Alan Greenspan, the World's Most Powerful Banker*. Hoboken, N.J.: John Wiley & Sons, 2002.

Waldron, Robert. *Oprah!* New York: St. Martin's Press, 1987.

Wall, Joseph Frazier. *Andrew Carnegie*. 1970. Reprint, Pittsburgh, Penn. Pittsburgh University Press, 1989.

Wallace, James. *Overdrive: Bill Gates and the Race to Control Cyberspace*. Hoboken, N.J.: John Wiley & Sons, 2001.

Walton, Sam. *Made in America: My Story*. New York: Bantam Books, 1993.

Welch, Jack, and John A. Byrne. *Jack: Straight from the Gut*. New York: Warner Business Books, 2001.

Wheen, Francis. *Karl Marx: A Life*. New York: W. W. Norton, 2001.

Whitelaw, Nancy. *Joseph Pulitzer and the New York World*. Greensboro, N.C.: Morgan Reynolds, 1999.

Woodward, Bob. *Maestro: Greenspan's Fed and the American Boom*. New York: Simon & Schuster, 2000.

Wright, Robert E. *Hamilton Unbound: Finance and the Creation of the American Republic*. Westport, Conn.: Greenwood Publishing, 2002.

Young, Jeffrey. *ForbesGreatest Business Technology Stories: Inspiring Tales of the Entrepreneurs and Inventors Who Revolutionized Modern Business*. New York: John Wiley & Sons, 1998.

Company Histories

Allen, Frederick. *Secret Formula: How Brilliant Marketing and Relentless Salesmanship Made Coca-Cola the Best-Known Product in the World*. New York: HarperBusiness, 1994.

Angel, Karen. *Inside Yahoo!: Reinvention for the Road Ahead*. Hoboken, N.J.: John Wiley & Sons, 2002.

Asakura, Reiji. *Revolutionaries at Sony: The Making of the Sony Playstation and the Visionaries Who Conquered the World of Video Games*. New York: McGraw-Hill, 2000.

Auletta, Ken. *World War 3.0: Microsoft and Its Enemies*. New York: Random House, 2001.

Beaton, Kendall. *Enterprise in Oil: A History of Shell in the United States*. New York: Appleton Century Crofts, 1957.

Beebe, Lucius, and Charles Clegg. *U.S. West, the Saga of Wells Fargo*. New York: E. P. Dutton, 1949.

Bender, Marylin, and Selig Altschul. *Chosen Instrument: Pan Am, Juan Trippe, the Rise and Fall of an American Entrepreneur*. New York: Simon & Schuster, 1982.

Brandt, E. N. *Growth Company: Dow Chemical's First Century*. East Lansing: Michigan State University Press, 1997.

Brill, Steven. *The Teamsters*. New York: Simon & Schuster, 1978.

Bryce, Robert. *Pipe Dreams: Greed, Ego, and the Death of Enron*. New York: Public Affairs, 2002.

Burrough, Bryan, and John Helyar. *Barbarians at the Gate: The Fall of RJR Nabisco*. New York: HarperCollins, 1991.

Byrne, Eleanor, and Martin McQuillan. *Deconstructing Disney*. London and Sterling, Va.: Pluto Press, 1999.

Byron, Christopher. *The Fanciest Dive: What Happened When the Media Empire of Time/Life Leaped without Looking into the Age of High-Tech*. New York: W. W. Norton, 1986.

Campbell-Smith, Duncan. *The British Airways Story: Struggle for Take-off*. London: Coronet Books, 1986.

Carson, Gerald. *Cornflake Crusade: From the Pulpit to the Breakfast Table*. New York: Ayer Company Publishers, Arno Press, 1976.

Clark, Jim, and Owen Edwards. *Netscape Time: The Making of the Billion-Dollar Start Up That Took on Microsoft*. New York: St. Martin's Press, 1999.

Cohen, Adam. *The Perfect Store: Inside eBay*. Boston: Little, Brown, 2003.

Coll, Steve. *The Deal of the Century: The Break-up of AT&T*. New York: Simon & Schuster, 1986.

Connellan, Tom. *Inside the Magic Kingdom: Seven Keys to Disney's Success*. Austin, Tex.: Bard Press, 1997.

Conrad, Barnaby. *Pan Am: An Aviation Legend*. Emeryville, Calif.: Woodford Publishing, 1999.

Corke, Alison. *British Airways: The Path to Profitability*. New York: St. Martin's Press, 1986.

Cotter, Arundel. *United States Steel: A Corporation with a Soul*. Garden City, N.J.: Doubleday, Page, 1921.

Dalzell, Robert F. *Enterprising Elite: The Boston Associates and the World They Made*. Cambridge, Mass.: Harvard University Press, 1987.

Davis, Shelley. *Unbridled Power: Inside the Secret Culture of the IRS*. New York: HarperBusiness, 1997.

Dealy, Francis X. *The Power and the Money Inside the* Wall Street Journal. Secaucus, N.J.: Carol Publishing Group, 1993.

Dennison, S. R., and Oliver MacDonagh. *Guinness 1886–1939: From Incorporation to the Second World War*. Cork, Ireland: Cork University Press, 1998.

Dorsey, David. *The Force*. New York: Random House 1994.

Downey, Lynn, Jill Novack, and Kathleen McDonough. *This Is a Pair of Levi's Jeans: The Official History of the Levi's Brand*. Corte Madera, Calif.: Gingko Press, 1995.

Eckes, George. *General Electric's Six Sigma Revolution: How General Electric and Others Turned Process into Profits*. New York: John Wiley & Sons, 2001.

Evans, David S., ed. *Breaking Up Bell: Essays on Industrial Organization and Regulation*. New York: North-Holland, 1983.

Finch, Christopher. *Of Muppets & Men: The Making of The Muppet Show*. New York: Muppet Press/Knopf, 1981.

Fine, Sidney. *Sit-Down: The General Motors Strike of 1936–1937*. Ann Arbor: University of Michigan Press, 1969.

Ford Motor Company. *Ford at Fifty, 1903–1953*. New York: Simon & Schuster, 1953.

Freiberg, Kevin, and Jackie Freiberg. *Nuts! Southwest Airlines' Crazy Recipe for Business and Personal Success*. Austin, Tex.: Bard Press International, 1996.

Friedman, Jon, and John Meehan. *House of Cards: Inside the Troubled Empire of American Express*. New York: Putnam, 1992.

Fusaro, Peter, and Ross Miller. *What Went Wrong at Enron: Everyone's Guide to the Largest Bankruptcy in U.S. History*. Hoboken, N.J.: John Wiley & Sons, 2002.

Gerretson, Frederick Carel. *History of the Royal Dutch*. 2nd ed. Leiden, the Netherlands: E. J. Brill, 1958.

Gerstner, Louis V., Jr. *Who Says Elephants Can't Dance?: Inside IBM's Historic Turnaround*. New York: HarperBusiness, 2003.

Gordy, Berry. *To Be Loved: The Music, the Magic, the Memories of Motown*. New York: Warner Books, 1994.

Henderson, Wayne, and Scott Benjamin. *Standard Oil: The First 125 Years*. St. Paul, Minn.: MBI Publishing, 1996.

Howarth, Stephen. *A Century in Oil: The "Shell" Transport and Trading Company 1897–1997*. London: Weidenfeld & Nicolson, 1997.

Jackson, Tim. *Inside Intel: Andy Grove and the Rise of the World's Most Powerful Chip Company*. Collingdale, Penn.: DIANE Publishing, 2002.

Kornberg, Arthur. *The Golden Helix: Inside Biotech Ventures*. Sausalito, Calif.: University Science Books, 1995.

Kraus, Henry, and Nelson Lichtenstein. *Heroes of Unwritten Story: The UAW, 1934–39*. Urbana: University of Illinois Press, 1994.

Kroc, Ray, with Robert Anderson. *Grinding It Out: The Making of McDonald's*. 1987. Reprint, New York: St. Martin's Paperbacks, 1997.

Lieber, James B. *Rats in the Grain: The Dirty Tricks and Trials of Archer Daniels Midland, the "Supermarket to the World."* New York: Four Walls Eight Windows, 2001.

Lipartito, Kenneth, and Carol Heher Peters. *Investing for Middle America: John Elliott Tappan and the Origins of American Express Financial Advisors*. New York: Palgrave Macmillan, 2001.

Love, John F. *McDonald's: Behind the Arches*. Rev. ed. New York: Bantam Books, 1995.

Lynch, Patrick. *Guinness's Brewery in the Irish Economy, 1759–1876*. London: Cambridge University Press, 1960.

Margolis, Stephen E., and Stanley J. Liebowitz. *Winners, Losers & Microsoft: Competition and Antitrust in High Technology*. Oakland, Calif.: Independent Institute, 2001.

Mishima, Yasuo. *The Mitsubishi: Its Challenge and Strategy*. Translated by Emiko Yamaguchi. Greenwich, Conn.: JAI Press, 1989.

Money, John. *The Destroying Angel: Sex, Fitness & Food in the Legacy of Degeneracy Theory: Graham Crackers, Kellogg's Corn Flakes, & American Health History*. Amherst, N.Y.: Prometheus Books, 1998.

Nathan, John. *Sony: The Private Life*. Boston: Houghton Mifflin, 1999.

Nelson, George. *Where Did Our Love Go? The Rise and Fall of the Motown Sound*. New York: St. Martin's Press, 1986.

Nelson, Walter Henry. *Small Wonder: The Amazing Story of the Volkswagen Beetle*. Cambridge, Mass.: Bentley Publishers, 1998.

Newman, Peter C. *Empire of the Bay*. New York: Penguin Books, 1998.

O'Boyle, Thomas F. *At Any Cost: Jack Welch, General Electric, and the Pursuit of Profit*. New York: Alfred A. Knopf, 1998.

Ogilvy, David. *Ogilvy on Advertising*. New York: Vintage Books, 1985.

Ohno, Taiichi. *Toyota Production System: Beyond Large-scale Production*. Portland, Ore.: Productivity Press, 1988.

Okrent, Daniel. *Fortune: The Art of Covering Business*. Salt Lake City, Utah: Gibbs Smith Publisher, 1999.

Ortega, Bob. *In Sam We Trust: The Untold Story of Sam Walton and How Wal-Mart Is Devouring America*. New York: Times Business, 1998.

Pendergrast, Mark. *For God, Country, and Coca-Cola: The Definitive History of the Great American Soft Drink and the Company That Makes It*. 2nd ed. New York: Basic Books, 2000.

Peters, Thomas J., and Robert H. Waterman, Jr. *In Search of Excellence: Lessons from America's Best-Run Companies*. New York: Warner Books, 1984.

Pugh, Emerson W. *Building IBM: Shaping an Industry and Its Technology*. Cambridge, Mass.: MIT Press, 1995.

Reed, Arthur. *Airline: The Inside Story of British Airways*. London: BBC Book Publishing, 1991.

Reid, Peter C. *Well Made in America: Lessons from Harley-Davidson on Being the Best*. New York: McGraw-Hill, 1990.

Rodgers, F. G., and Robert L. Shook. *The IBM Way: Insights into the World's Most Successful Marketing Organization*. New York: Harper & Row, 1987.

Rosenberg, Jerry Martin. *Inside the* Wall Street Journal: *The History and the Power of Dow Jones & Company and America's Most Influential Newspaper*. New York: Macmillan, 1982.

Schultz, Howard. *Pour Your Heart into It: How Starbucks Built a Company One Cup at a Time*. New York: Hyperion Press, 1998.

Shuler, Terry. *Volkswagen: Then, Now, and Forever*. Indianapolis, Ind.: Beeman Jorgensen, 1997.

Slater, Robert. *The GE Way Fieldbook: Jack Welch's Battle Plan for Corporate Revolution*. New York: McGraw-Hill, 2000.

Sloan, Alfred P., Jr. *My Years with General Motors*. New York: Doubleday, 1990.

Smith, Ralph Lee. *Self-Regulation in Action: Story of the Better Business Bureaus 1912–1962*. New York: Association of Better Business Bureaus, 1961.

Sorenson, Charles. *My Forty Years with Ford*. New York: W. W. Norton, 1956.

Spector, Robert. *Amazon.com: Get Big Fast*. New York: HarperInformation, 2002.

Stauffer, David M. *Big Shots, Business the Cisco Way: Secrets of the World's Fastest-Growing Company Ever*. Oxford: Capstone Publications, 2001.

Steenwyk, Elizabeth Van. *Levi Strauss: The Blue Jeans Man*. New York: Walker, 1998.

Stiles, Paul. *Riding the Bull: My Year in the Madness at Merrill Lynch*. New York: Times Business/Random House, 1998.

Strasser, J. B., and Laurie Becklund. *Swoosh: The Unauthorized Story of Nike and the Men Who Played There*. New York: HarperInformation, 1993.

Swisher, Kara. *AOL.com: How Steve Case Beat Bill Gates, Nailed the Netheads, and Made Millions in the War for the Web*. New York: Crown Publishing, 1999.

Tarbell, Ida M. *History of Standard Oil Company*. 1904. Reprint, Mineola, N.Y.: Dover Publications, 2003.

Vance, Sandra Stringer, and Roy V. Scott. *Wal-Mart: A History of Sam Walton's Retail Phenomenon*. New York: Twayne Publishers, 1994.

Vlamis, Anthony, and Bob Smith. *Do You? Business the Yahoo! Way*. Milford, Conn.: Capstone Publications, 2001.

Warren, Kenneth. *The First Century of the United States Steel Corporation, 1901–2001*. Pittsburgh, Penn.: University of Pittsburgh Press, 2001.

Watson, James L., ed. *Golden Arches East: McDonald's in East Asia*. Stanford, Calif.: Stanford University Press, 1997.

Watts, Steven. *The Magic Kingdom: Walt Disney and the American Way of Life*. Boston: Houghton Mifflin, 1997.

Wendt, Lloyd. *The Wall Street Journal: The Story of Dow Jones & the Nation's Business Newspaper*. Chicago: Rand McNally, 1982.

Whitehead, Don. *The Dow Story: The History of the Dow Chemical Company*. New York: McGraw-Hill, 1986.

Zell, Deone. *Changing by Design: Organizational Innovation at Hewlett-Packard*. Ithaca, N.Y.: ILR Press, 1997.

Historical Studies

Abrahamson David. *Magazine-Made America: The Cultural Transformation of the Postwar Periodical*. Cresskill, N.J.: Hampton Press, 1996.

Avrich, Paul. *The Haymarket Tragedy*. Princeton, N.J.: Princeton University Press, 1984.

Bean, Jonathan. *Big Government and Affirmative Action: The Scandalous History of the Small Business Administration*. Lexington: University of Kentucky Press, 2001.

Beatty, Jack, ed. *Colossus: How the Corporation Changed America*. New York: Broadway Books, 2001.

Bell, Gregory S. *In the Black: A History of African Americans on Wall Street*. Hoboken, N.J.: John Wiley & Sons, 2001.

Benson, Susan Porter. *Counter Cultures: Saleswomen, Managers, and Customers in American Department Stores, 1890–1940*. Urbana: University of Illinois Press, 1986.

Blackford, Mansel G. *A History of Small Business in America*. Chapel Hill: University of North Carolina Press, 2003.

Blackford, Mansel G., and K. Austin Kerr. *Business Enterprise in American History*. 3rd ed. Boston: Houghton Mifflin, 1994.

Bliss, Michael. *Northern Enterprises: Five Centuries of Canadian Business*. Toronto: McClelland and Stewart, 1987.

Brinkley, Alan. *The End of Reform*. New York: Alfred A. Knopf, 1995.

Bristo, Marca, ed. *Promises to Keep: A Decade of Federal Enforcement of the Americans with Disabilities Act*. Collingdale, Penn.: DIANE Publishing, 2001.

Brooks, John. *Telephone: The First Hundred Years*. New York: Harper & Row, 1976.

Brown, Stephen A. *Revolution at the Checkout Counter: The Explosion of the Bar Code*. Cambridge, Mass.: Harvard University Press, 1997.

Burstein, Paul. *Discrimination, Jobs, and Politics: The Struggle for Equal Employment Opportunity in the United States since the New Deal*. Chicago: University of Chicago Press, 1998.

Carrington, Timothy. *The Year They Sold Wall Street*. Boston: Houghton Mifflin, 1985.

Chancellor, Edward. *Devil Take the Hindmost: A History of Financial Speculation*. New York: Dutton/Plume, 2000.

Chandler, Alfred D., Jr. *Inventing the Electronic Century: The Epic Story of the Consumer Electronics and Computer Industries*. New York: Free Press, 2001.

Cochran, Thomas C. *Business in American Life: A History*. New York: McGraw-Hill, 1972.

Cohen, Lizabeth. *Making a New Deal: Industrial Workers in Chicago, 1919–1939*. New York: Cambridge University Press, 1990.

Commons, John R., Ulrich B. Phillips, Eugene A. Gilmore, Helen L. Sumner, and John B. Andrews, eds. *A Documentary History of American Industrial Society*. Vols.1–10. New York: Russell & Russell, 1958.

Corben, Herbert C. *The Struggle to Understand: A History of Human Wonder and Discovery*. New York: Prometheus Books, 1991.

Cringely, Robert X. *Accidental Empires: How the Boys of Silicon Valley Make Their Millions, Battle Foreign Competition, and Still Can't Get a Date*. New York: HarperInformation, 1996.

Dart, David. *The Santa Fe Trail*. New York: Alfred A. Knopf, 2001.

Davies, Glyn. *A History of Money from Ancient Times to the Present Day*. Cardiff, U.K.: University of Wales, 2002.

Doganis, Rigas. *The Airline Business in the 21st Century*. New York: Routledge, 2001.

Doris, Lillian, ed. *The American Way in Taxation: Internal Revenue, 1862–1963*. Englewood Cliffs, N.J.: Prentice-Hall, 1963.

Downing, David. *The Great Depression*. Chicago: Heinemann Library, 2001.

Dublin, Thomas. *Women at Work: The Transformation of Work and Community in Lowell, Massachusetts, 1826–1860*. 1979. Reprint, New York: Columbia University Press, 1993.

Dubofsky, Melvyn, and Foster Rhea Dulles. *Labor in America: A History*. 6th ed. Wheeling, Ill.: Harlan Davidson, 1999.

Dudley, Katherine Marie. *The End of the Line: Lost Jobs, New Lives in Postindustrial America*. Chicago: University of Chicago Press, 1994.

Economides, Michael, and Ronald Oligney. *The Color of Oil: The History, the Money, and the Politics of the World's Biggest Business*. Katey, Tex.: Round Oak Publishing, 2000.

Eliot, Thomas H. *Recollections of the New Deal*. Boston: Northeastern University Press, 1992.

Febvre, Lucien, and Henri-Jean Martin. *The Coming of the Book: The Impact of Printing 1450–1800*. London: Verso, 1997.

Filippelli, Ronald L. *Labor in the USA: A History*. New York: Knopf, 1984.

Foner, Philip S. *History of the Labor Movement in the United States: From Colonial Times to the Founding of the American Federation of Labor*. 2nd ed. New York: International Publishers, 1975.

————. *Women and the American Labor Movement: From the First Trade Unions to the Present*. New York: Free Press, 1982.

Fones-Wolf, Elizabeth. *Selling Free Enterprise: The Business Assault on Labor and Liberalism, 1945–1960*. Urbana: University of Illinois Press, 1994.

Fox, Stephen. *The Mirror Makers: A History of American Advertising and Its Creators*. Urbana: University of Illinois Press, 1997.

Freidman, Clara H. *Between Management and Labor: Oral Histories of Arbitration*. New York: Twayne Publishers; London: Prentice Hall International, 1995.

Friedman, Lawrence Meir. *American Law in the 20th Century*. New Haven, Conn.: Yale University Press, 2002.

Friedman, Milton, and Anna Jacobson Schwartz. *A Monetary History of the United States, 1867–1960*. Princeton, N.J.: Princeton University Press, 1971.

Gabin, Nancy. *Feminism in the Labor Movement: Women and the United Auto Workers, 1935–1975*. Ithaca, N.Y.: Cornell University Press, 1990.

Galbraith, John Kenneth. *The Great Crash, 1929*. Boston: Houghton Mifflin, 1997.

————. *A History of Economics*. London: H. Hamilton, 1987.

Galenson, Walter. *The CIO Challenge to the AFL: A History of the American Labor Movement*. Cambridge, Mass.: Harvard University Press, 1992.

Gallick, Rosemary, and Judith O'Sullivan. *Workers and Allies: Female Participation in the American Trade Union Movement, 1824–1976*. Washington, D.C.: Smithsonian Institution Press, 1975.

Goldstein, Paul. *Copyright's Highway: From Gutenberg to the Celestial Jukebox*. New York: Hill and Wang, 1996.

Gourley, Catherine. *Good Girl Work: Factories, Sweatshops, and How Women Changed Their Role in the American Workforce*. Brookfield, Conn.: Millbrook Press, 1999.

Graham, Gordon, and Richard Abel, eds. *The Book in the United States Today*. New Brunswick, N.J.: Transaction, 1996.

Grant, James. *Money of the Mind, Borrowing and Lending in America from the Civil War to Michael Milken*. New York: Farrar, Straus & Giroux, 1992.

Gras, N. S. B., and Henrietta M. Larson. *Casebook in American Business History*. New York: Appleton-Century-Crofts, 1939.

Green, Janet Wells. *From Forge to Fast Food: A History of Child Labor in New York State*. Troy, N.Y.: Council for Citizenship Education, 1995.

Green, Max. *Epitaph for American Labor: How Union Leaders Lost Touch with America*. Washington, D.C.: AEI Press, 1996.

Greene, L. *Child Labor: Then and Now*. New York: Franklin Watts, 1992.

Hall, Thomas, and J. David Ferguson. *The Great Depression: An International Disaster of Perverse Economic Policies*. Ann Arbor: University of Michigan Press, 2001.

Harrington, Michael. *Socialism: Past and Future*. New York: Arcade, 1989.

Homer, Sydney, and Richard Sylla. *A History of Interest Rates*. 3rd ed. New Brunswick, N.J.: Rutgers University Press, 1996.

Hounshell, David A. *From the American System to Mass Production, 1800–1932: The Development of Manufacturing Technology in the United States*. Baltimore, Md.: Johns Hopkins University Press, 1984.

Ingebretsen, Mark. *Nasdaq: A History of the Market That Changed the World*. Roseville, Calif: Forum, 2002.

IRS Historical Fact Book: A Chronology, 1646–1992. Washington, D.C.: Department of the Treasury, Internal Revenue Service, 1993.

Jarnow, Jesse. *Oil, Steel, and Railroads: America's Big Businesses in the Late 1800s*. New York: Rosen Publishing, 2003.

Kellor, Frances. *American Arbitration: Its History, Functions, and Achievements*. Washington, D.C.: Beard Books, 1999.

Kelly, Barbara M. *Expanding the American Dream: Building and Rebuilding Levittown*. New York: State University of New York Press, 1993.

Kessler-Harris, Alice. *Out to Work: A History of Wage-Earning Women in the United States*. New York: Oxford University Press, 1982.

Kimeldorf, Howard. *Battling for American Labor: Wobblies, Craft Workers, and the Making of the Union Movement*. Berkeley: University of California Press, 1999.

Kolko, Gabriel. *Railroads and Regulation, 1877–1916*. Princeton, N.J.: Princeton University Press, 1965.

Lewis, Michael. *The New New Thing: A Silicon Valley Story*. New York: W. W. Norton, 2000.

Lewis, Sinclair. *Cheap and Contented Labor: The Picture of a Southern Mill Town in 1929*. New York: United Textile Workers of America and Women's Trade Union League, 1929.

Lichtenstein, Nelson. *State of the Union: A Century of American Labor*. Princeton, N.J.: Princeton University Press, 2002.

Lipsitz, George. *Rainbow at Midnight: Labor and Culture in the 1940s*. Urbana: University of Illinois Press, 1994.

Markham, Jerry W. *The History of Commodity Futures Trading and Its Regulation*. New York: Praeger, 1987.

McElvaine, Robert. *The Great Depression: America 1929–1941*. New York: Times Books, 1984.

McIntosh, R. G. *Boys in the Pits: Child Labour in Coal Mining*. Montreal: McGill-Queen's University Press, 2000.

Micklethwaite, John, and Adrian Wooldridge. *The Company: A Short History of a Revolutionary Idea*. New York: Modem Books, 2003.

Montgomery, David. *Workers' Control in America: Studies in the History of Work, Technology, and Labor Struggles*. New York: Cambridge University Press, 1979.

Mueller, Milton. *Universal Service: Competition, Interconnection, and Monopoly in the Making of the American Telephone System*. Cambridge, Mass.: MIT Press, 1997.

Nardinelli, C. *Child Labor and the Industrial Revolution*. Bloomington: Indiana University Press, 1990.

Nelson, Daniel. *Shifting Fortunes: The Rise and Decline of American Labor, from the 1820's to the Present*. Chicago: Ivan R. Dee, 1998.

Orey, Michael. *Assuming the Risk: The Mavericks, the Lawyers, and the Whistle-Blowers Who Beat Big Tobacco*. New York: Little, Brown, 1999.

Paarlberg, Don. *An Analysis and History of Inflation*. Westport, Conn.: Praeger, 1993.

Pacelle, Mitchell. *Empire: A Tale of Obsession, Betrayal, and the Battle for an American Icon*. Hoboken, N.J.: John Wiley & Sons, 2001.

Paulsen, George E. *A Living Wage for the Forgotten Man: The Quest for Fair Labor Standards, 1933–1941*. London: Associated University Presses, 1996.

Prestbo, John A., ed. *Markets Measure: An Illustrated History of America Told through the Dow Jones Industrial Average*. New York: Dow Jones & Company, 1999.

Reid, Robert. *Architects of the Web: 1,000 Days That Built the Future of Business*. New York: John Wiley & Sons, 1997.

Roediger, David. *The Wages of Whiteness: Race and the Making of the American Working Class*. New York: Verso Books, 1991.

Roy, William G. *Socializing Capital: The Rise of the Large Industrial Corporation in America*. Princeton, N.J.: Princeton University Press, 1997.

Samuel, Charlie. *Money and Finance in Colonial America*. New York: Rosen Publishing, 2002.

Scheiber, Sylvester J., and John B. Shoven. *The Real Deal: The History and Future of Social Security*. New Haven, Conn.: Yale University Press, 1999.

Seligman, Joel. *The Transformation of Wall Street: A History of the Securities and Exchange Commission and Modern Corporate Finance*. Boston: Northeastern University Press, 1995.

Shachtman, Tom. *Skyscraper Dreams: The Great Real Estate Dynasties of New York*. Boston: Little Brown, 1991.

Sobel, Robert. *The Age of Giant Corporations: A Microeconomic History of American Business, 1914–1992*. 3rd ed. Westport, Conn.: Greenwood Press, 1993.

———. *The Curbstone Brokers: The Origins of the American Stock Exchange*. New York: Macmillan, 1970.

Taylor, Jack. *The Internal Revenue Service: A Short History*. Washington, D.C.: Congressional Research Service, Library of Congress, 1996.

Taylor, Ronald B. *Sweatshops in the Sun: Child Labor on the Farm*. Boston: Beacon Press, 1973.

Tomlins, Christopher. *The State and the Unions: Labor Relations, Law, and the Organized Labor Movement in America, 1880–1960*. New York: Cambridge University Press, 1985.

U.S. Department of Labor. *Important Events in Labor History: 1778–1978*. Washington, D.C.: U.S. Government Printing Office, 1978.

Vedder, Richard K., and Lowell Gallaway. *Out of Work: Unemployment and Government in Twentieth-Century America*. New York: New York University Press, 1997.

Ville, Simon P., and Gordon Boyce. *The Development of Modern Business*. New York: Palgrave Macmillan, 2002.

Weatherford, Jack. *The History of Money: From Sandstone to Cyberspace*. New York: Crown Publishers, 1997.

Weisman, JoAnne B., ed. *The Lowell Mill Girls: Life in the Factory*. Lowell, Mass.: Discover Enterprises, 1991.

Womack, James, Daniel T. Jones, and Daniel Roos. *The Machine That Changed the World*. New York: HarperPerennial, 1991.

Yellen, Samuel. *American Labor Struggles, 1877–1934*. New York: Arno, 1969.

Yergin, Daniel. *The Prize: The Epic Quest for Oil, Money, & Power*. New York: Simon & Schuster, 1992.

Economics and Industry

Anderson Terry L., and Peter J. Hill, eds. *The Privatization Process: A Worldwide Perspective*. Lanham, Md.: Rowman & Littlefield Publishers, 1996.

Armentano, Dominick T. *Antitrust and Monopoly: Anatomy of a Policy Failure*. 2nd ed. Oakland, Calif.: The Independent Institute, 1990.

Aronson, Robert L. *Self-Employment: A Labor Market Perspective*. Ithaca, N.Y.: ILR Press, 1991.

Auerbach, Paul. *Competition: The Economics of Industrial Change*. Oxford: B. Blackwell, 1988.

Bagby, Meredith. *Rational Exuberance: The Influence of Generation X on the New American Economy*. New York: Dutton, 1998.

Bailey Elizabeth E., and Janet Rothenberg Pack, eds. *The Political Economy of Privatization and Deregulation*. Brookfield, Vt.: Edward Elgar, 1995.

Beauchamp, Tom L., and Norman E. Bowie. *Ethical Theory and Business*. 6th ed. Upper Saddle River, N.J.: Prentice Hall, 2001.

Becker, Gary S. *Human Capital*. 3rd ed. Chicago: University of Chicago Press, 1993.

Benner, Chris. *Work in the New Economy: Flexible Labor Markets in Silicon Valley*. Malden, Mass.: Blackwell Publishers, 2002.

Bhagwati, Jagdish. *Free Trade Today*. Princeton, N.J.: Princeton University Press, 2002.

Blicksilver, Jack, ed. *Views on U.S. Economic and Business History: Molding the Mixed Enterprise Economy*. Atlanta: College of Business Administration, Georgia State University, 1985.

Bloom, Gordon F., and Herbert R. Northrup. *Economics of Labor Relations*. 4th ed. Homewood, Ill.: Richard D. Irwin, 1961.

Bork, R. H. *Antitrust Paradox: A Policy at War with Itself*. New York: Free Press, 1993.

Brazelton, Julia K., and Janice L. Ammons, eds. *Enron and Beyond: Technical Analysis of Accounting, Corporate Governance, and Security Issues*. Chicago: CCH, 2002.

Brennan, Troyen A., and Donald M. Berwick. *New Rules: Regulation, Markets, and the Quality of American Health Care*. San Francisco: Jossey-Bass Publishers, 1996.

Buderi, Robert. *Engines of Tomorrow: How the World's Best Companies Are Using Their Research Labs to Win the Future*. New York: Simon & Schuster, 2000.

Calderini, Mario, Paola Garrone, and Maurizio Sobrero, eds. *Corporate Governance, Market Structure and Innovation*. Cheltenham, U.K., and Northhampton, Mass.: Edward Elgar, 2003.

Card, David, ed. *Finding Jobs: Work to Welfare Reform*. New York: Russell Sage Foundation, 2000.

Carroll, Archie B., and Ann K. Buchholtz. *Business and Society: Ethics and Stakeholder Management*. Mason, Ohio: Thomson/South-Western, 2003.

Castells, Manuel. *The Power of Identity: The Information Age— Economy, Society, and Culture*. Malden, Mass.: Blackwell Publishers, 1997.

Caufield, Catherine. *Masters of Illusion: The World Bank and the Poverty of Nations*. New York: Henry Holt, 1996.

Chandler, Alfred D. *Scale and Scope: The Dynamics of Industrial Capitalism*. Cambridge, Mass.: Belknap Press, 1990.

———. *The Visible Hand: The Managerial Revolution in American Business*. Cambridge, Mass.: Belknap Press, 1977.

Coase, Ronald H. *The Firm, the Market, and the Law*. Chicago: University of Chicago Press, 1990.

Coplon, Jennifer Kane. *Single Older Women in the Workforce: By Necessity, or Choice?* New York: Garland Publishing, 1997.

Crosland, Anthony. *The Future of Socialism*. New York: Macmillan, 1957.

Davidson, D. Kirk. *The Moral Dimension of Marketing: Essays on Business Ethics*. Chicago: American Marketing Association, 2002.

Davis, Stan, and Christopher Meyer. *Blur: The Speed of Change in the Connected Economy*. Boston: Addison-Wesley Longman, 2000.

Deane, Phyllis. *The State and the Economic System*. New York: Oxford University Press, 1989.

Drivon, Laurence E., with Bob Schmidt. *The Civil War on Consumer Rights*. Berkeley, Calif., Conari Press, 1990.

Ehrenberg, Ronald, and Robert S. Smith, *Modern Labor Economics, Theory, and Public Policy*. 7th ed. Reading, Mass.: Addison Wesley, 2000.

Elkington, John. *Cannibals with Forks: The Triple Bottom Line of 21st Century Business*. Gabriola Island, British Columbia: New Society, 1998.

Etzkovitz, Henry, and Loet Leydesdorff, eds. *Universities and the Global Knowledge Economy*. New York: Continuum International Publishing Group, 2002.

Finkel, Gerald. *The Economics of the Construction Industry*. Armonk, N.Y.: M. E. Sharpe, 1997.

Florida, Richard. *The Rise of the Creative Class and How It's Transforming Work, Leisure, Community, and Everyday Life*. New York: Basic Books, 2002.

Fraser, Jill Andresky. *White-Collar Sweatshop: The Deterioration of Work and Its Rewards in Corporate America*. New York: W. W. Norton, 2001.

Friedman, Milton. *Capitalism and Freedom*. Chicago: University of Chicago Press, 1982.

Friedman, Thomas. *The Lexus and the Olive Tree. Understanding Globalization*. New York: Anchor Books, 2000.

Galbraith, John Kenneth. *The Affluent Society*. 1958. Reprint, New York: Houghton Mifflin, 1998.

Gates, Bill, with Nathan Myhrvold and Peter Rinearson. *The Road Ahead*. New York: Penguin, 1996.

Gilpin, Robert. *The Challenge of Global Capitalism: The World Economy in the Twenty-first Century*. Princeton, N.J.: Princeton University Press, 2000.

Gilpin, Robert, and Jean Gilpin. *Global Political Economy: Understanding the International Economic Order*. Princeton, N.J.: Princeton University Press, 2001.

Glover, John G., and Rudolph L. Lagai, eds. *The Development of American Industries: Their Economic Significance*. 4th ed. New York: Simmons-Boardman Publishing, 1959.

Goodale, Thomas L., and Peter A. Witt, eds. *Recreation and Leisure: Issues in an Era of Change*. 3rd ed. State College, Penn.: Venture Publishing, 1991.

Greco, Albert N. *The Book Publishing Industry*. Boston: Allyn and Bacon, 1997.

Hans, Valerie P. *Business on Trial: The Civil Jury and Corporate Responsibility*. New Haven, Conn.: Yale University Press, 2000.

Harvard Business Review on Corporate Governance. Boston: Harvard Business School Press, 2000.

Hayek, F. A. *The Road to Serfdom*. 1944. Reprint, Chicago: University of Chicago Press, 1994.

Heilbroner, Robert L., and James K. Galbraith. *The Economic Problem*. 9th ed. Englewood Cliffs, N.J.: Prentice Hall, 1990.

Heilbroner, Robert, and William Milberg. *The Making of Economic Society*. 11th ed. Upper Saddle River, N.J.: Prentice Hall, 2002.

Herzberg, Frederick. *Work and the Nature of Man*. Cleveland, Ohio: World Publishing, 1966.

Hoekman, Bernard M., and Michel M. Kostecki. *The Political Economy of the World Trading System: From GATT to WTO*. 2nd ed. Oxford: Oxford University Press, 2001.

Hoffman, Saul D. *Labor Market Economics*. Englewood Cliffs, N.J.: Prentice-Hall, 1986.

Hollander, Samuel. *The Economics of Thomas Robert Malthus*. Toronto and Buffalo, N.Y.: University of Toronto Press, 1997.

Hunter, Richard. *World without Secrets: Business, Crime and Privacy in the Age of Ubiquitous Computing*. New York: John Wiley & Sons, 2002.

Ide, Masasuke. *Japanese Corporate Finance and International Competition: Japanese Capitalism versus American Capitalism*. New York: St. Martin's Press, 1998.

Imparato, Nicholas, ed. *Capital for Our Time: The Economic, Legal, and Management Challenges of Intellectual Capital*. Stanford, Calif.: Hoover Institution Press, 1999.

Jackson, Paul J., and Jos M. van der Wielen, eds. *Teleworking: International Perspective—From Telecommuting to the Virtual Organization*. London: Routledge, 1998.

Kellison, Stephen. *Theory of Interest*. 2nd ed. Homewood, Ill.: Irwin, 1991.

Kelly, John R. *Recreation Business*. New York: John Wiley & Sons, 1985.

Keynes, John Maynard. *The General Theory of Employment, Interest, and Money*. 1935. Reprint, New York: Prometheus Books, 1997.

Kilpi, Jukka. *The Ethics of Bankruptcy*. New York: Routledge, 1998.

Krugman, Paul. *The Accidental Theorist*. New York: W. W. Norton, 1998.

Kwoka, John E., Jr., and Lawrence White, eds. *The Antitrust Revolution: Economics, Competition, and Policy*. 3rd ed. New York: Oxford University Press, 1999.

Landes, David. *The Wealth and Poverty of Nations: Why Some Are So Rich and Some So Poor*. New York: W. W. Norton, 1998.

Larson, Erik. *The Naked Consumer: How Our Private Lives Become Public Commodities*. New York: Henry Holt, 1992.

Laudon, Kenneth C., and Carol Guercio Traver. *E-Commerce: Business, Technology, Society*. Boston: Addison-Wesley Longman, 2003.

Leeds, Michael, and Peter Von Allmen. *The Economics of Sports*. Boston: Addison-Wesley Publishing, 2001.

Levy, Sidney M. *Build, Operate, Transfer: Paving the Way for Tomorrow's Infrastructure*. New York: John Wiley & Sons, 1996.

Litvin, Daniel B. *Empires of Profit: Commerce, Conquest, and Corporate Responsibility*. New York: Texere, 2003.

Loomis, John B., and Richard G. Walsh. *Recreation Economic Decisions: Comparing Benefits and Costs*. State College, Penn.: Venture Publishing, 1997.

Mansfield, Edwin, and Nariman Behravesh. *Economics U$A*. 5th ed. New York: W. W. Norton, 1998.

Marx, Karl, and Friedrich Engels. *The Communist Manifesto*. Edited and with an introduction by David McLellan. Oxford: Oxford University Press, 1992.

Matthews, John A. *Dragon Multinational: A New Model for Global Growth*. New York: Oxford University Press, 2002.

Maynard, Micheline. *The Global Manufacturing Vanguard: New Rules from the Industry Elite*. New York: John Wiley & Sons, 1998.

Meyers, William. *The Image Makers: Power and Persuasion on Madison Avenue*. New York: Times Books, 1984.

Micklethwaite, John, and Adrian Wooldridge. *A Future Perfect: The Challenge and Promise of Globalization*. New York: Random House, 2003.

Monks, Robert A. G., and Nell Minow. *Corporate Governance*. Oxford and Malden, Mass.: Blackwell Publishers, 2001.

Mooney, Peter J. *The Impact of Immigration on the Growth and Development of the U.S. Economy, 1890–1920*. New York: Garland Publishing, 1990.

Moore, James F. *The Death of Competition: Leadership & Strategy in the Age of Business Ecosystems*. New York: HarperBusiness, 1996.

Nader, Ralph, et al. *The Case against Free Trade: GATT, NAFTA, and the Globalization of Corporate Power*. Berkeley, Calif.: North Atlantic Books, 1993.

Newton, Lisa H., and Maureen M. Ford. *Taking Sides: Clashing Views on Controversial Issues in Business Ethics and Society*. Guilford, Conn.: McGraw-Hill/Dushkin, 2002.

Noll, Roger G., and Andrew Zimbalist, eds. *Sports Jobs and Taxes: The Economic Impact of Sports Teams and Stadiums*. Washington, D.C.: Brookings Institution Press, 1997.

O'Brien, Robert, et al. *Contesting Global Governance: Multilateral Economic Institutions and Global Social Movements*. Cambridge: Cambridge University Press, 2000.

Ohmae, Kenichi. *The End of the Nation State: The Rise of Regional Economies*. Collingdale, Penn.: DIANE Publishing, 1998.

Pava, Moses L. *Re-imagining Business Ethics: Meaningful Solutions for a Global Economy*. Amsterdam and Boston: Jai, 2002.

Pink, Daniel H. *Free Agent Nation: How America's New Independent Workers Are Transforming the Way We Live*. New York: Warner Books, 2001.

Powers, Treval C. *Leakage: The Bleeding of the American Economy*. New Canaan, Conn.: Benchmark Publications, 1996.

Quart, Alissa. *Branded: The Buying and Selling of Teenagers*. Cambridge, Mass.: Perseus Publishing, 2003.

Quirk, James, and Rodney D. Fort. *Pay Dirt: The Business of Professional Team Sports*. Princeton, N.J.: Princeton University Press, 1997.

Ratner, Sidney, James H. Soltow, and Richard Sylla. *The Evolution of the American Economy: Growth, Welfare, and Decision Making*. New York: Macmillan, 1993.

Reich, Robert B. *The Work of Nations: Preparing Ourselves for 21st Century Capitalism*. New York: Vintage Books, 1992.

Riddle, Dorothy I. *Service-Led Growth: The Role of the Service Sector in World Development*. New York: Praeger Publishers, 1986.

Ries, Al, and Laura Ries. *The Fall of Advertising and the Rise of PR*. New York: HarperBusiness, 2002.

Rifkin, Jeremy. *The End of Work: The Decline of the Global Labor Force and the Dawn of the Post-Market Era*. New York: G. P. Putnam's Sons, 1995.

Robbins, Richard. *Global Problems and the Culture of Capitalism*. Boston: Allyn and Bacon, 2002.

Roberts, Russell. *The Choice: A Fable of Free Trade and Protectionism*. Upper Saddle River, N.J.: Prentice Hall, 2001.

Roe, Mark J. *Political Determinants of Corporate Governance: Political Context, Corporate Impact*. Oxford and New York: Oxford University Press, 2003.

Rosentraub, Mark S. *Major League Losers: The Real Cost of Sports and Who's Paying for It*. New York: Basic Books, 1997.

Ryan, Mike H., Carl L. Swanson, and Rogene A. Buchholz. *Corporate Strategy, Public Policy, and the Fortune 500: How America's Major Corporations Influence Government*. Oxfordshire, U.K.: Blackwell Publishers, 1987.

Samuelson, Paul. *Economics*. 17th ed. Boston: McGraw-Hill, 2001.

Saracco, Roberto, et al. *The Disappearance of Telecommunications*. New York: IEEE Press, 2000.

Sargent, Thomas J. *The Conquest of American Inflation*. Princeton, N.J.: Princeton University Press, 1999.

Schor, Juliet B. *The Overspent American: Upscaling, Downshifting, and the New Consumer*. New York: Basic Books, 1998.

———. *The Overworked American: The Unexpected Decline of Leisure*. New York: HarperCollins, 1991.

Schudson, Michael. *Advertising, The Uneasy Persuasion: Its Dubious Impact on American Society*. New York: Basic Books, 1984.

Schumpeter, Joseph. *Business Cycles: A Theoretical, Historical, and Statistical Analysis of the Capitalist Process.* Philadelphia: Porcupine Press, 1982.

———. *Capitalism, Socialism, and Democracy.* Magnolia, Mass.: Peter Smith Publisher, 1983.

Shaw, William H., ed. *Ethics at Work: Basic Readings in Business Ethics.* New York: Oxford University Press, 2003.

Sheehan, Richard G. *Keeping Score: The Economics of Big-Time Sports.* South Bend, Ind.: Diamond Communications, 1996.

Shelp, Ronald Kent. *Beyond Industrialization: Ascendancy of the Global Service Economy.* New York: Praeger Publishers, 1981.

Shiller, Robert J. *Irrational Exuberance.* Princeton, N.J.: Princeton University Press, 2000.

———. *The New Financial Order: Risk in the Twenty-first Century.* Princeton, N.J.: Princeton University Press, 2003.

Sicilia, David B., and Jeffrey L. Cruikshank. *The Greenspan Effect: Words That Move the World's Markets.* New York: McGraw-Hill, 2000.

Smart, Barry. *Resisting McDonaldization.* Thousand Oaks, Calif.: Sage Publications, 1999.

Smith, Adam. *The Wealth of Nations.* 1776. Reprint, London: Penguin Books, 1999.

Southwick, Karen. *The Kingmakers: Venture Capital and the Money behind the Net.* New York: John Wiley & Sons, 2001.

Stone, Alan. *Economic Regulation and the Public Interest: The Federal Trade Commission in Theory and Practice.* Ithaca, N.Y.: Cornell University Press, 1977.

Tapscott, Don, David Ticoll, and Alex Lowy. *Digital Capital: Harnessing the Power of Business Webs.* London: Nicholas Brealey, 2000.

Taylor, Frederick W. *The Principles of Scientific Management.* 1911. Reprint, Westport, Conn.: Greenwood Press, 1972.

Turner, Adair. *Just Capital: The Liberal Economy.* London: Macmillan, 2001.

Tvede, Lars. *Business Cycles: The Business Cycle Problem from John Law to Chaos Theory.* Amsterdam: Harwood Academic Publishers, 1997.

Twitchell, James. *Lead Us into Temptation: The Triumph of American Materialism.* New York: Columbia University Press, 1999.

Underhill, Paco. *Why We Buy: The Science of Shopping.* New York: Simon & Schuster, 2000.

Van de Ven, Andrew H. *The Innovation Journey.* New York: Oxford University Press, 1999.

Wallach, Lori, and Michelle Sforza. *Whose Trade Organization?: Corporate Globalization and the Erosion of Democracy.* Washington, D.C.: Public Citizen, 1999.

Watkins, Steve. *The Black O: Racism and Redemption in an American Corporate Empire.* Athens: University of Georgia Press, 1997.

Weber, Max. *Max Weber: The Theory of Social and Economic Organization.* Translated by A. M. Henderson and Talcott Parsons. New York: Free Press, 1964.

Weiler, J. H. H., ed. *The EU, the WTO, and the NAFTA: Towards a Common Law of International Trade?* Oxford: Oxford University Press, 2000.

Weiss, Ann E. *The Glass Ceiling: A Look at Women in the Workforce.* Brookfield, Conn.: Twenty First Century Books, 1999.

Wihtol, Robert. *The Asian Development Bank and Rural Development: Policy and Practice.* New York: St. Martin's Press, 1988.

Woodstock Theological Center, Seminar in Business Ethics. *Ethical Considerations in Corporate Takeovers.* Washington, D.C.: Georgetown University Press, 1990.

World Trade Organization. *Trading into the Future.* Geneva: WTO, 2001.

Yeager, Leland. *International Monetary Relations: Theory, History, and Policy.* 2nd ed. New York: Harper & Row, 1976.

Zarnowitz, Victor. *Business Cycles: Theory, History, Indicators, and Forecasting.* Chicago: University of Chicago Press, 1992.

Practical Guides and Advice

Adair-Heeley, Charlene B. *The Human Side of Just-in-Time: How to Make the Techniques Really Work.* New York: AMACON, 1991.

Afuah, Allan. *Innovation Management: Strategies, Implementation, and Profits.* New York: Oxford University Press, 1998.

Anthony, Robert, and Leslie Pearlman. *Essentials of Accounting.* New York: Prentice Hall, 1999.

Boatright, John Raymond. *Ethics and the Conduct of Business.* Upper Saddle River, N.J.: Prentice Hall, 2003.

Bognanno, Mario, and Charles J. Coleman, eds. *Labor Arbitration in America: The Profession and Practice.* New York: Praeger, 1992.

Bolles, Richard N. *What Color Is Your Parachute? A Practical Manual for Job-Hunters and Career-Changers.* Berkeley, Calif.: Ten Speed Press, 2002.

Bouchard, Elizabeth. *Everything You Need to Know about Sexual Harassment.* New York: Rosen Publishing Group, 1997.

Burkett, Larry. *The Family Financial Workbook: A Practical Guide to Budgeting.* New York: Moody Press, 2002.

Burton, E. James. *Accounting and Finance for Your Small Business.* New York: John Wiley & Sons, 2001.

Cairncross, Frances. *Green Inc.: Guide to Business and the Environment.* London: Earthscan, 1995.

Cardis, Joel, et. al. *Venture Capital: The Definitive Guide for Entrepreneurs, Investors, and Practitioners.* New York: John Wiley & Sons, 2001.

Chapman, Jack. *Negotiating Your Salary: How to Make $1000 a Minute*. Berkeley, Calif.: Ten Speed Press, 2001.

Coke, Al. *Seven Steps to a Successful Business Plan*. New York: American Management Association, 2001.

Collins, James C., and Jerry I. Porras. *Built to Last: Successful Habits of Visionary Companies*. New York: HarperBusiness Essentials, 2002.

Costales, S. B., and Geza Szurovy. *The Guide to Understanding Financial Statements*. 2nd ed. New York: McGraw-Hill, 1994.

Crawford, Merle C., and C. Anthony Di Benedetto. *New Product Management*. 2nd ed. New York: McGraw-Hill, 1999.

Crouch, Margaret A. *Thinking about Sexual Harassment: A Guide for the Perplexed*. New York: Oxford University Press, 2001.

Cutlip, Scott M., Allen H. Center, and Glen M. Broom. *Effective Public Relations*. Upper Saddle River, N.J.: Prentice Hall, 1999.

Damico, Joan. *How to Be a Permanent Temp: Winning Strategies for Thriving in Today's Workplace*. Franklin Lakes, N.J.: Career Press, 2002.

Debelak, Don. *Entrepreneur Magazine: Bringing Your Product to Market*. New York: John Wiley & Sons, 1997.

De George, Richard T. *The Ethics of Information Technology and Business*. Malden, Mass.: Blackwell Publishers, 2003.

Dorfman, Mark S. *Introduction to Insurance*. 7th ed. Upper Saddle River, N.J.: Prentice Hall, 2002.

Duska, Ronald F., and Brenda Shay Duska. *Accounting Ethics*. Malden, Mass.: Blackwell Publishers, 2003.

Eberts, Marjorie, and Margaret Gisler. *Careers for Culture Lovers and Other Artsy Types*. New York: McGraw Hill Trade, 1999.

Fersh, Don. *Complying with the Americans with Disabilities Act*. Westport, Conn.: Quorum Books, 1993.

Fisher, C. M., and Alan Lovell. *Business Ethics and Values*. Harlow, U.K., and New York: Prentice Hall, 2003.

Fredman, Albert J., and Russ Wiles. *How Mutual Funds Work*. New York: New York Institute of Finance, 1998.

Fry, Ronald W. *Your First Resume: For Students and Anyone Preparing to Enter Today's Tough Job Market*. 5th ed. Franklin Lakes, N.J.: Career Press, 2001.

Garratt, Bob. *Thin on Top: Why Corporate Governance Matters and How to Measure and Improve Board Performance*. London and Yarmouth, Maine: Nicholas Brealey Publishing, 2003.

Godin, Seth, and Paul Lim. *If You're Clueless about Accounting and Finance and Want to Know More*. Chicago: Dearborn Financial Publishing, 1998.

Goodman, Jordan E. *Everyone's Money Book*. 2nd ed. Chicago: Dearborn Financial Publishing, 1998.

Grinblatt, Mark, et al. *Financial Markets and Corporate Strategy*. New York: McGraw-Hill, 2001.

Grove, Andrew. *Only the Paranoid Survive: How To Exploit the Crisis Points That Challenge Every Company and Career*. New York: Currency/Doubleday, 1996.

Gumpert, David E. *Inc. Magazine Presents How to Really Create a Successful Business Plan: Featuring the Business Plans of Pizza Hut, Software Publishing Corp., Celestial Seasonings, People Express, Ben & Jerry's*. 3rd ed. Boston: Inc. Publishers, 1996.

Hall, John A. *Bringing New Products to Market: The Art and Science of Creating Winners*. New York: AMACON, 1991.

Harmon, Steve. *Zero Gravity 2.0: Launching Technology Companies in a Tougher Venture Capital World*. Princeton, N.J.: Bloomberg Press, 2001.

Heller, Robert, and Tim Hinde. *Essential Managers Manual*. New York: Dorling Kindersley, 1998.

Higgins, Robert. *Analysis for Financial Management*. New York: McGraw-Hill Higher Education, 2000.

Hull, John C. *Options, Futures, and Other Derivatives*. 5th ed. Upper Saddle River, N.J.: Prentice Hall, 2003.

Hungelmann, Jack. *Insurance for Dummies*. New York: Hungry Minds, 2001.

Husch, Tony, and Linda Foust. *That's a Great Idea! The New Product Handbook*. Oakland, Calif.: Gravity Publishing, 1986.

Johnson, Mike. *Winning the People Wars: Talent and the Battle for Human Capital*. London: Financial Times, 2000.

Jones, Charles Parker. *Investments: Analysis and Management*. New York: John Wiley & Sons, 1998.

Jones, Ian W., and Michael G. Pollitt, eds. *Understanding How Issues in Business Ethics Develop*. New York: Palgrave Macmillan, 2002.

Kaen, Fred R. *A Blueprint for Corporate Governance: Strategy, Accountability, and the Preservation of Shareholder Value*. New York: AMACOM/American Management Association, 2003.

Kanbar, Maurice. *Secrets from an Inventor's Notebook*. San Francisco: Council Oaks Books, 2001.

Karwowski, Waldemar, and William S. Marras, eds. *The Occupational Ergonomics Handbook*. Boca Raton, Fla.: CRC Press, 2000.

Kennedy, Joyce Lane. *Job Interviews for Dummies*. 2nd ed. New York: Hungry Minds, 2000.

———. *Resumes for Dummies*. 3rd ed. New York: John Wiley & Sons, 2000.

Keup, Erwin J. *Franchise Bible: How to Buy a Franchise or Franchise Your Own*. Central Point, Ore.: Oasis Press, 2000.

Kiyosaki, Robert T., and Sharon Lechter. *Rich Dad, Poor Dad: What the Rich Teach Their Kids about Money—That the Poor and Middle Class Do Not!* New York: Warner Books, 2000.

Knesel, Dave. *Free Publicity: A Step by Step Guide.* New York: Sterling Publishing, 1982.

Lewis, Herschell Gordon, and Carol Nelson. *Advertising Age's Handbook of Advertising.* Lincolnwood, Ill.: NTC Business Books, 1999.

Lynch, Peter. *Beating the Street.* New York: Simon & Schuster, 1994.

Machan, Tibor R., and James E. Chesher. *A Primer on Business Ethics.* Lanham, Md.: Rowman & Littlefield, 2002.

Mauer, Michael. *The Union Member's Complete Guide: Everything You Want—and Need—to Know about Working Union.* Annapolis, Md.: Union Communications Services, 2001.

McLemore, Clinton W. *Street-smart Ethics: Succeeding in Business without Selling Your Soul.* Louisville, Ken.: Westminster John Knox Press, 2003.

Michaels, Ed, Helen Handfield-Jones, and Beth Axelrod. *The War for Talent.* Boston: Harvard Business School Press, 2001.

Minsky, Laurence, and Emily Thornton Calvo. *How to Succeed in Advertising When All You Have Is Talent.* Lincolnwood, Ill.: NTC Business Books, 1994.

Mullis, Darrell, and Judith Handler Orloff. *The Accounting Game: Basic Accounting Fresh from the Lemonade Stand.* Naperville, Ill.: Sourcebooks Trade, 1998.

Nilles, Jack M. *Managing Telework: Strategies for Managing the Virtual Workforce.* New York: John Wiley & Sons, 1998.

Oldman, Mark, and Samer Hamadeh, eds. *The Internship Bible.* New York: Random House, 2002.

Parkhurst, William. *How to Get Publicity.* New York: HarperBusiness, 2000.

Pinson, Linda. *Anatomy of a Business Plan: A Step-by-Step Guide to Building A Business and Securing Your Company's Future.* 5th ed. Chicago: Dearborn Trade Publishing, 2001.

Rachlin, Robert. *Handbook of Budgeting.* New York: John Wiley & Sons, 1999.

Reichheld, Frederick F. *Loyalty Rules! How Today's Leaders Build Lasting Relationships.* Boston: Harvard Business School Press, 2001.

Rejda, George E. *Principles of Insurance.* 3rd ed. Glenview, Ill.: Scott, Foresman, 1989.

Rosenburg, Arthur D., and David V. Hizer. *The Resume Handbook: How to Write Outstanding Resumes and Cover Letters for Every Situation.* 3rd ed. Avon, Mass.: Adams Media, 1996.

Schwab, Charles. *Charles Schwab's Guide to Financial Independence.* New York: Crown Publishers, 1998.

Shim, Jae K., and Joel G. Siegel. *Budget Basics and Beyond: A Step-by-Step Guide for Nonfinancial Managers.* New York: Prentice Hall, 1994.

Siegel, Jeremy. *Stocks for the Long-Run.* New York: McGraw-Hill, 1998.

Sitarz, D. *Debt Free: The National Bankruptcy Kit.* Carbondale, Ill.: Nova Publications, 1999.

Slemrod, Joel, and Jon Bakija. *Taxing Ourselves: A Citizen's Guide to the Great Debate over Tax Reform.* Cambridge, Mass.: MIT Press, 2000.

Stanley, Thomas J. *The Millionaire Mind.* Kansas City, Mo.: Andrews McMeel Publishing, 2001.

Stanley, Thomas J., and William D. Danko. *The Millionaire Next Door: The Surprising Secrets of America's Wealthy.* New York: Pocket Books, 1998.

Stephenson, James. *Entrepreneur's Ultimate Start-up Directory.* Irvine, Calif.: Entrepreneur Press, 2001.

Sveiby, K. E. *The New Organizational Wealth: Managing & Measuring Knowledge-Based Assets.* San Francisco: Berrett-Koehler Publishers, 1997.

Tracy, John A. *Accounting for Dummies.* Hoboken, N.J.: John Wiley & Sons, 2001.

———. *How to Read a Financial Report.* 5th ed. New York: John Wiley & Sons, 1999.

Trivoli, George W. *Personal Portfolio Management.* Upper Saddle River, N.J.: Prentice Hall, 2000.

U.S. Department of Labor. *Crossing the Bridge to Self-Employment.* Washington, D.C.: U.S. Government Printing Office, 2001.

Vick, Timothy P. *How to Pick Stocks Like Warren Buffet: Profiting from the Bargain Hunting Strategies of the World's Greatest Value Investor.* New York: McGraw-Hill, 2000.

Ward, Ralph D. *Improving Corporate Boards: The Boardroom Insider Guidebook.* New York: John Wiley & Sons, 2000.

Webb, Philip, and Sandra Webb. *The Small Business Handbook. The Entrepreneur's Definitive Guide to Starting and Growing a Business.* London: Financial Times/Prentice Hall, 2001.

Westhem, A. D. *Protecting Your Assets: How to Safeguard and Maintain Your Personal Wealth.* New York: Carol Publishing Group, 1996.

Wilcox, Dennis L. *Public Relations Writing and Media Techniques.* New York: Addison-Wesley Longman, 2001.

Wood, Lamont. *Your 24/7 Online Job Search Guide.* New York: John Wiley & Sons, 2002.

Woods, Saralee T. *Executive Temping: A Guide for Professionals.* New York: John Wiley & Sons, 1998.

Yate, Martin John. *Resumes That Knock 'Em Dead.* 4th ed. Holbrook, Mass.: Adams Media, 2000.

Yerkes, Leslie. *Fun Works: Creating Places Where People Love to Work.* San Francisco: Berrett-Koehler Publishers, 2001.

Zsolnai, Laszlo. *Ethics in the Economy: Handbook of Business Ethics.* Oxford and New York: Peter Lang, 2002.

Periodicals

Of the many business periodicals available, some of the most popular are listed below. Please note that URLs can change; all the publications below are also available in print. Some of the sites might charge a fee for information.

Magazines

Advertising Age
> www.adage.com/

Black Enterprise
> www.blackenterprise.com

Business 2.0
> www.business2.com

BusinessWeek
> www.businessweek.com

Consumer Reports
> www.consumerreports.org

Crain's Chicago Business
> www.crainschicagobusiness.com/

Crain's New York Business
> www.crainsnewyork.com/

Dollars & Sense
> www.dollarsandsense.org

The Economist
> www.economist.com

Entrepreneur
> www.entrepreneurmag.com

Fast Company
> www.fastcompany.com

Forbes
> www.forbes.com

Fortune
> www.fortune.com

Inc.
> www.inc.com

Information Week
> www.informationweek.com/

McKinsey Quarterly
> www.mckinseyquarterly.com

Money
> www.money.com

Red Herring
> www.redherring.com

SmartMoney
> www.smartmoney.com

Strategy + Business
> www.strategy-business.com

Newspapers

The most popular North American business newspapers include:

American Banker
> www.americanbanker.com

Barron's
> www.barrons.com

Financial Times
> www.news.ft.com/home/us

Investor's Business Daily
> www.investors.com/

Los Angeles Times (Business section)
> www.latimes.com/business/

New York Times (Business section)
> www.nytimes.com/pages/business/index.html

Wall Street Journal
> www.online.wsj.com/public/us

Washington Business Journal
> www.washington.bizjournals.com

Washington Post
> www.washingtonpost.com/wp-dyn/business/

Journals

American Economist
Business & Professional Ethics Journal
Business Ethics Quarterly
California Management Review
Corporate Conduct Quarterly
The GreenMoney Journal
Harvard Business Review
Journal of Business Ethics
Journal of Business and Professional Ethics
Journal of Modern Business
Long Range Planning
MIT Sloan Management Review
SAM Advanced Management Journal
Strategic Management Journal
Texas Business Review
The Wall Street Ethics & Policy Quarterly

Web Resources

The following World Wide Web sources feature information useful for students, teachers, and business professionals. By necessity, this list is only a representative sampling; most historical societies and professional organizations that are not listed have Web sites that are worth investigating as well. Other Internet resources, such as newsgroups, also exist and can be explored for further research. However, the World Wide Web offers the easiest access to the largest array of sources. Please note that all URLs have a tendency to change; addresses were functional and accurate as of June 2003.

Business Ethics and Corporate Governance

Business for Social Responsibility
www.bsr.org
Web site of a nonprofit organization that provides resources and news on business ethics and ethical companies.

Center for Applied Ethics
www.ethics.ubc.ca/resources/business
University of British Columbia's Web site features lists of business ethics resources online.

Corporate Governance
www.corpgov.net
Web site lists links to resources (online library, courses, conferences, and networks) on the subject of corporate governance.

The Corporate Library
www.thecorporatelibrary.com
Web site of a company that provides research in international corporate governance.

Council for Ethics in Economics
www.businessethics.org
Web site of a business ethics organization; it features the journal *Ethics in Economics.*

E-Center for Business Ethics
www.e-businessethics.com
Colorado State University's Web site on business ethics offers top business news stories and discussion of other news topics in the field of business ethics.

Encycogov
www.encycogov.com
Online encyclopedia of corporate governance.

Ethics Point
www.ethicspoint.com
Web-based hotline for reporting ethical issues.

Global Corporate Governance Forum
www.gcgf.org
The World Bank's multinational trust to foster academic research, improve policy, and finance corporate governance initiatives.

International Business Ethics Institute
www.business-ethics.org
Home page of the International Business Ethics Institute, with links to resources (education, professional, and publications) on business ethics.

International Corporate Governance Network
www.icgn.org
Home page of an international organization dedicated to discussing corporate governance and policy issues worldwide.

Investor Responsibility Research Center
www.irrc.com
Home page of an organization that aims to provide unbiased information on corporate governance and issues relevant to investors.

Society for Business Ethics
www.sba.luc.edu/centers/sbe
Web site and society sponsored by Loyola University–Chicago dedicated to the study of business ethics.

Transparency International
www.transparency.org
Home page of a nongovernmental organization dedicated to fighting corporate corruption worldwide.

Wharton Ethics Program
www.ethics.wharton.upenn.edu
Web site of a business ethics program sponsored by the University of Pennsylvania contains relevant financial news and information.

Business and Professional Organizations and Associations

Advertising Council, Inc.
www.adcouncil.org
Web site of the leading producer of public service announcements.

Asian Development Bank
www.adb.org
Home page of the Asian Development Bank.

Association of Chartered Accountants in the United States
www.acaus.org
Home page of the Association of Chartered Accountants; site also features an international history of accounting practices.

Better Business Bureau
www.bbb.org
Home page of the Better Business Bureau features product and policy news as well as consumer and business guidance.

International Labor Organization
www.ilo.org
Web site of the specialized agency of the United Nations that deals with international labor standards and labor rights.

International Monetary Fund
www.imf.org
Home page of the United Nations' International Monetary Fund has member information, evaluations, news, and resources.

International Organization for Standardization
www.iso.ch
Home page of the International Organization for Standardization provides news and information, including ISO 9000 and other management system standards.

National Black Chamber of Commerce
www.nationalbcc.org
Home page of the National Black Chamber of Commerce, an organization serving primarily African American–owned businesses.

National Commission of Entrepreneurship
www.ncoe.org
Home page of the National Commission of Entrepreneurship, with resources and information for entrepreneurs and those interested in public policy.

National Council on Economic Education
www.ncee.net
Web site features resources for improving education about economic and personal finance in the classroom.

National Society of Accountants
www.nsacct.org
Home page of the National Society of Accountants, whose Web site provides resources, news, and membership information to accountants nationwide.

Organization for Economic Cooperation and Development
www.oecd.org
Web site of an organization dedicated to preserving the market economy and helping develop member countries.

Organization of Petroleum Exporting Countries
www.opec.org
Official Web site of the Organization of Petroleum Exporting Countries (OPEC).

Rotary International
www.rotary.org
Home page of Rotary International, an organization of business and professional leaders who volunteer in community projects worldwide.

U.S. Chamber of Commerce
www.uschamber.com
Home page of the U.S. Chamber of Commerce.

United States Hispanic Chamber of Commerce
www.ushcc.com
Home page of the U.S. Hispanic Chamber of Commerce, a business organization serving primarily Latino-owned businesses.

World Bank
www.worldbank.org
Home page of the World Bank.

World Intellectual Property Organization
www.wipo.org
Home page of the United Nations' specialized agency dedicated to protecting intellectual property.

World Trade Organization
www.wto.org
Home page of the World Trade Organization.

Young Entrepreneurs Organization
www.yeo.org
Home page of the Young Entrepreneurs Organization, a nonprofit educational organization for business owners under 40.

Youth Tech Entrepreneurs.
www.yte.org
Web site of the Youth Tech Entrepreneurs, an organization that encourages students to use their technological and academic skills to pursue entrepreneurial opportunities.

Economic Theory and Economists

The Adam Smith Page
www.utdallas.edu/~harpham/adam.htm
Maintained by faculty at the University of Texas–Dallas, the Web site includes biographic and bibliographic information relevant to Adam Smith and his economic scholarship.

American Economics Association—Resources for Economists on the Internet
www.aeaweb.org/RFE
Site sponsored by the American Economics Association and compiled by faculty at SUNY–Oswego has links to Web-based resources on economics.

Archival Resources in the History of Economics
www.orbit.unh.edu/hes/archive.htm
This searchable Web site sponsored by the History of Economics Society contains multimedia archival materials on the history of economics.

Beige Book
www.federalreserve.gov/fomc/beigebook/2002
Web site of online economic data compiled by the Federal Reserve Board; published eight times annually.

Classic Works in Economics and Economic Thought
www.oswego.edu/~economic/oldbooks.htm
Web site of the State University of New York–Oswego's Economics Department lists and provides links to various transcribed and excerpted texts.

The Econometrics Hall of Fame
www.harold.econ.uiuc.edu/~roger/fame.html
Web site featuring portraits of internationally renowned economists. Sponsored by the University of Illinois–Urbana-Champaign Department of Econometrics.

The Economists' Papers Projects
www.scriptorium.lib.duke.edu/economists
Duke University library's Web site featuring special collection and archival texts of 30 modern economists.

EH.Net–Economic History Services
www.eh.net
Home page of a Web site dedicated to promoting communication between economic and business history researchers, educators, and students.

History of Economic Thought Web Site
www.cepa.newschool.edu/het/index.htm
Home page of the New School University's repository of links and information on economic history and theory.

The Joseph A. Schumpeter Page
www.utdallas.edu/~harpham/joseph.htm
Web site maintained by faculty at the University of Texas–Dallas has biographic and bibliographic information relevant to Joseph Schumpeter and his economic scholarship.

Labor Research Portal—Institute of Industrial Relations Library
www.iir.berkeley.edu/library/laborportal/index.html
Internet portal maintained by the University of California–Berkeley with links to labor research institutions, research guides, civil and state organizations, and bibliographic information.

Post Keynesian Thought Archive
www.csf.colorado.edu/pkt
Home page of a virtual community that participates in online discussions on economic theory and history.

Stanford Business School's Selected Business Web Sites
www.wesley.stanford.edu/library/links
Stanford's Jackson Library provides this Web site that lists general reference Web sites on many business topics, for example, accounting, human resources, and patents.

History of Business and Labor

AdFlip
www.adflip.com
Home page of a searchable database of print advertisements.

AFSCME's Labor Links—Women's Labor History
www.afscme.org/otherlnk/whlinks.htm
American Federation of State, County, and Municipal Employees sponsors this site containing links to resources on women's labor history in the United States.

Agricultural History Society
www.iastate.edu/~history_info/aghissoc.htm
Online site of a publication on U.S. agricultural history, sponsored by Iowa State University Center for Agricultural History.

Automotive History
www.mel.org/business/autos-history.html
State-sponsored Web site contains links to resources on Michigan and the history of the national automotive industry.

Best Business History Sites
www.prologuegroup.com/sites/sites-index.html
Sponsored by the Prologue Group, this Web page offers links to interesting company history sites.

BusinessHistory.Net
www.businesshistory.net
Home page features links to various company histories as well as histories of industries.

Business History at the University of Maryland
www.lib.umd.edu/MCK/GUIDES/business_history.html
Web site offers bibliographies and links to business history resources.

A Classification of American Wealth
www.raken.com/american_wealth/index.asp
Home page of a site featuring the history and genealogy of wealthy U.S. families.

CLIO Media Initiatives in U.S. History
www.albany.edu/history/histmedia
Sponsored by the Department of History of the State University of New York–Albany, the site offers multimedia projects on many topics, including some on the history of U.S. industry.

A Curriculum of United States Labor History for Teachers
www.kentlaw.edu/ilhs/curricul.htm
Web site offers a complete high school– and college-level teaching guide on U.S. labor history. Sponsored by the Illinois Historical Society.

Directory of Corporate Archives in the United States and Canada
www.hunterinformation.com/corporat.htm
Compiled by the Society of American Archivists, this Web site provides users with historical corporate information.

Financial Multimedia
www.fisher.osu.edu/fin/resources_education/clips.htm
Ohio State University's Fisher College of Business photo and video archive of materials relevant to U.S. economic history.

The Haymarket Affair Digital Collection
www.chicagohs.org/hadc
The Chicago Historical Society's site contains primary sources on the Haymarket Affair and its importance in U.S. labor history.

Historical Text Archive
www.historicaltextarchive.com
Mississippi State University's online archive of documents on a variety of historical topics, including business and labor history.

History at the Department of Labor
www.dol.gov/asp/programs/history/main.htm

The U.S. Department of Labor's site showcases the department's history and offers other historical materials.

History of Individual Companies
www.cohums.ohio-state.edu/history/co-hist.htm
Web site sponsored by Ohio State University features a collection of links to company biographies.

H-Labor
www2.h-net.msu.edu/~labor
Home page of a site dedicated to the discussion of international labor history.

Illinois Labor History Society
www.kentlaw.edu/ilhs
The society's home page contains links to resources on Illinois labor history as well as other historical materials.

International Cartel History Site
www.let.leidenuniv.nl/history/rtg/cartels/index.htm
This site, maintained by Leiden University, features historical documents, links, book reviews, and an international cartel database.

Labor and the Holocaust
www.nyu.edu/library/bobst/collections/exhibits/tam/JLC/
    opener.html
Online exhibit sponsored by New York University explores the Jewish Labor Committee's role in combating Nazi activity.

Labordoc
www.labordoc.ilo.org
Home page of the International Labor Organization's document archive.

Labor Management Conflict in American History
www.history.ohio-state.edu/projects/laborconflict
Sponsored by the Ohio State University's Department of History, the site offers research papers on major labor conflicts in U.S. history.

Life of the People
www.loc.gov/exhibits/goldstein
Library of Congress site contains prints and drawings from the collection of Ben and Beatrice Goldstein documenting the U.S. working class from 1912 to 1948.

Like a Family: The Making of a Southern Cotton Mill World
www.ibiblio.org/sohp
Site sponsored by the American Historical Association features oral histories collected for a print publication of the same name.

Lost Labor
www.lostlabor.com
Online site with a photo archive showcasing images of U.S. laborers from 1900 to 1980.

Nevada Labor History
www.nevadalabor.com/hist.html
Web site featuring primary documents and photographs highlighting Nevada's labor history.

New Deal Network
www.newdeal.feri.org
The Franklin and Eleanor Roosevelt Institute initially sponsored this site, which is now based at Columbia University. Material offered includes archival sources, as well as teaching resources, on the New Deal.

Organization of American Historians Labor History Bibliography
www.oah.org/pubs/magazine/labor/labor-bib.html
Online list of print resources, primarily journals, articles, and monographs, on the history of U.S. labor.

Pan American World Airways, Inc. Records
www.library.miami.edu/archives/panam/pan.html

The University of Miami's Richter Library hosts the Web site for Pan Am's archives. Selection of archival photographs available.

Prosperity and Thrift: The Coolidge Era and Its Consumer Economy
www.memory.loc.gov/ammem/coolhtml/coolhome.html
Library of Congress site linking to multimedia source materials on the Coolidge presidency and the evolving consumer economy.

Railroad History Archive
www.railroads.uconn.edu
Web site of University of Connecticut's archival collection of materials documenting the U.S. railroad industry.

The Samuel Gompers Papers: A Documentary History of the Working Class
www.history.umd.edu/Gompers/web1.html
Site featuring the University of Maryland–College Park's archival collection of resources on Samuel Gompers and U.S. labor history.

Sources in U.S. Women's Labor History
www.nyu.edu/library/bobst/research/tam/women/cover.html
Research guide sponsored by New York University's Bobst Library on U.S. women and the labor movement.

Tamient Library and Robert F. Wagner Labor Archives
www.nyu.edu/library/bobst/research/tam/resources
New York University's Bobst Library sponsors this online guide to U.S. labor history resources.

The Tax History Project
www.taxhistory.org/default.htm
Project and Web site sponsored by tax analysts provides information on the history, methods, and future of U.S. taxation.

Triangle Factory Fire
www.ilr.cornell.edu/trianglefire
Online exhibit sponsored by Cornell University on the Triangle factory fire of 1911.

U.S. Labor and Industrial History World Wide Web Audio Archive
www.albany.edu/history/LaborAudio
State University of New York–Albany's site showcases audio recordings of important speeches in U.S. labor history.

Unseen America
www.Bread-and-Roses.com/galleryindex.html
Department of Labor's photography exhibit, sponsored online by BreadandRoses.com, features photographs and quotes of working-class individuals.

World Wide Web Virtual Library–Labor History
www.iisg.nl/~w3vl
Online library of international labor history sources.

Online Business and Finance Information

American Stock Exchange
www.amex.com
Home page of the American Stock Exchange provides stock performance information, news, and market data.

@Brint
www.brint.com
A portal and network for business information, technology, book reviews, and related links.

Bloomberg.com
www.bloomberg.com
Online information service provides market data, business and finance news, and analysis.

Business.com
www.business.com
A search engine and directory for professionals and students.

Chicago Board of Trade
www.cbot.com
Home page of the Chicago Board of Trade offers stock performance information, news, and market data.

Conference Board
www.conference-board.org
Home page of a nonprofit organization that gives access to business information through such indexes as the Consumer Confidence Index and the Index of Leading Economic Indicators.

Dow Jones Indexes
www.djindexes.com
Web site with more than 3,000 stock indexes and other financial market information.

E Business World
www.e-businessworld.com
Web site on e-commerce features news, career advice, network and systems analysis, and technology information.

FinanceWise
www.financewise.com
Sponsored search engine for online finance-related content.

Fool.com
www.fool.com
Motley Fool's Web site features investment data and advice, discussion boards, and portfolio-tracking features.

Global Investor
www.global-investor.com
A U.K.-based Web site with online investment resources including worldwide conference schedules, finance courses, books, periodicals, and a financial dictionary.

Knowledge@Wharton
www.knowledge.wharton.upenn.edu
Biweekly online guide to financial markets sponsored by University of Pennsylvania's Wharton School of Business.

The Millenium: One Thousand Years of Finance
www.interactive.wsj.com/public/current/summaries/mill-1-f.htm
A *Wall Street Journal* educational site with information on 1,000 years of business history.

Morningstar
www.morningstar.com
Home page of Morningstar, a provider of information on mutual funds, stocks, and variable annuities.

Nasdaq
www.nasdaq.com
Home page of the Nasdaq market contains portfolio-tracking resources and other financial information and analysis.

New York Stock Exchange
www.nyse.com
Home page of the New York Stock Exchange offers news, finance and investment information, and market analysis.

Standard and Poor's
www.standardpoors.com
Online source of investment data, market analysis, and valuation information.

TheStreet.com
www.thestreet.com
Financial news Web site offers commentary, live chats, message boards, and investment trackers.

Visual Arts and Literature

Visual artists and writers of novels and plays often make business and industry—and the people who play a role in them—the subject of imaginative works of art. Although such portrayals are sometimes unflattering, these works can serve as the basis for fruitful discussion about the ways in which business and industry participate in society at large.

Former CEO and professor of literature Robert A. Brawer examines models of business leadership from Geoffrey Chaucer to John Updike in *Fictions of Business: Insights on Management from Great Literature* (New York: John Wiley and Sons, 1998). Ralph Windle has edited an anthology of poems about business from sacred scripture and classical literature to the writings of contemporary business leaders (*The Poetry of Business Life: An Anthology*, San Francisco: Berrett-Koehler Publishers, 1994). Studs Terkel's Pulitzer-Prize-winning oral history *Working: People Talk about What They Do All Day and How They Feel about What They Do* (New York: Pantheon Books, 1974) served as the basis for the musical play *Working* in 1978.

The particular works of art in the following lists are given in approximate chronological order of their creation and represent, especially for the photographers named here, only a few examples from large bodies of work on related themes.

Resources for Finding Works of Visual Art

deChassey, Eric, ed. *American Art, 1908–1947: From Winslow Homer to Jackson Pollock*. New York: Abrams, 2002.

Haskell, Barbara. *The American Century: Art and Culture, 1900–1950*. New York: W. W. Norton, 1999.

Hughes, Robert. *American Visions: The Epic History of Art in America*. New York: Knopf, 1997.

Joachimides, Christos M., and Norman Rosenthal, eds. *American Art in the Twentieth Century: Painting and Sculpture, 1913–1993*. Munich and New York: Prestel-Verlag, 1993.

Phillips, Lisa. *The American Century: Art and Culture, 1950–2000*. New York: W. W. Norton, 1999.

Rochfort, Desmond. *Mexican Muralists: Orozco, Rivera, Siqueiros*. San Francisco: Chronicle Books, 1998.

Artchive
www.artchive.com
Archive of visual resources categorized by name of artist.

ArtsEdNet
www.getty.edu/artsednet
Interdisciplinary lesson plans using visual resources.

Library of Congress, American Memory
www.memory.loc.gov
Farm Security Administration photographs and other visual resources. Click on Learning Page to access suggestions for using documentary photographs for investigation and study; click on Collection Finder for resources organized by subject and era.

The Phillips Collection
www.phillipscollection.org
Teaching resources and an interactive program on Jacob Lawrence.

Painting and Sculpture

Anshutz, Thomas. *The Ironworkers' Noontime*. 1880. Oil on canvas.

Bellows, George. *Pennsylvania Station Excavation*. 1909. Oil on canvas.

Ray, Man. *New York*. 1917. Chromed and painted bronze.

Stella, Joseph. *Brooklyn Bridge*. 1917-1918. Oil on canvas.

———. *The Quencher (Night Fires)*. c. 1919. Oil on canvas.

Davis, Stuart. *Lucky Strike*. 1921. Oil on canvas.

———. *Odol*. 1924. Oil on canvasboard.

Demuth, Charles. *Incense of a New Church*. 1921. Oil on board.

———. *My Egypt*. 1927. Oil on board.

———. *Buildings, Lancaster*. 1930. Oil on board.

Dickinson, Preston. *Industry*. c. 1923. Oil on canvas.

Dove, Arthur. *Sewing Machine*. 1927. Oil, cut and pasted linen and graphite on aluminum.

O'Keefe, Georgia. *East River from the Thirtieth Story of the Shelton Hotel*. 1928. Oil on canvas.

Sheeler, Charles. *Upper Deck*. 1929. Oil on canvas.

Benton, Thomas Hart. *America Today* murals. 1930. Distemper and egg tempera on gessoed linen with oil glaze.

———. *Social History of Missouri*. 1935. Egg tempera and oil on linen mounted on panel.

Hopper, Edward. *Early Sunday Morning*. 1930. Oil on canvas.

Wood, Grant. *American Gothic*. 1930. Oil on beadboard. (See also Gordon Parks)

————. *Study for Breaking the Prairie*. 1935-1939. Colored pencil, chalk, and graphite on paper.

Shahn, Ben. *The Passion of Sacco and Vanzetti*. 1931-1932. Tempera on canvas.

Rivera, Diego. *Allegory of California*. 1931. Fresco.

————. *The Making of a Fresco, Showing the Building of a City*. 1931. Fresco.

————. *Detroit Industry*. 1932-1933. Fresco.

————. *Portrait of America*.1933. Fresco.

————. *Man at the Crossroads*. 1934. Fresco.

Marsh, Reginald. *Locomotives Watering*. 1932. Oil and tempera on panel.

Siqueiros, David Alfaro. *Portrait of the Bourgeoisie*. 1939-1940. Pyroxaline on cement.

————. *Man the Master, Not the Slave, of Technology*. 1952. Pyroxaline on aluminum.

————. *For the Complete Safety of All Mexicans at Work*. 1952-1954. Vinylite and pyroxaline on plywood and fiberglass.

Lawrence, Jacob. *Great Migration* series. 1940-1941. Casein tempera on hardboard.

Bearden, Romare. *Factory Workers*. 1942. Gouache and casein on brown wrapping paper mounted on panel.

Warhol, Andy. *210 Coca Cola Bottles*. 1962. Silkscreen ink, acrylic, and pencil on canvas.

Oldenburg, Claes. *Soft Typewriter*. 1963. Vinyl, kapok, wood, plexiglass.

————. *Three Way Plug*. 1969. Wood and masonite.

Rauschenberg, Robert. *Retroactive II*. 1964. Oil and silkscreen ink on canvas.

Segal, George. *The Diner*. 1964-1966. Plaster, wood, chrome, plastic, masonite.

Koons, Jeff. *The New Hoovers Deluxe Shampoo Polishers*. 1980-1986. Three shampoo polishers, plexiglass, fluorescent lights.

Photographs

Riis, Jacob. *Lodgers in a Crowded Bayard Street Tenement: Five Cents a Spot*. 1890.

Stieglitz, Alfred. *The Steerage*. 1907.

Hine, Lewis. *Small Girl in Hosiery Mill, Cherokee*. 1913.

Lange, Dorothea. *Migrant Mother*. 1936.

Evans, Walker. *Waterfront Warehouse, Louisiana*. 1936.

Bourke-White, Margaret. *Fort Peck Dam, Montana*. 1936.

Parks, Gordon. *American Gothic, 1942*. 1942.

Novels

Swift, Jonathan. *Gulliver's Travels* (1726).

Dickens, Charles. *Dombey and Son* (1846-1848).

————. *Hard Times* (1854).

————. *Great Expectations* (1860-1861).

Gissing, George. *New Grub Street* (1891).

Dreiser, Theodore. *Sister Carrie* (1900).

Sinclair, Upton. *The Jungle* (1906).

Anderson, Sherwood. *Winesburg, Ohio* (1919).

Lewis, Sinclair. *Babbitt* (1922).

Fitzgerald, F. Scott. *The Great Gatsby* (1925).

Wilder, Laura Ingalls. *Little House on the Prairie* (1935).

Weidman, Jerome. *I Can Get It for You Wholesale* (1937).

Steinbeck, John. *The Grapes of Wrath* (1939).

Orwell, George. *Animal Farm* (1945).

Rand, Ayn. *Fountainhead* (1943).

————. *Atlas Shrugged* (1957).

Marquand, John P. *Point of No Return* (1949).

Wilson, Sloan. *The Man in the Grey Flannel Suit* (1956).

Wolfe, Tom. *Bonfire of the Vanities* (1987).

Plays

Ibsen, Henrik. *A Doll's House* (1879).

————. *An Enemy of the People* (1882).

Shaw, George Bernard. *Major Barbara* (1905).

Rice, Elmer. *The Adding Machine* (1923).

Brecht, Bertolt, with music by Kurt Weill. *The Threepenny Opera* (1928).

Hecht, Ben, and Charles MacArthur. *The Front Page* (1928).

Odets, Clifford. *Waiting for Lefty* (1935)

Kaufman, George, and Moss Hart. *You Can't Take It with You*. (1936).

Hellman, Lillian. *The Little Foxes* (1939).

Miller, Arthur. *All My Sons* (1947).

————. *Death of a Salesman* (1949).

Marchant, William. *The Desk Set* (1955).

Loesser, Frank L. (music and lyrics), and Abe Burrows (book). *How To Succeed in Business without Really Trying* (1961).

Mamet, David. *Glengarry Glen Ross* (1984).

Churchill, Caryl. *Serious Money* (1987).

Sterner, Jerry. *Other People's Money* (1989).

Baitz, Jon Robin. *The Substance of Fire* (1990).

Glossary

absolute prices Prices measured in dollars, unadjusted for the effects of inflation.

accounts receivable Debts owed to a business by its customers.

acquisition Purchase of a company by another firm. See encyclopedia entry, Merger and Acquisition.

affirmative action Set of policies designed to overcome the effects of past discrimination against members of minority groups. See encyclopedia entry. See also encyclopedia entries, Civil Rights Legislation; Women in the Workforce.

antitrust The process of encouraging business competition. See encyclopedia entry, Monopoly.

arbitration Method of resolving disputes by use of a neutral third party to hear arguments and make a ruling. See encyclopedia entry.

assembly line Production method wherein goods are made in a specified sequence by moving from one machine or worker to the next. See encyclopedia entry.

asset Something of value. See encyclopedia entry, Assets and Liabilities.

asset management Process of managing money and other items of value to make them grow in value.

auction market Stock market where a broker brings buyers and sellers together but never takes possession of the asset being traded.

audit Review of the finances of publicly owned companies.

balance of payments Record of all transactions between the residents of one nation and the residents of all foreign nations. See encyclopedia entry.

balance sheet Document that summarizes the assets and liabilities of a business at a given time. See encyclopedia entry.

bankruptcy Legal process that allows a company or individual to restructure debts. See encyclopedia entry.

bar code Series of vertical lines (bars) that represent a universal inventory number assigned to a given product. See encyclopedia entry.

barriers to entry Factors discouraging competition in a market.

bear market Period of declining stock prices. See encyclopedia entry, Recession.

benefits Noncash items of value provided, in part, by employers to employees, including insurance, pension plans, and so on.

best practice Standard of comparison used in businesses that takes companies or individuals who operate most efficiently as a benchmark.

blue chip Well-established company (or the stock of such company) considered to be a leader in its industry; Microsoft is a blue chip computer company.

bond A certificate stating that a firm or government will pay the holder regular interest payments and a set sum upon a specific maturity date. See encyclopedia entry, Stocks and Bonds.

bondholders Individuals or entities that own bonds.

brand Distinct symbol or phrase that distinguishes a good or service from competitors. See encyclopedia entry, Brand Names.

brand equity Value represented by a consumer's preference for a specific company's good or service. See encyclopedia entry, Brand Names.

branding Creating an image for a person or product. See encyclopedia entry, Brand Names.

broadband A range of communication methods, including cell phone, cable, and satellite, among others.

brokerage Business that sells investment vehicles and advice. See encyclopedia entry, Security Industry.

bull market Period of rising stock prices. See encyclopedia entry, Economic Growth.

capacity Requirement that parties have the legal ability to enter into a contract and to be bound by the terms of the contract.

capital Money or wealth that is put at risk to fund a business enterprise. See encyclopedia entry.

capital budgeting Process of selecting projects that a firm will undertake.

capital, human Skills and experience of workers.

capital, intellectual Knowledge used in production of a good or service.

capital intensity Measure of the amount of assets required to finance a given level of sales; for example, a high level of capital intensity is needed to build jet airliners.

capitalism Economic and social system based on private ownership of the means of production; goods and services are allocated through the coming together of supply and demand in the competitive free market. See encyclopedia entry.

capitalization The funding of business operations or growth.

capital management Decisions about optimal use of funds by a corporation.

capital, physical Tools used to produce and distribute goods and services.

capital structuring Combination of debt and equity financing that results in the lowest weighted average cost of capital.

cartel Group of producers in an industry that band together to coordinate output and prices, sometimes with government support. See encyclopedia entry.

cash flow analysis Process of examining the financial effects of different decisions. See encyclopedia entry, Cash Flow.

certificate of deposit Receipt of money by a bank that the bank contracts to repay with interest after a specified period.

Chapter 11 bankruptcy Legal proceeding that permits a business to continue to operate while restructuring finances and paying creditors. See encyclopedia entry, Bankruptcy.

citizen suit provision Legal concept that permits individual citizens to bring lawsuits against pollution sources for violations of environmental laws. See encyclopedia entry, Environmentalism.

Coase theorem Economic concept that states that given well-defined property rights and the ability to negotiate without costs, market participants and affected third parties will stabilize at the most efficient quantity.

cobranding Cooperation between at least two companies to sell or market a product or product line.

coincident index A measure of current economic activity.

collateral Assets used to guarantee the payment of a debt.

collective bargaining Negotiations between management and a union to establish a labor contract. See encyclopedia entry.

command-and-control System of government that makes specific and rigid rules that govern decisions by its citizens.

commercial paper Short-term loan made to businesses.

commodity Any natural resource or good that is traded.

commodity pricing Condition that exists when intense competition results in the price of a good being set only slightly above its cost of production. See encyclopedia entry, Supply and Demand.

communism Economic and social system based on group ownership of the means of production; goods and services are allocated by the central government. See encyclopedia entry.

comparative advantage One nation's ability to produce a good at a lower opportunity cost than can another nation. See encyclopedia entry.

compensation What a business gives employees in exchange for their labor.

compensatory damages Payments made by ruling of a court to injured parties in compensation for a loss; money paid to individuals for pain and suffering is a kind of compensatory damages.

compound interest The money earned on the original principal and on interest reinvested from prior periods. See encyclopedia entry, Interest.

conglomerate A company that grows by merging with or buying businesses in several different industries.

connectivity Degree to which computer systems can interact with each other.

conservationism Kind of environmentalism that focuses on protecting wild areas and species. See encyclopedia entry, Environmentalism.

consumer debt Debts incurred by the purchase of consumable goods that have little or no lasting value once purchased; food and clothes are examples. See encyclopedia entries, Consumerism; Debt.

consumerism Movement to inform consumers about what they buy, why they buy, and to develop a more regulated marketplace. See encyclopedia entry.

consumer price index (CPI) Measure of the overall price level of goods. See encyclopedia entry.

continuous processing Production method in which materials are moved automatically from one production process to another without human labor.

contract labor Employment arrangement that specifies the work to be done, the pay rate, and so on by contract; temporary workers are contract labor. See encyclopedia entries, Labor Market; Temporary Workers.

cooperative Corporation owned either by its employees or customers; credit unions are an example of a cooperative business.

copyright The exclusive ownership rights of authors, artists, or corporations to their works. See encyclopedia entry.

corporation Company owned by stockholders. See encyclopedia entry.

corporatism Economic and social system wherein national economic policy is negotiated between representatives of government, employers' organizations, and trade unions.

cost–benefit analysis Evaluating the monetary and nonmonetary gains and losses that ensue from making various choices. See encyclopedia entry, Cost.

cost-effectiveness Efficiency of using money in a particular way.

cost of living Index that reflects the average prices that consumers pay for common goods. See encyclopedia entry.

craft unionism The belief and practice that workers should be organized according to the specific job performed.

credit A promise to pay. See encyclopedia entry.

credit rating Assessment of likelihood of an individual, company, or government repaying its debts.

credit union Nonprofit financial institution owned by its members that functions as a bank.

day laborer Workers without permanent employment who work one day for a set wage; many farm workers are day laborers. See encyclopedia entry, Temporary Workers.

day trading Buying and selling stocks at a very rapid pace; usually done in the course of a day or one week. See encyclopedia entry.

dealer market Market in which those who trade stock actually take possession of the stock they trade.

debt (budgetary) Amount of money a government owes as a result of spending more than it receives in taxes and other revenues.

deficit Cash shortfall resulting from a government spending more than it takes in in taxes and other revenues.

demand Amount of a good or service consumers will purchase at different prices at a given time.

demographics The study of groups within a population, subdivided by age, gender, income, or other factors; related to marketing, the groups studied are buyers of specific products and services. See encyclopedia entry.

deposit insurance Insurance to protect depositors in financial institutions against loss if the financial institution fails.

depression Recession of unusual length and severity. See encyclopedia entries Great Depression; Recession.

deregulation Process of removing government restrictions on business.

derivatives market Trading of financial assets based on other instruments; futures and options are derivatives with their values determined by the movement of stock and commodities prices.

desktop publishing Using software to create professional quality publications. See encyclopedia entries, Computer Industry; Publishing Industry.

development economics Study of how a society can achieve high productivity and better living standards.

direct cost Costs to a business that can be precisely attributed to a specific product or service. See encyclopedia entry, Cost.

direct marketing Sending information about a good or service directly to the consumer.

disability insurance Public payments made to individuals who are unable to work because of physical or mental disabilities.

discount brokerage Business that specializes in trading stocks, bonds, and other financial instruments at low cost.

discount rate Interest rate at which banks may borrow funds for the short term from the Federal Reserve. See encyclopedia entry, Federal Reserve System.

disinvestment Decline of the total amount of capital goods in an economy.

distribution Getting a product to the right place at the right time. See encyclopedia entries, Distribution Channels; Just-in-Time Inventory.

distribution channel Choices that producers have for reaching consumers; this includes catalogs, commercials, and so on. See encyclopedia entry.

distribution of wealth How the assets of a society are divided among its members. See encyclopedia entry, Wealth Distribution.

distributive justice System of economic relationships among different groups in society; the communist view of distributive justice calls for resources to be allocated by degree of need.

diversification Allocation of money among different kinds of assets to minimize risk and maximize long-term results. See encyclopedia entries, Finance, Personal; Investment.

dividend The part of a corporation's profits paid to its stockholders.

double-entry accounting The practice of recording each financial transaction in a debit account and a credit account to maintain the basic accounting equation: assets = liabilities + owner's equity.

downsizing Process of laying off employees and shrinking operations to cut business expenses.

due diligence Researching a company to evaluate the benefits and risks of a merger. See encyclopedia entry, Merger and Acquisition.

dumping Sale of goods in a foreign country at prices below the production cost.

e-commerce Conducting business transactions over the Internet.

economic efficiency Using resources in such a way that any other use produces fewer goods or services.

economies of scale Declining average cost of production that results from increasing output. See encyclopedia entry.

elasticity Sensitivity of supply and demand to changes in a good's price. See encyclopedia entry, Supply and Demand.

embezzlement Unlawfully taking company property (usually money) for personal use.

encryption Encoding information.

entrepreneur Person who combines different resources to make goods or services available to others. See encyclopedia entry, Entrepreneurship.

entrepreneurship Combining different resources to make goods or services available to others. See encyclopedia entry.

environmentalism Set of political ideas based on people protecting and restoring the environment. See encyclopedia entry.

equilibrium price Occurs in a market in which quantity demanded by buyers equals the amount supplied by producers.

equity (owner's equity) The amount invested in a business by the owners, as well as the cumulative profits or losses from business operations.

equity (stock) A portion of ownership in a corporation. See encyclopedia entry, Stocks and Bonds.

ergonomics Science that studies how to design a tool or work environment to best fit the person using it. See encyclopedia entry.

e-signature Electronic equivalent of a person's signature.

exchange rates Price of one currency in terms of another.

excise tax Assessment based on the manufacture or sale of nonessential consumer goods; an alcohol tax is an excise tax. See encyclopedia entry, Taxation.

expense Cost of doing business.

export subsidy Payments made by governments to domestic producers of a good; intended to allow the producers to sell their products at low prices.

externalities Positive or negative effects of exchanges on those not directly involved in them. See encyclopedia entry.

fair market value Price at which property would change hands between a willing buyer and a willing seller when both are fully informed about the asset.

fair use Legal doctrine allowing limited use of materials under copyright to encourage the spread of knowledge. See encyclopedia entry, Copyright.

fascism Extreme political ideology that emphasizes aggressive nationalism and the superiority of the dominant ethnic group. See encyclopedia entry.

federal fund rate Interest rate at which banks lend each other federal funds.

Federal Reserve Central bank of the United States; it is responsible for the orderly operation of the banking system, monitoring the economy, and conducting monetary policy. See encyclopedia entry.

feudalism System of government wherein rulers granted land to nobles in exchange for loyalty; the nobles then allowed peasants residency in return for taxes and labor.

fiscal policy Process of managing economic expansions and contractions by adjusting government spending to stabilize incomes and economic performance. See encyclopedia entry.

fixed costs Charges to a business that are not directly affected by the amount of goods or services sold.

flexible specialization Production method whereby individuals or teams use technology to produce large amounts of specialized goods.

foreclosure Legal process that allows a lender to force the sale of a property if the buyer does not make timely payments on the debt that the property secures.

foreign exchange Financial instruments, including currency and checks, used for making payments between countries.

401(k) plans Method of saving for retirement that allows workers to set aside a portion of each paycheck for investment; no tax is imposed on the invested money or interest earned until withdrawal. See encyclopedia entry, Savings and Investment Options.

franchise License to operate a business that is part of a larger chain. See encyclopedia entry.

freelancing Self-employment in which an individual performs paid work for a client without belonging to the client's staff. See encyclopedia entry.

futures Financial arrangement where those involved agree on a set price, quantity, and date for an exchange in the future.

game theory Mathematical technique used to model (and predict) the behavior of individuals and firms in markets.

General Agreement on Tariffs and Trade (GATT) Influential series of agreements designed to encourage world trade. See encyclopedia entry.

globalization Expansion of international trade and increasing financial links between nations. See encyclopedia entry.

gold standard Basing a currency on a set amount of gold.

grant Public or private donated funds used to support groups or individuals in specific efforts.

gross domestic product (GDP) Estimate of the value of goods and services produced within a country over a given period. See encyclopedia entry.

gross national product (GNP) Estimate of the value of goods and services produced by a country over a given period, including those goods and services produced by national entities outside the nation's physical boundaries.

guild Association of individuals, usually skilled in a trade or craft, created for the mutual aid of its members. See encyclopedia entry, Labor Union.

hedging Method used by individuals or businesses to make financial transactions to protect against future price changes.

hyperinflation Period of dramatic price increases caused by an increase in the money supply. See encyclopedia entry, Inflation.

identity theft Fraudulent use of the name and personal information of someone else; for example, to apply for credit cards.

import substitution Encouraging economic development by limiting imports to encourage domestic production.

incentive-based regulation Government rules intended to attain policy goals through a system of rewards and penalties.

income distribution Measure of the equity of the allotment of a society's earnings among its members. See encyclopedia entry.

income inequality Differences in income between various groups. See encyclopedia entry, Income Distribution.

income statement Statement used by a business to report and assess its financial performance. See encyclopedia entry.

incorporate Legal process of becoming a corporation. See encyclopedia entry, Corporation.

incubator Private or publicly funded entity that provides facilities and support staff for small businesses.

independent contractor Self-employed person who offers services to the public. See encyclopedia entry, Freelancing.

index Mathematical measurement tool that uses a variety of data for input and comparison.

industrial espionage Act of stealing information about products or business practices from another company. See encyclopedia entry.

industrial unionism The belief and practice that all workers in a particular industry, regardless of skill level, should be eligible for union membership.

inflation Period of rising prices. See encyclopedia entry.

information technology Computer hardware and software used for storing and processing information, as well as the communications technology for transmitting it. See encyclopedia entry.

infrastructure Transportation, communication, education, and financial systems of a country. See encyclopedia entry.

initial public offering The first time a company sells stock to the public. See encyclopedia entry.

insider trading Buying or selling stock based on information not publicly available.

insolvency A financial condition in which an individual is unable to pay his or her debts as they come due or a condition in which liabilities exceed assets.

insurance Financial protection against loss. See encyclopedia entry, Insurance Industry.

integrated circuit A microchip; the part of a computer that processes information.

intellectual property Creations of the mind, for example, literary works and graphic designs. See encyclopedia entry.

interchangeable parts Components used in the production process that are identical. See encyclopedia entry.

interest Cost of borrowing money. See encyclopedia entry.

Internet service provider (ISP) Company that provides Internet access to its customers.

inventory The supply of goods held by a business. See encyclopedia entry.

investment Present use of resources to enable greater production in the future. See encyclopedia entry.

investment bank Financial entity that provides expertise in assisting companies selling stock to the public.

investment debt Debt, typically long term, that should increase a person's net worth over time; a home mortgage is an investment debt.

IRA Acronym for individual retirement account; a tax-advantaged account where money is invested until withdrawn at age 59½ or older.

joint-stock bank Group of individuals who pool their money in order to invest.

joint venture Two or more businesses cooperating to produce a good or service.

just-in-time Use of sophisticated computer inventory tracking software to lower business costs by minimizing inventory held and delivery times; both manufacturing and retail businesses use the technique. See encyclopedia entry, Just-in-Time Inventory.

keiretsu Japanese term for a group of companies that own shares in one another and support each other in business.

Keynesian principles Theories of economist John Maynard Keynes; the idea that governments can positively influence the business cycle through spending and taxation policies. See encyclopedia entry, Keynes, John Maynard.

knowledge workers People who use knowledge, rather than manual labor, to earn income.

labor market Buying and selling the services of workers. See encyclopedia entry.

labor union An organization of workers that represents its members in salary and other negotiations with management. See encyclopedia entry.

lagging index Measures of economic activity that change after the business cycle has turned.

laissez-faire Doctrine that the government should not interfere in the economy.

liabilities Debts of a business or individual. See encyclopedia entry, Assets and Liabilities.

liberalism In economics, the belief that a nation's wealth can achieve greatest increase by ensuring minimum government interference with trade.

license A kind of contract that grants permission to manufacture, copy, distribute, sell, or use intellectual property, for example, inventions or patents; or, government approval to take an action or engage in an activity. See encyclopedia entry.

limited liability Legal business structure whereby the business losses of owners are limited to their original investment. See encyclopedia entries, Liability; Partnership.

limited partnership Contract between an investor and a business that specifies how much money the investor will put into the business and the returns the investor can expect. See encyclopedia entry, Partnership.

liquidity The ease with which assets can be converted into cash without a decline in value. See encyclopedia entry, Assets and Liabilities.

liquidity event Conversion of a company into liquid assets like stock or cash.

litigation Process of bringing a lawsuit.

macroeconomics Study of an economy as a whole. See encyclopedia entry.

mainframe Mainframe computer; large computer that can be operated by multiple users at once.

management Work done by people responsible for guiding formal organizations toward their intended purposes. See encyclopedia entry.

marginal cost Cost of producing one more unit of a product.

market capitalization Total value of a corporation's outstanding shares.

market economy Economic system wherein decisions are made in markets and based on the forces of supply and demand.

market research The attempt to gain an understanding of customers in order to sell them products or services. See encyclopedia entry.

market segmentation Marketing method that focuses on groups of consumers that share specific characteristics, for example, age, sex, income.

market share Percentage of all dollars spent on a product or service that a specific company earns for that product or service; the proportion of a particular market dominated by a specific company.

mass media Any message produced by a small group intended for consumption by a large group; commercials are a form of mass media. See encyclopedia entry, Advertising Industry.

mass production Use of machines to produce goods in large numbers. See encyclopedia entry, Assembly Line.

mediation Method of dispute resolution in which a neutral third party hears the positions of both sides and assists them in reaching a settlement by offering expert opinion and suggestions. See encyclopedia entry, Arbitration.

Medicaid Government-subsidized medical care for most federally assisted welfare recipients See encyclopedia entry, Social Security and Medicare.

Medicare Hospital insurance and supplemental medical insurance; part of the U.S. social security program. See encyclopedia entry, Social Security and Medicare.

mercantilism Belief that wealth is the foundation of a powerful nation and that national economic policy should therefore be based on attempting to maximize exports and minimize imports. See encyclopedia entry.

merger Legal combining of two or more businesses to make one entity. See encyclopedia entry, Merger and Acquisition.

microcomputer Computer designed for personal use.

microeconomics Study of the decisions made by individuals and firms. See encyclopedia entry.

minicomputer Computer that is less powerful than a mainframe and is also smaller and less expensive.

minority interest Any share of ownership that is less than 50 percent.

mission statement Written statement that identifies the purpose of a business. See encyclopedia entry, Business Plan.

monetarism Economic theory that holds that government regulation of the money supply is key to stable economic growth.

monetary policy Government's use of its power over the money supply to influence economic growth and inflation. See encyclopedia entry.

money Asset that is accepted for payment of goods and services or for settling a debt. See encyclopedia entry.

money market fund A kind of mutual fund that specializes in purchasing money market certificates. See encyclopedia entry, Mutual Funds.

money supply Amount of money in an economy.

monopolistic competition Market with many producers, each of which sells its own unique product. See encyclopedia entry, Monopoly.

monopoly Type of market that involves only one seller. See encyclopedia entry.

monopsony Market with a single buyer of a good or service.

mortgage Debt in which the borrowing business retains ownership of the property and all of its inherent liabilities. See encyclopedia entry.

most-favored nation Designation that guarantees all nations accorded that status will receive equal treatment when trading with one another.

mutual fund Portfolio of stocks, bonds, or cash managed by an investment company on behalf of a group of investors. See encyclopedia entry.

NAICS (North American Industry Classification System) Six-digit coding system used to improve government collection of business data. See encyclopedia entry.

nanotechnology Field of science with the goal of constructing devices of extremely small size.

nationalization Government takeover of private industries.

natural monopoly Situation in which competition does not result in cheaper goods or services; rather one firm is able to provide a good or service at lowest cost to consumers. See encyclopedia entry, Monopoly.

negotiability Legal concept that requires an instrument (a check, for example) to be easily transferable without danger of being uncollectible.

negotiable instrument Signed document that contains a promise to pay an exact sum of money on demand on an exact future date.

net asset value (NAV) Price of shares in a mutual fund. See encyclopedia entry, Mutual Funds.

net present value Measure of the change in value of a firm that occurs when a project is undertaken.

networking Development of business relationships through personal contact; also process of connecting computers to transfer data.

nonprofit Self-governing organization dedicated to supporting some public purpose. See encyclopedia entry, Nonprofit Entities.

note payable A promissory note assuring payment of a debt.

note receivable An IOU owed to a business for a purchase.

oligopoly Market dominated by a few sellers.

open market operations Purchase or sale of government bonds by the Federal Reserve to influence the money supply.

operating system Program for managing the software on a computer.

opportunity cost Alternatives that are lost when a choice is made. See encyclopedia entry.

options Financial arrangement giving the owner the right to buy or sell a futures contract at a certain price for a limited time.

outsourcing Contracting with other companies for performance of specific production tasks. See encyclopedia entry.

overhead Expenses or costs associated with running a business but not directly linked to the process of producing a good or service; rent is part of overhead. See encyclopedia entry.

partnership Business structure with two or more individuals as owners. See encyclopedia entry.

patent Exclusive rights to a new product or invention for a set period. See encyclopedia entry.

payback Method used in the capital budgeting process to determine number of years required for a firm to recover its initial investment in a project.

pay equity Efforts to ensure that men and women are paid equally for similar work. See encyclopedia entry.

payroll A business's accounting of what it pays its employees. See encyclopedia entry.

pension Retirement savings plan offered through the employer.

per capita income Average income per person in a nation; determined by dividing the total wage and salary payments in a nation by the number of workers; an indicator of a nation's standard of living. See encyclopedia entry, Standard of Living.

perfect competition Theoretical market with many buyers and sellers, ease of entry and exit, and where all participants have knowledge of prices.

personal computer Computer designed for use by an individual.

philanthropy Contributing money to charitable causes.

pork barrel spending Legislation that subsidizes special projects for particular districts and states with the intention of serving the narrow interests of legislators or interest groups.

portfolio Investments owned by a person or group.

preferred stock Part ownership of a corporation that includes more voting rights and financial privileges than does ownership of common stock. See encyclopedia entry, Stocks and Bonds.

premiums Payments for insurance.

press release Document released to media outlets designed to shape public opinion about a company, person, product, or issue; companies frequently issue press releases about new products. See encyclopedia entry, Public Relations Industry.

price ceiling Legal maximum price that can be charged for a good or service. See encyclopedia entry, Pricing.

price fixing Attempt by a business or businesses to set artificially high prices for a good or service. See encyclopedia entry.

price floor Legal minimum that can be charged for a good or service. See encyclopedia entry, Pricing.

principal Money that is lent. See encyclopedia entry, Interest.

print-on-demand Publishing process in which books are printed only when customers place orders.

private property Property held by individuals either singly or in voluntary associations rather than being held by the state. See encyclopedia entry.

privatization Sale of government providers of goods and services to private sector. See encyclopedia entry.

procurement Process of businesses buying the materials they need.

productivity Amount of work that can be completed in a given time. See encyclopedia entry.

product liability Responsibility a manufacturer or seller incurs when a person or group has been injured by its product. See encyclopedia entry.

profit The amount left over after the cost of doing business has been subtracted. See encyclopedia entry, Profit and Loss.

profit and loss Feedback system for exchanges in a market economy; the size of either indicates how well resources are allocated, rewards efficiency, and provides incentives for innovation and risk taking. See encyclopedia entry.

profit sharing Annual or regular payment to employees based on the profitability of employer.

progressive tax Tax that is imposed at a higher percentage on individuals with higher incomes. See encyclopedia entry, Taxation.

promissory note Written IOU.

prospectus Public document containing accurate and complete financial information about a company selling stock to the public.

protectionism Government action that partly shields domestic industries from foreign competition; tariffs and quotas are forms of protectionism.

protocol Generally accepted method or standard.

prototype Working model of a product. See encyclopedia entry, Patent.

proved reserves Supplies of a natural resource such as oil confirmed by geologic study.

psychographics Part of market research involving lifestyle; where people live, age, marital status, and other factors are considered in psychographics. See encyclopedia entry, Demographics.

public goods Goods that everyone can enjoy equally and no one can be excluded from; fresh air and national defense are public goods. See encyclopedia entry.

public relations Process of creating a favorable public opinion of a person, product, concept, or organization See encyclopedia entry, Public Relations Industry.

public utility Range of industries owned by the state that provide services like transportation, communication, gas, power, and water.

punitive damages Payments mandated by a judge or jury in legal action; payments are meant to punish the payer for wrongdoing.

purchasing power Amount of goods and services that can be purchased with a given amount of money.

qualitative research Market research using in-person contact with the consumer; interviews and demonstrations are qualitative research. See encyclopedia entry, Market Research.

quantitative research Market research using mathematical or statistical methods; questionnaires are an example. See encyclopedia entry, Market Research.

quota A predetermined amount, for example, of a foreign product that can enter a country, or an expected level of productivity.

racketeering Conducting a business using dishonest or criminal methods.

rate of return Percentage by which revenues achieved exceed the cost of investment. See encyclopedia entry, Investment.

rationalism Belief that reason is the only means to pursue progress for humanity.

real estate investment trust (REIT) Investment vehicles, similar to mutual funds, that allow small investors to invest in real estate. See encyclopedia entries, Investment; Mutual Funds.

recession Period in which overall economic output declines. See encyclopedia entry.

reengineering Analyzing old software and making decisions about what should be kept and what should be restructured.

regressive tax Tax that places a greater proportional burden on people with lower incomes. Sales tax is an example. See encyclopedia entry, Taxation.

regulation Government action intended to promote fair trade practices and to safeguard citizens. See encyclopedia entry, Regulation of Business and Industry.

reserve requirements Percentage of deposits banks and other depository institutions must keep in cash or on account with the Federal Reserve.

residuals Payments made for each showing of an actor's work; commercials, television pay-per-view, and broadcasting of films on television can all result in residual payments.

residual value The value of an asset at the end of its expected usefulness.

resume Written summary of a person's career; a job hunter sends a resume to a potential employer in hopes of being hired. See encyclopedia entry.

retail Sellers of goods and services to the general public. See encyclopedia entry, Retail and Wholesale.

retained earnings Profits a business can use to fund further operations.

return on investment Percentage change in the value of an asset.

revenue Income earned during a specific period from the operations of a business.

reverse discrimination The argument that if certain individuals are favored in matters like employment and university admissions, others must necessarily be discriminated against.

reverse engineering Determining how to reproduce a product by studying an existing version. See encyclopedia entry.

risk management Process of identifying sources of potential losses, evaluating potential losses, and selecting means for responding to loss exposures. See encyclopedia entry.

royalty Payment made for the use of a resource—usually intellectual property. See encyclopedia entry, Intellectual Property.

rule of law When the laws governing a society are publicly known, understood by the public, and applied equally to all members of a society, a country is governed by rule of law. See encyclopedia entry.

scarcity Condition resulting from an inability to satisfy all of the wants of all members of society. See encyclopedia entry.

secondary market A stock exchange; the New York Stock Exchange is a secondary market.

securities Stocks, bonds, and other financial instruments. See encyclopedia entry, Stocks and Bonds.

service economy Economy in which the majority of employment and business revenues are generated by services. See encyclopedia entry.

sexual harassment Form of sexual discrimination involving unwanted sexual attention that humiliates or intimidates and is based on gender or sexual preference See encyclopedia entry.

shareholder Person who owns stock in a corporation. See encyclopedia entries, Investment; Stocks and Bonds.

SIC (Standard Industry Classification) Outdated coding system once used by the government to collect business data. See encyclopedia entry, NAICS Codes.

small business An independently owned and operated business that is not dominant in its field of operation. See encyclopedia entry.

smart card Credit-card-sized plastic card containing a microchip used for data storage and transactions.

socialism Economic system based on equality and group ownership of the means of production. See encyclopedia entry.

social security A complex collection of social programs designed to protect U.S. workers and their families from income losses associated with old age, illness, and death. See encyclopedia entry, Social Security and Medicare.

sole proprietorship A business owned by one person.

stagflation Condition of simultaneously rising unemployment and inflation.

stakeholders Active participants in corporate decisions.

standard deviation Statistical measure of the range of an investment's performance; the higher the number, the riskier the investment.

standard of living Quality of life. See encyclopedia entry.

stock Part ownership in a corporation. See encyclopedia entry, Stocks and Bonds.

stock options Right of employees (granted by employer) to buy shares in a company at a certain price at some point in the future.

strategic alliance Two or more businesses working together to produce a good or service or increase profits by seeking greater efficiencies; some companies form strategic alliances to order goods in bulk to reduce costs.

strategic planning System used by businesses and other organizations for planning for the long term. See encyclopedia entry.

subsidiary A business controlled by another business.

subsidize Financial payment from government to support a business endeavor. See encyclopedia entry.

subsidy Government financial support of a business endeavor. See encyclopedia entry.

supply Amount of a good or service producers will provide at different prices at a given time.

supply chain Series of businesses and transactions involved in producing a finished good or service.

surplus Positive difference in funds when a government spends less than it receives in taxes and other revenues.

sustainability Rate of economic growth that is compatible with planetary welfare and the needs of future generations. See encyclopedia entry, Sustainable Development.

sustainable agriculture A method of farming that attempts to minimize human impact on the environment.

sustainable development Promotion of economic growth in a manner that minimizes effect on the natural and cultural environment. See encyclopedia entry.

sweatshop Production facilities with poor working conditions and low pay.

tariff Tax on imported goods. See encyclopedia entry.

tax credit Legislation that reduces tax liabilities for specified expenses; for example, expenses associated with pollution reduction may be partly offset by a tax credit.

telecommuting Use of information and communication technologies to enable work to be done at sites away from a traditional workplace. See encyclopedia entry.

time value of money Money loses value over time; $1 of income today is more valuable than $1 of income five years from now.

tort Broad area of law imposing liability for intentional and unintentional conduct. See encyclopedia entry, Liability.

total quality management (TQM) Body of organizational and business theories and techniques that focus on ways to provide high-quality products and services. See encyclopedia entry.

tradable allowance Environmental policy that allows producers of pollution to buy and sell emissions credits to achieve an overall reduction in pollution.

trade deficit When a nation buys more from abroad than it sells. See encyclopedia entry, Balance of Trade.

trademark Legal ownership of a unique symbol or design associated with a product or service. See encyclopedia entry.

trade show Specific industry gatherings used to promote that industry and display goods and services.

trade surplus When a nation sells more goods to other nations than it buys from other nations.

trade union Association of workers created to improve their pay and working conditions. See encyclopedia entry, Labor Union.

tragedy of the commons Concept that explains the overuse of resources that are not privately owned. See encyclopedia entry.

transnational corporation Corporation that operates in many different countries. See encyclopedia entry, Multinational Corporation.

Treasury bills (T-bills) Bonds issued by the U.S. government.

trust Business structure that mandates all decisions in an industry be made by a central body for all producers in an attempt to raise prices and profitability. See encyclopedia entry, Monopoly.

unearned revenue An accounting liability created when a customer pays in advance for a good or service.

unemployment insurance Government payments to unemployed workers. See encyclopedia entry, Unemployment.

unemployment rate Percentage of people in the labor force who are willing to work but are not employed. See encyclopedia entry, Unemployment.

uniform commercial code Set of same laws passed by all states except Louisiana that govern commercial transactions.

unionism Support for labor unions. See encyclopedia entry, Labor Union.

valuation Process of estimating an asset's relative worth. See encyclopedia entry.

value added Method of calculating GDP by subtracting the cost of raw materials from the final sale price.

variable costs Charges to a business that are directly related to the amount of goods or services sold.

venture capital Private funds used to start or expand a business. See encyclopedia entry.

vertical integration Practice of combining all parts of the production process within a company.

virus Computer program designed to harm computers exposed to it.

vision statement Description of a business as it will exist at some point in the future. See encyclopedia entry, Business Plan.

vocational licensing Determination by the government or a professional association of who is qualified to practice a particular profession. See encyclopedia entry.

wage premium Higher rate of compensation; college graduates have a 50 percent wage premium compared with those who do not attend college.

warranty Guarantee by producer or seller of a product to make certain repairs within a set amount of time.

wealth distribution How the wealth of a society is divided among its members. See encyclopedia entry.

weighted average cost of capital Sum of after-tax costs of each source of funding multiplied by the proportion of each funding source in the capital structure.

welfare (or public assistance) Public assistance to the poor, which may include money payments, job training, food, or other benefits.

wholesale Set of activities directly associated with the sale of goods and services to businesses or other organizations for resale, use in production of goods or services, or operating an organization. See encyclopedia entry, Retail and Wholesale.

workers' compensation Publicly funded payments made to workers injured on the job.

working conditions Term encompassing a wide variety of on-the-job concerns, including worker safety, hours, benefits, and discrimination. See encyclopedia entry.

yield Return on an investment.

Statistics

Trade as a Percentage of Gross Domestic Product
1960 to 2000
(in percent)

Country	1960	1965	1970	1975	1980	1985	1990	1995	2000
Afghanistan	11.2	32.7	21.7	26.9	NA	NA	NA	NA	NA
Albania	NA	NA	NA	NA	45.8	34.7	38.1	47.0	59.3
Algeria	106.2	48.4	51.2	76.7	64.7	50.3	48.4	57.9	63.8
Angola	NA	NA	NA	NA	NA	61.1	59.8	NA	156.9
Antigua and Barbuda	NA	NA	NA	NA	154.0	167.9	175.9	171.5	145.7
Argentina	15.2	10.4	10.3	11.8	11.5	18.0	15.0	19.7	22.4
Armenia	NA	NA	NA	NA	NA	NA	81.3	86.1	73.9
Australia	29.4	29.2	27.2	28.2	33.0	34.7	33.5	39.8	45.6
Austria	48.0	49.5	59.6	61.5	74.1	79.4	78.0	74.4	101.2
Azerbaijan	NA	NA	NA	NA	NA	NA	83.1	85.9	78.6
Bahamas, the	NA	NA	NA	NA	133.3	124.1	NA	NA	NA
Bahrain	NA	NA	NA	NA	239.3	191.6	210.2	152.5	145.6
Bangladesh	19.3	23.0	20.8	11.0	24.1	25.8	19.9	27.9	33.3
Barbados	109.4	126.9	138.1	110.8	142.2	127.8	100.8	118.2	105.6
Belarus	NA	NA	NA	NA	NA	NA	89.6	103.7	141.6
Belgium	77.7	85.7	100.9	105.3	118.5	142.5	139.7	133.7	169.3
Belize	NA	NA	NA	NA	124.0	109.8	125.4	103.2	136.1
Benin	18.2	22.2	39.6	47.9	53.1	60.3	40.6	53.2	42.6
Bhutan	NA	NA	NA	NA	49.2	62.5	60.5	79.3	89.5
Bolivia	50.6	61.5	61.9	74.0	46.8	41.9	46.7	49.7	44.5
Bosnia and Herzegovina	NA	NA	NA	NA	NA	NA	NA	91.9	85.0
Botswana	58.2	72.7	143.7	107.4	119.5	117.5	104.8	89.0	94.3
Brazil	14.2	13.3	14.5	19.0	20.4	19.3	15.2	17.2	23.2
Bulgaria	NA	NA	NA	NA	66.4	86.0	69.8	90.9	116.8
Burkina Faso	22.2	17.3	23.2	40.1	43.1	44.6	38.4	44.5	38.7
Burundi	25.9	22.9	22.3	27.3	32.1	31.8	35.6	40.2	33.1
Cambodia	35.9	24.0	13.5	NA	NA	NA	18.9	80.0	110.0
Cameroon	NA	48.0	50.9	48.2	55.6	62.0	37.5	46.3	57.6
Canada	NA	37.6	42.6	47.0	54.6	54.7	52.0	72.3	86.8
Cape Verde	NA	NA	NA	NA	NA	NA	56.4	78.3	85.0
Central African Republic	57.5	64.8	73.5	61.1	66.3	53.0	42.4	48.1	29.4
Chad	30.4	31.3	38.3	40.3	45.8	43.2	41.4	56.5	48.6
Chile	29.2	26.2	28.6	52.8	49.8	53.9	66.0	59.3	58.5
China	NA	NA	3.7	8.4	15.5	24.1	31.9	45.7	49.1
Colombia	30.4	21.8	30.1	29.9	31.8	26.3	35.4	35.7	39.5
Comoros	NA	NA	NA	NA	60.6	67.1	48.9	64.3	44.5
Congo, Dem. Rep.	38.3	53.2	33.7	25.1	32.8	53.1	58.7	52.2	38.5
Congo, Rep.	106.1	89.1	92.5	99.6	120.1	112.8	99.5	128.3	123.9
Costa Rica	47.6	57.0	63.2	68.6	63.3	63.2	76.0	77.9	93.9
Côte d'Ivoire	57.1	66.9	64.9	73.3	76.2	79.2	58.8	76.9	72.9

Trade as a Percentage of Gross Domestic Product (cont.)
1960 to 2000
(in percent)

Country	1960	1965	1970	1975	1980	1985	1990	1995	2000
Croatia	NA	NA	NA	NA	NA	NA	NA	88.1	95.6
Cuba	NA	NA	NA	NA	NA	NA	NA	29.3	33.9
Cyprus	NA	NA	NA	92.2	108.3	107.6	108.6	96.6	NA
Czech Republic	NA	NA	NA	NA	NA	NA	87.8	112.0	142.5
Denmark	62.5	58.4	57.3	59.4	65.5	72.5	66.6	66.7	81.7
Djibouti	NA	NA	NA	NA	NA	NA	NA	98.4	107.4
Dominica	NA	NA	NA	NA	114.6	96.5	135.1	114.2	122.4
Dominican Republic	44.4	36.6	41.8	57.7	48.1	65.3	77.5	65.2	65.2
Ecuador	34.6	34.4	32.6	58.9	50.6	47.6	60.1	58.3	73.2
Egypt, Arab Rep.	39.6	38.9	32.9	61.5	73.4	52.0	52.8	50.0	39.2
El Salvador	45.0	55.2	49.4	71.3	67.4	52.2	49.8	59.4	69.8
Equatorial Guinea	NA	75.2	80.8	93.8	NA	69.7	101.7	159.4	NA
Eritrea	NA	NA	NA	NA	NA	NA	NA	111.3	95.1
Estonia	NA	NA	NA	NA	NA	NA	NA	152.1	191.7
Ethiopia	NA	NA	NA	NA	NA	24.3	20.3	35.7	46.3
Fiji	78.0	100.5	100.0	86.6	100.5	89.1	129.6	115.1	131.6
Finland	44.2	40.9	51.0	51.9	65.5	57.5	47.2	66.2	76.5
France	26.3	25.2	30.4	36.1	43.2	46.8	43.5	43.6	55.8
French Polynesia	NA	NA	NA	NA	NA	NA	NA	28.2	29.1
Gabon	66.8	80.5	87.7	97.4	96.4	119.9	76.9	91.4	71.8
Gambia, The	NA	NA	78.7	88.3	106.3	97.8	131.5	122.0	110.1
Georgia	NA	NA	NA	NA	NA	NA	85.6	67.8	63.4
Germany	NA	NA	NA	45.0	51.7	60.0	54.3	48.3	67.1
Ghana	63.6	43.8	44.0	37.8	17.6	24.2	42.7	57.4	118.8
Greece	24.0	27.1	26.4	40.6	51.4	46.4	45.9	42.6	57.9
Grenada	NA	NA	NA	NA	126.7	111.8	105.2	100.1	132.8
Guatemala	27.2	36.4	36.3	45.3	47.1	24.9	45.9	44.7	49.5
Guinea	NA	NA	NA	NA	NA	NA	61.5	45.3	53.2
Guinea-Bissau	NA	NA	34.2	31.1	54.5	67.5	47.0	46.8	90.0
Guyana	105.7	112.9	113.5	149.8	174.9	110.0	142.6	213.3	206.7
Haiti	41.5	30.8	31.5	37.5	52.1	45.2	37.5	40.6	46.1
Honduras	44.4	54.1	62.0	70.4	80.3	54.2	76.1	92.1	98.1
Hong Kong, China	178.5	143.7	181.5	163.7	180.6	208.6	260.1	303.2	295.4
Hungary	NA	NA	62.6	90.4	80.3	82.3	59.7	75.8	126.5
Iceland	85.6	69.7	86.4	73.4	69.5	80.3	66.9	68.5	76.5
India	NA	NA	8.1	12.9	16.0	14.2	17.2	25.6	30.5
Indonesia	26.9	11.0	28.4	45.0	54.4	43.0	49.1	54.0	74.1
Iran, Islamic Rep.	NA	NA	NA	76.0	29.7	16.0	45.5	39.0	38.2
Iraq	NA	NA	NA	NA	NA	NA	NA	NA	NA
Ireland	65.3	74.4	77.5	86.4	106.5	112.2	109.3	141.2	175.6
Israel	23.0	50.8	78.6	100.0	103.1	102.9	80.1	76.6	86.9
Italy	25.9	27.0	32.1	40.6	46.1	45.4	39.4	50.0	55.7
Jamaica	71.3	70.1	70.6	80.9	102.1	121.6	99.9	113.7	100.5
Japan	20.7	19.3	20.1	25.2	27.9	25.0	19.8	16.8	20.1
Jordan	NA	NA	NA	NA	124.1	113.1	154.6	123.0	110.4
Kazakhstan	NA	NA	NA	NA	NA	NA	NA	82.5	108.2
Kenya	64.8	62.1	60.5	64.3	67.0	51.7	57.0	71.4	62.3
Kiribati	NA	NA	NA	95.4	133.6	137.7	140.3	NA	NA
Korea, People's Dem. Rep. (North)	NA	NA	NA	NA	NA	NA	NA	NA	NA

Trade as a Percentage of Gross Domestic Product (cont.)
1960 to 2000
(in percent)

Country	1960	1965	1970	1975	1980	1985	1990	1995	2000
Korea, Rep. (South)	15.9	24.4	37.7	62.9	73.3	65.0	59.4	61.9	86.5
Kuwait	NA	90.8	83.9	106.5	112.6	96.4	103.0	96.6	91.2
Kyrgyz Republic	NA	NA	NA	NA	NA	NA	78.8	71.8	89.4
Lao PDR	NA	NA	NA	NA	NA	13.8	35.8	60.6	NA
Latvia	NA	NA	NA	NA	NA	NA	96.7	96.2	100.0
Lebanon	NA	NA	NA	NA	NA	NA	117.9	77.1	50.8
Lesotho	50.2	68.9	65.2	115.6	131.1	138.1	137.7	141.5	110.0
Libya	NA	86.1	89.2	98.4	97.6	NA	70.8	51.6	51.0
Lithuania	NA	NA	NA	NA	NA	NA	112.8	117.7	96.9
Luxembourg	176.5	177.0	181.1	198.9	195.9	233.5	220.9	205.6	290.7
Macao, China	NA	NA	NA	NA	NA	184.9	164.2	119.9	152.7
Macedonia, FYR	NA	NA	NA	NA	NA	NA	61.8	75.8	110.7
Madagascar	26.7	33.2	40.7	36.7	43.1	32.7	44.6	55.8	68.6
Malawi	60.5	52.7	63.4	75.0	63.6	54.1	57.2	76.7	64.9
Malaysia	89.0	79.4	78.7	85.6	111.0	103.2	147.0	192.1	229.6
Maldives	NA	NA	NA	NA	76.1	55.7	88.5	169.2	168.7
Mali	NA	NA	30.7	38.9	43.8	60.7	50.9	57.3	63.3
Malta	128.5	124.9	129.3	179.1	187.4	160.9	184.1	201.3	216.4
Marshall Islands	NA	NA	NA	NA	NA	83.1	84.0	93.5	NA
Mauritania	39.1	63.8	65.8	98.8	103.5	140.7	106.4	108.6	90.8
Mauritius	NA	NA	NA	NA	104.4	104.2	135.6	121.7	128.6
Mexico	20.1	17.2	17.4	16.5	23.7	25.7	38.3	58.2	64.1
Micronesia, Fed. Sts.	NA	NA	NA	NA	NA	NA	NA	116.7	NA
Moldova	NA	NA	NA	NA	NA	NA	100.0	130.3	125.4
Mongolia	NA	NA	NA	NA	NA	94.9	76.9	128.0	147.3
Morocco	46.3	35.1	39.2	55.8	45.3	59.7	58.9	61.5	68.6
Mozambique	NA	NA	NA	NA	38.2	14.3	44.2	55.1	52.3
Myanmar	40.4	34.9	14.0	12.0	22.0	13.2	7.5	3.1	NA
Namibia	NA	NA	NA	NA	NA	NA	100.7	109.5	107.0
Nepal	NA	21.7	13.2	22.3	30.3	31.5	31.6	58.8	55.7
Netherlands	91.8	84.8	89.7	94.6	103.8	118.0	104.6	109.0	129.6
New Caledonia	NA	NA	NA	NA	NA	NA	53.2	42.0	NA
New Zealand	NA	NA	NA	53.2	60.2	62.6	53.8	57.8	71.8
Nicaragua	49.8	61.7	55.9	65.0	67.5	36.6	71.3	91.6	NA
Niger	14.5	23.5	28.9	50.2	62.7	53.5	37.0	41.5	43.2
Nigeria	26.2	26.9	19.6	41.2	48.6	28.5	72.2	86.5	93.4
Norway	73.3	71.4	73.7	78.7	80.3	78.7	74.7	70.1	77.1
Oman	NA	NA	93.4	118.2	100.3	87.0	83.3	NA	NA
Pakistan	NA	NA	22.4	33.2	36.6	33.2	38.9	36.1	34.3
Palau	NA	NA	NA	NA	NA	NA	NA	78.0	117.3
Panama	NA	NA	NA	NA	99.1	69.5	72.2	76.1	72.7
Papua New Guinea	NA	56.0	72.4	86.1	96.5	94.6	89.6	105.6	NA
Paraguay	35.4	30.7	31.0	31.9	44.0	48.4	72.7	86.0	55.0
Peru	41.6	35.6	33.9	32.8	41.8	39.4	29.6	30.7	33.8
Philippines	21.0	34.4	42.6	48.1	52.0	45.9	60.8	80.5	106.5
Poland	NA	NA	NA	NA	NA	NA	50.2	48.4	65.6
Portugal	35.8	50.7	48.1	46.1	60.3	68.5	72.4	66.7	75.2
Puerto Rico	124.5	108.5	107.1	121.9	137.7	136.7	NA	168.9	173.2
Qatar	NA	NA	NA	NA	NA	NA	NA	87.7	NA

Trade as a Percentage of Gross Domestic Product (cont.)
1960 to 2000
(in percent)

Country	1960	1965	1970	1975	1980	1985	1990	1995	2000
Romania	NA	NA	NA	NA	NA	NA	42.9	60.8	71.7
Russian Federation	NA	NA	NA	NA	NA	NA	36.1	52.2	68.6
Rwanda	22.5	29.0	26.7	26.9	40.8	30.7	19.7	31.0	32.6
Samoa	NA	NA	NA	NA	NA	NA	NA	97.9	114.3
São Tomé and Príncipe	NA	NA	38.9	33.1	73.2	67.9	86.9	120.7	118.1
Saudi Arabia	72.0	86.6	89.0	99.2	101.0	80.0	82.4	74.3	68.5
Senegal	35.1	39.0	56.4	75.2	70.5	70.6	55.8	74.6	70.1
Seychelles	NA	NA	NA	NA	147.1	132.7	129.2	113.6	158.5
Sierra Leone	NA	60.1	60.3	59.6	61.1	31.4	46.2	42.2	50.7
Singapore	NA	NA	NA	NA	NA	NA	361.2	340.5	339.6
Slovak Republic	NA	NA	NA	NA	NA	NA	62.1	113.0	146.0
Slovenia	NA	NA	NA	NA	NA	NA	NA	112.4	121.8
Solomon Islands	NA	NA	NA	NA	170.3	123.6	119.6	NA	NA
Somalia	29.9	37.8	28.3	39.3	121.7	25.6	47.5	NA	NA
South Africa	55.5	53.5	46.4	57.1	62.2	53.5	43.0	45.1	54.3
South Asia	NA	NA	12.4	17.3	21.6	19.3	22.0	29.3	33.3
Spain	15.5	21.7	26.2	29.4	32.0	41.5	36.0	45.4	62.2
Sri Lanka	91.4	75.2	54.1	62.4	87.0	64.8	67.2	81.4	90.2
St. Kitts and Nevis	NA	NA	NA	NA	164.0	133.2	134.9	125.7	133.3
St. Lucia	NA	NA	NA	NA	161.2	132.4	156.7	136.9	126.0
St. Vincent and the Grenadines	NA	NA	NA	NA	160.1	151.7	142.6	117.8	112.9
Sub-Saharan Africa	50.3	50.5	47.8	55.8	61.8	53.8	52.7	59.0	63.4
Sudan	27.6	29.3	32.7	34.8	33.7	17.6	NA	NA	33.8
Suriname	118.2	123.9	114.6	132.2	143.0	76.6	55.5	41.9	152.9
Swaziland	74.5	106.8	128.9	129.7	179.0	141.6	148.9	168.1	142.3
Sweden	45.4	43.4	47.7	55.2	60.1	68.5	59.2	74.1	89.0
Switzerland	53.3	55.2	63.6	56.7	72.8	74.7	72.0	66.2	87.9
Syrian Arab Republic	49.2	34.1	39.4	56.5	54.8	38.0	56.3	69.0	68.4
Tajikistan	NA	NA	NA	NA	NA	NA	63.0	NA	169.5
Tanzania	NA	NA	NA	NA	NA	NA	50.1	59.3	37.7
Thailand	32.7	34.1	34.4	41.3	54.5	49.2	75.8	90.4	125.4
Timor-Leste	NA	NA	NA	NA	NA	NA	NA	55.2	57.6
Togo	62.7	63.1	88.4	97.1	107.4	105.5	78.8	69.8	81.9
Tonga	NA	NA	NA	112.1	97.8	102.4	92.7	NA	NA
Trinidad and Tobago	121.3	133.9	84.4	88.2	89.4	61.0	74.0	93.0	106.3
Tunisia	NA	33.4	46.7	64.0	85.8	70.2	94.2	93.4	91.6
Turkey	NA	NA	10.3	15.0	17.1	34.8	30.9	44.2	56.4
Turkmenistan	NA	NA	NA	NA	NA	NA	NA	71.1	113.2
Uganda	49.1	49.9	43.5	19.6	45.5	28.7	26.6	32.6	35.1
Ukraine	NA	NA	NA	NA	NA	NA	56.4	97.2	120.4
United Arab Emirates	NA	NA	NA	103.2	112.4	89.7	105.8	NA	NA
United Kingdom	41.8	37.9	43.8	52.4	52.0	56.5	50.6	57.1	57.9
United States	9.6	9.6	11.3	16.1	20.7	17.3	20.6	23.5	26.2
Uruguay	32.4	29.8	29.1	37.1	35.7	47.9	41.6	38.1	41.0
Uzbekistan	NA	NA	NA	NA	NA	NA	76.6	73.5	46.1
Vanuatu	NA	NA	NA	NA	74.9	123.3	123.0	97.8	NA
Venezuela	43.3	42.8	37.8	50.8	50.6	40.8	59.6	48.9	44.8
Vietnam	NA	NA	NA	NA	NA	NA	81.3	74.7	112.5
West Bank and Gaza	NA	NA	NA	NA	NA	NA	NA	76.8	84.6

Trade as a Percentage of Gross Domestic Product (cont.)
1960 to 2000
(in percent)

Country	1960	1965	1970	1975	1980	1985	1990	1995	2000
Yemen, Rep.	NA	NA	NA	NA	NA	NA	34.4	108.8	79.6
Yugoslavia, Fed. Rep.	NA	NA	NA	NA	NA	NA	NA	NA	81.2
Zambia	95.3	83.9	90.5	92.8	86.8	73.6	72.5	75.9	52.5
Zimbabwe	NA	NA	NA	47.2	49.9	44.2	45.7	79.2	56.5
World	24.9	24.9	27.1	34.2	39.3	39.4	39.7	42.8	50.8

Note: NA = Not available.

Source: World Bank, *World Development Indicators: 2003*, Washington, D.C., World Bank, 2003.

Global Growth of Output by Sector
(average annual percent growth)

	Agriculture		Industry		Manufacturing		Services	
	1980–90	1990–2001	1980–90	1990–2001	1980–90	1990–2001	1980–90	1990–2001
Afghanistan	NA	NA	NA	NA	NA	NA	NA	NA
Albania	1.9	5.7	2.1	1.0	NA	−5.0	−0.4	4.5
Algeria	4.1	3.7	2.6	1.9	4.1	−1.6	3.0	1.9
Angola	0.5	0.1	6.4	4.0	−11.1	0.6	1.3	−1.0
Argentina	0.7	3.2	−1.3	2.9	−0.8	1.9	0.0	3.9
Armenia	NA	1.0	NA	−6.1	NA	−3.2	NA	6.7
Australia	3.2	2.9	3.0	3.0	1.9	2.5	3.8	4.3
Austria	1.4	3.7	1.8	2.8	2.5	2.7	2.8	1.9
Azerbaijan	NA	−0.5	NA	−4.0	NA	−11.8	NA	10.3
Bangladesh	2.7	3.1	4.9	7.2	3.0	7.0	4.4	4.6
Belarus	NA	−3.5	NA	−0.7	NA	0.4	NA	0.5
Belgium	2.2	2.3	2.4	2.0	NA	NA	1.8	2.0
Benin	5.1	5.7	3.4	4.4	5.1	5.9	0.7	4.2
Bolivia	NA	2.8	NA	3.7	NA	3.6	NA	4.1
Bosnia and Herzegovina	NA	NA	NA	NA	NA	NA	NA	NA
Botswana	2.5	−1.3	11.4	4.2	11.4	4.4	15.9	8.1
Brazil	2.8	3.3	2.0	2.4	1.6	1.5	3.3	2.9
Bulgaria	−2.1	3.0	5.2	−4.0	NA	NA	4.7	−3.9
Burkina Faso	3.1	3.7	3.8	4.4	2.0	5.4	4.6	4.6
Burundi	3.1	−1.1	4.5	−4.3	5.7	−8.0	5.6	−1.5
Cambodia	NA	1.8	NA	10.2	NA	8.2	NA	6.2
Cameroon	2.2	5.5	5.9	0.0	5.0	2.0	2.1	0.5
Canada	2.3	1.1	2.9	3.1	3.8	4.3	3.2	2.9
Central African Republic	1.6	3.9	1.4	1.0	5.0	0.3	1.0	−0.5
Chad	2.3	4.0	8.1	2.8	NA	NA	6.7	1.7
Chile	5.9	1.9	3.5	5.7	3.4	4.1	2.9	4.9
China	5.9	4.0	11.1	13.1	10.8	12.1	13.5	8.9
Hong Kong, China	NA	NA	NA	NA	NA	NA	NA	NA
Colombia	2.9	−1.8	5.0	1.4	3.5	−1.9	3.1	3.9
Congo, Dem. Rep.	2.5	0.6	0.9	−7.8	1.6	NA	1.3	−10.9
Congo, Rep.	3.4	1.4	5.2	3.0	6.8	−1.8	2.2	−0.2
Costa Rica	3.1	3.9	2.8	5.8	3.0	6.2	3.3	4.6
Côte d'Ivoire	0.3	3.2	4.4	4.0	3.0	2.9	−0.3	2.7
Croatia	NA	−1.6	NA	−1.7	NA	−2.2	NA	2.5
Cuba	NA	5.2	NA	6.6	NA	6.3	NA	2.5

Global Growth of Output by Sector (cont.)
(average annual percent growth)

	Agriculture		Industry		Manufacturing		Services	
	1980–90	1990–2001	1980–90	1990–2001	1980–90	1990–2001	1980–90	1990–2001
Czech Republic	NA	3.5	NA	−0.3	NA	NA	NA	2.0
Denmark	2.6	2.7	2.0	2.2	1.3	2.2	1.9	2.5
Dominican Republic	−1.0	3.9	3.0	6.9	2.3	4.7	4.2	6.0
Ecuador	4.4	1.5	1.2	2.6	0.0	2.1	1.7	1.2
Egypt, Arab Rep.	2.7	3.4	3.3	4.6	NA	6.5	7.8	4.6
El Salvador	−1.1	1.1	0.1	5.1	−0.2	5.2	0.7	5.1
Eritrea	NA	1.2	NA	12.8	NA	8.8	NA	5.0
Estonia	NA	−2.8	NA	−1.9	NA	3.4	NA	2.2
Ethiopia	0.2	2.3	0.4	5.4	−0.9	5.4	3.1	7.2
Finland	−0.4	1.2	3.3	4.8	3.4	6.4	3.6	2.5
France	1.3	1.9	1.4	1.5	NA	2.1	3.0	2.0
Gabon	1.2	−1.0	1.5	2.4	1.8	0.6	0.1	3.4
Gambia, The	0.9	5.2	4.7	2.5	7.8	1.3	2.7	3.7
Georgia	NA	NA	NA	NA	NA	NA	NA	NA
Germany	1.7	1.7	1.1	0.0	NA	−0.1	3.1	2.4
Ghana	1.0	3.4	3.3	2.8	3.9	−2.2	5.7	5.5
Greece	−0.1	0.7	1.3	1.0	NA	NA	0.9	2.8
Guatemala	1.2	2.8	−0.2	4.1	0.0	2.7	0.9	4.6
Guinea	NA	4.2	NA	4.7	NA	4.3	NA	3.4
Guinea-Bissau	4.7	3.6	2.2	−3.1	NA	−2.2	3.5	−0.2
Haiti	−0.1	−2.8	−1.7	1.6	−1.7	−9.3	0.9	0.2
Honduras	2.7	1.9	3.3	3.6	3.7	4.1	2.5	3.7
Hungary	1.7	−2.2	0.2	3.8	NA	7.9	2.1	1.4
India	3.1	3.0	6.9	6.1	7.4	6.7	6.9	7.9
Indonesia	3.6	1.9	7.3	4.8	12.8	6.3	6.5	3.6
Iran, Islamic Rep.	4.5	4.0	3.3	−2.8	4.5	5.1	−1.0	8.5
Iraq	NA	NA	NA	NA	NA	NA	NA	NA
Ireland	NA	NA	NA	NA	NA	NA	NA	NA
Israel	NA	NA	NA	NA	NA	NA	NA	NA
Italy	−0.5	1.4	1.8	1.2	2.1	1.5	3.0	1.8
Jamaica	2.8	0.6	2.4	−0.4	2.7	−1.7	1.6	0.6
Japan	1.3	−3.1	4.1	−0.2	NA	0.7	4.2	2.3
Jordan	6.8	−2.0	1.7	4.7	0.5	5.4	2.3	5.0
Kazakhstan	NA	−6.5	NA	−6.9	NA	NA	NA	3.1
Kenya	3.3	1.2	3.9	1.6	4.9	2.0	4.9	3.1
Korea, Dem. People's Rep. (North)	NA	NA	NA	NA	NA	NA	NA	NA
Korea, Rep. (South)	3.0	2.0	11.4	6.3	12.1	7.6	8.4	5.6
Kuwait	14.7	NA	1.0	NA	2.3	NA	2.1	NA
Kyrgyz Republic	NA	2.1	NA	−8.5	NA	−14.1	NA	−3.9
Lao PDR	3.5	4.9	6.1	10.9	8.9	12.6	3.3	6.5
Latvia	2.3	−5.9	4.3	−6.7	4.4	−6.2	3.3	3.1
Lebanon	NA	1.8	NA	−1.6	NA	−4.3	NA	4.1
Lesotho	2.8	1.7	3.9	7.8	8.5	6.2	5.1	3.0
Liberia	NA	6.5	NA	−11.2	NA	NA	NA	−12.5
Libya	NA	NA	NA	NA	NA	NA	NA	NA
Lithuania	NA	−0.3	NA	2.8	NA	4.4	NA	4.3
Macedonia, FYR	NA	−0.3	NA	−2.3	NA	−4.5	NA	1.1
Madagascar	2.5	1.9	0.9	2.8	2.1	2.6	0.3	2.8
Malawi	2.0	7.2	2.9	1.8	3.6	0.4	3.3	2.3

Global Growth of Output by Sector (cont.)
(average annual percent growth)

	Agriculture		Industry		Manufacturing		Services	
	1980–90	1990–2001	1980–90	1990–2001	1980–90	1990–2001	1980–90	1990–2001
Malaysia	3.4	0.3	6.8	8.0	9.3	8.8	4.9	6.7
Mali	3.3	2.9	4.3	7.5	6.8	2.8	1.9	3.1
Mauritania	1.7	4.8	4.9	2.3	−2.1	0.0	0.4	5.2
Mauritius	2.6	−0.2	9.2	5.5	10.4	5.3	5.1	6.3
Mexico	0.8	1.6	1.1	3.7	1.5	4.2	1.4	3.0
Moldova	NA	−9.5	NA	−11.5	NA	−3.4	NA	0.3
Mongolia	1.4	3.2	6.6	−0.1	NA	NA	8.4	0.4
Morocco	6.7	−0.6	3.0	3.2	4.1	2.8	4.2	3.0
Mozambique	6.6	4.9	−4.5	15.2	NA	18.0	9.1	1.9
Myanmar	0.5	5.7	0.5	10.5	−0.2	7.9	0.8	7.2
Namibia	2.5	4.1	−0.2	2.1	3.1	2.6	2.2	4.3
Nepal	4.0	2.6	8.8	6.9	9.3	8.4	3.9	6.2
Netherlands	3.6	2.0	1.6	1.7	NA	NA	2.6	3.2
New Zealand	4.0	3.4	1.0	2.3	NA	2.4	2.1	3.5
Nicaragua	−2.2	5.2	−2.3	3.2	−3.2	1.3	−1.5	1.2
Niger	1.7	3.2	−1.7	2.1	−2.7	2.7	−0.7	2.2
Nigeria	3.3	3.5	−1.1	1.0	0.7	1.2	3.7	2.9
Norway	0.1	2.4	4.0	3.9	0.2	2.3	2.9	3.4
Oman	7.9	NA	10.3	NA	20.6	NA	5.9	NA
Pakistan	4.0	4.1	7.7	4.0	8.1	3.9	6.8	4.4
Panama	2.5	2.2	−1.3	4.7	0.4	1.8	0.7	3.8
Papua New Guinea	1.8	3.5	1.9	4.6	0.1	4.4	2.0	3.0
Paraguay	3.6	2.3	0.3	3.1	4.0	0.8	3.1	1.4
Peru	3.0	5.6	0.1	5.0	−0.2	3.5	−0.4	3.7
Philippines	1.0	1.8	−0.9	3.2	0.2	3.0	2.8	4.1
Poland	NA	−0.2	NA	4.2	NA	7.1	NA	4.2
Portugal	1.5	−0.2	3.4	3.0	NA	2.6	2.5	2.2
Puerto Rico	1.8	NA	3.6	NA	3.6	NA	4.6	NA
Romania	NA	NA	NA	NA	NA	NA	NA	NA
Russian Federation	NA	−4.5	NA	−6.1	NA	NA	NA	−0.3
Rwanda	0.5	3.4	2.5	−2.3	2.6	−4.8	3.6	−0.2
Saudi Arabia	13.4	NA	−2.3	NA	7.5	NA	1.3	NA
Senegal	2.8	2.3	4.3	5.1	4.6	4.2	2.8	4.0
Sierra Leone	3.1	−4.5	1.7	−4.6	NA	5.0	−0.9	−3.4
Singapore	−5.3	−2.1	5.2	7.2	6.6	6.5	7.6	7.6
Slovak Republic	1.6	1.6	2.0	−2.1	NA	4.3	0.9	5.6
Slovenia	NA	−0.1	NA	2.9	NA	4.0	NA	3.9
Somalia	3.3	NA	1.0	NA	−1.7	NA	0.9	NA
South Africa	2.9	0.8	0.7	1.0	1.1	1.2	2.4	2.7
Spain	3.1	1.0	2.7	2.3	NA	NA	3.3	2.9
Sri Lanka	2.2	1.7	4.6	6.5	6.3	7.5	4.7	5.7
Sudan	1.8	9.0	1.6	6.8	4.8	4.6	4.5	2.7
Swaziland	2.3	1.5	12.0	3.6	15.7	2.7	4.8	3.4
Sweden	1.4	0.0	2.8	3.6	NA	NA	2.4	1.8
Switzerland	NA	NA	NA	NA	NA	NA	NA	NA
Syrian Arab Republic	−0.6	4.9	6.6	9.3	NA	10.2	1.6	3.0
Tajikistan	−2.8	−5.8	5.5	−13.2	5.6	−12.6	3.4	−1.1
Tanzania	NA	3.3	NA	3.6	NA	3.0	NA	3.0
Thailand	3.9	1.7	9.8	5.4	9.5	6.5	7.3	3.8

Global Growth of Output by Sector (cont.)
(average annual percent growth)

	Agriculture 1980–90	1990–2001	Industry 1980–90	1990–2001	Manufacturing 1980–90	1990–2001	Services 1980–90	1990–2001
Togo	5.6	3.8	1.1	2.7	1.7	3.9	–0.3	0.4
Trinidad and Tobago	–5.9	3.4	–5.5	4.2	–10.1	6.7	6.7	3.1
Tunisia	2.8	2.4	3.1	4.7	3.7	5.6	3.5	5.4
Turkey	1.2	1.1	7.7	3.4	7.9	4.1	4.5	3.5
Turkmenistan	NA	–3.2	NA	–6.7	NA	NA	NA	–3.2
Uganda	2.1	3.8	5.0	11.9	3.7	12.8	2.8	7.7
Ukraine	NA	–4.9	NA	–9.5	NA	–9.0	NA	–0.9
United Arab Emirates	9.6	NA	–4.2	NA	3.1	NA	3.6	NA
United Kingdom	2.4	–1.0	3.3	1.3	NA	NA	3.1	3.4
United States	3.2	3.5	3.0	3.7	NA	4.3	3.4	3.7
Uruguay	0.1	2.0	–0.2	0.7	0.4	–0.5	1.0	4.0
Uzbekistan	NA	0.9	NA	–2.6	NA	NA	NA	1.6
Venezuela	3.1	1.4	1.7	2.6	4.4	0.8	0.5	0.5
Vietnam	2.8	4.2	4.4	11.6	1.9	11.2	7.1	7.3
West Bank and Gaza	NA	–4.2	NA	0.8	NA	3.6	NA	2.8
Yemen, Rep.	5.6	NA	7.5	NA	4.1	NA	5.0	NA
Yugoslavia, Fed. Rep.	NA	NA	NA	NA	NA	NA	NA	NA
Zambia	3.6	3.9	1.0	–3.6	4.1	1.1	–0.2	2.8
Zimbabwe	3.1	3.7	3.2	–0.4	2.8	–0.8	3.0	2.5

Note: NA = Not Available.
Source: World Bank, *World Development Indicators: 2003,* Washington, D.C., World Bank, 2003.

Selected Indexes of Manufacturing Activity by Country: 1980 to 2000
(1992=100)

Index	United States	Canada	Japan	Belgium	France	Germany	Italy	Netherlands	Norway	Sweden	United Kingdom
OUTPUT PER HOUR:											
1980	70.5	74.4	63.2	65.4	66.6	NA	69.6	68.7	76.7	73.1	54.3
1985	86.0	92.2	76.5	87.0	79.1	NA	84.1	88.4	90.2	86.2	71.1
1990	96.9	94.7	94.4	96.8	93.6	NA	92.2	98.4	96.6	94.6	89.1
1995	113.8	111.3	111.0	113.2	114.7	112.8	109.4	118.0	102.0	121.9	104.8
1999	135.1	114.9	125.8	128.9	132.9	122.4	111.8	127.7	103.1	143.5	110.8
2000	144.7	116.3	132.6	132.8	140.5	129.8	115.7	NA	104.2	150.4	116.4
AVERAGE ANNUAL PERCENT CHANGE:											
1979–85	3.5	3.4	3.5	6.0	3.0	NA	4.0	4.4	2.4	3.1	4.4
1985–90	2.4	0.5	4.3	2.2	3.4	NA	1.9	2.2	1.4	1.9	4.6
1990–2000	4.1	2.1	3.5	3.2	4.1	NA	2.3	NA	0.8	4.7	2.7
COMPENSATION PER HOUR, NATIONAL CURRENCY BASIS:[1]											
1980	55.6	47.6	58.5	52.5	40.8	NA	28.5	64.4	39.0	37.3	32.3
1985	75.1	71.9	72.4	75.3	72.8	NA	60.8	81.8	63.4	58.6	52.3
1990	90.8	88.3	90.5	90.1	90.6	NA	84.4	90.8	92.3	87.8	81.6
1995	107.9	106.0	108.3	109.2	108.5	118.2	112.7	110.6	109.2	106.5	107.8
1999	122.1	113.1	115.5	116.8	118.6	139.6	127.5	123.5	133.4	127.5	124.5
2000	130.1	117.0	115.5	119.8	124.9	134.2	131.2	NA	140.1	130.7	129.1
AVERAGE ANNUAL PERCENT CHANGE:											
1979–85	7.2	9.1	4.7	8.1	12.8	NA	16.5	5.0	10.0	9.8	11.8
1985–90	3.9	4.2	4.6	3.7	4.5	NA	6.8	2.1	7.8	8.4	9.3
1990–2000	3.7	2.9	2.5	2.9	3.3	NA	4.5	NA	4.3	4.1	4.7

Selected Indexes of Manufacturing Activity by Country: 1980 to 2000 (cont.)

Index	United States	Canada	Japan	Belgium	France	Germany	Italy	Netherlands	Norway	Sweden	United Kingdom
REAL HOURLY COMPENSATION:[1,2]											
1980	91.6	91.6	75.2	86.5	79.6	NA	80.0	87.4	86.0	87.7	67.2
1985	95.5	96.6	81.2	88.3	89.7	NA	89.6	90.7	90.8	87.4	76.6
1990	96.6	94.7	95.0	95.2	96.0	NA	94.3	96.6	97.7	97.6	89.7
1995	100.4	101.7	106.3	102.3	102.7	108.2	98.6	102.9	102.7	97.6	100.2
1999	104.6	102.4	110.9	103.3	107.6	113.2	101.4	105.7	115.6	109.4	104.2
2000	107.8	103.1	111.7	103.3	111.3	115.0	101.8	NA	117.7	115.8	105.0
AVERAGE ANNUAL PERCENT CHANGE:											
1979–85	0.8	1.1	1.1	1.1	2.3	NA	1.3	0.4	0.6	–0.5	2.6
1985–90	0.2	–0.4	3.2	1.5	1.4	NA	1.0	1.3	1.5	2.2	3.2
1990–2000	1.1	0.9	1.6	0.8	1.5	NA	0.8	NA	1.9	1.7	1.6
UNIT LABOR COSTS, NATIONAL CURRENCY:											
1980	78.8	63.9	92.5	80.3	61.3	NA	41.0	93.7	50.8	51.0	59.4
1985	87.3	78.0	94.6	86.5	92.0	NA	72.2	92.5	70.2	68.0	73.6
1990	93.7	93.3	95.9	93.0	96.8	NA	91.5	92.3	95.6	92.9	91.6
1995	94.8	95.2	97.6	96.4	94.6	104.7	103.0	93.7	107.0	87.4	102.9
1999	90.4	98.4	91.8	90.6	89.3	105.9	114.0	96.7	129.5	88.8	112.4
2000	89.9	100.6	87.1	90.2	88.9	103.4	113.4	NA	134.5	86.9	110.9
AVERAGE ANNUAL PERCENT CHANGE:											
1979–85	3.6	5.5	1.1	2.0	9.5	NA	12.0	0.5	7.4	6.5	7.1
1985–90	1.4	3.7	0.3	1.5	1.0	NA	4.8	–0.1	6.4	6.4	4.5
1990–2000	–0.4	0.8	–1.0	-0.3	–0.9	NA	2.2	NA	3.5	–0.7	1.9
UNIT LABOR COSTS, U.S. DOLLAR BASIS:[3]											
1980	78.8	66.1	51.8	88.3	76.7	NA	59.0	82.9	63.9	70.2	78.3
1985	87.3	69.0	50.3	46.9	54.2	NA	46.6	49.0	50.8	46.1	54.1
1990	93.7	96.6	83.8	89.5	94.0	NA	94.1	89.1	95.0	91.3	92.5
1995	94.8	83.8	131.7	105.2	100.4	114.2	77.9	102.7	105.0	71.3	91.9
1999	90.4	80.0	102.4	76.9	76.8	90.1	77.3	82.2	103.1	62.5	102.9
2000	89.9	81.8	102.5	66.4	66.2	76.2	66.6	NA	94.8	55.2	95.2
AVERAGE ANNUAL PERCENT CHANGE:											
1979–85	3.6	2.8	–0.3	–9.3	–3.3	NA	–2.5	–7.6	–1.7	–5.2	-1.3
1985–90	1.4	7.0	10.8	13.8	11.6	NA	15.1	12.7	13.3	14.7	11.3
1990–2000	–0.4	–1.6	2.0	–2.9	–3.5	NA	–3.4	NA	0.6	–4.9	0.3
EMPLOYMENT LEVELS IN MANUFACTURING:											
1980	111.6	115.1	88.9	119.3	125.0	NA	124.7	107.8	134.5	130.9	151.8
1985	106.0	106.8	93.5	104.0	110.3	NA	104.8	95.4	120.7	122.0	120.6
1990	105.4	113.2	97.5	102.5	105.4	NA	106.4	101.1	105.4	117.2	115.5
1995	102.5	104.8	90.1	91.9	92.1	86.2	97.2	91.3	107.2	97.9	98.8
1999	102.4	118.5	83.2	88.7	89.7	82.6	98.8	93.4	111.6	98.7	96.8
2000	101.7	123.7	81.7	90.3	90.8	83.2	98.9	NA	108.7	100.0	93.2
AVERAGE ANNUAL PERCENT CHANGE:											
1979–85	–1.4	–1.3	1.2	–2.6	–2.3	NA	–2.8	–2.2	–1.8	–1.2	-4.6
1985–90	–0.1	1.2	0.8	–0.3	–0.9	NA	0.3	1.2	–2.7	–0.8	-0.9
1990–2000	–0.4	0.9	–1.8	–1.3	–1.5	NA	–0.7	NA	0.3	–1.6	-2.1
AGGREGATE HOURS:											
1980	107.5	114.6	95.6	119.7	133.2	NA	121.3	111.8	135.0	124.0	160.5
1985	104.6	106.4	100.3	102.4	110.4	NA	100.8	96.7	120.2	119.4	125.2
1990	104.8	113.5	102.9	104.3	105.9	NA	107.8	101.5	103.7	116.4	118.1
1995	104.0	106.4	89.1	92.0	91.5	84.5	98.0	91.6	106.8	105.3	102.8
1999	104.3	122.6	80.3	91.3	88.3	79.6	98.6	93.0	110.6	107.1	99.4
2000	103.4	128.0	80.6	91.8	86.2	79.4	98.5	NA	106.4	108.6	96.1

Selected Indexes of Manufacturing Activity by Country: 1980 to 2000 (cont.)

Index	United States	Canada	Japan	Belgium	France	Germany	Italy	Netherlands	Norway	Sweden	United Kingdom
AVERAGE ANNUAL PERCENT CHANGE:											
1979–85	–1.2	–1.5	1.1	–3.2	–3.3	NA	–2.9	–2.5	–1.8	–0.8	–5.3
1985–90	Z	1.3	0.5	0.4	–0.8	NA	1.3	1.0	–2.9	–0.5	–1.2
1990–2000	–0.1	1.2	–2.4	–1.3	–2.0	NA	–0.9	NA	0.3	–0.7	–2.0

Notes: NA = Not available. Z = Represents or rounds to zero. Data relate to all employed persons (employees, self-employed workers, and unpaid family workers) in all countries except Belgium and Italy, where data relate only to wage and salary earners.

[1] Compensation includes, but real hourly compensation excludes, adjustments for payroll and employment taxes that are not compensation to employees, but are labor costs to employers. [2] Index of hourly compensation divided by the index of consumer prices to adjust for changes in purchasing power. [3] Indexes in national currency adjusted for changes in prevailing exchange rates.

Source: U.S. Bureau of Labor Statistics, *International Comparisons of Manufacturing Productivity and Unit Labor Cost Trends*, Revised Data for 1998, April 31, 2001.

U.S. Employment by Industry: 1980 to 2000
(in thousands)

Industry	1980	1990[1]	1995[1]	1999[1]	2000[1] Total	2000[1] Percent Female	2000[1] Percent Black	2000[1] Percent Hispanic[2]
Agriculture	3,364	3,223	3,440	3,281	3,305	26.4	4.2	22.5
Mining	979	724	627	565	521	13.7	5.2	8.3
Construction	6,215	7,764	7,668	8,987	9,433	9.7	6.7	14.9
Manufacturing	21,942	21,346	20,493	20,070	19,940	32.5	10.3	12.3
Transportation, communication, and other public utilities	6,525	8,168	8,709	9,554	9,740	28.7	15.7	9.4
Wholesale and retail trade	20,191	24,622	26,071	27,572	27,832	47.2	9.6	12.2
Wholesale trade	3,920	4,669	4,986	5,189	5,421	30.4	7.6	11.9
Retail trade	16,270	19,953	21,086	22,383	22,411	51.2	10.1	12.3
Finance, insurance, real estate	5,993	8,051	7,983	8,815	8,727	58.5	10.5	6.9
Services[3]	28,752	39,267	43,953	48,687	49,695	62.1	12.8	9.1
Business and repair services[3]	3,848	7,485	7,526	9,046	9,661	37.4	12.0	11.0
Advertising	191	277	267	284	280	55.2	6.6	6.6
Services to dwellings and buildings	370	827	829	820	862	51.6	16.3	27.0
Personnel supply services	235	710	853	1,066	1,063	59.9	22.8	11.2
Computer and data processing	221	805	1,136	2,079	2,496	31.8	7.4	3.6
Detective/protective services	213	378	506	593	574	25.6	24.3	10.6
Automobile services	952	1,457	1,459	1,583	1,626	14.9	11.0	16.2
Personal services[3]	3,839	4,733	4,375	4,488	4,515	70.0	13.8	18.6
Private households	1,257	1,036	971	940	894	92.1	15.7	29.8
Hotels and lodging places	1,149	1,818	1,495	1,541	1,443	57.9	16.7	21.0
Entertainment and recreation	1,047	1,526	2,238	2,649	2,582	42.3	9.9	9.6
Professional and related services[3]	19,853	25,351	29,661	32,370	32,784	70.0	13.2	7.1
Hospitals	4,036	4,700	4,961	5,117	5,028	76.3	17.5	6.4

U.S. Employment by Industry: 1980 to 2000 (cont.)
(in thousands)

Industry	1980	1990[1]	1995[1]	1999[1]	2000[1] Total	2000[1] Percent Female	2000[1] Percent Black	2000[1] Percent Hispanic[2]
Health services, except hospitals	3,345	4,673	5,967	6,529	6,569	79.7	15.4	7.8
Elementary, secondary schools	5,550	5,994	6,653	7,451	7,629	76.0	12.0	8.2
Colleges and universities	2,108	2,637	2,768	2,919	2,903	54.3	10.8	6.3
Social services	1,590	2,239	2,979	3,426	3,519	81.9	19.3	9.2
Legal services	776	1,215	1,335	1,365	1,362	58.5	6.7	6.5
Public administration [4]	5,342	5,627	5,957	5,958	6,015	44.9	16.6	7.3
Total employed	99,303	118,793	124,900	133,488	135,208	46.5	11.3	10.7

Note: For civilian noninstitutional population 16 years old and over. Annual averages of monthly figures.

[1] Data not strictly comparable with data for earlier years due to changes in industrial classification.

[2] Persons of Hispanic origin may be of any race. [3] Includes industries not shown separately. [4] Includes workers involved in uniquely governmental activities, e.g., judicial and legislative.

Source: U.S. Bureau of Labor Statistics, *Employment and Earnings*, monthly, January issues, and unpublished data.

Employment Status of the U.S. Civilian Population: 1970 to 2000
(in thousands)

	Civilian noninstitutional population	Civilian labor force Total	Civilian labor force Percent of population	Civilian labor force Employed	Civilian labor force Employment population ratio	Unemployed Number	Unemployed Percent of labor force	Not in labor force Number	Not in labor force Percent of population
TOTAL: [1]									
1970	137,085	82,771	60.4	78,678	57.4	4,093	4.9	54,315	39.6
1980	167,745	106,940	63.8	99,303	59.2	7,637	7.1	60,806	36.2
1985	178,206	115,461	64.8	107,150	60.1	8,312	7.2	62,744	35.2
1990[2]	189,164	125,840	66.5	118,793	62.8	7,047	5.6	63,324	33.5
1995	198,584	132,304	66.6	124,900	62.9	7,404	5.6	66,280	33.4
1998[2]	205,220	137,673	67.1	131,463	64.1	6,210	4.5	67,547	32.9
1999[2]	207,753	139,368	67.1	133,488	64.3	5,880	4.2	68,385	32.9
2000[2]	209,699	140,863	67.2	135,208	64.5	5,655	4.0	68,836	32.8
MALE:									
1970	64,304	51,228	79.7	48,990	76.2	2,238	4.4	13,076	20.3
1980	79,398	61,453	77.4	57,186	72.0	4,267	6.9	17,945	22.6
1985	84,469	64,411	76.3	59,891	70.9	4,521	7.0	20,058	23.7
1990[2]	90,377	69,011	76.4	65,104	72.0	3,906	5.7	21,367	23.6
1995	95,178	71,360	75.0	67,377	70.8	3,983	5.6	23,818	25.0
1998[2]	98,758	73,959	74.9	70,693	71.6	3,266	4.4	24,799	25.1
1999[2]	99,722	74,512	74.7	71,446	71.6	3,066	4.1	25,210	25.3
2000[2]	100,731	75,247	74.7	72,293	71.8	2,954	3.9	25,484	25.3
FEMALE:									
1970	72,782	31,543	43.3	29,688	40.8	1,855	5.9	41,239	56.7
1980	88,348	45,487	51.5	42,117	47.7	3,370	7.4	42,861	48.5
1985	93,736	51,050	54.5	47,259	50.4	3,791	7.4	42,686	45.5
1990[2]	98,787	56,829	57.5	53,689	54.3	3,140	5.5	41,957	42.5
1995	103,406	60,944	58.9	57,523	55.6	3,421	5.6	42,462	41.1

Employment Status of the U.S. Civilian Population: 1970 to 2000 (cont.)
(in thousands)

	Civilian noninstitutional population	Civilian labor force			Employment population ratio	Unemployed		Not in labor force	
		Total	Percent of population	Employed		Number	Percent of labor force	Number	Percent of population
FEMALE:									
1998[2]	106,462	63,714	59.8	60,771	57.1	2,944	4.6	42,748	40.1
1999[2]	108,031	64,855	60.0	62,042	57.4	2,814	4.3	43,175	40.0
2000[2]	108,968	65,616	60.2	62,915	57.7	2,701	4.1	43,352	39.8
WHITE:									
1970	122,174	73,556	60.2	70,217	57.5	3,339	4.5	48,618	39.8
1980	146,122	93,600	64.1	87,715	60.0	5,884	6.3	52,523	35.9
1985	153,679	99,926	65.0	93,736	61.0	6,191	6.2	53,753	35.0
1990[2]	160,625	107,447	66.9	102,261	63.7	5,186	4.8	53,178	33.1
1995	166,914	111,950	67.1	106,490	63.8	5,459	4.9	54,965	32.9
1998[2]	171,478	115,415	67.3	110,931	64.7	4,484	3.9	56,064	32.7
1999[2]	173,085	116,509	67.3	112,235	64.8	4,273	3.7	56,577	32.7
2000[2]	174,428	117,574	67.4	113,475	65.1	4,099	3.5	56,854	32.6
BLACK:									
1973	14,917	8,976	60.2	8,128	54.5	846	9.4	5,941	39.8
1980	17,824	10,865	61.0	9,313	52.2	1,553	14.3	6,959	39.0
1985	19,664	12,364	62.9	10,501	53.4	1,864	15.1	7,299	37.1
1990[2]	21,477	13,740	64.0	12,175	56.7	1,565	11.4	7,737	36.0
1995	23,246	14,817	63.7	13,279	57.1	1,538	10.4	8,429	36.3
1998[2]	24,373	15,982	65.6	14,556	59.7	1,426	8.9	8,391	34.4
1999[2]	24,855	16,365	65.8	15,056	60.6	1,309	8.0	8,490	34.2
2000[2]	25,218	16,603	65.8	15,334	60.8	1,269	7.6	8,615	34.2
HISPANIC:[3]									
1980	9,598	6,146	64.0	5,527	57.6	620	10.1	3,451	36.0
1985	11,915	7,698	64.6	6,888	57.8	811	10.5	4,217	35.4
1990[2]	15,904	10,720	67.4	9,845	61.9	876	8.2	5,184	32.6
1995	18,629	12,267	65.8	11,127	59.7	1,140	9.3	6,362	34.2
1998[2]	21,070	14,317	67.9	13,291	63.1	1,026	7.2	6,753	32.1
1999[2]	21,650	14,665	67.7	13,720	63.4	945	6.4	6,985	32.3
2000[2]	22,393	15,368	68.6	14,492	64.7	876	5.7	7,025	31.4
MEXICAN:									
1986	7,377	4,941	67.0	4,387	59.5	555	11.2	2,436	33.0
1990[2]	9,752	6,707	68.8	6,146	63.0	561	8.4	3,045	31.2
1995	11,609	7,765	66.9	7,016	60.4	750	9.7	3,844	33.1
1998[2]	13,216	9,096	68.8	8,431	63.8	664	7.3	4,121	31.2
1999[2]	13,582	9,267	68.2	8,656	63.7	611	6.6	4,315	31.8
2000[2]	14,386	9,955	69.2	9,364	65.1	591	5.9	4,430	30.8
PUERTO RICAN:									
1986	1,494	804	53.8	691	46.3	113	14.0	690	46.2
1990[2]	1,718	960	55.9	870	50.6	91	9.5	758	44.1
1995	1,896	1,098	57.9	974	51.4	123	11.2	798	42.1
1998[2]	2,080	1,249	60.0	1,145	55.0	104	8.3	832	40.0
1999[2]	2,058	1,269	61.6	1,165	56.6	104	8.2	789	38.3
2000[2]	2,025	1,278	63.1	1,196	59.1	82	6.4	747	36.9
CUBAN:									
1986	842	570	67.7	533	63.3	36	6.4	272	32.3
1990[2]	918	603	65.7	559	60.9	44	7.2	315	34.3

Employment Status of the U.S. Civilian Population: 1970 to 2000 (cont.)
(in thousands)

	Civilian noninstitutional population	Civilian labor force				Unemployed		Not in labor force	
		Total	Percent of population	Employed	Employment population ratio	Number	Percent of labor force	Number	Percent of population
CUBAN:									
1995	1,019	613	60.2	568	55.7	45	7.4	406	39.8
1998[2]	1,062	651	61.3	612	57.6	39	6.0	411	38.7
1999[2]	1,141	714	62.6	681	59.7	33	4.6	427	37.4
2000[2]	1,104	680	61.6	650	58.9	30	4.4	424	38.4

[1] Includes races not shown separately. [2] Due to statistical adjustments, data not strictly comparable to data in previous years.
[3] Persons of Hispanic origin may be of any race. Includes persons of other Hispanic origin, not shown separately.
Source: U.S. Bureau of Labor Statistics, Bulletin 2307, and *Employment and Earnings*, monthly, January issues.

Top 200 Rankings of Full-time Occupations: By Average Hourly Earnings
2000

Rank	Occupation	Mean ($)	Rank	Occupation	Mean ($)
1	Airplane pilots and navigators	95.80	33	Electrical and electronic engineers	33.94
2	Physicians	61.19	34	Financial managers	33.87
3	Economics teachers	54.47	35	Sales engineers	33.59
4	Physics teachers	52.95	36	Engineers, n.e.c.	33.51
5	Medical science teachers	51.20	37	Aerospace engineers	33.34
6	Law teachers	51.15	38	Nuclear engineers	33.24
7	Natural science teachers	44.37	39	Actuaries	33.00
8	Engineering teachers	42.29	40	Administrators, education and related fields	32.71
9	Physical education teachers	39.87	41	Managers and administrators, n.e.c.	32.64
10	Sociology teachers	39.74	42	Physicians' assistants	32.38
11	Education teachers	39.33	43	Chemists, except biochemists	31.23
12	Theology teachers	39.14	44	Art, drama, and music teachers	31.16
13	History teachers	39.07	45	Pharmacists	31.10
14	Lawyers	38.76	46	Surveyors and mapping scientists	31.05
15	Mathematical scientists	38.56	47	Social work teachers	30.83
16	Optometrists	38.53	48	Computer science teachers	30.73
17	Business, commerce, and marketing teachers	38.34	49	Teachers, special education	30.16
18	Judges	37.94	50	Managers, medicine and health	30.13
19	English teachers	37.85	51	Public transportation attendants	30.13
20	Mathematical science teachers	37.82	52	Securities and financial services sales occupations	30.11
21	Social science teachers	37.63	53	Personnel and labor relations managers	29.95
22	Chemistry teachers	37.52	54	Geologists and geodesists	29.85
23	Biological science teachers	37.46	55	Computer systems analysts and scientists	29.36
24	Earth, environmental, and marine science teachers	37.39	56	Secondary school teachers	29.16
25	Managers, marketing, advertising, and public relations	37.24	57	Economists	29.07
26	Petroleum engineers	36.75	58	Longshore equipment operators	28.91
27	Physicists and astronomers	36.66	59	Elementary school teachers	28.86
28	Chemical engineers	36.39	60	Metallurgical and materials engineers	28.78
29	Political science teachers	36.17	61	Physical scientists	28.56
30	Agriculture and forestry teachers	35.55	62	Musicians and composers	28.48
31	Health specialties teachers	35.22	63	Professional occupations	28.18
32	Psychology teachers	35.19	64	Operations and systems researchers and analysts	28.14

Rank	Occupation	Mean ($)
65	Athletes	28.13
66	Administrators and officials, public administration	27.80
67	Trade and industrial teachers	27.64
68	Actors and directors	27.49
69	Civil engineers	27.35
70	Managers, service organizations, n.e.c.	27.19
71	Dental hygienists	27.09
72	Psychologists	27.03
73	Elevator installers and repairers	26.88
74	Speech therapists	26.71
75	Industrial engineers	26.49
76	Teachers, n.e.c.	26.45
77	Mechanical engineers	26.20
78	Supervisors, police and detectives	26.20
79	Helpers, surveyors	25.56
80	Supervisors, plumbers, pipefitters, and steamfitters	25.35
81	Management analysts	25.33
82	Supervisors, electricians and power transmission installers	25.09
83	Medical scientists	25.03
84	Vocational and educational counselors	24.93
85	Purchasing agents and buyers	24.85
86	Editors and reporters	24.81
87	Atmospheric and space scientists	24.59
88	Management-related occupations	24.37
89	Foreign language teachers	24.22
90	Sales representatives, mining, manufacturing, and wholesale	24.22
91	Funeral directors	24.03
92	Urban planners	23.93
93	Other financial officers	23.92
94	Supervisors, carpenters and related workers	23.85
95	Librarians	23.76
96	Chief executives and general administrators, public administration	23.72
97	Supervisors, extractive occupations	23.65
98	Public relations specialists	23.60
99	Tile setters, hard and soft	23.55
100	Underwriters	23.45
101	Locomotive operating occupations	23.44
102	Biological and life scientists	23.36
103	Architects	23.22
104	Computer programmers	23.19
105	Supervisors, computer equipment operators	23.18
106	Power plant operators	23.09
107	Electrical power installers and repairers	23.06
108	Physical therapists	22.85
109	Real estate sales occupations	22.84
110	Occupational therapists	22.79
111	Supervisors, firefighters and fire prevention occupations	22.34
112	Forestry and conservation scientists	22.29
113	Painters, sculptors, craft artists, and artist printmakers	22.07
114	Buyers, wholesale and retail trade, except farm products	21.91
115	Insurance sales occupations	21.80
116	Personnel, training, and labor relations specialists	21.75
117	Sheetmetal duct installers	21.74
118	Advertising and related sales occupations	21.73
119	Registered nurses	21.69
120	Mining occupations	21.61
121	Agricultural and food scientists	21.53
122	Accountants and auditors	21.51
123	Archivists and curators	21.51
124	Stevedores	21.43
125	Inspectors and compliance officers, except construction	21.34
126	Telephone line installers and repairers	21.33
127	Social scientists	21.28
128	Camera, watch, and musical instrument repairers	21.28
129	Construction inspectors	21.19
130	Tool and die makers	21.19
131	Police and detectives, public service	21.01
132	Managers, properties and real estate	21.00
133	Brickmasons and stonemasons	20.91
134	Miscellaneous plant and system operators	20.91
135	Industrial engineering technicians	20.89
136	Railroad brake, signal and switch operators	20.81
137	Designers	20.80
138	Aircraft engine mechanics	20.75
139	Plumbers, pipefitters, and steamfitters	20.74
140	Mechanical engineering technicians	20.69
141	Aircraft mechanics, except engine	20.69
142	Sales occupations, other business services	20.67
143	Supervisors, construction trades, n.e.c.	20.43
144	Sales workers, motor vehicles and boats	20.32
145	Drywall installers	20.32
146	Supervisors, brickmasons, stonemasons, and tilesetters	20.26
147	Stationary engineers	20.16
148	Engineering technicians	20.12
149	Supervisors, production occupations	19.97
150	Electricians	19.81
151	Technical writers	19.78
152	Patternmakers and modelmakers, metal	19.77
153	Mechanical controls and valve repairers	19.72
154	Radiological technicians	19.66

Top 200 Rankings of Full-time Occupations: By Average Hourly Earnings (cont.)
2000

Rank	Occupation	Mean ($)
155	Electronic repairers, communications and industrial equipment	19.59
156	Precision inspectors, testers, and related workers	19.53
157	Technical and related occupations	19.42
158	Carpet installers	19.41
159	Drafters	19.18
160	Adjusters and calibrators	19.12
161	Fire inspection and fire prevention occupations	19.05
162	Telephone installers and repairers	18.98
163	Operating engineers	18.94
164	Millwrights	18.81
165	Respiratory therapists	18.69
166	Street and door-to-door sales workers	18.69
167	Supervisors, painters, paperhangers, and plasterers	18.69
168	Supervisors, financial records processing	18.57
169	Electrical and electronic technicians	18.53
170	Hoist and winch operators	18.50
171	Science technicians	18.49
172	Heavy equipment mechanics	18.48
173	Automobile body and related repairers	18.44
174	Supervisors, distribution, scheduling, and adjusting clerks	18.39
175	Purchasing agents and buyers, farm products	18.38
176	Chief communications operators	18.30

Rank	Occupation	Mean ($)
177	Ship captains and mates except fishing boats	18.22
178	Dietitians	18.21
179	Broadcast equipment operators	18.08
180	Supervisors, material moving equipment	18.08
181	Photographers	18.06
182	Chemical technicians	18.02
183	Prekindergarten and kindergarten teachers	17.94
184	Religious workers	17.87
185	Supervisors, agriculture-related workers	17.81
186	Industrial machinery repairers	17.80
187	Supervisors, motor vehicle operators	17.62
188	Locksmiths and safe repairers	17.57
189	Legal assistants	17.56
190	Precision grinders, filers, and tool sharpeners	17.55
191	Therapists	17.54
192	Tool programmers, numerical control	17.54
193	Supervisors, guards	17.54
194	Managers, food servicing and lodging establishments	17.52
195	Precision assemblers, metal	17.48
196	Plumbers, pipefitters and steamfitters apprentices	17.43
197	Carpenters	17.28
198	Insurance adjusters, examiners, and investigators	17.20
199	Clergy	17.17
200	Drillers, oil well	17.16

Notes: Earnings are straight-time hourly wages or salaries paid to employees. They include incentive pay, cost-of-living adjustments, and hazard pay. Excluded are premium pay for overtime, vacations, and holidays; nonproduction bonuses; and tips. The mean is computed by totaling the pay of all workers and dividing by the number of workers, weighted by hours. Survey covers all 50 states. Collection was conducted between June 1999 and April 2001. The average reference period was July 2000.

n.e.c. = not elsewhere classified.

Source: U.S. Department of Labor, *Monthly Labor Review*, March 2002.

Employment Projections by Industry: 1998 to 2008
(in thousands)

	1998	2008	Change 1998–2000	Average Annual Rate of Change 1998–2008
MOST RAPID GROWTH				
Computer and data processing services	1,599	3,472	1,872	8.1
Health services, n.e.c.	1,209	2,018	809	5.3
Residential care	747	1,171	424	4.6
Management and public relations	1,034	1,500	466	3.8
Personnel supply services	3,230	4,623	1,393	3.7
Miscellaneous equipment rental and leasing	258	369	111	3.6
Museums, botanical and zoological gardens	93	131	39	3.6
Research and testing services	614	861	247	3.4
Miscellaneous transportation services	236	329	94	3.4
Security and commodity brokers	645	900	255	3.4
Miscellaneous business services	2,278	3,172	893	3.4
Offices of health practitioners	2,949	4,098	1,150	3.3

Employment Projections by Industry: 1998 to 2008 (cont.)
(in thousands)

	1998	2008	Change 1998–2000	Average Annual Rate of Change 1998–2008
Automobile parking, repair, and services	944	1,300	356	3.2
Amusement and recreation services, n.e.c.	1,217	1,653	436	3.1
Water and sanitation	196	263	67	3.0
Local and interurban passenger transit	468	622	154	2.9
Individual and miscellaneous social services	923	1,223	300	2.9
Child day care services	605	800	196	2.8
Job training and related services	369	484	114	2.7
Landscape and horticultural services	460	603	142	2.7
Veterinary services	196	255	59	2.7
Producers, orchestras, and entertainers	176	225	49	2.5
Cable and pay television services	181	230	49	2.4
Commercial sports	127	160	34	2.4
Engineering and architectural services	905	1,140	235	2.3
Nondepository; holding and investment offices	906	1,141	235	2.3
Miscellaneous transportation equipment	76	96	20	2.3
Nursing and personal care facilities	1,762	2,213	451	2.3
Automotive rentals, without drivers	200	250	50	2.3
Services to buildings	950	1,187	237	2.3
MOST RAPID DECLINE				
Crude petroleum, natural gas, and gas liquids	143	77	-66	-6.0
Apparel	547	350	-197	-4.4
Coal mining	92	59	-32	-4.2
Footwear except rubber and plastic	38	25	-13	-4.1
Federal electric utilities	30	20	-10	-4.1
Metal cans and shipping containers	37	25	-12	-3.8
Watches, clocks and parts	7	5	-2	-3.7
Tobacco products	41	30	-11	-3.1
Metal mining	50	37	-13	-3.0
Luggage, handbags, and leather products, n.e.c.	45	34	-11	-2.7
Blast furnaces and basic steel products	232	177	-55	-2.7
Petroleum refining	96	75	-21	-2.5
Weaving, finishing, yarn and thread mills	320	251	-69	-2.4
Private households	962	759	-203	-2.3
Forestry, fishing, hunting, and trapping	48	38	-10	-2.3
Hydraulic cement	17	14	-4	-2.3
Electrical industrial apparatus	153	122	-31	-2.3
Railroad transportation	231	185	-46	-2.2
Knitting mills	159	128	-32	-2.2
Primary nonferrous smelting and refining	39	32	-8	-2.1
Service industries for the printing trade	50	41	-9	-2.0
Engines and turbines	84	69	-15	-1.9
Household appliances	117	96	-20	-1.9
Household audio and video equipment	82	67	-14	-1.9
Combined utilities	159	131	-27	-1.9
Jewelry, silverware, and plated ware	50	42	-8	-1.8
Ordnance and ammunition	41	34	-7	-1.8
Tires and inner tubes	79	66	-13	-1.8
Electric distribution equipment	82	70	-13	-1.7
Photographic equipment and supplies	81	69	-12	-1.6

Notes: X = Not applicable. *n.e.c.* = not elsewhere classified. Employment categories based on the 1987 Standard Industrial Classification.
Source: U.S. Bureau of Labor Statistics, *Monthly Labor Review*, November 1999.

Legal Documents

Americans with Disabilities Act

The Americans with Disabilities Act (ADA) was passed by the U.S. Congress in 1990 to open the doors of employment to millions of qualified people with disabilities. The act created new federal rights to protect people with disabilities from discrimination in employment (Title I), public services (Title II), public accommodations and services operated by private entities (Title III), and telecommunications (Title IV).

Congressional studies in the 1980s had shown that 66 percent of working-age people with disabilities in the United States were not employed. The cost to the nation was estimated at $300 billion per year, including welfare payments and lost taxes and productivity. Congress sought to ensure that people with disabilities could participate in society as members of the workforce. An excerpt of the act follows. For a complete transcript including amendments to the act, see the U.S. Department of Justice Web site at: www.usdoj.gov/crt/ada/pubs/ada.txt

Americans with Disabilities Act of 1990

S. 933

One Hundred First Congress of the United States of America

AT THE SECOND SESSION

Begun and held at the City of Washington on Tuesday, the twenty-third day of January, one thousand nine hundred and ninety

An Act

To establish a clear and comprehensive prohibition of discrimination on the basis of disability.

Be it enacted by the Senate and House of Representatives of the United States of America in Congress assembled

SEC. 2. FINDINGS AND PURPOSES.

(a) Findings.—The Congress finds that—

(1) some 43,000,000 Americans have one or more physical or mental disabilities, and this number is increasing as the population as a whole is growing older;

(2) historically, society has tended to isolate and segregate individuals with disabilities, and, despite some improvements, such forms of discrimination against individuals with disabilities continue to be a serious and pervasive social problem;

(3) discrimination against individuals with disabilities persists in such critical areas as employment, housing, public accommodations, education, transportation, communication,

recreation, institutionalization, health services, voting, and access to public services;

(4) unlike individuals who have experienced discrimination on the basis of race, color, sex, national origin, religion, or age, individuals who have experienced discrimination on the basis of disability have often had no legal recourse to redress such discrimination;

(5) individuals with disabilities continually encounter various forms of discrimination, including outright intentional exclusion, the discriminatory effects of architectural, transportation, and communication barriers, overprotective rules and policies, failure to make modifications to existing facilities and practices, exclusionary qualification standards and criteria, segregation, and relegation to lesser services, programs, activities, benefits, jobs, or other opportunities;

(6) census data, national polls, and other studies have documented that people with disabilities, as a group, occupy an inferior status in our society, and are severely disadvantaged socially, vocationally, economically, and educationally;

(7) individuals with disabilities are a discrete and insular minority who have been faced with restrictions and limitations, subjected to a history of purposeful unequal treatment, and relegated to a position of political powerlessness in our society, based on characteristics that are beyond the control of such individuals and resulting from stereotypic assumptions not truly indicative of the individual ability of such individuals to participate in, and contribute to, society;

(8) the Nation's proper goals regarding individuals with disabilities are to assure equality of opportunity, full participation, independent living, and economic self-sufficiency for such individuals; and

(9) the continuing existence of unfair and unnecessary discrimination and prejudice denies people with disabilities the opportunity to compete on an equal basis and to pursue those opportunities for which our free society is justifiably famous, and costs the United States billions of dollars in unnecessary expenses resulting from dependency and nonproductivity.

(b) Purpose.—It is the purpose of this Act—

(1) to provide a clear and comprehensive national mandate for the elimination of discrimination against individuals with disabilities;

(2) to provide clear, strong, consistent, enforceable standards addressing discrimination against individuals with disabilities;

(3) to ensure that the Federal Government plays a central role in enforcing the standards established in this Act on behalf of individuals with disabilities; and

(4) to invoke the sweep of congressional authority, including the power to enforce the fourteenth amendment and to regulate commerce, in order to address the major areas of discrimination faced day-to-day by people with disabilities. . . .

SEC. 102. DISCRIMINATION. [from Title I]

(a) General Rule.—No covered entity shall discriminate against a qualified individual with a disability because of the disability of such individual in regard to job application procedures, the hiring, advancement, or discharge of employees, employee compensation, job training, and other terms, conditions, and privileges of employment.

(b) Construction.—As used in subsection (a), the term "discriminate" includes—

(1) limiting, segregating, or classifying a job applicant or employee in a way that adversely affects the opportunities or status of such applicant or employee because of the disability of such applicant or employee;

(2) participating in a contractual or other arrangement or relationship that has the effect of subjecting a covered entity's qualified applicant or employee with a disability to the discrimination prohibited by this title (such relationship includes a relationship with an employment or referral agency, labor union, an organization providing fringe benefits to an employee of the covered entity, or an organization providing training and apprenticeship programs);

(3) utilizing standards, criteria, or methods of administration—

(A) that have the effect of discrimination on the basis of disability; or

(B) that perpetuate the discrimination of others who are subject to common administrative control;

(4) excluding or otherwise denying equal jobs or benefits to a qualified individual because of the known disability of an individual with whom the qualified individual is known to have a relationship or association;

(5)(A) not making reasonable accommodations to the known physical or mental limitations of an otherwise qualified individual with a disability who is an applicant or employee, unless such covered entity can demonstrate that the accommodation would impose an undue hardship on the operation of the business of such covered entity; or

(B) denying employment opportunities to a job applicant or employee who is an otherwise qualified individual with a disability, if such denial is based on the need of such covered entity to make reasonable accommodation to the physical or mental impairments of the employee or applicant;

(6) using qualification standards, employment tests or other selection criteria that screen out or tend to screen out an individual with a disability or a class of individuals with disabilities unless the standard, test or other selection criteria, as used

by the covered entity, is shown to be job-related for the position in question and is consistent with business necessity; and

(7) failing to select and administer tests concerning employment in the most effective manner to ensure that, when such test is administered to a job applicant or employee who has a disability that impairs sensory, manual, or speaking skills, such test results accurately reflect the skills, aptitude, or whatever other factor of such applicant or employee that such test purports to measure, rather than reflecting the impaired sensory, manual, or speaking skills of such employee or applicant (except where such skills are the factors that the test purports to measure).

(c) Medical Examinations and Inquiries.—

(1) In general.—The prohibition against discrimination as referred to in subsection (a) shall include medical examinations and inquiries.

(2) Preemployment.—

(A) Prohibited examination or inquiry.—Except as provided in paragraph (3), a covered entity shall not conduct a medical examination or make inquiries of a job applicant as to whether such applicant is an individual with a disability or as to the nature or severity of such disability.

(B) Acceptable inquiry.—A covered entity may make preemployment inquiries into the ability of an applicant to perform job-related functions.

(3) Employment entrance examination.—A covered entity may require a medical examination after an offer of employment has been made to a job applicant and prior to the commencement of the employment duties of such applicant, and may condition an offer of employment on the results of such examination, if—

(A) all entering employees are subjected to such an examination regardless of disability;

(B) information obtained regarding the medical condition or history of the applicant is collected and maintained on separate forms and in separate medical files and is treated as a confidential medical record, except that—

(i) supervisors and managers may be informed regarding necessary restrictions on the work or duties of the employee and necessary accommodations;

(ii) first aid and safety personnel may be informed, when appropriate, if the disability might require emergency treatment; and

(iii) government officials investigating compliance with this Act shall be provided relevant information on request; and

(C) the results of such examination are used only in accordance with this title.

(4) Examination and inquiry.—

(A) Prohibited examinations and inquiries.—A covered entity shall not require a medical examination and shall not make inquiries of an employee as to whether such employee is an individual with a disability or as to the nature or severity of the disability, unless such examination or inquiry

is shown to be job-related and consistent with business necessity.

(B) Acceptable examinations and inquiries.—A covered entity may conduct voluntary medical examinations, including voluntary medical histories, which are part of an employee health program available to employees at that work site. A covered entity may make inquiries into the ability of an employee to perform job-related functions.

(C) Requirement.—Information obtained under subparagraph (B) regarding the medical condition or history of any employee are subject to the requirements of subparagraphs (B) and (C) of paragraph (3).

SEC. 103. DEFENSES.

(a) In General.—It may be a defense to a charge of discrimination under this Act that an alleged application of qualification standards, tests, or selection criteria that screen out or tend to screen out or otherwise deny a job or benefit to an individual with a disability has been shown to be job-related and consistent with business necessity, and such performance cannot be accomplished by reasonable accommodation, as required under this title.

(b) Qualification Standards.—The term "qualification standards" may include a requirement that an individual shall not pose a direct threat to the health or safety of other individuals in the workplace. . . .

SEC. 302. PROHIBITION OF DISCRIMINATION BY PUBLIC ACCOMMODATIONS. [from Title III]

(a) General Rule.—No individual shall be discriminated against on the basis of disability in the full and equal enjoyment of the goods, services, facilities, privileges, advantages, or accommodations of any place of public accommodation by any person who owns, leases (or leases to), or operates a place of public accommodation.

(b) Construction.—

(1) General prohibition.—

(A) Activities.—

(i) Denial of participation.—It shall be discriminatory to subject an individual or class of individuals on the basis of a disability or disabilities of such individual or class, directly, or through contractual, licensing, or other arrangements, to a denial of the opportunity of the individual or class to participate in or benefit from the goods, services, facilities, privileges, advantages, or accommodations of an entity.

(ii) Participation in unequal benefit.—It shall be discriminatory to afford an individual or class of individuals, on the basis of a disability or disabilities of such individual or class, directly, or through contractual, licensing, or other arrangements with the opportunity to participate in or benefit from a good, service, facility, privilege, advantage, or accommodation that is not equal to that afforded to other individuals.

(iii) Separate benefit.—It shall be discriminatory to provide an individual or class of individuals, on the basis of a disability or disabilities of such individual or class, directly, or through contractual, licensing, or other arrangements with a good, service, facility, privilege, advantage, or accommodation that is different or separate from that provided to other individuals, unless such action is necessary to provide the individual or class of individuals with a good, service, facility, privilege, advantage, or accommodation, or other opportunity that is as effective as that provided to others.

(iv) Individual or class of individuals.—For purposes of clauses (i) through (iii) of this subparagraph, the term "individual or class of individuals" refers to the clients or customers of the covered public accommodation that enters into the contractual, licensing or other arrangement.

(B) Integrated settings.—Goods, services, facilities, privileges, advantages, and accommodations shall be afforded to an individual with a disability in the most integrated setting appropriate to the needs of the individual.

(C) Opportunity to participate.—Notwithstanding the existence of separate or different programs or activities provided in accordance with this section, an individual with a disability shall not be denied the opportunity to participate in such programs or activities that are not separate or different.

(D) Administrative methods.—An individual or entity shall not, directly or through contractual or other arrangements, utilize standards or criteria or methods of administration—

(i) that have the effect of discriminating on the basis of disability; or

(ii) that perpetuate the discrimination of others who are subject to common administrative control.

(E) Association.—It shall be discriminatory to exclude or otherwise deny equal goods, services, facilities, privileges, advantages, accommodations, or other opportunities to an individual or entity because of the known disability of an individual with whom the individual or entity is known to have a relationship or association.

(2) Specific prohibitions.—

(A) Discrimination.—For purposes of subsection (a), discrimination includes—

(i) the imposition or application of eligibility criteria that screen out or tend to screen out an individual with a disability or any class of individuals with disabilities from fully and equally enjoying any goods, services, facilities, privileges, advantages, or accommodations, unless such criteria can be shown to be necessary for the provision of the goods, services, facilities, privileges, advantages, or accommodations being offered;

(ii) a failure to make reasonable modifications in policies, practices, or procedures, when such modifications are necessary to afford such goods, services, facilities,

privileges, advantages, or accommodations to individuals with disabilities, unless the entity can demonstrate that making such modifications would fundamentally alter the nature of such goods, services, facilities, privileges, advantages, or accommodations;

(iii) a failure to take such steps as may be necessary to ensure that no individual with a disability is excluded, denied services, segregated or otherwise treated differently than other individuals because of the absence of auxiliary aids and services, unless the entity can demonstrate that taking such steps would fundamentally alter the nature of the good, service, facility, privilege, advantage, or accommodation being offered or would result in an undue burden;

(iv) a failure to remove architectural barriers, and communication barriers that are structural in nature, in existing facilities, and transportation barriers in existing vehicles and rail passenger cars used by an establishment for transporting individuals (not including barriers that can only be removed through the retrofitting of vehicles or rail passenger cars by the installation of a hydraulic or other lift), where such removal is readily achievable; and

(v) where an entity can demonstrate that the removal of a barrier under clause (iv) is not readily achievable, a failure to make such goods, services, facilities, privileges, advantages, or accommodations available through alternative methods if such methods are readily achievable.

(B) Fixed route system.—

(i) Accessibility.—It shall be considered discrimination for a private entity which operates a fixed route system and which is not subject to section 304 to purchase or lease a vehicle with a seating capacity in excess of 16 passengers (including the driver) for use on such system, for which a solicitation is made after the 30th day following the effective date of this subparagraph, that is not readily accessible to and usable by individuals with disabilities, including individuals who use wheelchairs.

(ii) Equivalent service.—If a private entity which operates a fixed route system and which is not subject to section 304 purchases or leases a vehicle with a seating capacity of 16 passengers or less (including the driver) for use on such system after the effective date of this subparagraph that is not readily accessible to or usable by individuals with disabilities, it shall be considered discrimination for such entity to fail to operate such system so that, when viewed in its entirety, such system ensures a level of service to individuals with disabilities, including individuals who use wheelchairs, equivalent to the level of service provided to individuals without disabilities.

(C) Demand responsive system.—For purposes of subsection (a), discrimination includes—

(i) a failure of a private entity which operates a demand responsive system and which is not subject to section

304 to operate such system so that, when viewed in its entirety, such system ensures a level of service to individuals with disabilities, including individuals who use wheelchairs, equivalent to the level of service provided to individuals without disabilities; and

(ii) the purchase or lease by such entity for use on such system of a vehicle with a seating capacity in excess of 16 passengers (including the driver), for which solicitations are made after the 30th day following the effective date of this subparagraph, that is not readily accessible to and usable by individuals with disabilities (including individuals who use wheelchairs) unless such entity can demonstrate that such system, when viewed in its entirety, provides a level of service to individuals with disabilities equivalent to that provided to individuals without disabilities.

(D) Over-the-road buses.—

(i) Limitation on applicability.—Subparagraphs (B) and (C) do not apply to over-the-road buses.

(ii) Accessibility requirements.—For purposes of subsection (a), discrimination includes (I) the purchase or lease of an over-the-road bus which does not comply with the regulations issued under section 306(a)(2) by a private entity which provides transportation of individuals and which is not primarily engaged in the business of transporting people, and (II) any other failure of such entity to comply with such regulations.

(3) Specific Construction.—Nothing in this title shall require an entity to permit an individual to participate in or benefit from the goods, services, facilities, privileges, advantages and accommodations of such entity where such individual poses a direct threat to the health or safety of others. The term "direct threat" means a significant risk to the health or safety of others that cannot be eliminated by a modification of policies, practices, or procedures or by the provision of auxiliary aids or services. . . .

SEC. 307. EXEMPTIONS FOR PRIVATE CLUBS AND RELIGIOUS ORGANIZATIONS.
The provisions of this title shall not apply to private clubs or establishments exempted from coverage under title II of the Civil Rights Act of 1964 (42 U.S.C. 2000-a(e)) or to religious organizations or entities controlled by religious organizations, including places of worship.

SEC. 308. ENFORCEMENT.
(a) In General.—

(1) Availability of remedies and procedures.—The remedies and procedures set forth in section 204(a) of the Civil Rights Act of 1964 (42 U.S.C. 2000a-3(a)) are the remedies and procedures this title provides to any person who is being subjected to discrimination on the basis of disability in violation of this title or who has reasonable grounds for believing that such person is about to be subjected to discrimination in

violation of section 303. Nothing in this section shall require a person with a disability to engage in a futile gesture if such person has actual notice that a person or organization covered by this title does not intend to comply with its provisions.

(2) Injunctive relief.—In the case of violations of sections 302(b)(2)(A)(iv) and section 303(a), injunctive relief shall include an order to alter facilities to make such facilities readily accessible to and usable by individuals with disabilities to the extent required by this title. Where appropriate, injunctive relief shall also include requiring the provision of an auxiliary aid or service, modification of a policy, or provision of alternative methods, to the extent required by this title.

(b) Enforcement by the Attorney General.—

(1) Denial of rights.—

(A) Duty to investigate.—

(i) In general.—The Attorney General shall investigate alleged violations of this title, and shall undertake periodic reviews of compliance of covered entities under this title.

(ii) Attorney general certification.—On the application of a State or local government, the Attorney General may, in consultation with the Architectural and Transportation Barriers Compliance Board, and after prior notice and a public hearing at which persons, including individuals with disabilities, are provided an opportunity to testify against such certification, certify that a State law or local building code or similar ordinance that establishes accessibility requirements meets or exceeds the minimum requirements of this Act for the accessibility and usability of covered facilities under this title. At any enforcement proceeding under this section, such certification by the Attorney General shall be rebuttable evidence that such State law or local ordinance does meet or exceed the minimum requirements of this Act.

(B) Potential violation.—If the Attorney General has reasonable cause to believe that—

(i) any person or group of persons is engaged in a pattern or practice of discrimination under this title; or

(ii) any person or group of persons has been discriminated against under this title and such discrimination raises an issue of general public importance, the Attorney General may commence a civil action in any appropriate United States district court.

(2) Authority of court.—In a civil action under paragraph (1)(B), the court—

(A) may grant any equitable relief that such court considers to be appropriate, including, to the extent required by this title—

(i) granting temporary, preliminary, or permanent relief;

(ii) providing an auxiliary aid or service, modification of policy, practice, or procedure, or alternative method; and

(iii) making facilities readily accessible to and usable by individuals with disabilities;

(B) may award such other relief as the court considers to be appropriate, including monetary damages to persons aggrieved when requested by the Attorney General; and

(C) may, to vindicate the public interest, assess a civil penalty against the entity in an amount—

(i) not exceeding $50,000 for a first violation; and

(ii) not exceeding $100,000 for any subsequent violation.

(3) Single violation.—For purposes of paragraph (2)(C), in determining whether a first or subsequent violation has occurred, a determination in a single action, by judgment or settlement, that the covered entity has engaged in more than one discriminatory act shall be counted as a single violation.

(4) Punitive damages.—For purposes of subsection (b)(2)(B), the term "monetary damages" and "such other relief" does not include punitive damages.

(5) Judicial consideration.—In a civil action under paragraph (1)(B), the court, when considering what amount of civil penalty, if any, is appropriate, shall give consideration to any good faith effort or attempt to comply with this Act by the entity. In evaluating good faith, the court shall consider, among other factors it deems relevant, whether the entity could have reasonably anticipated the need for an appropriate type of auxiliary aid needed to accommodate the unique needs of a particular individual with a disability.

SEC. 309. EXAMINATIONS AND COURSES

Any person that offers examinations or courses related to applications, licensing, certification, or credentialing for secondary or postsecondary education, professional, or trade purposes shall offer such examinations or courses in a place and manner accessible to persons with disabilities or offer alternative accessible arrangements for such individuals. . . .

The Fair Labor Standards Act

The Fair Labor Standards Act (FLSA) was passed by the U.S. Congress in 1938 to regulate how employers treated their employees in terms of compensation, hours, and the workplace environment. Over the years, various revisions and additions have been made to accommodate the changing workplace. The FLSA remains one of the most powerful laws in the employment sector, and it continues to regulate the flow of commerce by intervening at the production level. The act outlines the workweek, provides requirements for a minimum wage as well as overtime pay, and also includes statutes that regulate child labor. An excerpt of the act follows. For a complete transcript including amendments to the act, plus a brief history of the act, see the U.S. Department of Labor's Web site at: www.dol.gov/esa/whd/flsa/

The Fair Labor Standards Act of 1938, as amended
(29 U.S.C. 201, et seq.)
To provide for the establishment of fair labor standards in employments in and affecting interstate commerce, and for other

purposes. Be it enacted by the Senate and House of Representatives of the United States of America in Congress assembled, That this Act may be cited as the "Fair Labor Standards Act of 1938."

FINDING AND DECLARATION OF POLICY
SEC. 2.

(a) The Congress hereby finds that the existence, in industries engaged in commerce or in the production of goods for commerce, of labor conditions detrimental to the maintenance of the minimum standard of living necessary for health, efficiency, and general well-being of workers (1) causes commerce and the channels and instrumentalities of commerce to be used to spread and perpetuate such labor conditions among the workers of the several States; (2) burdens commerce and the free flow of goods in commerce; (3) constitutes an unfair method of competition in commerce; (4) leads to labor disputes burdening and obstructing commerce and the free flow of goods in commerce; and (5) interferes with the orderly and fair marketing of goods in commerce. The Congress further finds that the employment of persons in domestic service in households affects commerce.
(b) It is hereby declared to be the policy of this Act, through the exercise by Congress of its power to regulate commerce among the several States and with foreign nations, to correct and as rapidly as practicable to eliminate the conditions above referred to in such industries without substantially curtailing employment or earning power. . . .

MINIMUM WAGES
SEC. 6.

(a) Every employer shall pay to each of his employees who in any workweek is engaged in commerce or in the production of goods for commerce, or is employed in an enterprise engaged in commerce or in the production of goods for commerce, wages at the following rates:

(1) except as otherwise provided in this section, not less than $4.25 an hour during the period ending on September 30, 1996, not less than $4.75 an hour during the year beginning on October 1, 1996, and not less than $5.15 an hour beginning September 1, 1997; . . .
(d)(1) No employer having employees subject to any provisions of this section shall discriminate, within any establishment in which such employees are employed, between employees on the basis of sex by paying wages to employees in such establishment at a rate less than the rate at which he pays wages to employees of the opposite sex in such establishment for equal work on jobs the performance of which requires equal skill, effort, and responsibility, and which are performed under similar working conditions, except where such payment is made pursuant to (i) a seniority system; (ii) a merit system; (iii) a system which measures earnings by quantity or quality of production; or (iv) a differential based on any other factor other than sex: *Provided*, That an employer who is paying a wage rate differential in violation of this subsection shall not, in order to comply with the provisions of this subsection, reduce the wage rate of any employee.
(2) No labor organization, or its agents, representing employees of an employer having employees subject to any provisions of this section shall cause or attempt to cause such an employer to discriminate against an employee in violation of paragraph (1) of this subsection.
(3) For purposes of administration and enforcement, any amounts owing to any employee which have been withheld in violation of this subsection shall be deemed to be unpaid minimum wages or unpaid overtime compensation under this Act. . . .

MAXIMUM HOURS
SEC. 7

(a) (1) Except as otherwise provided in this section, no employer shall employ any of his employees who in any workweek is engaged in commerce or in the production of goods for commerce, or is employed in an enterprise engaged in commerce or in the production of goods for commerce, for a workweek longer than forty hours unless such employee receives compensation for his employment in excess of the hours above specified at a rate not less than one and one-half times the regular rate at which he is employed.
(2) No employer shall employ any of his employees who in any workweek is engaged in commerce or in the production of goods for commerce, or is employed in an enterprise engaged in commerce or in the production of goods for commerce, and who in such workweeks is brought within the purview of this subsection by the amendments made to this Act by the Fair Labor Standards Amendments of 1966. . . .

INVESTIGATIONS, INSPECTIONS, RECORDS, AND HOMEWORK REGULATIONS
SEC. 11.

(a) The Secretary of Labor or his designated representatives may investigate and gather data regarding the wages, hours, and other conditions and practices of employment in any industry subject to this Act, and may enter and inspect such places and such records (and make such transcriptions thereof), question such employees, and investigate such facts, conditions, practices, or matters as he may deem necessary or appropriate to determine whether any person has violated any provision of this Act, or which may aid in the enforcement of the provisions of this Act. Except as provided in section 12 and in subsection (b) of this section, the Secretary shall utilize the bureaus and divisions of the Department of Labor for all the investigations and inspections necessary under this section. Except as provided in section 12, the Secretary shall bring all actions under section 17 to restrain violations of this Act.
(b) With the consent and cooperation of State agencies charged with the administration of State labor laws, the Secretary of Labor may, for the purpose of carrying out his functions and duties under this Act, utilize the services of State and local

agencies and their employees and, notwithstanding any other provision of law, may reimburse such State and local agencies and their employees for services rendered for such purposes.

(c) Every employer subject to any provision of this Act or of any order issued under this Act shall make, keep, and preserve such records of the persons employed by him and of the wages, hours, and other conditions and practices of employment maintained by him, and shall preserve such records for such periods of time, and shall make such reports therefrom to the Secretary as he shall prescribe by regulation or order as necessary or appropriate for the enforcement of the provisions of this Act or the regulations or orders thereunder. . . .

(d) The Secretary is authorized to make such regulations and orders regulating, restricting, or prohibiting industrial homework as are necessary or appropriate to prevent the circumvention or evasion of and to safeguard the minimum wage rate prescribed in this Act, and all existing regulations or orders of the Administrator relating to industrial homework are hereby continued in full force and effect.

CHILD LABOR PROVISIONS
SEC. 12.

(a) No producer, manufacturer, or dealer shall ship or deliver for shipment in commerce any goods produced in an establishment situated in the United States in or about which within thirty days prior to the removal of such goods therefrom any oppressive child labor has been employed: *Provided,* That any such shipment or delivery for shipment of such goods by a purchaser who acquired them in good faith in reliance on written assurance from the producer, manufacturer, or dealer that the goods were produced in compliance with the requirements of this section, and who acquired such goods for value without notice of any such violation, shall not be deemed prohibited by this subsection: *And provided further,* That a prosecution and conviction of a defendant for the shipment or delivery for shipment of any goods under the conditions herein prohibited shall be a bar to any further prosecution against the same defendant for shipments or deliveries for shipment of any such goods before the beginning of said prosecution.

(b) The Secretary of Labor, or any of his authorized representatives, shall make all investigations and inspections under section 11(a) with respect to the employment of minors, and, subject to the direction and control of the Attorney General, shall bring all actions under section 17 to enjoin any act or practice which is unlawful by reason of the existence of oppressive child labor, and shall administer all other provisions of this Act relating to oppressive child labor.

(c) No employer shall employ any oppressive child labor in commerce or in the production of goods for commerce or in any enterprise engaged in commerce or in the production of goods for commerce.

(d) In order to carry out the objectives of this section, the Secretary may by regulation require employers to obtain from any employee proof of age. . . .

PROHIBITED ACTS
SEC. 15.

(a) After the expiration of one hundred and twenty days from the date of enactment of this Act, it shall be unlawful for any person—

(1) to transport, offer for transportation, ship, deliver, or sell in commerce, or to ship, deliver, or sell with knowledge that shipment or delivery or sale thereof in commerce is intended, any goods in the production of which any employee was employed in violation of section 6 or section 7, or in violation of any regulation or order of the Secretary of Labor issued under section 14; except that no provision of this Act shall impose any liability upon any common carrier for the transportation in commerce in the regular course of its business of any goods not produced by such common carrier, and no provision of this Act shall excuse any common carrier from its obligation to accept any goods for transportation; and except that any such transportation, offer, shipment, delivery, or sale of such goods by a purchaser who acquired them in good faith in reliance on written assurance from the producer that the goods were produced in compliance with the requirements of the Act, and who acquired such goods for value without notice of any such violation, shall not be deemed unlawful;

(2) to violate any of the provisions of section 6 or section 7, or any of the provisions of any regulation or order of the Secretary issued under section 14;

(3) to discharge or in any other manner discriminate against any employee because such employee has filed any compliant or instituted or caused to be instituted any proceeding under or related to this Act, or has testified or is about to testify in any such proceeding, or has served or is about to serve on an industry committee;

(4) to violate any of the provisions of section 12;

(5) to violate any of the provisions of section 11(c) or any regulation or order made or continued in effect under the provisions of section 11(d), or to make any statement, report, or record filed or kept pursuant to the provisions of such section or of any regulation or order thereunder, knowing such statement, report, or record to be false in a material respect.

PENALTIES
SEC. 16.

(a) Any person who willfully violates any of the provisions of section 15 shall upon conviction thereof be subject to a fine of not more than $10,000, or to imprisonment for not more than six months, or both. No person shall be imprisoned under this subsection except for an offense committed after the conviction of such person for a prior offense under this subsection.

(b) Any employer who violates the provisions of section 6 or section 7 of this Act shall be liable to the employee or employees affected in the amount of their unpaid minimum wages, or their unpaid overtime compensation, as the case may be, and in an additional equal amount as liquidated damages. Any

employer who violates the provisions of section 15(a)(3) of this Act shall be liable for such legal or equitable relief as may be appropriate to effectuate the purposes of section 15(a)(3), including without limitation employment, reinstatement, promotion, and the payment of wages lost and an additional equal amount as liquidated damages. An action to recover the liability prescribed in either of the preceding sentences may be maintained against any employer (including a public agency) in any Federal or State court of competent jurisdiction by any one or more employees for and in behalf of himself or themselves and other employees similarly situated. No employee shall be a party plaintiff to any such action unless he gives his consent in writing to become such a party and such consent is filed in the court in which such action is brought. The court in such action shall, in addition to any judgment awarded to the plaintiff or plaintiffs, allow a reasonable attorney's fee to be paid by the defendant, and costs of the action. . . .

Landrum–Griffin Act (Labor-Management Reporting and Disclosure Act)

In 1959 the U.S. Congress passed the Labor–Management Reporting and Disclosure Act, more commonly known as the Landrum–Griffin Act. The law resulted from a congressional investigation into the practices of several union officials, and was an attempt to make unions more responsive to the needs of their members. This landmark legislation gave the federal government the right to oversee the internal administration of labor unions, created a worker's "Bill of Rights" to promote democratic procedures and reduce union corruption, and placed severe restrictions on the ability of unions to conduct secondary boycotts and organizational picketing. Critics of the act argue that it tilted the playing field toward management and against labor. An excerpt of the act follows. For a complete transcript including amendments to the act, see the United Auto Workers Web site at: www.uaw.org/lmrda.html

The Labor–Management Reporting and Disclosure Act of 1959, As Amended

AN ACT
To provide for the reporting and disclosure of certain financial transactions and administrative practices of labor organizations and employers, to prevent abuses in the administration of trusteeships by labor organizations, to provide standards with respect to the election of officers of labor organizations, and for other purposes.

Be it enacted by the Senate and House of Representatives of the United States of America in Congress assembled, That this Act may be cited as the "Labor–Management Reporting and Disclosure Act of 1959."

Declaration of Findings, Purposes, and Policy
SEC. 2.
   (a) The Congress finds that, in the public interest, it continues to be the responsibility of the Federal Government to protect employees' rights to organize, choose their own representatives, bargain collectively, and otherwise engage in concerted activities for their mutual aid or protection; that the relations between employers and labor organizations and the millions of workers they represent have a substantial impact on the commerce of the Nation; and that in order to accomplish the objective of a free flow of commerce it is essential that labor organizations, employers, and their officials adhere to the highest standards of responsibility and ethical conduct in administering the affairs of their organizations, particularly as they affect labor–management relations.
   (b) The Congress further finds, from recent investigations in the labor and management fields, that there have been a number of instances of breach of trust, corruption, disregard of the rights of individual employees, and other failures to observe high standards of responsibility and ethical conduct which require further and supplementary legislation that will afford necessary protection of the rights and interests of employees and the public generally as they relate to the activities of labor organizations, employers, labor relations consultants, and their officers and representatives.
   (c) The Congress, therefore, further finds and declares that the enactment of this Act is necessary to eliminate or prevent improper practices on the part of labor organizations, employers, labor relations consultants, and their officers and representatives which distort and defeat the policies of the Labor Management Relations Act, 1947, as amended, and the Railway Labor Act, as amended, and have the tendency or necessary effect of burdening or obstructing commerce by (1) impairing the efficiency, safety, or operation of the instrumentalities of commerce; (2) occurring in the current of commerce; (3) materially affecting, restraining, or controlling the flow of raw materials or manufactured or processed goods into or from the channels of commerce, or the prices of such materials or goods in commerce; or (4) causing diminution of employment and wages in such volume as substantially to impair or disrupt the market for goods flowing into or from the channels of commerce. . . .

TITLE I — BILL OF RIGHTS OF MEMBERS OF LABOR ORGANIZATIONS
Bill of Rights
SEC. 101.
   (a)(1) EQUAL RIGHTS.— Every member of a labor organization shall have equal rights and privileges within such organization to nominate candidates, to vote in elections or referendums of the labor organization, to attend membership meetings and to participate in the deliberations and voting upon the business of such meetings, subject to reasonable rules and regulations in such organization's constitution and bylaws.
   (2) FREEDOM OF SPEECH AND ASSEMBLY.— Every member of any labor organization shall have the right to meet and assemble freely with other members; and to express any views, arguments, or opinions; and to express at meetings of

the labor organization his views, upon candidates in an election of the labor organization or upon any business properly before the meeting, subject to the organization's established and reasonable rules pertaining to the conduct of meetings: *Provided,* That nothing herein shall be construed to impair the right of a labor organization to adopt and enforce reasonable rules as to the responsibility of every member toward the organization as an institution and to his refraining from conduct that would interfere with its performance of its legal or contractual obligations.

(3) DUES, INITIATION FEES, AND ASSESSMENTS.— Except in the case of a federation of national or international labor organizations, the rates of dues and initiation fees payable by members of any labor organization in effect on the date of enactment of this Act shall not be increased, and no general or special assessment shall be levied upon such members, except—

    (A) in the case of a local organization,

        (i) by majority vote by secret ballot of the members in good standing voting at a general or special membership meeting, after reasonable notice of the intention to vote upon such question, or

        (ii) by majority vote of the members in good standing voting in a membership referendum conducted by secret ballot; or

    (B) in the case of a labor organization, other than a local labor organization or a federation of national or international labor organizations,

        (i) by majority vote of the delegates voting at a regular convention, or at a special convention of such labor organization held upon not less than thirty days' written notice to the principal office of each local or constituent labor organization entitled to such notice, or

        (ii) by majority vote of the members in good standing of such labor organization voting in a membership referendum conducted by secret ballot, or

        (iii) by majority vote of the members of the executive board or similar governing body of such labor organization, pursuant to express authority contained in the constitution and bylaws of such labor organization: *Provided,* That such action on the part of the executive board or similar governing body shall be effective only until the next regular convention of such labor organization.

(4) PROTECTION OF THE RIGHT TO SUE.— No labor organization shall limit the right of any member thereof to institute an action in any court, or in a proceeding before any administrative agency, irrespective of whether or not the labor organization or its officers are named as defendants or respondents in such action or proceeding, or the right of any member of a labor organization to appear as a witness in any judicial, administrative, or legislative proceeding, or to petition any legislature or to communicate with any legislator: *Provided,* That any such member may be required to exhaust reasonable hearing procedures (but not to exceed a four-month lapse of time) within such organization, before instituting legal or administrative proceedings against such organizations or any officer thereof: *And provided further,* That no interested employer or employer association shall directly or indirectly finance, encourage, or participate in, except as a party, any such action, proceeding, appearance, or petition.

(5) SAFEGUARDS AGAINST IMPROPER DISCIPLINARY ACTION.— No member of any labor organization may be fined, suspended, expelled, or otherwise disciplined except for nonpayment of dues by such organization or by any officer thereof unless such member has been:

    (A) served with written specific charges;

    (B) given a reasonable time to prepare his defense;

    (C) afforded a full and fair hearing.

(b) Any provision of the constitution and bylaws of any labor organization which is inconsistent with the provisions of this section shall be of no force or effect.

Civil Enforcement
SEC. 102.

Any person whose rights secured by the provisions of this title have been infringed by any violation of this title may bring a civil action in a district court of the United States for such relief (including injunctions) as may be appropriate. Any such action against a labor organization shall be brought in the district court of the United States for the district where the alleged violation occurred, or where the principal office of such labor organization is located. . . .

TITLE II — REPORTING BY LABOR ORGANIZANONS, OFFICERS AND EMPLOYEES OF LABOR ORGANIZATIONS, AND EMPLOYERS
Report of Labor Organizations
SEC. 201.

(a) Every labor organization shall adopt a constitution and bylaws and shall file a copy thereof with the Secretary, together with a report, signed by its president and secretary or corresponding principal officers, containing the following information—

    (1) the name of the labor organization, its mailing address, and any other address at which it maintains its principal office or at which it keeps the records referred to in this title;

    (2) the name and title of each of its officers;

    (3) the initiation fee or fees required from a new or transferred member and fees for work permits required by the reporting labor organization;

    (4) the regular dues or fees or other periodic payments required to remain a member of the reporting labor organization; and

    (5) detailed statements, or references to specific provisions of documents filed under this subsection which contain such statements, showing the provisions made and procedures followed with respect to each of the following:

(A) qualifications for or restrictions on membership,

(B) levying of assessments,

(C) participation in insurance or other benefit plans,

(D) authorization for disbursement of funds of the labor organization,

(E) audit of financial transactions of the labor organization,

(F) the calling of regular and special meetings,

(G) the selection of officers and stewards and of any representatives to other bodies composed of labor organizations' representatives, with a specific statement of the manner in which each officer was elected, appointed, or otherwise selected,

(H) discipline or removal of officers or agents for breaches of their trust,

(I) imposition of fines, suspensions, and expulsions of members, including the grounds for such action and any provision made for notice, hearing, judgment on the evidence, and appeal procedures,

(J) authorization for bargaining demands,

(K) ratification of contract terms,

(L) authorization for strikes, and

(M) issuance of work permits. Any change in the information required by this subsection shall be reported to the Secretary at the time the reporting labor organization files with the Secretary the annual financial report required by subsection (b).

(b) Every labor organization shall file annually with the Secretary a financial report signed by its president and treasurer or corresponding principal officers containing the following information in such detail as may be necessary accurately to disclose its financial condition and operations for its preceding fiscal year-

(1) assets and liabilities at the beginning and end of the fiscal year;

(2) receipts of any kind and the sources thereof,

(3) salary, allowances, and other direct or indirect disbursements (including reimbursed expenses) to each officer and also to each employee who, during such fiscal year, received more than $10,000 in the aggregate from such labor organization and any other labor organization affiliated with it or with which it is affiliated, or which is affiliated with the same national or international labor organization;

(4) direct and indirect loans made to any officer, employee, or member, which aggregated more than $250 during the fiscal year, together with a statement of the purpose, security, if any, and arrangements for repayment;

(5) direct and indirect loans to any business enterprise, together with a statement of the purpose, security, if any, and arrangements for repayment; and

(6) other disbursements made by it including the purposes thereof, all in such categories as the Secretary may prescribe.

(c) Every labor organization required to submit a report under this title shall make available the information required to be contained in such report to all of its members, and every such labor organization and its officers shall be under a duty enforceable at the suit of any member of such organization in any State court of competent jurisdiction or in the district court of the United States for the district in which such labor organization maintains its principal office, to permit such member for just cause to examine any books, records, and accounts necessary to verify such report. The court in such action may, in its discretion, in addition to any judgment awarded to the plaintiff or plaintiffs, allow a reasonable attorney's fee to be paid by the defendant, and costs of the action. . . .

Prohibition Against Certain Persons Holding Office
SEC. 504.

(a) No person who is or has been a member of the Communist Party or who has been convicted of, or served any part of a prison term resulting from his conviction of, robbery, bribery, extortion, embezzlement, grand larceny, burglary, arson, violation of narcotics laws, murder, rape, assault with intent to kill, assault which inflicts grievous bodily injury, or a violation of title II or III of this Act, any felony involving abuse or misuse of such person's position or employment in a labor organization or employee benefit plan to seek or obtain an illegal gain at the expense of the members of the labor organization or the beneficiaries of the employee benefit plan, or conspiracy to commit any such crimes or attempt to commit any such crimes, or a crime in which any of the foregoing crimes is an element, shall serve or be permitted to serve—

(1) as a consultant or adviser to any labor organization,

(2) as an officer, director, trustee, member of any executive board or similar governing body, business agent, manager, organizer, employee, or representative in any capacity of any labor organization,

(3) as a labor relations consultant or adviser to a person engaged in an industry or activity affecting commerce, or as an officer, director, agent, or employee of any group or association of employers dealing with any labor organization, or in a position having specific collective bargaining authority or direct responsibility in the area of labor–management relations in any corporation or association engaged in an industry or activity affecting commerce, or

(4) in a position which entitles its occupant to a share of the proceeds of, or as an officer or executive or administrative employee of, any entity whose activities are in whole or substantial part devoted to providing goods or services to any labor organization, or

(5) in any capacity, other than in his capacity as a member of such labor organization, that involves decisionmaking authority concerning, or decisionmaking authority over, or custody of, or control of the moneys, funds, assets, or property of any labor organization, during or for the period of thirteen years after such conviction or after the end of such imprisonment, whichever is later, unless the sentencing court on the motion of the person convicted sets a lesser period of at least three years after such conviction or after the end of such imprisonment, whichever is later, or unless prior to the end of such period, in the case of a person so convicted or imprisoned,

(A) his citizenship rights, having been revoked as a result of such conviction, have been fully restored, or (B) if the offense is a Federal offense, the sentencing judge or, if the offense is a State or local offense, the United States district court for the district in which the offense was committed, pursuant to sentencing guidelines and policy statements under section 994(a) of title 28, United States Code, determines that such person's service in any capacity referred to in clauses (1) through (5) would not be contrary to the purposes of this Act. Prior to making any such determination the court shall hold a hearing and shall give notice of such proceeding by certified mail to the Secretary of Labor and to State, county, and Federal prosecuting officials in the jurisdiction or jurisdictions in which such person was convicted. The court's determination in any such proceeding shall be final. No person shall knowingly hire, retain, employ, or otherwise place any other person to serve in any capacity in violation of this subsection.

(b) Any person who willfully violates this section shall be fined not more than $10,000 or imprisoned for not more than five years, or both.

(c) For the purpose of this section—

(1) A person shall be deemed to have been "convicted" and under the disability of "conviction" from the date of the judgment of the trial court, regardless of whether that judgment remains under appeal.

(2) A period of parole shall not be considered as part of a period of imprisonment.

(d) Whenever any person—

(1) by operation of this section, has been barred from office or other position in a labor organization as a result of a conviction, and

(2) has filed an appeal of that conviction, any salary which would be otherwise due such person by virtue of such office or position, shall be placed in escrow by the individual employer or organization responsible for payment of such salary. Payment of such salary into escrow shall continue for the duration of the appeal or for the period of time during which such salary would be otherwise due, whichever period is shorter. Upon the final reversal of such person's conviction on appeal, the amounts in escrow shall be paid to such person. Upon the final sustaining of such person's conviction on appeal, the amounts in escrow shall be returned to the individual employer or organization responsible for payments of those amounts. Upon final reversal of such person's conviction, such person shall no longer be barred by this statute from assuming any position from which such person was previously barred. . . .

TITLE VI — MISCELLANEOUS PROVISIONS
Investigations
SEC. 601.

(a) The Secretary shall have power when he believes it necessary in order to determine whether any person has violated or is about to violate any provision of this Act (except title I or amendments made by this Act to other statutes) to make an investigation and in connection therewith he may enter such places and inspect such records and accounts and question such persons as he may deem necessary to enable him to determine the facts relative thereto. The Secretary may report to interested persons or officials concerning the facts required to be shown in any report required by this Act and concerning the reasons for failure or refusal to file such a report or any other matter which he deems to be appropriate as a result of such an investigation.

(b) For the purpose of any investigation provided for in this Act, the provisions of sections 9 and 10 (relating to the attendance of witnesses and the production of books, papers, and documents) of the Federal Trade Commission Act of September 16, 1914, as amended (15 U.S.C. 49, 50), are hereby made applicable to the jurisdiction, powers, and duties of the Secretary or any officers designated by him.

Extortionate Picketing
SEC. 602.

(a) It shall be unlawful to carry on picketing on or about the premises of any employer for the purpose of, or as part of any conspiracy or in furtherance of any plan or purpose for, the personal profit or enrichment of any individual (except a bona fide increase in wages or other employee benefits) by taking or obtaining any money or other thing of value from such employer against his will or with his consent.

(b) Any person who willfully violates this section shall be fined not more than $10,000 or imprisoned not more than twenty years, or both.

Retention of Rights Under Other Federal and State Laws
SEC. 603.

(a) Except as explicitly provided to the contrary, nothing in this Act shall reduce or limit the responsibilities of any labor organization or any officer, agent, shop steward, or other representative of a labor organization, or of any trust in which a labor organization is interested, under any other Federal law or under the laws of any State, and, except as explicitly provided to the contrary, nothing in this Act shall take away any right or bar any remedy to which members of a labor organization are entitled under such other Federal law or law of any State.

(b) Nothing contained in titles I, II, III, IV, V, or VI of this Act shall be construed to supersede or impair or otherwise affect the provisions of the Railway Labor Act, as amended, or any of the obligations, rights, benefits, privileges, or immunities of any carrier, employee, organization, representative, or person subject thereto; nor shall anything contained in said titles (except section 505) of this Act be construed to confer any rights, privileges, immunities, or defenses upon employers, or to impair or otherwise affect the rights of any person under the National Labor Relations Act, as amended.

Effect on State Laws
SEC. 604. Nothing in this Act shall be construed to impair or diminish the authority of any State to enact and enforce general

criminal laws with respect to robbery, bribery, extortion, embezzlement, grand larceny, burglary, arson, violation of narcotics laws, murder, rape, assault with intent to kill, or assault which inflicts grievous bodily injury, or conspiracy to commit any of such crimes.

Service of Process
SEC. 605.

For the purposes of this Act, service of summons, subpena, or other legal process of a court of the United States upon an officer or agent of a labor organization in his capacity as such shall constitute service upon the labor organization.

Administrative Procedure Act
SEC. 606.

The provisions of the Administrative Procedure Act shall be applicable to the issuance, amendment, or rescission of any rules or regulations or any adjudication, authorized or required pursuant to the provisions of this Act.

Other Agencies and Departments
SEC. 607.

In order to avoid unnecessary expense and duplication of functions among Government agencies, the Secretary may make such arrangements or agreements for cooperation or mutual assistance in the performance of his functions under this Act and the functions of any such agency as he may find to be practicable and consistent with law. The Secretary may utilize the facilities or services of any department, agency, or establishment of the United States or of any State or political subdivision of a State, including the services of any of its employees, with the lawful consent of such department, agency, or establishment; and each department, agency, or establishment of the United States is authorized and directed to cooperate with the Secretary and, to the extent permitted by law, to provide such information and facilities as he may request for his assistance in the performance of his functions under this Act. The Attorney General or his representative shall receive from the Secretary for appropriate action such evidence developed in the performance of his functions under this Act as may be found to warrant consideration for criminal prosecution under the provisions of this Act or other Federal law.

Criminal Contempt
SEC. 608.

No person shall be punished for any criminal contempt allegedly committed outside the immediate presence of the court in connection with any civil action prosecuted by the Secretary or any other person in any court of the United States under the provisions of this Act unless the facts constituting such criminal contempt are established by the verdict of the jury in a proceeding in the district court of the United States, which jury shall be chosen and empaneled in the manner prescribed by the law governing trial juries in criminal prosecutions in the district courts of the United States.

Prohibition on Certain Discipline by Labor Organization
SEC. 609.

It shall be unlawful for any labor organization, or any officer, agent, shop steward, or other representative of a labor organization, or any employee thereof to fine, suspend, expel, or otherwise discipline any of its members for exercising any right to which he is entitled under the provisions of this Act. The provisions of section 102 shall be applicable in the enforcement of this section.

Deprivation of Rights Under Act by Violence
SEC. 610.

It shall be unlawful for any person through the use of force or violence, or threat of the use of force or violence, to restrain, coerce, or intimidate, or attempt to restrain, coerce, or intimidate any member of a labor organization for the purpose of interfering with or preventing the exercise of any right to which he is entitled under the provisions of this Act. Any person who willfully violates this section shall be fined not more than $1,000 or imprisoned for not more than one year, or both.

Separability Provisions
SEC. 611.

If any provision of this Act, or the application of such provision to any person or circumstances, shall be held invalid, the remainder of this Act or the application of such provision to persons or circumstances other than those as to which it is held invalid, shall not be affected thereby. . . .

North American Free Trade Agreement (NAFTA)

NAFTA is the trade pact signed in 1992 to gradually eliminate most tariffs and other trade barriers on products and services passing between the United States, Canada, and Mexico . The pact effectively creates a free-trade bloc among the three largest countries of North America. An excerpt of the agreement follows. For a complete transcript of the agreement, see the NAFTA Secretariat at www.nafta-sec-alena.org

North American Free Trade Agreement

Preamble

The Government of Canada, the Government of the United Mexican States and the Government of the United States of America, resolved to:

- STRENGTHEN the special bonds of friendship and cooperation among their nations;
- CONTRIBUTE to the harmonious development and expansion of world trade and provide a catalyst to broader international cooperation;
- CREATE an expanded and secure market for the goods and services produced in their territories;
- REDUCE distortions to trade;
- ESTABLISH clear and mutually advantageous rules governing their trade;

- ENSURE a predictable commercial framework for business planning and investment;
- BUILD on their respective rights and obligations under the General Agreement on Tariffs and Trade and other multilateral and bilateral instruments of cooperation;
- ENHANCE the competitiveness of their firms in global markets;
- FOSTER creativity and innovation, and promote trade in goods and services that are the subject of intellectual property rights;
- CREATE new employment opportunities and improve working conditions and living standards in their respective territories;
- UNDERTAKE each of the preceding in a manner consistent with environmental protection and conservation;
- PRESERVE their flexibility to safeguard the public welfare;
- PROMOTE sustainable development;
- STRENGTHEN the development and enforcement of environmental laws and regulations; and
- PROTECT, enhance and enforce basic workers' rights;

HAVE AGREED as follows:

Part One: General Part

Chapter One: Objectives

Article 101: Establishment of the Free Trade Area
The Parties to this Agreement, consistent with Article XXIV of the General Agreement on Tariffs and Trade, hereby establish a free trade area.

Article 102: Objectives
1. The objectives of this Agreement, as elaborated more specifically through its principles and rules, including national treatment, most-favored-nation treatment and transparency, are to:
   a. eliminate barriers to trade in, and facilitate the cross-border movement of, goods and services between the territories of the Parties;
   b. promote conditions of fair competition in the free trade area;
   c. increase substantially investment opportunities in the territories of the Parties;
   d. provide adequate and effective protection and enforcement of intellectual property rights in each Party's territory;
   e. create effective procedures for the implementation and application of this Agreement, for its joint administration and for the resolution of disputes; and
   f. establish a framework for further trilateral, regional and multilateral cooperation to expand and enhance the benefits of this Agreement.
2. The Parties shall interpret and apply the provisions of this Agreement in the light of its objectives set out in paragraph 1 and in accordance with applicable rules of international law. . . .

Part Two: Trade in Goods

Chapter Three: National Treatment and Market Access for Goods

Article 301: National Treatment
1. Each Party shall accord national treatment to the goods of another Party in accordance with Article III of the General Agreement on Tariffs and Trade (GATT), including its interpretative notes, and to this end Article III of the GATT and its interpretative notes, or any equivalent provision of a successor agreement to which all Parties are party, are incorporated into and made part of this Agreement.
2. The provisions of paragraph 1 regarding national treatment shall mean, with respect to a state or province, treatment no less favorable than the most favorable treatment accorded by such state or province to any like, directly competitive or substitutable goods, as the case may be, of the Party of which it forms a part. . . .

Article 302: Tariff Elimination
1. Except as otherwise provided in this Agreement, no Party may increase any existing customs duty, or adopt any customs duty, on an originating good.
2. Except as otherwise provided in this Agreement, each Party shall progressively eliminate its customs duties on originating goods in accordance with its Schedule to Annex 302.2.
3. On the request of any Party, the Parties shall consult to consider accelerating the elimination of customs duties set out in their Schedules. An agreement between two or more Parties to accelerate the elimination of a customs duty on a good shall supersede any duty rate or staging category determined pursuant to their Schedules for such good when approved by each such Party in accordance with its applicable legal procedures.
4. Each Party may adopt or maintain import measures to allocate in-quota imports made pursuant to a tariff rate quota set out in Annex 302.2, provided that such measures do not have trade restrictive effects on imports additional to those caused by the imposition of the tariff rate quota. . . .

Section F—Cooperation
Article 512: Cooperation
1. Each Party shall notify the other Parties of the following determinations, measures and rulings, including to the greatest extent practicable those that are prospective in application:
   (a) a determination of origin issued as the result of a verification conducted pursuant to Article 506(1);
   (b) a determination of origin that the Party is aware is contrary to
      (i) a ruling issued by the customs administration of another Party with respect to the tariff classification or value of a good, or of materials used in the production of a good, or the reasonable allocation of costs where calculating the net cost of a good, that is the subject of a determination of origin, or
      (ii) consistent treatment given by the customs administration of another Party with respect to the tariff classification or value of a good, or of materials used in the production of a good, or the reasonable allocation of costs where calculating the net cost of a good, that is the subject of a determination of origin;

(c) a measure establishing or significantly modifying an administrative policy that is likely to affect future determinations of origin, country of origin marking requirements or determinations as to whether a good qualifies as a good of a Party under the Marking Rules; and

(d) an advance ruling, or a ruling modifying or revoking an advance ruling, pursuant to Article 509.

2. The Parties shall cooperate:

(a) in the enforcement of their respective customs-related laws or regulations implementing this Agreement, and under any customs mutual assistance agreement or other customs-related agreement to which they are party;

(b) for purposes of the detection and prevention of unlawful transshipments of textile and apparel goods of a non-Party, in the enforcement of prohibitions or quantitative restrictions, including the verification by a Party, inaccordance with the procedures set out in this Chapter, of the capacity for production of goods by an exporter or a producer in the territory of another Party, provided that the customs administration of the Party proposing to conduct the verification, prior to conducting the verification

(i) obtains the consent of the Party in whose territory the verification is to occur, and

(ii) provides notification to the exporter or producer whose premises are to be visited, except that procedures for notifying the exporter or producer whose premises are to be visited shall be in accordance with such other procedures as the Parties may agree;

(c) to the extent practicable and for purposes of facilitating the flow of trade between them, in such customs-related matters as the collection and exchange of statistics regarding the importation and exportation of goods, the harmonization of documentation used in trade, the standardization of data elements, the acceptance of an international data syntax and the exchange of information; and

(d) to the extent practicable, in the storage and transmission of customs-related documentation. . . .

Part Three: Technical Barriers to Trade

Chapter Nine: Standards-Related Measures

Article 903: Affirmation of Agreement on Technical Barriers to Trade and Other Agreements
Further to Article 103 (Relation to Other Agreements), the Parties affirm with respect to each other their existing rights and obligations relating to standards-related measures under the *GATT Agreement on Technical Barriers to Trade* and all other international agreements, including environmental and conservation agreements, to which those Parties are party.

Article 904: Basic Rights and Obligations
Right to Take Standards-Related Measures

1. Each Party may, in accordance with this Agreement, adopt, maintain or apply any standards-related measure, including any such measure relating to safety, the protection of human, animal or plant life or health, the environment or consumers, and any measure to ensure its enforcement or implementation. Such measures include those to prohibit the importation of a good of another Party or the provision of a service by a service provider of another Party that fails to comply with the applicable requirements of those measures or to complete the Party's approval procedures.
Right to Establish Level of Protection
2. Notwithstanding any other provision of this Chapter, each Party may, in pursuing its legitimate objectives of safety or the protection of human, animal or plant life or health, the environment or consumers, establish the levels of protection that it considers appropriate in accordance with Article 907(2).
Non-Discriminatory Treatment
3. Each Party shall, in respect of its standards-related measures, accord to goods and service providers of another Party:

(a) national treatment in accordance with Article 301 (Market Access) or Article 1202 (Cross-Border Trade in Services); and

(b) treatment no less favorable than that it accords to like goods, or in like circumstances to service providers, of any other country.
Unnecessary Obstacles
4. No Party may prepare, adopt, maintain or apply any standards-related measure with a view to or with the effect of creating an unnecessary obstacle to trade between the Parties. An unnecessary obstacle to trade shall not be deemed to be created where:

(a) the demonstrable purpose of the measure is to achieve a legitimate objective; and

(b) the measure does not operate to exclude goods of another Party that meet that legitimate objective.

Article 905: Use of International Standards
1. Each Party shall use, as a basis for its standards-related measures, relevant international standards or international standards whose completion is imminent, except where such standards would be an ineffective or inappropriate means to fulfill its legitimate objectives, for example because of fundamental climatic, geographical, technological or infrastructural factors, scientific justification or the level of protection that the Party considers appropriate.
2. A Party's standards-related measure that conforms to an international standard shall be presumed to be consistent with Article 904(3) and (4).
3. Nothing in paragraph 1 shall be construed to prevent a Party, in pursuing its legitimate objectives, from adopting, maintaining or applying any standards related measure that results in a higher level of protection than would be achieved if the measure were based on the relevant international standard. . . .

Article 907: Assessment of Risk
1. A Party may, in pursuing its legitimate objectives, conduct an assessment of risk. In conducting an assessment, a Party may take into account, among other factors relating to a good or service:

(a) available scientific evidence or technical information;

(b) intended end uses;

(c) processes or production, operating, inspection, sampling or testing methods; or

(d) environmental conditions.

2. Where pursuant to Article 904(2) a Party establishes a level of protection that it considers appropriate and conducts an assessment of risk, it should avoid arbitrary or unjustifiable distinctions between similar goods or services in the level of protection it considers appropriate, where the distinctions:

(a) result in arbitrary or unjustifiable discrimination against goods or service providers of another Party;

(b) constitute a disguised restriction on trade between the Parties; or

(c) discriminate between similar goods or services for the same use under the same conditions that pose the same level of risk and provide similar benefits.

3. Where a Party conducting an assessment of risk determines that available scientific evidence or other information is insufficient to complete the assessment, it may adopt a provisional technical regulation on the basis of available relevant information. The Party shall, within a reasonable period after information sufficient to complete the assessment of risk is presented to it, complete its assessment, review and, where appropriate, revise the provisional technical regulation in the light of that assessment. . . .

Part Five: Investment, Services and Related Matters

Chapter Fifteen: Competition Policy, Monopolies and State Enterprises

Article 1501: Competition Law

1. Each Party shall adopt or maintain measures to proscribe anticompetitive business conduct and take appropriate action with respect thereto, recognizing that such measures will enhance the fulfillment of the objectives of this Agreement. To this end the Parties shall consult from time to time about the effectiveness of measures undertaken by each Party.

2. Each Party recognizes the importance of cooperation and coordination among their authorities to further effective competition law enforcement in the free trade area. The Parties shall cooperate on issues of competition law enforcement policy, including mutual legal assistance, notification, consultation and exchange of information relating to the enforcement of competition laws and policies in the free trade area.

3. No Party may have recourse to dispute settlement under this Agreement for any matter arising under this Article.

Article 1502: Monopolies and State Enterprises

1. Nothing in this Agreement shall be construed to prevent a Party from designating a monopoly.

2. Where a Party intends to designate a monopoly and the designation may affect the interests of persons of another Party, the Party shall:

(a) wherever possible, provide prior written notification to the other Party of the designation; and

(b) endeavor to introduce at the time of the designation such conditions on the operation of the monopoly as will minimize or eliminate any nullification or impairment of benefits in the sense of Annex 2004 (Nullification and Impairment).

3. Each Party shall ensure, through regulatory control, administrative supervision or the application of other measures, that any privately owned monopoly that it designates and any government monopoly that it maintains or designates:

(a) acts in a manner that is not inconsistent with the Party's obligations under this Agreement wherever such a monopoly exercises any regulatory, administrative or other governmental authority that the Party has delegated to it in connection with the monopoly good or service, such as the power to grant import or export licenses, approve commercial transactions or impose quotas, fees or other charges;

(b) except to comply with any terms of its designation that are not inconsistent with subparagraph (c) or (d), acts solely in accordance with commercial considerations in its purchase or sale of the monopoly good or service in the relevant market, including with regard to price, quality, availability, marketability, transportation and other terms and conditions of purchase or sale;

(c) provides non-discriminatory treatment to investments of investors, to goods and to service providers of another Party in its purchase or sale of the monopoly good or service in the relevant market; and

(d) does not use its monopoly position to engage, either directly or indirectly, including through its dealings with its parent, its subsidiary or other enterprise with common ownership, in anticompetitive practices in a non-monopolized market in its territory that adversely affect an investment of an investor of another Party, including through the discriminatory provision of the monopoly good or service, cross-subsidization or predatory conduct. . . .

Article 1504: Working Group on Trade and Competition

The Commission shall establish a Working Group on Trade and Competition, comprising representatives of each Party, to report, and to make recommendations on further work as appropriate, to the Commission within five years of the date of entry into force of this Agreement on relevant issues concerning the relationship between competition laws and policies and trade in the free trade area.

Part Six: Intellectual Property

Chapter Seventeen: Intellectual Property

Article 1701: Nature and Scope of Obligations

1. Each Party shall provide in its territory to the nationals of another Party adequate and effective protection and enforcement of intellectual property rights, while ensuring that measures to

enforce intellectual property rights do not themselves become barriers to legitimate trade.

2. To provide adequate and effective protection and enforcement of intellectual property rights, each Party shall, at a minimum, give effect to this Chapter and to the substantive provisions of:

(a) the *Geneva Convention for the Protection of Producers of Phonograms Against Unauthorized Duplication of Their Phonograms*, 1971 (Geneva Convention);

(b) the *Berne Convention for the Protection of Literary and Artistic Works*, 1971 (Berne Convention);

(c) the *Paris Convention for the Protection of Industrial Property*, 1967 (Paris Convention); and

(d) the *International Convention for the Protection of New Varieties of Plants*, 1978 (UPOV Convention), or the *International Convention for the Protection of New Varieties of Plants*, 1991 (UPOV Convention).

If a Party has not acceded to the specified text of any such Conventions on or before the date of entry into force of this Agreement, it shall make every effort to accede. . . .

Article 1702: More Extensive Protection

A Party may implement in its domestic law more extensive protection of intellectual property rights than is required under this Agreement, provided that such protection is not inconsistent with this Agreement.

Article 1703: National Treatment

1. Each Party shall accord to nationals of another Party treatment no less favorable than that it accords to its own nationals with regard to the protection and enforcement of all intellectual property rights. In respect of sound recordings, each Party shall provide such treatment to producers and performers of another Party, except that a Party may limit rights of performers of another Party in respect of secondary uses of sound recordings to those rights its nationals are accorded in the territory of such other Party.

2. No Party may, as a condition of according national treatment under this Article, require right holders to comply with any formalities or conditions in order to acquire rights in respect of copyright and related rights.

3. A Party may derogate from paragraph 1 in relation to its judicial and administrative procedures for the protection or enforcement of intellectual property rights, including any procedure requiring a national of another Party to designate for service of process an address in the Party's territory or to appoint an agent in the Party's territory, if the derogation is consistent with the relevant Convention listed in Article 1701(2), provided that such derogation:

(a) is necessary to secure compliance with measures that are not inconsistent with this Chapter; and

(b) is not applied in a manner that would constitute a disguised restriction on trade.

4. No Party shall have any obligation under this Article with respect to procedures provided in multilateral agreements concluded under the auspices of the World Intellectual Property Organization relating to the acquisition or maintenance of intellectual property rights.

Article 1704: Control of Abusive or Anticompetitive Practices or Conditions

Nothing in this Chapter shall prevent a Party from specifying in its domestic law licensing practices or conditions that may in particular cases constitute an abuse of intellectual property rights having an adverse effect on competition in the relevant market. A Party may adopt or maintain, consistent with the other provisions of this Agreement, appropriate measures to prevent or control such practices or conditions.

Article 1705: Copyright

1. Each Party shall protect the works covered by Article 2 of the Berne Convention, including any other works that embody original expression within the meaning of that Convention. In particular:

(a) all types of computer programs are literary works within the meaning of the Berne Convention and each Party shall protect them as such; and

(b) compilations of data or other material, whether in machine readable or other form, which by reason of the selection or arrangement of their contents constitute intellectual creations, shall be protected as such.

The protection a Party provides under subparagraph (b) shall not extend to the data or material itself, or prejudice any copyright subsisting in that data or material.

2. Each Party shall provide to authors and their successors in interest those rights enumerated in the Berne Convention in respect of works covered by paragraph 1, including the right to authorize or prohibit:

(a) the importation into the Party's territory of copies of the work made without the right holder's authorization;

(b) the first public distribution of the original and each copy of the work by sale, rental or otherwise;

(c) the communication of a work to the public; and

(d) the commercial rental of the original or a copy of a computer program.

Subparagraph (d) shall not apply where the copy of the computer program is not itself an essential object of the rental. Each Party shall provide that putting the original or a copy of a computer program on the market with the right holder's consent shall not exhaust the rental right.

3. Each Party shall provide that for copyright and related rights:

(a) any person acquiring or holding economic rights may freely and separately transfer such rights by contract for purposes of their exploitation and enjoyment by the transferee; and

(b) any person acquiring or holding such economic rights by virtue of a contract, including contracts of employment underlying the creation of works and sound recordings, shall be able to exercise those rights in its own name and enjoy fully the benefits derived from those rights. . . .

Sherman Antitrust Act

In 1890 the unprecedented growth of corporate power prompted Congress to pass the Sherman Antitrust Act, which was the first federal law in the antitrust field. Its goal was to preserve market competition and restrict anticompetitive economic behavior. The entire text of the act follows. For an online transcript of the act, see the U.S. Department of Justice Web site at: www.usdoj.gov/atr/foia/divisionmanual/ch2.htm

Sherman Antitrust Act, 15 U.S.C. 1-7

1. Trusts, etc., in restraint of trade illegal; penalty

Every contract, combination in the form of trust or otherwise, or conspiracy, in restraint of trade or commerce among the several States, or with foreign nations, is declared to be illegal. Every person who shall make any contract or engage in any combination or conspiracy hereby declared to be illegal shall be deemed guilty of a felony, and, on conviction thereof, shall be punished by fine not exceeding $10,000,000 if a corporation, or, if any other person, $350,000, or by imprisonment not exceeding three years, or by both said punishments, in the discretion of the court.

2. Monopolizing trade a felony; penalty

Every person who shall monopolize, or attempt to monopolize, or combine or conspire with any other person or persons, to monopolize any part of the trade or commerce among the several States, or with foreign nations, shall be deemed guilty of a felony, and, on conviction thereof, shall be punished by fine not exceeding $10,000,000 if a corporation, or, if any other person, $350,000, or by imprisonment not exceeding three years, or by both said punishments, in the discretion of the court.

3. Trusts in Territories or District of Columbia illegal; combination a felony

Every contract, combination in form of trust or otherwise, or conspiracy, in restraint of trade or commerce in any Territory of the United States or of the District of Columbia, or in restraint of trade or commerce between any such Territory and another, or between any such Territory or Territories and any State or States or the District of Columbia, or with foreign nations, or between the District of Columbia and any State or States or foreign nations, is declared illegal. Every person who shall make any such contract or engage in any such combination or conspiracy, shall be deemed guilty of a felony, and, on conviction thereof, shall be punished by fine not exceeding $10,000,000 if a corporation, or, if any other person, $350,000, or by imprisonment not exceeding three years, or by both said punishments, in the discretion of the court.

4. Jurisdiction of courts; duty of United States attorneys; procedure

The several district courts of the United States are invested with jurisdiction to prevent and restrain violations of sections 1 to 7 of this title; and it shall be the duty of the several United States attorneys, in their respective districts, under the direction of the Attorney General, to institute proceedings in equity to prevent and restrain such violations. Such proceedings may be by way of petition setting forth the case and praying that such violation shall be enjoined or otherwise prohibited. When the parties complained of shall have been duly notified of such petition the court shall proceed, as soon as may be, to the hearing and determination of the case; and pending such petition and before final decree, the court may at any time make such temporary restraining order or prohibition as shall be deemed just in the premises.

5. Bringing in additional parties

Whenever it shall appear to the court before which any proceeding under section 4 of this title may be pending, that the ends of justice require that other parties should be brought before the court, the court may cause them to be summoned, whether they reside in the district in which the court is held or not; and subpoenas to that end may be served in any district by the marshal thereof.

6. Forfeiture of property in transit

Any property owned under any contract or by any combination, or pursuant to any conspiracy (and being the subject thereof) mentioned in section 1 of this title, and being in the course of transportation from one State to another, or to a foreign country, shall be forfeited to the United States, and may be seized and condemned by like proceedings as those provided by law for the forfeiture, seizure, and condemnation of property imported into the United States contrary to law.

7. Conduct involving trade or commerce with foreign nations

Sections 1 to 7 of this title shall not apply to conduct involving trade or commerce (other than import trade or import commerce) with foreign nations unless—

1. such conduct has a direct, substantial, and reasonably foreseeable effect—

A. on trade or commerce which is not trade or commerce with foreign nations, or on import trade or import commerce with foreign nations; or

B. on export trade or export commerce with foreign nations, of a person engaged in such trade or commerce in the United States; and

C. such effect gives rise to a claim under the provisions of sections 1 to 7 of this title, other than this section.

If sections 1 to 7 of this title apply to such conduct only because of the operation of paragraph (1) (B), then sections 1 to 7 of this title shall apply to such conduct only for injury to export business in the United States.

8. "Person" or "persons" defined

The word "person," or "persons," wherever used in sections 1 to 7 of this title shall be deemed to include corporations and associations existing under or authorized by the laws of either the United States, the laws of any of the Territories, the laws of any State, or the laws of any foreign country.

Taft–Hartley Labor Act (Labor Management Relations Act of 1947)

Sponsored by Senator Robert Taft of Ohio and Representative Fred A. Hartley of New Jersey, the Labor Management Relations Act of 1947 (usually referred to as Taft–Hartley Act) amended the National Labor Relations Act of 1935; the goal of Taft–Hartley was to address perceived union abuses of power by, among other provisions, enlarging the National Labor Relations Board. Taft-Hartley expanded the power of the National Labor Relations Board to hear disputes between employees and employers, and it granted employees the right to collectively bargain under union auspices. Taft–Hartley also weakened labor unions significantly in a number of ways—in particular by setting strict limits on the use of strikes, and by giving employees the right not to join a labor union or to choose not to participate in collective bargaining. An excerpt of the act follows. For a complete transcript including amendments to the act, see www.nlrb.gov/publications/nlrb4.pdf (scroll to page 25 of the document).

LABOR MANAGEMENT RELATIONS ACT

Section 1. [Sec. 141.]
(a) This Act [chapter] may be cited as the Labor Management Relations Act, 1947. [Also known as the "Taft–Hartley Act."]
(b) Industrial strife which interferes with the normal flow of commerce and with the full production of articles and commodities for commerce, can be avoided or substantially minimized if employers, employees, and labor organizations each recognize under law one another's legitimate rights in their relations with each other, and above all recognize under law that neither party has any right in its relations with any other to engage in acts or practices which jeopardize the public health, safety, or interest.

It is the purpose and policy of this Act [chapter], in order to promote the full flow of commerce, to prescribe the legitimate rights of both employees and employers in their relations affecting commerce, to provide orderly and peaceful procedures for preventing the interference by either with the legitimate rights of the other, to protect the rights of individual employees in their relations with labor organizations whose activities affect commerce, to define and proscribe practices on the part of labor and management which affect commerce and are inimical to the general welfare, and to protect the rights of the public in connection with labor disputes affecting commerce. . . .

TITLE II
[Title 29, Chapter 7, Subchapter III, United States Code]
Conciliation of labor disputes in industries affecting commerce; national emergencies

Sec. 201. [Sec. 171. Declaration of purpose and policy] It is the policy of the United States that—
   (a) sound and stable industrial peace and the advancement of the general welfare, health, and safety of the Nation and of the best interest of employers and employees can most satisfactorily

be secured by the settlement of issues between employers and employees through the processes of conference and collective bargaining between employers and the representatives of their employees;
   (b) the settlement of issues between employers and employees through collective bargaining may by advanced by making available full and adequate governmental facilities for conciliation, mediation, and voluntary arbitration to aid and encourage employers and the representatives of their employees to reach and maintain agreements concerning rates of pay, hours, and working conditions, and to make all reasonable efforts to settle their differences by mutual agreement reached through conferences and collective bargaining or by such methods as may be provided for in any applicable agreement for the settlement of disputes; and
   (c) certain controversies which arise between parties to collective-bargaining agreements may be avoided or minimized by making available full and adequate governmental facilities for furnishing assistance to employers and the representatives of their employees in formulating for inclusion within such agreements provision for adequate notice of any proposed changes in the terms of such agreements, for the final adjustment of grievances or questions regarding the application or interpretation of such agreements, and other provisions designed to prevent the subsequent arising of such controversies.

Sec. 202. [Sec. 172. Federal Mediation and Conciliation Service]
   (a) [Creation; appointment of Director] There is created an independent agency to be known as the Federal Mediation and Conciliation Service (herein referred to as the ``Service,'' except that for sixty days after June 23, 1947, such term shall refer to the Conciliation Service of the Department of Labor). The Service shall be under the direction of a Federal Mediation and Conciliation Director (hereinafter referred to as the ``Director''), who shall be appointed by the President by and with the advice and consent of the Senate. The Director shall not engage in any other business, vocation, or employment.
   (b) [Appointment of officers and employees; expenditures for supplies, facilities, and services] The Director is authorized, subject to the civil service laws, to appoint such clerical and other personnel as may be necessary for the execution of the functions of the Service, and shall fix their compensation. . . and may, without regard to the provisions of the civil service laws, appoint such conciliators and mediators as may be necessary to carry out the functions of the Service. The Director is authorized to make such expenditures for supplies, facilities, and services as he deems necessary. Such expenditures shall be allowed and paid upon presentation of itemized vouchers therefor approved by the Director or by any employee designated by him for that purpose.
Functions of the service

Sec. 203. [Sec. 173. Functions of Service] (a) [Settlement of disputes through conciliation and mediation] It shall be the duty of the Service, in order to prevent or minimize interruptions of the

free flow of commerce growing out of labor disputes, to assist parties to labor disputes in industries affecting commerce to settle such disputes through conciliation and mediation.

(b) [Intervention on motion of Service or request of parties; avoidance of mediation of minor disputes] The Service may proffer its services in any labor dispute in any industry affecting commerce, either upon its own motion or upon the request of one or more of the parties to the dispute, whenever in its judgment such dispute threatens to cause a substantial interruption of commerce. The Director and the Service are directed to avoid attempting to mediate disputes which would have only a minor effect on interstate commerce if State or other conciliation services are available to the parties. Whenever the Service does proffer its services in any dispute, it shall be the duty of the Service promptly to put itself in communication with the parties and to use its best efforts, by mediation and conciliation, to bring them to agreement.

(c) [Settlement of disputes by other means upon failure of conciliation] If the Director is not able to bring the parties to agreement by conciliation within a reasonable time, he shall seek to induce the parties voluntarily to seek other means of settling the dispute without resort to strike, lockout, or other coercion, including submission to the employees in the bargaining unit of the employer's last offer of settlement for approval or rejection in a secret ballot. The failure or refusal of either party to agree to any procedure suggested by the Director shall not be deemed a violation of any duty or obligation imposed by this Act [chapter].

(d) [Use of conciliation and mediation services as last resort] Final adjustment by a method agreed upon by the parties is declared to be the desirable method for settlement of grievance disputes arising over the application or interpretation of an existing collective-bargaining agreement. The Service is directed to make its conciliation and mediation services available in the settlement of such grievance disputes only as a last resort and in exceptional cases.

(e) [Encouragement and support of establishment and operation of joint labor management activities conducted by committees] The Service is authorized and directed to encourage and support the establishment and operation of joint labor management activities conducted by plant, area, and industrywide committees designed to improve labor management relationships, job security and organizational effectiveness, in accordance with the provisions of section 205A [section 175a of this title]. . . .

Sec. 204. [Sec. 174. Co-equal obligations of employees, their representatives, and management to minimize labor disputes] (a) In order to prevent or minimize interruptions of the free flow of commerce growing out of labor disputes, employers and employees and their representatives, in any industry affecting commerce, shall—

(1) exert every reasonable effort to make and maintain agreements concerning rates of pay, hours, and working conditions, including provision for adequate notice of any proposed change in the terms of such agreements;

(2) whenever a dispute arises over the terms or application of a collective-bargaining agreement and a conference is requested by a party or prospective party thereto, arrange promptly for such a conference to be held and endeavor in such conference to settle such dispute expeditiously; and

(3) in case such dispute is not settled by conference, participate fully and promptly in such meetings as may be undertaken by the Service under this Act [chapter] for the purpose of aiding in a settlement of the dispute.

Sec. 205. [Sec. 175. National Labor–Management Panel; creation and composition; appointment, tenure, and compensation; duties]

(a) There is created a National Labor–Management Panel which shall be composed of twelve members appointed by the President, six of whom shall be elected from among persons outstanding in the field of management and six of whom shall be selected from among persons outstanding in the field of labor. Each member shall hold office for a term of three years, except that any member appointed to fill a vacancy occurring prior to the expiration of the term for which his predecessor was appointed shall be appointed for the remainder of such term, and the terms of office of the members first taking office shall expire, as designated by the President at the time of appointment, four at the end of the first year, four at the end of the second year, and four at the end of the third year after the date of appointment. Members of the panel, when serving on business of the panel, shall be paid compensation at the rate of $25 per day, and shall also be entitled to receive an allowance for actual and necessary travel and subsistence expenses while so serving away from their places of residence.

(b) It shall be the duty of the panel, at the request of the Director, to advise in the avoidance of industrial controversies and the manner in which mediation and voluntary adjustment shall be administered, particularly with reference to controversies affecting the general welfare of the country.

Sec. 205A. [Sec. 175a. Assistance to plant, area, and industrywide labor management committees]

(a) [Establishment and operation of plant, area, and industrywide committees] (1) The Service is authorized and directed to provide assistance in the establishment and operation of plant, area and industrywide labor management committees which—

(A) have been organized jointly by employers and labor organizations representing employees in that plant, area, or industry; and

(B) are established for the purpose of improving labor management relationships, job security, organizational effectiveness, enhancing economic development or involving workers in decisions affecting their jobs including improving communication with respect to subjects of mutual interest and concern.

(2) The Service is authorized and directed to enter into contracts and to make grants, where necessary or appropriate, to fulfill its responsibilities under this section.

(b) [Restrictions on grants, contracts, or other assistance]

(1) No grant may be made, no contract may be entered into and no other assistance may be provided under the provisions of this section to a plant labor management committee unless the employees in that plant are represented by a labor organization and there is in effect at that plant a collective bargaining agreement.

(2) No grant may be made, no contract may be entered into and no other assistance may be provided under the provisions of this section to an area or industrywide labor management committee unless its participants include any labor organizations certified or recognized as the representative of the employees of an employer participating in such committee. Nothing in this clause shall prohibit participation in an area or industrywide committee by an employer whose employees are not represented by a labor organization.

(3) No grant may be made under the provisions of this section to any labor management committee which the Service finds to have as one of its purposes the discouragement of the exercise of rights contained in section 7 of the National Labor Relations Act (29 U.S.C. Sec. 157) [section 157 of this title], or the interference with collective bargaining in any plant, or industry.

(c) [Establishment of office] The Service shall carry out the provisions of this section through an office established for that purpose.

(d) [Authorization of appropriations] There are authorized to be appropriated to carry out the provisions of this section $10,000,000 for the fiscal year 1979, and such sums as may be necessary thereafter. . . .

Sec. 207. [Sec. 177. Board of inquiry]

(a) [Composition] A board of inquiry shall be composed of a chairman and such other members as the President shall determine, and shall have power to sit and act in any place within the United States and to conduct such hearings either in public or in private, as it may deem necessary or proper, to ascertain the facts with respect to the causes and circumstances of the dispute.

(b) [Compensation] Members of a board of inquiry shall receive compensation at the rate of $50 for each day actually spent by them in the work of the board, together with necessary travel and subsistence expenses.

(c) [Powers of discovery] For the purpose of any hearing or inquiry conducted by any board appointed under this title [29 U.S.C.S. Sec. Sec. 171-183], the provisions of sections 9 and 10 (relating to the attendance of witnesses and the production of books, papers, and documents) of the Federal Trade Commission Act of September 16 [26], 1914, as amended (U.S.C. [19], title 15, secs. 49 and 50, as amended), are hereby

made applicable to the powers and duties of such board. (June 23, 1947, ch 120 Title II, Sec. 61 Stat. 155.)

Sec. 208. [Sec. 178. Injunctions during national emergency]

(a) [Petition to district court by Attorney General on direction of President] Upon receiving a report from a board of inquiry the President may direct the Attorney General to petition any district court of the United States having jurisdiction of the parties to enjoin such strike or lockout or the continuing thereof, and if the court finds that such threatened or actual strike or lockout—

(i) affects an entire industry or a substantial part thereof engaged in trade, commerce, transportation, transmission, or communication among the several States or with foreign nations, or engaged in the production of goods for commerce; and

(ii) if permitted to occur or to continue, will imperil the national health or safety, it shall have jurisdiction to enjoin any such strike or lockout, or the continuing thereof, and to make such other orders as may be appropriate.

(b) [Inapplicability of chapter 6] In any case, the provisions of sections 101 to 115 of title 29, United States Code [chapter 6 of this title] [known as the "Norris–LaGuardia Act"] shall not be applicable.

(c) [Review of orders] The order or orders of the court shall be subject to review by the appropriate circuit court of appeals [court of appeals] and by the Supreme Court upon writ of certiorari or certification as provided in sections 239 and 240 of the Judicial Code, as amended (U.S.C., title 29, secs. 346 and 347). (June 23, 1947, ch 120, Title II Sec. 208, 61 Stat. 155.) . . .

TITLE III
[Title 29, Chapter 7, Subchapter IV, United States Code]

Suits by and against labor organizations

Sec. 301. [Sec. 185.]

(a) [Venue, amount, and citizenship] Suits for violation of contracts between an employer and a labor organization representing employees in an industry affecting commerce as defined in this Act [chapter], or between any such labor organization, may be brought in any district court of the United States having jurisdiction of the parties, without respect to the amount in controversy or without regard to the citizenship of the parties.

(b) [Responsibility for acts of agent; entity for purposes of suit; enforcement of money judgments] Any labor organization which represents employees in an industry affecting commerce as defined in this Act [chapter] and any employer whose activities affect commerce as defined in this Act [chapter] shall be bound by the acts of its agents. Any such labor organization may sue or be sued as an entity and in behalf of the employees whom it represents in the courts of the United States. Any money judgment against a labor organization in a district court of the United States shall be enforceable only against the organization as an

entity and against its assets, and shall not be enforceable against any individual member or his assets.

(c) [Jurisdiction] For the purposes of actions and proceedings by or against labor organizations in the district courts of the United States, district courts shall be deemed to have jurisdiction of a labor organization (1) in the district in which such organization maintains its principal offices, or (2) in any district in which its duly authorized officers or agents are engaged in representing or acting for employee members.

(d) [Service of process] The service of summons, subpoena, or other legal process of any court of the United States upon an officer or agent of a labor organization, in his capacity as such, shall constitute service upon the labor organization.

(e) [Determination of question of agency] For the purposes of this section, in determining whether any person is acting as an "agent" of another person so as to make such other person responsible for his acts, the question of whether the specific acts performed were actually authorized or subsequently ratified shall not be controlling.

Restrictions on payments to employee representatives

Sec. 302. [Sec. 186.]

(a) [Payment or lending, etc., of money by employer or agent to employees, representatives, or labor organizations] It shall be unlawful for any employer or association of employers or any person who acts as a labor relations expert, adviser, or consultant to an employer or who acts in the interest of an employer to pay, lend, or deliver, or agree to pay, lend, or deliver, any money or other thing of value—

(1) to any representative of any of his employees who are employed in an industry affecting commerce; or

(2) to any labor organization, or any officer or employee thereof, which represents, seeks to represent, or would admit to membership, any of the employees of such employer who are employed in an industry affecting commerce;

(3) to any employee or group or committee of employees of such employer employed in an industry affecting commerce in excess of their normal compensation for the purpose of causing such employee or group or committee directly or indirectly to influence any other employees in the exercise of the right to organize and bargain collectively through representatives of their own choosing; or

(4) to any officer or employee of a labor organization engaged in an industry affecting commerce with intent to influence him in respect to any of his actions, decisions, or duties as a representative of employees or as such officer or employee of such labor organization.

(b) [Request, demand, etc., for money or other thing of value]

(1) It shall be unlawful for any person to request, demand, receive, or accept, or agree to receive or accept, any payment, loan, or delivery of any money or other thing of value prohibited by subsection (a) of this section.

(2) It shall be unlawful for any labor organization, or for any person acting as an officer, agent, representative, or employee of such labor organization, to demand or accept from the operator of any motor vehicle (as defined in section 13102 of title 49) employed in the transportation of property in commerce, or the employer of any such operator, any money or other thing of value payable to such organization or to an officer, agent, representative or employee thereof as a fee or charge for the unloading, or in connection with the unloading, of the cargo of such vehicle: *Provided*, That nothing in this paragraph shall be construed to make unlawful any payment by an employer to any of his employees as compensation for their services as employees.

(c) [Exceptions] The provisions of this section shall not be applicable

(1) in respect to any money or other thing of value payable by an employer to any of his employees whose established duties include acting openly for such employer in matters of labor relations or personnel administration or to any representative of his employees, or to any officer or employee of a labor organization, who is also an employee or former employee of such employer, as compensation for, or by reason of, his service as an employee of such employer; (2) with respect to the payment or delivery of any money or other thing of value in satisfaction of a judgment of any court or a decision or award of an arbitrator or impartial chairman or in compromise, adjustment, settlement, or release of any claim, complaint, grievance, or dispute in the absence of fraud or duress; (3) with respect to the sale or purchase of an article or commodity at the prevailing market price in the regular course of business; (4) with respect to money deducted from the wages of employees in payment of membership dues in a labor organization: *Provided*, That the employer has received from each employee, on whose account such deductions are made, a written assignment which shall not be irrevocable for a period of more than one year, or beyond the termination date of the applicable collective agreement, whichever occurs sooner; (5) with respect to money or other thing of value paid to a trust fund established by such representative, for the sole and exclusive benefit of the employees of such employer, and their families and dependents (or of such employees, families, and dependents jointly with the employees of other employers making similar payments, and their families and dependents): *Provided*, That

(A) such payments are held in trust for the purpose of paying, either from principal or income or both, for the benefit of employees, their families and dependents, for medical or hospital care, pensions on retirement or death of employees, compensation for injuries or illness resulting from occupational activity or insurance to provide any of the foregoing, or unemployment benefits or life insurance, disability and sickness insurance, or accident insurance; . . .

(C) such payments as are intended to be used for the purpose of providing pensions or annuities for employees are

made to a separate trust which provides that the funds held therein cannot be used for any purpose other than paying such pensions or annuities;

(6) with respect to money or other thing of value paid by any employer to a trust fund established by such representative for the purpose of pooled vacation, holiday, severance or similar benefits, or defraying costs of apprenticeship or other training programs: *Provided*, That the requirements of clause (B) of the proviso to clause (5) of this subsection shall apply to such trust funds;

(7) with respect to money or other thing of value paid by any employer to a pooled or individual trust fund established by such representative for the purpose of

(A) scholarships for the benefit of employees, their families, and dependents for study at educational institutions,

(B) child care centers for preschool and school age dependents of employees, or

(C) financial assistance for employee housing: *Provided*, That no labor organization or employer shall be required to bargain on the establishment of any such trust fund, and refusal to do so shall not constitute an unfair labor practice: *Provided further*, That the requirements of clause (B) of the proviso to clause (5) of this subsection shall apply to such trust funds;

(8) with respect to money or any other thing of value paid by any employer to a trust fund established by such representative for the purpose of defraying the costs of legal services for employees, their families, and dependents for counsel or plan of their choice: Provided, That the requirements of clause (B) of the proviso to clause (5) of this subsection shall apply to such trust funds: Provided further, That no such legal services shall be furnished:

(A) to initiate any proceeding directed (i) against any such employer or its officers or agents except in workman's compensation cases, or (ii) against such labor organization, or

its parent or subordinate bodies, or their officers or agents, or (iii) against any other employer or labor organization, or their officers or agents, in any matter arising under subchapter II of this chapter or this chapter; and

(B) in any proceeding where a labor organization would be prohibited from defraying the costs of legal services by the provisions of the Labor–Management Reporting and Disclosure Act of 1959 [29 U.S.C.A. Sec. 401 et seq.]; or

(9) with respect to money or other things of value paid by an employer to a plant, area or industrywide labor management committee established for one or more of the purposes set forth in section 5(b) of the Labor Management Cooperation Act of 1978.

(d) [Penalty for violations]

(1) Any person who participates in a transaction involving a payment, loan, or delivery of money or other thing of value to a labor organization in payment of membership dues or to a joint labor–management trust fund as defined by clause (B) of the proviso to clause (5) of subsection (c) of this section or to a plant, area, or industrywide labor–management committee that is received and used by such labor organization, trust fund, or committee, which transaction does not satisfy all the applicable requirements of subsections (c)(4) through (c)(9) of this section, and willfully and with intent to benefit himself or to benefit other persons he knows are not permitted to receive a payment, loan, money, or other thing of value under subsections (c)(4) through (c)(9) violates this subsection, shall, upon conviction thereof, be guilty of a felony and be subject to a fine of not more than $15,000, or imprisoned for not more than five years, or both; but if the value of the amount of money or thing of value involved in any violation of the provisions of this section does not exceed $1,000, such person shall be guilty of a misdemeanor and be subject to a fine of not more than $10,000, or imprisoned for not more than one year, or both. . . .

Thematic Indexes

Page numbers in **boldface type** indicate full articles on a subject. Page numbers in *italic type* indicate illustrations or other graphics. All numbers preceding colons indicate volume numbers.

Index of People

A

Adams, John, **8**:1137
Addams, Jane, **2**:200
Agricola, Georgius, **10**:1329
Aiken, Howard, **2**:250
Alberghetti, Anna Maria, **3**:*321*
Allen, Bill, **10**:1335
Allen, Paul, **3**:424, **4**:537, 538, **6**:803, **7**:873-74
Amos, Wally, **3**:426
Andersen, Terry L., **4**:*440*, 441-42
Andreas, Dwayne O., **1**:70, 71
Andreas, G. Allen, **1**:*70*, 71
Andreas, Michael D., **1**:71
Andreessen, Marc, **2**:215, *216*, **5**:711, 712
Andrews, Samuel, **8**:1128, 1129, **9**:1231
Annunziata, Robert, **3**:*295*
Arbenz, Jacobo, **2**:205
Arber, Werner, **4**:555
Archer, George P., **1**:*70*
Arevalo, Juan José, **2**:*204*, 205
Aristotle, **7**:980, **10**:1328
Arkwright, Richard, **5**:655, *657*
Armstrong, C. Michael, **1**:90
Armstrong, Edwin, **8**:1147-48
Aronson, Robert L., **4**:524
Ash, Mary Kay, **1**:76-77
Asner, Edward, **9**:1171
Austen, Jane, **2**:207
Avery, Clarence Willard, **1**:82
Avery, Oswald, **4**:555

B

Baade, Robert, **9**:1225-26
Babbage, Charles, **2**:249, **5**:663
Bacall, Lauren, **9**:1169, *1170*
Bachelier, Louis, **6**:728, 729
Bader, Edward L., **8**:*1068*
Baker, James, **9**:1267
Baker, Lorenzo Dow, **2**:204
Bakke, Allan, **1**:35, 36
Bakunin, Mikhail, **6**:839, **9**:1251
Baldwin, Jerry, **9**:1235
Ballmer, Steve, **4**:538
Barby, Abraham, **5**:*653*
Barrett, Colleen, **9**:*1221*
Barrett, Craig, **5**:686

Barrett, Matthew, **8**:*1132*
Barron, Clarence Walker, **10**:*1383*
Barron, Jessie, **10**:1384
Bartley, Robert, **10**:1386
Basinger, Kim, **2**:277-78, 279
Bast, James, **1**:*113*
Bayley, Charles, **5**:623
Beaver, Hugh, **5**:593
Beck, Dave, **9**:1275
Beckerman, Wilfred, **9**:1264, 1267
Becknell, William, **8**:*1142*, 1143-44
Bell, Alexander Graham, **1**:87, 88, **3**:400, **7**:912, **8**:1112, **9**:1285, 1286, **10**:1357
Bentham, Jeremy, **9**:1202
Bergstresser, Charles, **10**:1383, 1384
Berkley, Shelley, **2**:255
Bernays, Edward L., **8**:1066-67, 1068
Berners-Lee, Tim, **5**:663, 665, *667*, 711, 712, **8**:1112
Bernstein, Carl, **4**:572
Bernstein, Eduard, **9**:1208
Bezos, Jeffrey, **1**:49, 50
Bidzos, Jim, **5**:678
Bierce, Ambrose, **5**:609
Bina, Eric, **5**:711
Black, Eli, **2**:206
Blair, Tony, **9**:1209
Blake, William, **2**:200
Blodgett, Katherine, **4**:548
Boas, Franz, **10**:1365
Bogart, Humphrey, **1**:65, **9**:1169, *1170*
Bono, Sonny, **2**:284
Bosack, Len, **2**:207
Boulton, Matthew, **5**:653, *657*
Bové, Jose, **4**:566
Bowerman, Bill, **7**:950-52
Bowker, Gordon, **9**:1235
Bowker, R. R., **8**:1078
Boyer, Herbert, **4**:555, 556
Brady, Mathew, **7**:*910*
Brando, Marlon, **6**:786
Breedlove, Sarah. *See* Walker, Madame C. J.
Breyer, Stephen, **3**:358, 359
Brezhnev, Leonid, **2**:232
Bright, John, **2**:178
Brink, Washington Perry, **9**:1176
Bristol, William McLaren, **1**:121
Brooks, Edward W., **1**:115
Brown, Ann, **8**:*1109*
Brown, Helen Gurley, **8**:1077
Brown, Moses, **5**:657
Brown, Sarah, **5**:616

Brownstein, Michael, **6**:772
Brundtland, Gro Harlem, **9**:1265
Bryan, Richard, **2**:*255*
Buccleuch, duke of, **9**:1202-3
Buffett, Warren, **3**:*293*, **7**:948
Bugas, John, **2**:222
Burford, Anne, **4**:445
Burgdorf, Robert L., Jr., **1**:56-57
Burleson, Mary, **8**:*1144*
Burnett, Leo, **1**:139-40
Burns, Arthur, **4**:483
Burr, Aaron, **5**:597
Busby, Jheryl, **6**:857
Bush, George H. W., **3**:378, 402, **5**:586, **6**:764, **10**:1352
   Americans with Disabilities Act, **1**:56
   family leave veto, **4**:469
   NAFTA, **7**:*956*, 958
   presidential election (1992), **7**:999
Bush, George W., **4**:456, **5**:586, **7**:927, **9**:1262
   steel tariff, **8**:1056
Bush, Jeb, **1**:36, *37*
Bustamante, Cruz, **10**:*1359*

C

Cabell, James Branch, **4**:472
Cagney, James, **9**:1171
Cahsman, Brian, **6**:*815*
Cairncross, Frances, **9**:1265
Caligula, **8**:1137, 1139
Callaway, Ely, **9**:1200
Candler, Asa, **2**:217, 218
Capellas, Michael, **5**:*621*
Cardoza, Dennis, **10**:*1359*
Carey, Ronald R., **9**:1276
Carlson, Chester F., **10**:*1429*, *1430*
Carnegie, Andrew, **2**:184-86, **7**:906, 933, **8**:1050, **9**:1252
   Morgan deal, **9**:1168, **10**:1353, 1354
Carpentier, Georges, **8**:1147
Carson, Rachel, **2**:268, **3**:299-300, **4**:439, *440*, 443, 447
   Silent Spring, **9**:1194-95
Carter, Charles, **3**:*379*
Carter, Jimmy, **3**:358, **7**:937, **8**:1086, 1109, **9**:1215
Caruso, Enrico, **10**:1381
Cary, Frank T., **5**:634
Case, Steven, **1**:64, *65*, 66
Castro, Fidel, **2**:206, 229, 230
Cerf, Vinton, **3**:411
Chakrabarty, Ananda, **7**:*985*
Chan, Jackie, **2**:*193*
Chantarahesee, Darwan, **1**:79

Chapman, Gary, **7**:*945*
Charles II, **5**:622-23
Chavez, Cesar, **1**:69, **2**:194-96
Chiang Kai-Shek, **2**:229
Chino, Tadao, **1**:*79*
Chisholm, Shirley, **1**:115
Chouart, Medard, **5**:622
Chuck D (rapper), **2**:284
Churchill, Winston, **6**:749
Cicero, **6**:799-800
Citron, Jeffrey, **3**:342
Clare, David, **2**:*300*
Clark, Jim, **2**:215-16, **5**:*712*
Clark, Maurice, **8**:1128-29, **9**:1231
Cleghorn, John, **8**:*1132*
Clemenceau, Georges, **6**:749
Clinton, Bill, **3**:359, 395, **4**:533, **5**:586, 699, **6**:754
   affirmative action, **1**:36
   antitrust enforcement, **9**:1187
   family leave and, **4**:469
   minimum wage bill, **7**:*880*
   NAFTA, **7**:958
   National Black Chamber of Commerce, **7**:934
   political campaign, **8**:*1065*
   presidential elections (1992, 1996), **7**:999
   product liability bill veto, **8**:*1047*
   taxpayer advocate bill, **5**:699
   "Third Way" social policy, **9**:1209
   veto exercise, **2**:255
   Welfare Reform Act, **9**:1211, 1215-16
Clinton, George, **5**:595, 596
Coase, Ronald H., **4**:464-65, 528
Cobden, Richard, **2**:178
Codd, E. F., **3**:339
Cohen, Ben, **1**:106-8, **7**:945
Cohen, Stanley, **4**:555
Colbert, John-Baptiste, **6**:*849*, 850
Colt, Samuel, **5**:693, **6**:828
Columbus, Christopher, **5**:705, **6**:*849*, 850
Comer, Gary, **6**:769
Compton, Bill, **1**:*102*
Cook, Thomas, **10**:1312
Cooke, Jay, **7**:906
Cooley, Richard, **10**:1046
Coolidge, Calvin, **2**:*191*, **6**:858
Cooney, Joan Ganz, **5**:616
Cort, Henry, **5**:653
Cortés, Hernando, **6**:850
Cosby, Bill, **6**:792
Crane, Stephen, **5**:609
Crick, Francis, **4**:555

Crosby, Philip B., **10**:1309
Crosland, Anthony, **9**:1208-9
Cruger, Nicholas, **5**:595
Cudahy, Sheila, **4**:473
Cullinan, Joe ("Buckskin"),
    10:1305, *1307*
Curtiss, Glenn, **10**:1333

D

Daft, Doug, **2**:219, 220
D'Amato, Alphonse, **5**:674
Dana, Charles, **8**:1080-81
Daniels, John W., **1**:*70*
Darwin, Charles, **6**:817
Davidoff, Monte, **6**:803
Davidson, Arthur, **5**:598
Davidson, Walter, **5**:598
Davidson, William, **5**:598
Davidson, William G. (grandson),
    5:599-600
Davies, Marion, **5**:611-12
Davis, Angus, **10**:*1372*
Davis, Bette, **1**:65
Davis, Jacob, **6**:785, *786*
Davis, Marvin, **6**:773
Dean, James, **6**:786
Debs, Eugene, **4**:1083, **9**:*1209*,
    1210, 1252
Deere, Charles, **3**:348, 349
Deere, John, **3**:**347-49**, 348
De Gaulle, Charles, **4**:458
de Graff, Robert, **8**:1078
de Havilland, Olivia, **1**:65
Dell, Michael, **4**:*519*
Delligattia, Jim, **6**:848
DeLuca, Fred, **4**:523
Deming, W. Edwards, **10**:1309-10
Dempsey, Jack, **8**:1147
de Soto, Hernando, **8**:1138
Deterding, Henri Wilhelm August,
    8:1133, 1134
Disney, Roy, **10**:1391, 1392
Disney, Walt, **8**:1100, **10**:1391-92
Dodd, Christopher, **9**:*1173*
Dole, Bob, **7**:999
Donahue, Phil, **10**:1411
Donaldson, William H., **9**:*1174*
Dort, Josiah Dallas, **4**:550
Doughton, Robert, **9**:*1212*
Douglass, Benjamin, **3**:336
Douglass, Frederick, **10**:1382
Dow, Charles, **3**:376, 377, **7**:947,
    10:1383, 1384
Drake, Edwin, **8**:1128, **9**:1231,
    10:1305
Drake, Francis, **6**:*849*, 850
Dr. Dre (rapper), **2**:284
Dreyfuss, Richard, **9**:*1171*
Drucker, Peter, **3**:**380-81**
Duehl, David and Margaret, **6**:772
Duhalde, Eduardo, **5**:*701*
Duke, Patty, **9**:1171
Dun, Robert Graham, **3**:336
Dunlop, Gordon, **1**:125
Durant, William Crapo ("Billy"),
    4:550-51, *552*

E

Eastwood, Clint, **1**:*92*

Edison, Thomas Alva, **3**:**399-401**,
    414, 424, **4**:511, **7**:912
    General Electric, **3**:400,
        4:546-48
    mimeograph machine, **10**:1429
    persistence of, **8**:1112
Edward VII, king of Great Britain,
    7:1001
Ehrlich, Paul, **4**:437, *440*,
    6:817-18
Eisenhower, Dwight D., **9**:1200,
    1214
    military-industrial complex
        warning, **3**:351-52, 354
Eisner, Michael, **6**:*856*, **10**:*1392*,
    1393, 1394
Elizabeth I, queen of England,
    6:*849*, 850
Ellison, Lawrence, **2**:241
Emerson, Ralph Waldo, **4**:439
Engels, Friedrich, **2**:227, *228*,
    6:838, 839, 840, **9**:*1207*,
    1209, **10**:1365
Erasmus, Desiderius, **2**:281
Estrada Cabrera, Manuel, **2**:04
Evans, Christopher, **5**:665
Evans, Oliver, **5**:657, 658
Evers, Charles, **1**:115

F

Fahlman, Scott, **3**:412
Fanning, Shawn, **2**:284
Fargo, James Congdell, **1**:51
Fargo, William G., **1**:51, **10**:1405,
    1406
Farnsworth, Philo, **8**:1148
Farrar, John, **4**:472
Fayol, Henri, **6**:819, 824
Fenn, Sherilyn, **2**:278
Ferdinand, king of Aragon, **6**:850
Fielden, Samuel, **5**:602
Filo, David, **5**:711, **10**:1433, *1434*
Finn, Chester E., Jr., **3**:402
Fiorina, Carly, **4**:501-2, **5**:620-21
Fischer, Alice, **10**:*1348*
Flagg, Ella, **7**:936
Flagler, Henry M., **8**:1129, **9**:1231
Flint, Charles R., **5**:632
Flood, Curt, **6**:813, *815*
Follett, Ken, **7**:998
Fonda, Jane, **10**:1341
Ford, Edsel, **4**:*514*
Ford, Gerald, **5**:586, **8**:1130
Ford, Henry, **3**:299, 396,
    4:**511-14**, 551, **6**:728,
    8:1096
    antiunionization, **10**:1350
    assembly line, **1**:82, **5**:598,
        658, **6**:828-29
    entrepreneurship, **3**:424
    as Hitler idol, **10**:1377
Forster, E. M., **6**:749
Fourier, Charles, **9**:1206
Franco, Francisco, **4**:*475*, 476
Franklin, Benjamin, **1**:99, **5**:682,
    6:816, **8**:1074
Freud, Sigmund, **3**:380, **8**:1067
Friedman, Milton, **2**:182, **3**:358,
    360, **4**:**527-28**, **5**:661,
    6:751, 812

Fuggett, Carolyn E., **6**:*793*
Fulton, Robert, **5**:654, *657*

G

Gable, Clark, **6**:845
Galbraith, John Kenneth, **2**:267,
    4:**532-33**, **10**:1367
Gale, Leonard, **7**:911
Gandhi, Indira, **6**:818
Gandhi, Mohandas, **2**:195
Gantt, Henry L., **6**:824
Garrison, William Lloyd, **3**:337
Gary, Elbert H., **10**:1354
Gaskell, P., **10**:1417
Gates, Bill, **3**:424, **4**:**537-39**, 566,
    5:*651*, **6**:803, **7**:873-76,
    9:1292
    intellectual property, **5**:688,
        690
Gates, Melissa French, **4**:*538*, 539
Gelb, Lawrence M. and Joan,
    1:122-23
Gelb, Richard, **1**:123
Gerstner, Louis V., Jr., **5**:*633*, 637
Giambi, Jason, **6**:*815*
Gibbons, Thomas, **10**:1362
Gibson, Herb, **10**:1387
Gibson, Mel, **6**:774
Gilbreth, Frank B. and Lillian M.,
    6:825
Giroux, Robert, **4**:472, 473
Glass, David, **10**:1389
Goizueta, Roberto, **2**:219, 220
Goldberg, Arthur J., **7**:997
Goldwyn, Samuel, **2**:277
Gompers, Samuel, **1**:38, 39,
    7:936, **9**:1274
Gorbachev, Mikhail, **2**:*181*, 183,
    232
Gordon, Jeff, **8**:*1063*
Gordy, Berry, Jr., **4**:**568-69**
Gore, Al, **7**:*880*, 927
Gorman, Margaret, **8**:*1068*
Gott, Rodney C., **5**:599
Graham, Donald, **4**:572
Graham, Jennifer, **2**:*275*
Graham, Katharine, **4**:**570-72**
Graham, Philip, **4**:570-71
Grant, Johnny, **2**:*193*
Grasso, Richard, **7**:*949*
Graves, Earl, **1**:114, 115
Green, William, **1**:39, **7**:940
Greenfield, Jerry, **1**:106-8
Greenspan, Alan, **2**:152, **4**:483,
    5:586-87, 688, **6**:731
Grimes, Annie, **6**:858
Grove, Andrew, **5**:684, 686
Groza, Petra, **2**:*231*
Guevara, Che, **2**:230
Guinness, Arthur, **5**:592, *593*
Gutenberg, Johannes, **1**:31, **2**:281,
    8:1074
Gutierrez, Carlos, **6**:748
Gwynne, Ursula, **7**:945

H

Hadden, Briton, **1**:*64*, 66
Hagar, Daniel B., **7**:935
Halavais, Alexander, **7**:986
Halley, Edmund, **6**:728

Hamilton, Alexander, **2**:178,
    5:**595-97**, **6**:852
Harberger, Arnold C., **4**:528
Hardin, Garrett, **10**:1326, 1328
Hargreaves, James, **5**:654, *657*
Harkin, Tom, **1**:57
Harkness, Stephen, **8**:1129
Harley, William S., **5**:598
Harlow, Jean, **6**:*844*
Harrington, Michael, **9**:1210
Harris, Mildred, **6**:845
Harrison, Pat, **9**:*1212*
Hartley, Fred A., **9**:1268
Hastings, Warren, **6**:850
Hauser, Gaylord, **4**:473
Hawkins, John, **6**:*849*, 850
Hayek, Friedrich von, **3**:358
Hayes, Rutherford, **9**:1250
Headly, Jerrod, **2**:*208*
Heaney, Seamus, **4**:473
Hearst, George, **5**:609
Hearst, Phoebe, **5**:609, 611
Hearst, William Randolph,
    5:609-12, **8**:1075, 1081
Hegel, G. W. F., **6**:838
Heimbold, Charles, Jr., **1**:*123*
Heinz, Henry J., **5**:**613-15**
Henson, Brian, **5**:618
Henson, Jim, **5**:**616-18**
Henson, W. S., **10**:1331
Heston, Charlton, **9**:1171
Hewlett, William Redington,
    5:619, *620*, 621
Hiler, Bruce, **3**:*423*
Hill, Julia ("Butterfly"), **4**:518
Hine, Lewis W., **2**:*199*, 200
Hirono, Mazie, **10**:*1319*
Hitler, Adolf, **4**:474, *475*, 476,
    7:897, **10**:1377-79
Hobbes, Thomas, **8**:1026
Ho Chi Minh, **2**:229
Hoffa, James P. (son), **9**:*1274*,
    1276
Hoffa, James R. (father), **6**:765,
    767, **9**:*1274*, 1275
Hogate, Kenneth C., **10**:1384
Hollerith, Herman, **5**:632, *633*,
    663, 665, **6**:834
Holmes, Oliver Wendell, Sr.,
    5:604
Hoover, Herbert, **5**:581, 583, 584,
    585
Horsfall, William, **9**:1278
Hotchner, A. E., **7**:944
Hudson, Henry, **5**:622
Hughes, Charles Evans, **7**:940
Hume, David, **9**:1202
Hutcheson, Francis, **9**:1202

I

Ibuka, Masaru, **7**:908, **9**:1217,
    1218
Idei, Nobuyuki, **9**:1219
Igbi, Tai-ichi, **6**:741
Insull, Samuel, **3**:421
Isutani, Minoru, **1**:*92*
Iwasaki Hisaya, **7**:891
Iwasaki Koyata, **7**:891
Iwasaki Yanosuke, **7**:891

Iwasaki Yataro, 7:890-91
Iwerks, Ub, 10:1391

J

Jackson, Andrew, 10:1417
Jackson, Bo, 7:952
Jackson, Jesse, 1:37
Jackson, Michael, 4:569
Jackson, Shirley, 4:473
Jackson, Thomas Penfield, 7:875
Jaffe, Stanley, 6:773, 774
James, Etta, 4:568
Jay, John, 5:595, 596
Jefferson, Thomas, 5:597, 692-93,
    698, 6:851, 7:980
Jennings, O. B., 8:1129
Jobs, Steve, 3:426, 8:*1023*,
    10:1431
Johnson, Earvin ("Magic"), 6:857
Johnson, Edward C., II, 4:491,
    492
Johnson, Edward C., III ("Ned"),
    4:491
Johnson, John H., 6:739-40,
    8:1077
Johnson, Lyndon, 7:927, 8:1141
    affirmative action, 1:35
    civil rights bill, 2:211, *212*
    Economic Opportunity Act,
        3:394
    Great Society, 2:180, *181*
    labor unions, 1:39
    Medicare, 9:*1210*, 1214
Johnson, Robert, 10:*1351*
Jolson, Al, 1:*65*
Jones, Eddie, 10:1383
Jones, Edward T., 3:377
Jordan, Angelica, 3:*425*
Jordan, Michael, 1:*117*, 118,
    7:*950*, 952
Joyner, Russ, 2:*193*
Juran, Joseph M., 10:1309

K

Kahn, Alfred, 3:358, 359, 8:*1106*,
    1108-9
Kahn, Bob, 3:411
Kaneshige, Tom, 3:384
Kant, Immanuel, 2:153-54,
    9:1202
Kapur, Sumit, 3:*384*
Katzenberg, Jeffrey, 10:1394
Kawakami, Gen-ichi, 10:1435
Kay, John, 5:654, *657*
Kearny, Stephen Watts, 8:1144
Keith, Minor, 2:204
Kelleher, Hugh, 9:1220, 1221
Keller, Herb, 2:166
Kellogg, John Harvey, 6:745, 746
Kellogg, Will Keith, 6:745, 746-47
Kelly, Gene, 9:1169
Kelly, M. Clyde, 10:1333
Kelsey, Frances, 2:273
Kennedy, Edward, 9:*1257*
Kennedy, John F., 2:210-11, 230,
    4:532, 533, 8:1141, 9:1195,
    1210
    affirmative action, 1:34, 35
    civil rights, 8:1086
Kennedy, Robert F., 6:676, 9:*1275*

Kennedy, Ted, 3:358
Keppler, Joseph, 1:*67*
Kertzman, Mitchell, 7:874
Keynes, John Maynard, 6:749-51
    business cycle theory, 2:149,
        151
    Chicago School vs., 4:528
    economic model, 2:180, 182,
        3:364-65, 390
    key ideas of, 6:750
    macroeconomics, 6:*809*, 810,
        812, *812*
    recession theory, 8:1096
    Samuelson economics and,
        8:1140, 1141
Keynes, John Neville, 6:749
Keys, Alicia, 6:725
Khrushchev, Nikita, 2:232
Kilgore, Barney, 10:1384-85
King, Coretta Scott, 2:*196*
King, John, 1:125, 126
King, Martin Luther, Jr., 1:40,
    2:210, *212*, 8:1083, 1086
King, Martin Luther, III, 1:37
King, Stephen, 8:1078
Kirkland, Lane, 1:42
Klein, Naomi, 4:566
Kleinrock, Leonard, 5:*710*
Knight, Frank, 4:528
Knight, Phil, 7:950-52
Knudsen, William S., 4:552
Kohl, Helmut, 4:459
Kornei, Otto, 10:1429
Kovacevich, Dick, 10:1407
Kozlowski, L. Dennis, 2:*158*
Krause, Brad, 6:752
Kroc, Ray, 6:755-57, *846*, 847-48
Kropotkin, Pyotr, 4:441
Krugman, Paul, 8:1039
Kurata, Teruo, 9:*1217*

L

Lafayette, marquis de, 7:910
Landauer, Thomas, 5:665
Landis, James, 8:1105, 1107
Langbo, Arnold, 6:*748*
Langmuir, Irving, 4:548, 8:1110
Lansing, Sherry, 6:772-74
Lasker, Albert, 1:31, 32
Lauder, Estée, 6:775-77
Lauter, Joe, 6:775, 776
Lauter, Leonard, 6:775
Lauter, Ronald, 6:776
Lavagna, Roberto, 5:*701*
Lay, Kenneth L., 3:420, 421, 422
Leal, Donald R., 4:*440*, 441-42
Lee, Ang, 9:*1219*
Lee, Ivy, 8:1066, 1068
Leeson, Nicholas, 4:531
Leibniz, Gottfried, 5:663
Lenin, Vladimir, 2:179, 227-28,
    231, 232, 9:1207
Leonardo da Vinci, 9:1191,
    10:1331
Lerner, Sandy, 2:*207*
Leslie, Frank, 10:*1395*
Lessig, Lawrence, 2:165, 284,
    7:986
Levi, Carlo, 4:473
Levin, Gerald, 1:*65*, 66

Levine, Josh, 3:342
Levitt, Abe, 6:788
Levitt, Alfred, 6:788
Levitt, Arthur, Jr., 2:260
Levitt, William, 6:788-90
Lewis, David J., 9:*1212*
Lewis, John L., 1:39, 40
Lewis, Loida, 6:793
Lewis, Michael, 2:215
Lewis, Reginald, 6:791-93
Licklider, J. C. R., 5:*712*
Liebeck, Stella, 2:*161*, 8:1046
Lincoln, Abraham, 5:698, 6:781,
    7:912
Lingle, Linda, 10:*1319*
Lipton, Thomas, 8:1117
List, Friedrich, 2:178, 6:852
Lister, Joseph, 5:605
Livengood, Scott, 7:*949*
Lloyd, Henry Demerest, 9:1233
Lloyd, William Forster, 10:1328
Lloyd George, David, 6:749
Locke, John, 8:1026, 9:1203
López Arellano, Osvaldo, 2:206
Loudon, John Hugo, 8:1134-35
Louis XIV, king of France, 6:*849*,
    850
Lowell, Francis Cabot, 5:657,
    6:805, 807
Lowell, Robert, 4:473
Lucas, George, 1:75
Luce, Henry Robinson, 1:*64*, 66
Lynch, Edmund C., 6:858
Lynch, Peter, 4:491-92

M

Ma, Yo-Yo, 9:1219
Machado, Gerado, 10:1333
Madison, James, 5:595, 596
Madonna, 1:118
Major, John, 4:460
Mallet, Pierre and Paul, 8:1143
Malthus, Thomas Robert, 4:437,
    440, 6:816-18
Mandela, Nelson, 10:*1412*
Mao Zedong, 2:228, 229, 9:1208,
    1209
Marcuse, Herbert, 9:1165
Markowitz, Harry, 6:729
Marsh, George Perkins, 4:439, *440*
Marshall, Alfred, 6:749
Marshall, Colin, 1:*124*, 126
Marshall, John, 3:302, 304
Martin, Casey, 1:58
Martin, William McChesney,
    4:483
Marx, Karl, 2:227, *228*, 232,
    6:838-40, 8:1028, 9:1207,
    1208, *1209*, 1251, 10:1365,
    1396
Masih, Iqbal, 2:201
Maxim, Hiram, 10:1332
Mayer, Louis B., 6:844-45
McCarthy, Joseph, 8:1148
McCarthy, William, 9:1276
McDonald, Maurice, and Richard,
    6:756, 757, *846*, 847
McDonough, William, 4:442
McGowan, William, 3:360
McGuinn, Roger, 9:*1283*

McKinley, William, 3:350,
    5:610-11
McLaren, Wayne, 7:1003
McLean, David, 7:1003
McLuhan, Marshall, 5:667
McMurtie, Sandra Andreas, 1:71
McNally, Dave, 6:813
McNeely, P. J., 2:284
McWhirter, Norris and Ross,
    5:593
Meany, George, 1:40, 42, 8:1086
Meiggs, Henry, 2:204
Meili, Christoph, 10:*1346*, 1348
Melnick, Dan, 6:773
Melville, Herman, 9:1235
Merrill, Charles Edward, 6:858-59
Merrill, James, 6:858
Messersmith, Andy, 6:813
Meyer, Agnes, 4:570
Meyer, Eugene, 4:570, 571
Mfume, Kweisi, 6:793
Miescher, Johann Friedrich, 4:555
Miller, Daniel, Jr., 3:*425*
Miller, Marvin, 6:813
Miller, Ron, 10:1392
Mintzberg, Henry, 9:1247-48
Mitterrand, François, 4:459
Mngumi, Grace, 1:*123*
Monnet, Jean, 4:457, 460
Moody, Paul, 6:805-6, 807-8
Moore, G. E., 6:*749*
Moore, Gordon, 5:668, 684, 686
Moravia, Alberto, 4:473
Morgan, J. P., 1:88, 4:550, 5:583,
    7:905-7, 8:1051,
    10:1383-86
    Carnegie Steel and, 9:1168,
        10:1353, 1354
    General Electric and, 4:5
    U.S. Steel and, 2:186
Morgan, Junius Spencer, 7:905
Morgan, Lewis, 10:1365
Morgan, Ralph, 9:1169
Morita, Akio, 7:908-9, 9:1217,
    1218-19
Morris, Philip, 7:1000
Morrisey, George C., 9:1246
Morse, Leila Livingston, 7:*912*
Morse, Samuel, 5:657, 7:910-12,
    9:1284
Morse, Sidney, 7:910
Moynihan, Daniel Patrick, 7:925
Mulroney, Brian, 7:956
Mun, Thomas, 6:849, 851
Muris, Timothy J., 4:485, 487
Murray, Thorpe, and Lewis, 6:792
Muse, Lamar, 2:166
Musk, Elon, 7:*898*
Muskie, Edmund, 4:448
Mussa, Michael, 4:561-62
Mussolini, Benito, 4:474, *475*, *476*
Myers, John Ripley, 1:121

N

Nader, Ralph, 2:268, 274, 4:552,
    553, 6:794, 798, 7:925-27
Naisbitt, John, 5:665
Nally, E. J., 8:1146
Nebel, Jane, 5:616
Negroponte, Nicholas, 5:666-67

Nehru, Jawaharlal, **2**:181
Newcomen, Thomas, **5**:653, *657*
Newman, Nell, **7**:*944*, 946
Newman, Paul, **7**:944-46, **9**:*1171*
Newton, Isaac, **2**:177, **5**:688
Nicholas II, emperor of Russia, **2**:227
Niles, Jack, **9**:1290
Nixon, Richard, **2**:*181*, 182, **3**:316, 317, **5**:620, **8**:1130
   employment quotas, **1**:35
   EPA creation, **4**:*440*, 442, 448
   Greenspan and, **5**:586
   Samuelson and, **8**:1141
   Sarnoff and, **8**:1148
   social security COLAs, **9**:1215
   visit to China, **2**:230
   wage and price controls, **8**:1016
   Watergate scandal, **4**:571-72, **5**:699
Noble, L. Clarence, **5**:613, 614
Nordhoff, Heinz, **10**:1378
Noyce, Robert, **5**:684, 685

O

Ohga, Norio, **9**:1219
Ohno, Tai-ichi, **6**:741
Olds, Ransom E., **4**:550
Omidyar, Pierre, **10**:1408
Orfalea, Paul, **6**:752, 753-54
Orwell, George, **6**:837
Outcault, R. G., **5**:609
Ovitz, Michael, **10**:1394
Owen, Chandler, **8**:1083
Owen, Robert, **2**:227, **9**:1206, *1209*
Oz, Frank, **1**:75

P

Packard, David, **5**:619, 620, 621
Packard, Vance, **2**:267
Paley, William, **6**:816
Palmer, Arnold, **1**:92
Papa, David, **9**:*1186*
Parker, James, **9**:*1221*
Parks, Rosa, **2**:*210*
Parlin, Charles Coolidge, **6**:833
Pascal, Blaise, **5**:663, **6**:728
Pasteur, Louis, **5**:605
Paterson, Tim, **7**:874
Pegler, Arthur James, **5**:610
Pemberton, John Styth, **2**:217
Perkins, Frances, **7**:994-97, **9**:*1212*
Perón, Juan, **4**:476
Perot, H. Ross, **7**:**998-1000**
Phillips, A. W., **5**:661
Picasso, Pablo, **8**:*1020*
Pierce, E. A., **6**:859
Pinkerton, Allan, **9**:1176
Pinochet, Augusto, **4**:476
Pipes, Richard, **8**:1026
Pitt, Harvey, **9**:*1173*
Pitt, William the Younger, **6**:*816*, 817
Piuze, Michael, **7**:*1004*
Pizarro, Francisco, **6**:850
Podell, Jules, **3**:*321*
Pol Pot, **2**:230
Poole, Arthur F., **7**:*982*

Porsche, Ferdinand, **10**:1377
Porter, Michael, **9**:1247
Post, C. W., **6**:746
Presley, Elvis, **6**:786
Presser, Jackie, **9**:1276
Prince, Earl, **6**:756
Proudhon, Pierre-Joseph, **6**:838, **8**:1028
Pulitzer, Joseph, **5**:609, **8**:1075, **1080-82**
Pullman, George, **3**:298, 299, **9**:1252
Putnam, Samuel, **6**:728

Q

Quesnay, François, **9**:1203

R

Radclyffe, Charles, **10**:1378
Radisson, Pierre-Esprit, **5**:622
Ramazinni, Bernardino, **4**:454
Randolph, A. Philip, **8**:**1083-86**
Rasheed, Abdul, **2**:202
Ratner, Brett, **2**:*193*
Reagan, Ronald, **3**:300, **5**:699, **6**:751, 764, **10**:1339, 1352
   air traffic controllers strike, **9**:1254, 1268
   antitrust enforcement, **9**:1187
   capitalism and, **2**:*181*, 182-83
   defense industry and, **3**:352
   deregulation, **3**:358, **8**:1109
   EPA and, **4**:445
   Greenspan and, **5**:586
   military spending, **4**:478
   monetarism, **4**:527
   Screen Actors Guild presidency, **9**:*1169*, 1171
   tax policy, **5**:699
Reichardt, Carl, **10**:1046, *1407*
Reid, Harry, **2**:255
Remington, Frederick, **5**:610
Resor, Stanley, **1**:32
Reuther, Walter, **1**:40, **2**:*222*, **10**:1351
Reverend Billy (Bill Talen), **2**:267
Ricardo, David, **2**:178, **6**:851
Rice, Linda Johnson, **6**:*739*, 740
Ridge, Tom, **3**:403
Rifkin, Jeremy, **8**:1042
Rigas, John, **3**:297
Roberts, Julia, **6**:*799*
Robinson, Harriet H., **6**:806
Robinson, James, **1**:52
Robinson, Smokey, **4**:568-69
Roche, James M., **4**:553
Rockefeller, David, **7**:945
Rockefeller, John D., **2**:186, **5**:583, **8**:**1128-30**
   National Black Chamber of Commerce, **7**:933
   oil refining, **10**:1305
   profit and loss, **8**:1050, 1051, 1133
   public relations, **8**:1066
   Standard Oil, **7**:901, *902*, **8**:1133, 1134, **9**:1231-34
   vertical integration, **7**:972
Rockefeller, John D., Jr., **8**:1130, **9**:*1232*

Rockefeller, Nelson Aldrich, **8**:1130
Rockefeller, William, **8**:1129, **9**:1231
Rodriguez, Alex, **9**:1227
Rodriguez, Arturo, **1**:*69*
Rogers, Richard, **1**:77
Rollins, Hugh, **9**:1220
Roosevelt, Eleanor, **6**:740
Roosevelt, Franklin D., **3**:360, 365, **5**:698, **10**:1384
   bank closure by, **9**:1172
   capitalism and, **2**:179, 180, *181*
   environmental projects, **4**:439, *440*
   fair employment practices, **8**:1085
   farm program, **1**:47
   labor relations, **1**:39, **6**:763, **7**:939, **9**:1252, 1274
   minimum wage, **7**:878-79
   New Deal, **5**:585, **6**:750, **7**:941, 943, 996, **9**:1210
   Perkins and, **7**:994, 995, 996
   regulatory legislation, **8**:107, 1104, *1105*
   social security, **9**:*1211*, 1212
Roosevelt, Theodore, **1**:67, **4**:439, *440*, **5**:615, **7**:907
Root, Elihu, **3**:350
Root, Elisha King, **5**:693
Ross, Diana, **4**:569
Ross, Steve, **1**:65
Rossotti, Charles O., **5**:700
Rousseau, Jean-Jacques, **2**:199
Ruckelshaus, William D., **4**:445
Russell, Bertrand, **6**:749
Rustin, Bayard, **8**:1086

S

Saint-Simon, Henri de, **9**:1206, 1207
Salazar, Antonio, **4**:475, 476
Salinas de Gortari, Salinas, **7**:*956*
Samuel, Marcus, **8**:1133, *1134*
Samuelson, Paul, **8**:**1140-41**
Sanitas Nut Food Company, **6**:745
Sarandon, Susan, **9**:*1171*
Sarbanes, Paul, **9**:*1173*
Sarnoff, David, **8**:**1146-48**
Saro-Wiwa, Ken, **7**:920, **8**:1135
Satterlee, Herbert, **4**:550
Savery, Thomas, **5**:653
Say, Jean-Baptiste, **6**:750
Scalia, Antonin, **1**:58
Schlaet, Arnold, **10**:1305, *1307*
Schlender, Brent, **7**:874
Schneider, Ralph, **3**:*321*
Schotz, John, **6**:775, 776
Schultz, Howard, **9**:1235, *1237*
Schultz, Theodore, **5**:625
Schumacher, E. F., **4**:441, **9**:1264
Schuman, Robert, **4**:457
Schumpeter, Joseph A., **5**:690, **9**:**1164-65**
Schwab, Charles, **9**:**1166-68**
Schwab, Michael, **5**:601, 602
Schwartz, Robert, **2**:*152*
Schwarzenbach, Ernest B., **9**:*1217*
Scott, Thomas A., **2**:184, 185

Scripps, Edward W., **8**:1075
Seitz, Peter, **6**:813
Selden, George, **4**:511-12
Selig, Bud, **9**:1227
Selig, William N., **5**:611
Sen, Amartya, **6**:818
Shannon, Claude Elwood, **5**:*663*, 665
Sherman, John, **9**:*1187*
Shewhart, Walter, **10**:1310
Shi Guangsheng, **10**:*1427*
Siegel, Jeremy, **9**:1159
Siegel, Zev, **9**:1235
Sikorsky, Igor, **9**:**1191-93**
Sinclair, Upton, **2**:267
Singer, Isaac, **6**:828
Skilling, Jeffrey, **3**:422, *423*
Slater, Samuel, **5**:657
Sloan, Alfred P., **4**:551, *552*
Smith, Adam, **9**:**1202-5**
   capitalism, **2**:156, 177-78, *181*
   copyright, **2**:281
   on division of labor, **3**:370
   economic growth, **3**:388-89
   entrepreneurship, **3**:424
   free market theory, **1**:92, **5**:705-6, **6**:851, **7**:901, **9**:1203-4, **10**:1396, 1400-1401
   "invisible hand" concept, **2**:156, **3**:358, 361, **5**:690
   key ideas of, **9**:*1204*
   Malthusian theory vs., **6**:816, 817
   mercantilist theory vs., **6**:*849*, 851
   as microeconomics founder, **7**:869
   Veblen's consumer-influenced theory and, **10**:1365
   Wealth of Nations, The, **10**:1400-1401
Smith, Al, **7**:994
Smith, Fred, **4**:488, 489
Smith, Frederick (father), **4**:488
Smith, Hamilton, **4**:555
Smith, William A., **9**:1231, **10**:1305
Smits, H. N. J., **9**:1265
Solow, Robert, **8**:1039, 1110
Sontag, Susan, **4**:473
Sorenson, Charles, **1**:82
Spector, Robert, **3**:335
Spencer, Herbert, **6**:817
Spielberg, Steven, **10**:1411
Spies, August, **5**:601, 602
Spitzer, Eliot, **6**:860, **8**:1018
Squibb, Charles and Edward, **1**:122
Squibb, Edward Robinson, **1**:122
Stalin, Joseph, **2**:179, 228, 229, **9**:1207, *1209*
Stanley brothers, **10**:1330
Stearns, Dick, **6**:769
Steinbeck, John, **5**:584
Steinem, Gloria, **8**:1077
Stephenson, George and Robert, **5**:654, *657*
Stern, Richard, **2**:278-79

Stevenson, Adlai, **4**:533
Stewart, Martha, **1**:118, **8**:1100, **9**:*1238-40*
Stewart, Meredith, **3**:*422*
Stigler, George, **3**:358, 359, **4**:528
Stillman, Charles B., **7**:936
Strachey, Lytton, **6**:749
Straus, Robert W., Jr., **4**:472, *473*
Strauss, Levi, **6**:785, *786*
Summers, Lawrence, **3**:359-60
Sun Yat-sen, **2**:229
Sweeney, John J., **1**:*38*, 42
Sylvis, William H., **10**:1413

T

Taft, Robert, **9**:1268
Taft, William Howard, **10**:1418
Talen, Bill (Reverend Billy), **2**:267
Tandy, Vertner Woodson, **10**:1381
Tappan, Lewis, **3**:*336*, 337
Tarbell, Ida, **9**:*1231*, 1233, 1234
Tartikoff, Brandon, **6**:774
Tate, John, **7**:*949*
Tatum, Donn, **10**:1392
Taylor, Frederick, **4**:454, **6**:823-24
Taylor, Hobart, Jr., **1**:35
Taylor, Michael, **10**:1326
Terman, Frederick, **5**:619
Tesla, Nikola, **4**:547
Thatcher, Margaret, **2**:*181*, 182-83, **3**:358, **4**:459-60, **6**:751, **8**:*1031*, 1032
Thiel, Peter, **7**:898
Thomas, Clarence, **2**:257
Thomson, J. Edgar, **2**:184, 185
Thomson, William Curtis, **7**:1000
Thoreau, Henry David, **4**:439
Tito, Dennis, **10**:1315
Tito, Josip, **2**:230
Tobin, Daniel J., **9**:1274, 1275
Toffler, Alvin, **5**:*663*, 665, **9**:1290
Toman, Ed, **6**:846
Tomlinson, Ray, **3**:411, **5**:*712*
Townsend, William, **5**:*586*
Townshend, Charles, **9**:1202
Toyoda, Eiji, **6**:830
Trevithick, Richard, **5**:*657*, **10**:1329
Trippe, Juan, **10**:1333-35
Trotsky, Leon, **2**:228, **9**:1207
Truman, Harry, **5**:698-99, **7**:996, **10**:1384
armed forces desegregation, **8**:1085
social security, **9**:1214
Taft–Hartley and, **9**:*1268*
Trump, Donald, **8**:193, **10**:1336-38
Tsai, Gerald, **4**:491
Tsunoda, Yuji, **9**:*1237*
Tucker Anthony Sutro, **8**:1132
Tull, Jethro, **5**:*657*
Turner, Ted, **1**:*65*, **10**:1339-41
Twain, Mark, **5**:609

U

Ubico, Jorge, **2**:*204*, 205
Ulrich, Lars, **9**:*1283*
Utyke, Dennis, **6**:752

V

Vail, Alfred, **7**:911
Valentine, Don, **2**:207
Valentine, Thomas W., **7**:935
Van Buren, Martin, **10**:1417
Vanderbilt, Cornelius, **10**:1362-64
Vargas, Getúlio, **4**:476
Veblen, Thorstein, **3**:358, **10**:1365-67
Venable, Willis, **2**:217
Verne, Jules, **9**:1191
Viner, Jacob, **4**:528
Volcker, Paul, **4**:483, **7**:945

W

Wagner, Ray, **6**:772
Wagner, Robert F., Sr., **7**:939, **9**:*1212*
Walcott, Derek, **4**:473
Walker, A'Lelia, **10**:1381, *1382*
Walker, Madame C. J., **10**:1380-82
Walton, Sam, **3**:424, **6**:744, **10**:1387-88
"Ten Rules for Building a Business," **10**:1388, 1390
Warner, Abe, **1**:*64*, 65
Warner, Harry, **1**:*64*, 65
Warner, Jack, **1**:*64*, 65
Warner, Kate, **9**:1176
Warner, Sam, **1**:*64*, 65
Washington, Booker T., **7**:933, *934*
Washington, Derrick, **2**:*214*
Washington, George, **5**:*595*, *596*, 597
Watford, Odessa, **3**:*404*
Watkins, Sherron, **3**:*423*
Watson, James, **4**:555
Watson, Thomas J., **5**:632-33, 634
Watson, Thomas J., Jr., **5**:634
Watson, Tom, **9**:1226-27
Watt, James, **5**:*653*, 656, *657*, 665
Webber, J. Leroy, **1**:121
Weber, Max, **6**:820, 823
Webster, William, **5**:700
Wedgwood, Josiah, **5**:656
Weinstein, Bob, **7**:888-89
Weinstein, Harvey, **7**:888-89
Weiss, Bernard, **4**:555
Welch, Carolyn, **10**:1402
Welch, Jack, **3**:379, 420, **4**:547, 549, **10**:1402-4
Weldon, Fay, **1**:30
Welles, Orson, **5**:*611*, 612
Wells, Frank, **10**:*1392*, 1393, 1394
Wells, H. G., **9**:1282
Wells, Henry, **1**:51, **10**:1405, *1406*
Wells, Mary, **4**:569
Westinghouse, George, **4**:547, 548
Wheeler, Harry C., **9**:1252
Whitacre, Mark, **1**:71
White, Ellen G., **6**:745
Whitehead, A. N., **6**:749
Whitehead, John, **7**:945
Whitehead, Mary Beth, **2**:278-79
Whitman, Christie Todd, **4**:*444*
Whitman, Meg, **10**:1408-9

Whitney, Eli, **1**:81, **5**:655, *657*, 658, 693, **6**:828
Whiton, Alexander, **4**:511
Whittle, Christopher, **3**:402, *403*, 404
Wiley, Ralph, **3**:*373*, 374
Wilkins, Roy, **6**:739
Williams, Roy, **9**:1275
Willson, Millicent, **5**:611-12
Wilson, Charles E., **4**:552
Wilson, Edmund, **4**:473
Wilson, Jackie, **4**:568
Wilson, Owen, **2**:*193*
Wilson, Terrance, **1**:71
Wilson, Woodrow, **4**:485, **9**:1252
Winfrey, Oprah, **1**:115, **8**:1078, **9**:*1236*, **10**:1410-12
Wolfe, Tom, **4**:473
Wonder, Stevie, **4**:569
Woodruff, Paul, **2**:219
Woods, Mel, **6**:*856*
Woods, Tiger, **1**:115, **7**:*952*, **9**:*1223*, 1227
Woodward, Bob, **4**:572
Wright, Orville and Wilbur, **10**:1331, 1333

Y

Yamaha, Torakusu, **10**:1435
Yang, Jerry, **5**:711, **10**:1433, *1434*
Yergin, Daniel, **3**:359
Yersai, Raj, **3**:*384*
Young, Stanley, **4**:472, 473

Z

Zell, Sam, **8**:1095
Zworykin, Vladimir, **8**:1148

Index of Companies and Organizations

A

A&P, **8**:1115
ABC (television), **1**:66
A. B. Dick, **3**:400
Accessory Transit Company, **10**:1362-63
Adelphia Communications, **3**:297
Adidas, **7**:951
ADM. *See* Archer Daniels Midland Company
Admiralty Bancorp, Incorporated, **8**:1132
Advanced Research Projects Agency, **5**:710, *712*
Advance Group, **8**:1075, 1077
Aeon Group, **8**:1118
AEW Capital Management LP, Boston, **8**:1095
Agricultural Adjustment Administration, **7**:941, **9**:1255
Agriculture Department, U.S., **2**:272, **4**:559, **9**:1195
Air France, **1**:126
Alcoa, **7**:900, *903*
Altria Group, **7**:*1001*, 1004

Amazon.com, **1**:49-50, **3**:382, **5**:*712*, 714, **8**:1077, 1079
customer service, **3**:335
eBay contrasted with, **10**:1408
"one-click" shopping patent, **7**:986
venture capital investment return, **10**:1370
American Arbitration Association, **1**:68
American Bar Association, **6**:783, **8**:*1048*
American Booksellers Association, **8**:1077, 1079
American Chamber of Commerce Researchers Association, **3**:312-13
American Chambers of Commerce, **2**:192
American Economic Association, **8**:1141
American Express Company, **1**:51-53, **3**:320, **5**:637
athlete endorsement, **9**:1227
Wells Fargo and, **10**:1405, *1406*
American Football League, **9**:1224
American Gaming Association, **4**:534, 536
American Heart Association, **7**:954
American Institute of Certified Public Accountants, **8**:*1048*
American Library Association, **2**:279, **8**:*1048*
American Machinery and Foundry, **5**:599
American Management Association, **8**:*1048*
American Marconi Wireless Telegraph Company, **8**:1146, *1147*
American Medical Association, **8**:1048
American Motors, **10**:1351
American Normal School Association, **7**:935
American Pulp and Paper Association, **4**:517
American Railway Express, **10**:1405
American Research and Development, **10**:1369
American Telephone & Telegraph. *See* AT&T
American Tobacco Company, **3**:376
American Trust Company, **10**:1406
America Online. *See* AOL Time Warner
AmEx. *See* American Express Company
Amgen, **7**:931
AMK-John Morrell, **2**:*204*, 206
Amoco. *See* BP Amoco
Ampex Corporation, **9**:1218
Amtrak, **10**:1330
Anchor Books, **8**:1078
Anchor Brand, **5**:613, *614*
Andersen Worldwide, **2**:259-60
Andrews, Clark & Company, **8**:1128-29, **9**:1231

Anglo-Persian Oil Company, **10**:1306

Anglo-Saxon Petroleum Company, **8**:1134

Anheuser-Busch, **8**:1069

Anti-Corn Law League, **2**:178

AOL Time Warner, **1**:64-66, **4**:521
  merger of, **6**:853, 854, 855
  Microsoft and, **7**:875, 876
  Netscape and, **2**:216, **5**:*712*, **8**:1025
  price fixing and, **8**:1019-20
  TBS merger, **1**:64, **10**:*1339*, 1341

A. Philip Randolph Institute, **8**:1086

Apollo Group, **3**:405

Apple Computer, **2**:251, **5**:635, 636, **6**:753, **7**:874-75, **10**:1433
  pricing, **8**:1023-24
  product development, **8**:1034
  venture capital, **10**:1370

Aramco, **10**:1306, *1307*

Arbitration Foundation, **1**:68

Arbitration Society of America, **1**:68

Archer Daniels Midland Company, **1**:70-71

Archor Brand food products, **5**:613

Arthur Andersen, **2**:260, **3**:379, 422

Asian Development Bank, **1**:78-80

Asian Wall Street Journal, **10**:1386

Aspen Education Group, **3**:405

Aspen Skiing Company, **9**:1190

Associated Advertising Clubs of America, **1**:112

Associated Newspapers of Britain, **3**:402

Associated Press, **8**:1075

Association for Computing Machinery, **2**:279, **8**:*1049*

Association of Licensed Automobile Manufacturers, **4**:512

Association to Advance Collegiate Schools of Business, **6**:841

AT&T, **1**:87-90, **8**:1147, **10**:1357
  breakup of, **1**:89-90, **2**:246, **3**:360-61, **7**:904, **9**:1188, 1234, 1286-89, **10**:1359
  browser, **2**:216
  competition and, **2**:246
  deregulation of, **3**:*359*
  Fiorina and, **4**:501, *502*
  monopoly status, **9**:1285-86
  racial discrimination suit, **2**:213
  regulation effects, **9**:1286

Atari, **1**:65, **10**:1433

Atlanta Braves (baseball), **10**:1339, *1340*

Atlanta Hawks (basketball), **10**:1339

Atlantic Oil (ARCO), **9**:1234

Atlantic records, **1**:64

Audubon Society, **9**:1195

Aviation Corporation of America, **10**:1333, *1334*

Ayershire Farms, **2**:207

B

Baby Bells, **1**:89, 90, **9**:1188, 1286-89

Bahrain Petroleum, **10**:1306, *1307*

Baltimore & Ohio Railroad, **9**:1250, **10**:1330

Bankers Trust, **1**:49

Bank in Winterthur, **10**:1346-47

Bank of America, **9**:*1166*, 1167, **10**:1406

Bank of Montreal, **8**:*1132*

Bank of the United States, **5**:595, 596

Bantam Books, **8**:1078

Barclays Bank of California, **10**:1406

Barings Bank, **4**:531

Barnard College, **9**:1238

Barnes & Noble, **3**:382, **8**:1079, **10**:1389

Basler Bankverein, **10**:1346-47

Battelle Development Corporation, **10**:1429, 1430

Battle Creek Toasted Corn Flake Company, **6**:746

Bavarian Petroleum Company, **8**:1133-34

Beatrice Foods International, **6**:792-93

Bell Laboratories, **1**:90, **8**:1111

BellSouth Corp., **1**:90, **9**:1288

Bell Telephone, **1**:87, 89, **6**:825, **9**:1285, **10**:1357

Ben & Jerry's Homemade, Inc., **1**:106-8, **7**:946

Benchmark Capital, **10**:1370

Berkshire Hathaway, **3**:*293*, **7**:948

Bertelsmann, **8**:1018, 1079

Bethlehem Steel, **4**:454, **9**:1168

Better Business Bureau, **1**:32, 112-13, **2**:274

Bill and Melinda Gates Foundation, **4**:*538*, 539

Biological Service, U.S., **9**:1194

Black Enterprise, **1**:114-15

Blockbuster, **10**:1389

Blue Ribbon Sports. *See* Nike

BMG Music, **8**:1018

Boeing, **3**:353, **5**:651, **10**:1332
  McDonnell Douglass merger, **8**:1104

Bolt, Beranek, and Newman, **3**:411, 412

Bon Marché (Paris), **8**:1115

Book-of-the-Month Club, **8**:1078

Booz-Allen & Hamilton, Inc., **2**:258

Borders, **8**:1079

Boston Associates, **6**:805, 807, 808

Boston Bank of Commerce, **6**:857

Boston Fruit Company, **2**:204

Boston Manufacturing Company, **6**:805

Boston Red Sox, **9**:1223

Boston University, **8**:1067

Boulton and Watt, **5**:653, *657*

Bowery Savings Bank, **3**:*315*

Boy Scouts of America, **8**:1100

BP Amoco, **3**:416, **9**:1234, **10**:1307

Breyer's, **9**:1236

Bridgestone-Firestone, **2**:*160*, **8**:1045

Bright Horizons Family Solutions, **3**:405

Brinks Express Company, **9**:*1175*

Bristol-Myers Squibb, **1**:121-23

British Airways, **1**:124-26

British Telecommunications, **7**:986

Brooklyn (N.Y.) Chamber of Commerce, **2**:191

BSA Company, **10**:1435

Budweiser, **1**:29-30

Buick Company, **4**:550

Bureau of Labor Statistics, **3**:311, **5**:659, **8**:1072
  Consumer Price Index, **2**:269-71
  productivity data, **8**:1043
  unemployment data, **10**:1345

Business for Social Responsibility, **1**:108

Business Information Centers, **9**:1201

Business Software Alliance, **2**:279

Butterfield & Wasson, **1**:51

C

Cadillac Motor Car Company, **1**:139

California-Texas Oil Company (Caltex), **10**:1306, 1307

Cambridge University, **4**:555, **6**:749, 750, 816

Campbell Soup, **5**:687

Canadian Southern Railroad, **10**:1364

Capella University, **3**:406, 408

Capital Cities/ABC, **10**:*1392*, 1394

Capoten, **1**:*121*, 123

Cargill Co., **1**:70, **2**:214

Carnegie Company, **2**:185-86

Carnegie Steel. *See* United States Steel Corporation

Cartoon Network, **10**:1340

Caterpillar, **6**:763, **10**:1351

CBS (television), **8**:1148

CBS/Sony Group, **9**:1218

Census Bureau, U.S., **5**:632, *633*, *663*, 665
  market research and, **6**:834, 836
  per capita income, **9**:1228

Center for the Study of Responsive Law, **7**:927

Centers for Disease Control, **7**:961

Central Pacific Railroad, **10**:1330

Central Railroad, **10**:1363

Centura Banks Incorporated, **8**:1132

Century 21, **8**:1091, 1092, 1095

Charles E. Merrill and Company, **6**:858

Charles Schwab and Company, **9**:1166-68

Chase Manhattan Bank, **3**:378

Cheplin Laboratories, **1**:122

Chevrolet Motor Company, **4**:551

Chevron (Socal), **3**:376, **9**:1234, **10**:1306, 1307

Chevron Texaco, **7**:*921*, **10**:1307

Childcraft, **10**:1392

Chiquita, **1**:118, **2**:204-6

Christie's, **8**:1019, 1020

Chrysler Corp., **10**:1350, 1352

Church of Stop Shopping, **2**:267

Circadia Coffee House, **9**:1237

Cisco Systems, **2**:207-9, **3**:409, **5**:670, **7**:931, **10**:1433

Citicorp, **5**:599, 600

Citigroup, **7**:948

Citizens Loan Corporation, **6**:739

Civil Aeronautics Board, **3**:358, 359

Civil Aeronautics Authority, **8**:1105, 1109

Civilian Conservation Corps, **2**:180, **4**:439, *440*, **6**:750, **7**:*941*, **9**:1255

Civil Service Commission, **7**:996

Civil Works Administration, **7**:*941*

Clairol, **1**:*121*, 122-23

Clayton, Dubliner & Rice, **6**:753-54

Clinique, **6**:777

Clinton Pharmaceutical Company, **1**:121

Club of Rome, **4**:439, **6**:818, **9**:1264

CNN (cable channel), **1**:64, 66, **10**:1339, *1341*, 1358

Coca-Cola Company, **2**:217-20
  market research, **6**:833
  stock returns, **9**:1241, 1242
  trade secret protection, **2**:164, 218

Coleman Co., **7**:933

Colonial Air Transport, **10**:1333

Columbia Pictures, **6**:773, **7**:709, 909, **9**:1218-19

Columbia Records, **9**:*1218*

Columbia University, **4**:527, *528*, **7**:994
  Hamilton and, **5**:595
  Pulitzer Prizes, **8**:1082
  School of Journalism, **8**:1080, 1081

Commerce Department, U.S., **6**:778, 836, **10**:1312-13

Commercial Cable Company, **8**:1146

Committee against Jim Crow in Military Service and Training, **8**:1085

Committee for the First Amendment, **9**:1169, *1170*

Committee on Economic Security, **9**:1212

Commodore International, **2**:251

Communist League, **6**:838

Community Action Agencies, **3**:394, 395

Community School 66 (N.Y.C.), **3**:*404*

Community Service Organization, **2**:195

Community Services Administration, **3**:395

Compaq Computer, **2**:251, **4**:502, **5**:621, 636, **8**:1112

Computer Center Corporation, **7**:873

Computer Literacy (online bookseller), **1**:49

Computing Scale Company of America, **5**:632, 633

Computing-Tabulating-Recording Company (C-T-R), **5**:632, *633*

Confederation Paysanne, **4**:566

Conference Board, **2**:261-63, **6**:778

Consolidated Edison, **3**:377

Consumer Product Safety Commission, **2**:272, 273, **3**:300, **8**:*1106*, 1107, *1109*

Consumer Protection Agency, **2**:268

Consumer Reports, **2**:267, *274*, **10**:1378

Consumer Research Center, **2**:261

Consumers Union, **2**:267

Continental Oil (Conoco), **9**:1234

Convention and Visitors Bureau, **2**:192

Cookman Institute, **8**:1083

Cornell University, **4**:559, **7**:*995*, 997

Corning Glass, **3**:374

Corporate Accountability Research Group, **7**:927

Cosmopolitan Productions, **5**:611

Council of Better Business Bureaus, Inc., **1**:60

Council of Economic Advisors, **5**:586, **8**:1141

Council on Environmental Quality, **8**:*1106*, 1107

Covansys, **5**:670

Credit Union National Association, **8**:1048

Crocker National Bank, **10**:1406, 1407

Crown Publishing, **9**:1230

CSNET (Computer and Science Network), **3**:412

CSPAN (cable channel), **10**:1358

Curtis Publishing Company, **6**:833

D

Dabney, Morgan and Company, **7**:906

DaimlerChrysler, **7**:*891*, 892

Dain Rauscher Corporation, **8**:1132

Daughters of the American Revolution, **8**:1145

Dayton Hudson, **10**:1387

Dayton Wright Company, **4**:551

Deere & Company, **3**:348-49

Defenders of Wildlife, **4**:450

Defense Department, U.S., **3**:411, 412, **4**:552-53, **7**:998
industrial R&D spending, **8**:*1112*

Delaware Association of Nonprofit Agencies, **8**:1049

Dell Computer, **2**:252, **4**:501, **6**:743, **8**:1112

Deloitte Touche Tohmatsu, **2**:259-60

Democratic Socialists of America, **9**:1210

D. E. Shaw & Co., **1**:49

Deutsche Bank, **8**:1095

Digital Equipment Corp., **2**:251

Dimension Films, **7**:889

Diners' Club, **1**:51, 52, **3**:316, *317*, 320, *321*

Disney Company. *See* Walt Disney Company

Disneyland, **10**:1392

Disneyland Paris, **10**:1393

Disney Press, **10**:1393

Disney Stores, **2**:267, **10**:1392

Dixie Greyhound Lines, **4**:488

DKW motorcycle, **10**:1435

DNA Sciences, **2**:216

Doctors without Borders, **1**:123

Dole, **1**:118

Domino's Pizza, **7**:918, **9**:*1186*

DoubleClick, **5**:671, **10**:1370

Douglas, Aircraft, **4**:552

Dow, Jones & Company, **10**:1383-86

Dow Chemical Company, **3**:350, **373-75**

DowElanco, **3**:374

Dow Process Company, **3**:373

Doyle Dane Bernbach, **10**:1379

Dreamworks Studio, **10**:1394

Duke University, **6**:841

Dupont Dow Elastomers, **3**:374

Durant-Dort Carriage Company, **4**:550

Durant Motors, **4**:551

Dynergy, **3**:421

E

Eagle Bancshares Incorporated, **8**:1132

E. A. Pierce & Cassatt, **6**:859

Eastern Airlines, **3**:358, **4**:552

Eastern Air Transport, **4**:552, **10**:1333

Eastman Kodak, **3**:378

eBay, **3**:382, **5**:*712*, 714, **9**:1280
venture capital investment return, **10**:1370
Whitman and, **10**:1408-9

eBay Premier, **10**:1409

eBay Professional Services, **10**:1409

Ebony, **6**:739, 740, **8**:1077

EC. *See* European Community

Eco-Mart, **4**:442

Economic Development Institute, **10**:*1421*, 1422

Economic Policy Advisory Board, **4**:527

Edison General Electric Company, **4**:547, 548

Edison Machine Works, **4**:548

Edison Schools, Inc. **3**:402-4, 405

Education Alternatives, Inc., **3**:402

EEC. *See* European Economic Community

EEOC. *See* Equal Employment Opportunity Commission

Elektra records, **1**:64

Eli Lilly, **3**:374, **7**:900, *903*

El Paso Southwestern Railroad, **9**:1252

EMI Group, **4**:569, **8**:1018

Empire State Development Corporation, **2**:274

End Child Prostitution in Asian Tourism, **10**:1315

Energy Department, U.S., **5**:650, **8**:*1112*

Enron, **3**:297, **420-23**, **4**:521
Arthur Andersen collapse, **2**:260

bankruptcy, **1**:101, **3**:306, 420, 422-23

business ethics, **2**:153, **3**:*296*, **8**:1053

SEC and, **9**:*1173*, 1174

Enron Energy Services, **3**:422

EnronOnline, **3**:*420*, 421, 422

Environmental Protection Agency, **3**:300, **4**:439, *440*, 442, **443-46**, 447, 449, 450, 465, **6**:797, 798, **8**:*1106*, 1107
genetically modified crops and, **4**:559
OSHA and, **7**:961
time line, **4**:444
toxic waste cleanup liability, **6**:797, 798
water standards, **10**:1358

Equal Employment Opportunity Commission, **2**:212, 213, **3**:300, **4**:452-53, **7**:987, **8**:*1106*, 1107
Americans with Disabilities Act compliance, **1**:58
pay equity and, **7**:987
sexual harassment and, **9**:1184, 1185, *1186*
Title VII enforcement, **1**:35

Equifax, **3**:325

Equity Office Properties Trust, **8**:1095

ERA (realtor), **8**:1091

Erie Railroad, **10**:1363-64

Ernst & Young International, **2**:259-60

Erwin Wasey and Company, **1**:139

ESPN (cable channel), **9**:1224

Estée Lauder, Inc., **6**:775, 776-77

Ethyl Dow Company, **3**:374

European Atomic Energy Community, **4**:457

European Central Bank, **4**:459

European Coal and Steel Community, **4**:457

European Community, **4**:457-59

European Economic Community, **4**:457, 458

European Parliament, **4**:457, 460

European Union, **1**:94, **4**:457-60, **5**:707-8, **6**:853, **7**:921, 956, 967, **10**:1347
banana trade war, **2**:*204*, 206
pharmaceutical cartel fine, **2**:188
steel subsidy, **8**:1056
sustainable development, **9**:1265
telecommuting guidelines, **9**:1291
trade policy, **10**:1325
U.S. disputes, **10**:1323

Experian (formerly TRW), **3**:325

Exxon, **1**:117, **7**:948, **9**:1234

ExxonMobil, **3**:416, **4**:521, **6**:854, **10**:1307
profitability, **8**:1052, *1053*

F

Faber & Faber, Inc., **4**:473

Fair Employment Practices Committee, **8**:1085

FAO. *See* Food and Agriculture Organization

Fargo & Co., **10**:1406, *1407*

Farrar, Straus & Giroux, **4**:472-73, **8**:1078

Fashion Fair Cosmetics, **6**:739, 740

Fawcett World Library, **8**:1078

FDA. *See* Food and Drug Administration

Federal Aeronautics Administration, **9**:1254

Federal Aviation Administration, **10**:1332

Federal Bureau of Investigation, **1**:71, **5**:651-52

Federal Commission on Industrial Relations, **1**:38

Federal Communications Commission, **1**:27, 88, 89, **2**:246, **7**:*941*, 943, **8**:1105, *1106*, 1148, **9**:1289, **10**:1358

Federal Deposit Insurance Corporation, **3**:315, *317*, **7**:941, *941*, **8**:1105, **9**:1157, 1158

Federal Emergency Relief Administration, **7**:*941*

Federal Energy Regulatory Commission, **10**:1358

Federal Housing Administration, **6**:790, **7**:*941*, **8**:1105, *1106*

Federal Mediation Commission, **9**:1252

Federal Mediation Service, **9**:1269

Federal Open Market Committee, **4**:482, 483

Federal Power Commission, **8**:1105

Federal Reserve Board, **4**:482-83

Federal Steel Company, **10**:1354

Federal Trade Commission, **4**:484-87
Clayton Act and, **2**:*245*
consumer protection, **2**:272, 273, 275
deceptive advertising, **1**:32, **2**:158, **8**:1104, 1105
franchises, **4**:523
identity theft, **3**:328
price fixing, **8**:1020
Xerox and, **10**:1431

FedEx, **3**:377, **4**:488-90
bar code, **1**:105
customer service, **3**:334-35

FHA. *See* Federal Housing Administration

Fidelity Investments, **4**:491-92

Financial Women's Association, **8**:1048

First Interstate Bancorp, **10**:*1406*, 1407

First National Bank of Chicago, **6**:739

Fish and Wildlife Service, **9**:1194

Fisher Body Company, **4**:551, **10**:1349-50

Food and Agriculture Organization, **4**:506, 509

Food and Drug Administration, **2**:272-74, **4**:559, **6**:796, 798, **9**:1195

Food Network (cable), **8**:1100

Forbes, **10**:1386
richest Americans list, **6**:*739*, 740

Ford Motor Company, **10**:1330, 1379
assembly line, **1**:81, 82, **4**:512-13, **5**:598
collective bargaining, **2**:222
equal employment complaints, **4**:*452*, 453
Ford's business philosophy, **4**:511-14
General Motors and, **4**:550, 551, 552
mass production, **6**:829, 830
product liability, **8**:1045
quality control, **10**:*1308*
stock certificate, **6**:*728*
sustainable design, **4**:442
United Auto Workers, **10**:*1349*, 1350, 1352

Ford Service Department, **10**:1350

Forestry Stewardship Council, **4**:517, **9**:1265

Forest Service, U.S., **4**:*440*, 515

Fortune, **1**:66, **2**:219, **4**:519-21, **6**:786, **7**:874, 889, **8**:1077
"America's 25 Most Influential People," **9**:1240
"best companies for minority employees," **6**:786
"best companies to work for," **6**:754

Fox (television), **7**:889

Franklin National Bank, **1**:51-52

Free Software Foundation, **6**:804

Friends for Life, **1**:*123*

Friends of the Earth, **9**:1258

Frigidaire Corporation, **4**:551, 552

FTC. *See* Federal Trade Commission

Fujitsu, **5**:685

F. W. Woolworth, **8**:1117, **10**:1387

G

Gannett (newspaper chain), **8**:1075

Gap, brand recognition, **1**:*118*

GE. *See* General Electric

GE Capital, **4**:548

Genentech Inc., **4**:556

General Accounting Office, **5**:700

General Electric, **3**:353, 376, 420, **4**:546-49, **5**:619
downsizing, **3**:378-79
Edison and, **3**:400, **4**:546-48
employment discrimination complaints, **4**:453
first publicity department, **8**:1066
Fortune 500 listing, **4**:521
Honeywell merger blockage, **6**:853
Morgan financing, **7**:905
NYSES listing, **7**:948
RCA and, **8**:1146-47, 1148
research and development, **8**:1111

Welch and, **4**:*547*, 549, **10**:1402-4

General Foods, **7**:1002

General Mills, **6**:747

General Motors, **4**:512, **550-54**, **5**:600
bond issuance, **9**:1242
collective bargaining, **1**:39
Electronic Data Systems, **7**:*998*, 999
employment discrimination complaints, **4**:453
global locations, **4**:564, *565*
just-in-time inventory, **6**:*742*
manufacturing system, **6**:829-30
market research, **6**:833
Nader case, **7**:925-27
Perot and, **7**:*998*, 999
stock issuance, **9**:1241
strike against (1937), **9**:1252-53
United Auto Workers, **10**:1349, 1352

General Motors Acceptance Corporation, **4**:551, 553

GeoCities, **10**:1434

George H. Burr & Company, **6**:858

Getty Oil, **10**:1307

GG&E Corporation, **3**:377

Girl Scouts of America, **8**:1100

Global Climate Coalition, **9**:1267

Global Crossing Ltd., **3**:*295*

Global Knowledge, **3**:405

GM. *See* General Motors

GMAC, **4**:551, 553

Gnutella, **2**:284

Goodyear, **3**:376

Grameen Bank, **5**:668

Great Atlantic and Pacific Tea Company, **8**:1115

Guinness, **5**:592-94

Gulf Oil, **9**:1234

H

H&R Block, **3**:427

Hachette Filipacchi, **8**:1077

Haloid Company, **10**:1429-30

Hamburger University, **6**:*756*, 757, 847

Hans Seidel Foundation, **1**:80

Harley-Davidson, **1**:116, **5**:598-600, **6**:743

Harper (publisher), **8**:1078

Harvard Business School, **6**:841, 842, 843, **10**:1408

Harvard Law School, **6**:781, 791, 792, 793, **7**:925, 986

Harvard Medical School, **4**:555

Harvard University, **4**:538, **7**:873
electronic calculators, **2**:250
as first nonprofit entity, **7**:954
Galbraith and, **4**:532, *533*
Mark I computer, **5**:633-34
Samuelson and, **8**:1140, 1141
Schumpeter and, **9**:1164, *1165*

Harvester, **10**:1351, 1352

Hasbro, **9**:*1280*, **10**:1408

Hawaii Technology and Trade Association, **10**:*1319*

HBO (cable channel), **1**:64, 66, **10**:1357-58

Health Care Financing Administration, **9**:1214

Healtheon Corp., **2**:*215*, 216

Hearst King Features, **5**:612

Hearst publishing, **8**:1075, 1077, 1079

Heinz, Noble & Company, **5**:613

Heller Financial Corporation, **5**:600

Hershey's, **8**:*1047*

Hewitt & Tuttle, **8**:1128

Hewlett-Packard, **3**:424, **5**:619-21
Fiorina as CEO, **4**:501-2, **5**:620-21
research and development, **8**:1111

Hill and Knowlton, **8**:1068

Hill and Wang, **4**:*472*, 473

Hitachi, **5**:685

H. J. Heinz Company, **5**:614-15

Hollywood Chamber of Commerce, **2**:*193*

Hollywood Pictures, **10**:1393

Holtzbrinck (publisher), **8**:1079

Home Box Office. *See* HBO

Home Depot, **3**:376, **8**:1100

Home Owners Loan Corporation, **7**:*941*

Homer Mckee Company, **1**:139

Homestead Works, **2**:185

Honda, **4**:564, **5**:599, 600

Honeywell, **6**:853, **7**:909

Hong Kong and Shanghai Banking Corporation, **10**:1406

Houghton Mifflin, **8**:1078

House Un-American Activities Committee, **9**:1169

Housing Authority, **8**:1105

Houston Natural Gas, **3**:420

Houston Texans (football), **9**:1224-25, 1227

Howard Johnson's motels, **10**:1312

HP. *See* Hewlett-Packard

Hudson's Bay Company, **5**:622-24

Hughes Aircraft Company, **4**:554

Hughes Electronics, **3**:353

Human Rights Watch, **2**:201, **7**:958

Hyperion Books for Children, **10**:1393

I

Ibbotson Associates, Inc., **2**:247

IBM, **5**:632-37
antitrust, **8**:1104, *1106*
bar codes, **1**:103
bundling, **1**:138
computers, **2**:249-51, **7**:874, **10**:1432
employee outsourcing, **10**:1304
history of, **5**:663, 665, 679, **6**:834
Intel and, **5**:635, 636, 684, 685
Microsoft and, **6**:802, **7**:873-74
Perot and, **7**:998
research and development, **8**:1111
Xerox lawsuit, **10**:1431-32

IBM Global Services, **5**:670

IBRD. *See* World Bank

ICC. *See* Interstate Commerce Commission

I. G. Farbeindustrie, **2**:187

IKEA, **8**:1118

ImClone, **9**:1240

IMF. *See* International Monetary Fund

Independent Grocers' Alliance, **3**:369

Industrial Commission of the State of New York, **7**:994, *995*

Industrias de Chocolate Lacta S.A., **7**:1002

Insignia/ESG, New York, **8**:1095

Institute for Social Research, **2**:262

Institute of Electrical and Electronic Engineers, **8**:*1048*

Intel Corporation, **3**:376, **5**:684-86, **9**:1200
IBM and, **5**:635, 636, 684, 685
Information Revolution and, **5**:680
lack of competition, **2**:244
Nasdaq trading, **5**:677, **7**:931
strategic innovation of, **5**:680, 684
venture capital, **10**:1370

Internal Revenue Service, **5**:697-700, **7**:990-93
audit rate, **5**:700
payroll functions, **7**:990, *991*, 992-93
small business information, **9**:1199
valuation ruling, **10**:1360

International Air Transport Association, **10**:1335

International Bank for Reconstruction and Development. *See* World Bank

International Business Machines Corp. *See* IBM

International Center for Settlement of Investment Disputes, **10**:*1421*, 1422

International Chamber of Commerce, **9**:1265

International Civil Aviation Organization, **10**:1313

International Conference on Computer Communications, **5**:*712*

International Data Corporation, **5**:669

International Development Association, **10**:*1421*, 1422

International Ecotourism Society, **10**:1313-14

International Finance Corporation, **10**:*1421*, 1422

International Graduate School of Management (Spain), **6**:841

International Monetary Fund, **2**:180, *181*, **4**:563, **5**:701-3, **6**:751, **10**:1425
information technology, **5**:671
international trade, **5**:708-9
recession and, **8**:1098
subsidy and, **9**:1256-57
World Bank and, **10**:1324, 1421, 1423

International News Service, **5**:611, **8**:1075

International Organization for Standardization, **6**:732-34

International Picture Service, **5**:611

International Telework Association and Council, **9**:1290

International Time Recording Company, **5**:632, *633*

International Trade Commission, **5**:600

International Trade Organization, **10**:1425

International Union for the Conservation of Nature, **1**:80

Interstate Commerce Commission, **1**:88, **3**:359, **8**:1103, 1105, 1109, **10**:1330

Investment Company Institute, **7**:922

IRS. *See* Internal Revenue Service

ITT Corp., **6**:*788*, 790

J

Jaffe-Lansing Productions, **6**:773-74

Japanese Musical Instrument Company, **10**:1435

Jaycees, **2**:192-93

Jet, **6**:*739*, 740

Jim Henson Company, **5**:617-18

Joel Popkin and Company, **9**:1196

John M. Bradstreet Company, **3**:336

Johns Hopkins University, **4**:555

Johnson & Johnson, **2**:214, **3**:300

Johnson Publishing Company, **6**:*739*, 740

Jolly Green Giant Company, **1**:139

Jones Lang LaSalle, Inc., **8**:1095

Junior Chamber of Commerce, **2**:192-93

Justice Department, U.S., **3**:360, 422, **5**:633, **7**:874, 875, 902
  consumer protection, **2**:272
  merger and acquisition approval, **6**:853, 854, **8**:1106
  Teamsters and, **9**:*1274*, 1276

K

Kaplan Learning Center, **3**:*406*, 407

Kashi Company, **6**:*746*, 748

Kawasaki, **5**:599

Kdf-Wagen, **10**:1377

KDKA (radio station), **8**:1147

Keebler, **6**:*746*, 748

Kellogg Company, **6**:**745-48**

Kentucky Fried Chicken, **8**:1037

Keystone Bridge Company, **2**:185

Kiernan News Agency, **10**:1383

KinderCare Learning Centers, **3**:405

King Features, **5**:611

Kinko's, **6**:**752-54**

Kinney National, **1**:*64*, 65

Kiwanis, **3**:299

Kleenex, **1**:116, **8**:1037

Kleiner Perkins Caulfield & Byers, **10**:1373

Kmart, **3**:*364*, **9**:1240, **10**:1387

Kodak, **1**:117

Kondratiev, N. D., **9**:1164

KPMG International, **2**:259-60

Kraft Foods, **7**:1000, 1002, 1004, **8**:*1047*

Krispy Kreme Doughnuts, **7**:*949*

L

Labor Department, U.S.
  affirmative action, **1**:34
  Consumer Price Index, **2**:269
  founding of, **10**:1418, 1420
  minimum wage, **7**:877
  Nader and, **7**:925
  OSHA and, **7**:960, 961
  pay equity, **7**:987
  Perkins as secretary of, **7**:994, 995, 996, 997
  small businesses, **9**:1199
  workplace diversity, **1**:37
  See also Equal Employment Opportunity Commission

Lake Shore Railroad, **10**:1364

Lands' End, **6**:769-71

League for Non-Violent Civil Disobedience Against Military Segregation, **8**:1085

Learning Tree, **3**:405

Leavitt and Sons, **6**:780

Lee (jeans company), **6**:786

Lender's Bagels, **6**:748

Lend Lease Real Estate Investment Management, Inc., **8**:1095

Leo Burnett Agency, **1**:139-40, **7**:1003

Leo Burnett Worldwide, **1**:140

Levi Strauss & Co., **6**:**785-87**

Levitt and Sons, **6**:788-90

Liberate Technologie, **7**:874

Liberty Live and Liberty Insurance Services, **8**:1132

Library of Congress, **5**:687

Lily Tulip Cup Company, **6**:755-56

Limited, The, **1**:53

Literary Guild, **8**:1078

Little, Brown (publisher), **1**:64, **8**:1078

Liverpool and Manchester Railway, **5**:654, *657*

Livingston, Fargo & Company, **1**:51, **10**:1405

Lloyd's of London, **6**:728, **8**:*1125*, **10**:1409

Lockheed Martin, **2**:214, **3**:352, 353

Lockheed Missile and Space, **3**:351

Long Island Airways, **10**:1333

Louis B. Mayer Company, **6**:845

Lowell Mills, **6**:805-8, **10**:1417

Lowell National Historic Park, **6**:805, 808

Lowe's, **8**:1100

Lucent Technologies, **1**:89, 90, **4**:501, *502*, **5**:670

M

Ma Bell. *See* AT&T

Macy's. *See* R. H. Macy's

Madame C. J. Walker Hair Culturists Union, **10**:1381

Madame C. J. Walker Manufacturing Company, **10**:1380-82

Magazine Publishers of America, **8**:1076

Maggioni Canning Company, **2**:*199*

Main Line Pictures, **2**:277-78, 279

Major League Baseball, **9**:1224

Major League Soccer, **9**:1224, *1225*

Manufacturing.Net, 386

Marathon Oil Company, **10**:*1353*, 1355

Maritime Commission, **8**:1105

Marshall Field's, **2**:*264*, 265, **3**:333, **8**:1115

Marsh's (Troy, Ohio, supermarket), **1**:103

Martha Stewart Living, **9**:*1238*, 1240

Martha Stewart Omnimedia, **9**:1238-40

Martin Marietta, **3**:353

Mary Kay Inc., **1**:76, 77

Massachusetts Institute of Technology, **7**:986, **8**:1110
  Samuelson and, **8**:1140-41
  Sloan School, **6**:843

Massachusetts Investors Trust, **4**:491

Materials Transportation Bureau, **8**:*1106*, 1107

Matsushita Electric, **8**:1019, **9**:1218

Maxwell-Briscoe, **4**:550

MCA, **4**:569

McCall Pattern Company, **6**:792

McCormick Harvester Company, **5**:601

McDonald's, **2**:232, **3**:427, **4**:566, **6**:**846-48**, **7**:918
  cultural differences and, **3**:331, **7**:918
  discount bundling, **1**:136
  Kroc and, **6**:755, 756-57
  liability suit, **2**:*161*, **8**:1046

McDonnell Douglass, **3**:353, **5**:651

McGraw-Hill (publisher), **8**:1078

McGraw Hill Education, **3**:406

MCI, **1**:89, **3**:360

McKinsey & Co., **2**:258

Mead Johnson, **1**:123

Médecins sans Frontiéres, **1**:123

Merchants Bank of Halifax, **8**:1131, *1132*

Merchants Union Express Company, **1**:51, *52*

Merck & Company, **1**:121

Meredith (publisher), **8**:1077

Merriam (publisher), **8**:1078

Merrill Lynch, **6**:**858-60**

Metallica, **2**:284, **9**:*1283*

METRO AG, **8**:1118

Metro-Goldwyn-Mayer. *See* MGM

Metromail, **6**:836

Metro Pictures Corporation, **6**:845

MGM, **6**:773, 845

MGM/United Artists, **10**:1340

Michigan Central Railroad, **10**:1364

Michigan Southern Railroad, **10**:1364

Microsoft, **3**:339, **5**:670, 677, **7**:**873-76**
  antitrust case, **1**:138, **3**:361, **8**:1051, 1104, *1106*, **9**:1190

breakup reversal, **7**:874, 875

browser, **2**:216

browser price war, **8**:1025

bundling, **1**:138

certification, **10**:1376

corporate security, **5**:*651*

in Dow Jones Average, **3**:376

education division, **3**:407

Gates and, **4**:537, 538-39

globalization and, **4**:566

human capital, **5**:625-26

IBM and, **2**:252, **5**:635, 636

independent contractors, **10**:1304

intellectual property, **5**:688, 689, 690

licenses, **6**:802, 804

monopoly charges, **7**:873, 874, 875, 902, *903*

multinationalism, **7**:*919*

Nasdaq trading, **7**:931

racial discrimination suit, **2**:214

stock returns, **9**:1242

Windows, **1**:138, **5**:636, 689, 690

Microsystems, **2**:216

Microwave Communications, Inc. *See* MCI

Midas Mufflers, **3**:427

Midland Chemical Company, **3**:373

Midland Linseed Products Company, **1**:70

Miller Brewing Company, **7**:1001, 1002, 1004

Mining Enforcement and Safety Administration, **8**:*1106*, 1107

Minnesota Valley Canning Company, **1**:139

Miramax Films, **7**:888-89, **10**:1393

Mitsubishi Motors, **5**:649, **7**:890-92

Mobil, 7.948, 9.123, 6.854. *See also* ExxonMobil

Montgomery Improvement Association, **2**:210

Montgomery Ward, **2**:265, **9**:1274

Mosaic Communications, 5.711, 5.712. *See also* Netscape

Motion Picture Academy, **7**:888, 889

Motion Picture Association of America, **7**:888

Motown Records, **1**:115, **4**:568-69

Mount Holyoke College, **7**:994, *995*

MSNBC (cable channel), **7**:876

Multilateral Investment Guarantee Agency, **10**:*1421*, 1422

Multimixer, **6**:756, 847

N

NAACP, **6**:739-40, **10**:1381, 1382

Napster, **2**:165, 283, 284, **6**:803

National Academy of Design, **7**:910, *911*

National Advertising Review Board, **1**:112

National Aeronautics and Space Administration, **5**:710, **8**:1059, *1112*

National Archives, **7**:1000

National Association for Stock Car Auto Racing, 9:1224

National Association for the Advancement of Colored People, 6:739-40, 10:1381, 1382

National Association for the Promotion of Labor Unionism among Negroes, 8:1083

National Association of Colored Women, 10:1382

National Association of Elementary School Principals, 8:1048

National Association of Home Builders, 1:133-34, 8:1048

National Association of Independent Schools, 8:1049

National Association of Realtors, 8:1048, 1090-91

National Association of School Superintendents, 7:935

National Association of Securities Dealers, 1:54, 55, 3:342

National Association of Securities Dealers Automatic Quotation System. See Nasdaq

National Basketball Association, 9:1224

National Better Business Bureau. See Better Business Bureau

National Black Chamber of Commerce, 2:193, 7:933-34

National Broadcasting Company. See NBC

National Business Coalition on Health, 2:172

National Cancer Institute, 1:123

National Cash Register Co., 5:632

National Child Labor Committee, 2:200

National Collegiate Athletic Association, 9:1224, 1226

National Consumers League, 2:267, 7:994

National Council of Better Business Bureaus, 1:112

National Council on Disability, 1:60

National Council on Disability Congress, 1:56

National Credit Union Administration, 2:272, 273

National Education Association, **7:935-38**

National Farm Workers Association, 2:194, 195

National Football League, 9:1223, 1224, 1226, 1227

National Forestry Association, 4:517

National Foundation for Teaching Entrepreneurship, 3:425

National Gambling Impact Study Commission, 4:536

National Guard, U.S., 3:350-53

National Highway Traffic Safety Administration, 2:272, 273, 8:1106, 1107

National Hockey League, 9:1226, 10:1393

National Institute for Occupational Safety and Health, 7:961

National Institutes of Health, 8:1059

National Marine Fisheries Service, 4:509

National Negro Business League, 7:933, 934

National Organization for Women, 9:1184

National Park Service, 6:808

National Railroad Passenger Corporation, 10:1330

National Recovery Administration, 7:940, 941, 941

National Refiners Association, 9:1231, 1232

National Science Foundation, 5:714, 8:1059

National Society of Fund Raising Executives, 8:1049

National Transportation Safety Board, 8:1106, 1107

National Vigilance Committee, 1:112

National War Labor Board, 10:1414

National Youth Administration, 7:941

NBC (television), 4:549, 8:1147, 1148

NBCC. See National Black Chamber of Commerce

NCR Corp., 1:89, 90

NEA. See National Education Association

Negro American Labor Council, 8:1086

Nestlé, 3:332, 8:1047

Netscape, 5:678, 712, 10:1433
  Navigator browser, 2:215-16, 5:711, 7:875
  Navigator price war, 8:1025

Nevada National Bank, 10:1405

New American Library, 8:1078

Newman's Organics, 7:944, 946

Newman's Own, **7:944-46**

New School for Social Research, 2:267

News Corporation, 8:1075, 1079

Newspaper Association of America, 8:1074-75

New York City Consumer's League, 7:994, 995

New York Public Service Commission, 8:1108-9

New York Yankees, 6:814, 815, 9:1223

Nike, 3:346, 4:565-66, 7:918, **950-53**, 9:1227

Nippon Gakki Company, 10:1435

Nistevo, 3:386

Nobel Learning Centers, 3:405

Nordstrom, 3:335

North American Aviation, 10:1350

Northeastern University, 2:284

Northrop Grumman, 3:352

Northwest Airlines, 2:224, 3:377, 7:931

North West Company, 5:624

Northwestern Telephone, 9:1285

Northwestern University, 6:772, 773, 843

Nucor Steel Corporation, 5:679, 680

O

Occupational Safety and Health Administration, 6:759, 796, 798, 7:960-63, 8:1106, 1107
  ergonomics and, 4:456
  founding of, 10:1418
  small businesses and, 9:1199

OECD. See Organization for Economic Cooperation and Development

Office of Economic Opportunity, 3:393

Office of Management and Budget, 7:928

Office of Production Management, 4:552

Office of Strip Mining Regulation and Enforcement, 8:1107

Old Navy, 1:118

OPEC. See Organization of Petroleum Exporting Countries

Oracle Corp., 2:216, 241, 10:1433

Organization for Economic Cooperation and Development, 7:966-67

Organization of Banana Exporting Countries, 2:206
  Origins, 6:777

OSHA. See Occupational Safety and Health Administration

Oxygen Media, 10:1411-12

P

Pabst brewery, 7:1002

Pacific Gas and Electric, 1:37, 6:796, 8:1016, 10:1356

Paine Webber, 10:1346

Palmer Memorial Institute, 10:1382

Palo Alto Research Center (Calif.), 10:1429, 1430-32

Pan American Airways, 3:358, 9:1192, 10:1333-35

Pantheon, 8:1078

Paralyzed Veterans of America, 1:56

Paramount Pictures, 6:773, 774, 10:1393

PARC (Palo Alto Research Center), 10:1429, 1430-32

Patent Office, U.S., 5:687, 7:984, 8:1036

Patent Office Board of Appeals, U.S., 7:986

Paul Newman Foundation, 7:944, 945, 946

Paul Weiss (law firm), 6:791-92

Pearson (publisher), 8:1079

Pearson Education, 3:406

Pemex, 3:418

Pennsylvania Railroad, 2:184, 185, 8:1066, 9:1250

Pennzoil, 10:1307

Pentax, 7:909

PeopleSoft, 5:670

PepsiCo, 9:1236

Permanent Court of International Arbitration, 1:67

Perma Soft, 3:374

Perot Systems, 7:998, 999

Phelps Dodge, 9:1252

Philadelphia Electric Company, 7:901

Philip Morris Companies, 7:**1001-4**
  General Mills-Kellogg price war, 747
  Leo Burnett Advertising, 1:139
  liability suits, 8:1046

Philip Morris International, 7:1004

Philip Morris Research Center, 7:1003

Philip Morris USA, 7:1004

Philips Electronics NV, 3:402

Pillsbury Doughboy, 1:140

Pinkerton National Detective Agency, 9:1176, 1250, 1251

PIRGs (Public Interest Research Groups), 9:1258

Plato (education firm), 3:407

Pocket Books, Inc., 8:1078

Pricewaterhouse Coopers, 2:259-60

Princeton Review, 3:407

Princeton University, 4:532, 533

Prism Financial Corporation, 8:1132

Procter & Gamble, 1:37

Prodigy, 10:1406

Professional Golfers Association, 9:1224

Public Citizen, Inc., 2:274, 7:926, 927

Public Interest Research Group, 7:927

Public Relations Consultants Association (Britain), 8:1067

Public Relations Society of America, 8:1067

Public Safety Research Institute, 7:927

Public Works Administration, 2:180, 6:750, 7:941, 943

Pullman Company, 8:1083-84

Q

Qwest Communications International, 1:90, 9:1288

R

Radio Corporation of America. See RCA

Random House, 8:1078

Raytheon Corporation, 3:352, 353, 5:651

RBC. See Royal Bank of Canada

RCA, 1:103, 4:549, 8:1146-48, 9:1218

RCA Laboratories, 8:1148

Reconstruction Finance Corporation, 9:1200, 1201

Recording Industry Association of America, 2:284

Reebok, 7:952

Reginald Lewis International Law Center, 6:793

Reliant Energy Company, **9:**1224-25
RE/MAX (realtor), **8:**1091
Remington Rand Corp., **2:**250, **5:**633
Renaissance Learning, **3:**407
Renaissance Software, Inc., **5:**648
REO (auto company), **4:**550
Research & Polling, Inc., **6:**837
Resettlement Administration, **7:***941*
Reuters, **10:**1434
R. G. Dun & Company, **3:**336, *337*
R. H. Macy's, **3:**333, **8:**1115
Rice Broadcasting, **10:**1339
R. J. Reynolds, **7:**1004, **8:**1046
RJR Nabisco, **5:**637, **7:***1001*, 1002
Rockefeller & Andrews, **9:**1231
Rockefeller, Andres & Flagler, **8:**1129
Rockefeller Foundation, **8:**1130
Rockefeller Institute, **4:**555, **8:**1130
Rockefeller University, **8:**1130
Rockwell International, **3:**353, **10:**1350
Royal Bank of Canada, **8:1131-32**
Royal Dutch/Shell, **3:**416, **7:**719-20, 0.1133-36, **10:**1307
Rural Electrification Administration, **7:***941*

S

Sanyo, **7:**909
Sarah's Kitchen, **9:***1198*
Sarnoff Corporation, **8:**1148
Saudi Arabian Oil Company, **10:**1307
SBA. *See* Small Business Administration
SBC. *See* Swiss Banking Corporation
SBC Communications, **1:**90, **3:**376, **9:**1288
Schweizerische Bangesellschart, **10:**1347
Scientific Data Systems, **10:**1430-32
Scott Newman Foundation, **7:**945
Scripps Howard, **8:**1075
Sears, **3:**376, **4:**513, **5:**679, **7:**909, **10:**1389
  catalog sales, **2:**265
  credit card, **3:**319
  employment discrimination complaints, **4:**453
  Lands' End acquisition by, **6:**770, 772
Seattle Computer Products, **7:**874
Securities Industry Association, **7:**930
Securities Investor Protection Corporation, **9:**1157, 1173
Sequoia Capital, **10:**1433
Service Corps of Retired Executives, **9:**1198, 1201
Seven Arts Productions, Ltd., **1:**65
Seven-Up, **7:**1002
Shell Oil. *See* Royal Dutch/Shell
Shell Transport & Trading Company, **8:**1133, *1134, 1136*
Shuttlefly, **2:**216
Sierra Club, **4:**516, **7:**958
Sikorsky Aircraft Corporation, **9:**1193

Sikorsky Manufacturing Corporation, **9:**1192
Silicon Graphics, **2:***215*, 216
Simon & Schuster, **8:**1078
Simon Property Group, Inc., **8:**1095
Singer Sewing Machine Company, **4:**522, **7:**916
SkillSoft, **3:**406
Sloan School, **6:**843
Small Business Administration, **1:**60, **6:**792, 836, **7:**934, **9:**1197-98, **1200-1201**, **10:**1370
Small Business Development Centers, **9:**1201
Small Defense Plants Administration, **9:**1201
Smaller War Plants Corporation, **9:**1200-1201
Socal. *See* Chevron
Social Science Research Council, **8:**1140
Social Security Administration, **9:**1199, 1214
Social Security Board, **9.**1212, 1214
Sohio, **9:**1234
Sony Corporation, **7:**889, 908-9, **9:1217-19**
Sony Music, **8:**1018, **9:**1219
Sony Pictures China, **9:**1219
Sony Pictures Classics, **9:**1219
Sotheby's, **8:**1019, 1020
South Improvement Company, **9:**1231-32
Southwest Airlines, **2:**169, **3:**334, **8:**1127, **9:1220-22**
Springfield System, **6:**828
Squibb. *See* Bristol-Myers Squibb
SRI International, **8:**1148
S. S. Kresge, **10:**1387
Standard Oil, **8:**1104, **9:1231-34**
  breakup of, **7:***902*, 904, **9:**1188, 1234, **10:**1305
  as monopoly, **7:**901, *902*, 904
  Rockefeller and, **8:***1128*, 1129-30
  Shell competition, **8:**1133, 1134
  Texaco and, **10:**1305
  vertical integration, **7:**972, **8:**1129
Stanford University, **2:**215, **3:**424, **4:**528, **5:**619, 620, **9:**1166, **10:**1433
  Fiorina and, **4:**501, *502*
  genetic engineering, **4:**555
  Yahoo! search engine, **5:**711, *712*
Stanley Home Products, **1:**76
Stanley Steamers, **10:**1330
Staples, **9:**1200
Starbucks, **2:**267, **9:1235-37**
Star Enterprise, **10:**1307
Star-Kist Tuna, **1:**139-40
StarLink, **4:**559
Stockton and Darlington Railway, **5:**654, *657*
Stringfellow, **10:**1331-32
Stroh brewery, **7:**1002
Subway, **3:**427, **4:**523
Sunkist, Inc., **1:**31

Sun Microsystems, **4:**501, **5:**670
  browser, **2:**216
  inventory overhang, **6:**727
  Java programming language, **5:**711, 712
  team-up strategy, **5:**680
Supreme Liberty Life Insurance Company, **6:**739
Survey Research Center, **2:**261-62, **6:**779
Suzuki Motor Company, **4:**554, **5:**599
Swift Company, **1:**81
Swiss Banking Corporation, **10:***1346*
Sylvan Learning, **3:**407

T

Tabulating Machine Company, **5:**632, *633*
Target, **8:**1018, **10:**1387
Taxpayers for Common Sense, **9:**1258
Technicon, **3:**386
Tecolote Research, **3:**352
Teenage Research Unlimited, **3:**355-56
Tellme Networks, Inc., **10:***1372*
Tengelmann, **8:**1118
Tennessee Valley Authority, **7:**941, 943, *943*, **9:**1255-56
Tesco, **8:**1118
Texaco, **2:**157, **9:**1234, **10:1305-7**
Texas Instruments, **5:**636
Texas Oil Company, **10:**1305, *1307*
Texas Rangers (baseball), **9:**1227
Texas Utilities Company, **3:**377
Thomson-Houston Company, **4:**547, 548
Thomson Learning, **3:**406
Time Warner, **3:**301, 402, **8:**1075, 1077, 1079, **9:**1240
  merger with America Online, **6:**853, 854
  See also AOL Time Warner
TLC (The Lewis Company), **6:**792
TLC Beatrice, **6:**792
Tokyo Telecommunications Engineering Corporation, **9:**1217, *1218*
Tokyo Telecommunications Research Institute, **7:**908
Tokyo Tsushin Kogyo K.K. *See* Sony Corporation
Touchstone Pictures, **10:**1393
Toyota, **6:**741, 743, 830-31
Toys R Us, **3:**382
Traf-O-Data, **7:**873, *874*
Trammell Crow Co., **8:**1095
Transco Energy Company, **3:**420
Transcontinental and Western Air, Inc., **4:**552
Trans Union Corporation, **3:**325
Treasury Department, U.S., **5:**697, **8:**1092
  Federal Reserve and, **4:**482
  Hamilton as first secretary of, **5.**595, 596
  Samuelson and, **8:**1141
Tribune Company, **8:**1075

Trump Organization, **10:**1336
Trump Plaza Hotel and Casino (Atlantic City), **10:**1336
Trump Shuttle Airline, **10:**1336, 1337
Turner Broadcasting System, **1:**64, **10:**1339, 1341
Turner Classic Movies, **10:**1341
Turner Communications, **10:**1339
Turner Foundation, **10:**1341
Tuskegee Institute, **7:**933, **10:**1382
TWA, **1:**101, *102*, **4:**552
20th Century-Fox, **6:**772, 773
Tyco International, **2:**153, *158*

U

UBS AB. *See* Union Bank of Switzerland
UBS Asset Management, **10:**1346
UBS Warburg, **10:**1346
U-Matic, **9:**1218
Unilever PLC, **1:***106*, 108
Union Bank of Switzerland, **10:**1346, **1346-48**
Union Carbide, **3:**373, 374, *376*, **4:**441, **9:***1264*, 1266
Unión de Países Exportadores de Banano, **2:**06
Union Iron Works, **2:**185
Union of Swiss Banks, **10:**1347
Union Pacific Railroad, **3:**377, **8:**1144, **10:**1330
Union Trust Company, **10:**1405-6
Unisys, **7:**986
United Brands, **2:***204*, 206
United Fruit, **2:**204, *205*, 206
United Negro College Fund, **4:**539
United Parcel Service (UPS)
  MaxiCode, **1:**105
  strike, **2:***221*, **9:**1253, 1254, 1276
  temporary workers, **10:**1301
United Press Association, **8:**1075
United Press International, **8:**1075
United States Chamber of Commerce, **2:**191-92, **8:***1048*
United States Football League, **10:**1336
United States Hispanic National Chamber of Commerce, **2:**193
United States Junior Chamber of Commerce, **2:**192-93
United States Steel Corporation, **2:**186, **5:**673, 679, **9:**1168, 1251-52, **10:1353-55**
  collective bargaining, **1:**39
  Morgan and, **7:**905, 906
United Technologies Corporation, **9:**1193
Universal Music, **8:**1018
Universal Studios, **7:**889
University of Chicago, **2:**182, **3:**358, **6:**841
  economics Nobel laureates, **4:**528
  Friedman and, **4:**527, 528
  Graham and, **4:**572
  Rockefeller philanthropy and, **8:**1130
  Samuelson and, **8:**1140, 1141
  Veblen and, **10:**1365

University of Michigan
Index of Consumer Sentiments, 2:261-62, 263
Survey Research Center, 2:261-62, 6:779
University of Pennsylvania, 6:843, 7:994, 10:1336
University of Phoenix Online, 3:406
UPS. See United Parcel Service
U.S. See also under United States
USAA (insurance/financial services), 3:335
U.S. Freightways, 3:377
U.S. Rubber Company, 3:376

V

Vanderbilt University, 10:1364
Verizon Communications, 1:90, 9:1288
Verlagsgruppe Georg von Holtzbrinck, 4:472
Viacom, 8:1079
Videx, 1:123
Vivendi, 8:1019-20
Volkswagen, 10:1377-79

W

Wage and Hour Administration, 7:961
Walker Club, 10:1382
Wall Street Journal, 3:376, 377, 381, 8:1075, 10:1383-86
corporate image ranking, 1:108
Wall Street Journal Europe, 10:1386
Wal-Mart, 10:1387-90
blocking strategy, 5:679-80
bond issuance, 9:1242
competition, 8:1018
credit card antitrust suit, 1:53
entrepreneurial innovation, 3:424
environmentalism and, 4:442
globalization, 4:564-65, 8:1118
innovation, 5:679
just-in-time inventory, 6:744, 9:1280, 10:1389
stock issuance, 9:1241
technology, 9:1280
vertical marketing system, 3:369
Walt Disney Company, 1:66, 2:267, 6:856, 7:888-89, 10:1391-94
Walt Disney Studio Entertainment, 5:619-21, 10:1393
Walt Disney World, 10:1392, 1393
Walton's Five and Dime, 10:1387
Warburg Dillon Read. See UBS Warburg
Warner Books, 1:64
Warner Bros., 1:64, 65
Warner Bros.-Seven Arts, 1:64, 65
Warner Communications. See AOL Time Warner
Warner Music, 8:1018
Washington Post, 4:570-72, 8:1075
W. Atlee Burpee Company, 1:23
WB (television network), 1:64, 66
W. Edwards Deming Institute, 10:1310
Wells & Co., 1:51
Wells Fargo, 1:51, **10:1405-7**

Western Electric Company, 1:87-88, 89, 90, 6:825, 10:1310
Western Health Reform Institute, 6:745
Western Union, 1:88, 3:399, 400, 9:1284, 1285
Westinghouse, 3:371, 8:1147
Wharton School, 6:843, 10:1336
Whitaker & Baxter, 8:1068
Whittle Communications, 3:402
Winn-Dixie, 1:105
Woolco, 10:1387
Works Progress Administration, 7:941, 942, 943
World Bank, 1:78, 2:180, 181, 4:563, 565, 567, 6:751, 10:1421-24, 1425
information technology, 5:671
International Monetary Fund and, 5:702, 703
international trade, 5:708-9
privatization studies, 8:1031
recession and, 8:1098
"Rule of Law and Development," 8:1139
sustainable development and, 9:1267
World Bank Group, 10:1422
World Business Council on Sustainable Development, 9:1265, 1266, 1267
WorldCom, 1:89, 3:297, 306
business ethics, 2:153
World Gift Co., 1:76-77
World Health Organization, 10:1313
World Hunger Relief, Inc., 5:715
World Tourism Organization, 10:1313, 1315
World Trade Organization, 1:95, 2:181, 232, 5:708, 10:1425-28
antiglobalization protests, 4:566, 7:967
fair trade complaints, 10:1325
GATT as forerunner, 4:540, 543, 563
member nations, 2:232, 10:1426
Worthington Foods, 6:746, 748
Wrangler, 6:786
WTO. See World Trade Organization

X

Xerox Corporation, 1:37, 9:1292, 10:1429-32
downsizing, 3:378
research and development, 8:1111
XKL (company), 2:207
Xlibris, 8:1078

Y

Yahoo!, 4:492, 5:711, 712, 7:876, 10:1433-34
Yale University, 4:488, 10:1333, 1365, 1366
Yamaha Corporation, **10:1435-36**
Yamaha de Mexico, 10:1436

Yamaha International Corporation, U.S., 10:1436
York Factory, 5:623

Z

Zenith, 8:1019

Index of Laws, Court Cases, and Public Policy

A

Act to Regulate Commerce (1887), 8:1103, 1106
ADA. See Americans with Disabilities Act
Adamson Act (1916), 10:1418
Adarand Constructors v. Pena (1995), 1:36
affirmative action, 1:34-37, 135, 5:630
Age Discrimination in Employment Act (1967), 1:34, 2:213, 4:452-53, 10:1418
Age Discrimination in Employment Act (1975), 1:34
Agricultural Labor Relations Act (Calif.), 2:195, 196
Aid to Dependent Children, 9:1212
Aid to the Blind, 9:1212
Alcoa case (1945), 9:1189
Americans with Disabilities Act (1990), 1:56-60, 2:213, 4:452-53
Anti-Chain–Store Act (1936). See Robinson–Patman Act
Architectural Barriers Act (1968), 1:56

B

Banking Act (1935), 3:315, 316, 317
Bill of Rights, U.S., 2:256, 7:1000
Bono Copyright Extension Act (1998), 2:284
Brown v. Board of Education (1954), 7:936, 8:1085
Budget and Accounting Act (1921), 4:477
business law, 2:160-65
affirmative action, 1:34
business ethics and, 2:154, 157, 159, 160-62, 6:782
contracts, 2:160-61, 276-79
copyright, 2:164, 165, 280-84
corporations, 3:302
e-business, 3:384
employment discrimination, 2:213-14
family leave, 4:468-71
human resources department, 5:630-31
initial public offering, 5:677

intellectual property, 5:688-89
legal services, 6:781-84
liability, 6:794-800
licenses, 6:802-3
partnership, 7:976
product liability, 8:1045-47
risk management, 8:1127
rule of law and, 8:1137, 1138-39
trademark, 10:1320, 1321

C

Cellar–Kefauver Antimerger Act (1950), 7:900
Civil Aeronautics Act (1938), 8:1105, 1106
Civil Rights Act (1964), 1:56, 2:210-13, 3:300, 7:987
affirmative action, 1:34, 35
disabilities extension, 1:59
equal employment, 4:452-53
excerpt, 2:211
sexual harassment, 9:1184, 1185
workplace conditions, 10:1418
Civil Rights Act (1991), 2:212, 213, 214
civil rights legislation, 2:210-14, 7:987
affirmative action vs., 1:34
Americans with Disabilities Act, 1:56-60
arbitration, 1:68
corporate social responsibility and, 3:300
disparate impact theory, 2:212-13
EEOC and, 4:452-53
immigrant groups and, 5:639-43
key laws, 2:213
pay equity, 2:236, 7:987
sexual harassment and, 9:1184, 1184-86
Texaco discrimination lawsuit, 10:1307
working conditions, 10:1417, 1418
working women and, 10:1414, 1415, 1416, 1418
Civil Service Reform Act (1978), 2:213
Clayton Antitrust Act (1914), 4:485, 553, 6:762, 9:1197
provisions, 2:245, 7:900, 904
Clean Air Act (1927), 7:927
Clean Air Act (1955), 4:448
Clean Air Act Amendments (1970), 2:268, 4:443, 444, 447, 448, 449, 450
Clean Air Act Amendments (1990), 4:444, 446, 447, 448, 449
Clean Water Act (1948), 4:448
Clean Water Act (1977), 4:447, 448, 450
Community Service Amendments (1974), 3:395
Comprehensive Environmental Response, Compensation, and Liability Act (1970). See Superfund

Constitution, U.S., **2:**253-57, **7:**980, 1000
  affirmative action rulings, **1:**36
  civil rights guarantees, **2:**210
  contract protection, **2:**277
  copyright provision, **2:**281, **8:**1112
  corporation rights, **3:**302
  Hamilton and, **5:**595, 596, 597
  implied powers doctrine, **5:**596
  income tax amendment, **5:**697
  intellectual property, **5:**687
  patent provision, **7:**980, **8:**1112
  as rule of law, **8:**1137, 1138
  taxing power, **5:**698
  See also specific amendments
Consumer Credit Protection Act (1968), **3:**325
Consumer Leasing Act, **2:**275
Consumer Lending Act, **4:**485
Consumer protection, **2:**267-68, **272-75**, **7:**925-27
  advertising and, **1:**32, 112, 113
  AT&T monopoly and, **9:**1286
  Better Business Bureau and, **1:**112-13
  business ethics and, **2:**158
  business law and, **2:***160*
  contract law and, **2:**279
  corporate social responsibility, **3:**300
  credit cards, **3:**320, 321
  e-business, **2:**279
  federalism and, **2:**255-56
  FTC and, **4:**484-87, **8:**1104, 1105
  genetically modified food and, **4:**559
  GM Corvair and, 553, **4:**552
  identity theft and, **3:**326, 328
  liability law and, **6:**794-800
  Nader and, **7:**925-27
  product liability and, **8:**1045-47
  regulatory activity, **6:**796, **8:**1104-9
Consumer Protection Act (1969), **3:**321
contracts and contract law, **2:**160-61, **276-79**
  bankruptcy, **1:**99-102
  corporations and, **3:**302
  credit repair, **3:**326
  e-business and, **3:**384
  liability and, **6:**794, 795
  license and, **6:**801-4
  outsourcing and, **7:**972-93
  rule of law and, **8:**1137, 1138, 1139
Convention on the Elimination of All Forms of Discrimination Against Women, **4:**468
Convention on the Law and the Sea (1982), **4:**509
Convention on the Rights of the Child (1989), **2:**201

copyright, **2:**280-84, **7:**874
  amortization, **1:**61, 63
  business law, **2:**164, 165
  e-business and, **3:**384
  information technology, **9:**1282, 1283
  as intangible asset, **1:***84*, 85
  intellectual property, **5:**687
  Internet, **5:**710
  limited duration, **2:**165
  materials covered by, **2:***281*, 283
  patent vs., **7:**980
  piracy, **6:**803, *804*
  as property right, **8:**1029
  reverse engineering and, **8:**1122, 1123
  small business, **9:**1199
  as writer protection, **8:**1112
  WTO and, **10:**1427
Corning Glass Works v. Brennan (1974), **10:**1415
Credit Repair Organization Act, **3:**326
Current Tax Payment Act (1943), **5:**697, 698
cyberlaw, **2:**165

D
Davis–Bacon Act (1933), **6:**763
Declaration of Independence, **6:**851, 852, **10:**1401
Diamond v. Diehr, **7:**986
Digital Millennium Copyright Act (1998), **2:**283-84

E
Earth Summit (1992), **1:***78*, **4:***440*
Economic Opportunity Act (1964), **3:**393-95
Economic Recovery Tax Act (1981), **8:**1094
Education for All Handicapped Children Act (1975), **1:**56
Eighth Amendment, **2:**257
Electronic Signatures in Global and National Commerce Act (2000), **3:**412
Ellereth case (1998), **9:**1185-86
Emergency Banking Relief Act (1933), **7:**941, **8:**1104, *1105*, *1106*
Employment Act (1946), **7:**893
Endangered Species Act (1973), **4:**447, *448*, 450
Energy Policy Act (1992), **4:**485
environmentalism, **4:**437-42
  agricultural production and, **1:**45, 46, 48
  Asian Development Bank and, **1:**78, 79-80
  automobile ownership and, **9:**1230
  business ethics and, **2:**154, 157-58
  consumerism and, **2:**268
  corporate responsibility and, **3:**299-301
  Dow Chemical hazards, **3:**373, 375

economic growth balanced with, **3:***391*, 392
  ecotourism and, **10:**1313-14
  energy industry and, **3:**418
  EPA controls, **4:**443, 444, 447, *448*, 450
  European Union and, **4:***460*
  externalities and, **4:**437-38, 463-64, 465
  federal budget and, **4:**479
  fields of interest, **4:**437, 443
  forest products and, **4:**515-16, *518*
  GATT rounds and, **4:**545
  genetically modified crops and, **4:**559
  GM catalytic converter, **4:**552
  key principles of, **4:**437
  liability and, **6:**795, 796
  Malthusian theory and, **6:**816, 817-18
  mining industry and, **7:**884, 884-85, 885
  multinationals and, **7:**919
  Nader and, **7:**927
  NAFTA and, **7:**958-59
  as negative production externality, **4:**463-64
  Nike and, **7:**952-53
  OSHA standards and, **7:**960, 962
  public goods and, **8:**1059, 1060
  regulation problems, **4:**450-51
  Royal Dutch/Shell and, **8:**1135-36
  Silent Spring and, **9:**1195
  subsidies and, **9:**1258
  sustainable development and, **4:**442, **9:**1264-67
  Texaco and, **10:**1307
  tragedy of the commons and, **10:**1326-28
  Turner and, **10:**1341
  World Bank and, **10:**1324, *1421*
environmental regulation, **4:**439, *440*, **447-51**, **8:***1106*, 1107, 1109
  externalities and, **4:**465
  forest products and, **4:**515-16
  key provisions, **4:**448
  mining industry and, **7:**884-85
  OSHA and, **7:**960, 961, 962
  politics of, **4:**441-42
  private property and, **8:**1029
  profit and loss and, **8:**1051
  rule of law and, **8:**1139
  sustainable development and, **9:**1266-67
Equal Credit Opportunity Act (1974), **3:**320
Equal Pay Act (1963), **1:***34*, **2:***213*, **4:**452-53, 467, **7:***987*, **10:**1414, 1418
equal protection, **1:**36, **2:**210, **8:**1138

F
Fair Credit Reporting Act (1968), **3:**325-26, **4:**485

Fair Labor Standards Act (1938), **3:**299, **4:**466-67, **7:**996, **10:**1418
  child labor, **2:***200*, 201, 203, **4:**466
  minimum wage, **4:**466, **7:**877, 879-80, 943
Fair Packaging and Labeling Act, **2:**275
Fair Trade Act (1937), **9:**1197
fair use rules, **2:**284, **5:**687, 690, **9:**1282
Family and Medical Leave Act (1993), **4:**468, 469-71, **5:**630
Faragher case (1998), **9:**1185-86
Federal Arbitration Act (1925), **1:**67-68
federal budget, **4:**477-79, 503, 505
Federal Cigarette Labeling and Advertising Act (1966), **4:**485, **7:**1003
Federal Food, Drug, and Cosmetic Act (1938). *See* Food, Drug, and Cosmetic Act
Federal Insecticide, Fungicide and Rodenticide Act (1972), **4:***448*
Federal Insurance Contributions Act, **9:**1212-13
Federal Reserve Act (1913), **3:**315
Federal Reserve System, **4:**480-83, 503
  consumer protection, **2:***272*
  district banks, **4:**481, 482
  economic growth and, **3:**390, 391
  Greenspan and, **5:**586-87
  inflation measures, **5:**661
  interest rates and, **5:**695, 696
  investment and, **6:**730-31
  Leading Economic Index and, **6:**778
  macroeconomics and, **6:**812
  monetary policy, **3:**315-16, 390, 391, **4:**480-83, 527, 528, **7:**893-95
  Morgan and, **7:**905, 907
  real estate brokerage, **8:**1092
  recession measures, **8:**1098
Federal Trade Commission Act (1914), **4:**485, **8:**1104, *1106*
  provisions, **2:**245, **7:***900*
FICA. *See* social security and Medicare
Fifth Amendment, **2:***256*
Financial Services Modernization Act (1999), **5:**683
First Amendment, **2:**210-14, *256*, 257
  corporation rights, **3:**302
fiscal policy, **4:**503-5
  exchange rate, **4:**461
  federal budget, **4:**477-79, 503
  Friedman monetarism and, **4:**528
  Galbraith theory and, **4:**532, 533

fiscal policy (cont.)
  Keynesian macroeconomics and, 6:750, 812
  macroeconomics, 6:750, 810, 811, 812
  recession, 8:1098
  subsidy, 9:1255-58
  wealth distribution, 10:1399
FLSA. *See* Fair Labor Standards Act
Food, Drug, and Cosmetic Act (1938), 2:275, 4:*448*, 8:1105, *1106*
Food and Drug Act (1906), 2:275
Food Quality Protection Act (1996), 4:448
Foreign Corrupt Practices Act (1977), 2:*156*, 159
Fourteenth Amendment, 2:210, 3:302
  corporation rights, 3:302
Fourth Amendment, 2:256, 257
Freedom of Information Act (1966), 2:268, 5:649, 7:927
Full Employment Act (1946), 2:152
Full Employment and Balanced Growth Act (1978), 7:893

G

Garn–St. Germain Act (1982), 8:1094
Glass–Steagall Act (1933), 7:941, 8:1105, *1106*
Gottschalk v. Benson (1972), 7:986
government regulation. *See* regulation of business and industry
government spending. *See* federal budget; fiscal policy
Great Depression, 5:581-85, 7:947
  American Stock Exchange, 1:55
  blue jeans market, 6:785, *786*
  business cycle theory, 2:149, 150-51
  as capitalism threat, 2:179-80, *181*
  child labor effects, 2:201
  corporate responsibility, 3:299
  credit, 3:315, 317-18
  Dow Jones Industrial Average, 2:*151*
  economic effects of, 8:1097
  environmental projects, 4:439, *440*
  Fair Labor Standards Act, 4:466-67
  farm programs, 1:47
  fascism, 4:474
  Federal Reserve, 4:480-81
  General Motors, 4:551
  Harley-Davidson, 5:598
  IBM, 5:632-33
  Keynesian economics, 3:364-65, 390, 6:750, 810
  labor unions, 1:40, 6:762-63
  minimum wage, 7:878, 8:1014
  National Labor Relations Act, 7:939, 940
  Perkins and, 7:994-97

protectionism, 4:563, 10:1428
regulation of business and industry, 3:359
regulatory activity, 8:1104-5, 1107
Royal Bank of Canada, 8:1131-32
Samuelson theory, 8:1140, 1141
Schumpeter theory, 9:1164
SEC founding, 9:1172
small business failures, 9:1197
small business loans, 9:1200
stock market, 7:947
strikes, 9:1252-53
subsidies, 9:1255-56
Teamsters, 9:1274
women workers, 10:1413
Great Society, 2:180, *181*, 9:1214
Griswold v. Connecticut (1965), 2:257

H

Hart–Cellar Act (1965), 5:638
Hart–Scott–Rodino Notification Act (1976), 7:900
Hepburn Act (1906), 8:1103, *1106*
Highway Safety Act (1970), 2:273
Homestead Act, 1:47
Hudson v. McMillian (1992), 2:257

I

Immigration Act (1990), 5:641
Immigration and Nationality Act (1965), 5:638
Immigration Reform and Control Act (1986), 5:639-40, 641
Indian Gaming Regulatory Act (1989), 4:535
Industrial Espionage Act (1996), 5:652
intellectual property, 5:687-91
  business law, 2:160, 164-65
  Coca-Cola, 2:164, 218
  copyright, 2:280-84
  early laws, 2:280-81
  industrial espionage, 5:648-52
  license, 6:801-4
  as property right, 8:1029
  R&D protection, 8:1112
  trademark, 10:1320
  World Trade Organization and, 10:1427, 1428
  See also copyright; patent
Internal Revenue Service Restructuring and Reform Act (1998), 5:699-700

K

Keating–Owen Act (1916), 2:200
Kefauver–Harris bill, 2:273
Kelly Act (1925), 10:1333

L

Labor–Management Relations Act (1947). *See* Taft–Hartley Act
Labor–Management Reporting and Disclosure Act (1959). *See* Landrum–Griffin Act

La Follette Seaman's Act (1915), 10:1418
Landrum–Griffin Act (1959), 6:767-68, 9:1269, 1275
liability, 6:794-800
  contract law, 2:276-79
  corporate protections from, 3:302
  credit, 3:314
  risk management, 8:1124-25
  strict principles, 8:1045
  tort law, 2:161-62
  See also product liability
license, 6:801-4
  as competition entry barrier, 7:900
  contract law, 2:279
  copyright, 2:280, 281, 282
  Disney characters, 10:1391-92
  import procedures, 4:543
  Intel 8088 chip, 5:635, 636
  Internet film downloading, 7:889
  Microsoft, 5:635, 636, 7:874
  negative externality control, 4:465
  of patents, 8:1112
  product development, 8:1036
  by Small Business Administration, 9:1201
  Sony, 9:1218
  sports merchandise, 9:1223
  vocational, 10:1374-76
Lucas v. South Carolina Coastal Commission (1992), 2:256

M

Magna Carta (1215), 7:999-1000
Main Line Pictures v. Basinger (1993), 2:277-78, 279
McCulloch v. Maryland, 5:596
Medicaid, 2:180, 5:606, 607, 9:1214
Medicare, 2:180, 5:606, 608, 9:*1210*, 1211, 1214-15
  federal budget, 4:478-79
Merchant Marine Act (1936), 8:1105, *1106*
Meritor Savings Bank, FSB v. Vinson (1986), 9:1184, 1185
Microsoft Corp v. Vizcaino (1992), 10:1304
Miller–Tydings Act (1937), 9:1197
Motor Carrier Act (1935), 8:1105, *1106*, 1109
Motor Vehicle Information and Cost Savings Act (1972), 2:273
Munn v. Illinois (1877), 8:1103, *1106*

N

NAICS codes, 7:928-29, 8:1115, 1116
National Bank Act (1864), 3:3.115, *317*
National Currency Act (1863), 3:314-15, *317*
National Environmental Policy Act (1969), 4:*448*

National Industrial Recovery Act (1933), 7:878, 940, 996
National Labor Relations Act (1935), 2:196, 4:552, 6:763, 767, 7:938, **939-40**, 943, 9:1252, 1272-73
  Taft-Hartley Act and, 9:1268, 1269
National Labor Relations Board v. Jones and Laughlin Steel Company (1937), 7:940
National Traffic and Motor Vehicle Safety Act (1966), 2:274
Navigation Acts, British (1651-1849), 6:850-51
New Deal, **7:941-43**
  capitalism and, 2:179-80, *181*
  environmental projects, 4:439, *440*
  Fair Labor Standards Act, 4:467
  farm programs, 1:47
  government regulation, 3:360
  government spending, 3:365
  Great Depression, 5:581-85
  Keynesian theory, 2:180, 6:750
  labor unions, 1:39, 40, 8:1084, 9:1252-53, 1274
  minimum wage, 7:878-79, 943, 996
  National Labor Relations Act, 7:939-40
  Perkins and, 7:994, 996, 997
  regulatory agencies, 8:1104-7
  social democracy and, 9:*1209*, 1210
  social security, 9:1211, 1212
  strikes, 9:1252-53
  subsidy legislation, 9:1255-56
  wage standards, 3:299
  Wall Street Journal view of, 10:1384-85
NLRA. *See* National Labor Relations Act
Norris–La Guardia Act (1932), 6:763, 7:939
Nuclear Waste Policy Act (1982), 4:*448*
Nuclear Waste Policy Amendments Act (2000), 2:255

O

Occupational Safety and Health Act (1970), 7:960
Ocean Dumping Ban Act (1988), 4:*448*
Oil Pollution Act (1990), 4:448

P

patent, **7:980-86**
  amortization of, 1:61, 63
  for Bell's telephone, 1:87, 88
  business law on, 2:160, 164, 165
  as competitive entry barrier, 7:900, *903*, 904
  Edison grants, 3:400, 4:547
  for gasoline engine, 4:511-12
  industrial espionage and, 5:649

Industrial Revolution, **5**:653, 654-55
as intangible asset, **1**:*84*, 85
intellectual property and, **2**:280, **5**:687, 689
Levi Strauss grant, **6**:785, *786*
license and, **6**:801
product development and, **8**:1036-37
property rights and, **8**:1029
RCA sharing agreement, **8**:1147
for revolver, **5**:693
television claims, **8**:1148
types and duration, **8**:1112
for water frame, **5**:*657*
World Trade Organization and, **10**:1427
Xerox grants, **10**:1429, 1430
Patent Act (1790, 1793), **7**:980
Patent Act and Amendments (1952, 1995) (1995), **7**:980
Pollock v. Farmers' Loan and Trust Company, **5**:697, 698
Pregnancy Discrimination Act (1978), **1**:34
privatization, **8**:1030-33
British Airways, 126, **1**:125
capitalism, **2**:182, 183
deregulation, **3**:358, 362
Edison Schools, **3**:402-4, 405
education industry, **3**:402-4, 405-10
energy industry, **3**:418
subsidy and, **9**:1256
product liability, **6**:791, **8**:1045-47
"lemon laws," **2**:272
Philip Morris, **7**:*1001*, 1004
risk management, **8**:1125, 1127
tort actions, **6**:796
Public Utility Holding Company Act (1935), **8**:1105, *1106*
Pure Food and Drug Act (1906), **1**:*121*, 122, **4**:*448*, **5**:*614*, 615

R

Rail Passenger Service Act (1970), **10**:1330
Regents of the University of California v. Bakke (1978), **1**:36-37
regulation of business and industry, **8**:1103-9
advertising, **1**:32
affirmative action, **1**:34-37
agriculture, **1**:47-48, 70
airline ticket prices, **8**:1024
arbitration, **1**:67-68
AT&T, **1**:88-89
automobile safety, **7**:927
business cycles and, **2**:151, 180
business ethics and, **2**:157-58
business law and, **2**:160-65
capitalism and, **2**:179-83
chemical toxins, **9**:1194, 1195
civil rights law, **1**:56-60
competition and, **2**:245, 246
Constitution (U.S.) and, **2**:254, 255-57

consumer protection, **2**:268, 272-75, **6**:796
corporate social responsibility and, **3**:300, 301
corporations and, **3**:300, 301, 302
credit, **3**:315-16, 318
credit card loans, **3**:320-21
disability provisions, **1**:56-60
e-business, **3**:384
economic growth and, **3**:389-90
energy industry, **3**:416-17, 418
Enron collapse and, **3**:423
environmentalism, **4**:439-51
equal employment opportunity, **4**:452-53
ergonomics, **4**:456
externalities, **4**:465
Fair Labor Standards Act, **4**:466-67
family leave, **4**:469-71
Federal Trade Commission, **4**:484-87
fishing industry, **4**:508-10
food processing, **5**:614-15
franchises, **4**:523
futures market, **4**:531
gaming industry, **4**:536
genetically modified foods, **4**:559
as Great Depression measure, **5**:585
human resources compliance, **5**:630-31
inflation and, **5**:663, **8**:1021
insurance companies, **5**:683
intellectual property, **5**:687-88
legal services, **6**:781-84
liability, **6**:797-99, **8**:1046-47
licenses, **6**:801-4
merger and acquisition, **6**:853, 854
microeconomics and, **7**:869, 871
minimum wage, **4**:466, **7**:877-82, **8**:1013, 1014-15, **10**:1417, 1418
mining, **7**:885
monopolies, **7**:902, 903-4
Nader campaign for, **7**:917
natural monopolies, **8**:1015-16, 1021
New Deal, **2**:180, **7**:941-42, 943
price controls, **8**:1013-16, 1021
privatization vs., **8**:1030-33
profit and loss and, **8**:1051
rule of law and, **8**:1138
securities market, **1**:55, **9**:1172-74
Smith's free market vs., **9**:1204-5, **10**:1400
smoking bans, **7**:1003
sustainability and, **9**:1266-67
telecommunications, **1**:66, **2**:246, **8**:1105, **9**:1286
time line, **8**:*1106*

as tragedy of the commons solution, **10**:1328
utilities, **8**:1105, *1106*, 1107-9, **10**:1356, 1358-59
vocational licensing, **10**:1374-76
working conditions, **7**:960-63, **10**:1417
Rehabilitation Act (1973), **1**:*34*, 56, **2**:*213*, **4**:452-53
Resource Conservation and Recovery Act (1976), **4**:*448*
Robinson–Patman Act (1936), **4**:485, **7**:*900*, **9**:1197
Roe v. Wade (1973), **2**:257
rule of law, **8**:1137-39
business law, **2**:160-65
components of, **8**:1137-38
Constitution as, **2**:253-57
contract law, **2**:276-79
copyright, **2**:280-84
corporations and, **3**:302
private property and, **8**:1026
privatization and, **8**:1032

S

Safe Drinking Water Act (1974), **4**:*448*
Santa Clara County v. Southern Pacific Railroad (1886), **3**:302
Sarbanes–Oxley Act (2002), **2**:157, 159
Schultz v. Wheaton Glass Company (1970), **10**:1414-15
Sea Around Us, The (Carson), **9**:1194
Securities Act (1933), **9**:1172
Securities Exchange Act (1934), **7**:943, **8**:1105, *1106*, **9**:1172-73
Sherman Antitrust Act (1890), **2**:*181*, **6**:762, **9**:1187-90, 1197
AT&T and, **1**:88, 89
General Motors and, **4**:553
Microsoft and, **7**:874, 875
passage, **8**:1104, *1106*, *1128*, 1130
price fixing illegality, **8**:1018, 1019, 1051
provisions, **2**:245, **7**:*900*, 903-4
Standard Oil and, **7**:*902*, 904, **8**:1130, **9**:*1231*, 1234
Silent Spring (Carson), **2**:268, 3:299-300, **4**:439, *440*, 443, 447, **9**:1194-95
Single European Act (1986), **4**:457, 459
Sixteenth Amendment, **5**:697, 698
Small Business Administration Act, **9**:1196
Social Security Act (1935), **5**:633, **7**:942-43, **9**:1211, 1212
Amendments (1954), **9**:1214
Amendments (1980), **9**:1215
Perkins and, **7**:996, 997
social security and Medicare, **2**:180, **9**:1211-16
Consumer Price Index, **2**:271

cost-of-living adjustment, **3**:*311*, **5**:662
human resources department, **5**:630
IBM contract, **5**:633
identity theft and, **3**:328
payroll and, **7**:990, 992-93
wealth distribution and, **10**:1396
Sonny Bono Copyright Extension Act (1998), **2**:165, 284
Staggers Rail Act (1980), **8**:1109
Stamp Act (1765), **6**:851
Standard Oil Co. v. United States (1911), **7**:902
State Street v. Signature (1998), **7**:986
subsidy, **4**:477, **9**:1255-58
agriculture, **1**:47, 70, **7**:941, **9**:1255, 1257, *1258*
competition vs., **2**:245
microeconomics and, **7**:871
price controls and, **8**:1013, 1016
sports facilities, **9**:1225-26
steel industry, **8**:1056, **9**:*1262*, 1263
trade policy, **1**:95, **4**:543, **5**:706, **8**:1056, **10**:*1323*, 1324-25
Sugar Act (1764), **6**:851
Superfund, **4**:444-45, *446*, *448*

T

Taft–Hartley Act (1947), **1**:*38*, 40, **6**:764, 767, 768, **7**:940, **9**:1268-69, **10**:1351
anticommunist loyalty oath, **9**:1170
provisions, **9**:1253, *1269*
takings clause (Fourth Amendment), **2**:256
Telecommunications Act (1996), **9**:1287-88, 1289
Telemarketing and Consumer Fraud and Abuse Prevention Act, **2**:275
Terminal Railroad Association case (1912), **9**:1189
Third Amendment, **2**:256
Thirteenth Amendment, **2**:210
Ticket to Work and Work Incentives Improvement Act (1999), **9**:1216
Title VII. *See* Civil Rights Act (1964)
tort law, **2**:161-62, **6**:795-99, **8**:1045
Townsend Acts (1767), **6**:851
Toxic Substances Control Act (1976), **4**:*448*
Trade Name Registration Act, **9**:1198
Trade-Related Aspects of Intellectual Property Rights, **10**:*1427*
Truth–in–Lending Act, **3**:320, 321, **4**:485

U

Uniform Computer Information Transactions Act (1999), **2**:279, **6**:803-4
Uniform Partnership Act, **7**:976
United States Airline Deregulation Act, **8**:*1106*, 1109
United States v. Addyston Pipe and Steel Co. (1898), **8**:1019
United States v. Morrison (1994), **2**:253-54
United States v. The Amistad (1841), **3**:337
United States v. Topco Associates, Inc. (1972), **2**:245

V

Violence against Women Act (1994), **2**:253-54
Voting Rights Act (1965), **1**:56, **2**:*213*

W

Wabash, St. Louis and Pacific Railway Company v. Illinois (1886), **8**:1103
Wagner Act (1935). *See* National Labor Relations Act
Wagner–Steagall Act (1936), **8**:1105, *1106*
Walsh–Healey Act (1936), **10**:1418
Wards Cove Packing Co. v. Antonio (1989), **2**:212, 213
Welfare Reform Act (1996), **9**:*1211*, 1215-16
Wheeler–Lea Act (1938), **4**:485
Whelan v. Jaslow (1986), **7**:986
Wholesome Meat Act (1967), **2**:268
Workmen's Compensation Act, **7**:994-95

Index of Business Operations and Industries

A

accounting and bookkeeping, **1**:23-26
  amortization and depreciation, **1**:61-63
  assets and liabilities, **1**:83-86
  balance sheet, **1**:96-98
  basic accounting equation, **1**:*25*, 96
  bookkeeping functions, **1**:23-25
  breakeven point, **1**:119-20
  budget, **1**:127-30
  business ethics, **2**:153, 157, **3**:296-97, *379*, 422, **8**:1053
  cash flow, **2**:189, *190*
  consulting service, **2**:259-60, **3**:297
  corporate governance, **3**:294, 296-97
  data management, **3**:338-39
  debt and, **3**:343-46
  Enron and, **3**:422, 423
  income statement, **1**:25, 26, 61, **5**:647
  management and, **6**:822
  partnership, **7**:976
  payroll, **7**:990-93
  professional associations, **8**:*1048*
  profit and loss, **8**:*1051*, 1052-53
  small business, **9**:1198
  spreadsheets, **3**:338-39
  stock options, **3**:296
  temporary workers, **10**:1301
acquisition. *See* merger and acquisition
advertising, business practice, **1**:27-30
  actors' residuals, **9**:*1169*, 1171
  African Americans and, **6**:740
  Better Business Bureau and, **1**:112, 113
  brand loyalty and, **8**:1051
  business ethics. *See* false advertising
  business law and, **2**:164-65
  by Coca-Cola, **2**:217-18, 219
  commercial speech protection, **2**:257
  compact disc price-fixing, **8**:1018
  consumers and, **2**:*175*, 265-67, 272, 274
  copyright and, **2**:283
  demand creation by, **8**:1051
  demographics and, **3**:356, *357*
  by Estée Lauder, **6**:776
  Federal Trade Commission and, **1**:32, **4**:485, **8**:1104, 1105
  by Guinness, **5**:594
  by Harley-Davidson, **5**:600
  by Heinz, **5**:613, 614, *615*
  by Intel, **5**:686
  by Kellogg, **6**:746
  of law firms, **6**:782
  of Levi jeans, **6**:786, 787
  market research and, **6**:833
  Marlboro Man image, **7**:1003
  in newspapers, **8**:1075
  by Nike, **7**:952
  pricing and, **8**:1024
  public relations and marketing and, **8**:1061-63, 1066
  spammed e-mail, **3**:413
  sports industry, **9**:1223, 1227
  by Volkswagen, **10**:1379
  by Wells Fargo, **10**:1407
advertising industry, **1**:31-33
  Burnett Agency, **1**:139-40
  careers in, **1**:32
  expenditures by medium, **1**:*33*
  Leo Burnett Agency, **1**:139-40
agriculture industry, **1**:43-48
  agrarian age and, **9**:1277
  Archer Daniels Midland, **1**:70-71
  assembly line, **1**:81
  careers in, **1**:45
  child migrant labor, **2**:201, 203
  Chiquita, **2**:204-6
  commodities trading, **2**:225-26
  corporate profits, **3**:*305*
  Deere products, **3**:347-49
  Dow Chemical products, **3**:375
  economic theory and, **9**:1203
  environmentalism and, **1**:48, **4**:437-41, 443, **9**:1194, 1195
  federal budget and, **4**:477
  futures market, **2**:197, 198, *225*, **4**:530
  GATT failure with, **4**:545
  genetic engineering, **1**:48, **3**:375, **4**:555, 556-58
  Great Depression and, **5**:583-84
  import restrictions, **10**:1323-24
  Industrial Revolution and, **5**:657
  labor organization, **1**:69, **2**:194, 195-96, **6**:764
  Malthusian theory and, **6**:818
  migrant workers, **5**:639, **10**:1301, 1420
  NAFTA protests, **7**:958
  New Deal measures, **7**:941, 943
  price supports, **8**:1013, 1014, 1105
  principal crops (1990-2000), **1**:*44*
  private property and, **8**:1027
  productivity, **8**:1041-42
  raw materials, **8**:1087-88
  scarcity and, **9**:1162, *1163*, *1256*
  seasonal workers, **10**:1303
  small business criteria, **9**:1196
  social security coverage, **9**:1214
  Soviet collectivization, **2**:228
  subsidies, **1**:47, 70, **7**:941, **9**:1255, 1257, *1258*
  water competition, **10**:1358
  wealth distribution and, 1395
  World Bank loans, **10**:1423, 1424
amortization and depreciation, **1**:61-63
arbitration, **1**:40, **67-69**, **9**:1252
  liability and, **6**:799
arts and entertainment industry, **1**:71-75
  AOL Time Warner, **1**:64-66
  careers in, **1**:74, 75
  contract law, **2**:277-78, 279
  copyright, **2**:280-83, *281*, *282*, 283
  Gordy and, **4**:568-69
  Hearst and, **5**:611, 612
  Henson and, **5**:616-18
  Lansing and, **6**:772-74
  licensing, **6**:801, *802*
  Mayer and, **6**:844-45
  Miramax, **7**:888-89
  pricing, **8**:1024
  public relations and, **8**:1068
  Sarnoff and, **8**:1146
  Screen Actors Guild, **9**:1169-71
  Sony Corporation, **7**:909, **9**:1217, 1218-19
  Stewart and, **9**:1238-40
  Trump and, **10**:1337
  Turner and, **10**:1339-41
  Walt Disney Company, **10**:1391-94
  Winfrey and, **10**:1410-12
assembly line, **1**:81-82
  automobile industry, **3**:424, **4**:512-13, **6**:828-29
  defense industry, **10**:1329
  division of labor, **3**:371, 372
  as economy of scale, **3**:396
  Ford, **1**:81, 82, **4**:512-13, **5**:598, 658, **6**:828-29
  just-in-time concept and, **6**:741-43
  Levitt home construction, **6**:788-89
  McDonald's fast-food, **6**:846
  productivity and, **8**:*1040*
  service economy and, **9**:1182
  Toyota, **6**:831
assets and liabilities, **1**:83-86
  amortization and depreciation, **1**:61-63
  annual report, **8**:1052
  asset types, **1**:*84*
  balance of payments, **1**:91-92, 93
  balance sheet, **1**:83-86, 96-97, *128*
  bankruptcy, **1**:99
  bookkeeping equation, **1**:23-24, 25, 83
  book value, **1**:61, *62*, 63
  cash flow, **2**:189
  cost, **3**:307
  credit, **3**:318
  debt, **3**:343-46
  human capital, **5**:625-28
  investments, **6**:728-31
  liability types, **1**:*86*
  merger and acquisition, **6**:853
  money, **7**:896, 897
  partnership, **7**:977-78
  privatization, **8**:1032-33
  valuation, **10**:1360, 1361

B

balance sheet, **1**:96-98
  accounting and, **1**:25, 26
  amortization and depreciation, **1**:61-63, 63
  assets and liabilities, **1**:83-86, 96-97
  breakeven point, **1**:119-20
  budget, **1**:*128*
  business finances, **4**:493-96
  corporation, **3**:*303*
  debt and, **3**:343-44
  human capital and, **5**:625
  income statement, **5**:647
  partnership, **7**:*978*
  personal finances, **4**:499-500
  profit and loss, **8**:*1051*, 1052-53
  small business, **9**:1198
bar codes, **1**:103-5, **6**:726, 744
benchmarking, **1**:109-11, 127
benefits. *See* compensation
bookkeeping. *See* accounting and bookkeeping
brand names, **1**:116-18
  advertising image, **1**:29, 30, 32, 139-40, **8**:1051
  Coca-Cola, **2**:217-18
  Martha Stewart, **9**:1240
  Nike, **7**:950, 952
  pricing and, **8**:1021, 1025

product development and,
8:1037
public relations and marketing
campaigns, 8:1063
Sony, 7:909
Starbucks, 9:1236
trademarks, 10:1320
breakeven point, 1:119-20
budget, 1:127-30
advertising, 1:28
capital, 4:493-94, 495, 496
cash flow, 2:189-90
federal, 4:477-79, 503, 505
income statement, 5:647
personal, 4:498-99
standard of living and, 9:1229
U.S. defense, 3:354
building trades, 1:131-35
affirmative action, 1:35, 135
careers in, 1:134
corporate profits, 3:305
forest products and, 4:517
Levitt and, 6:788-90
licensed workers, 10:1374
new construction, 8:1092, 1094
bundling, 1:136-38, 8:1109
business ethics, 2:153-59
accounting firm consultants,
2:260
advertising, 1:32, 112, 113
American Stock Exchange, 1:55
Archer Daniels Midland, 1:70-71
Better Business Bureau, 1:112-13
business law and, 2:154, 157,
159, 160-62, 6:782
consumerism and, 2:267
corporate, 3:293, 296-97, 298,
306, 379
day trading, 3:342
Edison Schools, 3:403-4
Enron, 3:296, 420, 422-23
fraud arbitration, 1:68
industrial espionage, 5:648-52
information technology, 9:1283
pharmaceuticals, 1:121, 122
profit and loss reports, 8:1053
reverse engineering and,
8:1122-23
Stewart stock deal, 9:1240
tobacco industry, 7:1001, 1002-4
Union Bank of Switzerland,
10:1346, 1348
United Brands, 2:206
workplace guidelines, 2:155
business finance. See finance,
business
business law, 2:160-65
affirmative action, 1:34
business ethics and, 2:154, 157,
159, 160-62, 6:782
contracts, 2:160-61, 276-79
copyright, 2:164, 165, 280-84
corporations, 3:302
e-business, 3:384
employment discrimination,
2:213-14
family leave, 4:468-71
human resources department,
5:630-31

initial public offering, 5:677
intellectual property, 5:688-89
legal services, 6:781-84
liability, 6:794-800
licenses, 6:802-3
partnership, 7:976
product liability, 8:1045-47
risk management, 8:1127
rule of law and, 8:1137, 1138-39
trademark, 10:1320, 1321
business plan, 2:166-68, 3:427
entrepreneurship and, 3:427
Kroc and, 6:755, 756-67
Lands' End and, 6:769-71
Leading Economic Index and,
6:778
product development, 8:1034,
1036
small business, 9:1198
strategic planning, 9:1246-48
business-to-business sales, 2:169-72
benchmarking, 1:111
contract law, 2:276-77
distribution channels, 3:366-69
e-business, 3:383, 384-87, 420,
421, 5:713
Enron, 3:420, 421, 422
farm products, 1:46-47, 70-71
just-in-time concept, 6:741, 743,
744
Lands' End, 6:770
Levitt and Sons, 6:789
wholesalers, 8:1118-20

C

cash flow, 2:189-90
accounting statement, 1:25, 26
debt and, 3:343-44, 345
small business, 9:1198, 1199
taxation and, 9:1273
chain stores. See retail and wholesale
chambers of commerce, 2:191-93,
8:1048
ergonomic regulations, 4:456
market research, 6:836
National Black Chamber of
Commerce, 7:933-34
small businesses and, 9:1198
commodities, 2:225-26
Archer Daniels Midland, 1:70-71
Chicago Board of Trade,
2:197-98, 225, 226
energy industry, 3:418
Enron trading, 3:420, 421
futures market, 2:225, 226,
4:529-31
pricing, 8:1021-23
risk management, 8:1127
compensation, 2:236-41
benefit plans, 3:299
benefits by industry, 2:237
benefits equity, 7:989
benefits lowering, 10:1420
budget and, 1:129
building trade, 1:134, 135
as business liability, 1:86, 97
CEO, 2:241, 3:294-96, 10:1404
CEO vs. average worker, 2:296
collective bargaining for,
2:221-24

components, 2:236
corporate management, 3:295-96
Ford Motor policy, 4:513, 6:829
freelance vs. salaried employees,
7:993
government employees,
8:1071-73
government workers, 8:1072
health insurance, 5:606
Heinz policy, 5:614
Hewlett-Packard innovations,
5:619-20
human resources department
and, 5:630
IBM policy, 5:633
income distribution, 5:644-46
inflation-adjustment, 2:271
internship, 5:715
job search and, 6:737, 738
labor unions and, 6:763, 764-66
Lands' End policy, 6:770
Levi Strauss policy, 6:786
major league baseball, 6:813-14,
815
minimum wage, 7:874-76
partnership, 7:978
paycheck deductions, 7:990-91
payroll, 7:990-93
productivity and, 8:1039, 1042
professional athletes, 9:1227
Southwest Airlines policy,
9:1220-21
standard of living and, 9:1228-29
Starbucks policy, 9:1236
as strike issue, 9:1252
telecommuters, 9:1290
temporary workers, 10:1302,
1303, 1420
United Automobile Workers,
10:1351
vacation time and, 8:1101
Wal-Mart policy, 10:1390
computer industry, 2:249-52
Amazon.com, 1:49-50
antitrust cases, 8:1106
assembly line, 1:82
assets and liabilities, 1:85
browser price war, 8:1025
bundling, 1:138
business law, 2:165
careers in, 2:252
Cisco Systems, 2:207-9
Clark and, 2:215-16
Clark graphics development,
2:215
competition barriers, 2:244
consultants, 2:259, 260
contract law, 2:279, 283, 284
corporate training, 3:406
customer service records, 3:335
data management, 3:338-40
day trading, 3:342
development cycles, 8:1037-38
development in India, 5:670
digital imaging, 1:74
economies of scale and, 7:901
energy industry, 3:418
engineering career, 2:252
engineers, 2:252

entrepreneurship, 3:424, 427
Fiorina and, 4:501-2
Gates and, 4:537-39, 566
globalization and, 4:566
gross domestic income, 2:249
Hewlett-Packard and, 5:619-21
IBM and, 5:632-37, 7:873-74
immigrant workers, 5:642
industrial espionage and,
5:648-49, 651
information technology and,
5:668-72, 9:1277, 1280-82,
1280-83, 1282
intellectual property law, 2:165
Intel microprocessor, 5:684, 685,
686
Kinko rentals, 6:753
labor market and, 6:759
license, 6:801, 802, 803, 804
Microsoft and, 7:873-76, 902,
903, 8:1051
monopoly charge, 7:873, 874,
875, 902, 903
Nasdaq stock, 7:930, 931-32
patents, 7:981, 986
Perot and, 7:998, 999, 1000
personal computer, 2:251-52
personal computer pricing,
8:1023-24
piracy, 2:282, 8:1122
product development, 8:1034
professional association, 8:1049
programmers, 2:252
raw materials, 8:1088
research and development,
8:1112
reverse engineering, 8:1122,
1122-23, 1123
Sarnoff and, 8:1148
security systems and, 9:1175,
1176
service economy and, 9:1182,
1183
Silicon Valley, 3:424, 427
software copyright, 2:283-84,
5:687-90
software development cycles,
8:1037-38
software patents, 7:980, 986
stock trading technology and,
9:1245
telephone lines and, 9:1284,
10:1357
temporary workers, 10:1303,
1304
wealth and, 10:1397-98
working conditions, 10:1420
Xerox and, 10:1429, 1430-32
Yamaha and, 10:1436
See also data management;
Internet
conglomerate. See merger and
acquisition
consulting, 2:258-60, 3:297,
9:1181, 1182, 10:1302
continuous processing. See assembly
line
contractors. See building trades
corporate ethics. See business ethics

corporate governance, **3:**293-97, 303-4
  compensation policy, **2:**236-41
  cultural differences and, **3:**31
  discrimination suits and, **2:**213-14
  of Enron, **3:**420-23
  ethics and, **2:**153-59, 160-62, **3:**293, 296-97, 306
  Galbraith's views on, **4:**532-33
  of General Electric, **4:**549, **10:**1403-4
  of General Motors, **4:**550-52
  in Great Depression, **5:**581
  of Hewlett-Packard, **5:**619-20
  human capital and, **5:**626
  human resources and, **5:**626-27, 629-31
  of IBM, **5:**633, 634
  management, **6:**819-22, **9:**1281
  management theory, **3:**380-81
  MBA degree, **6:**841-43
  merger or acquisition and, **6:**853, 856
  risk management, **8:**1127
  of Standard Oil, **8:**1129-30
corporate social responsibility, **3:**298-301, 306
  affirmative action, **1:**34, 35, 37
  Ben & Jerry's and, **1:**107, 108
  business ethics, **2:**154-57
  Carnegie projects, **2:**184, 185-86
  Dow Chemical and, **3:**373, 374
  environmentalism and, **4:**442
  Levi Strauss and, **6:**786
  Madame C. J. Walker and, **10:**1382
  minority venture capital firms, **6:**792
  Nader activism for, **7:**927
  National Black Chamber of Commerce and, **7:**933
  Newman's Own and, **7:**944, 946
  Nike campaign, **7:**953
  Wal-Mart and, **10:**1390
corporation, **3:**302-6
  agency of, **2:**163
  annual report, **8:**1052-53
  balance sheet, **1:**128
  bankruptcy, **1:**101-2
  benchmarking, **1:**110
  bond issuance, **3:**317, **9:**1242
  budget, **1:**127-28
  capital, **2:**173-74
  capital gains, **2:**175-76
  data management, **3:**338-40
  debt, **3:**303, 306, 317
  dissolution, **3:**305-6
  downsizing, **3:**378-79
  employee education, **3:**405, 406
  equal employment complaints, **4:**452-53
  Fair Employment Standards Act, **4:**467
  federal regulations of, **8:**1107
  first billion-dollar, **10:**1353
  Fortune 500, **4:**519-21
  health and safety standards, **6:**796
  human capital, **5:**625-28

inflation theory, **5:**661, 662
information technology, **5:**669-70, 671
initial public offering, **5:**676-78
legal services, **6:**782
liability principle, **6:**796-98
Morgan financing, **7:**905, 906
nonprofit, **7:**954-55
outsourcing, **7:**971, 972-73
overhead, **7:**974-75
partnership vs., **7:**976-79
profit and loss, **8:**1050-53
public relations and marketing, **8:**1061-65
racial bias suit payments, **2:***214*
real estate investment trusts, **8:**1094-95
research and development, **8:**1110-12
shareholders. *See* stocks and bonds
by size and industry (1998), **2:***304*
small business, **9:**1198
structure. *See* corporate governance
subsidy, **9:**1257-58
tax structure, **3:**317, **5:**698, **9:**1272
trade associations, **10:**1317
vertical integration, **2:**185, 186, **7:***971*, 972, **8:**1129, **9:**1189
See also multinational corporation
cost, **3:**307-10
  amortization and depreciation, **1:**61
  breakeven point, **1:**119-20
  comparative advantage, **2:**233
  competition and, **2:**246
  of economic growth, **3:**391-92
  economies of scale and, **3:**395-98
  of employee, **2:***239, 240*, **7:**993
  externalities and, **4:**463-65
  of federal regulation, **8:***1108*
  food industry, **1:**48
  Industrial Revolution and, **5:**653
  inflation and, **5:**660, 661-62
  infrastructure breakdown, **5:**673, 674-75
  intellectual property, **5:**690
  interest rate and, **5:**695
  inventory, **6:**725, 726
  just-in-time principles, **6:**741
  minimum wage and, **7:**880
  mining industry, **7:**884
  opportunity cost, **3:**309, **7:**964-65
  outsourcing, **7:**972
  overhead, **7:**974-75
  pricing and, **8:**1021, 1025
  profit or loss, **8:**1050
  protectionism, **8:**1054-57
  public goods, **8:**1058, 1060
  retail and wholesale, **8:**1120
  of rule of law absence, **8:**1138-39
  scarcity and, **9:**1161-63
  of software product development, **8:**1037
  subsidies and, **8:**1056

supply and demand effects, **9:**1260-61
of tragedy of the commons, **10:**1326, 1328
of unemployed disabled people, **1:**56
cultural difference, **3:**329-32
  demographics and, **3:**356-57
  immigration and, **3:**356-57
  McDonald's and, **7:**918
  Morita and, **7:**908-9
  multinationals and, **7:**917, 918, 921
  as standard of living influence, **9:**1229
  Wal-Mart and, **10:**1389
customer service, **3:**333-35
  e-business, **3:**383-84, 385
  e-commerce, **5:**713
  Kinko's, **6:**753
  Lands' End, **6:**770-71
  McDonald's, **6:**756, 757
  Southwest Airlines, **3:**334, **9:**1220, 1221
  Starbucks, **9:**1236, 1237

D

data management, **3:**338-40
  bar codes, **1:**103, 104
  bookkeeping, **1:**23-25
  census, **6:**834
  e-business, **3:**383, 385
  information technology for, **5:**668, 669-70
  inventory system, **6:**726, 727
  just-in-time applications, **6:**744
  as management aids, **6:**819, 826
  market research, **6:**834, 836
  Perot and, **7:**998
  real estate multiple listings, **8:**1091
  security systems, **9:**1175
  software development, **8:**1038
  Wal-Mart, **10:***1387*, 1388-89
defense industry, **3:**350-54
  armed forces desegregation, **8:**1085
  assembly line, **10:**1329
  careers in, **3:**352
  Dow Chemical contracts, **3:**350, 373-74
  equal employment, **8:**1084, 1085
  federal budget and, **4:**477, 478, 505
  General Electric contracts, **4:**548, 549
  General Motors contracts, **4:**552, 554
  in Germany, **10:**1377
  Harley-Davidson and, **5:**598-99
  IBM and, **5:**633-34
  interchangeable parts, **1:**81, **5:***657*, 658, 692-93, **6:**828
  Internet and, **5:**710
  in Japan, **7:**891, 908
  public goods and, **8:**1059
  reverse engineering, **8:**1122
  Sikorsky contracts, **9:***1193*
  small business procurement, **9:**1200-1201

United Automobile Workers and, **10:**1350
women workers, **10:**1414
demographics, **3:**355-57
  advertising, **1:**27-28, 32
  economic growth, **6:**816
  immigration, **5:**638-40
  Malthus and, **6:**816-18
  market research, **6:**833, 834, 835
  public relations, **8:**1068
  suburbanization, **6:**790
  tourism, **10:**1315-16
depreciation. *See* amortization and depreciation
distribution channels, **3:**366-69
  agricultural products, **1:**46
  business-to-business sales, **2:**171
  e-business, **3:**382-87
  franchises, **4:**522-23
  Guinness, **5:**592-93
  just-in-time concept, **6:**744
  product development, **8:**1034, 1036
  retail and wholesale, **8:**1117, 1118-20
downsizing, **3:**378-79, 422
  British Airways, **1:**125
  General Electric, **4:**549
  Kellogg Company, **6:**748
  labor market and, **6:**759
  from merger or acquisition, **6:**853
  minimum wage and, **7:**877
  productivity and, **8:**1041
  women workers and, **10:**1413

E

e-business, **3:**382-87, **5:***712*, 713-14
  Amazon.com, **1:**49-50
  business-to-business sales, **2:**171, 172
  chambers of commerce, **2:**193
  consumerism, **2:**267
  consumer protection, **2:**279
  contract law, **2:**279
  credit card use, **3:**323
  customer service, **3:**333, 335
  e-commerce vs., **3:**382, **5:**713
  EnronOnline, **3:**420, 421
  information technology and, **9:**1280, 1282
  intellectual property law, **2:**165
  Kinko's, **6:**754
  Lands' End, **6:**770-71
  licenses, **6:**803, 804
  retail sales, **8:**1116-17, *1119*
  Whitman and, **10:**1408-9
  Yahoo!, **10:**1433-34
e-commerce, **5:**665, 713-14
  business law, **2:**165
  e-business vs., **3:**382, **5:**713
  information age and, **5:**665
  just-in-time concept and, **6:**744
  retail and wholesale, **8:**1120
education industry, **3:**405-10
  affirmative action, **1:**35-36
  agricultural research, **1:**47
  alternate dispute resolution, **1:**69
  arts incorporation into, **1:**74

Asian Development Bank and, 1:79
careers in, 3:408
child labor and, 2:200, 201, 202
disabilities provision, 1:56
Economic Opportunity Act and, 3:393, 394, 395
Edison Schools, 3:402-4
federal budget and, 4:479
information technology access and, 5:671
lawyer training, 6:781, 783
licensing or certification, 10:1375, 1376
master of business administration, 6:841-43
National Education Association, 7:935-38
outsourcing, 7:973
positive externality and, 4:463
privatization, 8:1031, 1033
professional associations, 8:1048, 1049
as public good, 8:1059
public vs. private ownership, 8:1031
Rockefeller philanthropy, 8:1130
school desegregation, 7:936, 8:1085
as service economy sector, 9:1180
unionism, 8:1070
wealth potential and, 10:1397
e-mail, 1:75, 2:252, 3:411-13, 5:710, 711, 712, 713, 9:1284
copyright, 2:283
number of users, 5:663
productivity from, 5:670, 671, 8:1040
energy industry, 3:414-19
careers in, 3:415
deregulation, 10:1359
Enron, 3:420-23
environmental regulation, 4:437, 439, 440, 449, 465
externalities, 4:464, 465
futures market, 2:225
Industrial Revolution, 5:653-55, 656
mineral mining, 7:883-87
subsidy, 9:1257-58
sustainable development, 9:1265, 1266
U.S. Steel and, 10:1355
utilities, 10:1356-59

F
fishing industry, 4:506-10
aquaculture, 1:45, 48, 4:508, 510
corporate profits, 3:305
forest products and, 4:516
Native American rights, 1:45
sustainable development, 9:1267
tragedy of the commons, 10:1326, 1327-28
forest products industry, 4:515-18
corporate profits, 3:305
Industrial Revolution, 5:653, 656
sustainable development, 9:1265-66

Fortune 500, 4:519-21, 5:670
list of companies, 4:520
franchise, 4:522-23
Coca-Cola, 2:217
Disney, 10:1393
as distribution channel, 3:369
entrepreneurship and, 3:427
government, 7:900, 903
McDonald's, 6:755, 756-57, 846, 847, 848
realtor, 8:1091, 1092, 1095
retailing, 8:1117, 1118
sports, 9:1224, 1225, 1227
Starbucks, 9:1235-37

G
gaming industry, 4:534-36, 9:1223, 1224, 10:1335
genetic engineering, 4:555-59
agriculture, 1:48, 3:375, 4:555, 556-58
information technology and, 5:669
intellectual property and, 5:689, 691
Kellogg Company and, 6:748
patent, 7:981, 985

H
health care services industry, 5:603-8
Asian Development Bank, 1:79
Bristol-Myers Squibb, 1:121-23
business-to-business sales, 2:170-71, 172
Clark venture, 2:215, 216
Economic Opportunity Act, 3:393
employee benefits, 2:237-38, 3:299, 9:1229, 1236
federal budget, 4:478-79
genetically engineered products, 4:556, 558
income level, 10:1397
information technology, 5:669
insurance, 2:237-38, 5:603, 604-7, 619, 630, 682
nonprofits, 7:955
patents, 5:689
pay inequities, 7:989
product liability, 8:1047
professional associations, 8:1048
professional licensing, 10:1374-75, 1376
as service economy sector, 9:1180
skills compensation, 2:239
smoking risk warnings, 7:1002-4
standard of living, 9:1229
tourism, 10:1314-15
unionism, 8:1070, 1072
human resources, 5:629-31
Asian Development Bank, 1:78, 79
job applicants, 6:737
resume, 8:1113-14
security industry, 9:1175, 1177
temporary workers, 10:1301-4

I
income statement, 5:647
accounting, 1:25, 26, 61
balance sheet, 1:97
breakeven point, 1:119-20
budget, 1:127, 128, 129
cash flow, 2:189-90
Fortune 500, 4:521
overhead, 7:974-75
payroll deductions, 7:990-91
small business, 9:1198
industrial espionage, 5:648-52
security industry, 9:1175, 1176, 1177
information technology, 5:668-72, 9:1277, 1279-81
census data, 6:834
Cisco Systems, 2:207-9
Clark ventures, 2:215-16
copyright, 2:281, 283
data management, 3:338-40
e-mail, 3:411-13
entrepreneurship, 9:1165
Hewlett-Packard, 5:621
human capital, 5:625-28
IBM, 5:632-37
innovation, 5:679
Intel, 5:684-86
intellectual property, 5:687-91
investment pace, 5:663
licenses, 6:803-4
Nasdaq stock, 7:931
New York Stock Exchange, 7:948-49
productivity, 8:1039-42
publishing industry, 8:1078
reverse engineering, 8:1122-23
security systems, 9:1175, 1176
strategic alliances, 5:680
telecommuting, 9:1290-92
temporary workers, 10:1301
working conditions, 10:1420
Yahoo!, 10:1433-34
See also computer industry; Internet
innovation, 5:679-80
assembly line, 1:81-82
Carnegie and, 2:184, 185, 186
competition by, 2:242, 246
copyright, 2:165, 280
Deere products, 3:349
division of labor and, 3:370, 372, 10:1400
eBay, 10:1409
e-business, 3:382-87
economic growth from, 3:391
Edison and, 3:399-401, 424, 4:458, 546-47
e-mail, 3:411-13
entrepreneurship and, 3:424, 425, 426, 9:1164
Ford, 4:512-14
genetic engineering, 4:555-59
Hewlett-Packard, 5:619-20
IBM, 5:632, 635, 636
Industrial Revolution, 5:653-55, 657
information, 5:663-72, 679
Intel, 5:680, 684

intellectual property rights, 5:688, 690
interchangeable parts, 5:692-93
international trade and, 5:705
invention vs., 5:679
labor unions and, 6:764
Lands' End, 6:770, 771
license, 6:801
McDonald's, 6:756
microeconomics and, 7:871
Microsoft monopoly and, 7:875
monopoly vs., 9:1285-86
Morse and, 7:910, 911-12, 9:1284
Nike, 7:952
patents for, 2:165, 5:687, 7:980-86, 8:1112
pricing, 8:1024
printing press, 1:31
product development, 8:1036, 1037
productivity, 8:1040
profit incentive for, 8:1050
research and development, 8:1111-12
rule of law and, 8:1139
Southwest Airlines, 9:1221, 1222
telephone, 9:1285, 1286
transportation, 10:1329
Wal-Mart, 10:1388-90
wealth and, 10:1397
Wells Fargo, 10:1406
Xerox, 10:1429
Yamaha, 10:1435
insurance industry, 5:681-83
bank deposits, 7:941, 1105
building trades, 1:133-34
corporate benefits, 5:619, 633
corporate profits, 3:305
liability premiums, 6:796
nontradable financial securities, 9:1157, 1158, 1159
probability theory, 6:728
real estate industry, 8:1092
risk management, 8:1124, 1125, 1126-27
interchangeable parts, 5:657, 658, 692-93, 6:828
ISO 9000 standards, 6:732-34
Internet, 5:710-14
as activist contact means, 4:566
advertising, 1:29, 32, 33
airline ticket sales, 9:1220, 1222
Amazon.com, 1:49, 49-50, 50
anticonsumption movement, 2:267
AOL Time Warner, 1:64-65, 66
auctions via, 10:1408-9
banking online, 10:1406
bankruptcy resources, 1:102
Better Business Bureau, 1:113
browser price war, 8:1025
bubble and burst, 1:50, 2:209, 3:424, 5:678, 6:759
business ethics resources, 2:157
business law, 2:165
business plan resources, 2:167
business uses, 5:670
chambers of commerce, 2:193

Internet (*cont.*)
Cisco Systems and, **2**:207-9
Clark enterprises, **2**:215-16
competition, **2**:246
computer manufacture, **2**:252
conferencing online, **5**:713
consumerism, **2**:267
copyright, **2**:283, 283-84
corporate responsibility, **3**:299
credit, **3**:318
data mining, **3**:340
day trading, **3**:341-42
defense industry use, **3**:352
demand-driven economy and, **9**:1281
discount brokers, **9**:1245
eBay, **10**:1408-9
e-business, **3**:382-87, 387, *420*, *421*
e-learning, **3**:406, 408, 409
e-mail, **3**:411-13
energy deals, **3**:418, 421
Enron and, **3**:*420*, 421, 422
entrepreneurship, **3**:424, 427, 428
feature film distribution, **7**:*788*, 889
Fortune 500 companies, **4**:521
gaming online, **9**:1219
globalization and, **4**:564
government regulation, **2**:246
health care system links, **2**:216
high-speed acess, **9**:1288
households with access to, **5**:*668*, *672*, *713*, *714*
identity theft, **3**:328
intellectual property law, **2**:165, **5**:690
internship, **5**:716
investment sites, **6**:731
job search resources, **5**:627, **6**:738
just-in-time concept, **6**:744
labor market and, **6**:759
Lands' End sales, **6**:770-71
laws and statutes, **8**:1137
license agreements, **6**:803
market research, **6**:836
Microsoft and, **7**:874, 875-76, 902
mortgage applications, **7**:915
Nasdaq stock, **7**:931-92
Netscape Navigator, **2**:215-16
newspapers online, **8**:1075-76, **10**:*1383*, 1386
number of users, **5**:663, 670
patent sites, **7**:980
payments online, **7**:898
privacy and, **5**:671
productivity and, **8**:1039, 1040, 1043
raw materials information sites, **8**:1089
real estate transactions and, **8**:1092
research and development, **8**:1111
retail sales, **2**:267, **8**:1116-17, *1119*

reverse engineering, **8**:1122-23
savings and investments sites, **9**:1160
SEC and, **9**:1174
security industry and, **9**:1176
sex tourism and, **10**:1315
software patents and, **7**:986
Sony wireless data-transmission, **9**:1219
Starbucks and, **9**:1237
start-up firms, **3**:424
stock trading online, **9**:*1166*, 1167, 1168
stock values, **3**:341
telecommunications and, **9**:1286, 1287, 1288
telecommuting and, **9**:1291, *1292*
ticket service online, **10**:1316
trade association uses, **10**:1318-19
venture capital, **3**:346, **10**:1370
wealth and, **10**:1397-98
Whitman and, **10**:1408-9
World Wide Web development, **5**:*663*, 665, 711, *712*
World Wide Web inventor, **8**:1112
Yahoo!, **5**:711, **10**:1433-34
internship, **5**:715-16
inventory, **6**:725-27, **8**:1116, 1118
Amazon.com, **1**:49
as asset or liability, **1**:83, 84, *96*, *97*
bar codes, **1**:103
debt and, **3**:343, 344, 346
investment and, **6**:729, 730, 731
just-in-time, **6**:726-27, 741-44, 831
Leading Economic Index and, **6**:778
price floor, **8**:1014
Wal-Mart computerized, **10**:*1387*, 1388-89
ISO 9000, **6**:732-34, **10**:1318
benchmarking, **1**:110-11

J
job search, **6**:735-38
human capital and, **5**:626-27
human resources department, **5**:629, *631*
internship, **5**:715-16
resume, **8**:1113-14
just-in-time inventory, **4**:565, **6**:726-27, **741-44**, 831
Wal-Mart, **6**:744, **9**:1280, **10**:1389

L
legal services, **6**:781-84
arbitration and mediation vs., **1**:68-69
careers in, **6**:783
contract law, **2**:276-79, **6**:794-95
frivolous liability suits, **8**:1047
income level, **10**:1397
lawyer training, **8**:1138
Lewis and, **6**:791-92
liability cases, **6**:794-800
licenses and, **6**:802-3

partnership, **7**:976
pay inequities, **7**:989
professional associations, **8**:*1048*
professional licensing, **10**:1374-75
real estate industry, **8**:1092
suits against tobacco companies, **7**:1001, 1002-4
liabilities. *See* assets and liabilities
liability, **6**:794-800
contract law, **2**:276-79
corporate protections from, **3**:302
risk management, **8**:1124-25
strict principles, **8**:1045
tort law, **2**:161-62

M
management, **6**:819-22
accounting reports, **1**:25
affirmative action, **1**:36
agricultural industry, **1**:45
Archer Daniels Midland skills, **1**:70
assembly line, **1**:82
benchmarking, **1**:110-11
budget control, **1**:128, 130
business ethics, **3**:296-97
business finance, **4**:493-96
collective bargaining, **2**:221-24
consulting, **2**:258-60
corporate governance, **3**:293-97
division of labor structure, **3**:372
downsizing, **3**:378-79
entrepreneurship, **3**:426
franchise format, **4**:522-23
General Electric, **10**:1403
General Motors, **4**:551
government employment, **8**:1071
Hewlett-Packard style, **5**:619-20
human capital, **5**:626, 627, 628, **9**:1281
innovation, **5**:679
ISO 9000 standard, **1**:110-11
just-in-time approach, **6**:741-42, 743
labor relations, **6**:763-64, **9**:1253
law firms, **6**:782
MBA degree, **6**:841-43
ownership relations, **3**:294-95
performance reviews by, **2**:240-41
principles of, **6**:824
quality control, **10**:1308-10
sexual harassment by, **9**:1185-86
top-down structure, **6**:829-30
management theory, **6**:819, 820, **823-27**
Drucker and, **3**:380-81
small business, **9**:1197
Total Quality Management, **10**:1308-10
manufacturing industry, **6**:828-32
assembly line, **1**:81-82, **4**:512, 513
benchmarking, **1**:109
brand names, **1**:118
business cycles, **2**:149
business ethics, **2**:159

business-to-business sales, **2**:169-70, 172
capital gains, **2**:175, *176*
careers in, **6**:832
child labor, **2**:200, 201
consumerism and, **2**:265
consumer safety standards, **2**:275
corporate profits, **3**:*305*
defense contracts, **3**:352-53
division of labor, **3**:370-72, **10**:1400
economic growth's social costs, **3**:391-92
economies of scale and, **3**:396, 397-98
environmentalism, **3**:*391*, **4**:437, 438, *440*, 441, 442
environmental regulations, **4**:444-45, *448*
ergonomics, **4**:454
first modern factory, **5**:655
franchises, **4**:522
globalization effects, **4**:564-65, **10**:1397, *1398*
Great Depression effects, **5**:582-83
income distribution, **5**:644, *645*
Industrial Revolution, **5**:653-58, **9**:1277-78
interchangeable parts, **5**:692-93
inventory, **6**:725
ISO 9000 standards, **6**:732, 733
just-in-time approach, **6**:741-44
knowledge workers, **5**:625
labor unions, **1**:40, 42, **6**:760-64, **10**:1452
as Leading Economic Index component, **6**:778-79
Lowell Mills, 805-8, **6**:805-8
mass production, **4**:513
multinationals, **7**:917-18, 919
overhead, **7**:974, *975*
patents, **7**:980-81
product development, **8**:1034-38
raw materials, **8**:1087-89
service economy and, **9**:1178, 1181-82, 1183
small business component, **9**:1196
strikes, **9**:1250, 1251
supply and demand, **9**:1260-61
sustainable design, **4**:442
sustainable development, **9**:1266-67
Total Quality Management, **10**:1308
value of goods by state, **6**:*829*
wholesale operations, **8**:1118
women workers, **10**:1413
working conditions, **4**:466, **10**:1417, 1418
market research, **6**:833-37
ad campaign, **1**:27, 28, 32
on cultural differences, **3**:330-31
on customer service, **3**:334
demographics, **3**:356
e-business, **3**:383
pricing and, **8**:1024
product development, **8**:1034

master of business administration,
    6:841-43
merger and acquisition, **6:853-57**
    airlines, **1:**124, **7:**1001-2
    book publishers, **8:**1079
    business law, **2:**160
    as competition reduction, **8:**1052
    consumer protection and, **2:**272
    corporation, **3:**306
    defense industry, **3:**353
    entertainment, **7:**909, **9:**1218-19,
        10:*1339*, 1341, *1392*
    global competition, **8:**1104
    Internet companies, **5:***712*
    monopolistic, **7:**901-2
    oil companies, **8:**1133-34,
        9:1234, **10:**1307
    Rockefeller and, **8:**1129
    Schwab, **9:**1167, 1168
    telephone industry, **9:**1288
    venture capital, **6:**792
mining industry, **7:883-87**
    Bisbee deportation, **9:**1252
    careers in, **7:**887
    child labor, **2:**200, 201
    commodity markets, **2:**223
    corporate profits, **3:***305*
    futures and options market,
        2:198
    labor unions, **1:**39, 40
    public relations, **8:**1066
    raw materials, **8:***1087, 1088,*
        1089
    regulatory activity, **8:***1106*, 1107
    small business component,
        9:1196
multinational corporation, **3:**306,
    7:916-21
    Amazon.com as, **1:**50
    book publishing, **8:**1079
    business ethics, **2:**154, 156,
        158-59
    corporate social responsibility,
        3:301
    Enron as, **3:**420, 421
    globalization, **2:**183, **4:**561,
        565-66, **5:**709
    intellectual property and, **5:**690
    labor unions and, **1:**42
    mining, **7:**886-87
    outsourcing, **7:**918, 952, 972
    petroleum industry, **10:**1306
    Philip Morris as, **7:**1002
    product development, **8:**1037
    retailers, **8:**1118
    Royal Dutch/Shell as, **8:**1133-36
    Sony as, **9:**1217-19

N

nonprofit entities, **7:954-55,**
    10:1369

O

overhead, **7:974-75**

P

partnership, **3:**346, 427, **7:976-79,**
    9:1198
    vertical integration, **2:**185, 186

payroll, **7:990-93**
    FICA deductions, **9:**1212-13
personnel management. *See* human
    resources
pricing, **8:1021-25**
    airline tourist class, **10:***1334,*
        1335
    breakeven point, **1:**119
    breakfast cereal war, **6:**746, 7457
    bundling and, **1:**136-38
    business cycles, **2:**149, 151
    competition by, **2:**242, 246
    conspicuous consumption and,
        10:1366-67
    Consumer Price Index, **2:**269-71
    cost of living, **3:**311-12
    costs and, **3:**308
    division of labor and, **3:**372, 388
    Dow Jones Average stocks, **3:**376,
        377
    dumping, **10:**1325
    e-business, **3:**383
    environmentalism and, **4:**441-42
    factors in, **8:***1021*
    farm products, **1:**47-48, 70
    futures market, **1.**16, **1.**530, 531
    gasoline, **10:**1352
    globalization effects, **4:**564-65
    Guinness, **5:**593
    inflation, **5:**659, 660, 661, 662
    initial public offering, **5:**676, 677,
        678
    innovation and, **5:**690
    insurance policy basis, **5:**681
    market economy, **8:**1103
    mass production, **6:**829
    microeconomics and, **7:**869, 870,
        872
    mined products, **7:**885-87
    mining and, **7:**885-87
    of Model T, **4:**513
    monetary policy and, **7:**893
    monopoly and, **7:**870, *901,*
        902-3, *904*
    Nike, **7:**952
    oil, **8:**1135, **9:**1234
    OPEC, **7:**968, 969-70
    overhead and, **7:**974-75
    of personal computers, **2:**252,
        5:635
    petroleum, **7:**968, **9:**1231
    pharmaceuticals, **1:**122
    product liability threat and,
        8:1047
    profit and loss and, **8:**1050, 1052
    protectionism and, **5:**706,
        8:1054-56, 1057
    psychology of, **8:**1024-25
    public goods and, **8:**1060
    sales tax and, **9:**1273
    small business, **9:**1198
    Southwest Airlines, **9:**1221, 1222
    Standard Oil, **9:**1232
    state public service commissions,
        8:1108-9
    steel, **10:**1353
    of stocks, **3:**341-42, 376, 377
    supply and demand, **8:**1050,
        9:1259-63, **10:**1360, 1400

    tariff and, **9:**1270, 1271
    telephone service, **9:**1289,
        10:1359
    Wal-Mart, **10:**1387
product development, **8:1034-38**
    advertising and, **1:**31
    brand names and, **1:**116-18
    genetic engineering and,
        4:555-59
    information technology, **5:**668-72
    innovation and, **5:**679-80
    research and development, **8:**111
    reverse engineering and, **8:**1122
professional associations, **8:1048-49**
    five largest, **8:***1048*
    licensing, **10:**1375
    National Black Chamber of
        Commerce, **7:**933-34
    public relations, **8:**1067
    realtors, **8:**1090-91
    trade associations vs., **10:**1317
public relations and marketing,
        business practice, **8:1061-65,**
        1066, 1068-69
    demand creation, **8:**1051
    demographics, **8:**555-57
    distribution channels, **3:**366-69
    goals of, **8:***1069*
    market research, **6:**835-36
    process phases, **8:***1066*
    Southwest Airlines, **9:**1221
public relations industry, **8:1066-69**
    careers in, **8:**1067
    responsibilities, **8:***1064*
    tools of, **8:***1061*
publishing industry, **8:1074-79**
    advertising, **1:**31-33
    Amazon.com, **1:**49-50, **8:**1077,
        1079
    AOL Time Warner, **1:**64, 65, 66
    Black Enterprise, **1:**114-15
    careers in, **8:**1077
    copyright, **2:**280-83, **8:**1112
    Disney and, **10:**1393
    e-business, **3:**382
    Farrar, Straus & Giroux,
        4:472-73
    Graham and, **4:**570-72
    Guinness Book of Records, **5:**593,
        594
    Hearst and, **5:**609-12, **8:**1075,
        1081
    international trade show, **2:***171*
    Johnson and, **6:**739-40
    Kinko's and, **6:**754
    market channels, **2:***171*
    Martha Stewart Omnimedia,
        9:*1238*, 1239, 1240
    Merrill and, **6:**859
    Pulitzer empire, **8:**1075, 1080-82
    Time Inc., **1:**66
    Wall Street Journal, **10:**1383-86
    Winfrey and, **10:**1410-12

R

R&D. *See* research and development
raw materials, **8:1087-89**
    competition entry barrier, **7:**900,
        903

economic growth and, **3:***388,*
    389
energy industry, **3:**414-19
environmentalism and, **4:**437,
    439
forest products industry,
    4:617-18
gross domestic product vs., **3:***388*
population growth and, **6:**817-18
real estate industry, **8:1090-95**
    capital gains, **2:**175
    careers in, **8:**1095
    contract law, **2:**279
    corporate profits, **3:***305*
    debt and, **3:**345, 346
    lending rules, **3:**314, 316
    as market research source, **6:**836
    mortgages, **7:**913-15
    private property and, **8:**1027-28
    professional associations, **8:***1048*
    Trump and, **10:**1335-38
    valuation, **10:**1360, 1361
recreation industry, **8:1099-1102**
    arts and entertainment, **1:**72-75
    careers in, **8:**1102
    gambling, **4:**554-56
    motorcycles, **5:**598
    sports, **9:**1223-27
    tourism, **10:**1311-16
    Yamaha products, **10:**1436
research and development,
    8:1110-12
    Dow Chemical, **3:**374, *375*
    Edison projects, **3:**399-401
    expenditures (1960-2000),
        8:*1110*
    General Electric, **4:**548
    genetic engineering, **4:**555-59
    IBM, **5:**632-37
    information technology, **5:**669,
        670
    innovation and, **5:**679-80
    intellectual property costs, **5:**690
    by multinationals, **7:**919
    patent rights, **8:**1112
    product development, **8:**1034,
        1037
    productivity and, **8:**1041
    public good and, **8:**1059
    reverse engineering, **8:**1121-23
    Xerox, **10:***1429*, 1430-32
resume, **5:**627, 629, 716, **6:**735,
    736, **8:1113-14**, **10:**1302
retail and wholesale, **8:1115-20**
    bar codes, **1:**103-5
    Better Business Bureau, **1:**112
    book superstores, **8:**1079
    brand names, **1:**116-18
    Consumer Price Index, **2:**269-71
    corporate profits, **3:***305*
    credit cards, **1:**52, 53, **3:**319
    credit history, **3:**324
    customer service, **3:**333-35
    distribution channels, **3:**366-69
    e-business, **3:**382-85
    entrepreneurship, **3:**424
    innovation, **5:**679
    inventory, **6:**725
    just-in-time industry and, **6:**744

retail and wholesale (*cont.*)
  minimum wage, 7:880, 881
  NAICS codes, 7:928-29
  online sales, 1:49-50
  pricing, 8:1018, 1024, 1025
  retail, 8:1115-18, 1119
  small business component,
    9:1196
  temporary workers, 10:1301
  Wal-Mart, 3:424, 10:1387-90
  wholesale, 8:1118-20
reverse engineering, 5:636, 649,
  8:1121-23

S

security industry, **9:1175-77**
  industrial espionage and,
    5:648-52
  strike breaking by, 9:1250, 1251,
    1252
small business, **9:1196-99**, 1200-01
  Americans with Disabilities Act
    impact, 1:59-60
  Black Enterprise and, 1:114, 115
  chambers of commerce,
    2:191-93
  credit history, 3:326
  Economic Opportunity Act and,
    3:393
  entrepreneurship, 3:425-27
  as Fair Labor Standards Act
    exemptions, 4:467
  freelancing vs., 4:524
  Lewis law firm and, 6:792
  management, 6:822
  minimum wage and, 7:877, 881
  National Black Chamber of
    Commerce, 7:933-34
  partnership, 7:976
  public relations, 8:1069
  retail sales, 8:1117
  social security coverage, 9:1214
  venture capital, 10:1368-70
sports industry, **9:1223-27**
  Americans with Disabilities Act
    ruling, 1:58
  careers in, 9:1224
  collective bargaining, 2:225
  consumer demographics, 3:355
  Disney hockey franchise,
    10:1393
  Major League Baseball Players
    Association, 6:813-15
  Nike and, 7:950-53
  television broadcasts, 10:1339
  Turner and, 10:1339, *1340*
strategic planning, **9:1246-48**

T

technology, **9:1277-83**
  agriculture, 1395
  arts and entertainment, 1:74-75
  assembly line, 1:81-82
  bar codes, 1:103-5, **103-5**
  bundling, 1:137
  capitalism and, 2:177
  certification, 10:1376
  child labor and, 2:201
  Clark and, 2:215-16
  comparative advantage, 2:233

competition and, 2:246
credit card transaction, 3:321-22
data management, 3:338-40
day trading, 3:341-42
defense industry, 3:350-53
division of labor and, 3:370
Dow Chemical, 3:373-75
downsizing from, 3:378
e-business, 3:383
economies of scale and, 3:396
Edison and, 3:399-401, 4:546-48
education industry, 3:408-9
energy industry, 3:418, 419
entrepreneurship and, 3:424
environmental laws and,
  4:449-50
ergonomics and, 4:454-56
fishing industry, 4:508
forest products industry,
  4:516-17
freelancing and, 4:526
futures markets, 2:197, 198
General Electric, 4:548, 549
General Motors, 4:553-54
genetic engineering, 4:555-59
globalization and, 4:563-64,
  566-67
gross national product linked
  with, 8:1110-11
health care, 5:605, 606
Heinz, 5:614
Hewlett-Packard, 5:619-21
IBM, 5:632-37
income gaps and, 4:561
industrial espionage and,
  5:648-52
Industrial Revolution, 5:653-58
innovation and, 2:246, 5:679,
  680
Intel, 5:684-85
intellectual property and,
  2:164-65
labor market and, 6:759
licenses and, 6:802, 803, 804
Lowell Mills, 6:808
market research, 6:834
Microsoft, 7:874-76
mining industry, 7:86, 883
monopoly and, 3:361
Nasdaq stock, 7:931-32
New York Stock Exchange,
  7:948-49
product development and,
  8:1037
productivity and, 8:1039, 1040,
  1041, 1044
raw materials, 8:1088
reverse engineering, 8:1121-23
security industry and, 9:1177
service economy and, 9:1181-82
Southwest Airlines, 9:1222
standards, 9:1281
stock trading and, 1:54, 9:1245
structural unemployment and,
  10:1344
telecommunications, 9:1284,
  1286-89, 10:1357
temporary workers and,
  10:1301, 1302

tourism and, 10:1316
trade associations and,
  10:1318-19
training programs in use of,
  3:406-7
transportation, 10:1329, 1332
venture capital and, 10:1368,
  1369
wealth distribution and,
  10:1397-98
Wells Fargo, 10:1406-7
Xerox, 10:1429-32
See also computer industry;
  information technology;
  Internet
telecommunications industry,
  9:1284-89
  Americans with Disabilities Act
    compliance, 1:58-59
  antitrust and, 9:1188
  AT&T, 1:87-90
  bundling, 1:137, 8:1109
  business travel effects, 10:1316
  careers in, 9:1289
  cash flow, 2:190
  cellular telephones, 5:663, *664*
  Cisco Systems, 2:209
  competition, 2:246
  corporate profits, 3:*305*
  customer service, 3:*334*
  deregulation, 2:246, 3:358, *359*,
    360-61, 8:1109, 10:1359
  economies of scale and, 3:398
  e-mail, 3:411-13
  information technology and,
    5:663, *664*, 671, 9:*1282*
  as infrastructure, 5:673, 674
  as monopoly, 9:1285-86
  monopoly vs. competition,
    2:245, 246
  Morse and, 7:910, 911-12
  NAICS codes, 7:928, *929*
  Nasdaq stock and, 7:931
  as natural monopoly, 1:89,
    2:245, 8:1103, 1109
  regulation of, 1:66, 2:246,
    8:1105, 9:1286
  Sarnoff and, 8:1146-48
  security industry and, 9:1176
  Sony, 9:1217-19
  utilities industry, 10:1356-57
Total Quality Management, 6:826,
  10:1308-10
  ISO 9000 standards, 6:732-33
  Japanization and, 6:830-31
  just-in-time inventory and,
    6:741, 742-43, 744
  Xerox, 10:*1429*, 1432
tourism industry, **10:1311-16**
  airlines and, 1:124, 125, 126,
    8:1024, 9:1221, 10:1334-35
  American Express services, 1:51,
    52, 53
  chambers of commerce and,
    2:*193*
  credit cards and, 3:320
  exchange rate and, 4:462
  recreation and, 8:*1099*, 1100,
    1101

TQM. *See* Total Quality
  Management
trade associations, **10:1317-19**
  five largest, 8:*1048*
trademark, 5:630, **10:1320-21**
  amortization of, 1:61, 63
  brand names as, 1:117
  business law, 2:160, 164
  Coca-Cola protection, 2:218
  copyright vs., 2:283
  franchise, 4:522-23
  as intangible asset, 1:*84*, 85
  license and, 6:801
  patent vs., 7:980
  product development, 8:1037
  property rights and, 8:1029
  Royal Dutch/Shell, 8:1133, 1134
  small business, 9:1199
  Wells Fargo, 10:1405, 1407
  Xerox, 10:1429
transportation industry, **10:1329-32**
  as advertising venue, 1:32
  American Express Company,
    1:51
  British Airways, 1:125-26
  civil rights law and, 1:58, 2:210
  deregulation, 3:358, 8:1109
  Dow Jones Average companies,
    3:377
  federal regulation, 8:1105, *1106*,
    1107
  FedEx, 4:488-90
  Industrial Revolution and,
    5:653-54
  as infrastructure, 5:673, *675*
  Mitsubishi, 7:890-91
  natural monopolies and, 8:1103
  New Deal measures, 7:941
  petroleum product fuels,
    3:415-16
  pricing, 8:1024
  productivity, 8:1040
  Santa Fe Trail, 8:1142-45
  Sikorsky and, 9:1192
  Southwest Airlines, 9:1220-22
  standard of living and, 9:1229-30
  Standard Oil and, 9:1231-32
  Teamsters and, 9:1274-76
  technology and, 9:1279
  tourism and, 10:1311, 1311-12,
    1313, 1316, 1334-35
  Vanderbilt and, 10:1362-64
  Wells Fargo and, 10:1405
travel industry. *See* tourism industry

U

utilities industry, **10:1356-59**
  careers in, 10:1357
  corporate profits, 3:*305*
  deregulation, 2:246
  Dow Jones Average, 3:376, 377
  economies of scale, 3:397, 398
  as infrastructure, 5:673
  municipal ownership, 8:1031
  as natural monopoly, 2:245, 246,
    7:900-901, 904, 8:1015-16,
    1021, 1103, 1107-8
  New Deal measures, 7:941, 943
  price controls, 8:1016
  price discrimination, 7:903

privatization, 8:1032
state regulation, 8:1105, *1106*,
1107-9

W

wholesale. *See* retail and wholesale

Index of Economic Theory

A

antitrust
arbitration, 1:.68
AT&T, 1:87, 88-90, 2:246,
3:360-61, 9:1188, 1286,
1289, 10:1359
baseball exception, 6:813,
9:1224
Better Business Bureau and,
1:112
broadcast industry, 8:1147
bundling, 1:136, 138
capitalism and, 2:179, *181*
cartels, 2:188
FTC and, 4:484-85
General Motors, 4:553
IBM, 5:633, 8:*1106*
innovation and, 5:690
institutionalist inflation theory,
5:663
key acts, 2:*245*, 7:*900*,
9:1187-90
labor unions, 6:762
legal services, 6:782
merger or acquisition, 6:854,
8:1052
microeconomics and, 7:871
Microsoft, 1:138, 3:361, 4:539,
5:690, 7:873, *874*, 875, 902,
8:1051, 1104, *1106*, 9:1190
monopolies and, 8:1022, 1051
price fixing and, 8:1018, 1019,
1020, 1022
regulation of business and
industry and, 8:1104, *1106*
restraint of trade rulings, 8:*1104*
as small business protection,
9:1197
Smith's *Wealth of Nations* and,
10:1401
sports industry, 9:1224
Standard Oil, 7:902, *902*, 904,
8:134, 1130, 9:1188, *1231*,
1234, 10:1305
United Fruit, 2:205
U.S. Steel, 10:1353
Visa/MasterCard, 1:52-53
Xerox, 10:1431
See also deregulation;
monopoly; Sherman
Antitrust Act

B

business cycles, 2:149-52
balance sheet, 1:96
building trades, 1:133

capitalism and, 2:149-51, 178,
181, 182
Consumer Confidence Index,
2:261-63
economic growth, 3:390, 392
income statement, 5:647
Keynesian model, 2:151, 180,
182, 3:364-65, 6:750, 810
Leading Economic Index,
6:778-80
macroeconomics and, 6:810-12
outsourcing, 7:972-93
real estate, 8:1091, 1094, 1095
recession and, 8:1096-98
Schumpeter theory, 9:1164
strikes and, 9:1250
unemployment, 10:1343, 1344
United States (1854-2001),
1:*150*
wealth distribution and,
10:1396, 1397

C

capitalism, 2:177-83
AFL and, 1:38
business cycles, 2:149-52, 178,
182
business ethics, 2:156, 3:297
cartels, 2:187-88
Chinese communism and,
2:183, 232
competition and, 2:245-46
consumerism and, 2:264-68
contract law, 2:277
corporate social responsibility,
3:298-301
deregulation and, 3:358, 359,
361
economic growth and,
3:388-89, 391
entrepreneurship and,
3:424-28, 9:1164
environmentalism and, 4:*440*,
441-42
fascism vs., 4:474
Friedman monetary theory,
4:527-28
government regulation vs.,
3:359
historical landmarks in, 2:*181*
intellectual property and, 5:690
international trade, 5:705-6,
709
Japanese form of, 7:890
Keynesian critique of, 2:151
Marxist critique of, 6:838, 839,
10:1365
mercantilism and, 6:849-52
monopoly and, 7:901
New Deal welfare state and,
7:941
New York Stock Exchange and,
7:947
private property and, 8:1026,
1028, 1050
profit and loss and, 8:1050-53
Samuelson economics and,
8:1140
Schumpeter theory and,
9:1164-65

Smith as original theoretician
of, 6:851, 9:1202-5,
10:1400-1402
socialism vs., 9:1164, 1165,
1206, 1207, 1208-9
wealth distribution and,
10:1397
See also free market
cartel, 2:187-88, 7:900, *903*,
9:1189
airfare, 10:1335
competition vs., 2:244-45
credit card, 1:53
German bromine, 3:373
mining, 7:885-86
petroleum, 2:187, 7:968-70,
9:1230
price fixing and, 8:1017-18,
1022
common ownership. *See* tragedy
of the commons
communism, 2:227-32
capitalism vs., 2:179, 180-82,
232, 9:1165
economic liberalism and, 2:*181*,
183
failure of, 2:231-32, 3:359,
4:563, 9:1208, *1209*, 1210
fascist opposition to., 4:474
labor unions and, 1:40
Landrum–Griffin Act and,
9:1269
private property and, 8:1028
privatization and, 8:1033
Sarnoff campaign against,
8:1148
Screen Actors Guild and,
9:1169, 1170
socialism and, 9:1207-8, 1210
spread of, 2:181-82, 228, 229-31
strikes and, 9:1251
Taft–Hartley Act and, 9:1268,
1269
timeline, 2:*228*
United Fruit holdings and,
2:205, 206
See also Marxism
comparative advantage, 2:233-35
benchmarking, 1:109-11
international trade and, 5:704
microeconomics and, 7:869-70
NAFTA and, 7:958, 959
outsourcing and, 7:971-73
competition, 2:242-46
athletic shoes, 7:952
automobile industry, 10:1352
brand names, 1:118
breakfast cereals, 6:747
British Airways, 1:125, 126
capitalism and, 2:178
cartel vs., 2:187-88, 244-45
computer industry, 7:875
credit card companies, 1:52, 53
deregulation and, 3:300,
358-62
education industry, 3:408
entry barriers, 7:900, *903*, 904
Federal Trade Commission and,
4:484-87

four types of, 7:899
Friedman economic theory and,
4:528
globalization and, 4:560
industrial espionage and,
5:648-52
as inflation antidote, 5:662
Information Revolution and,
5:663-67
innovation and, 3:372,
5:679-80
intellectual property and, 5:690
Intel strategy, 5:684
just-in-time concept and,
6:743
labor unions and, 6:762, 763,
764-65
major league baseball players,
6:813
Malthusian theory and, 6:817
media companies, 1:66
merger and acquisition and,
6:854, 8:1104
monopoly vs., 2:178-79, 225,
244, 246, 7:899, 904
multinationals and, 7:921
Nike and, 7:950, 962
outsourcing and, 7:972
patents and, 8:1112
petroleum industry, 10:1305
price controls and, 8:1015-16
price fixing and, 8:1017-20
pricing and, 8:1021
privatization and, 8:1032-33
productivity, 8:1041
profit and loss and, 8:1050,
1051-52
protectionism and, 8:1054-57
regulatory activity and, 8:1104,
1107
research and development and,
8:1111-12
restraint of trade and, 8:1104
reverse engineering and, 8:1122
Sherman Antitrust Act and,
9:1187-90
small business, 9:1197, 1198
Smith theory and, 9:1203,
1204
sports industry limitations,
9:1224
stock exchanges, 1:55
supply and demand and, 7:870
sustainable development and,
9:1265
telephone service, 3:359,
360-61, 9:1285-86, 1289
Total Quality Management and,
10:1308, 1309
trade barriers vs., 1:94, 95
trade policy and, 10:1324-25
unfair business practices and,
8:1104
utilities industry, 10:1359
Web server software, 7:876
See also antitrust; monopoly
Consumer Confidence Index,
2:261-63, 6:778, 779

consumerism, **2:**264-68
  advertising and, **1:**27, 29, 32, 33, 112, 139-40
  African Americans and, 740, **6:**740
  agriculture industry and, **1:**43, 46, 48
  AT&T breakup and, **9:**1286
  black market, **1:**115
  brand names and, **1:**116-18, **8:**1021, 1025, 1037, 1051
  competition and, **2:**246
  computer market, **2:**251-52
  confidence indexes, **2:**261-63
  conspicuous consumption and, **10:**1366-67
  cost of living and, **3:**311-13
  costs, **3:**307, 308
  credit and, **3:**315, 316-18, 346
  credit and debit cards, **3:**319-23, 346
  credit history, **3:**325-26, 328
  customer service and, **3:**333-35
  data mining and, **3:**340
  debt and, **3:**346, **4:**498-99
  demographics and, **3:**355-57
  disposable income and, **3:**363-65
  distribution channels and, **3:**366
  division of labor benefits for, **3:**388
  e-business and, **3:**382-83
  entrepreneurship and, **3:**424
  environmentalism and, **4:**437, 438, 439
  franchises and, **4:**523
  Friedman theory on, **4:**528
  Galbraith theory on, **4:**532-33
  grape boycott, **2:**195
  inflation and, **3:**390
  macroeconomics and, **6:**810
  market research on, **6:**833, 836
  microeconomics and, **7:**869, 870
  monetary policy and, **7:**893
  personal expenditures (1930-2000), **2:**265
  price ceiling and, **8:**1013, 1016
  price fixing and, **8:**1017, 1018
  pricing and, **8:**1021, 1022, 1024
  protectionism and, **8:**1054-55, 1057
  recession and, **8:**1097
  recreation projects, **8:**1100, 1101
  retail sales and, **8:**1116-18, 1119
  sales tax and, **9:**1273
  service economy and, **9:**1179
  standard of living and, **9:**1229, 1229-30
  supply and demand and, **8:**1050, **9:**1259, 1281
  tariffs and, **9:**1270-71
  technology and, **9:**1281
  Total Quality Management and, **10:**1308-10

  trade policies and, **1:**92, 94
  Veblen theory and, **10:**1365-67
Consumer Price Index, **2:**269-71, **8:**1021
  cost of living, **3:**311
  as inflation indicator, **5:**659, 662
  Leading Economic Indicators and, **6:**780
  macroeconomics and, **6:**810
  social security benefits and, **9:**1215
corporatist economy, **2:**180, **4:**474, 476
cost-benefit analysis, **3:**308, 309
  benchmarking, **1:**109-10, *111*
  of federal regulation, **8:***1108*
  market behavior, **7:**870, 872
  protectionism, **1:**95
  public goods, **8:**1060
cost of living, **3:**311-13
  Consumer Price Index, **2:**269-71
  GM-UAW contract, **4:**552
  inflation and, **5:**660, 663
  Silicon Valley, **4:**566-67
  standard of living and, **9:**1228
CPI. *See* Consumer Price Index

D
demand. *See* supply and demand
deregulation, **3:**358-62, **8:***1106*
  banking, **8:**1109, 1132
  brokerage firms, **9:**1166
  cable television, **10:**1359
  competition and, **2:**246
  corporate social responsibility and, **3:**300
  mergers and acquisitions, **6:**853
  natural gas, **3:**420, **10:**1359
  privatization and, **8:**1030-33
  productivity and, **8:**1040
  Securities and Exchange Commission and, **9:**1174
  trucking, **3:**358, **8:**1109
  wholesale power market, **8:**1016
division of labor, **3:**370-72
  assembly line, **1:**82
  capitalism and, **2:**177, 178
  economic gains from, **7:***870*
  economic growth and, **3:**370-71, 388
  economies of scale and, **3:**396
  family leave and, **4:**468
  free trade and, **9:**1270
  manufacturing industry, **6:**828, 829
  Smith theory of, **6:**851, **9:**1203, 1204, 10.1400

E
economic growth, **3:**388-92
  Asian Development Bank, **1:**78
  business cycle, **3:**390, 392
  credit, **3:**315, 316, 318
  disposable income, **3:**364-65
  division of labor, **3:**370-71, 388
  entrepreneurship, **3:**428
  environmentalism, **4:**437, 439, 441-42

  European Union, **5:**708
  Great Depression slowdown, **5:**581
  gross domestic product, **5:**588-91
  income distribution, **5:**644
  inflation rate, **5:**659, 661
  innovation, **5:**679
  labor market, **8:**1096
  Leading Economic Index, **6:**778
  macroeconomics, **6:**811, 812
  manufacturing industry, **6:**828
  microeconomics, **7:**869-72
  monetary policy, **3:**390, **7:**893-95
  population growth, **6:**816-17, 818
  productivity, **8:**1039, 1040, 1042
  profit and loss, **8:**1050
  recession vs., **8:**1096-98
  retailing, **8:**1116
  rule of law, **8:***1137*
  savings and investments, **3:**363-64
  service economy, **9:**1178, *1183*
  Smith's free market, **6:**851, **9:**1203, 1204, **10:**1400, 1401
  sustainable development, **9:**1264-67
  technology, **9:**1277-83
  trade policy, **10:**1322
economies of scale, **3:**396-98
  cartels as, **2:**187-88
  Edison Schools, **3:**402-3
  electricity industry, **3:**421
  NAFTA and, **7:**958
  as natural monopoly, **7:**900-901, *903*, **8:**1103, 1107
  outsourcing and, **7:**972
  retail chains, **8:**1117
  service economy, **9:**1180-81
  small business, **9:**1197
  Soviet "diseconomies," **2:**231
entrepreneurship, **3:**424-28
  Ben & Jerry's, **1:**106-8
  Black Enterprise, **1:**114-15
  breakfast cereals, **6:**745-46
  building trades, **1:**133
  business plan, **2:**166-69
  chambers of commerce, **2:**191-93
  Clark and, **2:**215-16
  consultants, **2:**258
  costs, **3:**308
  Deere and, **3:**347-49
  division of labor benefits for, **3:**388
  eBay and, **10:**1408-9
  Edison and, **3:**400-401, 424
  Ford and, **3:**424, **4:**511-14
  free-rider problem and, **8:**1058
  Gates and, **4:**537, 538-39
  Gordy and, **4:**568-69
  Guinness, **5:**592-93
  Harley-Davidson, **5:**598-600
  Hewlett-Packard, **5:**619-21

  information technology, **2:**207, 215-16
  innovation and, **5:**679
  Johnson and, **6:**739-40
  Kellogg Company, **6:**745-47
  Kinko's, **6:**752-54
  knowledge workers, **9:**1280-81
  Kroc and, **6:**755-57
  Lauder and, **6:**775-77
  Leo Burnett Agency, **1:**139-40
  Levitt and, **6:**788-90
  Lewis and, **6:**792-93
  management and, **6:**822
  Mary Kay Inc., **1:**76-77
  monopoly and, **7:**901
  National Black Chamber of Commerce, **7:**933-34
  Nike, **7:**950
  Perot and, **7:**998
  product development, **8:**1036
  retail sales, **8:**1117
  Rockefeller and, **8:**1128-30
  savings and investment and, **3:**363
  Schumpeter theory on, **9:**1164
  Schwab and, **9:**1166-68
  small business, **9:**1196-99, 1200-1201
  Southwest Airlines, **9:**1220
  Starbucks empire, **9:**1235-37
  Stewart and, **9:**1238-40
  Trippe and, **10:**1333-35
  Trump and, **10:**1336-38
  Vanderbilt and, **10:**1362-64
  venture capital, **10:**1368-73
  Walker and, **10:**1380-82
  Walton and, **10:**1387-88
  wealth distribution and, **10:**1396, 1397, 1398
  Winfrey and, **10:**1410-12
external benefits. *See* public goods externalities, **4:**437-38, 463-65

F
fascism, **4:**474-76, **5:**612
  private property and, **8:**1028-29
  See also Nazism
free market
  balance of payments, **1:**92
  balance of trade, **1:**94
  business cycles, **1:**149-52, **2:**178, 182
  business ethics, **2:**156, **3:**297
  capitalism and, **2:**177, 179
  cartel disfavor, **2:**188
  Chicago School, **4:**528
  economic growth, **3:**388-92
  former communist state conversions to, **9:**1207, 1208
  FTC and, **4:**484
  government regulation and, **8:**1103
  "invisible hand" of, **2:**156, **3:**358, 361, **5:**690, **9:**1203-4, **10:**1400
  liberalism and, **10:**1396
  macroeconomics, **6:**812
  mercantilism vs., **6:***849*

minimum wage vs., **7**:880-81
monopoly and, **7**:901
population growth and, **6**:816
price controls and, **8**:1013, 1014, 1016
price fixing and, **8**:1017-19
privatization and, **8**:1032
public goods and, **8**:1058-59, 1060
rule of law and, **8**:1137, 1138
self-interest and, **5**:690, **7**:869
Smith theory of, **1**:92, **5**:705-6, **6**:851, **7**:901, **9**:1203-4, **10**:1396, 1400-1401
supply and demand, **9**:1259-63, **10**:1365
tariff effects on, **9**:1270
"Third Way" and, **9**:1209
valuation, **10**:1360-61

G

gross domestic product, **5**:588-91
economic growth and, **3**:388, 392
food processing chain, **1**:47
GDP Deflator, **2**:271
globalization effects, **4**:562, 567
Great Depression years, **5**:583
health care services, **5**:603
Leading Economic Index, **6**:779, 780
macroeconomics, **6**:810, 811
manufacturing's percentage, **6**:832
price index, **2**:271
productivity, **8**:1039, 1043, 1044
recession, **8**:1096
gross national product, **8**:1110-11

H

human capital, **5**:625-28
building trades, **1**:131, 133, 134
as business asset, **1**:85
compensation, **2**:239
as economic growth factor, **3**:389
energy industry, **3**:417
information technology, **5**:668
intellectual property, **5**:687-91
labor market, **6**:758-59
productivity, **8**:1041, 1051
service economy, **9**:1178-83
technology, **9**:1280-81

I

income distribution, **5**:644-46
African Americans, **1**:36, **8**:1085
aggregate of selected nations, **10**:1398, 1399
aggregate of U.S., **10**:1396
by educational attainment, **10**:1397
farming, **1**:47-48
globalization, **4**:561, 565-66, 567
per capita, **4**:561, **9**:1228, 1229
by race and sex, **1**:36

Silicon Valley, **4**:566
taxation and, **9**:1272
See also wealth distribution
Industrial Revolution, **5**:653-58, **9**:1277-78, 1281
assembly line, **1**:81-82
capitalism, **2**:178, 181
child labor, **2**:199, 200
division of labor, **3**:370-72
Information Age shift, **5**:625
interchangeable parts, **5**:657, 658, 692-93
Lowell Mills, **6**:805-8, **10**:1417
management concepts, **6**:819
manufacturing industry, **6**:828
Morgan financing, **7**:905, 906
socialism, **9**:1206
social security, **9**:1211-12
steam power, **5**:655-58, 665, 668
strikes, **9**:1249-50
wealth distribution, **10**:1395-96
women in the workforce, **10**:1413
working conditions, **10**:1417
inflation, **5**:659-62
business cycles, **2**:182
consumer consumption, **4**:532
Consumer Price Index, **2**:269, 270-71
cost of living, **3**:311-12
economic growth, **3**:390-91
Federal Reserve, **4**:480, 483, 527
fiscal policy, **4**:503-4
income distribution, **5**:644
interest rates, **5**:661, 695, **8**:1021
Keynesian macroeconomics, **6**:750, 751, 810-12
minimum wage, **7**:881, 882
monetary policy, **2**:182, **7**:893
money supply, **8**:1098
money's value, **7**:897
national debt, **3**:315
price controls for, **8**:1013, 1016
social security benefits, **9**:1214, 1215
stagflation, **6**:751
stock returns, **9**:1159
T-bill returns, **9**:1242-43
trade policy, **1**:92
unemployment, **10**:1342-43
wealth distribution, **10**:1397, 1398
Information Revolution, **5**:663-67, 668
Industrial Age vs., **5**:625
manufacturing decline, **6**:832
wealth distribution, **10**:1397, 1398
infrastructure, **5**:673-75
economic growth, **3**:389
highways, **5**:674, **10**:1312
World Bank loans, **10**:1423
intellectual capital. See human capital

L

labor market, **6**:758-59
business ethics, **2**:159

Consumer Confidence Index, **2**:263
demographics, **3**:357
disabled people, **1**:56-60
economic growth, **3**:392, **8**:1096
EEOC and, **4**:452-53
entrepreneurship, **3**:425-26, 427
ethnicity and, **3**:357
Fair Labor Standards Act, **4**:466-67
farm goods processing, **1**:47
freelancing, **4**:524-26
globalization effects, **4**:564-66
immigrant workers, **5**:639-43
job search, **6**:736
knowledge workers, **5**:625, 668
labor unions and, **6**:762, 763, 766
macroeconomics, **6**:810
manufacturing jobs, **6**:832
microeconomics, **7**:869
minimum wage, **8**:1014-15
monopsonistic, **6**:762
NAFTA effects, **7**:959
pay equity, **7**:987-89
population growth and, **6**:816
productivity, **8**:1039-44, 1051
protectionism and, **8**:1054-56, 1057
public sector unionism and, **8**:1070-71
Say's Law, **8**:750
service economy, **9**:1178-80
temporary workers, **10**:1301-4
unemployment, **10**:1342-45
union membership, **6**:763, 766
women and, **10**:1413-16, 1415
Leading Economic Index, **2**:262, **5**:696, **6**:778-80
macroeconomics and, **6**:810, 811
liberalism
free-trade policy, **5**:705-6
mercantilism vs., **6**:849, 851, 852, **9**:1203, 1204
Smith's Wealth of Nations, The, **10**:1400-1401
wealth distribution and, **10**:1396

M

macroeconomics, **6**:809-12
business cycles, **2**:149-51
Keynesian, **2**:180, **6**:712, 749, 750-51, 809, 810
microeconomics vs., **7**:869
Samuelson and, **8**:1141
schools of, **6**:812
managed economy, **1**:92, **4**:474.
See also communism
market economy. See capitalism; free market
market forces. See supply and demand
Marxism, **9**:1207-8, 1209, 1210
Veblen critique of, **10**:1365-66

wealth distribution and, **10**:1396
See also communism
mercantilism, **6**:849-52, **7**:901
balance of payments, **1**:92
capitalism vs., **2**:177
liberalism vs., **5**:705-6, **9**:1203, 1204, **10**:1401
microeconomics, **6**:809, **7**:869-72
externalities, **4**:463-64
macroeconomics vs., **7**:869
public goods, **8**:1058-60
Samuelson and, **8**:1141
mixed economies, **9**:1208
monetarism, **2**:182-83, **4**:527
inflation theory, **5**:660-61, 662
macroeconomics, **6**:812
monetary policy and, **7**:893-95
business cycles, **2**:151, 180
credit, **3**:316
economic growth, **3**:390
exchange rate, **4**:461
Federal Reserve and, **3**:315-16, 390, 391, **4**:480-83, 527, 528
fiscal policy, **4**:503
Friedman monetarism and, **4**:527-28, **6**:812
gold/gold-exchange standards, **3**:315, 316, 317
inflation, **2**:182, **3**:390, **5**:659-61
international economy, **2**:180, 181, 182
Keynes macroeconomics and, **2**:180, **6**:749, 750, 810-12
Leading Economic Index, **6**:778, 779
national debt, **3**:315
price controls, **8**:1016
recession, **8**:1097, 1098
tools of, **7**:893
trade policies and, **5**:706
monopoly, **7**:899-904
AT&T, **1**:87, 88-89, **2**:246, **3**:359, 360-61, 398, **9**:1188, 1234, 1285-86, **10**:1357
Baby Bells, **9**:1289
bundling and, **1**:138
cartel as, **2**:188
competition vs., **2**:178-79, 225, 244, 245, 246
consumer protection from, **2**:272
copyright as, **2**:165, 280, 281
economies of scale and, **3**:398
electricity industry, **3**:360, 361-62, 398, 417
FTC and, **4**:484
inflation theory and, **5**:661-662
innovation and, **5**:679
institutionalist inflation theory and, **5**:661, 663
labor unions seen as, **6**:762, 764-65
license restrictions, **6**:804
mercantilist, **1**:92, **6**:850, **9**:1203

monopoly (*cont.*)
microeconomics and, **7:**870, 871
Microsoft charges, **3:**361, **4:**539, **7:**874, 875
Mitsubishi, **7:**891
Morgan and, **7:**906
natural vs. unnatural, **1:**88, 89
pricing, **8:**1022
privatization and, **8:**1032
profit and loss and, **8:**1051
Sherman Antitrust Act, **2:***245*, **9:**1187, 1189-90
Standard Oil, **8:**1129-30, **9:***1231*, 1232, 1234
state ownership as preventive, **8:**1031
U.S. Steel clearance, **10:**1353
utilities, **8:**1015-16, 1021, **10:**1356, 1359
Xerox, **10:**1430, 1431
See also antitrust

N

natural monopoly, **2:**245, **3:**360, 361, 398, **7:**900-901, 904
AT&T as, **1:**88, 89
deregulation, **8:**1109
prices and, **8:**1015-16, 1021
state regulation, **8:**1103, 1107-9
Nazism, **2:**179, **3:**380, **5:**612, **10:**1346, 1348
fascist ideology, **4:**474, *475*, 476
Volkswagen design, **10:**1377

O

oligopoly, **7:**870, 899, **8:**1017, 1032
opportunity cost, **3:**309, **7:964-65**
inventory excess as, **6:**725

P

per capita income. *See* income distribution
perfect competition theory, **2:**244
Phillips Curve, **5:**661
physiocrats, **2:**177, **9:**1203, **10:**1400
planned economy. *See* communism; socialism
price controls, **4:**533, **8:1013-16**, 1021
ceilings, **8:***1013*, *1014*, 1016
fair trade and, **8:**1103, *1106*
floors, **8:***1013*, 1014
Galbraith and, **4:**533
inflation and, **5:**661-62
New Deal, **8:**1105
profit and loss and, **8:**1051
supply and demand, **9:**1263
price fixing, **8:1017-20**, 1022, 1104, 1133, 1135
as anticompetitive, **2:**244, 245
Archer Daniels Midland, **1:**70, 71
cartel, **2:**187-88, 244
illegality of, **9:**1189
institutionalist view of inflation and, **5:**661
small business, **9:**1197

Standard Oil, **9:**1231-32
supply and demand vs., **9:**1259
trade association restraints, **10:**1318
private property, **8:1026-29**
constitutional protection, **2:**256-57
contractual transfer, **2:**279
copyright, **2:**280-84, **8:**1112
corporate ownership, **3:**302
economic growth and, **3:**389
entrepreneurship, **3:**428
environmentalism and, **4:**441-42, 450
fair market value, **10:**1360
intellectual property, **5:**687-91
land wealth and, **9:**1277
legal protection, **8:**1138, 1139
license coverage, **6:**801-4
opposition to, **8:**1028-29
patent law, **7:**980-86, **8:**1112
privatization and, **8:**1032
profits and, **8:**1050
public goods vs., **8:**1058
real estate industry and, **8:**1090-95
renting vs. owning, **3:**345
risk management, **8:***1124*, 1125, 1139
tort liability, **6:**795
as tragedy of the commons solution, **10:**1328
productivity, **8:1039-44**
agriculture, **1:**43, *44*, *47*, 48
assembly line, **1:**81, 82, **6:**829
business cycles, **2:**149, 151
division of labor, **3:**370-72, **10:**1400
economic growth and, **3:**388, 391
ergonomics and, **4:**454
Industrial Revolution, **5:**658
information technology and, **5:**669-70, 671-72
just-in-time concept and, **6:**741, 742
labor unions and, **6:**763-64
as Leading Economic Index component, **6:**778, 779
management theory and, **6:**824, 825
NAICS codes and, **7:**928
privatization and, **8:**1032
profit and loss and, **8:**1051
recreation and, **8:**1101
robotics and, **1:***110*
service economy and, **9:**1178
Smith division of labor theory and, **9:**1204
Southwest Airlines, **9:**1221
tariff effects, **9:**1270
telecommuting, **9:**1291
unemployment effects, **10:**1342
profit and loss, **8:1050-53**
Amazon.com, **1:**50
balance sheet, **1:**97
breakeven point, **1:**119-20
British Airways, **1:**124
cartels and, **2:**187-88

cash flow and, **2:**190
competition and, **2:**244, 246
corporate, **3:**301, 302, *305*
corporate social responsibility vs., **3:**301
costs and, **3:**310
customer service and, **3:**334
division of labor and, **3:**372, 388
e-commerce companies, **5:**714
economic growth and, **3:**389
economies of scale and, **3:**396-98
education industry, **3:**404, 410
Enron accounting and, **3:**422
entrepreneurship, **3:**424
Fortune 500 and, **4:**521
futures market, **2:**226, **4:**530
Hewlett-Packard divisions, **5:**620
IBM losses, **5:**637
income statement, **1:**26, **5:**647
minimum wage and, **7:**880
monopoly and, **7:**902-3, *904*
overhead, **7:**974-75
partnership, **7:**978
price fixing and, **8:**1017, 1018, 1133
pricing and, **8:**1021, 1022
research and development and, **8:**1111-12
small business, **9:**1198
supply and demand factors, **8:**1050-51
Wal-Mart, **10:**1387
property rights. *See* private property
public goods, **8:1058-60**
microeconomics and, **7:**871-72
recreation industry and, **8:**1100, *1101*
Smith on, **9:**1204, **10:**1400
tragedy of the commons and, **10:**1326
types of, **8:***1059*

R

recession, **8:1096-98**
business cycles, **2:**152, 178
Consumer Confidence Index, **2:**261
General Motors losses, **4:**554
government policy, **3:**390
income distribution, **5:**644
inflation slowed by, **5:**659
interest rates and, **3:**316, 391
inventory overhangs, **6:**726-27, 731
investment and, **6:**729-30, 731
Keynesian macroeconomics and, **6:**750, 812
labor market, **6:**759
mid-1970s, **7:**947
strikes and, **9:**1250

S

Say's Law, **6:**750
scarcity, **9:1161-63**
intellectual property and, **5:**689
microeconomics and, **7:**869-72

opportunity cost and, **7:**964
price controls and, **8:**1016
valuation and, **10:**1360
service economy, **9:1178-83**
bundling and, **1:**137-38
corporate profits, **3:***305*
cost and, **3:**307
e-business and, **3:**382, 384
economic growth and, **3:**392
immigrant labor and, **5:**642
income distribution and, **5:**644, *645*
information technology and, **9:***1282*
labor unions and, **1:**42
pay equity, **7:**987, 989
small business component, **9:**1196, 1197
tourism and, **10:**1312-16
wealth distribution and, **10:**1397
socialism, **9:1206-10**
capitalism and, **2:**178, 183, **9:**1164, 1165
energy industry, **3:**418
Marx and, **6:**838
private property and, **8:**1028
privatization and, **8:**1033
Schumpeter theory and, **9:**1164, 1165
strikes and, **9:**1252
utopian communities, **2:**227
specialization. *See* division of labor
stagflation, **2:**182, **5:**661, **6:**751
standard of living, **9:1228-30**
cost of living, **3:**311, 313
economic growth, **3:**388, 392
entrepreneurship, **3:**428
foreign worker wages, **4:**565
income distribution, **5:**645
Industrial Revolution, **5:**653
international trade, **5:**708
liberal economic theory, **10:**1396-97, 1400
personal finance, **4:**497-98, 500
worker demands, **3:**372
supply and demand, **9:1259-63**
business cycles, **2:**149, 150
capital gains and, **2:**175
capitalism and, **2:**177
commodities market, **2:**225-26
comparative advantage, **2:**233-35
competition and, **2:**242-46
demand pull inflation theory, **5:**660-61
elasticity, **9:**1263
exchange rates, **4:**461
externalities, **4:**463, 464, *465*
free market and, **6:**816, **9:**1203-4, **10:**1400
Great Depression, **5:**582-83
inventory and, **6:**725-26
just-in-time inventory and, **6:**741-44
Keynesian economics and, **6:**750
labor market and, **6:**758-59
labor unions and, **6:**765

Leading Economic Index and, **6**:778

microeconomics and, **7**:869-70

monopolistic pricing and, **7**:903

oil prices and, **7**:970

population growth and, **6**:816

price controls and, **8**:1013, 1014, 1016

price fixing and, **8**:1018

pricing and, **7**:903, 970, **8**:1021-22, 1025, 1050, 1103

profit and loss and, **8**:1050-51

property rights and, **8**:1026

Say's Law and, **6**:750

scarcity and, **9**:1161-63

technology and, **9**:1281

valuation, **10**:1360-61

Veblen theory and, **10**:1365

supply-side economics, **6**:751

sustainable development, **3**:301, **9:1264-67**

  economic growth and, **3**:390

  energy industry and, **3**:418

  environmentalism and, 4:442

  fishing industry and, **4**:510

  WTO and, **4**:545

T

"Third Way" social policy, **9**:*1209*, 1210

totalitarianism, **9**:1207, *1209*

tragedy of the commons, **4**:441, **8**:1027 **10:1326-28**

U

utilitarianism, **2**:153, **9**:1202

utopianism, **2**:227, **9**:1206, *1209*

W

wage-price controls, **5**:661-62, **8**:1016

wealth distribution, **10:1395-99**

  business estimates by firm size, **9**:*1199*

  economic growth and, **3**:392

  Economic Opportunity Act, **3**:393-95

  entrepreneurship and, **3**:426

  Forbes richest Americans list, **6**:*739*, 740

  Great Depression and, **5**:581, 583

  income distribution, **5**:644, 645

  intellectual property and, **5**:687

  Internet access and, **5**:*714*

  mercantilist theory of, **2**:177, **6**:849, 850, **9**:1203

  monopoly and, **9**:1234

  private property and, **8**:1028

  redistribution of, **9**:1209

  Rockefeller and, **9**:1233

  service economy and, **9**:1178

  Smith's theory of, **9**:1203, 1204, **10**:1400

  Stewart and, **9**:1234

  taxation and, **9**:1272

  technology and, **9**:1277, 1280-81

Trump and, **10**:1336

Veblen leisure class theory and, **10**:1366

Walker and, **10**:1380

Walton and, **10**:1390

Winfrey and, **10**:1412

Wealth of Nations, The (Smith), **2**:177-78, *181*, **5**:705-6, **6**:*849*, 851, **9**:1202, 1203-4, **10:1400-1401**

  division of labor example, **3**:370-71

  economic growth concept, **3**:388

  excerpt, **10**:1401

  key ideas of, **10**:*1400*

  microeconomics and, **7**:869

welfare capitalism, **2**:180, *181*, **3**:299

welfare state, **7**:941, **9**:1208

workforce. *See* labor market

Index of Labor Organizations and Issues

A

Actors' Equity Association, **1**:68

affirmative action, **1**:34-37, 135, **5**:630

AFL-CIO, **1:38-42**

  American Federation of Teachers, **7**:936, 938

  corruption allegations, **6**:764

  labor movement and, **5**:601, 602

  membership (1979-1998), **1**:*41*

  Perkins and, **7**:996

  Randolph and, **8**:*1083*, 1084, 1085-86

  strikes, **9**:1252

  United Automobile Workers, **10**:1349

  United Farm Workers, **2**:195

AFT. *See* American Federation of Teachers

Agricultural Workers Organizing Committee, **2**:195

air traffic controllers strike (1981), **9**:1254, 1268

American Federation of Film and Television Actors, **9**:1171

American Federation of Labor. *See* AFL-CIO

American Federation of State, County, and Municipal Employees, **8**:1070, *1072*, *1073*

American Federation of Teachers, **3**:403, **7**:936, 938, **8**:1070

American Railway Union, **9**:1252

American Teachers Association, **7**:938

arbitration, **1**:40, 67-69, *69*, **9**:1252

B

Brotherhood of Electrical Workers, **10**:1375

Brotherhood of Professional Baseball Players, **6**: 813, *815*

Brotherhood of Sleeping Car Porters, **8**:1083-84, *1085*, 1086

C

California Farm Labor Board, **2**:196

child labor, **2**:178, **199-203**, **3**:371

  Fair Labor Standards Act, **4**:466

  Industrial Revolution, **5**:*656*

  Lowell Mills, **6**:*806*, 807

  minimum wage, **7**:877

  minimum working age, **7**:879

  Perkins reforms, **7**:994, 995, 996

  prohibition of, **10**:1418

  reforms, **10**:1396

  workday limits, **10**:1417

CIO. *See* AFL-CIO

closed shop, 1268, **9**:1269

collective bargaining, **2:221-24**, **6**:760

  California farm workers, **2**:196

  family leave, **4**:468

  General Electric, **4**:552

  Lewis and, **1**:39

  major league baseball, **6**:813, 814, 815

  National Education Association, **7**:938

  National Labor Relations Act, **7**:939, 943, **9**:1252, 1274-75

  National Labor Relations Board, **8**:1105

  pattern bargaining, **6**:763

  public sector unionism, **8**:1070

  Randolph and, **8**:1084

  Screen Actors Guild, **9**:1169

  Taft–Hartley Act and, **9**:1268

  temporary workers, **10**:1304

  United Automobile Workers, **10**:*1349*, 1350

  United Fruit, **2**:205

Communication Workers of America, **1**:40, 50

Congress of Industrial Organization. *See* AFL-CIO

craft unionism, **1**:38, 39

D

downsizing, **3:378-79**, 422

  British Airways, **1**:125

  General Electric, **4**:549

  Kellogg Company, **6**:748

  labor market and, **6**:759

  from merger or acquisition, **6**:853

  minimum wage and, **7**:877

  productivity and, **8**:1041

  women workers and, **10**:1413

  See also unemployment

E

equal employment opportunity affirmative action, **1**:34, 35

Americans with Disabilities Act, **1**:58, 59-60

Asian Development Bank, **1**:79

  building trades set-asides, **1**:135

  civil rights legislation, **2**:212-13

  legal services, **6**:783

  as Levi Strauss policy, **6**:786

  management theory, **6**:827

  as Randolph cause, **8**:1084-85

  women and, **10**:1414-15

equal pay. *See* pay equity

ergonomics, **4**:454-56, **7**:960, 961, 962, 963, **10**:1419-20

F

family leave, **3**:357, **4:468-71**

Federation of Organized Trade and Labor, **5**:601

flexible work schedules, **1**:60, **9**:1290

free agency, **6**:813, 814, *815*, **9**:1224, 1227

freelancing, **4:524-26**

  as independent contractor, **10**:1302-3

  publishing industry, **8**:1077

  social security tax payment, **7**:993

G

glass ceiling, **6**:773, **10**:1415

government employees

  equal opportunity, **8**:1084-85

  strikes, **9**:1254, 1260

  unionism, **8**:1070-73

H

Haymarket Square riot, **5**:601-2

human capital, **5:625-28**

  building trades, **1**:131, 133, 134

  as business asset, **1**:85

  compensation, **2**:239

  as economic growth factor, **3**:389

  energy industry, **3**:417

  information technology, **5**:668

  intellectual property, **5**:687-91

  labor market, **6**:758-59

  productivity, **8**:1041, 1051

  service economy, **9**:1178-83

  technology, **9**:1280-81

I

immigration, **5:638-43**

  demographic shifts, **3**:356-57

  labor laws, **5**:630

  labor unions, **1**:42

  Lowell Mills, **6**:807, 808

  women workers, **10**:1413

  working conditions, **10**:1418, 1419-20

  See also migrant workers

independent contractor. *See* freelancing

International Brotherhood of Teamsters. *See* Teamsters Union

International Labor Organization, **2:**201, *202*
International Ladies Garment Workers Union, **1:**40
International Workers of the World, **1:**38, **9:***1209*, 1252

J

job loss. *See* downsizing; unemployment

K

Knights of Labor, **1:**38, **5:**601, 602

L

Labor Hall of Fame, **7:**997
labor union, **6:**760-66
  AFL-CIO, **1:**38-42
  Amazon.com and, **1:**50
  arbitration, **1:**40, *69*
  automobile industry, **4:**550, 552, *553*, **10:**1349-52
  building trades, **1:**133-35
  capitalism and, **2:**178, 180
  Chavez and, **2:**194, 195-96
  child labor and, **2:**200
  collective bargaining, **2:**221-24
  division of labor and, **3:**371-72
  Guatemalan banana workers, **2:**205
  Haymarket Square riot, **5:**601-2
  institutionalist inflation theory, **5:**661
  International Workers of the World, **9:***1209*, 1210
  legislation, **7:**939-40, 943
  legislative curbs, **6:**767-68, **9:**1268-69, 1275
  Lowell Mills, **6:**807
  major league baseball, **6:**813-15, **9:**1227
  minimum wage and, **7:**877, 878, 943
  multinationals and, **7:**719
  NAFTA and, **7:**958, 959
  National Education Association, **7:**935-38
  New Deal measures, **7:**943, **8:**1105
  open vs. closed shop, **9:**1269
  OSHA and, **7:**963
  outsourcing objections, **7:**973
  Perkins and, **7:**994
  public sector, **8:**1070-73
  Randolph and, **8:**1083-86
  Screen Actors Guild, **9:**1169-71
  social democracy and, **9:**1208
  tariffs and, **1:**95
  Teamsters, **9:**1274-76
  temporary workers, **10:**1304
  wealth distribution, **10:**1397, *1398*
  women workers, **1:**38, 39, **10:**1413, 1414
  working conditions and, **10:**1420
  See also strikes
layoffs. *See* downsizing; unemployment
Lowell Mills, **6:**805-8, **10:**1417

Ludlow massacre, **8:**1066

M

Major League Baseball Players Association, **6:**813-15, **9:**1227
migrant workers, **5:**639, **10:**1301
  child workers, **2:**201, 203
  unionization, **2:**194, 195-96
  working conditions, **10:**1420
minimum wage, **7:**877-82, **10:**1417
  legislation, **4:**466, **10:**1418
  microeconomics and, **7:**872
  New Deal, **7:**878-79, 943, 996
  profit and loss and, **8:**1051
  pros and cons, **8:**1013, 1014-15
  small business and, **9:**1199
  strikes and, **9:**1252
  unconstitutionality ruling, **5:**583
  United Auto Workers, **10:**1349
Molly Maguires, **9:**1250
mommy track, **4:**471, **10:**1415
monopsony, **6:**762, **10:**1324

N

National Education Association, **7:**935-38
National Labor Relations Board, **7:**939, 940, *941*, 943, **8:**1105, *1106*
  collective bargaining, **2:**221-23
  labor unions and, **6:**764
  Taft–Hartley Act and, **9:**1268
  temporary worker unionization, **10:**1304
  United Automobile Workers and, **10:**1350
National Labor Union, **10:**1413
National Teachers' Association, **7:**935, 936
National Women's Trade Union League, **1:**39, **2:***221*

O

open shop, **9:**1269
organized labor. *See* labor union

P

pay equity, **7:**987-89
  CEO vs. average worker, **3:***296*
  civil rights cases, **2:**214
  collective bargaining, **2:**223
  compensation policy, **2:**236
  corporate social responsibility, **3:**299, 300
  Equal Employment Opportunity Commission, **4:**452-53
  Equal Pay Act, **10:**1418
  Fair Labor Standards Act, **4:**466, 467
  Ford $5 day, **3:**299
  human resources department, **5:**630
  immigrant inequities, **5:**642-43
  income differences, **10:**1397
  relevant cost, **3:**309-10

service sector, **9:***1181*, 1183
  temporary workers, **10:**1303
  women's inequities, **10:**1413, 1414-15, 1418
public sector unionism, **6:**763, **8:**1070-73
  strikes, **9:**1254, 1268
  Taft–Hartley Act and, **9:**1268
  teachers and, **7:**937-38

S

Screen Actors Guild, **9:**1169-71
seasonal unemployment, **10:**1343, 1344
seasonal workers, **10:**1303
secondary boycotts, **6:**768, **9:**1269
seniority system, **2:**237, 238, 239
Service Employees International Union, **1:**42
sexual harassment, **2:**213, **5:**630, **9:**1170, **1184-86**, **10:**1414, 1415, 1416
sit-down strike, **1:**38, 40, **4:**550, 552, *553*, **9:**1253, **10:**1349
strikes, **9:**1249-54
  AFL-CIO history, **1:**38, 39, 40
  banana workers, **2:**205
  California farm workers, **2:**196
  collective bargaining, **2:**221, 223
  colonial-era printers, **10:**1417
  corporate responsibility and, **3:**299
  Haymarket Square riot, **5:**601-2
  legal restraints, **6:**764, 767, 768, **9:**1268
  professional sports, **6:**814, *815*, **9:**1227
  Screen Actors Guild, **9:**1169, 1171
  as socialist agenda, **9:**1210
  Teamster, **9:**1276
  textile mills, **10:**1417
  United Auto Workers, **10:**1349-50, *1352*
sweatshops, **4:***564*, 565-66, **10:**1418, 1420

T

Teacher's International Union of America, **7:**936
Teamsters Union, **1:**38, 40, **6:***765*, **9:**1274-76
  corruption and, **6:**764, 767
  farm workers and, **2:**195
  strikes, **9:**1254
telecommuting, **5:**620, 670, **9:**1290-92
  Kinko's services, **6:**754
  principles of, **9:**1291
  working conditions, **10:**1420
temporary workers, **10:**1301-4, 1420
  freelancers vs., **4:**524
  outsourcing, **7:**973
trade union. *See* labor union

U

unemployment, **10:**1342-45
  business cycles, **2:**149, 151, 152, 178

downsizing, **3:**378-79
  excess inventory and, **6:**726
  fiscal policy and, **4:**503
  freelancing and, **4:**525
  Great Depression, **4:**466, **5:**581, 584, 585, **8:**1097
  income distribution and, **5:**644
  inflation and, **5:**661
  Keynesian model, **3:**364, 365, 390, **6:**750, 810
  labor market and, **6:**759
  as Leading Economic Index component, **6:**778, 779
  macroeconomics and, **6:**810-11, 812
  measurement of, **10:**1345
  from merger or acquisition, **6:**853
  minimum wage and, **7:**881, **8:**1014, 1015
  monetary policy and, **7:**893
  New Deal measures, **7:**940, 941-42, 996
  recession and, **8:**1096
  as social cost of economic growth, **3:**391-92
  stagflation and, **2:**182, **6:**751
  subsidy programs and, **9:**1255-56
  temporary workers and, **10:**1303
unemployment insurance, **2:**180, **5:**630, **7:**942, 995, 996, **9:***1211*, 1212, **10:**1345
  small business tax, **9:**1199
  wealth distribution and, **10:**1396
unionization. *See* labor union
union shop, **9:**1269
United Automobile Workers of America, **1:**38, 40, **6:**766, **10:**1349-52
  collective bargaining, **2:**222
  General Motors and, **4:**552, *553*
  pattern bargaining, **6:**763
United Farm Workers, **1:***69*, **2:**194, 195, 196
United Mine Workers, **1:**39, 40
United Steelworkers of America, **1:**40, **6:**813

V

vocational licensing, **10:1374-76**

W

wage gap. *See* pay equity
wildcat strike, **9:**1254, 1268
Wobblies. *See* International Workers of the World
women in the workforce, **10:1413-16**
  affirmative action, **1:**34
  Ash's career, **1:**76-77
  Asian Development Bank program, **1:***78*, 79
  benefits programs, **2:**238
  building trades, **1:**135
  civil rights law, **2:**210, 212-13, 236

corporate social responsibility, 3:300
demographics, 3:355, 357
equal employment opportunity, 4:453
Fair Labor Standards Act, 4:467
family leave, 4:468-71
Fiorina as first Fortune 500 CEO, 4:501-2
first bond saleswoman, 6:858
freelancers, 4:525-26
Graham's *Washington Post* role, 4:570, 571-72
income distribution, 5:645
income median, 1:36
information technology and, 5:670
labor unions and, 1:38, 39, 40, 42, 2:221
Lansing's career, 6:772, 773
Lauder's career, 6:775-77
legal services, 6:783
management theory and, 6:827
Mary Kay sales by, 1:77
mill and sweatshop workers, 6:806-8, 10:1417, 1418
minimum wage, 7:877, 878, 879, *881*, 882
pay inequities, 2:236, 4:467, 7:987-90, 10:1413, 1414-15
Perkins's career, 7:994, 995
professional associations, 8:1048
Screen Actors Guild and, 9:1170
sexual harassment, 9:1184-86
Small Business Administration and, 9:1201
Stewart's career, 9:1238-40
teachers' union and, 7:935-36
Walker's career, 10:1380-82
wealth distribution, 10:1397
Whitman's career, 10:1408-9
Winfrey's career, 10:1410-12
Women's Business Centers, 9:1198, 1201
working conditions, 10:**1417-20**
affirmative action and, 1:34, 35, 36-37
AFL-CIO and, 1:39
arbitration and, 1:68
assembly line, 4:513
Ben & Jerry's employees, 1:108
building trades, 1:133
business ethics, 2:154, 155, 157, 158
Chavez and, 2:194-96
child labor and, 2:200-203
civil rights laws, 2:213-14
collective bargaining for, 2:221-24
compensation and, 2:236-41
corporate responsibility, 3:298, 299-300, 301, 306
disability provisions, 1:56-60
division of labor benefits, 3:370-72, 388

downsizing and, 3:378-79
economic growth and, 3:389
eight-hour day, 5:601
employer-provided health insurance, 5:606
equal opportunity and, 4:452-53
ergonomics, 4:454-56, 10:1419-20
Fair Labor Standards Act, 4:466, 467
family leave, 4:468-71
farm workers, 2:194-96
fatal injuries (2000), 10:*1419*, 1420
flexible schedules, 1:60
Ford employees, 4:513, 6:829
Haymarket Square riot, 5:601, 602
Heinz employees, 5:614
Hewlett-Packard innovations, 5:619-20
human resources department and, 5:630
IBM employees, 5:633
information technology and, 5:671-72
Japanese workers, 6:831
labor market and, 6:759
labor unions and, 6:766
legislation, 10:1418
Levi Strauss employees, 6:786
liberal economics and, 10:1396
Lowell Mills, 6:806, 807
management theory and, 6:823, 825-26
manufacturing jobs, 6:832
minimum wage, 7:877-82, 879, 943
multinationals and, 7:918, 919, 921
Nader safety campaign, 7:927
Nike employees, 7:918, 952-53
OSHA and, 7:960
overtime, 4:466, 5:630
Perkins reforms, 7:994-95
regulatory activity, 8:*1106*, 1107
retirement plans, 4:499
sexual harassment and, 9:1185-86, 10:1414-16
social reform, 2:178
Southwest Airlines employees, 9:1220-21
stress factors, 7:962
strikes and, 9:1249-51, 1252
telecommuting and, 9:1290-92
tort liability and, 6:796
trade policies and, 1:94
United Auto Workers, 10:1349
women workers, 10:1413
Workingman's Party, 1:38, 9:1251
work-to-rules strategy, 6:764

Y
Yellow-Dog Contract, 7:939-40

Index of Finance and Trade

A
American Stock Exchange, 1:**54-55**
Nasdaq contrasted with, 7:930-31
amortization and depreciation, 1:**61-63**

B
balance of payments, 1:**91-92**, 93
exchange rates, 4:461-62
IMF and, 5:701, 702
balance of trade, 1:91, **93-95**
cotton subsidies, 10:*1325*
exchange rates, 4:461-62
GATT requirements, 4:545
inflation and, 5:660
mercantilism and, 6:849, 850, 852
mercantilism vs. Smith theory, 9:1203
NAFTA and, 7:959
recession and, 8:1098
surplus creation, 5:708
bankruptcy, 1:**99-102**
business cycles, 2:149
California utilities, 8:1016
cash flow and, 2:190
Chrysler bailout, 10:1352
corporation, 3:297, 306
credit history, 3:324, 325, 326
from day trading, 3:342
debt and, 3:344
Durant and, 4:551
as economic growth cost, 3:391
Enron, 1:101, 3:306, 420, 422-23
as futures market risk, 4:529
Heinz and, 5:614
profit and loss and, 8:1053
savings and loan, 8:1094
small business, 9:1197
telecommunications, 9:1288
Texaco, 10:1307
Trump and, 10:*1336*, 1337, 1338
bonds. *See* stocks and bonds

C
Canadian and United States Trade Agreement (1989), 7:956
capital, 2:**173-74**
business finances, 4:493-96
debt and, 3:343, *344*, 345-46
economic growth and, 3:389
energy industry, 3:417
entrepreneurship and, 3:427
exports as, 5:708
financial managers, 4:493-96
interest rates, 4:504
investment, 6:729-30
Morgan and, 7:905
natural monopolies, 8:1103
small business, 9:1197-98, 1199, 1200

stock and bond issuance for, 9:1241, 1242, 1245
taxation and, 9:1272-73
World Bank, 10:1423
See also venture capital
capital gains, 2:**175-76**, 9:1158-59
Chicago Board of Trade, 1:46, 2:**197-98**, 225, *226*, 4:*529*, 8:1127, 9:*1243*
Chicago Mercantile Exchange, 2:225
common stock, 3:302, 345
definition of, 9:1241
compound interest, 2:**247-48**, 5:694
savings growth with, 9:1157, *1158*
Consolidated Stock Exchange, 1:55
credit, 3:**314-18**
accounting definition of, 1:24-25
Asian Development Bank, 1:78
balance of payments, 1:91-92
bankruptcy and, 1:99, 101-2
cash flow and, 2:189-90
commercial real estate and, 8:1094-95
compound interest and, 2:247-48
consumer, 2:265, 266, 3:315, 316-18, 346
consumer protection, 2:272
corporate, 3:303, 306, 317
debt and, 3:343-46
entrepreneurship and, 3:427
federally guaranteed housing loans, 6:790
Federal Reserve and, 4:480, 481, 482
FTC consumer alerts, 4:486, *487*
GE Capital, 4:548
GMAC, 4:551, 553
Great Depression and, 5:581
Hamilton's views on, 5:596
IMF loans, 5:703, 709
income statement and, 5:647
inflation and, 5:660
as Leading Economic Index component, 6:728-31
loans as long-term liabilities, 1:86, 97
monetary policy and, 7:893, 894-95
mortgage, 7:913-15
personal finance and, 4:498-99
professional associations, 8:1048
promissory note, 1:84, 86
secured loan, 3:319
small business, 9:1200, 1201
time line, 3:*317*
World Bank, 10:1423
See also interest
credit cards and debit cards, 3:318, **319-23**
American Express, 1:51-52

credit cards and debit cards (*cont.*)
bank, **1**:51-52
credit history and, **3**:324
debit cards, **3**:323
debt and, **1**:101, **3**:346
history of, **3**:316, *317*, 320-21
identity theft and, **3**:326, 328
personal finance and, **4**:498-99
theft of, **5**:671
credit history, **3**:324-28
D&B reports, **3**:326, 336-37
data mining, **3**:340
private property and, **8**:1029

D

D&B, **3**:326, **336-37**
day trading, **3**:341-42, **9**:1245
debit cards. *See* credit cards and debit cards
debt, **3**:343-46
accounting, **1**:24-25
alternatives to, **3**:345-46
balance of payments, **1**:91, 92
bankruptcy, **1**:99-102
bond issuance as, **9**:1241, 1242
British Airways, **1**:125
business, **3**:343-46, **4**:494-95
business vs. personal, **3**:346
cash flow and, **2**:189-90
consumer, **2**:265, **4**:533
corporate, **3**:303, 306, 317
cost and, **3**:307
credit and, **3**:314-18
credit history, **3**:324-28
D&B reports, **3**:336-37
from day trading, **3**:342
Enron, **3**:422
IMF and, **5**:702-3
inflation and, **5**:660
as liability, **1**:83, 86, 97
liquidity ratios, **3**:343, 344
macroeconomics and, **6**:811
money as settlement of, **7**:896, 897
mortgage, **7**:913
national, **3**:315, **4**:478, 503, *504*
personal, **3**:316, 318, 345, 346, **4**:498-99, 500
war, **5**:583
World Bank, **10**:1423-24
See also credit
discount brokerage, **4**:491-92, **9**:1167-68, 1245
discount rate, **4**:482, **7**:893, 894-95
disposable income, **3**:363-65
standard of living and, **9**:1228-30
Dow Jones Averages, **2**:198, **3**:376-77, **4**:548, **5**:581, **7**:947
business cycles, **2**:149, *151*, 152
futures market, **2**:225
dumping, **4**:540, **8**:1056, **10**:*1323*, 1325

E

Eurex (European Derivatives Market), **2**:198
euro (currency), **4**:457, 459, 460, **5**:707-8
European Free Trade Area, **4**:458
European Monetary System, **4**:459
exchange rates, **2**:180, **4**:461-62, **5**:710
exports. *See* international trade

F

finance, business, **4**:493-96
accounting and bookkeeping, **1**:23-26
accounting firm consulting, **2**:260
assets and liabilities, **1**:83-86
balance sheet, **1**:96-98
bankruptcy, **1**:99-102
breakeven point, **1**:119-20
budget, **1**:127-28, 129-30
capital, **2**:173-74
capital gains, **2**:175-76
cash flow, **2**:189-90
corporations, **3**:302-3
credit, **3**:314-18
credit card, **3**:319
credit history, **3**:326-27, 328
D&B reports, **3**:336-37
debt, **3**:343-46
employee-compensation costs, **2**:239, *240*
entrepreneur funding, **3**:427
Fortune 500 listing, **4**:520-21
human capital, **5**:625-28
income statement, **5**:647
interest, **5**:695, 696
investments, **6**:729-31
IRS and, **5**:697-700
management and, **6**:822
multinational revenues, **7**:*917*
small business, **9**:1199
finance, personal, **4**:497-500
bankruptcy, **1**:99, 100
budget, **1**:127, 128-29, *130*
capital gains, **2**:175-76
cash flow, **1**:189
compound interest, **2**:247-48
credit, 316-18, **3**:315
credit card transactions, **3**:319-23
credit history, **3**:324-25
debt, **3**:316, 318, 343, 345, 346
disposable income, **3**:363-65
interest, **5**:695, 696
IRS and, **5**:697-700
mortgage, **7**:913-15
savings and investment options, **4**:491-92, **6**:729, 730, 858-60, **7**:922-24, **9**:1157-60, 1241-45
standard of living and, **9**:1229-30
wealth distribution and, **10**:1397-98
foreign trade. *See* international trade
free trade, **7**:928, 956-59, **10**:1325, 1337
arguments for, **1**:92, 94

capitalism and, **2**:178, 179, 180, *181*
common markets, **5**:707-8
competition and, **2**:246
European Union, **4**:457, 458, 459, 460
GATT rounds, **4**:543, 545
globalization and, **4**:563
mercantilism vs., **6**:849, 850, 851, 852
NAFTA and, **7**:956-59
NAICS codes, **7**:928
protectionism vs., **8**:1054
restrictions vs., **5**:706-7, **9**:1270-71
Smith case for, **1**:92, **5**:705-6, **9**:1203, 1204
WTO and, **10**:1425, 1427
futures markets, **4**:529-31, **9**:*1243*
business cycles, **2**:*152*
Chicago Board of Trade, **2**:197-98, 225
commodities, **1**:46, **2**:225, 226

G

General Agreement on Tariffs and Trade, **1**:95, **2**:180, 183, **4**:540-45, 563, **5**:708, **9**:1270, **10**:1425, 1427, 1428
signatories and year signed, **4**:541-42, *544*
globalization, **4**:560-67
Asian Development Bank, **1**:78-80
business cycles, **2**:152
business ethics, **2**:158-59
capitalism, **2**:178, 180, 183
child labor, **2**:201-3
Coca-Cola, **2**:217, 219-20
consumerism, **2**:268
contract law, **2**:279
corporate social responsibility, **3**:301
cultural differences, **3**:329-32
eBay, **10**:1409
e-business-to-business, **3**:384
economic growth, **3**:391-92
environmental regulation, **4**:451
financial markets, **9**:1241, 1245
forest products, **4**:517-18
free trade, **10**:1325
General Agreement on Tariffs and Trade, **4**:540-45, **10**:1425
immigrant workers, **5**:643
income distribution, **5**:645-46
Information Revolution, **5**:663, 665
information technology, **5**:670-71, **9**:1282
innovation, **5**:679-80
intellectual property, **5**:689-90
International Monetary Fund, **5**:701-3
international trade, **5**:709
ISO 9000 standards, **6**:732-34
Keynesian policy, **2**:180
Kinko's, **6**:754

labor unions, **1**:42
manufacturing, **6**:831-32
MBA programs, **6**:841
McDonald's, **6**:846, 847, 848
mergers and acquisitions, **6**:853, *856*
Mitsubishi, **7**:892
Morita, **7**:909
multinationals, **3**:306, **7**:916-21
Organization for Economic Cooperation and Development, **7**:966-67
protests against, **2**:*183*, **4**:561, 566, **5**:702, **7**:967, **10**:*1424*, *1428*
recession, **8**:1098
research and development, **8**:1111
retailing, **8**:1117-18
Sony, **7**:908, 909
Starbucks, **9**:1236-37
sustainable development, **9**:1265-67
tourism, **10**:1311, 1312, 1313-14
Wal-Mart stores, **10**:1389
wealth distribution, **10**:1397-99
Welch on, **10**:1403
working conditions, **10**:1417, 1420
World Bank, **10**:1421-24
Yamaha, **10**:1435, 1436

I

imports. *See* international trade
initial public offering, **5**:676-78
Electronic Data Systems, **7**:998
Healtheon, **2**:216
Martha Stewart Omnimedia, **9**:*1238*, *1239*, 1240
Microsoft, **7**:874
Nasdaq, **7**:930
Netscape, **2**:215, 216
Nike, **7**:952
Time Inc., **1**:66
venture capital, **10**:1368, 1371, 1373
Wal-Mart, **10**:*1387*
insider information, **9**:1173, 1240
interest, **5**:694-96
bond payments, **9**:1242
compound vs. simple, **2**:247, *248*
credit, **3**:314, 317, 318
credit card, **1**:52, **3**:319, 320, **4**:498
Federal Reserve rate-setting, **4**:480, 482, **5**:695, 696, **6**:731, **8**:1098
fiscal policy and, **4**:503, 504
gold standard and, **3**:316
government borrowing and, **9**:1273
inflation and, **3**:391, **5**:661, 695, **8**:1021
investment, **6**:731
Keynesian macroeconomics, **6**:750, 811

Leading Economic Index, **6**:778, 779
monetary policy, **4**:503, **7**:893, 894-95
as money supply control, **5**:661
mortgage, **7**:913, 914-15
national debt, **3**:315
savings and investment options, **9**:1157, 1158-59
Swiss, **10**:1347
taxation of, **9**:159
as tax deduction, **3**:317
International Securities Exchange, **1**:*54*, 55
international trade, **5**:**704-9**
 agricultural controls, **1**:47, 48, 70
 balance of payments, **1**:91-92, 93
 balance of trade, **1**:91, 93-95
 bananas, **2**:*204*, 206
 barriers to, 8.*1054. See also* protectionism; tariff
 brand names, **1**:117, *118*
 cartels, **2**:187
 chambers of commerce, **2**:192, 193
 comparative advantage, **2**:233, 235
 cultural differences, **3**:329-32
 European Union, **4**:457-60, **5**:707-8
 exchange rates, **4**:461-62
 globalization and, **4**:560-67
 Great Depression roots in, **5**:583
 IMF and, **5**:701, 703
 Industrial Revolution and, **5**:653
 inflation effects, **5**:660
 intellectual property piracy, **6**:*804*
 ISO 9000 standards, **6**:732-34
 mining industry, **7**:884
 Morita and, **7**:909
 multinationals and, **7**:916-21
 NAFTA and, **7**:956-59
 NAICS codes, **7**:928-29
 price controls, **8**:1016
 trademarked goods, **10**:1321
 trade policy, **10**:1322-25
 WTO and, **10**:1425-28
 See also free trade; General Agreement on Tariffs and Trade
investment, **6**:**728-31**
 breakeven point, **1**:119-20
 business cycles, **2**:149, 151, 152
 business finance, **4**:493-96
 business plan, **2**:166-69
 capital, **2**:173-74
 capital gains, **2**:173-74
 cash flow indications, **2**:190
 compound interest, **2**:247-48
 debt, **3**:343, **4**:498
 Dow Jones Average, **3**:376-77
 economic growth, **3**:389
 Enron problems, **3**:422, 423

financial management, **4**:493-96
fiscal policy and, **4**:503
Fortune 500 listing, **4**:520-21
futures market, **4**:529-31
globalization, **4**:564
Great Depression effects, **5**:581-83
in human capital, **5**:627, 628
initial public offering, **5**:676-78
Leading Economic Index, **6**:778, 780
mutual funds, **7**:922-24
Nasdaq, **7**:930-32
New York Stock Exchange, **7**:947-49
in private infrastructure, **5**:673
SEC and, **9**:1172-74
Silicon Valley, **3**:424
in small business, **9**:1200
socially responsible, **3**:301
trade deficit and, **1**:91-92, 93
valuation and, **10**:1360-61
venture capital, **10**:1368-73
World Bank, **10**:*1421*, 1422
See also savings and investment options; stocks and bonds
IPO. *See* initial public offering

L

liquidity, **5**:676, **10**:1370-71, 1373
 ratios, **3**:*343*, 344
London International Futures and Options Exchange, **2**:198
London Metal Exchange, **2**:225

M

margin buying, **3**:341, **4**:529, **5**:581-82
money, **7**:**896-98**
 as asset, **1**:84, 96
 breakeven point, **1**:120
 as capital, **2**:173
 cash flow, **2**:189-90
 commodity futures, **2**:225
 credit card vs., **3**:319
 debit card vs., **3**:323
 euro, **4**:457, 459, 460, **5**:707-8
 exchange rates, **4**:461-62
 Federal Reserve and, **4**:480, 481-82
 gold standard, **3**:316
 inflation, **5**:659
 as investment, **6**:728-31
 negotiable instrument substitutes, **2**:162-63
 valuation, **10**:1360
money market funds, **4**:491, **9**:1158
mortgage, **3**:316, 318, **7**:**913-15**, **8**:1091
 as debt, **3**:345, 346, **4**:498
 federally guaranteed, **6**:790
 most-favored-nation (MFN) status, **4**:543
mutual funds, **7**:**922-24**, 948
 diversification, **2**:293-94
 Fidelity, **4**:491-92

as investment option, **9**:1158, 1241
Schwab and, **9**:1167
socially responsibile investing, **3**:301
stockholders, **3**:293-94, 297

N

NAFTA. *See* North American Free Trade Agreement
Nasdaq, **2**:*152*, *173*, **5**:677, **7**:930-32, **9**:*1243*
 Amazon.com stock, **1**:50
 American Stock Exchange and, **1**:*54*, *55*
 day trading, **3**:341-42
 Edison Schools listing, **3**:404
 futures market, **2**:2252
 initial public offering, **5**:677
 Level II screen, **3**:*341*
 tradable securities, **9**:1157
New York Commodity Exchange, **2**:225
New York Cotton Exchange, **2**:225
New York Curb Agency. *See* American Stock Exchange
New York Mercantile Exchange, **2**:225
New York Metal Exchange, **2**:225
New York Stock Exchange, **5**:677, *678*, **7**:930-31, **947-49**
 American Stock Exchange and, **1**:*54*, *55*
 Bristol-Meyers listing, **1**:121
 computer technology, **9**:1245
 daily shares traded (1900-2000), **7**:*947*
 Dow Jones Average stocks, **3**:376
 initial public offering, **5**:677, *678*
 Nasdaq contrasted with, **7**:930-31
 risk management, **8**:1127
 Royal Bank of Canada listing, **8**:1132
 Securities and Exchange Commission and, **9**:1172
 Stewart and, **9**:*1239*
 tradable securities, **9**:1157
 trading volumes, **7**:948, **9**:1244-45
 UBS AG shares, **10**:*1346*, 1348
 valuation and, **10**:1360
New York Stock Exchange Index, **2**:*152*, *225*
New York Sugar Exchange, **2**:225
North American Free Trade Agreement, **1**:94, **2**:*181*, 183, **5**:707, 708, **7**:**956-59**
 NAICS codes, **7**:928-29
 UAW opposition, **10**:1352
North American Free Trade Area, **10**:1325
NYSE. *See* New York Stock Exchange

O

Organization of Petroleum Exporting Countries, **7**:886, **968-70**, **10**:1349, 1352
 as cartel, **2**:187, **7**:968-70, **9**:1230
 price fixing, **8**:1022, 1135
 pricing, **9**:1259

P

preferred stock, **3**:302, 345
promissory note, **1**:84, 86, **2**:163, **3**:343
protectionism, **8**:**1054-57**
 arguments for, **10**:1324-25
 balance of trade and, **1**:94-95
 capitalism and, **2**:178, 179
 competition vs., **2**:245, 246
 European Union and, **4**:460
 GATT and, **4**:540, 543, 545, **10**:1425
 Great Depression, **4**:563, **5**:581, 583
 mercantilism and, **6**:850, 851, 852
 tariffs, **1**:94-95, **6**:850-52, **8**:1016, **9**:1270
 as trade policy, **5**:706-7

R

reserve requirements, **7**:893, *894*, 895
risk management, **8**:**1124-27**
 bonds vs. stocks, **9**:1242
 capital gains and, **2**:176
 credit history, **3**:326
 credit ratings, **3**:317, 328, 337
 debt and, **3**:344
 Enron, **3**:421
 futures market, **2**:197-98, 226, **4**:529, 530, 531
 insurance industry, **5**:681-83
 interest rate, **5**:696
 investment, **3**:294, **6**:728, 729
 labor market, **6**:759
 returns and, **9**:1159, 1241-43
 rule of law and, **8**:1139
 supply and demand factors, **8**:1050
 venture capital, **10**:1368

S

S&P 400 Index, Domini 400 Social Index vs., **3**:*301*
S&P 500 Index, **1**:54, **2**:152, *225*, **4**:521, **6**:779
 mutual index funds and, **7**:923
 Nasdaq Composite index vs., **7**:931
Santa Fe Trail, **8**:**1142-45**
savings and investment options, **9**:**1157-60**
 business cycles, **2**:149, 151, 152
 capital gains, **2**:175-76
 compound interest, **2**:247-48
 consumer confidence, **3**:315, 318, 364
 disposable, **3**:363-65

savings and investment options (*cont.*)
  diversification, **9:**1158, 1159, 1160, 1243
  economic growth and, **3:**363-64
  Fidelity Investments and, **4:**491-92
  initial public offering, **5:**676-78
  Merrill Lynch and, **6:**858, 859-60
  mutual funds, **3:**293-94, 301, **7:**922-24
  personal finances and, **4:**499
  risk and returns, **9:**1158-59, 1241-43, 1246
  Schwab and, **9:**1166-68
  stocks and bonds, **3:**302, **9:**1241-45
  wealth from, **10:**1398
Securities and Exchange Commission, **1:**55, **3:**403-4, **4:**519, **7:**930, **8:**1105, **9:1172-74**
  accounting industry oversight, **2:**260
  commissioners, **9:**1173
  day trading and, **3:**342
  initial public offering and, **5:**677
  merger and acquisition filing, **6:**853
  New Deal and, **7:**943, **9:***941*
  securities prospectus approval by, **9:**1244
  United Brands ethics charge, **2:**206
Standard & Poor's 500. *See* S&P 500 Index
stock options, **2:**241, **3:**296, **9:**1229, 1236, **10:**1390, 1398
stocks and bonds, **9:1241-45**
  accountant audits, **2:**260
  American Stock Exchange, **1:**54-55
  as assets, **1:**84, 196
  bond issuance, **3:**317
  bonds vs. stocks, **9:**1242, 1245
  bull markets, **7:**947-48
  business cycles and, **2:**149, 151-52, 180, *181*, **3:**364
  business ethics and, **2:**153
  as capital, **2:***173*, 174
  capital gains, **2:**175-76
  Chicago Board of Trade traders, **2:**198
  compound interest return, **2:**247
  corporate financing with, **3:**302
  corporate governance and, **3:**293-97, 303-4

corporate scandal effects, **3:**297
day trading, **3:**341-42, **9:**1245
debt claims, **3:**344-45
discount brokers, **9:**1167, 1245
dividends, **3:**302, 304, 317
Dow Jones Average, **3:**376-77
e-business and, **3:**382
exchange rates and, **4:**462
federal regulation, **7:**941, 943, **8:**1105, **9:**1172-74
Federal Reserve and, **4:**480, 482
Fidelity Investments and, **4:**491-92
financial managers and, **4:**493-96
fraud arbitration, **1:**68
futures market, **2:**198, *225*
Great Depression and, **5:**581, 582, 583
income statement, **5:**647
initial public offering, **5:**676-78
investment analysis, **6:**728
as investment option, **9:**1157-58, 1159
as Leading Economic Index component, **6:**778, 779
margin buying, **5:**581-82
mergers and acquisitions and, **6:**853, 854-55
Merrill Lynch and, **6:**858-60
monetary policy and, **7:**894
Morgan and, **7:**906, *906*, 907
mutual funds, **7:**922-24
Nasdaq, **7:**930-32
New York Stock Exchange, **7:**947-49
risk management, **8:**1127
risks and returns, **9:**1158-59, *1241*, 1242-43, 1245
Schwab and, **9:**1166-68
socially responsible investing, **3:**301
as Southwest Airlines employee benefits, **9:**1221
stockholder reports, **4:***493*
stocks vs. bonds, **9:**1158-59
valuation d, **10:**1360
wealth generation from, **10:**1398

T
tariff, **9:1270-71**
  balance of payment, **1:**92
  balance of trade, **1:**94
  business cycles and, **2:**151
  as competition barrier, **2:**245, 246
  countries with highest-lowest barriers, **8:***1056*

free trade vs., **2:**178, 179, 180, 245
GATT rounds, **4:**540, 543, 545, **10:**1425
Great Depression, **5:**581, 583
as import limitation, **10:**1322
intellectual property piracy, **6:**803
Latin American banana exports, **2:**206
mercantilism and, **6:**849, 850, 851, 852
NAFTA and, **7:**956
as price control, **8:**1016
protectionism, **1:**94-95, **8:**1054-57
steel industry, **1:**95, **2:**246, **4:**460, **8:**1056, *1057*, **9:***1262*
as trade restriction, **5:**706, 707
types of, **8:**1054
See also protectionism
taxation, **9:1272-73**
  business cycles, **2:**150, 151, 152, 180
  as business liability, **1:**86, 97
  of capital gains, **2:**175-76, **9:**1158-59
  debt deductibility, **3:**317, 346
  earned income tax credit, **6:**759, **7:**881
  on entrepreneurs, **3:**428
  federal budget and, **4:**477, 479
  fiscal policy and, **4:**503
  Hamilton's views on, **5:**595, 596
  income distribution and, **5:**644, 645-46
  information technology and, **9:**1282
  Internal Revenue Service, **5:**697-700
  international travel receipts, **10:***1312*
  Keynesian economics and, **2:**180, **3:**390, **6:**750
  mercantilism and, **6:**851
  microeconomics and, **7:**872
  nonprofits' exemption, **7:**954, 955
  on partnerships, **7:**978
  payroll functions, **7:**990, *991*, 992-93
  per capita disposable income and, **9:**1228
  personal deductions, **4:**500
  price controls and, **8:**1016
  for public goods, **8:**1059, 1060
  real estate write-offs, **8:**1094-95
  recession and, **8:**1098

savings and investments and, **9:**1158-60
small business and, **9:**1199
social security and Medicare, **9:**1211-16
subsidy payments from, **9:**1255-58
Swiss law on, **10:**1347
wealth distribution and, **10:**1396, 1397
See also tariff
Tokyo Stock Exchange, **6:**850, *858*
trade policy, **9:**1270-71, **10:1322-25**
  capitalism and, **2:**178-81
  comparative advantage, **2:**233-35
  European Union, **4:**457, 458, 459, 460
  exchange rates, **4:**461-62
  Hudson's Bay Company, **5:**622-24
  interstate commerce regulation, **8:**1103-4, 1105
  mercantilism, **5:**705, **6:**849-52
  protectionism, **8:**1054-57
  Smith economic theory, **9:**1203
  types of, **10:***1323*
  unfair practices, **8:**1056
  WTO and, **10:**1427-28
  See also free trade; international trade
Treasury bills (T-bills), **9:**1158, 1159
Treasury bonds, **3:***314*, 315, **6:**779, **7:**894, 906, **9:**1241, 1242

V
valuation, **10:1360-61**
  amortization and depreciation, **1:**61-63
  formulas, **10:**1360
  intellectual property, **5:**689
  money as unit of, **7:**897
  opportunity cost, **7:**964, 965
  price acceptance and, **8:**1024-25, 1060
  private property, **8:**1026, 1028
  scarcity and, **9:**1162
  Smith economic theory and, **9:**1203
  of trademark, **10:**1321
venture capital, **2:***173*, **3:**346, 427, **10:1368-73**
  for Cisco Systems, **2:**207
  Clark enterprises, **2:**215, 216
  Lewis's minority firms, **6:**792
  for small businesses, **9:**1200
  for Yahoo!, **10:**1433

Comprehensive Index

Page numbers in **boldface type** indicate full articles on a subject. Page numbers in *italic type* indicate illustrations or other graphics. All numbers preceding colons indicate volume numbers.

A

A&P, **8:**1115
ABC (television), **1:**66
A. B. Dick, **3:**400
absolute advantage, **2:**233-35
Accessory Transit Company, **10:**1362-63
accident insurance, **5:**682
accounting and bookkeeping, **1:23-26**
  amortization and depreciation, **1:**61-63
  assets and liabilities, **1:**83-86
  balance sheet, **1:**96-98
  basic accounting equation, **1:**25, 96
  bookkeeping functions, **1:**23-25
  breakeven point, **1:**119-20
  budget, **1:**127-30
  business ethics, **2:**153, 157, **3:**296-97, *379*, 422, **8:**1053
  cash flow, **2:**189, 190
  consulting service, **2:**259-60, **3:**297
  corporate governance, **3:**294, 296-97
  data management, **3:**338-39
  debt, **3:**343-46
  Enron methods, **3:**422, 423
  income statement, **1:**25, 26, 61, **5:***647*
  management and, **6:**822
  partnership and, **7:**976
  payroll, **7:**990-93
  professional associations, **8:***1048*
  profit and loss, **8:***1051*, 1052-53
  small business, **9:**1198
  spreadsheets, **3:**338-39
  stock options, **3:**296
  temporary workers, **10:**1301
a/c/e (Alliance/CBOT/Eurex) system, **2:***197*, 198
acquisition. *See* merger and acquisition
activity ratios, **3:**344
Actors' Equity Association, **1:**68
Act to Regulate Commerce (1887), **8:**1103, *1106*
actuaries, **6:**728

ADA. *See* Americans with Disabilities Act
Adams, John, **8:**1137
Adamson Act (1916), **10:**1418
Adarand Constructors v. Pena (1995), **1:**36
Addams, Jane, **2:**200
Adelphia Communications, **3:**297
Adidas, **7:**951
adjustable-rate mortgage, **7:**914, 915
ADM. *See* Archer Daniels Midland Company
Admiralty Bancorp, Inc., **8:**1132
ad valorem tariff, **8:***1054*, **9:**1270
Advanced Research Projects Agency, **5:**710, *712*
Advance Group, **8:**1075, 1077
advertising, business practice, **1:27-30**
  actors' residuals, **9:***1169*, 1171
  African Americans and, **6:**740
  Better Business Bureau and, **1:**112, 113
  brand loyalty and, **8:**1051
  business ethics. *See* false advertising
  business law and, **2:**164-65
  by Coca-Cola, **2:**217-18, 219
  commercial speech protection, **2:**257
  compact disc price-fixing, **8:**1018
  consumers and, **2:***175*, 265-67, 272, 274
  copyright and, **2:**283
  demand creation by, **8:**1051
  demographics and, **3:**356, *357*
  by Estée Lauder, **6:**776
  Federal Trade Commission and, **1:**32, **4:**485, **8:**1104, 1105
  by Guinness, **5:**594
  by Harley-Davidson, **5:**600
  by Heinz, **5:**613, 614, *615*
  by Intel, **5:**686
  by Kellogg, **6:**746
  of law firms, **6:**782
  of Levi jeans, **6:**786, *787*
  market research and, **6:**833
  Marlboro Man image, **7:**1003
  in newspapers, **8:**1075
  by Nike, **7:**952
  pricing and, **8:**1024
  public relations/marketing and, **8:**1061-63, 1066
  spammed e-mail, **3:**413
  sports industry, **9:**1223, 1227
  by Volkswagen, **10:**1379
  by Wells Fargo, **10:**1407

advertising industry, **1:31-33**
  Burnett Agency, **1:**139-40
  careers in, **1:**32
  expenditures by medium, **1:***33*
  Leo Burnett Agency, **1:**139-40
Aeon Group, **8:**1118
aerospace industry
  collective bargaining, **10:**1350
  defense industry, **3:**351-53
  Dow Chemical, **3:**374
  General Motors, **4:**550, 552, 554
  industrial espionage, **5:**651
  Sikorsky, **9:**1191-93
AEW Capital Management LP, Boston, **8:**1095
AFFECT (Americans For Fair Electronic Commerce Transactions), **6:**803-4
affirmative action, **1:34-37**, 135, **5:**630
Affluent Society, The (Galbraith), **2:**267, **4:**532, 533, **10:**1367
AFL-CIO, **1:38-42**
  auto workers and, **10:**1349
  corruption allegations, **6:**764
  farm workers and, **2:**195
  labor movement and, **5:**601, 602
  membership (1979-1998), **1:***41*
  Perkins and, **7:**996
  Randolph and, **8:***1083*, 1084, 1085-86
  strikes, **9:**1252
  teachers' union and, **7:**936, 938
African Americans
  affirmative action, **1:**34-37
  Black Enterprise, **1:**114-15
  building trades, **1:**135
  civil rights laws, **2:**210-14, **8:**1083-86
  cosmetics market, **6:***739*, 740, **10:**1380-82
  cultural differences, **3:**332
  demographics, **3:***356*
  EEOC and, **4:**452, 453
  entrepreneurs, **3:**426
  Equal Employment Opportunity Commission and, **4:**452, 453
  first national bank, **6:**857
  immigrant labor competition, **5:**641, 642
  income, **1:**36, **8:**1085
  information technology and, **5:**670
  Internet access, **5:***714*
  labor unions and, **1:**38, 40, 42, **6:**763, **8:**1083-86

  legal profession discrimination, **6:**783
  Lewis enterprises, **6:**791-93
  Motown and, **4:**568-69
  National Black Chamber of Commerce, **2:**193, **7:**933-34
  National Education Association members, **7:**936
  National Education Association membership, **7:**936
  New Deal measures, **7:**943
  pay equity, **3:**300
  publishing industry, **1:**114-15, **6:**739-40, **8:**1075, 1077, 1083
  slavery abolishment, **2:**210
  Walker enterprises, **10:**1380-82
  Winfrey enterprises, **10:**1410-12
  See also equal employment opportunity
AFT. *See* American Federation of Teachers
Age Discrimination in Employment Act (1967), **1:**34, **2:**213, **4:**452-53, **10:***1418*
Age Discrimination in Employment Act (1975), **1:**34
"Agenda for America" (AFL-CIO), **1:***38*, 42
agribusiness. *See* agriculture industry
Agricola, Georgius, **10:**1329
Agricultural Adjustment Administration, **7:**941, **9:**1255
Agricultural Labor Relations Act (Calif.), **2:**195, 196
Agricultural Workers Organizing Committee, **2:**195
Agriculture Department, U.S., **2:**272, **4:**559, **9:**1195
agriculture industry, **1:43-48**
  agrarian age and, **9:**1277
  Archer Daniels Midland, **1:**70-71
  assembly line, **1:**81
  careers in, **1:**45
  child migrant labor, **2:**201, 203
  Chiquita, **2:**204-6
  commodities trading, **2:**225-26
  corporate profits, **3:**305
  Deere products, **3:**347-49
  Dow Chemical products, **3:**375
  economic theory and, **9:**1203
  environmentalism and, **1:**48, **4:**437-41, 443, **9:**1194, 1195
  federal budget and, **4:**477
  futures market, **2:**197, 198, 225, **4:**530
  GATT failure with, **4:**545

agriculture industry (cont.)
    genetic engineering, 1:48, 3:375,
        4:555, 556-58
    Great Depression and, 5:583-84
    import restrictions, 10:1323-24
    Industrial Revolution and, 5:657
    labor organization, 1:69, 2:194,
        195-96, 6:764
    Malthusian theory and, 6:818
    migrant workers, 5:639,
        10:1301, 1420
    NAFTA protests, 7:958
    New Deal and, 1:47, 7:941, 943
    price supports, 8:1013, 1014,
        1105
    principal crops (1990-2000),
        1:44
    private property and, 8:1027
    productivity, 8:1041-42
    raw materials, 8:1087-88
    scarcity and, 9:1162, 1163, 1256
    seasonal workers, 10:1303
    small business criteria, 9:1196
    social security coverage, 9:1214
    Soviet collectivization, 2:228
    subsidies, 1:47, 70, 7:941,
        9:1255, 1257, 1258
    water competition, 10:1358
    wealth distribution and, 1395
    World Bank loans, 10:1423,
        1424
    See also food industry; livestock
Agriculture Research Service,
    9:1195
AIDS, 3:332, 5:646, 689, 6:786
    drugs, 1:121, 123, 2:273
Aid to Dependent Children, 9:1212
Aid to the Blind, 9:1212
Aiken, Howard, 2:250
aircraft manufacture. See aerospace
    industry
Air France, 1:126
airline industry, 10:1331-32
    bankruptcy filing, 1:101, 102
    British Airways, 1:125-26
    business plan, 2:169
    customer service, 3:333, 334
    deregulation, 2:246, 3:358, 359,
        8:1041, 1106, 1109
    federalized security, 3:362
    FedEx and, 4:488-90
    General Motors and, 4:552
    Southwest Airlines, 9:1220-22
    strikes, 2:221, 224, 9:1254, 1268
    subsidy, 9:1256
    ticket pricing, 7:903, 8:1024,
        10:1334, 1334
    tourism and, 10:1311, 1313,
        1316, 1334-35
    unionized pilots and, 6:765,
        8:1070
airmail, 10:1333, 1334
air pollution. See environmentalism
air traffic controllers strike (1981),
    9:1254, 1268
airwave rights, 8:1028
Alaimo, Carol Ann, as contributor,
    4:534-36, 560-67, 5:681-83
Alberghetti, Anna Maria, 3:321

Alcoa, 7:900, 903
Alcoa case (1945), 9:1189
Allen, Bill, 10:1335
Allen, Paul, 3:424, 4:537, 538,
    6:803, 7:873-74
Alles, Peter, as contributor, 2:169-72,
    3:382-87
Alm, Rick, as contributor, 6:813-15,
    9:1223-27
Altair (computer), 4:538, 6:803,
    7:873, 874
Alto (computer), 10:1430-31
Altria Group, 7:1001, 1004
Aluminum Company of America.
    See Alcoa
Amazon.com, 1:49-50, 3:382,
    5:712, 714, 8:1077, 1079
    customer service, 3:335
    eBay contrasted with, 10:1408
    "one-click" shopping patent,
        7:986
    venture capital investment return,
        10:1370
American Arbitration Association,
    1:68
American Bar Association, 6:783,
    8:1048
American Booksellers Association,
    8:1077, 1079
American Chamber of Commerce
    Researchers Association,
    3:312-13
American Chambers of Commerce,
    2:192
American Economic Association,
    8:1141
American Express Company,
    1:51-53, 3:320, 5:637
    athlete endorsement, 9:1227
    Wells Fargo and, 10:1405, 1406
American Express Money Order,
    1:51
American Express Travelers Cheque,
    1:51
American Federation of Film and
    Television Actors, 9:1171
American Federation of Labor. See
    AFL-CIO
American Federation of State,
    County, and Municipal
    Employees, 8:1070, 1072,
    1073
American Federation of Teachers,
    3:403, 7:936, 938, 8:1070
American Football League, 9:1224
American Gaming Association,
    4:534, 536
American Heart Association, 7:954
American Institute of Certified
    Public Accountants, 8:1048
American Library Association,
    2:279, 8:1048
American Machinery and Foundry,
    5:599
American Management Association,
    8:1048
American Marconi Wireless
    Telegraph Company, 8:1146,
    1147

American Medical Association,
    8:1048
American Motors, 10:1351
American Normal School
    Association, 7:935
American Pulp and Paper
    Association, 4:517
American Railway Express, 10:1405
American Railway Union, 9:1252
American Research and
    Development, 10:1369
American Stock Exchange, 1:54-55
    Nasdaq contrasted with,
    7:930-31
American System, 6:828
American Teachers Association,
    7:938
American Telephone & Telegraph.
    See AT&T
American Tobacco Company, 3:376
American Trust Company, 10:1406
America Online. See AOL Time
    Warner
Americorps, 3:395
AmEx. See American Express
    Company
Amex. See American Stock
    Exchange
Amgen, 7:931
AMK-John Morrell, 2:204, 206
Amoco. See BP Amoco
amortization and depreciation,
    1:61-63
Amos, Wally, 3:426
Ampex Corporation, 9:1218
Amtrak, 10:1330
anarchism, 5:601-2, 9:1251, 1252
Anchor Books, 8:1078
Anchor Brand, 5:613, 614
Andersen, Terry L., 4:440, 441-42
Andersen Worldwide, 2:259-60
Anderson, Curt, as contributor,
    2:233-35, 4:463-65,
    8:1058-60
Andreas, Dwayne O., 1:70, 71
Andreas, G. Allen, 1:70, 71
Andreas, Michael D., 1:71
Andreessen, Marc, 2:215, 216,
    5:711, 712
Andrews, Samuel, 8:1128, 1129,
    9:1231
Andrews, Clark & Company,
    8:1128-29, 9:1231
angel investors, 10:1368
Anglo-Persian Oil Company,
    10:1306
Anglo-Saxon Petroleum Company,
    8:1134
Anheuser-Busch, 8:1069
Annecy Round, 4:540
annual improvement factor, 4:552
annual percentage rate, 3:319
annual report, 8:1052-53
    Merrill Lynch, 6:858, 859
Annual Retail Trade Survey, 8:1116

Annual Wholesale Trade Survey,
    8:1119
Annunziata, Robert, 3:295
Anti-Chain–Store Act (1936). See
    Robinson–Patman Act
anticommunism. See communism
Anti-Corn Law League, 2:178
antidiscrimination policies,
    affirmative action vs., 1:34
anti-Semitism
    fascism and, 4:474, 476
    Ford statements, 4:512, 514
    Nazi confiscations, 10:1348
antitrust
    arbitration, 1:68
    AT&T, 1:87, 88-90, 2:246,
        3:360-61, 9:1188, 1286,
        1289, 10:1359
    baseball exception, 6:813,
        9:1224
    Better Business Bureau and,
        1:112
    broadcast industry, 8:1147
    bundling, 1:136, 138
    capitalism and, 2:179, 181
    cartels, 2:188
    FTC and, 4:484-85
    General Motors, 4:553
    IBM, 5:633, 8:1106
    innovation and, 5:690
    institutionalist inflation theory,
        5:663
    key acts, 2:245, 7:900, 9:1187-90
    labor unions, 6:762
    legal services, 6:782
    merger or acquisition, 6:854,
        8:1052
    microeconomics and, 7:871
    Microsoft, 1:138, 3:361, 4:539,
        5:690, 7:873, 874, 875, 902,
        8:1051, 1104, 1106, 9:1190
    monopolies and, 8:1022, 1051
    price fixing and, 8:1018, 1019,
        1020, 1022
    regulation of business and
        industry and, 8:1104, 1106
    restraint of trade rulings, 8:1104
    as small business protection,
        9:1197
    Smith's Wealth of Nations, The,
        and, 10:1401
    sports industry, 9:1224
    Standard Oil, 7:902, 902, 904,
        8:134, 1130, 9:1188, 1231,
        1234, 10:1305
    United Fruit, 2:205
    U.S. Steel, 10:1353
    Visa/MasterCard, 1:52-53
    Xerox, 10:1431
    See also deregulation; monopoly;
        Sherman Antitrust Act
AOL Time Warner, 1:64-66, 4:521
    merger of, 6:853, 854, 855
    Microsoft and, 7:875, 876
    Netscape and, 2:216, 5:712,
        8:1025
    price fixing, 8:1019-20
    TBS merger, 1:64, 10:1339,
        1341

apartment buildings
  as commercial real estate, **8:**1090, 1093, 1095
  rent controls, **8:**1013-14, *1015*
  Trump and, **10:**1336
A. Philip Randolph Institute, **8:**1086
Apollo Group, **3:**405
Apple Computer, **2:**251, **5:**635, 636, **6:**753, **7:**874-75, **10:**1433
  pricing, **8:**1023-24
  product development, **8:**1034
  venture capital, **10:**1370
aquaculture, **1:**45, *48*, **4:**508, *510*
Aramco, **10:**1306, *1307*
Arbenz, Jacobo, **2:**205
Arber, Werner, **4:**555
arbitration, **1:**40, **67-69**, **6:**799, **9:**1252
Arbitration Foundation, **1:**68
Arbitration Society of America, **1:**68
Archer, George P., **1:***70*
Archer Daniels Midland Company, **1:71-71**
Architectural Barriers Act (1908), **1:**56
architectural copyright, **2:***281*
Archor Brand food products, **5:**613
Arevalo, Juan José, **2:***201*, 205
Aristotle, **7:**980, **10:**1328
Arkwright, Richard, **5:**655, *657*
arms manufacture. *See* defense industry
Armstrong, C. Michael, **1:***90*
Armstrong, Edwin, **8:**1147-48
Aronson, Robert L., **4:**524
ARPA. *See* Advanced Research Projects Agency
ARPANET, **3:**411, 412, **5:**710, *712*
Arthur Andersen, **2:**260, **3:**379, 422
arts and entertainment industry, **1:71-75**
  AOL Time Warner, **1:**64-66
  careers in, **1:**74, 75
  copyright, **2:**280-83
  Gordy and, **4:**568-69
  Henson and, **5:**616-18
  Lansing and, **6:**772-74
  licensing, **6:**801, *802*
  pricing, **8:**1024
  public relations and, **8:**1068
  Sarnoff and, **8:**1146
  Screen Actors Guild, **9:**1169-71
  Sony Corporation, **7:**909, **9:**1217, 1218-19
  Stewart and, **9:**1238-40
  Trump and, **10:**1337
  Turner and, **10:**1339-41
  Walt Disney Company, **10:**1391-94
  Winfrey and, **10:**1410-12
  See also film industry; television
Ash, Mary Kay, **1:76-77**
Asian Development Bank, **1:78-80**
Asian Wall Street Journal, **10:**1386
Asner, Edward, **9:**1171
Aspen Education Group, **3:**405
Aspen Skiing Company, **9:**1190

assembly line, **1:81-82**
  automobile industry, **3:**424, **4:**512-13, **6:**828-29
  defense industry, **10:**1329
  division of labor, **3:**371, 372
  as economy of scale, **3:**396
  as Ford innovation, **1:**81, 82, **4:**512-13, **5:**598, 658, **6:**828-29
  just-in-time concept, **6:**741-43
  Levitt home construction, **6:**788-89
  McDonald's fast-food, **6:**846
  productivity from, **8:***1040*
  service economy, **9:**1182
  Toyota, **6:**831
assets and liabilities, **1:83-86**
  amortization and depreciation, **1:**61-63
  annual report, **8:**1052
  asset types, **1:***84*
  balance of payments, **1:**91-92, 93
  balance sheet, **1:**83-86, 96-97, *128*
  bankruptcy, **1:**99
  bookkeeping equation, **1:**23-24, 25, 83
  book value, **1:**61, *62*, 63
  cash flow, **2:**189
  cost, **3:**307
  credit, **3:**318
  debt, **3:**343-46
  human capital, **5:**625-28
  investments, **6:**728-31
  liability types, **1:**86
  merger and acquisition, **6:**853
  money, **7:**896, 897
  partnership, **7:**977-78
  privatization, **8:**1032-33
  valuation, **10:**1360, 1361
Associated Advertising Clubs of America, **1:**112
Associated Newspapers of Britain, **3:**402
Associated Press, **8:**1075
Association for Computing Machinery, **2:**279, **8:***1049*
Association of Licensed Automobile Manufacturers, **4:**512
associations. *See* professional associations; *specific names*
Association to Advance Collegiate Schools of Business, **6:**841
AT&T, **1:87-90**, **8:**1147, **10:**1357
  breakup of, **1:**89-90, **2:**246, **3:**360-61, **7:**904, **9:**1188, 1234, 1286-89, **10:**1359
  browser, **2:**216
  competition, **2:**246
  deregulation of, **3:***359*
  Fiorina and, **4:**501, *502*
  monopoly status, **9:**1285-86
  racial discrimination suit, **2:**213
  regulation effects, **9:**1286
Atari, **1:**65, **10:**1433
Atlanta Braves (baseball), **10:**1339, *1340*
Atlanta Hawks (basketball), **10:**1339

Atlantic Oil (ARCO), **9:**1234
Atlantic records, **1:**64
ATMs (automated teller machines), **3:**322, 323, **10:**1406
  international protocols, **6:**732
auctions
  eBay, **10:**1408-9
  price fixing, **8:**1019, 1020
  pricing, **8:**1025
Audubon Society, **9:**1195
Austen, Jane, **2:**207
authoritarianism, **8:**1028, 1137, 1139
automation, **5:**634, **6:**831, 832
  labor unions and, **6:**766
  Nasdaq, **7:**930
  productivity and, **8:**1039, 1042
  service economy and, **9:**1181-82
  telephone service, **10:**1357
automobile industry, **10:**1330-31
  assembly line, **1:**81–82, **3:**424, **4:**512-13, **5:**598, 658, **6:**828-29
  automation, **6:**766
  bundling, **1:**136, *137*
  business-to-business sales, **2:***169*, 172
  car ownership cost, **3:***307*, 308, *309*, 318
  collective bargaining, **2:**222
  consumer "lemon laws," **2:**272
  Consumer Price Index, **2:**271
  current status, **6:**832
  downsizing, **3:**378
  e-business and, **3:**382
  economies of scale and, **3:**396, 397-98
  emissions controls, **4:**444, 448-49, 450, 552, 554
  entrepreneurship in, **3:**424
  ethanol fuel, **1:**45, 70
  Ford innovations, **4:**511-14
  gas economy models, **4:**554
  gasoline needs, **8:**1134
  General Motors, **4:**550-54
  globalization and, **4:**564, *565*
  GM strike, **9:**1252-53
  Harley-Davidson and, **5:**598, 600
  import quotas, **5:**706
  interchangeable parts, **5:**692
  ISO 9000 standards, **6:**732
  Japanese voluntary export restraints, **10:***1322*, 1323
  just-in-time inventory, **6:**741, 742-43
  market research, **6:**833
  Mitsubishi Motors, **7:**890-92
  1920s growth, **5:**582
  outsourcing objections, **7:**973
  pattern bargaining, **6:**763
  planned obsolescence, **4:**551
  productivity, **8:***1040*
  protectionism, **8:**1057
  recession effects, **8:**1096
  robotics, **1:***110*
  safety issues, **2:**268, *271*, 273, 274, **7:**925-27
  standard of living and, **9:**1229-30
  sustainable design, **4:**442

Total Quality Management, **10:**1308
tourism and, **10:**1311, 1312, 1313, 1316
Toyota Production System, **6:**830-31
United Automobile Workers, **1:**39, 40, **10:**1349-52
Volkswagen, **10:**1377-79
automobile insurance, **5:***681*, 682-83
Avery, Clarence Willard, **1:**82
Avery, Oswald, **4:**555
aviation. *See* aerospace industry; airline industry
Aviation Corporation of America, **10:**1333, *1334*
Ayershire Farms, **2:**207
Ayres, Karen, *as contributor*, **1:**31-33, **4:**452-53, **6:**828-32, **7:**998-1000, **8:**1061-65, 1080-82, 1146-48, **10:**1329-32, 1336-38, 1339-41, 1362-64

B

Baade, Robert, **9:**1225-26
Babbage, Charles, **2:**249, **5:**663
Baby Bells, **1:**89, 90, **9:**1188, 1286, 1287, 1288, 1289
Bacall, Lauren, **9:**1169, *1170*
Bachelier, Louis, **6:**728, 729
Bader, Edward L., **8:***1068*
Baghdad Copper Mine (Ariz.), **2:**221
Bahrain Petroleum, **10:**1306, *1307*
Baker, James, **9:**1267
Baker, Lorenzo Dow, **2:**204
Bakke, Allan, **1:**35, 36
Bakunin, Mikhail, **6:**839, **9:**1251
balance of payments, **1:91-92**, 93
  exchange rates, **4:**461-62
  IMF and, **5:**701, 702
balance of trade, **1:**91, **93-95**
  cotton subsidies, **10:***1325*
  exchange rates, **4:**461-62
  GATT requirements, **4:**545
  inflation and, **5:**660
  mercantilism and, **6:**849, 850, 852
  mercantilism vs. Smith theory, **9:**1203
  NAFTA and, **7:**959
  recession and, **8:**1098
  surplus creation, **5:**708
balance sheet, **1:96-98**
  accounting and, **1:**25, 26
  amortization and depreciation, **1:**61-63, 63
  assets and liabilities, **1:**83-86, 96-97
  breakeven point, **1:**119-20
  budget, **1:***128*
  business finances, **4:**493-96
  corporation, **3:***303*
  debt and, **3:**343-44
  human capital, **5:**625
  income statement, **5:**647
  partnership, **7:***978*
  personal finances, **4:**499-500

balance sheet (cont.)
profit and loss, **8**:*1051*, 1052-53
small business, **9**:1198
Baldwin, Jerry, **9**:1235
Ballmer, Steve, **4**:538
Baltimore & Ohio Railroad, **9**:1250, **10**:1330
Bankers Trust, **1**:49
Banking Act (1935), **3**:315, 316, *317*
banking industry, **3**:314-17
American Express services, **1**:51-52
Asian Development Bank, **1**:78-80
ATMs, **3**:322, 323, **6**:732, **10**:1406
bankruptcy law and, **1**:101
business ethics, **3**:296-97
computer use, **2**:251
consumer confidence, **3**:318
credit and debit cards, **1**:51-52, **3**:314-16, 319-23
currency trading, **4**:462
deregulation, **8**:1109, 1132
European Union, **4**:459
Great Depression failures, **2**:149, **3**:315, *317*, **5**:581, 584, **7**:941, **8**:1097, **9**:1172
Hamilton and, **5**:595, 596
history of, **3**:314-16
insurance industry and, **5**:683
interest rates, **5**:*695-96*
investment and, **6**:729
ISO 9000 standards, **6**:732
macroeconomics and, **6**:811
mergers, **6**:857
monetary policy and, **7**:893, 894-95
Morgan and, **7**:905-7
mortgage issuance, **7**:913
New Deal measures, **7**:941, 943
nontradable securities, **9**:1157
online services, **3**:382
paycheck direct deposit, **7**:990, 992
real estate brokerage, **8**:1092
recession and, **8**:1097-98
regulation of, **8**:1104-5, *1106*
Royal Bank of Canada, **8**:1131-32
savings interest, **2**:247
security industry and, **9**:*1175*
Union Bank of Switzerland, **10**:1346-48
Wells Fargo, **10**:1405-7
See also Federal Reserve System; World Bank
Bank in Winterthur, **10**:1346-47
Bank of America, **9**:*1166*, 1167, **10**:1406
Bank of Montreal, **8**:*1132*
Bank of the United States, **5**:595, 596
bankruptcy, **1**:**99-102**
business cycles, **2**:149
California utilities, **8**:1016
cash flow and, **2**:190
Chrysler bailout, **10**:1352
corporation, **3**:297, 306

credit history, **3**:324, 325, 326
from day trading, **3**:342
debt and, **3**:344
Durant and, **4**:551
as economic growth cost, **3**:391
Enron, **1**:101, **3**:306, 420, 422-23
as futures market risk, **4**:529
Heinz and, **5**:614
profit and loss and, **8**:1053
savings and loan, **8**:1094
small business, **9**:1197
telecommunications, **9**:1288
Texaco, **10**:1307
Trump and, **10**:*1336*, 1337, 1338
Bantam Books, **8**:1078
Barby, Abraham, **5**:653
Barclays Bank of California, **10**:1406
bar codes, **1**:103-5, **6**:726, 744
Barings Bank, **4**:531
Barnard College, **9**:1238
Barnes & Noble, **3**:382, **8**:1079, **10**:1389
Barrett, Colleen, **9**:*1221*
Barrett, Craig, **5**:686
Barrett, Matthew, **8**:*1132*
Barron, Clarence Walker, **10**:*1383*
Barron, Jessie, **10**:1384
barter, **3**:345, **7**:896
Bartley, Robert, **10**:1386
baseball, **9**:1223, *1226*, 1227
collective bargaining, **2**:221
players union, **6**:813-15
Turner team ownership, **10**:1339, *1340*
basic accounting equation, **1**:25, 96
Basinger, Kim, **2**:277-78, 279
basketball, **6**:814, **9**:1223, 1224, *1226*, 1227, **10**:1339
Basler Bankverein, **10**:1346-47
Bast, James, **1**:*113*
Battelle Development Corporation, **10**:1429, 1430
Battle Creek Toasted Corn Flake Company, **6**:746
Baughn, Gary, *as contributor*, **1**:139-40, **3**:399-401, **4**:488-90, 511-14, **5**:592-94, **6**:791-93, **7**:910-12
Bavarian Petroleum Company, **8**:1133-34
Bayley, Charles, **5**:623
Bean, Jonathan J., *as contributor*, **10**:1383-86
Beatrice Foods International, **6**:792-93
Beaver, Hugh, **5**:593
Beck, Dave, **9**:1275
Beckerman, Wilfred, **9**:1264, 1267
Becknell, William, **8**:*1142*, 1143-44
beer, **7**:1001-2, **8**:1069
advertising, **1**:29-30
Guinness, **5**:592-94
Bell, Alexander Graham, **1**:87, 88, **3**:400, **7**:912, **8**:1112, **9**:1285, 1286, **10**:1357
Bell Laboratories, **1**:90, **8**:1111
BellSouth Corp., **1**:90, **9**:1288

Bell Telephone, **1**:87, *89*, **6**:825, **9**:1285, **10**:1357
Ben & Jerry's Homemade, Inc., **1**:**106-8**, **7**:946
Benchmark Capital, **10**:1370
benchmarking, **1**:**109-11**, 127
benefits. *See* compensation
Bentham, Jeremy, **9**:1202
Bergstresser, Charles, **10**:1383, 1384
Berkley, Shelley, **2**:255
Berkshire Hathaway, **3**:293, **7**:948
Bernays, Edward L., **8**:1066-67, 1068
Berners-Lee, Tim, **5**:*663*, 665, 667, 711, *712*, **8**:1112
Bernstein, Carl, **4**:572
Bernstein, Eduard, **9**:1208
Bernstein, Lynne, *as contributor*, **9**:1175-77
Bernstein, Michael, *as contributor*, **9**:1184-86
Bertelsmann, **8**:1018, 1079
Bethlehem Steel, **4**:454, **9**:1168
Better Business Bureau, **1**:32, **112-13**, **2**:274
Bezos, Jeffrey, **1**:49, 50
Bidzos, Jim, **5**:678
Bierce, Ambrose, **5**:609
Big Five (accounting firms), **2**:260
Bill and Melinda Gates Foundation, **4**:*538*, 539
billboards, **1**:28, 32, *33*
Bill of Rights, U.S., **2**:256, **7**:1000
Bina, Eric, **5**:711
Biological Service, U.S., **9**:1194
biometrics, **9**:1177
biotechnology
genetic engineering, **4**:555, 556
intellectual property rights, **5**:689, 691
Nasdaq stock, **7**:931
patents, **7**:981, *985*
BITNET (Because It's Time Network), **3**:412
Black, Eli, **2**:206
Black Enterprise, **1**:**114-15**
Blair, Tony, **9**:1209
Blake, William, **2**:200
Blockbuster, **10**:1389
blocking strategy, **5**:679-80
Blodgett, Katherine, **4**:548
Blue Ribbon Sports. *See* Nike
BMG Music, **8**:1018
BOAC. *See* British Airways
board of directors, **3**:293, 294-95, 303-4
Boas, Franz, **10**:1365
Boehme, Karen, *as contributor*, **6**:732-34
Boeing, **3**:353, **5**:651, **10**:1332
McDonnell Douglass merger, **8**:1104
Bogart, Humphrey, **1**:65, **9**:1169, *1170*
Bolden, Scarlet, *as contributor*, **1**:71-75
Bolt, Beranek, and Newman, **3**:411, 412

bonded labor, **2**:202-3
bonds. *See* stocks and bonds
Bon Marché (Paris), **8**:1115
Bono, Sonny, **2**:284
Bono Copyright Extension Act (1998), **2**:284
bonuses, **2**:239, 241
book clubs, **8**:1078, **10**:1410, 1411
bookkeeping. *See* accounting and bookkeeping
Book-of-the-Month Club, **8**:1078
book value, **1**:61, *62*, 63
Booz-Allen & Hamilton, Inc., **2**:258
Borders, **8**:1079
borrowers. *See* credit; debt
Bosack, Len, **2**:207
Boston Associates, **6**:805, 807, 808
Boston Bank of Commerce, **6**:857
Boston Fruit Company, **2**:204
Boston Manufacturing Company, **6**:805
Boston Red Sox, **9**:1223
Boston University, **8**:1067
Boulton, Matthew, **5**:653, *657*
Boulton and Watt, **5**:653, *657*
Bové, Jose, **4**:566
Bowerman, Bill, **7**:950-52
Bowery Savings Bank, **3**:*315*
Bowker, Gordon, **9**:1235
Bowker, R. R., **8**:1078
Boyer, Herbert, **4**:555, 556
Boy Scouts of America, **8**:1100
BP Amoco, **3**:416, **9**:1234, **10**:1307
Bradley, Rob, *as contributor*, **3**:414-19, 420-23
Brady, Mathew, **7**:*910*
brand equity, **10**:1321
brand mark, brand name vs., **1**:116
brand names, **1**:**116-18**
advertising image, **1**:29, 30, 32, 139-40, **8**:1051
Coca-Cola, **2**:217-18
Martha Stewart, **9**:1240
Nike, **7**:950, 952
pricing and, **8**:1021, 1025
product development and, **8**:1037
public relations/marketing campaigns, **8**:1063
Sony, **7**:909
Starbucks, **9**:1236
trademarks, **10**:1320
Brando, Marlon, **6**:786
Brannon, J. Isaac, *as contributor*, **6**:758-59, 760-66, **8**:1070-73
breach of contract, **2**:278-79
breakeven point, **1**:**119-20**
Breedlove, Sarah. *See* Walker, Madame C. J.
Bretton Woods Conference (1944), **2**:180, *181*, 182, **5**:701-3, **6**:*750*, 751, **10**:1421
brewery industry, **5**:592-94, **7**:1001-2
Breyer, Stephen, **3**:358, 359
Breyer's, **9**:1236
Brezhnev, Leonid, **2**:232
bribery. *See* business ethics

Bridgestone-Firestone, **2:***160*,
    8:1045
Bright, John, **2:**178
Bright Horizons Family Solutions,
    3:405
Brink, Washington Perry, **9:**1176
Brinks Express Company, **9:***1175*
Bristol, William McLaren, **1:**121
Bristol-Myers Squibb, **1:**121-23
British Airways, **1:**124-26
British Telecommunications, **7:**986
broadband, **1:**64-65, **8:**1031,
    9:1219
brokerage firms
    Fidelity, **4:**491-92
    Merrill Lynch, **6:**858-60
    Schwab, **9:**1166-68
    SEC regulation of, **9:**1172
    securities exchange seat, **9:**1245
    wholesale, **8:**1119
Brooklyn (N.Y.) Chamber of
    Commerce, **2:***191*
Brooks, Edward W., **1:**115
Brotherhood of Electrical Workers,
    10:1375
Brotherhood of Professional Baseball
    Players, **6:** 813, *815*
Brotherhood of Sleeping Car
    Porters, **8:**1083-84, *1085*,
    1086
Brown, Ann, **8:***1109*
Brown, Helen Gurley, **8:**1077
Brown, Moses, **5:**657
Brown, Sarah, **5:**616
Brownstein, Michael, **6:**772
Brown v. Board of Education (1954),
    7:936, **8:**1085
browsers (Internet), **2:**215-16,
    5:711, **7:**874, 875, *902*
    price war, **8:**1025
Brundtland, Gro Harlem, **9:**1265
Bryan, Richard, **2:***255*
BSA Company, **10:**1435
Buccleuch, duke of, **9:**1202-3
Buckles, Stephen, *as contributor*,
    6:809-12, **7:**869-72
Buckwalter, Stephanie, *as*
    contributor, **2:**191-93,
    3:314-18, 324-28, 343-46,
    4:497-500, **5:**625-28, 629-31,
    710-14, **6:**735-38, 741-44,
    7:833-37, 990-93, **8:**1034-38,
    1110-12, 1113-14,
    9:1277-83, **10:**1301-4
budget, **1:**127-30
    advertising, **1:**28
    capital, **4:**493-94, *495*, 496
    cash flow, **2:**189-90
    federal, **4:**477-79, 503, 505
    income statement, **5:**647
    personal, **4:**498-99
    standard of living and, **9:**1229
    U.S. defense, **3:**354
Budget and Accounting Act (1921),
    4:477
Budweiser, **1:**29-30
Buffett, Warren, **3:***293*, **7:**948
Bugas, John, **2:**222
Buick Company, **4:**550

building trades, **1:**131-35
    affirmative action, **1:**35, 135
    careers in, **1:**134
    corporate profits, **3:***305*
    forest products and, **4:**517
    Levitt and, **6:**788-90
    licensed workers, **10:**1374
    new construction, **8:***1092*, *1094*
bullionism, **6:**849
bull market, **9:**1241, 1245
bundling, **1:**136-38, **8:**1109
Bureau of Census. *See* Census
    Bureau, U.S.
Bureau of Labor Statistics, **3:**311,
    5:659, **8:**1072
    Consumer Price Index, **2:**269-71
    productivity data, **8:**1043
    unemployment data, **10:**1345
Burford, Anne, **4:**445
Burgdorf, Robert L., Jr., **1:**56-57
Burleson, Mary, **8:***1144*
Burnett, Leo, **1:**139-40
Burns, Arthur, **4:**483
Burr, Aaron, **5:**597
Busby, Jheryl, **6:**857
Bush, George H. W., **5:***378, 402*,
    5:586, **6:**764, **10:**1352
    Americans with Disabilities Act,
       1:56
    family leave veto, **4:**469
    NAFTA, **7:***956*, 958
    presidential election (1992),
       7:999
Bush, George W., **4:**456, **5:**586,
    7:927, **9:**1262
    steel tariff, **8:**1056
Bush, Jeb, **1:**36, *37*
Business Charter for Sustainable
    Development, **9:**1265
business confidence, **6:**730, 778,
    779
business cycles, **2:**149-52
    balance sheet, **1:**96
    building trades, **1:**133
    capitalism and, **2:**149-51, 178,
       181, 182
    Consumer Confidence Index,
       2:261-63
    economic growth, **3:**390, 392
    income statement, **5:**647
    Keynesian model, **2:**151, 180,
       182, **3:**364-65, **6:**750, 810
    Leading Economic Index,
       6:778-80
    macroeconomics and, **6:**810-12
    outsourcing, **7:**972-93
    real estate, **8:**1091, 1094, 1095
    recession and, **8:**1096-98
    Schumpeter theory, **9:**1164
    strikes and, **9:**1250
    unemployment, **10:**1343, 1344
    United States (1854-2001), **1:***150*
    wealth distribution and, **10:**1396,
       1397
Business Cycles (Schumpeter),
    9:1164, *1165*
business ethics, **2:**153-59
    accounting firm consultants,
       2:260

advertising, **1:**32, 112, 113
American Stock Exchange, **1:**55
Archer Daniels Midland, **1:**70-71
Better Business Bureau, **1:**112-13
business law and, **2:**154, 157,
    159, 160-62, **6:**782
consumerism and, **2:**267
corporate, **3:**293, 296-97, *298*,
    306, *379*
day trading, **3:**342
Edison Schools, **3:**403-4
Enron, **3:***296*, 420, 422-23
fraud arbitration, **1:**68
industrial espionage, **5:**648-52
information technology, **9:**1283
pharmaceuticals, **1:**121, 122
profit and loss reports, **8:**1053
reverse engineering and,
    8:1122-23
Stewart stock deal, **9:**1240
tobacco industry, **7:***1001*, 1002-4
Union Bank of Switzerland,
    10:*1346*, 1348
United Brands, **2:**206
workplace guidelines, **2:**155
business finance. *See* finance,
    business
Business for Social Responsibility,
    1:108
Business Information Centers,
    9:1201
business law, **2:**160-65
    affirmative action, **1:**34
    business ethics and, **2:**154, 157,
       159, 160-62, **6:**782
    contracts, **2:**160-61, 276-79
    copyright, **2:**164, 165, 280-84
    corporations, **3:**302
    e-business, **3:**384
    employment discrimination,
       2:213-14
    family leave, **4:**468-71
    human resources department,
       5:630-31
    initial public offering, **5:**677
    intellectual property, **5:**688-89
    legal services, **6:**781-84
    liability, **6:**794-800
    licenses, **6:**802-3
    partnership, **7:**976
    product liability, **8:**1045-47
    risk management, **8:**1127
    rule of law and, **8:***1137*, 1138-39
    trademark, **10:**1320, *1321*
business plan, **2:**166-68, **3:**427
    entrepreneurship, **3:**427
    Kroc and, **6:**755, 756-67
    Lands' End and, **6:**769-71
    Leading Economic Index and,
       6:778
    product development, **8:**1034,
       1036
    small business, **9:**1198
    strategic planning, **9:**1246-48
Business Software Alliance, **2:**279
business-to-business sales, **2:**169-72
    benchmarking, **1:**111
    contract law, **2:**276-77
    distribution channels, **3:**366-69

e-business, **3:***383*, 384-87, *420*,
    421, **5:**713
Enron, **3:***420*, 421, 422
farm products, **1:**46-47, 70-71
just-in-time concept, **6:**741, 743,
    744
Lands' End, **6:**770
Levitt and Sons, **6:**789
wholesalers, **8:**1118-20
Bustamante, Cruz, **10:***1359*
Butterfield & Wasson, **1:**51

C

Cabell, James Branch, **4:**472
cable television, **1:**74-75, **3:**297,
    9:1287, 1288, **10:**1356,
    1357-58
    24-hour news, **10:**1339
    advertising, **1:**32, *33*, 74
    AOL Time Warner and, **1:**64,
       65-66
    AT&T and, **1:**90
    competition, **2:**246
    deregulation of, **10:**1359
    sports broadcasts, **9:**1224
    Winfrey and, **10:***1412*
Cadillac Motor Car Company, **1:**139
Cagney, James, **9:**1171
Cahsman, Brian, **6:**815
Cairncross, Frances, **9:**1265
Caldwell, Jean, *as contributor*,
    2:184-86, **5:**595-97, 613-15,
    622-24, 653-58, **6:**775-77,
    805-8, **8:**1142-45
California Farm Labor Board, **2:**196
California Fruit Growers Exchange,
    1:31
California-Texas Oil Company
    (Caltex), **10:**1306, *1307*
Caligula, emperor of Rome, **8:**1137,
    1139
Callaway, Ely, **9:**1200
Cambridge University, **4:**555, **6:**749,
    750
Campbell, Christina, *as contributor*,
    10:1408-9
Campbell Soup, **5:***687*
Canada
    commodity market, **2:**226
    fishing industry, **4:**508
    free trade agreement, **2:***181*, 183
    graduate business education,
       6:841
    Hudson's Bay Company,
       5:622-24
    Kellogg Company, **6:**746
    lumber industry, **4:**517-18
    NAFTA, **5:**708, **7:**956-59
    NAICS codes, **7:**928-29,
       8:1115
    oil reserve, **8:**1132
    Royal Bank of, **8:**1131-32
    Trump real estate, **10:**1337
    United Automobile Workers,
       10:1352
    Wal-Mart, **10:**1389
Canadian and United States Trade
    Agreement (1989), **7:**956
Canadian Southern Railroad,
    10:1364

canal system, **6**:805, 807
cancer
  carcinogens, **3**:375
  drugs, **1**:123, **2**:273
  tobacco industry suits, **7**:1002, 1003-4
Candler, Asa, **2**:217, 218
Capellas, Michael, **5**:*621*
Capella University, **3**:406, 408
capital, **2**:173-74
  business finances, **4**:493-96
  debt and, **3**:343, *344*, 345-46
  economic growth and, **3**:389
  energy industry, **3**:417
  entrepreneurship and, **3**:427
  exports as, **5**:708
  financial managers, **4**:493-96
  interest rates and, **4**:504
  investment, **6**:729-30
  Morgan and, **7**:905
  natural monopolies, **8**:1103
  small business, **9**:1197-98, 1199, 1200
  stock and bond issuance for, **9**:1241, 1242, 1245
  taxation and, **9**:1272-73
  World Bank, **10**:1423
  See also human capital; venture capital
Capital (Marx), **6**:*838*, 839, 840
Capital Cities/ABC, **10**:*1392*, 1394
capital gains, **2**:175-76, **9**:1158-59
capitalism, **2**:177-83
  AFL and, **1**:38
  business cycles, **2**:149-52, 178, 182
  business ethics, **2**:156, **3**:297
  cartels, **2**:187-88
  Chinese communism and, **2**:183, 232
  competition and, **2**:245-46
  consumerism and, **2**:264-68
  contract law, **2**:277
  corporate social responsibility, **3**:298-301
  deregulation and, **3**:358, 359, 361
  economic growth and, **3**:388-89, 391
  entrepreneurship and, **3**:424-28, **9**:1164
  environmentalism and, **4**:*440*, 441-42
  fascism vs., **4**:474
  Friedman monetary theory, **4**:527-28
  government regulation vs., **3**:359
  historical landmarks in, **2**:*181*
  intellectual property and, **5**:690
  international trade, **5**:705-6, 709
  Japanese form of, **7**:890
  Keynesian critique of, **2**:151
  Marxist critique of, **6**:838, 839, **10**:1365
  mercantilism and, **6**:849-52
  monopoly and, **7**:901
  New Deal welfare state and, **7**:941

New York Stock Exchange and, **7**:947
  private property and, **8**:1026, 1028, 1050
  profit and loss and, **8**:1050-53
  Samuelson economics, **8**:1140
  Schumpeter theory, **9**:1164-65
  Smith theory, **6**:851, **9**:1202-5, **10**:1400-1402
  socialism vs., **9**:1164, 1165, 1206, 1207, 1208-9
  wealth distribution and, **10**:1397
  See also free market
Capitalism, Socialism, and Democracy (Schumpeter), **9**:1164, *1165*
Capitalism and Freedom (Friedman), **4**:527, *528*
Capoten, **1**:*121*, 123
Cardoza, Dennis, **10**:*1359*
careers
  in advertising, **1**:32
  in agriculture, **1**:45
  in arts and entertainment, **1**:74, 75
  in building trade, **1**:134
  in computer industry, **2**:252
  in defense industry, **3**:352
  in education industry, **3**:408
  in energy industry, **3**:415
  in fishing industry, **4**:509
  in forest products industry, **4**:518
  in gaming industry, **4**:536
  in health care industry, **5**:606
  in insurance industry, **5**:682
  internships, **5**:715-16
  job search, **6**:735-38
  in legal services, **6**:783
  in manufacturing, **6**:832
  in mining industry, **7**:887
  in public relations, **8**:1067
  in publishing industry, **8**:1077
  in real estate industry, **8**:1095
  in recreation industry, **8**:1102
  in security industry, **9**:1176
  in sports industry, **9**:1224
  in telecommunications industry, **9**:1289
  in tourism, **10**:1315
  in utilities industry, **10**:1357
Career World magazine, **5**:671
Carey, Ronald R., **9**:1276
Cargill Co., **1**:70, **2**:214
Carlson, Chester F., **10**:*1429*, *1430*
Carnegie, Andrew, **2**:184-86, **7**:906, 933, **8**:1050, **9**:1252
  Morgan deal, **9**:1168, **10**:1353, 1354
Carnegie Company, **2**:185-86
Carnegie Hall (N.Y.C.), **2**:186
Carnegie libraries, **2**:*185*, 186
Carnegie Steel. *See* United States Steel Corporation
carpal tunnel syndrome, **4**:455, **7**:962
Carpentier, Georges, **8**:1147
Carr, Kay J., *as contributor*, **7**:935-38
Carson, Rachel, **2**:268, **3**:299-300, **4**:439, *440*, 443, 447, **9**:1194-95

cartel, **2**:187-88, **7**:900, *903*, **9**:1189
  airfare, **10**:1335
  competition vs., **2**:244-45
  credit card, **1**:53
  German bromine, **3**:373
  mining, **7**:885-86
  petroleum, **2**:187, **7**:968-70, **9**:1230
  price fixing and, **8**:1017-18, 1022
Carter, Charles, **3**:379
Carter, Jimmy, **3**:358, **7**:937, **8**:1086, 1109, **9**:1215
Cartoon Network, **10**:1340
Caruso, Enrico, **10**:1381
Cary, Frank T., **5**:634
Case, Steven, **1**:64, *65*, 66
cash. *See* money
cash flow, **2**:189-90
  accounting statement, **1**:25, 26
  debt and, **3**:343-44, 345
  small business, **9**:1198, 1199
  taxation and, **9**:1273
cash merger, **6**:854-55
casinos, **4**:534, 535-36
  Trump and, **10**:1336, *1338*
Castro, Fidel, **2**:206, 229, 230
catalog sales. *See* mail-order sales
catalytic converter, **4**:552, 554, 559
Caterpillar, **6**:763, **10**:1351
CBS (television), **8**:1148
CBS/Sony Group, **9**:1218
ceiling price. *See* price controls
celebrity endorsements, **1**:32, **7**:952
Cellar–Kefauver Antimerger Act (1950), **7**:900
cellular phones, **5**:663, *664*, 668, **7**:876, **9**:1219, 1286, 1288, **10**:1357, 1420
Census Bureau, U.S., **5**:632, *633*, *663*, 665
  market research and, **6**:834, 836
  per capita income, **9**:1228
Center for the Study of Responsive Law, **7**:927
Centers for Disease Control, **7**:961
central banking system, 3.315, 3.390. *See also* Federal Reserve System
Central Pacific Railroad, **10**:1330
Central Railroad, **10**:1363
Centura Banks Incorporated, **8**:1132
Century 21 (realtor), **8**:1091, 1092, 1095
CEO (chief executive officer), **3**:304
  accounting practices, **3**:297
  compensation, **2**:241, **3**:294-95, 296, **10**:1404
  Fiorina as first woman Fortune 500, **4**:501-2, **5**:620-21
  temporary jobs for, **10**:1304
  Welch's GE policies, **4**:547, 549
Cerf, Vinton, **3**:411
certificate of deposit, **2**:163, **9**:1157
certification, **10**:1376
certification mark, **2**:164-65
chain stores. *See* retail and wholesale

Chakrabarty, Ananda, **7**:985
chambers of commerce, **2**:191-93, **8**:*1048*
  ergonomic regulations, **4**:456
  market research, **6**:836
  National Black Chamber of Commerce, **7**:933-34
  small businesses and, **9**:1198
Chan, Jackie, **2**:*193*
Chantarahesee, Darwan, **1**:79
Chapman, Gary, **7**:*945*
Chapter 7 bankruptcy, **1**:99-100, 101
Chapter 11 bankruptcy, **1**:99, 101-2
  Texaco filing, **10**:1307
charge cards. *See* credit cards and debit cards
Charles E. Merrill and Company, **6**:858
Charles II, king of England, **5**:622-23
Charles Schwab and Company, **9**:1166-68
charter schools, **7**:938
Chase Manhattan Bank, **3**:378
Chavez, Cesar, **1**:*69*, **2**:194-96
checks, **4**:482, **7**:898
cheese import quotas, **8**:1054, 1055
chemical industry
  compound patents, **7**:980, 981
  Dow products, **3**:350, 373-75
  sustainable development, **9**:1266
  textile industry and, **5**:655-56
  toxic hazards, **9**:1194-95
  See also hazardous waste; pesticides
Cheplin Laboratories, **1**:122
Chernobyl nuclear accident (Ukraine), **4**:439, *440*
Chevrolet Motor Company, **4**:551
Chevron (Socal), **3**:376, **9**:1234, **10**:1306, 1307
Chevron Texaco, **7**:*921*, **10**:1307
Chiang Kai-Shek, **2**:229
Chicago Board of Trade, **1**:46, **2**:197-98, 225, 226, **4**:529, **8**:1127, **9**:*1243*
Chicago Mercantile Exchange, **2**:225
Chicago School of Economics, **4**:528, **6**:751
child care, **2**:238, **3**:357, 405, **10**:1415
Childcraft, **10**:1392
child labor, **2**:178, **199-203**, **3**:371
  Fair Labor Standards Act, **4**:466
  Industrial Revolution, **5**:656
  Lowell Mills, **6**:806, 807
  minimum wage, **7**:877
  minimum working age, **7**:879
  Perkins reforms, **7**:994, 995, 996
  prohibition of, **10**:1418
  reforms, **10**:1396
  workday limits, **10**:1417
China
  American Express ad, **1**:53
  Asian Development Bank, **1**:78
  communism, **2**:181, *228*, 229-30, 232, **9**:1208, *1209*

economic espionage, 5:649
globalization, 4:567
Hewlett-Packard joint venture, 5:620
market socialism, 2:183, 232
Merrill Lynch office, 6:850, 858
Nixon visit, 2:230
retailing, 8:1115, 1118
reverse engineering, 8:1122
Starbucks, 9:1236
World Trade Organization, 10:1427
Chino, Tadao, 1:79
Chiquita, 1:118, 2:204-6
Chisholm, Shirley, 1:115
chocolate products liability suit, 8:1047
Chouart, Medard, 5:622
Christie's, 8:1019, 1020
Chrysler Corp., 10:1350, 1352
Chuck D (rapper), 2:284
Churchill, Winston, 6:749
Church of Stop Shopping, 2:267
Cicero, 6:799-800
cigarettes. See tobacco industry
CIO. See AFL-CIO
Circadia Coffee House, 9:1237
Cisco Systems, 2:207-9, 3:409, 5:670, 7:931, 10:1433
Citicorp, 5:599, 600
cities. See urban areas
Citigroup, 7:948
Citizens Loan Corporation, 6:739
Citron, Jeffrey, 3:342
Civil Aeronautics Act (1938), 8:1105, 1106
Civil Aeronautics Authority, 8:1105, 1109
Civil Aeronautics Board, 3:358, 359
Civilian Conservation Corps, 2:180, 4:439, 440, 6:750, 7:941, 9:1255
Civil Rights Act (1964), 1:56, 2:210-13, 3:300, 7:987
   affirmative action, 1:34, 35
   disabilities extension, 1:59
   equal employment, 4:452-53
   excerpt, 2:211
   sexual harassment, 9:1184, 1185
   workplace conditions, 10:1418
Civil Rights Act (1991), 2:212, 213, 214
civil rights legislation, 2:210-14, 7:987
   affirmative action vs., 1:34
   Americans with Disabilities Act, 1:56-60
   arbitration, 1:68
   corporate social responsibility and, 3:300
   disparate impact theory, 2:212-13
   EEOC and, 4:452-53
   immigrant groups and, 5:639-43
   key laws, 2:213
   pay equity, 2:236, 7:987
   sexual harassment and, 9:1184, 1184-86
   Texaco discrimination lawsuit, 10:1307

working conditions, 10:1417, 1418
working women and, 10:1414, 1415, 1416, 1418
civil rights movement
   initiation of, 2:210
   labor unions and, 1:40, 42
   Motown sound and, 4:568
   nonviolent tactics, 2:195, 210
   Randolph and, 8:1083, 1085-86
   Walker and, 10:1381
Civil Service Commission, 7:996
Civil Service Reform Act (1978), 2:213
Civil War, U.S., 3:314-15, 317, 349, 5:693, 698
   press coverage, 8:1075
   Pulitzer and, 8:1080
   railroad use, 10:1330
   Santa Fe Trail use, 8:1144, 1145
   telegraph use, 7:912
   Wells Fargo and, 10:1405
Civil Works Administration, 7:941
Clairol, 1:121, 122-23
Clare, David, 2:300
Clark, Jim, 2:215-16, 5:712
Clark, Maurice, 8:1128-29, 9:1231
class
   Marx conflict theory, 2:227, 9:1207, 10:1365
   socialism and, 9:1207, 1210
   standard of living and, 9:1230
   Veblen's leisure class theory, 10:1365-66
   wealth distribution and, 10:1395-96, 1397
class-action suits, 6:796
classical management theory, 6:824, 825
Clayton, Dubliner & Rice, 6:753-54
Clayton Antitrust Act (1914), 4:485, 553, 6:762, 9:1197
   provisions, 2:245, 7:900, 904
Clean Air Act (1927), 7:927
Clean Air Act (1955), 4:448
Clean Air Act Amendments (1970), 2:268, 4:443, 444, 447, 448, 449, 450
Clean Air Act Amendments (1990), 4:444, 446, 447, 448, 449
Clean Water Act (1948), 4:448
Clean Water Act (1977), 4:447, 448, 450
Cleghorn, John, 8:1132
Clemenceau, Georges, 6:749
Clinique, 6:777
Clinton, Bill, 3:359, 395, 4:533, 5:586, 699, 6:754
   affirmative action, 1:36
   antitrust enforcement, 9:1187
   family leave policy, 4:469
   minimum wage bill, 7:880
   NAFTA and, 7:958
   National Black Chamber of Commerce and, 7:934
   political campaign, 8:1065
   presidential elections (1992, 1996), 7:999
   product liability bill veto, 8:1047

taxpayer advocate bill, 5:699
   "Third Way" social policy, 9:1209
   veto exercise, 2:255
   Welfare Reform Act, 9:1211, 1215-16
Clinton, George, 5:595, 596
Clinton Pharmaceutical Company, 1:121
closed shop, 1268, 9:1269
clothing industry
   beaver hats, 5:622
   brand name, 1:118
   consumer demographics, 3:355
   downsizing, 3:378
   immigrant workers, 5:642
   labor unions, 1:40, 42
   Lands' End, 6:769-71
   Levi Strauss, 6:785-87
   manufacturing output, 6:832
   NAFTA and, 7:958
   strikes, 9:1252
   working conditions, 10:1417, 1418, 1420
Club of Rome, 4:439, 6:818, 9:1264
CNN (cable channel), 1:64, 66, 10:1339, 1341, 1358
coal industry, 1:39, 3:414-15, 417, 418, 7:884, 8:1087
   Great Depression and, 5:583
   Industrial Revolution and, 5:653, 665
   strikes, 9:1250
Coase, Ronald H., 4:464-65, 528
Coase theorem, 4:464-65
Cobden, Richard, 2:178
Coca-Cola Company, 2:217-20
   market research, 6:833
   stock returns, 9:1241, 1242
   trade secret protection, 2:164, 218
Codd, E. F., 3:339
Cohen, Ben, 1:106-8, 7:945
Cohen, Stanley, 4:555
coins, 7:898
Coke. See Coca-Cola Company
COLAs. See cost-of-living adjustments
Colbert, John-Baptiste, 6:849, 850
cold war
   capitalism and, 2:180-81
   communism and, 2:228, 229-31
   computers and, 2:250
   defense industry and, 3:351, 352
   European Union and, 4:457
   federal budget and, 4:478
   Internet and, 5:710, 712
   labor unions and, 1:40
   protectionism and, 4:563
   Sarnoff and, 8:1148
   Screen Actors Guild and, 9:1169
   socialism and, 9:1210
Coleman Co., 7:933
collaborative product development, 8:1037-38
collective bargaining, 2:221-24, 6:760, 7:938, 939, 943, 8:1070
   California farm workers, 2:196

family leave, 4:468
General Electric, 4:552
Lewis and, 1:39
major league baseball, 6:813, 814, 815
National Education Association, 7:938
National Labor Relations Act, 7:939, 943, 9:1252, 1274-75
National Labor Relations Board, 8:1105
pattern bargaining and, 6:763
public sector unionism, 8:1070
Randolph and, 8:1084
Screen Actors Guild, 9:1169
Taft–Hartley Act and, 9:1268
temporary workers, 10:1304
United Automobile Workers, 2:222, 10:1349, 1350
United Fruit, 2:205
collective goods. See public goods
collective mark (trade symbol), 2:164, 165
collectivization, 2:179, 227-28
collusion, 8:1017-20, 1022, 1104
   Wealth of Nations on, 10:1400-1401
Colonial Air Transport, 10:1333
colonialism, 6:849-51
Colt, Samuel, 5:693, 6:828
Columbia Pictures, 6:773, 7:909, 9:1218-19
Columbia Records, 9:1218
Columbia University, 4:527, 528, 7:994
   Hamilton and, 5:595
   Pulitzer Prizes, 8:1082
   School of Journalism, 8:1080, 1081
Columbus, Christopher, 5:705, 6:849, 850
Comer, Gary, 6:769
commerce clause, 2:253
Commerce Department, U.S., 6:778, 836, 10:1312-13
Commercial Cable Company, 8:1146
commercial paper, 3:314, 316
commercial real estate, 8:1090, 1093-95
Committee against Jim Crow in Military Service and Training, 8:1085
Committee for the First Amendment, 9:1169, 1170
Committee on Economic Security, 9:1212
commodities, 2:225-26
   Archer Daniels Midland, 1:70-71
   Chicago Board of Trade, 2:197-98, 225, 226
   energy industry, 3:418
   Enron trading, 3:420, 421
   futures market, 2:225, 226, 4:529-31
   pricing, 8:1021-23
   risk management, 8:1127
Commodity Futures Trading Commission, 4:531

Commodore International, **2**:251
common ownership. *See* tragedy of the commons
common stock, **3**:302, 345
definition of, **9**:1241
Communication Workers of America, **1**:40, 50
communism, **2:227-32**
capitalism vs., **2**:179, 180-82, 232, **9**:1165
economic liberalism and, **2**:*181*, 183
failure of, **2**:231-32, **3**:359, **4**:563, **9**:1208, *1209*, 1210
fascist opposition to, **4**:474
labor unions and, **1**:40
Landrum–Griffin Act and, **9**:1269
private property and, **8**:1028
privatization and, **8**:1033
Sarnoff campaign against, **8**:1148
Screen Actors Guild and, **9**:1169, 1170
socialism and, **9**:1207-8, 1210
spread of, **2**:181-82, 228, 229-31
strikes and, **9**:1251
Taft–Hartley Act and, **9**:1268, 1269
time line, **2**:*228*
United Fruit holdings and, **2**:205, 206
See also Marx, Karl; Marxism
Communist League, **6**:838
Communist Manifesto, The (Marx and Engels), **2**:227, *228*, **6**:838, **9**:1207, *1209*
excerpts, **6**:840
Community Action Agencies, **3**:394, 395
Community School 66 (N.Y.C.), **3**:*404*
Community Service Amendments (1974), **3**:395
Community Service Organization, **2**:195
Community Services Administration, **3**:395
compact discs, price fixing, **8**:1018
Compaq Computer, **2**:251, **4**:502, **5**:621, 636, **8**:1112
comparative advantage, **2:233-35**
benchmarking, **1**:109-11
international trade and, **5**:704
microeconomics and, **7**:869-70
NAFTA and, **7**:958, 959
outsourcing and, **7**:971-73
compensation, **2:236-41**
benefit plans, **3**:299
benefits by industry, **2**:*237*
benefits equity, **7**:989
benefits lowering, **10**:1420
budget and, **1**:129
building trade, **1**:134, 135
as business liability, **1**:86, 97
CEO, **2**:241, **3**:294-96, **10**:1404
CEO vs. average worker, **2**:296
collective bargaining for, **2**:221-24
components, **2**:236

corporate management, **3**:295-96
Ford Motor policy, **4**:513, **6**:829
freelance vs. salaried employees, **7**:993
government employees, **8**:1071-73
government workers, **8**:1072
health insurance, **5**:606
Heinz policy, **5**:614
Hewlett-Packard innovations, **5**:619-20
human resources department and, **5**:630
IBM policy, **5**:633
income distribution, **5**:644-46
inflation-adjustment, **2**:271
internship, **5**:715
job search and, **6**:737, 738
labor unions and, **6**:763, 764-66
Lands' End policy, **6**:770
Levi Strauss policy, **6**:786
major league baseball, **6**:813-14, *815*
minimum wage, **7**:877-82
partnership, **7**:978
paycheck deductions, **7**:990-91
payroll, **7**:990-93
productivity and, **8**:1039, 1042
professional athletes, **9**:1227
Southwest Airlines policy, **9**:1220-21
standard of living and, **9**:1228-29
Starbucks policy, **9**:1236
as strike issue, **9**:1252
telecommuters, **9**:*1290*
temporary workers, **10**:1302, 1303, 1420
United Automobile Workers, **10**:1351
vacation time and, **8**:1101
Wal-Mart policy, **10**:1390
See also pay equity; stock options; working conditions
compensatory damages, **6**:796
competition, **2:242-46**
athletic shoes, **7**:952
automobile industry, **10**:1352
brand names, **1**:118
breakfast cereals, **6**:747
British Airways, **1**:125, 126
capitalism and, **2**:178
cartel vs., **2**:187-88, 244-45
computer industry, **7**:875
credit card companies, **1**:52, 53
deregulation and, **3**:300, 358-62
education industry, **3**:408
entry barriers, **7**:900, *903, 904*
Federal Trade Commission and, **4**:484-87
four types of, **7**:899
Friedman economic theory and, **4**:528
globalization and, **4**:560
industrial espionage and, **5**:648-52
as inflation antidote, **5**:662
Information Revolution and, **5**:663-67
innovation and, **3**:372, **5**:679-80

intellectual property and, **5**:690
Intel strategy, **5**:684
just-in-time concept and, **6**:743
labor unions and, **6**:762, 763, 764-65
major league baseball players, **6**:813
Malthusian theory and, **6**:817
media companies, **1**:66
merger and acquisition and, **6**:854, **8**:1104
monopoly vs., **2**:178-79, 225, 244, 246, **7**:899, *904*
multinationals and, **7**:921
Nike and, **7**:950, 962
outsourcing and, **7**:972
patents and, **8**:1112
petroleum industry, **10**:1305
price controls and, **8**:1015-16
price fixing and, **8**:1017-20
pricing and, **8**:1021
privatization and, **8**:1032-33
productivity, **8**:1041
profit and loss and, **8**:1050, 1051-52
protectionism and, **8**:1054-57
regulatory activity and, **8**:1104, 1107
research and development and, **8**:1111-12
restraint of trade and, **8**:1104
reverse engineering and, **8**:1122
Sherman Antitrust Act and, **9**:1187-90
small business, **9**:1197, 1198
Smith theory of, **9**:1203, 1204
sports industry limitations, **9**:1224
stock exchanges, **1**:55
supply and demand and, **7**:870
sustainable development and, **9**:1265
telephone service, **3**:*359*, 360-61, **9**:1285-86, 1289
Total Quality Management and, **10**:1308, 1309
trade barriers vs., **1**:94, 95
trade policy and, **10**:1324-25
unfair business practices and, **8**:1104
utilities industry, **10**:1359
Web server software, **7**:876
See also antitrust; free market
compound interest, **2:247-48**, **5**:694
savings growth with, **9**:1157, *1158*
Comprehensive Environmental Response, Compensation, and Liability Act (1970). *See* Superfund
Compton, Bill, **1**:*102*
computer age. *See* Information Revolution
Computer Center Corporation, **7**:873
computer industry, **2:249-52**
Amazon.com, **1**:49-50
antitrust cases, **8**:*1106*

assembly line, **1**:82
assets and liabilities, **1**:*85*
browser price war, **8**:1025
bundling, **1**:138
business law., **2**:165
careers in, **2**:252
Cisco Systems, **2**:207-9
Clark and, **2**:215-16
Clark graphics development, **2**:215
competition barriers, **2**:244
consultants, **2**:259, *260*
contract law, **2**:279, 283, 284
corporate training, **3**:406
customer service records, **3**:335
day trading, **3**:342
development cycles, **8**:1037-38
development in India, **5**:670
digital imaging, **1**:74
economies of scale and, **7**:901
energy industry, **3**:418
engineering career, **2**:252
engineers, **2**:252
entrepreneurship, **3**:424, 427
Fiorina and, **4**:501-2
Gates and, **4**:537-39, 566
globalization and, **4**:566
gross domestic income, **2**:*249*
Hewlett-Packard and, **5**:619-21
IBM and, **5**:632-37, **7**:873-74
immigrant workers, **5**:642
information technology and, **5**:668-72, **9**:1277, 1280-83
intellectual property law, **2**:165
Intel microprocessor, **5**:684, 685, 686
Kinko rentals, **6**:753
labor market and, **6**:759
license, **6**:801, 802, 803, 804
Microsoft and, **7**:873-76, 902, *903*, **8**:1051
monopoly charge, **7**:873, *874*, 875, 902, *903*
Nasdaq stock, **7**:*930*, 931-32
patents, **7**:981, 986
Perot and, **7**:998, 999, 1000
personal computer, **2**:251-52
personal computer pricing, **8**:1023-24
piracy, **2**:282, **8**:1122
product development, **8**:1034
professional association, **8**:*1049*
programmers, **2**:252
raw materials, **8**:1088
research and development, **8**:1112
reverse engineering, **8**:1122, 1122-23, 1123
Sarnoff and, **8**:1148
security systems and, **9**:1175, *1176*
service economy and, **9**:1182, 1183
Silicon Valley, **3**:424, 427
software copyright, **2**:283-84, **5**:687-90
software development cycles, **8**:1037-38
software patents, **7**:980, 986

stock trading technology and, **9**:1245

telephone lines and, **9**:1284, **10**:1357

temporary workers, **10**:1303, 1304

wealth and, **10**:1397-98

working conditions, **10**:1420

Xerox and, **10**:1429, 1430-32

Yamaha and, **10**:1436

See also data management; e-business; Internet

Computer Literacy (online bookseller), **1**:49

computers

accounting systems and, **1**:26

census data and, **6**:834

early meaning of term, **2**:250

ergonomics, **4**:455-56

file-sharing, **2**:283, 284

first programmable, **5**:663

freelancing and, **4**:526

futures trading, **2**:198

human capital and, **5**:625, 628

industrial espionage and **5**:648-49, *651*

Information Revolution and, **5**:63, 665, 668

inventory system, **6**:726, 727

just-in-time applications, **6**:744

management aids and, **6**:819, 826

MLS database system, **8**:1091

modems, **9**:1206

multiuses, **2**:249, 251, 252

Nasdaq network, **7**:930, 931

ownership, **5**:666, *672*

productivity and, **5**:658, **8**:1039, *1042*, 1043

stock trading, **1**:54

Wal-Mart use of, **10**:*1387*, 1388-89

See also computer industry; Internet

Computing Scale Company of America, **5**:632, *633*

Computing-Tabulating-Recording Company (C-T-R), **5**:632, *633*

Concept of the Corporation, The (Drucker), **3**:380, *381*

Confederation Paysanne, **4**:566

Conference Board, **2**:261, 262, 263, **6**:778

conglomerate. *See* merger and acquisition

Congress of Industrial Organization. *See* AFL-CIO

conservationism, environmentalism vs., **4**:443

conservatism

economic liberalism vs., **10**:1396

Wall Street Journal, **10**:1383, 1384, 1385, 1386

Consolidated Edison, **3**:377

Consolidated Stock Exchange, **1**:55

conspicuous consumption, **10**:1366, 1367

Constitution, U.S., **2**:253-57

affirmative action rulings and, **1**:36

civil rights guarantees, **2**:210

contract protection, **2**:277

copyright provision, **2**:281, **8**:1112

corporation rights, **3**:302

Hamilton and, **5**:595, 596, 597

implied powers doctrine, **5**:596

income tax amendment, **5**:697

intellectual property and, **5**:687

patent provision, **7**:980, **8**:1112

as rule of law, **8**:1137, 1138

taxing power, **5**:698

See also specific amendments

construction industry. *See* building trades

consulting, **2**:258-60, **3**:297, **9**:1181, *1182*, **10**:1302

Consumer Confidence Index, **2**:261-63, **6**:778, 779

Consumer Credit Protection Act (1968), **3**:325

consumerism, **2**:264-68

advertising and, **1**:*27*, *29*, *32*, *33*, 112, 139-40

African Americans and, **6**:740

agriculture industry and, **1**:43, 46, 48

AT&T breakup and, **9**:1286

black market, **1**:115

brand names and, **1**:116-18, **8**:1021, 1025, 1037, 1051

competition and, **2**:246

computer market and, **2**:251-52

confidence indexes, **2**:261-63

conspicuous consumption and, **10**:1366-67

cost of living and, **3**:311-13

costs, **3**:307, 308

credit and, **3**:315, 316-18, 346

credit and debit cards, **3**:319-23, 346

credit history, **3**:325-26, 328

customer service and, **3**:333-35

data mining and, **3**:340

debt and, **3**:346, **4**:498-99

demographics and, **3**:355-57

disposable income and, **3**:363-65

distribution channels and, **3**:366

division of labor benefits for, **3**:388

e-business and, **3**:382-83

entrepreneurship and, **3**:424

environmentalism and, **4**:437, 438, 439

franchises and, **4**:523

Friedman theory on, **4**:528

Galbraith theory on, **4**:532-33

grape boycott, **2**:195

inflation and, **3**:390

macroeconomics, **6**:810

market research on, **6**:833, 836

microeconomics, **7**:869, 870

monetary policy and, **7**:893

personal expenditures (1930-2000), **2**:*265*

price ceiling and, **8**:1013, 1016

price fixing and, **8**:1017, 1018

pricing and, **8**:1021, 1022, 1024

protectionism and, **8**:1054-55, 1057

recession and, **8**:1097

recreation projects, **8**:1100, 1101

retail sales and, **8**:1116-18, 1119

sales tax and, **9**:1273

service economy and, **9**:1179

standard of living and, **9**:1229, 1229-30

supply and demand and, **8**:1050, **9**:1259, 1281

tariffs and, **9**:1270-71

technology and, **9**:1281

Total Quality Management and, **10**:1308-10

trade policies and, **1**:92, 94

Veblen theory of, **10**:1365-67

Consumer Leasing Act, **2**:275

Consumer Lending Act, **4**:485

Consumer Price Index, **2**:269-71, **8**:1021

cost of living, **3**:311

as inflation indicator, **5**:659, *662*

Leading Economic Indicators, **6**:*780*

macroeconomics, **6**:810

social security benefits, **9**:1215

Consumer Product Safety Commission, **2**:272, 273, **3**:300, **8**:*1106*, 1107, *1109*

consumer protection, **2**:267-68, **272-75**, **7**:925-27

advertising, **1**:32, 112, 113

AT&T monopoly, **9**:1286

Better Business Bureau, **1**:112-13

business ethics, **2**:158

business law, **2**:*160*

contract law, **2**:279

corporate social responsibility, **3**:300

credit cards, **3**:320, 321

e-business, **2**:279

federalism, **2**:255-56

Federal Trade Commission, **4**:484-87, **8**:1104, 1105

genetically modified food, **4**:559

GM Corvair, 553, **4**:*552*

identity theft, **3**:326, 328

liability law, **6**:794-800

Nader and, **7**:925-27

product liability, **8**:1045-47

regulatory activity, **6**:796, **8**:1104-9

Consumer Protection Act (1969), **3**:321

Consumer Protection Agency, **2**:268

Consumer Reports, **2**:267, *274*, **10**:1378

Consumer Research Center, **2**:261

Consumers Union, **2**:267

consumption

definition of, **3**:363

disposable income and personal expenditures, **3**:*363*

externalities, **4**:463

Keynesian economic model, **3**:364-65

See also consumerism

Continental Oil (Conoco), **9**:1234

contingent workers. *See* temporary workers

continuous processing. *See* assembly line

contractionary fiscal policy, **4**:503, 504

contractors. *See* building trades

contracts and contract law, **2**:160-61, **276-79**

bankruptcy, **1**:99-102

corporations and, **3**:302

credit repair, **3**:326

e-business and, **3**:384

liability and, **6**:794, 795

license and, **6**:801-4

outsourcing and, **7**:972-93

rule of law and, **8**:1137, 1138, 1139

contracts of adhesion, **6**:795

convenience, pricing and, **8**:1024-25

Convention and Visitors Bureau, **2**:192

Convention on the Elimination of All Forms of Discrimination Against Women, **4**:468

Convention on the Law and the Sea (1982), **4**:509

Convention on the Rights of the Child (1989), **2**:201

conveyor belt. *See* assembly line

Cook, Thomas, **10**:1312

Cooke, Jay, **7**:906

Cookman Institute, **8**:1083

Cooley, Richard, **10**:1046

Coolidge, Calvin, **2**:*191*, **6**:858

Cooney, Joan Ganz, **5**:616

copyright, **2**:280-84, **7**:874

amortization, **1**:61, 63

business law, **2**:164, 165

e-business and, **3**:384

information technology, **9**:1282, 1283

as intangible asset, **1**:*84*, 85

intellectual property, **5**:687

Internet, **5**:710

limited duration, **2**:165

materials covered by, **2**:*281*, 283

patent vs., **7**:980

piracy, **6**:803, *804*

as property right, **8**:1029

reverse engineering and, **8**:1122, 1123

small business, **9**:1199

World Trade Organization and, **10**:1427

as writer protection, **8**:1112

Cornell University, **4**:559, **7**:*995*, 997

Corning Glass, **3**:374

Corning Glass Works v. Brennan (1974), **10**:1415

Corn Laws (Britain), **2**:178

Corporate Accountability Research Group, **7**:927

corporate ethics. *See* business ethics

Cullinan, Joe ("Buckskin"),
  10:1305, *1307*
cultural difference, **3**:329-32
  demographics and, **3**:356-57
  immigration and, **3**:356-57
  McDonald's and, **7**:918
  Morita and, **7**:908-9
  multinationals and, **7**:917, 918,
    921
  as standard of living influence,
    9:1229
  Wal-Mart and, **10**:1389
curbstone brokers, **1**:54-55
currency. *See* money
Current Tax Payment Act (1943),
  5:697, 698
Curtis Publishing Company, **6**:833
Curtiss, Glenn, **10**:1333
customer relationship management,
  3:383-84, 385
customer service, **3**:333-35
  e-business, **3**:383-84, 385
  e-commerce, **5**:713
  Kinko's, **6**:753
  Lands' End, **6**:770-71
  McDonald's, **6**:756, 757
  Southwest Airlines, **3**:334,
    9:1220, 1221
  Starbucks, **9**:1236, 1237
customs duty. *See* tariff
cyberlaw, **2**:165
cyclical unemployment, **10**:1343
CYPNET, **3**:411

D
D&B, **3**:326, 336-37
Dabney, Morgan and Company,
  7:906
Daft, Doug, **2**:219, 220
DaimlerChrysler, **7**:*891*, 892
Dain Rauscher Corporation, **8**:1132
dairy industry, **8**:1013, 1054, 1055
damages. *See* liability; product
  liability
D'Amato, Alphonse, **5**:674
Dana, Charles, **8**:1080-81
Daniels, John W., **1**:*70*
Darwin, Charles, **6**:817
data management, **3**:338-40
  bar codes, **1**:103, 104
  bookkeeping, **1**:23-25
  census, **6**:834
  e-business, **3**:383, 385
  information technology for,
    5:668, 669-70
  inventory system, **6**:726, 727
  just-in-time applications, **6**:744
  as management aids, **6**:819, 826
  market research, **6**:834, 836
  Perot and, **7**:998
  real estate multiple listings,
    8:1091
  security systems, **9**:1175
  software development, **8**:1038
  Wal-Mart, **10**:*1387*, 1388-89
data mining, **3**:340
Data Universal Numbering System,
  3:336-37
data warehouses, **3**:338, 340

Daughters of the American
  Revolution, **8**:1145
Davidoff, Monte, **6**:803
Davidson, Arthur, **5**:598
Davidson, Walter, **5**:598
Davidson, William, **5**:598
Davidson, William G. (grandson),
  5:599-600
Davies, Marion, **5**:611-12
Davies, Thomas H., *as contributor*,
  8:1087-89
Davis, Angus, **10**:*1372*
Davis, Bette, **1**:65
Davis, Denise, *as contributor*,
  9:1196-99
Davis, Jacob, **6**:785, *786*
Davis, Marvin, **6**:773
Davis–Bacon Act (1933), **6**:763
Dayton Hudson, **10**:1387
Dayton Wright Company, **4**:551
day trading, **3**:341-42, **9**:1245
DDT (pesticide), **4**:439, *440*,
  450-51, **9**:1194-95
Dean, James, **6**:786
DeBeers diamond cartel, **7**:886,
  900, 903
debit cards. *See* credit cards and
  debit cards
Debs, Eugene, **8**:1083, **9**:*1209*,
  1210, 1252
debt, **3**:343-46
  accounting, **1**:24-25
  alternatives to, **3**:345-46
  balance of payments, **1**:91, 92
  bankruptcy, **1**:99-102
  bond issuance as, **9**:1241, 1242
  British Airways, **1**:125
  business, **3**:343-46, **4**:494-95
  business vs. personal, **3**:346
  cash flow and, **2**:189-90
  consumer, **2**:265, **4**:533
  corporate, **3**:*303*, 306, 317
  cost and, **3**:307
  credit history, **3**:324-28
  D&B reports, **3**:336-37
  from day trading, **3**:342
  Enron, **3**:422
  inflation and, **5**:660
  International Monetary Fund,
    5:702-3
  as liability, **1**:83, 86, 97
  liquidity ratios, **3**:*343*, 344
  macroeconomics and, **6**:811
  money as settlement of, **7**:896,
    897
  mortgage, **7**:913
  national, **3**:315, **4**:478, 503, *504*
  personal, **3**:316, 318, 345, 346,
    4:498-99, 500
  war, **5**:583
  World Bank, **10**:1423-24
  See also credit
debt capital, **2**:173-74
debt financing, **6**:792
debt labor, **2**:202
debtors' prison, **1**:99
DECA program, **5**:651-52
deceptive advertising. *See* false
  advertising

Declaration of Independence,
  6:851, 852, **10**:1401
declining balance method
  (depreciation), **1**:62-63
Deere, Charles, **3**:348, 349
Deere, John, **3**:347-49, 348
Deere & Company, **3**:348-49
defective products. *See* product
  liability
Defenders of Wildlife, **4**:450
Defense Department, U.S., **3**:411,
  412, **4**:552-53, **7**:998
  industrial R&D spending, **8**:*1112*
defense industry, **3**:350-54
  armed forces desegregation,
    8:1085
  assembly line, **10**:1329
  careers in, **3**:352
  Dow Chemical contracts, **3**:350,
    373-74
  equal employment, **8**:1084, 1085
  federal budget and, **4**:477, 478,
    505
  General Electric contracts, **4**:548,
    549
  General Motors contracts, **4**:552,
    554
  in Germany, **10**:1377
  Harley-Davidson and, **5**:598-99
  IBM and, **5**:633-34
  interchangeable parts, **1**:81,
    5:657, 658, 692-93, **6**:828
  Internet and, **5**:710
  in Japan, **7**:891, 908
  public goods and, **8**:1059
  reverse engineering, **8**:1122
  Sikorsky contracts, **9**:*1193*
  small business procurement,
    9:1200-1201
  United Automobile Workers and,
    10:1350
  women workers, **10**:1414
deficit, national, **4**:478, 503, **6**:811,
  812
deficit, trade, **1**:91, 92, 93, **5**:660
De Gaulle, Charles, **4**:458
de Graff, Robert, **8**:1078
de Havilland, Olivia, **1**:65
Delaware Association of Nonprofit
  Agencies, **8**:1049
Dell, Michael, **4**:*519*
Dell Computer, **2**:252, **4**:501,
  6:743, **8**:1112
Delligattia, Jim, **6**:848
Deloitte Touche Tohmatsu,
  2:259-60
DeLuca, Fred, **4**:523
demand. *See* supply and demand
demand pull inflation, **5**:660-61,
  662
Deming, W. Edwards, **10**:1309-10
Democratic Party
  environmentalism and, **4**:448
  Galbraith economics and, **4**:532,
    533
  labor support, **7**:943
  National convention (1948),
    8:*1084*
  Perkins and, **7**:995

democratic socialism, **9**:1208-9
Democratic Socialists of America,
  9:1210
demographics, **3**:355-57
  advertising, **1**:27-28, 32
  economic growth, **6**:816
  immigration, **5**:638-40
  Malthus and, **6**:816-18
  market research, **6**:833, 834, 835
  public relations, **8**:1068
  suburbanization, **6**:790
  tourism, **10**:1315-16
Dempsey, Jack, **8**:1147
department stores, **3**:424, **8**:1115
  consumerism, **2**:264, 265
  customer service, **3**:333, 335
  Estée Lauder cosmetics and,
    6:776, 777
  Hudson's Bay Company, **5**:622,
    624
depreciation. *See* amortization and
  depreciation
depression of the 1930s. *See* Great
  Depression
deregulation, **3**:358-62, **8**:*1106*
  banking, **8**:1109, 1132
  brokerage firms, **9**:1166
  cable television, **10**:1359
  competition and, **2**:246
  corporate social responsibility
    and, **3**:300
  mergers and acquisitions, **6**:853
  natural gas, **3**:420, **10**:1359
  privatization and, **8**:1030-33
  productivity and, **8**:1040
  SEC and, **9**:1174
  trucking, **3**:358, **8**:1109
  wholesale power market, **8**:1016
derivatives markets, **2**:197-98
D. E. Shaw & Co., **1**:49
de Soto, Hernando, **8**:1138
Deterding, Henri Wilhelm August,
  8:1133, 1134
Deutsche Bank, **8**:1095
developing nations
  Asian Development Bank,
    1:78-80
  child labor, **2**:201-3
  communism, **2**:229-30, 231,
    9:1208
  consumption, **2**:268
  debt crisis, **10**:1424
  fishing industry, **4**:507
  GATT policies, **4**:545
  globalization and, **4**:560-61, 563
  globalization effects, **4**:560-61,
    563
  human capital potential, **5**:625
  IMF loans, **5**:703, 708-9
  infant formula controversy, **3**:332
  information technology, **5**:668,
    670-71, 708-9
  international trade, **5**:707, 708
  mercantilist policies, **6**:852
  OPEC policies, **7**:968-70
  piracy, **8**:1122
  population growth, **4**:437
  reverse engineering, **8**:1122-23
  rule of law, **8**:1139

developing nations (cont.)
 sustainable development, 9:1265-67
 tariff purpose, 10:1322
 tariff use, 10:1322
 wealth distribution, 10:1398-99
 World Bank and, 10:1421-22
Development of Espionage, Counterintelligence, and Counterterrorism Awareness, 5:651-52
Diamond v. Diehr, 7:986
Dicker, Dawn, *as contributor*, 8:1066-69
Digital Equipment Corp., 2:251
Digital Millennium Copyright Act (1998), 2:283-84
digital technology, 1:29, 74-75, 105
 copyright, 2:283, 284
Dillon Round, 4:540
Dimension Films, 7:889
Diners' Club, 1:51, 52, 3:316, *317*, 320, *321*
direct cost, overhead vs., 7:974
direct deposit form, 7:990, *992*
direct mail, 1:31-32, *33*, 8:1061, 1063
disability
 affirmative action law, 1:*34*
 civil rights law, 1:56-60
 definition of, 1:57-58
 EEOC and, 4:452-53
 information technology and, 5:669
disability insurance, 9:1211, 1214, 1215, 1216
discount brokerage, 4:491-92, 9:1167-68, 1245
discount rate, 4:482, 7:*893*, 894-95
discount sales, 8:1021, 1024, 1025, 1116
 bundling, 1:136
 price fixing and, 8:1018-19, 1020
 price floors and, 8:1014
 Wal-Mart, 10:1387-90
disk storage, 5:634
Disney, Roy, 10:1391, 1392
Disney, Walt, 8:1100, 10:1391-92
Disney Company. *See* Walt Disney Company
Disneyland, 10:1392
Disneyland Paris, 10:1393
Disney Press, 10:1393
Disney Stores, 2:267, 10:1392
disposable income, 3:**363-65**
 standard of living and, 9:1228-30
dispute resolution. *See* arbitration; mediation
distribution channels, 3:**366-69**
 agricultural products, 1:46
 business-to-business sales, 2:171
 e-business, 3:382-87
 franchises, 4:522-23
 Guinness, 5:592-93
 just-in-time concept, 6:744
 product development, 8:1034, 1036
 retail and wholesale, 8:1117, 1118-20

dividends, 3:302, 304, 9:1158-59, 1242
 taxes on, 3:317
division of labor, 3:**370-72**
 assembly line, 1:82
 capitalism and, 2:177, 178
 economic gains from, 7:*870*
 economic growth and, 3:370-71, 388
 economies of scale and, 3:396
 family leave and, 4:468
 free trade and, 9:1270
 manufacturing industry, 6:828, 829
 productivity, 3:370-72, 9:1204, 10:1400
 Smith theory of, 6:851, 9:1203, 1204, 10:1400
Dixie Greyhound Lines, 4:488
DKW motorcycle, 10:1435
DNA Sciences, 2:216
doctors. *See* health care services industry
Doctors without Borders, 1:123
Dodd, Christopher, 9:*1173*
Dole (company), 1:118
Dole, Bob, 7:999
dollar, 3:316
Domain Name System, 5:710-11, *712*
domestic content requirements, 10:1322, *1323*
Domino's Pizza, 7:918, 9:*1186*
Donahue, Phil, 10:1411
Donaldson, William H., 9:1174
Dort, Josiah Dallas, 4:550
DoubleClick, 5:671, 10:1370
double-entry accounting, 1:24
Doughton, Robert, 9:*1212*
Douglas Aircraft, 4:552
Douglass, Benjamin, 3:336
Douglass, Frederick, 10:1382
Dow, Charles, 3:376, 377, 7:947, 10:*1383*, 1384
Dow Chemical Company, 3:350, **373-75**
DowElanco, 3:374
Dow, Jones & Company, 10:1383-86
Dow Jones Averages, 2:198, 3:376-77, 4:548, 5:581, 7:947
 business cycles, 2:149, *151*, 152
 futures market, 2:225
downsizing, 3:**378-79**
 British Airways, 1:125
 Enron, 3:422
 General Electric, 3:378-79, 4:549, 10:1404
 Kellogg Company, 6:748
 labor market and, 6:759
 from merger or acquisition, 6:853
 minimum wage and, 7:877
 productivity and, 8:1041
 women workers and, 10:1413
 See also unemployment
Dow Process Company, 3:373
Doyle Dane Bernbach, 10:1379

Drago, Will, *as contributor*, 5:679-80, 9:1246-48
Drake, Edwin, 8:1128, 9:1231, 10:1305
Drake, Francis, 6:*849*, 850
Dr. Dre (rapper), 2:284
Dreamworks Studio, 10:1394
Dreyfuss, Richard, 9:*1171*
Drucker, Peter, 3:**380-81**
drugs. *See* pharmaceutical industry
Duehl, David and Margaret, 6:772
Duhalde, Eduardo, 5:*701*
Duke, Patty, 9:*1171*
Duke University, 6:841
dumping, 4:540, 8:1056, 10:*1323*, 1325
Dun, Robert Graham, 3:336
Dun & Bradstreet. *See* D&B
Dunlop, Gordon, 1:125
D-U-N-S Number, 3:336-37
Dupont Dow Elastomers, 3:374
Durant, William Crapo ("Billy"), 4:550-51, *552*
Durant-Dort Carriage Company, 4:550
Durant Motors, 4:551
DVD (digital videodisk), 1:74, 75, 2:282
DVR (digital video recorder), 1:29
Dynamic Random-Access-Memory (DRAM), 5:*684*, 685
Dynergy, 3:421

E

Eagle Bancshares Incorporated, 8:1132
EAN (European Article Numbering) system, 1:104
E. A. Pierce & Cassatt, 6:859
Earned Income Tax Credit, 7:881
earnings, 1:97, 129
 Fortune 500 companies, 4:519-21
Earth Summit (1992), 1:78, 4:*440*
Eastern Airlines, 3:358, 4:552
Eastern Air Transport, 4:552, 10:1333
Eastman Kodak, 3:378
Eastwood, Clint, 1:92
eBay, 3:382, 5:*712*, 714, 9:1280
 venture capital investment return, 10:1370
 Whitman and, 10:1408-9
eBay Premier, 10:1409
eBay Professional Services, 10:1409
Ebony (magazine), 6:739, 740, 8:1077
e-business, 3:**382-87**, 5:*712*, 713-14
 Amazon.com, 1:49-50
 business-to-business sales, 2:171, 172
 chambers of commerce, 2:193
 consumerism, 2:267
 consumer protection, 2:279
 contract law, 2:279
 credit card use, 3:323
 customer service, 3:333, 335
 e-commerce vs., 3:382, 5:713
 EnronOnline, 3:*420*, 421

information technology, 9:1280, 1282
intellectual property law, 2:165
 Kinko's, 6:754
 Lands' End, 6:770-71
 licenses, 6:803, 804
 retail sales, 8:1116-17, *1119*
 Whitman and, 10:1408-9
 Yahoo!, 10:1433-34
EC. *See* European Union
Eco-Mart, 4:442
e-commerce, 5:665, 713-14
 business law, 2:165
 e-business vs., 3:382, 5:713
 information age and, 5:665
 just-in-time concept and, 6:744
 retail and wholesale, 8:1120
Economic Development Institute, 10:*1421*, 1422
economic efficiency, 7:869, 870, 871, 896
economic growth, 3:**388-92**
 Asian Development Bank, 1:78
 business cycle, 3:390, 392
 credit, 3:315, 316, 318
 disposable income, 3:364-65
 division of labor, 3:370-71, 388
 entrepreneurship, 3:428
 environmentalism, 4:437, 439, 441-42
 European Union, 5:708
 Great Depression slowdown, 5:581
 gross domestic product, 5:588-91
 income distribution, 5:644
 inflation rate, 5:659, 661
 innovation, 5:679
 labor market, 8:1096
 Leading Economic Index, 6:778
 macroeconomics, 6:811, 812
 manufacturing industry, 6:828
 microeconomics, 7:869-72
 monetary policy, 3:390, 7:893-95
 population growth, 6:816-17, 818
 productivity, 8:1039, 1040, 1042
 profit and loss, 8:1050
 recession vs., 8:1096-98
 retailing, 8:1116
 rule of law, 8:*1137*
 savings and investments, 3:363-64
 service economy, 9:1178, *1183*
 Smith's free market, 6:851, 9:1203, 1204, 10:1400, 1401
 sustainable development, 9:1264-67
 technology, 9:1277-83
 trade policy, 10:1322
economic indicators, 6:778-80, 810, 811
economic mobility, 10:1397
Economic Opportunity Act (1964), 3:**393-95**
Economic Policy Advisory Board, 4:527
Economic Recovery Tax Act (1981), 8:1094

Economics: An Introductory Analysis (Samuelson), 8:1141
economies of scale, **3:396-98**
  cartels as, 2:187-88
  Edison Schools, 3:402-3
  electricity industry, 3:421
  NAFTA and, 7:958
  as natural monopoly, 7:900-901, *903*, 8:1103, 1107
  outsourcing, 7:972
  retail chains, 8:1117
  service economy, 9:1180-81
  small business, 9:1197
  Soviet "diseconomies," 2:231
ecosystems, 3:299, 4:438-39, 443
ecotourism, 10:1313-14
Edge of the Sea, The (Carson), 9:1194
Edison, Thomas Alva, **3:399-401**, *414*, 424, 4:511, 7:912
  General Electric, 3:400, 4:546-48
  mimeograph machine, 10:1429
  persistence of, 8:1112
Edison General Electric Company, 4:547, 548
Edison Machine Works, 4:548
Edison Schools, 3:402-4, 405
EDS. *See* Electronic Data Systems
educational achievement-wealth potential, 10:1397
Education Alternatives, Inc., 3:402
Education for All Handicapped Children Act (1975), 1:56
education industry, **3:405-10**
  affirmative action, 1:35-36
  agricultural research, 1:47
  alternate dispute resolution, 1:69
  arts incorporation into, 1:74
  Asian Development Bank and, 1:79
  careers in, 3:408
  child labor and, 2:200, 201, 202
  disabilities provision, 1:56
  Economic Opportunity Act and, 3:393, 394, 395
  Edison Schools, 3:402-4
  federal budget and, 4:479
  information technology access and, 5:671
  lawyer training, 6:781, *783*
  licensing or certification, 10:1375, 1376
  master of business administration, 6:841-43
  National Education Association, 7:935-38
  outsourcing, 7:973
  positive externality, 4:463
  privatization, 8:1031, 1033
  professional associations, 8:1048, 1049
  as public good, 8:1059
  public vs. private ownership, 8:1031
  Rockefeller philanthropy, 8:1130
  school desegregation, 7:936, 8:1085
  as service economy sector, 9:1180
  unionism, 8:1070

education savings accounts, 7:938
Edward VII, king of Great Britain, 7:1001
EEOC. *See* Equal Employment Opportunity Commission
e-50 Index of Internet companies, 4:521
Ehrle, Karen, *as contributor*, 1:106-8, 3:298-301, 378-79, 4:570-72, 5:581-85, 586-87, 616-18, 6:769-71, 781-84, 844-45, 9:1166-68, 1228-30, 1238-40, 10:1353-55, 1402-4, 1410-12
Ehrlich, Paul, 4:437, *440*, 6:817-18
Eighth Amendment, 2:257
8088 chip, 5:635, 636
Eisenhower, Dwight D., 9:1200, 1214
  on military-industrial complex, 3:351-52, 354
Eisner, Michael, 6:856, 10:*1392*, 1393, 1394
elasticity, demand, 6:765, 9:1263
e-learning, 3:405, 408, 409
electricity, 3:411-19, 5:673, 8:1016
  competition and, 2:246
  deregulation, 3:360, 361-62
  Dow Jones Average stocks, 3:377
  economies of scale, 3:397, 398
  Edison inventions, 3:400-401, 424, 7:912
  General Electric, 4:546-48
  Industrial Revolution, 5:658
  Insull and, 3:421
  monopoly, 7:900-901, 903
  pricing, 8:1021
  privatization, 8:1032
  productivity and, 8:1039
  regulation, 8:1105
  state public service commissions, 8:1108-9
  technology, 9:1278
  telegraph, 7:*910*, 911, *912*
  Tennessee Valley Authority, 7:941, 943
  utilities, 10:1356, 1358
electronic business. *See* e-business
Electronic Communication Networks, 3:342
electronic copying
  copyright, 2:282, 283
  intellectual property law, 2:165
  Xerox, 10:1429-30, 1431, 1432
Electronic Data Systems, 3:382, 7:998, 10:1304
electronic funds transfer, 4:481-82, 7:898
electronic mail. *See* e-mail
electronic publishing, 8:1078
Electronic Signatures in Global and National Commerce Act (2000), 3:412
electronics industry
  downsizing, 3:378
  Hewlett-Packard, 5:619-21
  Perot and, 7:998, 1000
  price fixing, 8:1019
  Sony, 7:908-9, 9:1217-19

Elektra records, 1:64
Eli Lilly, 3:374, 7:900, *903*
Elizabeth I, queen of England, 6:*849*, 850
Ellereth case (1998), 9:1185-86
Ellison, Lawrence, 2:241
El Paso Southwestern Railroad, 9:1252
e-mail, 1:75, 2:252, 3:411-13, 5:710, 711, *712*, 713, 9:1284
  copyright, 2:283
  number of users, 5:663
  productivity, 5:670, 671, 8:1040
embezzlement. *See* business ethics
Emergency Banking Relief Act (1933), 7:941, 8:1104, *1105*, *1106*
Emerson, Ralph Waldo, 4:439
EMI Group, 4:569, 8:1018
Emory, John D., Jr., *as contributor*, 5:676-78, 10:1360-61
Empire State Development Corporation, 2:274
employee benefits. *See* compensation
employee handbook, 5:629-30
Employment Act (1946), 7:893
encryption, 3:413, 8:1122-23
endangered species, 1:45, 48, 4:439, 447, 450
  fishing industry and, 4:506, 508, 509-10
  forest products industry and, 4:515-16
  sustainable development and, 9:1267
  tragedy of the commons analysis, 10:1327, 1328
Endangered Species Act (1973), 4:447, *448*, 450
End Child Prostitution in Asian Tourism, 10:1315
Energy Department, U.S., 5:650, 8:*1112*
energy industry, **3:414-19**
  careers in, 3:415
  deregulation, 10:1359
  Enron, 3:420-23
  environmental regulation, 4:437, 439, *440*, 449, 465
  externalities, 4:464, 465
  futures market, 2:225
  Industrial Revolution, 5:653-55, 656
  mineral mining, 7:883-87
  subsidy, 9:1257-58
  sustainable development, 9:1265, 1266
  U.S. Steel and, 10:1355
  utilities, 10:1356-59
  See also electricity; natural gas; petroleum industry
Energy Policy Act (1992), 4:485
Engels, Friedrich, 2:227, *228*, 6:838, 839, 840, 9:1207, *1209*, 10:1365
Enron, 3:297, 420-23, 4:521
  Arthur Andersen collapse, 2:260

bankruptcy, 1:101, 3:306, 420, 422-23
business ethics, 2:153, 3:*296*, 8:1053
  SEC and, 9:*1173*, 1174
Enron Energy Services, 3:422
EnronOnline, 3:*420*, 421, 422
entrepreneurship, **3:424-28**
  Ben & Jerry's, 1:106-8
  Black Enterprise, 1:114-15
  breakfast cereals, 6:745-46
  building trades, 1:133
  business plan, 2:166-69
  chambers of commerce, 2:191-93
  Clark and, 2:215-16
  consultants, 2:258
  costs, 3:308
  Deere and, 3:347-49
  division of labor and, 3:388
  eBay, 10:1408-9
  Edison and, 3:400-401, 424
  Ford and, 3:424, 4:511-14
  free-rider problem, 8:1058
  Gates and, 4:537, 538-39
  Gordy and, 4:560-69
  Guinness, 5:592-93
  Harley-Davidson, 5:598-600
  Hewlett-Packard, 5:619-21
  information technology, 2:207, 215-16
  innovation and, 5:679
  Johnson and, 6:739-40
  Kellogg Company, 6:745-47
  Kinko's, 6:752-54
  knowledge workers, 9:1280-81
  Kroc and, 6:755-57
  Lauder and, 6:775-77
  Leo Burnett Agency, 1:139-40
  Levitt and, 6:788-90
  Lewis and, 6:792-93
  management and, 6:822
  Mary Kay Inc., 1:76-77
  monopoly and, 7:901
  National Black Chamber of Commerce, 7:933, *934*
  Nike, 7:950
  Perot and, 7:998
  product development, 8:1036
  retail sales, 8:1117
  Rockefeller and, 8:1128-30
  savings and investment and, 3:363
  Schumpeter theory on, 9:1164
  Schwab and, 9:1166-68
  small business, 9:1196-99, 1200-1201
  Southwest Airlines, 9:1220
  Starbucks empire, 9:1235-37
  Stewart and, 9:1238-40
  Trippe and, 10:1333-35
  Trump and, 10:1336-38
  Vanderbilt and, 10:1362-64
  venture capital, 10:1368-73
  Walker and, 10:1380-82
  Walton and, 10:1387-88
  wealth distribution, 10:1396, 1397, 1398
  Winfrey and, 10:1410-12

environmentalism, **4**:437-42
　agricultural production and, **1**:45, 46, 48
　Asian Development Bank, **1**:78, 79-80
　automobile ownership and, **9**:1230
　business ethics and, **2**:154, 157-58
　consumerism and, **2**:268
　corporate responsibility and, **3**:299-301
　Dow Chemical hazards, **3**:373, 375
　economic growth balanced with, **3**:*391*, 392
　ecotourism and, **10**:1313-14
　energy industry and, **3**:418
　EPA controls, **4**:443, 444, 447, *448*, 450
　European Union and, **4**:*460*
　externalities and, **4**:437-38, 463-64, 465
　federal budget and, **4**:479
　fields of interest, **4**:437, 443
　forest products and, **4**:515-16, *518*
　GATT rounds and, **4**:545
　genetically modified crops and, **4**:559
　GM catalytic converter, **4**:*552*
　key principles of, **4**:437
　liability and, **6**:795, 796
　Malthusian theory and, **6**:816, 817-18
　mining industry and, **7**:884, 884-85, 885
　multinationals and, **7**:919
　Nader and, **7**:927
　NAFTA and, **7**:958-59
　as negative production externality, **4**:463-64
　Nike and, **7**:952-53
　OSHA standards and, **7**:960, 962
　public goods and, **8**:1059, 1060
　regulation problems, **4**:450-51
　Royal Dutch/Shell and, **8**:1135-36
　Silent Spring and, **9**:1195
　subsidies and, **9**:1258
　sustainable development and, **4**:442, **9**:1264-67
　Texaco and, **10**:1307
　tragedy of the commons and, **10**:1326-28
　Turner and, **10**:1341
　World Bank and, **10**:1324, *1421*
Environmental Protection Agency, **3**:300, **4**:439, *440*, 442, **443-46**, 447, 449, 450, 465, **6**:797, 798, **8**:*1106*, 1107
　genetically modified crops and, **4**:559
　OSHA and, **7**:961
　time line, **4**:444
　toxic waste cleanup liability, **6**:797, 798
　water standards, **10**:1358

environmental regulation, **4**:439, *440*, **447-51**, **8**:*1106*, 1107, 1109
　externalities and, **4**:465
　forest products and, **4**:515-16
　key provisions, **4**:448
　mining industry and, **7**:884-85
　OSHA and, **7**:960, 961, 962
　politics of, **4**:441-42
　private property and, **8**:1029
　profit and loss and, **8**:1051
　rule of law and, **8**:1139
　sustainable development and, **9**:1266-67
　See also Environmental Protection Agency
EPA. *See* Environmental Protection Agency
e-publishing, **8**:1078
equal access, **1**:56, 58, 60
Equal Credit Opportunity Act (1974), **3**:320
equal employment opportunity
　affirmative action, **1**:34, 35
　Americans with Disabilities Act, **1**:58, 59-60
　Asian Development Bank, **1**:79
　building trades set-asides, **1**:135
　civil rights legislation, **2**:212-13
　legal services, **6**:783
　as Levi Strauss policy, **6**:786
　management theory, **6**:827
　as Randolph cause, **8**:1084-85
　women and, **10**:1414-15
Equal Employment Opportunity Commission, **2**:212, 213, **3**:300, **4**:452-53, **7**:987, **8**:*1106*, 1107
　Americans with Disabilities Act compliance, **1**:58
　pay equity and, **7**:987
　sexual harassment and, **9**:1184, 1185, *1186*
　Title VII enforcement, **1**:35
equal pay. *See* pay equity
Equal Pay Act (1963), **1**:34, **2**:*213*, **4**:452-53, 467, **7**:987, **10**:1414, 1418
equal protection, **1**:36, **2**:210, **8**:1138
Equifax (credit bureau), **3**:325
equilibrium price, **9**:*1261*, 1262
Equity Office Properties Trust, **8**:1095
ERA (realtor), **8**:1091
Erasmus, Desiderius, **2**:281
ergonomics, **4**:454-56, **7**:960, 961, 962, 963, **10**:1419-20
Erie Railroad, **10**:1363-64
Ernst & Young International, **2**:259-60
Erwin Wasey and Company, **1**:139
ESPN (cable channel), **9**:1224
"Essay on the Principle of Population, An" (Malthus), **4**:437, *440*, **6**:816
Estée Lauder, Inc., **6**:775, 776-77
estimated price, valuation and, **10**:1360

Estrada Cabrera, Manuel, **2**:04
Ethernet, **10**:1431, 1432
Ethyl Dow Company, **3**:374
E*TRADE, **5**:714
Eurex (European Derivatives Market), **2**:198
euro (currency), **4**:*457*, 459, 460, **5**:707-8
European Atomic Energy Community, **4**:457
European Central Bank, **4**:459
European Coal and Steel Community, **4**:457
European Community, **4**:457-59
European Economic Community, **4**:457, 458
European Free Trade Area, **4**:458
European Monetary System, **4**:459
European Parliament, **4**:457, 460
European Union, **1**:94, **4**:**457-60**, **5**:707-8, **6**:853, **7**:921, 956, 967, **10**:1347
　banana trade war, **2**:*204*, 206
　pharmaceutical cartel fine, **2**:188
　steel subsidy, **8**:1056
　sustainable development, **9**:1265
　telecommuting guidelines, **9**:1291
　trade policy, **10**:1325
　U.S. product standards disputes, **10**:1323
Evans, Christopher, **5**:665
Evans, Oliver, **5**:657, 658
Evers, Charles, **1**:115
Exchange Alley (London), **1**:54
Exchange Rate Mechanism, **4**:459
exchange rates, **2**:180, **4**:**461-62**, **5**:710
expansionary fiscal policy, **4**:503, 504
expense accounts, **1**:26
Experian (formerly TRW), **3**:325
Explorer (Ford vehicle), **8**:1045
Explorer (Microsoft browser), **2**:216, **7**:874, 875, **8**:1025
exports. *See* international trade
external benefits. *See* public goods
externalities, **4**:437-38, **463-65**
Exxon, **1**:117, **7**:948, **9**:1234
ExxonMobil, **3**:416, **4**:521, **6**:854, **10**:1307
　profitability, **8**:1052, *1053*

F

Faber & Faber, Inc., **4**:473
facsimile machines. *See* fax machines
factories. *See* manufacturing industry
factors of production, **3**:398
Fahlman, Scott, **3**:412
Fair Credit Reporting Act (1968), **3**:325-26, **4**:485
Fair Employment Practices Committee, **8**:1085
Fair Labor Standards Act (1938), **3**:299, **4**:466-67, **7**:996, **10**:1418
　child labor, **2**:*200*, 201, 203, **4**:466

minimum wage, **4**:466, **7**:877, 879-80, 943
fair market value, **10**:1360, 1361
Fair Packaging and Labeling Act, **2**:275
Fair Trade Act (1937), **9**:1197
fair trade practices. *See* regulation of business and industry
fair use rules (copyright), **2**:284, **5**:687, 690, **9**:1282
false advertising, **1**:32, 112, 113
　business ethics, **2**:154, 158, 267
　consumer protection, **2**:267, 272, 274, 275
　FTC and, **8**:1104, 1105
Family and Medical Leave Act (1993), **4**:468, 469-71, **5**:630
family budget. *See* finance, personal
family businesses, **9**:1196
family economy, **2**:200
family fortunes, **10**:1398
family leave, **3**:357, **4**:468-71
Famous Amos cookies, **3**:426
Fanning, Shawn, **2**:284
Faragher case (1998), **9**:1185-86
Fargo, James Congdell, **1**:51
Fargo, William G., **1**:51, **10**:1405, *1406*
Fargo & Co., **10**:1406, *1407*
farming. *See* agriculture industry; aquaculture
Farnsworth, Philo, **8**:1148
Farrar, John, **4**:472
Farrar, Straus & Giroux, **4**:**472-73**, **8**:1078
Farrell, Walter C., Jr., *as contributor*, **2**:210-14, **3**:355-57, 393-95, **4**:466-67, **5**:638-43, **7**:933-34, **9**:1268-69
fascism, 4.474-76, 5.612, 8.1028-29. *See also* Nazism
Fashion Fair Cosmetics, **6**:739, 740
fast-food chains
　cultural differences and, **3**:331
　discount bundling, **1**:136
　franchises, **4**:523
　McDonald's, **6**:755, 756-57, 846-48
Fawcett World Library, **8**:1078
fax machines, **9**:1284, 1286, **10**:1432
Fayol, Henri, **6**:819, 824
FBI. *See* Federal Bureau of Investigation
FCC. *See* Federal Communications Commission
FDA. *See* Food and Drug Administration
FDIC. *See* Federal Deposit Insurance Corporation
Federal Aeronautics Administration, **9**:1254
Federal Arbitration Act (1925), **1**:67-68
Federal Aviation Administration, **10**:1332
federal budget, **4**:477-79, 503, 505
Federal Bureau of Investigation, **1**:71, **5**:651-52

Federal Cigarette Labeling and Advertising Act (1966), **4:**485, **7:**1003
Federal Commission on Industrial Relations, **1:**38
Federal Communications Commission, **1:**27, 88, 89, **2:**246, **7:***941*, 943, **8:**1105, *1106*, 1148, **9:**1289, **10:**1358
Federal Deposit Insurance Corporation, **3:**315, *317*, **7:***941*, *941*, **8:**1105, **9:**1157, 1158
Federal Emergency Relief Administration, **7:***941*
Federal Energy Regulatory Commission, **10:**1358
Federal Food, Drug, and Cosmetic Act (1938). *See* Food, Drug, and Cosmetic Act
federal funds rate, **7:**893, 894
Federal Housing Administration, **6:**790, **7:***941*, **8:**1105, *1106*
Federal Insecticide, Fungicide and Rodenticide Act (1972), **4:***448*
Federal Insurance Contributions Act, **9:**1212-13
Federal Mediation Commission, **9:**1252
Federal Mediation Service, **9:**1269
Federal Open Market Committee, **4:**482, 483
Federal Power Commission, **8:**1105
federal regulatory agencies. *See* regulation of business and industry
Federal Reserve Act (1913), **3:**315
Federal Reserve Board, **4:**482-83
Federal Reserve System, **4:480-83**
consumer protection, **2:**272
district banks, **4:**481, 482
economic growth and, **3:**390, 391
fiscal policy and, **4:**503
Greenspan and, **5:**586-87
inflation measures, **5:**661
interest rates and, **5:**695, 696
investment and, **6:**730-31
Leading Economic Index and, **6:**778
macroeconomics and, **6:**812
monetary policy, **3:**315-16, 390, 391, **4:**480-83, 527, 528, **7:**893-95
Morgan and, **7:**905, 907
real estate brokerage, **8:**1092
recession measures, **8:**1098
Federal Steel Company, **10:**1354
Federal Trade Commission, **4:484-87**
Clayton Act and, **2:***245*
consumer protection, **2:**272, 273, 275
deceptive advertising, **1:**32, **2:***158*, **8:**1104, 1105
franchises, **4:**523
identity theft, **3:**328
price fixing, **8:**1020
Xerox and, **10:**1431

Federal Trade Commission Act (1914), **4:**485, **8:**1104, *1106*
provisions, **2:**245, **7:***900*
Federation of Organized Trade and Labor, **5:**601
FedEx, **3:**377, **4:488-90**
bar code, **1:**105
customer service, **3:**334-35
Fenn, Sherilyn, **2:***278*
Ferdinand, king of Aragon, **6:**850
Fersh, Don, *as contributor*, **1:**56-60
feudalism, **8:**1026, **10:**1395
FHA. *See* Federal Housing Administration
fiber-optic cable, **1:***90*, **7:**887, **9:**1286-87, 1288, **10:**1358
FICA. *See* social security and Medicare
Fidelity Investments, **4:491-92**
Fielden, Samuel, **5:**602
Fifth Amendment, **2:**256
film industry
AOL Time Warner, **1:**64, 65
blue jean image, **6:**785
colorization, **10:**1341
computer created special effects, **2:**215
contract law, **2:**277-78, 279
copyright, **2:***281*, *282*, 283
digital technology, **1:**74, *75*
Hearst and, **5:**611, 612
Henson and, **5:**618
Hollywood Chamber of Commerce, **2:***193*
intellectual property law, **2:**157, **5:**690-91
Lansing and, **6:**772-74
liability case portrayal, **6:***699*, 796
license, **6:**801
Mayer and, **6:**844-45
Miramax films, **7:**888-89
product placement, **1:**29, *30*
Screen Actors Guild, **9:**1169-71
Sony-Columbia Pictures deal, **7:**909, **9:**1219
soundtrack oscillators, **5:**619
subliminal advertising, **1:**27
Turner and, **10:**1340, 1341
tying (bundling), **1:**138
Walt Disney Company, **10:**1391-94
Warner Bros., **1:**64, 65
Winfrey and, **10:***1410*
Filo, David, **5:**711, **10:**1433, *1434*
finance, business, **4:493-96**
accounting and bookkeeping, **1:**23-26
accounting firm consulting, **2:**260
assets and liabilities, **1:**83-86
balance sheet, **1:**96-98
bankruptcy, **1:**99-102
breakeven point, **1:**119-20
budget, **1:**127-30
capital, **2:**173-74
capital gains, **2:**175-76
cash flow, **2:**189-90
corporations, **3:**302-3
credit, **3:**314-18

credit card, **3:**319
credit history, **3:**326-27, 328
D&B reports, **3:**336-37
debt, **3:**343-46
employee-compensation costs, **2:***239*, *240*
entrepreneur funding, **3:**427
Fortune 500 listing, **4:**520-21
human capital, **5:**625-28
income statement, **5:**647
interest, **5:**695, 696
investments, **6:**729-31
IRS and, **5:**697-700
management and, **6:**822
multinational revenues, **7:***917*
small business, **9:**1199
finance, personal, **4:497-500**
bankruptcy, **1:**99, 100
budget, **1:**127, 128-29, *130*
capital gains, **2:**175-76
cash flow, **1:**189
compound interest, **2:**247-48
credit, 316-18, **3:**315
credit card transactions, **3:**319-23
credit history, **3:**324-25
debt, **3:**316, 318, 313, 315, 316
disposable income, **3:**363-65
interest, **5:**695, 696
IRS and, **5:**697-700
mortgage, **7:**913-15
savings and investment options, **4:**491-92, **6:**729, 730, 858, 859-60, **7:**922-24, **9:**1157-60, 1241-45
standard of living, **9:**1229-30
wealth distribution, **10:**1397-98
Financial Services Modernization Act (1999), **5:**683
financial statement. *See* balance sheet
Financial Women's Association, **8:**1048
Finn, Chester E., Jr., **3:**402
Fiorina, Carly, **4:**501-2, **5:**620-21
fire insurance, **5:**682
First Amendment, **2:**210-14, *256*, 257
corporation rights, **3:**302
First Interstate Bancorp, **10:***1406*, 1407
First National Bank of Chicago, **6:**739
fiscal policy, **4:503-5**
exchange rate, **4:**461
federal budget, **4:**477-79, 503
Friedman monetarism, **4:**528
Galbraith theory, **4:**532, 533
Keynesian macroeconomics, **6:**750, 810, 811, 812
recession, **8:**1098
subsidy, **9:**1255-58
wealth distribution, **10:**1399
See also monetary policy
Fischer, Alice, **10:***1348*
Fish and Wildlife Service, **9:**1194
Fisher Body Company, **4:**551, **10:**1349-50
fishing industry, **4:506-10**
aquaculture, **1:**45, *48*, **4:**508, *510*

corporate profits, **3:***305*
forest products and, **4:**516
Native American rights, **1:**45
sustainable development, **9:***1267*
tragedy of the commons, **10:**1326, 1327-28
Flagg, Ella, **7:**936
Flagler, Henry M., **8:**1129, **9:**1231
flexible work schedules, **1:**60, **9:**1290
Flint, Charles R., **5:**632
Flint (Mich.) auto plants, **10:**1349-50
Flood, Curt, **6:**813, *815*
FLSA. *See* Fair Labor Standards Act
Follett, Ken, **7:**998
Fonda, Jane, **10:**1341
Food, Drug, and Cosmetic Act (1938), **2:**275, **4:***448*, **8:**1105, *1106*
Food and Agriculture Organization, **4:**506, 509
Food and Drug Act (1906), **2:**275
Food and Drug Administration, **2:**272-71, **4:**559, **6:**796, 790, **9:**1195
food industry
advertising, **1:**31, 139-40, **8:**1105
Archer Daniels Midland, **1:**70-71
Ben & Jerry's, **1:**106-8
consumer protection, **2:**272, 275
cultural differences, **7:***918*
discount bundling, **1:**136
franchises, **4:**523
Heinz products, **5:**613-15
Kellogg Company, **6:**745-48
labels, **2:**255-56
minimum wage, **7:**881
multinationals, **7:***918*
Newman's Own, **7:**944-46
Philip Morris, **7:**1001, 1002
processing assembly line, **1:**81
processing chain, **1:**46-47, 70-71
public relations, **8:**1066
real costs, **1:**48
retail outlets, **8:**1116
safety, **4:**440, 441, *448*, **5:**614-15
tourism and, **10:**1312
unionization, **6:***766*
See also fast-food chains; grocery industry
Food Network, **8:**1100
Food Quality Protection Act (1996), **4:***448*
Forbes (magazine), **10:**1386
richest Americans list, **6:***739*, 740
Ford, Edsel, **4:***514*
Ford, Gerald, **5:**586, **8:**1130
Ford, Henry, **3:**299, 396, **4:**511-14, 551, **6:***728*, **8:**1096
antiunionization, **10:**1350
assembly line, **1:**82, **5:**598, 658, **6:**828-29
entrepreneurship, **3:**424
as Hitler idol, **10:**1377
Fordism, **6:**829, 830

Ford Motor Company, **10**:1330, 1379
  assembly line, **1**:81, 82, **4**:512-13, **5**:598
  collective bargaining, **2**:222
  equal employment complaints, **4**:452, 453
  Ford's business philosophy, **4**:511-14
  General Motors and, **4**:550, 551, 552
  mass production, **6**:829, 830
  product liability, **8**:1045
  quality control, **10**:*1308*
  stock certificate, **6**:*728*
  sustainable design, **4**:442
  United Auto Workers, **10**:*1349*, 1350, 1352
Ford Service Department, **10**:1350
Foreign Corrupt Practices Act (1977), **2**:156, 159
foreign investment, **1**:91-92, 93, **2**:192
foreign trade. *See* international trade
forest products industry, **4**:515-18
  corporate profits, **3**:305
  Industrial Revolution, **5**:653, 656
  sustainable development, **9**:1265-66
Forestry Stewardship Council, **4**:517, **9**:1265
Forest Service, U.S., **4**:*440*, 515
Fortune (magazine), **1**:66, **2**:219, **4**:519-21, **6**:786, **7**:874, 889, **8**:1077
  "America's 25 Most Influential People," **9**:1240
  "best companies for minority employees," **6**:786
  "best companies to work for," **6**:754
Fortune 500, **4**:519-21
  list of companies, **4**:*520*
  software outsourcing, **5**:670
forward triangular merger, **6**:855
Foundations of Economic Analysis (Samuelson), **8**:1140
Fourier, Charles, **9**:1206
401(k) plan, **4**:492, 499, **8**:1072, **9**:1159-60, 1241
403(b) plan, **9**:1241
Fourteenth Amendment, **2**:210, **3**:302
Fourth Amendment, **2**:256, 257
Fox (television), **7**:889
France
  antiglobalization activist, **4**:566
  contract law, **2**:277
  Disneyland Paris, **10**:1393
  economic espionage, **5**:649, 650
  European Union, **4**:457, 458, 459, 460
  graduate business education, **6**:841
  Hudson's Bay Company, **5**:622, 623-24
  mercantilism, **6**:*849*, 850
  physiocrats, **2**:177, **9**:1203, **10**:1400

railroads, **10**:1329
tourism, **10**:1311
franchise, **4**:522-23
  Coca-Cola, **2**:217
  Disney, **10**:1393
  as distribution channel, **3**:369
  entrepreneurship and, **3**:427
  government, **7**:900, *903*
  McDonald's, **6**:755, 756-57, *846*, 847, 848
  realtor, **8**:1091, 1092, 1095
  retailing, **8**:1117, 1118
  sports, **9**:1224, 1225, 1227
  Starbucks, **9**:1235-37
Franco, Francisco, **4**:475, 476
Franklin, Benjamin, **1**:99, **5**:682, **6**:816, **8**:1074
Franklin National Bank, **1**:51-52
fraud. *See* business ethics
free agency, **6**:813, 814, *815*, **9**:1224, 1227
Freedom of Information Act (1966), **2**:268, **5**:649, **7**:927
free enterprise. *See* capitalism
free gift with purchase, **6**:776
freelancing, **4**:524-26
  as independent contractor, **10**:1302-3
  publishing industry, **8**:1077
  social security tax payment, **7**:993
free market
  balance of payments, **1**:92
  balance of trade and, **1**:94
  business cycles, **1**:149-52, **2**:178, 182
  business ethics, **2**:156, **3**:297
  capitalism and, **2**:177, 179
  cartel disfavor, **2**:188
  Chicago School, **4**:528
  economic growth, **3**:388-92
  Federal Trade Commission and, **4**:484
  former communist state conversions to, **9**:1207, 1208
  government regulation and, **8**:1103
  "invisible hand" of, **2**:156, **3**:358, 361, **5**:690, **9**:1203-4, **10**:1400
  liberalism and, **10**:1396
  macroeconomics, **6**:812
  mercantilism vs., **6**:*849*
  minimum wage vs., **7**:880-81
  monopoly and, **7**:901
  population growth and, **6**:816
  price controls and, **8**:1013, 1014, 1016
  price fixing and, **8**:1017-19
  privatization and, **8**:1032
  public goods and, **8**:1058-59, 1060
  rule of law and, **8**:1137, 1138
  self-interest and, **5**:690, **7**:869
  Smith theory of, **1**:92, **5**:705-6, **6**:851, **7**:901, **9**:1203-4, **10**:1396, 1400-1401
  supply and demand, **9**:1259-63, **10**:1365

tariff effects on, **9**:1270
"Third Way" and, **9**:1209
valuation, **10**:1360-61
See also free trade
Free Market Environmentalism (Andersen and Leal), **4**:*440*, 441-42
Freenet, **2**:284
free-rider problem, **8**:1058, 1059
Free Software Foundation, **6**:804
free speech, **2**:210-14, 256-57, **6**:768
free trade, **10**:1325, 1337
  arguments for, **1**:92, 94
  capitalism and, **2**:178, 179, 180, *181*
  common markets, **5**:707-8
  competition and, **2**:246
  European Union, **4**:457, 458, 459, 460
  GATT rounds, **4**:543, 545
  globalization and, **4**:563
  mercantilism vs., **6**:849, 850, 851, 852
  NAFTA and, **7**:956-59
  NAICS codes, **7**:928
  protectionism vs., **8**:1054
  restrictions vs., **5**:706-7, **9**:1270-71
  Smith case for, **1**:92, **5**:705-6, **9**:1203, 1204
  WTO and, **10**:1425, 1427
Freud, Sigmund, **3**:380, **8**:1067
frictional unemployment, **10**:1343-44
Friedman, Ken, *as contributor*, **2**:280-84, **10**:1320-21
Friedman, Milton, **2**:182, **3**:358, 360, **4**:527-28, **5**:661, **6**:751, 812
Friends for Life, **1**:*123*
Friends of the Earth, **9**:1258
Frigidaire Corporation, **4**:551, 552
FTC. *See* Federal Trade Commission
Fuggett, Carolyn E., **6**:793
Fujitsu, **5**:685
Full Employment Act (1946), **2**:152
Full Employment and Balanced Growth Act (1978), **7**:893
Fulton, Robert, **5**:654, *657*
fur trade, **5**:622-24
future generations, **4**:439, **9**:1264
Future of Socialism, The (Crosland), **9**:1208-9
Future Shock (Toffler), **5**:*663*, 665
futures markets, **4**:529-31, **9**:*1243*
  business cycles, **2**:*152*
  Chicago Board of Trade, **2**:197-98, 225
  commodities, **1**:46, **2**:225, 226
F. W. Woolworth, **8**:1117, **10**:1387

G

Gable, Clark, **6**:845
Galbraith, John Kenneth, **2**:267, **4**:532-33, **10**:1367
Gale, Leonard, **7**:911
gambling. *See* gaming industry
game theory, **7**:870
gaming industry, **4**:534-36, **9**:1223, 1224, **10**:1335

Gandhi, Indira, **6**:818
Gandhi, Mohandas, **2**:195
Gannett newspapers, **8**:1075
Gantt, Henry L., **6**:824
Gantt chart, **6**:824, 825
Gap, brand recognition, **1**:*118*
gap analysis, **1**:109, 111
garment industry. *See* clothing industry
Garn–St. Germain Act (1982), **8**:1094
Garrison, William Lloyd, **3**:337
Gary, Elbert H., **10**:1354
Gaskell, P., **10**:1417
gasoline, **8**:1134, **10**:1305, 1349, 1352
  diesel fuel, **8**:1087
  ethanol, **1**:45, 70
  tourism and, **10**:1312
  See also oil crisis
gasoline engine, **4**:511-12
Gates, Bill, **3**:424, **4**:537-39, 566, **5**:*651*, **6**:803, **7**:873-76, **9**:1292
  intellectual property, **5**:688, 690
Gates, Melissa French, **4**:*538*, 539
GATT. *See* General Agreement on Tariffs and Trade
GDP. *See* gross domestic product
GE. *See* General Electric
GE Capital, **4**:548
Gelb, Lawrence M. and Joan, **1**:122-23
Gelb, Richard, **1**:123
Genentech Inc., **4**:556
General Accounting Office, **5**:700
General Agreement in Trade and Services, **10**:1427
General Agreement on Tariffs and Trade, **1**:95, **2**:180, 183, **4**:540-45, 563, **5**:708, **9**:1270, **10**:1425, 1427, 1428
  signatories and year signed, **4**:541-42, *544*
General Electric, **3**:353, 376, 420, **4**:546-49, **5**:619
  downsizing, **3**:378-79, **4**:549, **10**:1404
  Edison and, **3**:400, **4**:546-48
  employment discrimination complaints, **4**:453
  first publicity department, **8**:1066
  Fortune 500 listing, **4**:521
  Honeywell merger blockage, **6**:853
  Morgan financing, **7**:905
  NYSES listing, **7**:948
  RCA and, **8**:1146-47, 1148
  research and development, **4**:548, **8**:1111
  Welch and, **4**:547, 549, **10**:1402-4
General Foods, **7**:1002
General Mills, **6**:747
General Motors, **4**:512, **550-54**, **5**:600
  bond issuance, **9**:1242
  collective bargaining, **1**:39

Electronic Data Systems, **7**:*998*, 999
employment discrimination complaints, **4**:453
global locations, **4**:564, *565*
just-in-time inventory, **6**:*742*
manufacturing system, **6**:829-30
market research, **6**:833
Nader case, **7**:925-27
Perot and, **7**:*998*, 999
stock issuance, **9**:1241
strike against (1937), **9**:1252-53
United Auto Workers, **10**:1349, 1352
General Motors Acceptance Corporation, **4**:551, 553
general strikes, **9**:1249, 1250-51, 1252
General Theory of Employment, Interest, and Money (Keynes), **6**:750, 810
genetically modified crops, **3**:375
genetic engineering, **4**:**555-59**
agriculture, **1**:48, **3**:375, **4**:555, 556-58
information technology, **5**:669
intellectual property, **5**:689, 691
Kellogg Company, **6**:748
patent, **7**:981, *985*
Geneva Rounds, **4**:540
GeoCities, **10**:1434
George H. Burr & Company, **6**:858
Gerber, Barbara, *as contributor*, **6**:788-90, **7**:939-40, 994-97, **9**:1169-71, 1211-16
German Social Democratic Party, **9**:1209
Germany
automobile industry, **6**:832, **10**:1330, 1331
Berlin Wall, **2**:228, 230, 232
cartels, **2**:187, **3**:373
European Union, **4**:457, 459
Green parties, **4**:441
historical retailing, **8**:1115, 1117
inflation, **5**:659, **7**:897
manufacturing output decline, **6**:832
neo-Nazism, **4**:476
productivity, **8**:*1039*, *1043*, 1956
quality control, **10**:1308
tourism, **10**:1311
Volkswagen, **10**:1377-79
World War I reparations, **6**:749
See also Nazism
Gerstner, Louis V., Jr., **5**:*633*, 637
Getty Oil, **10**:1307
GG&E Corporation, **3**:377
Giambi, Jason, **6**:*815*
Gibbons, Thomas, **10**:1362
Gibson, Herb, **10**:1387
Gibson, Mel, **6**:774
Gilbreth, Frank B. and Lillian M., **6**:825
Girl Scouts of America, **8**:1100
Giroux, Robert, **4**:*472*, 473
Glass, David, **10**:1389
glass ceiling, **6**:773, **10**:1415

Glass–Steagall Act (1933), **7**:941, **8**:1105, *1106*
Global 500, **4**:521
Global Climate Coalition, **9**:1267
Global Crossing Ltd., **3**:*295*
globalization, **4**:**560-67**
Asian Development Bank, **1**:78-80
business cycles, **2**:152
business ethics, **2**:158-59
capitalism, **2**:178, 180, 183
child labor, **2**:201-3
Coca-Cola, **2**:217, 219-20
consumerism, **2**:268
contract law, **2**:279
corporate social responsibility, **3**:301
cultural differences, **3**:329-32
eBay, **10**:1409
e-business-to-business, **3**:384
economic growth, **3**:391-92
environmental regulation, **4**:451
financial markets, **9**:1241, 1245
forest products, **4**:517-18
free trade, **10**:1325
GATT and, **4**:540-45, **10**:1425
IMF and, **5**:701-3
immigrant workers, **5**:643
income distribution, **5**:645-46
Information Revolution, **5**:663, 665
information technology, **5**:670-71, **9**:1282
innovation, **5**:679-80
intellectual property, **5**:689-90
international trade, **5**:709
ISO 9000 standards, **6**:732-34
Keynesian policy, **2**:180
Kinko's, **6**:754
labor unions, **1**:42
manufacturing, **6**:831-32
MBA programs, **6**:841
McDonald's, **6**:846, 847, 848
mergers and acquisitions, **6**:853, *856*
Mitsubishi, **7**:892
Morita, **7**:909
multinationals, **3**:306, **7**:916-21
OECD and, **7**:966-67
protests against, **2**:*183*, **4**:561, 566, **5**:*702*, **7**:967, **10**:*1424*, *1428*
recession and, **8**:1098
research and development, **8**:1111
retailing, **8**:1117-18
Sony, **7**:908, 909
Starbucks, **9**:1236-37
sustainable development, **9**:1265-67
tourism, **10**:1311, 1312, 1313-14
Wal-Mart stores, **10**:1389
wealth distribution, **10**:1397-99
Welch on, **10**:1403
working conditions, **10**:1417, 1420
World Bank, **10**:1421-24
Yamaha, **10**:1435, 1436

Global Knowledge, **3**:405
global warming, **1**:80, **3**:300, 418-19, **4**:438, 451
GM. *See* General Motors
GMAC, **4**:551, 553
Gnutella, **2**:284
Goizueta, Roberto, **2**:219, 220
gold, **5**:701, **8**:1087
coins, **7**:898
exchange standard, **3**:315, 316, *317*, **5**:710, **6**:749
Federal Reserve, **4**:*480*
futures, **2**:198, **4**:529
mercantilism, **1**:92, **6**:849, 850
mining of, **7**:883, **8**:*1089*
Wells Fargo shipments, **10**:*1405*, *1406*
Goldberg, Arthur J., **7**:997
Gold Rush (1849), **8**:*1142*, **10**:1362-63, 1405
Goldwyn, Samuel, **2**:277
golf, **9**:1223, 1224, 1226-27
disability decision, **1**:58
Pebble Beach ownership, **1**:92
Gompers, Samuel, **1**:38, 39, **7**:936, **9**:1274
Goodwill Games, **10**:*1339*, 1340
Goodyear, **3**:376
Gorbachev, Mikhail, **2**:*181*, 183, 232
Gordon, Jeff, **8**:*1063*
Gordy, Berry, Jr., **4**:**568-69**
Gorman, Margaret, **8**:*1068*
Gore, Al, **7**:*880*, 927
Gott, Rodney C., **5**:*599*
Gottschalk v. Benson (1972), **7**:986
government bonds. *See* Treasury bonds
government employees
equal opportunity, **8**:1084-85
strikes, **9**:1254, 1268
unionism, **8**:1070-73
government regulation. *See* regulation of business and industry
government spending. *See* federal budget; fiscal policy
Graham, Donald, **4**:572
Graham, Jennifer, **2**:275
Graham, Katharine, **4**:**570-72**
Graham, Philip, **4**:570-71
grain crops, **1**:46, 81, **2**:197, 198, *225*, 226, **4**:530
Grameen Bank, **5**:668
Grant, Johnny, **2**:*193*
grape boycott, **2**:195, 196
graphical user interface, **7**:874, **10**:1431
Grasso, Richard, **7**:*949*
Graves, Earl, **1**:114, 115
Great Atlantic and Pacific Tea Company, **8**:1115
Great Britain
airlines, **1**:124-25
capitalism, **2**:178, *180*, 182-83
cartels, **2**:188
coal energy, **3**:414
commodities markets, **2**:225
contract law, **2**:277, **6**:795

copyright law, **2**:281
Corn Laws controversy, **2**:178
debtors' prison, **1**:*99*
environmentalism, **4**:439
European Community, **4**:*457*, 458
European Union, **4**:459-60
futures trading, **2**:198
Guinness, **5**:592-94
historical retailing, **8**:1117
Hudson's Bay Company, **5**:622-24
Industrial Revolution, **2**:178, **3**:370-71, **5**:653-57, 658
Kellogg Company, **6**:746
Keynes and, **6**:749-51
liability law, **6**:799
Luddites, **9**:1278
mad-cow epidemic, **4**:*440*
Malthus and, **6**:816-18
manufacturing, **6**:828, 832
meat standards, **10**:*1324*
mercantilism, **6**:849, 850, 850-51
monopoly, **7**:902
neoliberalism, **2**:*181*, 182-83
patent law, **7**:980
Philip Morris, **7**:1000
privatization, **8**:1031, 1032
property rights, **8**:1026
public relations, **8**:1067
railroads, **10**:1329
rule of law, **8**:1138
Smith and, **9**:1202-5
stock market, **1**:54
textile workers, **10**:1417
"Third Way" socialism, **9**:*1209*
tourism, **10**:1311, 1312
unwritten constitution, **2**:253
urban conditions, **10**:1395
Great Depression, **5**:**581-85**
American Stock Exchange, **1**:55
blue jeans market, **6**:785, *786*
business cycle theory, **2**:149, 150-51
as capitalism threat, **2**:179-80, *181*
child labor effects, **2**:201
corporate responsibility, **3**:299
credit, **3**:315, 317-18
Dow Jones Industrial Average, **2**:*151*
economic effects of, **8**:1097
environmental projects, **4**:439, *440*
Fair Labor Standards Act, **4**:466-67
farm programs, **1**:47
fascism, **4**:474
Federal Reserve, **4**:480-81
General Motors, **4**:551
Harley-Davidson, **5**:598
IBM, **5**:632-33
Keynesian economics, **3**:364-65, 390, **6**:750, 810
labor unions, **1**:40, **6**:762-63
minimum wage, **7**:878, **8**:1014
National Labor Relations Act, **7**:939, 940
Perkins and, **7**:994-97

Great Depression (cont.)
  protectionism, 4:563, **10**:1428
  regulatory activity, 3:359, 5:585,
    8:1104-5, 1107
  Royal Bank of Canada,
    8:1131-32
  Samuelson theory, 8:1140, 1141
  Schumpeter theory, 9:1164
  SEC founding, 9:1172
  small business failures, 9:1197
  small business loans, 9:1200
  stock market, 7:947
  strikes, 9:1252-53
  subsidies, 9:1255-56
  Teamsters, 9:1274
  women workers, 10:1413
  See also New Deal
Great Society, 2:180, *181*, 9:1214
Green, William, 1:39, 7:940
Greenfield, Jerry, 1:106-8
greenhouse effect, 3:418, 4:438, 451
Green parties, 4:441, 7:927
Greenspan, Alan, 2:152, 4:483,
    5:586-87, 688, 6:*731*
Gribben, Donald, *as contributor,*
    3:307-10
Grimes, Annie, 6:858
Griswold v. Connecticut (1965),
    2:257
grocery industry
  bar codes, 1:103, 105
  brand names, 1:117, 118
  Consumer Price Index, 2:271
  credit-card puchases, 3:323
  food processing chains, 1:46-47
  retail chains, 8:1115, 1116
gross domestic product, **5:588-91**
  economic growth, 3:388, 392
  food processing chain, 1:47
  GDP Deflator, 2:271
  globalization effects, 4:*562*, 567
  Great Depression years, 5:583
  health care services, 5:603
  Leading Economic Index, 6:779,
    780
  macroeconomics, 6:810, 811
  manufacturing's percentage, 6:832
  price index, 2:271
  productivity, 8:1039, *1043*, 1044
  recession, 8:1096
gross national product, 8:1110-11
gross private domestic investment,
    6:*730*
Grosvenor, Peter C., *as contributor,*
    2:177-83, 227-32, 4:437-42,
    457-60, 474-76, 6:749-51,
    816-18, 838-40, 849-52,
    8:1131-32, 9:1164-65,
    1202-5, 1206-10,
    10:1365-67, 1400-1401
group life insurance, 5:633
Grove, Andrew, 5:684, 686
Groza, Petra, 2:*231*
guest workers, 10:1303
Guevara, Che, 2:230
guilds, 3:370, 6:760, 7:901
  history of, 9:1170
  marks, 10:1320
  working conditions, 10:1417

Guinness, **5:592-94**
Guinness, Arthur, 5:592, *593*
Gulf Oil, 9:1234
Gustaitis, Joseph, *as contributor,*
    1:34-37, 49-50, 2:225-26,
    3:302-6, 4:527-28, 532-33,
    5:659-62, 697-700, 6:728-31
Gutenberg, Johannes, 1:31, 2:281,
    8:1074
Gutierrez, Carlos, 6:748
Gwynne, Ursula, 7:945

H

H&R Block, 3:427
Haacke, Carl, *as contributor,*
    4:477-79, 503-5, 7:877-82,
    987-89, 10:1342-45
Hachette Filipacchi, 8:1077
Hadden, Briton, 1:*64*, 66
Haessler, Stephen, *as contributor,*
    1:81-82, 2:149-52
Hagar, Daniel B., 7:935
hair care products, 1:122-23,
    10:1380-82
Halavais, Alexander, 7:986
Halley, Edmund, 6:728
Haloid Company, 10:1429-30
Hamburger University, 6:*756*, 757,
    847
Hamilton, Alexander, 2:178,
    5:595-97, 6:852
Hammurabi's Code, 5:604
Hans Seidel Foundation, 1:80
Hantula, Richard, *as contributor,*
    1:103-5
Harberger, Arnold C., 4:528
Hardin, Garrett, 10:1326, 1328
Hargreaves, James, 5:654, *657*
Harkin, Tom, 1:57
Harkness, Stephen, 8:1129
Harley, William S., 5:598
Harley-Davidson, 1:116,
    5:598-600, 6:743
Harlow, Jean, 6:*844*
Harper (publisher), 8:1078
Harrington, Michael, 9:1210
Harris, Mildred, 6:845
Harrison, Pat, 9:*1212*
Hart–Cellar Act (1965), 5:638
Hartley, Fred A., 9:1268
Hart–Scott–Rodino Notification Act
    (1976), 7:900
Harvard Business School, 6:841,
    842, 843, 10:1408
Harvard Law School, 6:781, 791,
    792, 793, 7:925, 986
Harvard Medical School, 4:555
Harvard University, 4:538, 7:873
  electronic calculators, 2:250
  as first nonprofit entity, 7:954
  Galbraith and, 4:532, *533*
  Mark I computer, 5:633-34
  Samuelson and, 8:1140, 1141
  Schumpeter and, 9:1164, *1165*
Harvester, 10:1351, 1352
Hasbro, 9:*1280*, 10:1408
Hastings, Warren, 6:850
Hauser, Gaylord, 4:473
Hawkins, John, 6:*849*, 850
Hayek, Friedrich von, 3:358

Hayes, Rutherford, 9:1250
Haymarket Square riot, **5:601-2**
hazardous waste
    corporate social responsibility,
      3:300
    Dow Chemical, 3:375
    EPA controls, 4:444-45, *448*
    liability, 6:797, *800*
HBO (cable channel), 1:64, 66,
    10:1357-58
Headly, Jerrod, 2:*208*
Head Start, 3:393
Health Care Financing
    Administration, 9:1214
health care services industry,
    5:603-8
    Asian Development Bank, 1:79
    Bristol-Myers Squibb, 1:121-23
    business-to-business sales,
      2:170-71, *172*
    Clark venture, 2:*215*, 216
    Economic Opportunity Act,
      3:393
    employee benefits, 2:237-38,
      3:299, 9:1229, 1236
    federal budget, 4:478-79
    genetically engineered products,
      4:556, 558
    income level, 10:1397
    information technology, 5:669
    insurance, 2:237-38, 5:603,
      604-7, 619, 630, 682
    nonprofits, 7:955
    patents, 5:689
    pay inequities, 7:989
    product liability, 8:1047
    professional associations,
      8:1048
    professional licensing,
      10:1374-75, 1376
    as service economy sector,
      9:1180
    skills compensation, 2:239
    smoking risk warnings, 7:1002-4
    standard of living, 9:1229
    tourism, 10:1314-15
    unionism, 8:*1070*, *1072*
Healtheon Corp., 2:*215*, 216
health foods, 6:745-46
Heaney, Seamus, 4:473
Hearst, George, 5:609
Hearst, Phoebe, 5:609, 611
Hearst, William Randolph,
    5:609-12, 8:1075, 1081
Hearst King Features, 5:612
Hearst publishing, 8:1075, 1077,
    1079
Heavily Indebted Poor Countries
    (HIPC) Initiative, 10:1423-24
hedging, 2:225, 4:530
Hegel, G. W. F., 6:838
Heimbold, Charles, Jr., 1:*123*
Heinz, Henry J., **5:613-15**
Heinz, Noble & Company, 5:613
Heller Financial Corporation, 5:600
Henson, Brian, 5:618
Henson, Jim, **5:616-18**
Henson, W. S., 10:1331

Hentschke, Guilbert, *as contributor,*
    3:405-10
Hepburn Act (1906), 8:1103, *1106*
Hershey's, 8:*1047*
Heston, Charlton, 9:1171
Hewitt & Tuttle, 8:1128
Hewlett, William Redington, 5:619,
    620, 621
Hewlett-Packard, 3:424, **5:619-21**
    Fiorina as CEO, 4:501-2,
      5:620-21
    research and development,
      8:1111
Highway Safety Act (1970), 2:273
Hiler, Bruce, 3:423
Hill, Julia ("Butterfly"), 4:518
Hill and Knowlton, 8:1068
Hill and Wang, 4:472, 473
Hine, Lewis W., 2:*199*, 200
Hirono, Mazie, 10:*1319*
History of the Standard Oil Company
    (Tarbell), 9:*1231*, 1233, 1234
Hitachi, 5:685
Hitler, Adolf, 4:474, 475, 476,
    7:897, 10:1377-79
H. J. Heinz Company, 5:614-15
HMOs, 5:607
Hobbes, Thomas, 8:1026
Hobbs, Bradley, *as contributor,*
    4:540-45, 9:1270-71
Ho Chi Minh, 2:229
Hofer, Tracy, *as contributor,*
    8:1054-57
Hoffa, James P. (son), 9:*1274*, 1276
Hoffa, James R. (father), 6:765, 767,
    9:*1274*, 1275
Hogate, Kenneth C., 10:1384
Hollerith, Herman, 5:632, 633, *663*,
    665, 6:834
Hollywood. *See* film industry
Hollywood Chamber of Commerce,
    2:*193*
Hollywood Pictures, 10:1393
Holmes, Oliver Wendell, Sr., 5:604
Holtzbrinck (publisher), 8:1079
Home Box Office. *See* HBO
Home Depot, 3:376, 8:1100
home improvements, 8:*1100*, 1101,
    1117
Home Owners Loan Corporation,
    7:*941*
Homer Mckee Company, 1:139
Homestead (Pa.) strike, 9:1251
Homestead Act, 1:47
Homestead Works, 2:185
Honda, 4:564, 5:599, 600
Honeywell, 6:853, 7:909
Hong Kong and Shanghai Banking
    Corporation, 10:1406
Hoover, Herbert, 5:581, 583, 584,
    585
horizontal integration, 9:1189
Horsfall, William, 9:1278
hospitals. *See* health care services
    industry
hostile takeover, 6:853, 856
hostile work environment, 9:1185
Hotchner, A. E., 7:944
hotels, 10:1336, 1337

Houghton Mifflin, **8:**1078
hours of work. *See* working conditions
household finance. *See* finance, personal
House Un-American Activities Committee, **9:**1169
housework, **10:**1416
Housing Authority, **8:**1105
Houston Natural Gas, **3:**420
Houston Texans, **9:**1224-25, 1227
Howard Johnson's motels, **10:**1312
HP. *See* Hewlett-Packard
HR. *See* human resources
Hudson, Henry, **5:**622
Hudson's Bay Company, **5:**622-24
Hudson v. McMillian (1992), **2:**257
Huerta, Dolores, **1:**69
Hughes, Charles Evans, **7:**940
Hughes Aircraft Company, **4:**554
Hughes Electronics, **3:**353
Hull House, **7:**994
human capital, **5:**625-28
    building trades, **1:**131, 133, 134
    as business asset, **1:**85
    compensation, **2:**239
    as economic growth factor, **3:**389
    energy industry, **3:**417
    information technology, **5:**668
    intellectual property, **5:**687-91
    labor market, **6:**758-59
    productivity, **8:**1041, 1051
    service economy, **9:**1178-83
    technology, **9:**1280-81
human resources, **5:**629-31
    Asian Development Bank, **1:**78, 79
    job applicants, **6:**737
    resume, **8:**1113-14
    security industry, **9:**1175, 1177
    temporary workers, **10:**1301-4
human rights, **2:**201, **8:**1135, 1136
    business ethics, **2:**159
    child labor, **2:**201
    rule of law, **8:***1137*
Human Rights Watch, **2:**201, **7:**958
Hume, David, **9:**1202
Hurst, Blake, *as contributor*, **1:**43-48
Hutcheson, Francis, **9:**1202
hydroelectric power, **3:***414*, 415, **7:***903*, 941, *943*, **10:**1358, *1421*, 1424
hyperinflation, **5:**659
Hyperion Books for Children, **10:**1393
hypertext markup language (HTML), **5:**711

I

Ibbotson Associates, Inc., **2:**247
IBM, **5:**632-37
    antitrust, **8:**1104, *1106*
    bar codes, **1:**103
    bundling, **1:**138
    computers, **2:**249-51, **7:**874, **10:**1432
    employee outsourcing, **10:**1304
    history of, **5:**663, 665, 679, **6:**834
    Intel and, **5:**635, 636, 684, 685

Microsoft and, **6:**802, **7:**873-74
    Perot and, **7:**998
    research and development, **8:**1111
    Xerox lawsuit, **10:**1431-32
IBM Global Services, **5:**670
IBRD. *See* World Bank
Ibuka, Masaru, **7:**908, **9:**1217, *1218*
ICC. *See* Interstate Commerce Commission
Idei, Nobuyuki, **9:**1219
Igbi, Tai-ichi, **6:**741
I. G. Farbeindustrie, **2:**187
IKEA, **8:**1118
ILO. *See* International Labor Organization
ImClone, **9:**1240
IMF. *See* International Monetary Fund
immigration, **5:**638-43
    demographic shifts, **3:**356-57
    labor laws, **5:**630
    labor unions, **1:**42
    Lowell Mills, **6:**807, 808
    women workers, **10:**1413
    working conditions, **10:**1418, 1419-20
    See also migrant workers
Immigration Act (1990), **5:**641
Immigration and Nationality Act (1965), **5:**638
Immigration Reform and Control Act (1986), **5:**639-40, 641
implied powers doctrine, **5:**596
imports. *See* international trade
import-substitution industrialization, **6:**852
incentives
    economic growth, **3:**389
    economic mobility, **10:**1397
    environmental controls, **4:**449
    microeconomics, **7:**872
income-based valuation, **10:**1361
income distribution, **5:**644-46
    African Americans, **1:**36, **8:**1085
    aggregate of selected nations, **10:***1398*, 1399
    aggregate of U.S., **10:***1396*
    by educational attainment, **10:**1397
    farming, **1:**47-48
    globalization, **4:**561, 565-66, 567
    per capita, **4:***561*, **9:**1228, *1229*
    by race and sex, **1:***36*
    Silicon Valley, **4:**566
    taxation and, **9:**1272
    See also wealth distribution
income statement, **5:**647
    accounting, **1:**25, 26, 61
    balance sheet, **1:**97
    breakeven point, **1:**119-20
    budget, **1:***127*, 128, 129
    cash flow, **2:**189-90
    Fortune 500, **4:**521
    overhead, **7:**974-75
    payroll deductions, **7:**990-91
    small business, **9:**1198
income tax. *See* taxation
incorporation. *See* corporation

independent contractor. *See* freelancing
Independent Grocers' Alliance, **3:**369
indexed stocks, **1:**54, **2:**152
index funds, **7:**923, 924
Index of Consumer Expectations, **2:**262, **6:**779
Index of Consumer Sentiments, **2:**261-62, 263
Indian Gaming Regulatory Act (1989), **4:**535
Individual Retirement Account, **4:**499, **9:**1159, *1160*, 1167, 1241
individual rights, **2:**256-57, **8:**1026
Industrial Commission of the State of New York, **7:**994, *995*
industrial espionage, **5:**648-52
    security industry, **9:**1175, 1176, 1177
Industrial Espionage Act (1996), **5:**652
industrial property, intellectual property vs., **5:**688
Industrial Revolution, **5:**653-58
    assembly line, **1:**81-82
    capitalism, **2:**178, *181*
    child labor, **2:**199, 200
    division of labor, **3:**370-72
    Information Age shift, **5:**625, 665, 668
    interchangeable parts, **5:**657, 658, 692-93
    Lowell Mills, **6:**805-8, **10:**1417
    management concepts, **6:**819
    manufacturing industry, **6:**828
    Morgan financing, **7:**905, 906
    socialism, **9:**1206
    social security, **9:**1211-12
    steam power, **5:**655-56, *657*, 658
    strikes, **9:**1249-50
    technology, **9:**1277-78, 1281
    wealth distribution, **10:**1395-96
    women in workforce, **10:**1413
    working conditions, **10:**1417
Industrias de Chocolate Lacta S.A., **7:**1002
inelastic demand, **8:**1018
infant formula controversy, **3:**332
inflation, **5:**659-62
    business cycles, **2:**182
    consumer consumption, **4:**532
    Consumer Price Index, **2:**269, 270-71
    cost of living, **3:**311-12
    economic growth, **3:**390-91
    Federal Reserve, **4:**480, 483, 527
    fiscal policy, **4:**503-4
    income distribution, **5:**644
    interest rates, **5:**661, 695, **8:**1021
    Keynesian macroeconomics, **6:**750, 751, 810-12
    minimum wage, **7:**881, 882
    monetary policy, **2:**182, **7:**893
    money supply, **8:**1098
    money's value, **7:**897
    national debt, **3:**315
    price controls for, **8:**1013, 1016

social security benefits, **9:**1214, 1215
stagflation, **6:**751
stock returns, **9:**1159
T-bill returns, **9:**1242-43
trade policy, **1:**92
unemployment, **10:**1342-43
wealth distribution, **10:**1397, *1398*
Information Revolution, **5:**663-67, 668
    Industrial Age vs., **5:**625
    manufacturing decline, **6:**832
    wealth distribution, **10:**1397, *1398*
information technology, **5:**668-72, **9:**1277, 1279-81
    census data, **6:**834
    Cisco Systems, **2:**207-9
    Clark ventures, **2:**215-16
    copyright, **2:**281, 283
    data management, **3:**338-40
    e-mail, **3:**411-13
    entrepreneurship, **9:**1165
    Hewlett-Packard, **5:**621
    human capital, **5:**625-28
    IBM, **5:**632-37
    innovation, **5:**679
    Intel, **5:**684-86
    intellectual property, **5:**687-91
    investment pace, **5:**663
    licenses, **6:**803-4
    Nasdaq stock, **7:**931
    New York Stock Exchange, **7:**910-19
    productivity, **8:**1039-42
    publishing industry, **8:**1078
    reverse engineering, **8:**1122-23
    security systems, **9:**1175, 1176
    strategic alliances, **5:**680
    telecommuting, **9:**1290-92
    temporary workers, **10:**1301
    working conditions, **10:**1420
    Yahoo!, **10:**1433-34
    See also computer industry; Information Revolution; Internet
information theft. *See* industrial espionage
information theory, **5:**665
infrastructure, **5:**673-75
    economic growth, **3:**389
    highways, **5:**674, **10:**1312
    World Bank loans, **10:**1423
initial public offering, **5:**676-78
    Electronic Data Systems, **7:**998
    Healtheon, **2:**216
    Martha Stewart Omnimedia, **9:***1238*, *1239*, 1240
    Microsoft, **7:**874
    Nasdaq, **7:**930
    Netscape, **2:***215*, 216
    Nike, **7:**952
    Time Inc., **1:**66
    venture capital, **10:**1368, 1371, 1373
    Wal-Mart, **10:***1387*
injunction, **7:**939
injury. *See* liability

innovation, **5:**679-80
  assembly line, **1:**81-82
  Carnegie and, **2:**184, 185, 186
  competition by, **2:**242, 246
  copyright, **2:**165, *280*
  Deere products, **3:**349
  division of labor and, **3:**370, 372,
    10:1400
  eBay, **10:**1409
  e-business, **3:**382-87
  economic growth from, **3:**391
  Edison and, **3:**399-401, 424,
    4:458, 546-47
  e-mail, **3:**411-13
  entrepreneurship and, **3:**424,
    425, 426, **9:**1164
  Ford and, **4:**512-14
  genetic engineering, **4:**555-59
  Hewlett-Packard, **5:**619-20
  IBM, **5:**632, 635, 636
  Industrial Revolution, **5:**653-55,
    657
  information, **5:**663-72, 679
  Intel, **5:**680, 684
  intellectual property rights,
    5:688, 690
  interchangeable parts, **5:**692-93
  international trade and, **5:**705
  invention vs., **5:**679
  labor unions and, **6:**764
  Lands' End, **6:**770, 771
  license, **6:**801
  McDonald's, **6:**756
  microeconomics and, **7:**871
  Microsoft monopoly and, **7:**875
  monopoly vs., **9:**1285-86
  Morse and, **7:***910*, 911-12,
    9:1284
  Nike, **7:**952
  patents for, **2:**165, **5:**687,
    7:980-86, **8:**1112
  pricing, **8:**1024
  printing press, **1:**31
  product development, **8:**1036,
    1037
  productivity, **8:**1040
  profit incentive for, **8:***1050*
  research and development,
    8:1111-12
  rule of law and, **8:**1139
  Southwest Airlines, **9:**1221, 1222
  telephone, **9:**1285, 1286
  transportation, **10:**1329
  Wal-Mart, **10:**1388-90
  wealth and, **10:**1397
  Wells Fargo, **10:**1406
  Xerox, **10:**1429
  Yamaha, **10:**1435
insider information, **9:**1173, 1240
Insignia/ESG, New York, **8:**1095
Institute for Social Research, **2:**262
Institute of Electrical and Electronic
  Engineers, **8:***1048*
Institutional Party of the Revolution
  (Mexico), **2:**182, **6:**852
Insull, Samuel, **3:**421
insurance industry, **5:**681-83
  bank deposits, **7:**941, **8:**1105
  building trades, **1:**133-34

corporate benefits, **5:**619, 633
corporate profits, **3:***305*
liability premiums, **6:**796
nontradable financial securities,
  9:1157, 1158, 1159
probability theory, **6:**728
real estate industry, **8:**1092
risk management, **8:**1124, 1125,
  1126-27
intangible assets, **1:***84*, 85
  amortization of, **1:**61, 63
Intel Corporation, **3:**376, **5:**684-86,
  9:1200
  IBM and, **5:**635, 636, 684, 685
  Information Revolution and,
    5:680
  lack of competition, **2:**244
  Nasdaq trading, **5:**677, **7:**931
  strategic innovation, **5:**680, 684
  venture capital, **10:**1370
intellectual capital. *See* human
  capital
intellectual property, **5:**687-91
  business law, **2:**160, 164-65
  Coca-Cola, **2:**164, 218
  copyright, **2:**280-84
  early laws, **2:**280-81
  industrial espionage, **5:**648-52
  license, **6:**801-4
  as property right, **8:**1029
  R&D protection, **8:**1112
  trademark, **10:**1320
  WTO and, **10:**1427, 1428
  See also copyright; patent;
    trademark
interchangeable parts, **5:**657, 658,
  692-93, **6:**828
ISO 9000 standards, **6:**732-34
interest, **5:**694-96
  bond payments, **9:**1242
  compound vs. simple, **2:**247, *248*
  credit, **3:**314, 317, 318
  credit card, **1:**52, **3:**319, 320,
    4:498
  Federal Reserve rate-setting,
    4:480, 482, **5:**695, 696,
    6:731, **8:**1098
  fiscal policy and, **4:**503, 504
  gold standard and, **3:**316
  government borrowing and,
    9:1273
  inflation and, **3:**391, **5:**661, 695,
    8:1021
  investment, **6:**731
  Keynesian macroeconomics,
    6:750, 811
  Leading Economic Index, **6:**778,
    779
  monetary policy, **4:**503, **7:**893,
    894-95
  as money supply control, **5:**661
  mortgage, **7:**913, 914-15
  national debt, **3:**315
  savings and investment options,
    9:1157, 1158-59
  Swiss, **10:**1347
  taxation of, **9:**159
  as tax deduction, **3:**317

internal rate of return, **4:**493-94,
  495
Internal Revenue Service,
  5:697-700, **7:**990-93
  audit rate, **5:**700
  payroll functions, **7:**990, *991*,
    992-93
  small business information,
    9:1199
  valuation ruling, **10:**1360
Internal Revenue Service
  Restructuring and Reform Act
  (1998), **5:**699-700
International Air Transport
  Association, **10:**1335
International Bank for
  Reconstruction and
  Development. *See* World Bank
International Brotherhood of
  Teamsters. *See* Teamsters
  Union
International Business Machines
  Corp. *See* IBM
International Center for Settlement
  of Investment Disputes,
  10:*1421*, 1422
International Chamber of
  Commerce, **9:**1265
International Civil Aviation
  Organization, **10:**1313
International Conference on
  Computer Communications,
  5:*712*
International Conference on
  Straddling Fish Stocks and
  Highly Migratory Fish Stocks,
  4:509
International Data Corporation,
  5:669
International Development
  Association, **10:***1421*, 1422
International Ecotourism Society,
  10:1313-14
International Finance Corporation,
  10:*1421*, 1422
International Graduate School of
  Management (Spain), **6:**841
International Intellectual Property
  Alliance, **6:***804*
International Labor Organization,
  2:201, *202*
International Ladies Garment
  Workers Union, **1:**40
International Monetary Fund,
  2:180, *181*, **4:**563, **5:**701-3,
  6:751, **10:**1425
  information technology, **5:**671
  international trade, **5:**708-9
  recession and, **8:**1098
  subsidy and, **9:**1256-57
  World Bank and, **10:**1324, 1421,
    1423
International News Service, **5:**611,
  8:1075
International Organization for
  Standardization, **6:**732-34
International Picture Service, **5:**611
International Securities Exchange,
  1:54, 55

International Standard Book
  Number. *See* ISBN
International Standard Industrial
  Classification System, **7:**928
International Telework Association
  and Council, **9:**1290
International Time Recording
  Company, **5:**632, *633*
international trade, **5:**704-9
  agricultural controls, **1:**47, 48, 70
  balance of payments, **1:**91-92, 93
  balance of trade, **1:**91, 93-95
  bananas, **2:***204*, 206
  barriers to, 8.*1054*. *See also*
    protectionism; quotas; tariff
  brand names, **1:**117, *118*
  cartels, **2:**187
  chambers of commerce, **2:**192,
    193
  comparative advantage, **2:**233,
    235
  cultural differences, **3:**329-32
  European Union, **4:**457-60,
    5:707-8
  exchange rates, **4:**461-62
  globalization and, **4:**560-67
  Great Depression roots in, **5:**583
  IMF and, **5:**701, 703
  Industrial Revolution and, **5:**653
  inflation effects, **5:**660
  intellectual property piracy, **6:***804*
  International Monetary Fund,
    5:701, 703
  ISO 9000 standards, **6:**732-34
  mining industry, **7:**884
  Morita and, **7:**909
  multinationals and, **7:**916-21
  NAFTA and, **7:**956-59
  NAICS codes, **7:**928-29
  price controls, **8:**1016
  trademarked goods, **10:**1321
  trade policy, **10:**1322-25
  WTO and, **10:**1425-28
  See also free trade; General
    Agreement on Tariffs and
    Trade
International Trade Commission,
  5:600
International Trade Organization,
  10:1425
International Union for the
  Conservation of Nature, **1:**80
International Workers of the World,
  1:38, **9:***1209*, 1252
International Year of Ecotourism,
  10:1313
International Year of the Ocean,
  4:510
Internet, **5:**710-14
  activist contact via, **4:**566
  advertising, **1:**29, 32, *33*
  airline ticket sales, **9:***1220*, 1222
  Amazon.com, **1:**49, 49-50, 50
  anticonsumption movement,
    2:267
  AOL Time Warner, **1:**64-65, 66
  auctions via, **10:**1408-9
  banking via, **10:**1406
  bankruptcy resources, **1:**102

Better Business Bureau, 1:*113*
browser price war, 8:1025
bubble and burst, 1:50, 2:209, 3:424, 5:678, 6:759
business ethics resources, 2:157
business law, 2:165
business plan resources, 2:167
business uses, 5:670
chambers of commerce, 2:193
Cisco Systems and, 2:207-9
Clark enterprises, 2:215-16
competition, 2:246
computer manufacture, 2:252
conferencing via, 5:713
consumerism, 2:267
copyright, 2:283, 283-84
corporate responsibility, 3:299
credit, 3:318
data mining, 3:340
day trading, 3:341-42
defense industry use, 3:352
demand-driven economy and, 9:1281
discount brokers, 9:1245
eBay, 10:1408-9
e-business, 3:382-87, 387, 420, 421
e-learning, 3:406, 408, 409
e-mail, 3:411-13
energy deals, 3:418, 421
Enron and, 3:420, 421, 422
entrepreneurship, 3:424, 427, 428
feature film distribution, 7:788, 889
Fortune 500 companies, 4:521
gaming via, 9:1219
globalization and, 4:564
government regulation, 2:246
health care system links, 2:216
high-speed access, 9:1288
households with access to, 5:668, *672, 713, 714*
identity theft, 3:328
intellectual property law, 2:165, 5:690
internship, 5:716
investment sites, 6:731
job search resources, 5:627, 6:738
just-in-time concept, 6:744
labor market and, 6:759
Lands' End sales market, 6:770-71
laws and statutes, 8:1137
license agreements, 6:803
market research, 6:836
Microsoft and, 7:874, 875-76, 902
mortgage applications, 7:915
Nasdaq stock, 7:931-92
Netscape Navigator, 2:215-16
newspapers online, 8:1075-76, 10:*1383*, 1386
number of users, 5:663, 670
patent sites, 7:980
payments online, 7:898
privacy concerns, 5:671

productivity and, 8:1039, 1040, 1043
raw materials information sites, 8:1089
real estate transactions via, 8:1092
research and development, 8:1111
retail sales, 2:267, 8:1116-17, *1119*
reverse engineering, 8:1122-23
savings and investments sites, 9:1160
SEC and, 9:1174
security industry and, 9:1176
sex tourism and, 10:1315
software patents and, 7:986
Sony wireless data-transmission, 9:1219
Starbucks and, 9:1237
start-up firms, 3:424
stock trading online, 9:*1166*, 1167, 1168
stock values, 3:341
telecommunications and, 9:1286, 1287, 1288
telecommuting and, 9:1291, *1292*
ticket service online, 10:1316
trade association uses, 10:1318-19
venture capital, 3:346, 10:1370
wealth and, 10:1397-98
Whitman and, 10:1408-9
World Wide Web development, 5:*663*, 665, 711, 712
World Wide Web inventor, 8:1112
Yahoo!, 5:711, 10:1433-34
Internet2, 5:712, 714
internship, 5:715-16
interstate commerce, 2:200, 7:904, 940, 8:1103-4, 1105
trucking deregulation, 3:358, 8:1109
Interstate Commerce Commission, 1:88, 3:359, 8:1103, 1105, 1109, 10:1330
inventory, 6:**725-27**, 8:1116, 1118
Amazon.com, 1:49
as asset or liability, 1:83, 84, *96, 97*
bar codes, 1:103
debt and, 3:343, 344, 346
investment and, 6:729, 730, 731
just-in-time, 6:726-27, 741-44, 831
Leading Economic Index and, 6:778
price floor, 8:1014
Wal-Mart computerized, 10:*1387*, 1388-89
investment, 6:**728-31**
breakeven point, 1:119-20
business cycles, 2:149, 151, 152
business finance, 4:493-96
business plan, 2:166-69
capital, 2:173-74
capital gains, 2:173-74

cash flow indications, 2:190
compound interest, 2:247-48
debt, 3:343, 4:498
Dow Jones Average, 3:376-77
economic growth, 3:389
Enron problems, 3:422, 423
financial management, 4:493-96
fiscal policy and, 4:503
Fortune 500 listing, 4:520-21
futures market, 4:529-31
globalization, 4:564
Great Depression effects, 5:581-83
in human capital, 5:627, 628
initial public offering, 5:676-78
Leading Economic Index, 6:778, 780
mutual funds, 7:922-24
Nasdaq, 7:930-32
New York Stock Exchange, 7:947-49
in private infrastructure, 5:673
SEC and, 9:1172-74
Silicon Valley, 3:424
in small business, 9:1200
socially responsible, 3:301
trade deficit and, 1:91-92, 93
valuation and, 10:1360-61
venture capital, 10:1368-73
World Bank, 10:*1421*, 1422
See also savings and investment options; stocks and bonds
investment banking, 3:296-97, 314, 316, 7:906-7, 941, 9:1243-44
initial public offering, 5:677
Merrill and, 6:859
Morgan and, 7:906-7
separation of, 8:1105
Investment Company Institute, 7:922
"invisible hand" metaphor, 2:156, 3:358, 361, 5:690, 9:1203-4, 10:1400
involuntary servitude, 1:99
IP addresses, 5:710, 711
IPO. *See* initial public offering
IRA. *See* Individual Retirement Account
iron industry, 2:186, 5:653, 655, 656, 658, 8:1087
IRS. *See* Internal Revenue Service
ISO 9000, 6:732-34, 10:1318
benchmarking, 1:110-11
Isutani, Minoru, 1:92
ITT Corp., 6:788, 790
Iwasaki Hisaya, 7:891
Iwasaki Koyata, 7:891
Iwasaki Yanosuke, 7:891
Iwasaki Yataro, 7:890-91
Iwerks, Ub, 10:1391

J

Jackson, Andrew, 10:1417
Jackson, Bo, 7:952
Jackson, Jesse, 1:37
Jackson, Michael, 4:569
Jackson, Shirley, 4:473
Jackson, Thomas Penfield, 7:875
Jaffe, Stanley, 6:773, 774
Jaffe-Lansing Productions, 6:773-74

James, Etta, 4:568
JAN (Japanese Article Numbering) system, 1:104
Japan
Asian Development Bank, 1:78
automobile industry, 4:554, 564, 5:706, 6:741, 830-31, 8:*1040*, 10:1331
automobile voluntary export restraints, 10:*1322*, 1323
balance of trade, 5:708
capitalist model, 2:183
commodity exchanges, 2:223
competitive business practices, 7:951
cultural difference, 3:329
high-technology comparative advantage, 2:233
immigrant workers in, 5:643
industrial espionage, 5:649, 651
international retailers, 8:1118
investments in U.S., 1:92
just-in-time delivery, 6:741, 831
manufacturing, 6:832
memory chips, 5:685-86
Microsoft sales subsidiary, 7:873, 875
Mitsubishi, 7:890-92
Morita ventures, 7:908-9
motorcycles, 5:599, *600*
multinationals, 7:918, 921
OECD and, 7:967
pricing, 8:1050
Sony, 9:1217-19
Starbucks, 9:1237
television set price fixing, 8:1019
Tokyo Disneyland, 10:1393
total quality management, 6:830-31, 10:1308, 1309, 1310
Yamaha, 10:1435-36
Japanese Musical Instrument Company, 10:1435
Japanization, 6:831
Japan That Can Say No, A (Morita), 7:909
Java (programming language), 5:670, 711
Jay, John, 5:595, 596
Jaycees, 2:192-93
Jefferson, Thomas, 5:597, 692-93, 698, 6:851, 7:980
Jennings, O. B., 8:1129
Jet (magazine), 6:*739*, 740
jet airplane, 4:548, 10:1332, 1333, 1335
Jim Henson Company, 5:617-18
JIT. *See* just-in-time inventory
Job Accommodation Network, 1:60
Job Corps, 3:394, 395
job loss. *See* downsizing; unemployment
job market. *See* labor market
Jobs, Steve, 3:426, 8:*1023*, 10:1431
job search, 6:735-38
human capital and, 5:626-27
human resources and, 5:629, *631*
internship, 5:715-16
resume, 8:1113-14

jobs program, 3:365, 6:750
Joel Popkin and Company, 9:1196
John M. Bradstreet Company, 3:336
Johns Hopkins University, 4:555
Johnson, Earvin ("Magic"), 6:857
Johnson, Edward C., II, 4:491, 492
Johnson, Edward C., III ("Ned"),
  4:491
Johnson, John H., 6:739-40,
  8:1077
Johnson, Lyndon, 7:927, 8:1141
  affirmative action, 1:35
  civil rights bill, 2:211, 212
  Economic Opportunity Act,
    3:394
  Great Society, 2:180, 181
  labor unions, 1:39
  Medicare, 9:1210, 1214
Johnson, Robert, 10:1351
Johnson & Johnson, 2:214, 3:300
Johnson Publishing Company,
  6:739, 740
joint-stock banks, 10:1346
joint-stock companies, 3:302
Jolly Green Giant Company, 1:139
Jolson, Al, 1:65
Jones, Eddie, 10:1383
Jones, Edward T., 3:377
Jones Lang LaSalle, Inc., 8:1095
Jordan, Angelica, 3:425
Jordan, Michael, 1:117, 118, 7:950,
  952
journalism. See publishing industry
Joyner, Russ, 2:193
judiciary, 9:1204, 10:1400
  independence of, 8:1138
Jungle, The (Sinclair), 2:267
Junior Chamber of Commerce,
  2:192-93
Juran, Joseph M., 10:1309
Justice Department, U.S., 3:360,
  422, 5:633, 7:874, 875, 902
  consumer protection, 2:272
  merger and acquisition approval,
    6:853, 854, 8:1106
  Teamsters and, 9:1274, 1276
  See also antitrust
just-in-time inventory, 4:565,
  6:726-27, 741-44, 831
  Wal-Mart, 6:744, 9:1280,
    10:1389
JVC (Japan Victor Company),
  9:1218

K

Kahn, Alfred, 3:358, 359, 8:1106,
  1108-9
Kahn, Bob, 3:411
Kaneshige, Tom, 3:384
Kant, Immanuel, 2:153-54, 9:1202
Kaplan Learning Center, 3:406, 407
Kapur, Sumit, 3:384
Kashi Company, 6:746, 748
Katzenberg, Jeffrey, 10:1394
Kawakami, Gen-ichi, 10:1435
Kawasaki, 5:599
Kay, John, 5:654, 657
Kdf-Wagen, 10:1377
KDKA radio, 8:1147
Kearny, Stephen Watts, 8:1144

Keating–Owen Act (1916), 2:200
Keckhaver, John, as contributor,
  2:272-75, 4:468-71, 484-87
Keebler, 6:746, 748
Kefauver–Harris bill, 2:273
keiretsu system, 7:890, 891
Keith, Minor, 2:204
Kelleher, Hugh, 9:1220, 1221
Keller, Herb, 2:166
Kellogg, John Harvey, 6:745, 746
Kellogg, Will Keith, 6:745, 746-47
Kellogg Company, 6:745-48
Kelly, Gene, 9:1169
Kelly, M. Clyde, 10:1333
Kelly Act (1925), 10:1333
Kelsey, Frances, 2:273
Kennedy, Edward, 9:1257
Kennedy, John F., 2:210-11, 230,
  4:532, 533, 8:1141, 9:1195,
  1210
  affirmative action, 1:34, 35
  civil rights, 8:1086
Kennedy, Robert F., 6:676, 9:1275
Kennedy, Ted, 3:358
Kennedy Round, 4:540, 543
Kentucky Fried Chicken, 8:1037
Keppler, Joseph, 1:67
Kertzman, Mitchell, 7:874
Keynes, John Maynard, 6:749-51
  business cycle theory, 2:149, 151
  Chicago School vs., 4:528
  economic model, 2:180, 182,
    3:364-65, 390
  key ideas of, 6:750
  macroeconomics, 6:809, 810,
    812, 812
  recession theory, 8:1096
  Samuelson economics and,
    8:1140, 1141
Keynes, John Neville, 6:749
Keys, Alicia, 6:725
Keystone Bridge Company, 2:185
Khrushchev, Nikita, 2:232
kibbutz movement, 9:1207
kickbacks, 2:244, 245
Kiernan News Agency, 10:1383
Kilgore, Barney, 10:1384-85
KinderCare Learning Centers, 3:405
King, Coretta Scott, 2:196
King, John, 1:125, 126
King, Martin Luther, Jr., 1:40,
  2:210, 212, 8:1083, 1086
King, Martin Luther, III, 1:37
King, Stephen, 8:1078
King Features syndicate, 5:611
Kinko's, 6:752-54
Kinney National, 1:64, 65
Kirkland, Lane, 1:42
Kiwanis, 3:299
Kleenex, 1:116, 8:1037
Klein, Naomi, 4:566
Kleiner Perkins Caulfield & Byers,
  10:1373
Kleinrock, Leonard, 5:710
Kmart, 3:364, 9:1240, 10:1387
Knight, Frank, 4:528
Knight, Phil, 7:950-52
"knight" metaphors, 6:853
Knights of Labor, 1:38, 5:601, 602

knowledge workers. See human
  capital
Knudsen, William S., 4:552
Kodak, 1:117
Kohl, Helmut, 4:459
Kondratiev, N. D., 9:1164
Korb, Andréa, and David Korb, as
  contributors, 1:23-26, 61-63,
  96-98, 109-11, 119-20,
  127-30, 5:647, 694-96,
  7:913-15, 974-75
Kornei, Otto, 10:1429
Kouliavtsev, Mikhail, as contributor,
  2:187-88, 5:598-600,
  7:899-904, 968-70,
  8:1017-20
Kovacevich, Dick, 10:1407
Kozlowski, L. Dennis, 2:158
KPMG International, 2:259-60
Kraft Foods, 7:1000, 1002, 1004,
  8:1047
Kraig, Beth, as contributor, 2:194-96,
  5:601-2, 9:1194-95
Krause, Brad, 6:752
Krispy Kreme Doughnuts, 7:949
Kroc, Ray, 6:755-57, 846, 847-48
Kropotkin, Pyotr, 4:441
Krugman, Paul, 8:1039
K12 (online education), 3:408, 409
Kumar, Anil, as contributor,
  3:338-40, 5:668-72
Kurata, Teruo, 9:1217
Kuwait, 4:438, 6:848, 7:968, 969,
  970

L

labeling, 2:272
Labor Department, U.S.
  affirmative action, 1:34
  Consumer Price Index, 2:269
  founding of, 10:1418, 1420
  minimum wage, 7:877
  Nader and, 7:925
  OSHA and, 7:960, 961
  pay equity, 7:987
  Perkins as secretary, 7:994, 995,
    996, 997
  small businesses, 9:1199
  workplace diversity, 1:37
  See also Equal Employment
    Opportunity Commission
Labor Hall of Fame, 7:997
Labor–Management Relations Act
  (1947). See Taft–Hartley Act
Labor–Management Reporting and
  Disclosure Act (1959). See
  Landrum–Griffin Act
labor market, 6:758-59
  business ethics, 2:159
  Consumer Confidence Index,
    2:263
  demographics, 3:357
  disabled people, 1:56-60
  economic growth, 3:392, 8:1096
  EEOC and, 4:452-53
  entrepreneurship, 3:425-26, 427
  ethnicity and, 3:357
  Fair Labor Standards Act,
    4:466-67
  farm goods processing, 1:47

  freelancing, 4:524-26
  globalization effects, 4:564-66
  immigrant workers, 5:639-43
  job search, 6:736
  knowledge workers, 5:625, 668
  labor unions and, 6:762, 763,
    766
  macroeconomics, 6:810
  manufacturing jobs, 6:832
  microeconomics, 7:869
  minimum wage, 8:1014-15
  monopsonistic, 6:762
  NAFTA effects, 7:959
  pay equity, 7:987-89
  population growth and, 6:816
  productivity, 8:1039-44, 1051
  protectionism and, 8:1054-56,
    1057
  public sector unionism and,
    8:1070-71
  Say's Law, 6:750
  service economy, 9:1178-80
  temporary workers, 10:1301-4
  unemployment, 10:1342-45
  union membership, 6:763, 766
  women and, 10:1413-16, 1415
labor union, 6:760-66
  AFL-CIO, 1:38-42
  Amazon.com and, 1:50
  arbitration, 1:40, 69
  automobile industry, 4:550, 552,
    553, 10:1349-52
  building trades, 1:133-35
  capitalism and, 2:178, 180
  Chavez and, 2:194, 195-96
  child labor and, 2:200
  collective bargaining, 2:221-24
  division of labor and, 3:371-72
  Guatemalan banana workers,
    2:205
  Haymarket Square riot, 5:601-2
  institutionalist inflation theory,
    5:661
  International Workers of the
    World, 9:1209, 1210
  legislation, 7:939-40, 943
  legislative curbs, 6:767-68,
    9:1268-69, 1275
  Lowell Mills, 6:807
  major league baseball, 6:813-15,
    9:1227
  minimum wage and, 7:877, 878,
    943
  multinationals and, 7:719
  NAFTA and, 7:958, 959
  National Education Association,
    7:935-38
  New Deal measures, 7:943,
    8:1105
  open vs. closed shop, 9:1269
  OSHA and, 7:963
  outsourcing objections, 7:973
  Perkins and, 7:994
  public sector, 8:1070-73
  Randolph and, 8:1083-86
  Screen Actors Guild, 9:1169-71
  social democracy and, 9:1208
  tariffs and, 1:95
  Teamsters, 9:1274-76

temporary workers, **10**:1304
wealth distribution, **10**:1397, *1398*
women workers, **1**:38, 39, **10**:1413, 1414
working conditions and, **10**:1420
See also strikes
Labour Party (Britain), **9**:1209
Lafayette, marquis de, **7**:910
La Follette Seaman's Act (1915), **10**:1418
Lagging Index, **6**:778, 779
laissez-faire policy. *See* free market
Lake Shore Railroad, **10**:1364
Lambert, Laura, *as contributor*, **3**:333-35, 402-4, **8**:1090-95, **10**:1311-16, 1405-7, 1417-20
LAN (local area network), **10**:1430-31
Landauer, Thomas, **5**:665
Landis, James, **8**:1105, 1107
land ownership, **1**:61, 85, 96, **8**:1027-29, **9**:1277
Landrum-Griffin Act (1959), **6**:767-68, **9**:1269, 1275
Lands' End, **6**:769-71
Langbo, Arnold, **6**:748
Langmuir, Irving, **4**:548, **8**:1110
Lansing, Sherry, **6**:772-74
laptops, **5**:648-49
laser printer, **10**:1431, 1432
Lasker, Albert, **1**:31, 32
Lauder, Estée, **6**:775-77
Lauter, Joe, **6**:775, 776
Lauter, Leonard, **6**:775
Lauter, Ronald, **6**:776
Lavagna, Roberto, **5**:701
Lavin, Angeline, *as contributor*, **2**:197-98, 247-48, **3**:376-77, **7**:922-24, 930-32, 947-49, **9**:1157-60, 1241-45
Lavin, Marilyn, *as contributor*, **3**:366-69, **6**:841-43, **7**:928-29, 941-43, **8**:1103-9, 1115-20
law schools, **6**:781, 783
Lay, Kenneth L., **3**:420, 421, 422
layoffs. *See* downsizing; unemployment
Leading Economic Index, **2**:262, **5**:696, **6**:778-80
macroeconomics and, **6**:810, 811
League for Non-Violent Civil Disobedience Against Military Segregation, **8**:1085
Leal, Donald R., **4**:*440*, 441-42
Learning Tree, **3**:405
Leavitt and Sons, **6**:780
Lee (jeans company), **6**:786
Lee, Ang, **9**:*1219*
Lee, Ivy, **8**:1066, 1068
Leeson, Nicholas, **4**:531
legal aid societies, **6**:784
legal services, **6**:781-84
arbitration/mediation vs., **1**:68-69
careers in, **6**:783
contract law, **2**:276-79, **6**:794-95
frivolous liability suits, **8**:1047

income level, **10**:1397
lawyer training, **8**:1138
Lewis and, **6**:791-92
liability cases, **6**:794-800
licenses and, **6**:802-3
partnership, **7**:976
pay inequities, **7**:989
professional associations, **8**:1048
professional licensing, **10**:1374-75
real estate industry, **8**:1092
suits against tobacco companies, **7**:1001, 1002-4
tort law, **2**:161-62, **6**:795-99, **8**:1045
Leibniz, Gottfried, **5**:663
leisure class, **10**:1365-66
leisure industry. *See* recreation industry
"lemon laws," **2**:272
lender of last resort, **4**:480, 481
Lender's Bagels, **6**:748
Lend Lease Real Estate Investment Management, Inc., **8**:1095
Lenin, Vladimir, **2**:179, 227-28, *231, 232,* **9**:*1207*
Leo Burnett Agency, **1**:139-40, **7**:1003
Leo Burnett Worldwide, **1**:140
Leonardo da Vinci, **9**:1191, **10**:1331
Lerner, Sandy, **2**:207
Leslie, Frank, **10**:*1395*
Lessig, Lawrence, **2**:165, 284, **7**:986
leveraged buyout, **1**:77, **9**:1167
Levi, Carlo, **4**:473
Levin, Gerald, **1**:65, 66
Levine, Josh, **3**:342
Levi Strauss & Co., **6**:785-87
Levitt, Abe, **6**:788
Levitt, Alfred, **6**:788
Levitt, Arthur, Jr., **2**:260
Levitt, William, **6**:788-90
Levitt and Sons, **6**:788-90
Levittowns, **6**:788-90
Lewis, David J., **9**:*1212*
Lewis, John L., **1**:39, 40
Lewis, Loida, **6**:793
Lewis, Michael, **2**:215
Lewis, Reginald, **6**:791-93
liabilities. *See* assets and liabilities
liability, **6**:794-800
contract law, **2**:276-79
corporate protections from, **3**:302
credit, **3**:314
risk management, **8**:1124-25
strict principles, **8**:1045
tort law, **2**:161-62
See also product liability
liberal environmentalism, **4**:441, 442
liberalism
free-trade policy, **5**:705-6
mercantilism vs., **6**:*849,* 851, 852, **9**:1203, 1204
Smith's *Wealth of Nations*, **10**:1400-1401
wealth distribution and, **10**:1396

Liberate Technologie, **7**:874
libertarianism, **9**:1206-7
Liberty Live and Liberty Insurance Services, **8**:1132
libraries
Carnegie, **2**:*185,* 186
disability accessibility, **1**:58, *60*
unionism, **8**:*1070*
Library of Congress, **5**:687
license, **6**:801-4
as competition entry barrier, **7**:900
contract law, **2**:279
copyright, **2**:280, 281, 282
Disney characters, **10**:1391-92
import procedures, **4**:543
Intel 8088 chip, **5**:635, 636
Internet film downloading, **7**:889
Microsoft, **5**:635, 636, **7**:874
negative externality control, **4**:465
of patents, **8**:1112
product development, **8**:1036
by Small Business Administration, **9**:1201
Sony, **9**:1218
sports merchandise, **9**:1223
vocational, **10**:1374-76
Licklider, J. C. R., **5**:*712*
Liebeck, Stella, **2**:*161,* **8**:1046
life-cycle marketing, **6**:837
life insurance, **5**:633, 682, 683
life tables, **6**:728
lifestyle. *See* standard of living
Lily Tulip Cup Company, **6**:755-56
Limited, The, **1**:53
limited partnership, **3**:346, **7**:979, **10**:1369
Limits to Growth (report), **4**:439, **6**:818, **8**:1264
Lincoln, Abraham, **5**:698, **6**:781, **7**:912
Lingle, Linda, **10**:*1319*
Lipton, Thomas, **8**:1117
liquid assets, **1**:83-84
liquidity, **5**:676, **10**:1370-71, 1373
ratios, **3**:*343,* 344
liquidity crisis, **2**:189-90
List, Friedrich, **2**:178, **6**:852
Lister, Joseph, **5**:605
literary copyright, **2**:280, 281-82, 283
Literary Guild, **8**:1078
Little, Brown (publisher), **1**:64, **8**:1078
Livengood, Scott, **7**:*949*
Liverpool and Manchester Railway, **5**:654, *657*
livestock, **1**:43-46
futures market, **2**:225
meatpacking industry, **1**:81
trade policy, **10**:1323-24
Livingston, Fargo & Company, **1**:51, **10**:1405
Lloyd, Henry Demerest, **9**:1233
Lloyd, William Forster, **10**:1328
Lloyd George, David, **6**:749
Lloyd's of London, **6**:728, **8**:*1125,* **10**:1409

loans. *See* credit; interest
Locke, John, **8**:1026, **9**:1203
Lockheed Martin, **2**:214, **3**:352, 353
Lockheed Missile and Space, **3**:351
logo
Coca-Cola, **2**:218
franchise, **8**:1117
Nike, **7**:952
Shell Oil, **8**:1133, 1134
Starbucks, **9**:1236
Wells Fargo, **10**:1497
London International Futures and Options Exchange, **2**:198
London Metal Exchange, **2**:225
Long, David, *as contributor*, **1**:91-92, 93-95, **3**:293-97, 347-49, 363-65, 370-72, 388-92, 424-28, **4**:461-62, 529-31, **5**:644-46, 704-9, **7**:905-7, 950-53, **8**:1050-53, 1096-98, **9**:1220-22, **10**:1395-99
Long Island Airways, **10**:1333
long-range planning, **9**:1246-47
long-term capital gains, **2**:176
Long Term Capital Management fund, **10**:1347
López Arellano, Osvaldo, **2**:206
Lotus 1-2-3, **3**:339
Loudon, John Hugo, **8**:1134-35
Louis XIV, king of France, **6**:*849,* 850
Louis B. Mayer Company, **6**:845
Love Canal (N.Y.), **3**:300, **4**:444
Lowell, Francis Cabot, **5**:657, **6**:805, 807
Lowell, Robert, **4**:473
Lowell Mills, **6**:805-8, **10**:1417
Lowe's chain, **8**:1100
Lucas, George, **1**:75
Lucas v. South Carolina Coastal Commission (1992), **2**:256
Luce, Henry Robinson, **1**:64, 66
Lucent Technologies, **1**:89, 90, **4**:501, *502,* **5**:670
Luddites, **9**:1278
Ludlow massacre, **8**:1066
lumbering. *See* forest products industry
luxury goods
pricing, **8**:*1024,* 1025
standard of living, **9**:1229
Veblen's theory, **10**:1366
Lynch, Edmund C., **6**:858
Lynch, Peter, **4**:491-92

M
Ma, Yo-Yo, **9**:1219
Maastricht Treaty (1991), **4**:*457,* 459, 460
Ma Bell. *See* AT&T
"macaroni defense" metaphor, **6**:853
MacDonald, Rich, *as contributor*, **4**:480-83, **7**:893-95, 896-98
Machado, Gerado, **10**:1333
machinery
as child labor replacement, **2**:201
division of labor, **3**:370-71
Industrial Revolution, **6**:828
interchangeable parts, **5**:692-93

machinery (cont.)
   knowledge vs., 5:625
   Lowell Mills, 6:807-8
   manufacturing, 6:828
   patents, 7:980
Macintosh computer, 5:636, 6:753, 7:874-75, 10:1431
macroeconomics, 6:809-12
   business cycles, 2:149-51
   Keynesian, 2:180, 6:712, 749, 750-51, 809, 810
   microeconomics vs., 7:869
   Samuelson and, 8:1141
   schools of, 6:812
Macy's. See R. H. Macy's
Madame C. J. Walker Hair Culturists Union, 10:1381
Madame C. J. Walker Manufacturing Company, 10:1380-82
Madison, James, 5:595, 596
Madonna, 1:118
Magazine Publishers of America, 8:1076
Magellan Fund, 4:491-92
Maggioni Canning Company, 2:199
Magloff, Lisa, as contributor, 1:51-53, 121-23, 2:204-6, 207-9, 217-20, 3:341-42, 373-75, 411-13, 4:454-56, 491-92, 519-21, 522-23, 546-49, 550-54, 5:609-12, 619-21, 632-37, 648-62, 6:745-48, 752-54, 755-57, 785-87, 846-48, 858-60, 7:873-76, 888-89, 908-9, 944-46, 1001-4, 8:1083-86, 1128-30, 9:1191-93, 1217-19, 1231-34, 1235-37, 10:1305-7, 1333-35, 1346-48, 1349-52, 1377-79, 1380-82, 1387-90, 1391-94, 1413-16, 1429-32, 1433-34, 1435-36
Magna Carta (1215), 7:999-1000
mail-order sales, 2:265, 6:837, 8:1078, 1116
   Lands' End, 6:769-71
mainframe computers, 2:250-51, 5:632-34
Main Line Pictures, 2:277-78, 279
Main Line Pictures v. Basinger (1993), 2:277-78, 279
Major, John, 4:460
Major League Baseball, 9:1224
Major League Baseball Players Association, 6:813-15, 9:1227
Major League Soccer, 9:1224, 1225
Mallet, Pierre and Paul, 8:1143
Mall of America, 2:266, 267
malls. See shopping malls
Malthus, Thomas Robert, 4:437, 440, 6:816-18
managed economy, 1.92, 4.474. See also communism
management, 6:819-22
   accounting reports, 1:25
   affirmative action, 1:36
   agricultural industry, 1:45

Archer Daniels Midland skills, 1:70
assembly line, 1:82
benchmarking, 1:110-11
budget control, 1:128, 130
business ethics, 3:296-97
business finance, 4:493-96
collective bargaining, 2:221-24
consulting, 2:258-60
corporate governance, 3:293-97
division of labor structure, 3:372
downsizing, 3:378-79
entrepreneurship, 3:426
franchise format, 4:522-23
General Electric, 10:1403
General Motors, 4:551
government employment, 8:1071
Hewlett-Packard style, 5:619-20
human capital, 5:626, 627, 628, 9:1281
innovation, 5:679
ISO 9000 standard, 1:110-11
just-in-time approach, 6:741-42, 743
labor relations, 6:763-64, 9:1253
law firms, 6:782
MBA degree, 6:841-43
ownership relations, 3:294-95
performance reviews by, 2:240-41
principles of, 6:824
quality control, 10:1308-10
sexual harassment by, 9:1185-86
top-down structure, 6:829-30
Management by Walking Around (MBWA), 5:619
management consulting, 2:258-60
management theory, 6:819, 820, 823-27
   Drucker and, 3:380-81
   small business, 9:1197
   Total Quality Management, 10:1308-10
Mandela, Nelson, 10:1412
manufacturers' agents, 3:367, 8:1119
manufacturing industry, 6:828-32
   assembly line, 1:81-82, 4:512, 513
   benchmarking, 1:109
   brand names, 1:118
   business cycles, 2:149
   business ethics, 2:159
   business-to-business sales, 2:169-70, 172
   capital gains, 2:175, 176
   careers in, 6:832
   child labor, 2:200, 201
   consumerism and, 2:265
   consumer safety standards, 2:275
   corporate profits, 3:305
   defense contracts, 3:352-53
   division of labor, 3:370-72, 10:1400
   economic growth's social costs, 3:391-92
   economies of scale, 3:396, 397-98

environmentalism, 3:391, 4:437, 438, 440, 441, 442
environmental regulations, 4:444-45, 448
ergonomics, 4:454
first modern factory, 5:655
franchises, 4:522
globalization effects, 4:564-65, 10:1397, 1398
Great Depression effects, 5:582-83
income distribution, 5:644, 645
Industrial Revolution, 5:653-58, 9:1277-78
interchangeable parts, 5:692-93
inventory, 6:725
ISO 9000 standards, 6:732, 733
just-in-time approach, 6:741-44
knowledge workers, 5:625
labor unions, 1:40, 42, 6:760-64, 10:1452
as Leading Economic Index component, 6:778-79
Lowell Mills, 805-8, 6:805-8
mass production, 4:513
multinationals, 7:917-18, 919
overhead, 7:974, 975
patents, 7:980-81
product development, 8:1034-38
raw materials, 8:1087-89
service economy and, 9:1178, 1181-82, 1183
small business component, 9:1196
strikes, 9:1250, 1251
supply and demand, 9:1260-61
sustainable design, 4:442
sustainable development, 9:1266-67
Total Quality Management, 10:1308
value of goods by state, 6:829
wholesale operations, 8:1118
women workers, 10:1413
working conditions, 4:466, 10:1417, 1418
See also automobile industry; textile industry
Manufacturing.Net, 386
Mao Zedong, 2:228, 229, 9:1208, 1209
maquiladoras, 10:1420
Marathon Oil Company, 10:1353, 1355
March on Washington (1963), 1:40, 8:1083, 1086
Marcuse, Herbert, 9:1165
marginal cost, 9:1260-61
marginal propensity to consume, 3:364, 365
margin buying, 3:341, 4:529, 5:581-82
Maritime Commission, 8:1105
marketability discounts, 10:1361
market basket, 2:269, 3:312, 6:810
market economy. See capitalism; free market
market forces. See supply and demand

marketing. See advertising, business practice; market research; public relations and marketing, business practice
marketing channels. See distribution channels
market research, 6:833-37
   ad campaign, 1:27, 28, 32
   on cultural differences, 3:330-31
   on customer service, 3:334
   demographics, 3:356
   e-business, 3:383
   pricing and, 8:1024
   product development, 8:1034
market segments, 8:1024-25
market share, 1:27
market value. See valuation
Mark I computer, 2:250, 5:633-34
Markowitz, Harry, 6:729
Marlboro Man, 1:139, 7:1003
Marsh, George Perkins, 4:439, 440
Marshall, Alfred, 6:749
Marshall, Colin, 1:124, 126
Marshall, John, 3:302, 304
Marshall Field's, 2:264, 265, 3:333, 8:1115
Marsh's supermarket (Troy, Ohio), 1:103
Martha Stewart Living (magazine), 9:1238, 1240
Martha Stewart Omnimedia, 9:1238-40
Martin, Casey, 1:58
Martin, William McChesney, 4:483
Martin Marietta, 3:353
Martinsburg (W. Va.) strike, 9:1250
Marx, Karl, 2:227, 228, 232, 6:838-40, 8:1028, 9:1207, 1208, 1209, 1251, 10:1365, 1396
Marxism, 9:1207-8, 1209, 1210
   Veblen critique of, 10:1365-66
   wealth distribution and, 10:1396
   See also communism
Mary Kay Inc., 1:76, 77
Masih, Iqbal, 2:201
Mason, David, as contributor, 3:336-37, 6:767-68, 9:1172-74, 10:1356-59
Massachusetts Institute of Technology, 7:986, 8:1110
   Samuelson and, 8:1140-41
   Sloan School, 6:843
Massachusetts Investors Trust, 4:491
mass production
   consumption relationship, 3:316-17
   division of labor, 3:371, 372
   Ford and, 3:424, 4:513
   Industrial Revolution, 5:656, 658
   interchangeable parts, 5:693
   Levitt houses, 6:788-90
   manufacturing industry, 6:828-29
   strikes and, 9:1250
   See also assembly line
MasterCard, 1:52-53, 3:23, 321

master of business administration, **6**:841-43

Materials Transportation Bureau, **8**:*1106*, 1107

maternity leave, **4**:468, 471

Matsushita Electric, **8**:1019, **9**:1218

Maxim, Hiram, **10**:1332

maximum price. *See* price controls

Maxwell-Briscoe, **4**:550

Mayer, Louis B., **6**:844-45

MBA. *See* master of business administration

MCA, **4**:569

McCall Pattern Company, **6**:792

McCarthy, Joseph, **8**:1148

McCarthy, William, **9**:1276

McCormick Harvester Company, **5**:601

McCulloch v. Maryland, **5**:596

McDonald, Maurice and Richard, **6**:*756, 757, 846, 847*

McDonald's, **2**:232, **3**:427, **4**:566, **6**:846-48, **7**:918
　cultural differences and, **3**:331, 7:918
　discount bundling, **1**:136
　Kroc and, **6**:755, 756-57
　liability suit, **2**:*161*, **8**:1046

McDonnell Douglass, **3**:353, **5**:651

McDonough, William, **4**:442

McGowan, William, **3**:360

McGraw-Hill, **8**:1078

McGraw Hill Education, **3**:406

McGuinn, Roger, **9**:*1283*

McHugh, Rich, *as contributor*, **2**:264-68

MCI, **1**:89, **3**:360

McKinley, William, **3**:350, **5**:610-11

McKinsey & Co., **2**:258

McLaren, Wayne, **7**:1003

McLean, David, **7**:1003

McLennon, Mary Ann, *as contributor*, **4**:501-2, 568-69

McLuhan, Marshall, **5**:667

McMurtie, Sandra Andreas, **1**:71

McNally, Dave, **6**:813

McNeely, P. J., **2**:284

McWhirter, Norris and Ross, **5**:593

Mead Johnson, **1**:123

Meany, George, **1**:40, 42, **8**:1086

Médecins sans Frontiéres, **1**:123

media
　as advertising outlets, **1**:27, 28, 29, 31, 32, *33*
　AOL Time Warner, **1**:64-66
　arts and entertainment, **1**:71-75
　Disney acquisitions, **10**:1394
　market research, **6**:833
　public relations and marketing campaign, **8**:1063-64, 1066, 1068-69
　Winfrey and, **10**:1410-12
　See also specific types

mediation, **1**:68-69, 95, **2**:223

Medicaid, **2**:180, **5**:606, 607, **9**:1214

medical care. *See* health care services industry

medical schools, **5**:604-5

Medicare, **2**:180, **5**:606, 608, **9**:*1210*, 1211, 1214-15
　federal budget, **4**:478-79

Meiggs, Henry, **2**:204

Meili, Christoph, **10**:*1346*, 1348

Melnick, Dan, **6**:773

Melville, Herman, **9**:1235

mercantilism, **6**:849-52, **7**:901
　balance of payments, **1**:92
　capitalism vs., **2**:177
　liberalism vs., **5**:705-6, **9**:1203, 1204, **10**:1401

Merchant Marine Act (1936), **8**:1105, *1106*

Merchants Bank of Halifax, **8**:1131, *1132*

Merchants Union Express Company, **1**:51, *52*

merchant wholesalers, **8**:1118-19, *1120*

Merck & Company, **1**:121

Meredith (publisher), **8**:1077

merger and acquisition, **6**:853-57
　airlines, **1**:124, **7**:1001-2
　book publishers, **8**:1079
　business law, **2**:160
　as competition reduction, **8**:1052
　consumer protection and, **2**:272
　corporation, **3**:306
　defense industry, **3**:353
　entertainment, **7**:909, **9**:1218-19, **10**:*1339*, 1341, *1392*
　global competition, **8**:1104
　Internet companies, **5**:*712*
　monopolistic, **7**:901-2
　oil companies, **8**:1133-34, **9**:1234, **10**:1307
　Rockefeller and, **8**:1129
　Schwab, **9**:1167, 1168
　telephone industry, **9**:1288
　venture capital, **6**:792

Meritor Savings Bank, FSB v. Vinson (1986), **9**:1184, 1185

merit raises, **2**:236

Merriam (book publisher), **8**:1078

Merrill, Charles Edward, **6**:858-59

Merrill, James, **6**:858

Merrill Lynch, **6**:858-60

Messersmith, Andy, **6**:813

Metallica, **2**:284, **9**:*1283*

METRO AG, **8**:1118

Metro-Goldwyn-Mayer. *See* MGM

Metromail, **6**:836

Metro Pictures Corporation, **6**:845

Mexico
　economic planning, **2**:182
　globalization, **4**:567
　illegal immigrant labor, **5**:640, 641, 642
　IMF loan, **5**:703
　international retailers, **8**:1118
　multinationals, **7**:921
　NAFTA, **2**:*181*, 183, **5**:708, **7**:956-59
　NAICS codes, **7**:928-29, **8**:1115
　Santa Fe Trail, **8**:1142, 1143-44
　seasonal workers, **10**:1303
　Volkswagen factory, **10**:1379
　Wal-Mart in, **10**:1389

working conditions, **10**:1420
　Yamaha subsidiary, **10**:1436

Meyer, Agnes, **4**:570

Meyer, Eugene, **4**:570, 571

Mfume, Kweisi, **6**:*793*

MGM, **6**:773, 845

MGM/United Artists, **10**:1340

Michigan Central Railroad, **10**:1364

Michigan Southern Railroad, **10**:1364

microeconomics, **6**:809, **7**:869-72
　externalities, **4**:463-64
　macroeconomics vs., **7**:869
　public goods, **8**:1058-60
　Samuelson and, **8**:1141

microfinance, **5**:668

microprocessor, **2**:244, **5**:621, 684, 685, 686, *710*

Microsoft, **3**:339, **5**:670, 677, **7**:873-76
　antitrust case, **1**:138, **3**:361, **8**:1051, 1104, *1106*, **9**:1190
　breakup reversal, **7**:*874*, 875
　browser, **2**:216, **7**:*874*, 875
　browser price war, **8**:1025
　bundling, **1**:138
　certification, **10**:1376
　corporate security, **5**:*651*
　in Dow Jones Average, **3**:376
　education division, **3**:407
　Gates and, **4**:537, 538-39
　globalization and, **4**:566
　human capital, **5**:625-26
　IBM and, **2**:252, **5**:635, 636
　independent contractors, **10**:1304
　intellectual property, **5**:688, 689, 690
　licenses, **6**:802, 804
　monopoly charges, **7**:873, *874*, 875, 902, *903*
　multinationalism, **7**:*919*
　Nasdaq trading, **5**:677, **7**:931
　racial discrimination suit, **2**:214
　stock returns, **9**:1242
　Windows, **1**:138, **5**:636, 689, 690

Microsoft Corp v. Vizcaino (1992), **10**:1304

Microsystems, **2**:216

Microwave Communications, Inc. *See* MCI

Midas Mufflers, **3**:427

middleman's markup, **3**:366

Midland Chemical Company, **3**:373

Midland Linseed Products Company, **1**:70

Miescher, Johann Friedrich, **4**:555

migrant workers, **5**:639, **10**:1301
　child workers, **2**:201, 203
　unionization, **2**:194, 195-96
　working conditions, **10**:1420

military-industrial complex, **3**:351-54

milk price supports, **8**:1013

Miller, Daniel, Jr., **3**:425

Miller, Donna, *as contributor*, **2**:261-63, 269-71, **6**:778-80

Miller, Marvin, **6**:813

Miller, Ron, **10**:1392

Miller Brewing Company, **7**:1001, 1002, 1004

Miller-Tydings Act (1937), **9**:1197

mimeograph machine, **3**:400, **10**:1429

minimum price. *See* price controls

minimum wage, **7**:877-82, **10**:1417
　legislation, **4**:466, **10**:1418
　microeconomics and, **7**:872
　New Deal, **7**:878-79, 943, 996
　profit and loss and, **8**:1051
　pros and cons, **8**:1013, 1014-15
　small business and, **9**:1199
　strikes and, **9**:1252
　unconstitutionality ruling, **5**:583
　United Auto Workers, **10**:1349

Mining Enforcement and Safety Administration, **8**:*1106*, 1107

mining industry, **7**:883-87
　Bisbee deportation, **9**:1252
　careers in, **7**:887
　child labor, **2**:200, 201
　commodity markets, **2**:225
　corporate profits, **3**:*305*
　futures and options market, **2**:198
　labor unions, **1**:39, 40
　public relations, **8**:1066
　raw materials, **8**:1087, *1088*, 1089
　regulatory activity, **8**:*1106*, 1107
　small business component, **9**:1196

Minnesota Valley Canning Company, **1**:139

Mintzberg, Henry, **9**:1247-48

Miramax Films, **7**:888-89, **10**:1393

mission statement, **2**:167, **9**:1246

Mitsubishi Motors, **5**:649, **7**:890-92

Mitterrand, François, **4**:459

mixed economies, **9**:1208

Mngumi, Grace, **1**:*123*

Mobil, 7.948, 9.123, 6.854. *See also* ExxonMobil

Model T (car), **1**:*81*, 82, **3**:424, **4**:512, 513-14, **5**:598, **6**:829, **10**:1379

Molly Maguires, **9**:1250

"mom and pop" stores, **8**:1117

mommy track, **4**:471, **10**:1415

monetarism, **2**:182-83, **4**:527
　inflation theory, **5**:660-61, 662
　macroeconomics, **6**:812

monetary policy, **7**:893-95
　business cycles, **2**:151, 180
　credit, **3**:316
　economic growth, **3**:390
　exchange rate, **4**:461
　Federal Reserve and, **3**:315-16, 390, 391, **4**:480-83, 527, 528
　fiscal policy and, **4**:503
　Friedman monetarism, **4**:527-28, **6**:812
　gold and gold-exchange standards, **3**:315, 316, *317*
　inflation, **2**:182, **3**:390, **5**:659-61
　international economy, **2**:180, *181*, 182

monetary policy (cont.)
Keynes macroeconomics, **2**:180, **6**:749, 750, 810-12
Leading Economic Index, **6**:778, 779
national debt, **3**:315
price controls, **8**:1016
recession, **8**:1097, 1098
tools of, **7**:*893*
trade policies and, **5**:706
money, **7**:**896-98**
as asset, **1**:84, 96
breakeven point, **1**:120
as capital, **2**:173
cash flow, **2**:189-90
commodity futures, **2**:225
credit card vs., **3**:319
debit card vs., **3**:323
euro, **4**:*457*, 459, 460, **5**:707-8
exchange rates, **4**:461-62
Federal Reserve and, **4**:480-82
gold standard, **3**:316
inflation, **5**:659
as investment, **6**:728-31
negotiable instrument substitutes, **2**:162-63
valuation, **10**:1360
money laundering, **10**:1346, 1347
money market funds, **4**:491, **9**:1158
money multiplier, **3**:*364*, 365
money orders, **1**:51
money supply. *See* monetary policy
Monnet, Jean, **4**:457, 460
monopoly, **7**:**899-904**
AT&T, **1**:87, 88-89, **2**:246, **3**:*359*, 360-61, 398, **9**:1188, 1234, 1285-86, **10**:1357
Baby Bells, **9**:1289
bundling and, **1**:138
cartel as, **2**:188
competition vs., **2**:178-79, 225, 244, 245, 246
consumer protection from, **2**:272
copyright as, **2**:165, 280, 281
economies of scale and, **3**:398
electricity industry, **3**:*360*, 361-62, 398, 417
Federal Trade Commission and, **4**:484
inflation theory and, **5**:661-662
innovation and, **5**:679
institutionalist inflation theory and, **5**:661, 663
labor unions seen as, **6**:762, 764-65
license restrictions and, **6**:804
mercantilist, **1**:92, **6**:850, **9**:1203
microeconomics and, **7**:870, 871
Microsoft charges, **3**:361, **4**:539, **7**:874, 875
Mitsubishi, **7**:891
Morgan and, **7**:906
natural vs. unnatural, **1**:88, 89
pricing, **8**:1022
privatization and, **8**:1032
profit and loss and, **8**:1051
Sherman Antitrust Act, **2**:*245*, **9**:1187, 1189-90

Standard Oil, **8**:1129-30, **9**:*1231*, 1232, 1234
state ownership as preventive, **8**:1031
U.S. Steel clearance, **10**:1353
utilities, **8**:1015-16, 1021, **10**:1356, 1359
Xerox, **10**:1430, 1431
See also antitrust
monopsony, **6**:762, **10**:1324
Montgomery Improvement Association, **2**:210
Montgomery Ward, **2**:265, **9**:1274
Monthly Retail Trade Survey, **8**:1116
Monthly Wholesale Survey, **8**:1119
Moody, Paul, **6**:805-6, 807-8
Moore, G. E., **6**:749
Moore, Gordon, **5**:668, 684, 686
Moore's Law, **5**:684
Moravia, Alberto, **4**:473
Morgan, J. P., **1**:88, **4**:550, **5**:583, **7**:*905-7*, **8**:1051, **10**:1383-86
Carnegie Steel and, **9**:1168, **10**:1353, 1354
General Electric and, **4**:547, 548
United States Steel and, **2**:186
Morgan, Junius Spencer, **7**:905
Morgan, Lewis, **10**:1365
Morgan, Ralph, **9**:1169
Morita, Akio, **7**:**908-9**, **9**:1217, 1218-19
Morris, Philip, **7**:1000
Morrisey, George C., **9**:1246
Morriss, Andrew, *as contributor*, **2**:253-57, **4**:447-51, **7**:960-63, **8**:1026-29, 1030-33, 1137-39
Morse, Leila Livingston, **7**:*912*
Morse, Samuel, **5**:*657*, **7**:**910-12**, **9**:1284
Morse, Sidney, **7**:910
Morse code, **7**:911, 912, **9**:1284
mortgage, **3**:316, 318, **7**:**913-15**, **8**:1091
as debt, **3**:345, 346, **4**:498
federally guaranteed, **6**:790
Mosaic Communications, 5.711, 5.*712*. See also Netscape
most-favored-nation (MFN) status, **4**:543
motels, **10**:1312
Motion Picture Academy, **7**:888, 889
Motion Picture Association of America, **7**:888
Motor Carrier Act (1935), **8**:1105, *1106*, 1109
Motor Vehicle Information and Cost Savings Act (1972), **2**:273
Motown Records, **1**:115, **4**:568-69
Mount Holyoke College, **7**:994, *995*
mouse (computer), **10**:1431, 1432
Moynihan, Daniel Patrick, **7**:925
MP3 computer file format, **2**:284
MS-DOS, **5**:635, 636, **7**:873-74
MSNBC (cable channel), **7**:876
Mulroney, Brian, **7**:*956*
Multilateral Investment Guarantee Agency, **10**:*1421*, 1422

multilateralism, **10**:1428
Multimixer, **6**:756, 847
multinational corporation, **3**:306, **7**:**916-21**
Amazon.com as, **1**:50
book publishing, **8**:1079
business ethics, **2**:154, 156, 158-59
corporate social responsibility, **3**:301
Enron as, **3**:420, 421
globalization, **2**:183, **4**:561, 565-66, **5**:709
intellectual property and, **5**:690
labor unions and, **1**:42
mining, **7**:886-87
outsourcing, **7**:918, 952, 972
petroleum industry, **10**:1306
Philip Morris as, **7**:1002
product development, **8**:1037
retailers, **8**:1118
Royal Dutch/Shell as, **8**:1133-36
Sony as, **9**:1217-19
multiple listing services, **8**:1091, 1092
Mun, Thomas, **6**:*849*, 851
municipal services
privatization, **8**:1031-32, 1033
as public good, **8**:1059-60
public sector unionism, **8**:1070, 1071
Munn v. Illinois (1877), **8**:1103, *1106*
Muris, Timothy J., **4**:*485*, 487
Murray, Alan, *as contributor*, **3**:358-62, **5**:687-91
Murray, Thorpe, and Lewis, **6**:792
Muse, Lamar, **2**:166
music industry, **1**:72, 73
advertising jingles, **1**:29
AOL Time Warner, **1**:64, 66
black enterprise, **1**:115
CD price fixing, **8**:1018, 1019-20
copyright, **2**:280, *281*, *282*, 283, 284
digital copying, **9**:*1283*
intellectual property, **2**:157, 165, **5**:688, 689
Internet downloading, **1**:74
license agreements, **6**:801, 802
Motown, **1**:115, **4**:568
recordings, **1**:64, 65, 66, 74
Warner Bros., **1**:64, 65
Yamaha instruments, **10**:1435, 1436
Musk, Elon, **7**:*898*
Muskie, Edmund, **4**:448
Mussa, Michael, **4**:561-62
Mussolini, Benito, **4**:474, *475*, *476*
mutual funds, **7**:**922-24**, 948
diversification, **2**:293-94
Fidelity, **4**:491-92
as investment option, **9**:1158, 1241
Schwab and, **9**:1167
socially responsible investing, **3**:301
stockholders, **3**:293-94, 297
Myers, John Ripley, **1**:121

N
NAACP, **6**:739-40, **10**:1381, 1382
Nader, Ralph, **2**:268, 274, **4**:*552*, 553, **6**:794, 798, **7**:**925-27**
NAFTA. *See* North American Free Trade Agreement
NAICS codes, **7**:928-29, **8**:1115, 1116
Naisbitt, John, **5**:665
Nally, E. J., **8**:1146
Napster, **2**:165, 283, 284, **6**:803
Nasdaq, **2**:173, **5**:677, **7**:**930-32**, **9**:*1243*
Amazon.com stock, **1**:50
American Stock Exchange and, **1**:54, *55*
day trading, **3**:341-42
Edison Schools listing, **3**:404
futures market, **2**:*152*
initial public offering, **5**:677
Level II screen, **3**:*341*
tradable securities, **9**:1157
Nasdaq Composite Index, **7**:931, 932
Nasdaq MarketSite, **7**:*930*, 931
Nasdaq National Market, **7**:931
Nasdaq SmallCap Market, **7**:931
National Academy of Design, **7**:910, *911*
National Advertising Review Board, **1**:112
National Aeronautics and Space Administration, **5**:710, **8**:1059, *1112*
National Archives, **7**:1000
National Association for Stock Car Auto Racing, **9**:1224
National Association for the Advancement of Colored People, **6**:739-40, **10**:1381, 1382
National Association for the Promotion of Labor Unionism among Negroes, **8**:1083
National Association of Colored Women, **10**:1382
National Association of Elementary School Principals, **8**:1048
National Association of Home Builders, **1**:133-34, **8**:*1048*
National Association of Independent Schools, **8**:1049
National Association of Realtors, **8**:*1048*, 1090-91
National Association of School Superintendents, **7**:935
National Association of Securities Dealers, **1**:54, *55*, **3**:342
National Association of Securities Dealers Automatic Quotation System. *See* Nasdaq
National Bank Act (1864), **3**:115, *317*
National Basketball Association, **9**:1224
National Better Business Bureau. *See* Better Business Bureau
National Black Chamber of Commerce, **2**:193, **7**:*933-34*

National Broadcasting Company. *See* NBC

National Business Coalition on Health, **2**:172

National Cancer Institute, **1**:123

National Cash Register Co., **5**:632

National Child Labor Committee, **2**:200

National Collegiate Athletic Association, **9**:1224, *1226*

National Consumers League, **2**:267, **7**:994

National Council of Better Business Bureaus, **1**:112

National Council on Disability, **1**:56, 60

National Credit Union Administration, **2**:272, 273

National Currency Act (1863), **3**:314-15, *317*

National Education Association, **7**:935-38

National Environmental Policy Act (1969), **4**:*448*

National Farm Workers Association, **2**:*194*, 195

National Football League, **9**:1223, 1224, *1226*, 1227

National Forestry Association, **4**:517

National Foundation for Teaching Entrepreneurship, **3**:425

National Gambling Impact Study Commission, **4**:536

National Guard, U.S., **3**:350-53

National Highway Traffic Safety Administration, **2**:272, 273, **8**:*1106*, 1107

National Hockey League, **9**:*1226*, **10**:1393

national identification card, **9**:1177

National Industrial Recovery Act (1933), **7**:878, 940, 996

National Institute for Occupational Safety and Health, **7**:961

National Institutes of Health, **8**:1059

National Labor Relations Act (1935), **2**:196, **4**:552, **6**:763, 767, **7**:938, **939-40**, 943, **9**:1252, 1272-73

  Taft–Hartley Act and, **9**:1268, 1269

National Labor Relations Board, **7**:939, 940, *941*, 943, **8**:1105, *1106*

  collective bargaining, **2**:221-23

  labor unions and, **6**:764

  Taft–Hartley Act and, **9**:1268

  temporary worker unionization, **10**:1304

  United Automobile Workers and, **10**:1350

National Labor Relations Board v. Jones and Laughlin Steel Company (1937), **7**:940

National Labor Union, **10**:1413

National Marine Fisheries Service, **4**:509

National Negro Business League, **7**:933, 934

National Organization for Women, **9**:1184

national parks and forests, **4**:157, 439, *440*, 515-16, **8**:1100

National Park Service, **6**:808

National Railroad Passenger Corporation, **10**:1330

National Recovery Administration, **7**:940, 941, *941*

National Refiners Association, **9**:*1231*, 1232

National Science Foundation, **5**:714, **8**:1059

national security

  defense industry and, **3**:350-54

  deregulation vs., **3**:362

  government provision of, **9**:1204, **10**:1400

  protectionism and, **8**:1056

  as public good, **8**:1059, 1060

  reverse engineering, **8**:1122

National Society of Fund Raising Executives, **8**:1049

National Teachers' Association, **7**:935, 936

National Traffic and Motor Vehicle Safety Act (1966), **2**:274

National Transportation Safety Board, **8**:*1106*, 1107

National Vigilance Committee, **1**:112

National War Labor Board, **10**:1411

National Women's Trade Union League, **1**:39, **2**:*221*

National Youth Administration, **7**:*941*

natural gas, **3**:*415*, 416, *417*, 418

  deregulation, **8**:1109, **10**:1359

  Enron system, **3**:420-21

  federal regulation, **8**:1105

  Royal Dutch/Shell, **8**:1135

  utilities industry, **10**:1356, 1358

natural monopoly, **2**:245, **3**:360, 361, 398, **7**:900-901, 904

  AT&T as, **1**:88, 89

  deregulation, **8**:1109

  prices and, **8**:1015-16, 1021

  state regulation, **8**:1103, 1107-9

Navigation Acts, British (1651-1849), **6**:850-51

Navigator (browser). *See* Netscape Navigator

Nazism, **2**:179, **3**:380, **5**:612, **10**:*1346*, 1348

  fascist ideology, **4**:474, *475*, 476

  Volkswagen design, **10**:1377

NBC (television), **4**:549, **8**:1147, 1148

NBCC. *See* National Black Chamber of Commerce

NCR Corp., **1**:89, 90

NEA. *See* National Education Association

Nebel, Jane, **5**:616

negligence claims, **2**:161-62, **8**:1046

negotiation, **2**:221-24, **6**:738

Negro American Labor Council, **8**:1086

Negroponte, Nicholas, **5**:666-67

Nehru, Jawaharlal, **2**:181

neoliberalism, **2**:*181*, 182-83

Nestlé, **3**:332, **8**:*1047*

net income, **1**:26, **5**:647

net present value, **4**:493, *495*

Netscape, **5**:678, 712, **10**:1433

  Navigator browser, **2**:215-16, **5**:711, **7**:875

  Navigator price war, **8**:1025

Nevada National Bank, **10**:1405

New American Library, **8**:1078

Newcomen, Thomas, **5**:653, *657*

New Deal, **7**:941-43

  capitalism and, **2**:179-80, *181*

  environmental projects, **4**:439, *440*

  Fair Labor Standards Act, **4**:467

  farm programs, **1**:47, **7**:941, 943

  government regulation, **3**:360

  government spending, **3**:365

  Great Depression, **5**:581-85

  Keynesian theory, **2**:180, **6**:750

  labor unions, **1**:39, 40, **8**:1084, **9**:1252-53, 1274

  minimum wage, **7**:878-79, 943, 996

  National Labor Relations Act, **7**:939-40

  Perkins and, **7**:994, 996, 997

  regulatory agencies, **8**:1104-7

  social democracy and, **9**:*1209*, 1210

  social security, **9**:1211, 1212

  strikes, **9**:1252-53

  subsidy legislation, **9**:1255-56

  wage standards, **3**:299

  Wall Street Journal view of, **10**:1384-85

Newman, Nell, **7**:*944*, 946

Newman, Paul, **7**:944-46, **9**:*1171*

Newman's Organics, **7**:*944*, 946

Newman's Own, **7**:944-46

New School for Social Research, **2**:267

News Corporation, **8**:1075, 1079

Newspaper Association of America, **8**:1074-75

newspapers. *See* publishing industry

Newton, Isaac, **2**:177, **5**:688

New York City Consumer's League, **7**:994, 995

New York Commodity Exchange, **2**:225

New York Cotton Exchange, **2**:225

New York Curb Agency. *See* American Stock Exchange

New York Mercantile Exchange, **2**:225

New York Metal Exchange, **2**:225

New York Public Service Commission, **8**:1108-9

New York Stock Exchange, **7**:947-49

  American Stock Exchange and, **1**:54, 55

  Bristol-Meyers listing, **1**:121

  computer technology, **9**:1245

  daily shares traded (1900-2000), **7**:*947*

  Dow Jones Average stocks, **3**:376

  initial public offering, **5**:677, *678*

  Nasdaq contrasted with, **7**:930-31

  risk management, **8**:1127

  Royal Bank of Canada listing, **8**:1132

  Securities and Exchange Commission and, **9**:1172

  Stewart and, **9**:*1239*

  tradable securities, **9**:1157

  trading volumes, **7**:948, **9**:1244-45

  UBS AG shares, **10**:*1346*, 1348

  valuation, **10**:1360

New York Stock Exchange Index, **2**:152, 225

New York Sugar Exchange, **2**:225

New York Yankees, **6**:*814*, *815*, **9**:1223

Next Generation Internet, **5**:714

niche market, **0**.1024 25

  magazines, **8**:1077

  tourism, **10**:1313-14

Nicholas II, emperor of Russia, **2**:227

Nike, **3**:346, **4**:565-66, **7**:918, **950-53**, **9**:1227

Niles, Jack, **9**:1290

Nippon Gakki Company, **10**:1435

Nistevo, **3**:386

Nixon, Richard, **2**:*181*, 182, **3**:316, 317, **5**:620, **8**:1130

  employment quotas, **1**:35

  EPA creation, **4**:*440*, 442, 448

  Greenspan and, **5**:586

  Samuelson and, **8**:1141

  Sarnoff and, **8**:1148

  social security COLAs, **9**:1215

  visit to China, **2**:230

  wage and price controls, **8**:1016

  Watergate scandal, **4**:571-72, **5**:699

NLRA. *See* National Labor Relations Act

Nobel Learning Centers, **3**:405

Nobel Prize in economics

  corporate researcher winners, **8**:1110, 1111

  Friedman and, **4**:528

  human capital concept, **5**:625

  Samuelson and, **8**:1140, *1141*

Noble, L. Clarence, **5**:613, 614

no-down-payment loans, **3**:316, 318

Non-Acceleration Interest Rate of Unemployment, **5**:661

nonprofit entities, **7**:954-55, **10**:1369

nontariff barriers (NTBs), **4**:543

Nordhoff, Heinz, **10**:1378

Nordstrom, **3**:335

Norris-La Guardia Act (1932), **6**:763, **7**:939

North American Agreement on Environmental Cooperation, 7:958

North American Aviation, 10:1350

North American Free Trade Agreement, 1:94, 2:181, 183, 5:707, 708, 7:956-59
  NAICS codes, 7:928-29
  UAW opposition, 10:1352

North American Free Trade Area, 10:1325

North American Industry Classification System. See NAICS codes

Northeastern University, 2:284

Northrop Grumman, 3:352

Northwest Airlines, 2:224, 3:377, 7:931

North West Company, 5:624

Northwestern Telephone, 9:1285

Northwestern University, 6:772, 773, 843

notebook computers, 5:637

Noyce, Robert, 5:684, 685

nuclear energy, 3:414, 415, 4:439, 440, 457

Nuclear Waste Policy Act (1982), 4:448

Nuclear Waste Policy Amendments Act (2000), 2:255

Nucor Steel Corporation, 5:679, 680

NYSE. See New York Stock Exchange

O

Occupational Safety and Health Act (1970), 7:960

Occupational Safety and Health Administration, 6:759, 796, 798, 7:960-63, 8:1106, 1107
  ergonomics and, 4:456
  founding of, 10:1418
  small business and, 9:1199

Ocean Dumping Ban Act (1988), 4:448

OECD. See Organization for Economic Cooperation and Development

Office of Economic Opportunity, 3:393

Office of Management and Budget, 7:928

Office of Production Management, 4:552

Office of Strip Mining Regulation and Enforcement, 8:1107

Ohga, Norio, 9:1219

Ohno, Tai-ichi, 6:741

oil. See petroleum industry

oil crisis (1973), 2:182, 7:970
  automobile industry effects, 4:554, 10:1349, 1352
  prices, 8:1134, 1135
  recession, 8:1096

Oil Pollution Act (1990), 4:448

oil spills, 3:300, 4:438, 439, 440, 448
  genetically engineered bacterium cleanup, 7:981, 985

old-age insurance. See social security and Medicare

Old Navy (company), 1:118

Olds, Ransom E., 4:550

oligopoly, 7:870, 899, 8:1017, 1032

Omidyar, Pierre, 10:1408

One Stop Capital Shops, 9:1201

OPEC. See Organization of Petroleum Exporting Countries

open shop, 9:1269

opportunity cost, 3:309, 7:964-65
  inventory excess as, 6:725

options contract. See futures market

Oracle Corp., 2:216, 241, 10:1433

Orfalea, Paul, 6:752, 753-54

Organization for Economic Cooperation and Development, 7:966-67

Organization of Banana Exporting Countries, 2:206

Organization of Petroleum Exporting Countries, 7:886, 968-70, 10:1349, 1352
  as cartel, 2:187, 7:968-70, 9:1230
  1973 oil embargo. See oil crisis
  price fixing, 8:1022, 1135
  pricing, 9:1259

organized labor. See labor union

Origins, 6:777

Orwell, George, 6:837

OSHA. See Occupational Safety and Health Administration

Our Common Future (1987 report), 9:1265

Outcault, R. G., 5:609

outsourcing, 7:971-73
  education services, 3:408
  by multinationals, 7:918, 919, 921, 972
  NAFTA and, 7:959
  by Nike, 7:952-53

Overbey, Theresa, as contributor, 4:506-10

overhead, 7:974-75

overnight delivery, 4:488-90

over-the-counter (OTC) market, 7:930

overtime, 4:466, 5:630

Ovitz, Michael, 10:1394

Owen, Chandler, 8:1083

Owen, Robert, 2:227, 9:1206, 1209

Oxygen Media, 10:1411-12

Oz, Frank, 1:75

P

Pabst brewery, 7:1002

Pacific Gas and Electric, 1:37, 6:796, 8:1016, 10:1356

Pacini, Carl, as contributor, 1:83-86, 99-102, 2:160-65, 221-24, 7:966-67, 980-86, 8:1124-27, 9:1189-90

Packard, David, 5:619, 620, 621

Packard, Vance, 2:267

"Pacman defense" metaphor, 6:853

PACs. See political action committees

Paine Webber, 10:1346

Paley, William, 6:816

Palmer, Arnold, 1:92

Palmer Memorial Institute, 10:1382

Palo Alto Research Center (Calif.), 10:1429, 1430-32

Pan American Airways, 3:358, 9:1192, 10:1333-35

Pantheon, 8:1078

Papa, David, 9:1186

paper currency. See money

Paralyzed Veterans of America, 1:56

Paramount Pictures, 6:773, 774, 10:1393

PARC. See Palo Alto Research Center

Paris Convention for the Protection of Industrial Property, 7:986

Parker, James, 9:1221

Parks, Rosa, 2:210

parks and recreation areas, 8:1100-1102

Parlin, Charles Coolidge, 6:833

partnership, 3:346, 427, 7:976-79, 9:1198
  vertical integration, 2:185, 186

Pascal, Blaise, 5:663, 6:728

Pascal, Donna, as contributor, 4:472-73

Pasteur, Louis, 5:605

patent, 7:980-86
  amortization of, 1:61, 63
  for Bell's telephone, 1:87, 88
  business law on, 2:160, 164, 165
  as competitive entry barrier, 7:900, 903, 904
  Edison grants, 3:400, 4:547
  for gasoline engine, 4:511-12
  industrial espionage and, 5:649
  Industrial Revolution, 5:653, 654-55
  as intangible asset, 1:84, 85
  intellectual property and, 2:280, 5:687, 689
  Levi Strauss grant, 6:785, 786
  license and, 6:801
  product development and, 8:1036-37
  property rights and, 8:1029
  RCA sharing agreement, 8:1147
  for revolver, 5:693
  television claims, 8:1148
  types and duration, 8:1112
  for water frame, 5:657
  World Trade Organization and, 10:1427
  Xerox grants, 10:1429, 1430

Patent Act (1790, 1793), 7:980

Patent Act and Amendments (1952, 1995) (1995), 7:980

Patent Office, U.S., 5:687, 7:984, 8:1036
  Board of Appeals, 7:986

Paterson, Tim, 7:874

Paul Newman Foundation, 7:944, 945, 946

Paul Weiss (law firm), 6:791-92

payday loans, 4:486, 487

pay equity, 7:987-89
  CEO vs. average worker, 3:296
  civil rights cases, 2:214

collective bargaining, 2:223

compensation policy, 2:236

corporate social responsibility, 3:299, 300

Equal Employment Opportunity Commission, 4:452-53

Equal Pay Act, 10:1418

Fair Labor Standards Act, 4:466, 467

Ford $5 day, 3:299

human resources department, 5:630

immigrant inequities, 5:642-43

income differences, 10:1397

relevant cost, 3:309-10

service sector, 9:1181, 1183

temporary workers, 10:1303

women's inequities, 10:1413, 1414-15, 1418

See also income distribution

payroll, 7:990-93
  FICA deductions, 9:1212-13

Peace Corps, 3:395

Pearson (publishing), 8:1079

Pearson Education, 3:406

Pebble Beach (Calif.), 1:92

Pegler, Arthur James, 5:610

Pemberton, John Styth, 2:217

Pemex, 3:418

Pennsylvania Railroad, 2:184, 185, 8:1066, 9:1250

Pennzoil, 10:1307

pension and retirement plans
  corporate social responsibility, 3:299
  401(k), 4:492, 499, 8:1072, 9:1159-60, 1241
  gender equity, 7:989
  government workers, 8:1072
  human resources department, 5:630
  income distribution and, 5:645
  inflation effects, 5:660, 663
  payroll deductions, 7:990, 9:1212-13
  personal finances and, 4:499
  standard of living and, 9:1229
  See also social security and Medicare

Pentax, 7:909

PeopleSoft, 5:670

PepsiCo, 9:1236

per capita income. See income distribution

perfect competition theory, 2:244

performance-based compensation, 2:238-41

Perkins, Frances, 7:994-97, 9:1212

Permanent Court of International Arbitration, 1:67

Perma Soft, 3:374

Perón, Juan, 4:476

Perot, H. Ross, 7:998-1000

Perot Systems, 7:998, 999

personal computer. See computer industry

personal expenditures. See finance, personal

personnel management. *See* human resources
pesticides, **1**:43, 48, **3**:375, **4**:438, 439, *440*, 443, *448*, 450-51, **9**:1194-95
  environmentalism, **10**:1424
  Silent Spring on, **9**:1194-95
petrochemical industry, **8**:1087
petroleum industry, **3**:414-15, **4**:554
  cartel, **2**:187, 188, **7**:886, 968-70, **9**:1230
  defense industry and, **3**:350
  externalities, **4**:437-38
  foreign sources, **10**:1306
  genetic engineering patent, **7**:981, *985*
  major oil reserves, **3**:*418*
  Middle East upheavals, **4**:437-38, 554
  mining and, **7**:883, 884
  multinationals, **7**:919-20, *921*
  offshore drilling, **8**:*1133*, 1134
  oil consumption (1980-1995), **3**:*416*
  oil crisis (1973), **2**:182, **4**:554, **7**:970, **10**:*1349*, 1352
  oil spills, **3**:300, **4**:438, 439, *440*, *448*, **7**:871, *985*
  OPEC and, **7**:886, 968-70, **10**:1349, 1352
  price fixing, **8**:1022, 1135
  pricing, **8**:1135, **9**:1234, 1259
  products, **10**:1305
  raw materials, **8**:1087
  recession and, **8**:1096
  Rockefeller and, **8**:1128-30
  Royal Bank of Canada funding, **8**:1132
  Royal Dutch/Shell, **8**:1133-36
  Standard Oil, **7**:901, *902*, **9**:1231-34
  Standard Oil vertical integration, **7**:971
  strikes, **9**:1251
  Texaco, **10**:1305-7
  U.S. Steel and, **10**:1355
  See also gasoline
pharmaceutical industry
  Bristol-Myers Squibb, **1**:121-23
  cartel, **2**:188
  consumer protection, **2**:272, 273, 275
  corporate social responsibility, **3**:300
  FTC and, **8**:1105
  genetic engineering, **4**:556, 558
  health care services, **5**:605, 608
  intellectual property, **5**:689, 690, 691
  multinationals, **7**:919
  patents, **7**:900, *903*, 904
  retail outlets, **8**:1117
  reverse engineering, **5**:649, **8**:1122, *1123*
Phelps Dodge, **9**:1252
Philadelphia Electric Company, **7**:901
philanthropy
  Carnegie and, **2**:184, *185*, 186

chambers of commerce, **2**:193
  corporate, **3**:299, 301
  Gates Foundation, **4**:*538*
  Gordy and, **4**:569
  Newman's Own, **7**:944-45
  nonprofit entities, **7**:955
  Perot and, **7**:999
  personal finance and, **4**:500
  Rockefeller and, **8**:1128, 1130
  Turner and, **10**:1339, 1341
  Vanderbilt and, **10**:1364
  Walker and, **10**:1382
  Wal-Mart, **10**:1390
Philip Morris Companies, **7**:**1001**-4
  General Mills-Kellogg price war, **6**:747
  Leo Burnett Advertising, **1**:139
  liability suits, **8**:1046
Philip Morris International, **7**:1004
Philip Morris Research Center, **7**:1003
Philip Morris USA, **7**:1004
Philips Electronics NV, **3**:402
Phillips, A. W., **5**:661
Phillips Curve, **5**:661
photocopying, **10**:1429-32
  Kinko's, **6**:752-54
physiocrats, **2**:177, **9**:1203, **10**:1400
Picasso, Pablo, **8**:*1020*
picketing, **6**:768, **8**:*1084*, **9**:1269
Pierce, E. A., **6**:859
Pillsbury Doughboy, **1**:140
pin factory (Smith example), **3**:370-71, 388, 389, **9**:1204, **10**:1400
Pinkerton, Allan, **9**:1176
Pinkerton National Detective Agency, **9**:1176, 1250, 1251
Pinochet, Augusto, **4**:476
Pipes, Richard, **8**:1026
piracy, **2**:282, 284
  intellectual property, **6**:801-4
  reverse engineering and, **8**:1122, 1123
  trademark, **10**:1321
PIRG. *See* Public Interest Research Group
Pitt, Harvey, **9**:*1173*
Pitt, William the Younger, **6**:*816*, 817
Piuze, Michael, **7**:*1004*
Pizarro, Francisco, **6**:850
planned economy. *See* communism; socialism
planned obsolescence, **4**:551
plant patents, **7**:980, 983, **8**:1112
plastics, **3**:374, **4**:*441*, *442*, **8**:1089
Plato (education infrastructure firm), **3**:407
Pocket Books, Inc., **8**:1078
Podell, Jules, **3**:*321*
political action committees, **3**:300, **10**:1317
political parties
  advertising campaigns, **1**:31
  AFL-CIO and, **1**:38-39, 40, 42
  Archer Daniels Midlands and, **1**:71-72
  See also specific parties

Pollock v. Farmers' Loan and Trust Company, **5**:697, 698
Pol Pot, **2**:230
Poole, Arthur F., **7**:*982*
Population Bomb, The (Ehrlich), **4**:437, *440*, **6**:817-18
population growth, **4**:437, *440*
  Malthusian theory, **6**:816-18
  sustainable development and, **9**:1267
Porsche, Ferdinand, **10**:1377
Porter, Michael, **9**:1247
portfolio manager, **8**:1095
Post, C. W., **6**:746
predatory pricing, **9**:1189
preferred stock, **3**:302, 345
Pregnancy Discrimination Act (1978), **1**:*34*
Presley, Elvis, **6**:786
Presser, Jackie, **9**:1276
price controls, **8**:**1013**-16, 1021
  fair trade and, **8**:1103, *1106*
  Galbraith and, **4**:533
  inflation and, **5**:661-62
  minimum wage and, **8**:1013, 1014-15
  New Deal, **8**:1105
  profit and loss and, **8**:1051
  supply and demand vs., **9**:1263
  See also protectionism
price discrimination, **7**:903
price fixing, **8**:**1017**-20, 1022, 1104, 1133, 1135
  as anticompetitive, **2**:*244*, 245
  Archer Daniels Midland, **1**:70, 71
  cartel, **2**:187-88, 244
  illegality of, **9**:1189
  inflation and, **5**:661
  small business, **9**:1197
  Standard Oil, **9**:1231-32
  supply and demand vs., **9**:1259
  trade association restraints, **10**:1318
Priceline.com, **3**:382
price squeezes, **9**:1189
price wars, **8**:1021-23, 1025
Pricewaterhouse Coopers, **2**:259-60
pricing, **8**:**1021**-25
  airline tourist class, **10**:*1334*, 1335
  breakeven point, **1**:119
  breakfast cereal war, **6**:746, 7457
  bundling, **1**:136-38
  business cycles, **2**:149, 151
  competition by, **2**:242, 246
  conspicuous consumption and, **10**:1366-67
  Consumer Price Index, **2**:269-71
  cost of living, **3**:311-12
  costs and, **3**:308
  division of labor and, **3**:372, 388
  Dow Jones Average stocks, **3**:376, 377
  dumping, **10**:1325
  e-business, **3**:383
  environmentalism and, **4**:441-42
  factors in, **8**:*1021*
  farm products, **1**:47-48, 70
  futures markets, **1**:46, **4**:530, 531

gasoline, **10**:1352
globalization effects, **4**:564-65
Guinness, **5**:593
inflation, **5**:659, 660, 661, 662
initial public offering, **5**:676, 677, 678
innovation and, **5**:690
insurance policy basis, **5**:681
market economy, **8**:1103
mass production, **6**:829
microeconomics and, **7**:869, 870, 872
mined products, **7**:885-87
of Model T, **4**:513
monetary policy and, **7**:893
monopoly and, **7**:870, *901*, 902-3, *904*
Nike, **7**:952
oil, **8**:1135, **9**:1234, 1259
OPEC, **7**:968, 969-70
Organization of Petroleum Exporting Countries, **7**:968, 969-70
overhead and, **7**:974-75
of personal computers, **2**:252, **5**:635
petroleum, **7**:968, **9**:1231
pharmaceuticals, **1**:122
product liability threat and, **8**:1047
profit and loss and, **8**:1050, 1052
protectionism and, **5**:706, **8**:1054-56, 1057
psychology of, **8**:1024-25
public goods and, **8**:1060
sales tax and, **9**:1273
small business, **9**:1198
Southwest Airlines, **9**:1221, 1222
Standard Oil, **9**:1232
state public service commissions, **8**:1108-9
steel, **10**:1353
of stocks, **3**:341-42, 376, 377
supply and demand, **8**:1050, **9**:1259-63, **10**:1360, 1400
tariff and, **9**:1270, 1271
telephone service, **9**:1289, **10**:1359
Wal-Mart, **10**:1387
Priest, Ty, *as contributor*, **8**:1133-36
prime interest rate, **5**:696
Prince, Earl, **6**:756
Princeton Review, **3**:407
Princeton University, **4**:532, *533*
Prism Financial Corporation, **8**:1132
privacy
  constitutional rulings, **2**:257
  credit history, **3**:326
  data mining and, **3**:340
  e-business, **3**:384
  e-mail, **3**:412-13
  information technology, **5**:671, **9**:1283
  market research and, **6**:837
  personal property and, **8**:*1027*
  security industry and, **9**:1177
  taxpayer, **5**:699
  workplace safety and, **2**:158

private property, **8:**1026-29
  constitutional protection,
    2:256-57
  contractual transfer, **2:**279
  copyright, **2:**280-84, **8:**1112
  corporate ownership, **3:**302
  economic growth and, **3:**389
  entrepreneurship, **3:**428
  environmentalism and, **4:**441-42,
    450
  fair market value, **10:**1360
  intellectual property, **5:**687-91
  land wealth and, **9:**1277
  legal protection, **8:**1138, 1139
  license coverage, **6:**801-4
  opposition to, **8:**1028-29
  patent law, **7:**980-86, **8:**1112
  privatization and, **8:**1032
  profits and, **8:**1050
  public goods vs., **8:**1058
  real estate industry and,
    8:1090-95
  renting vs. owning, **3:**345
  risk management, **8:***1124*, 1125,
    1139
  tort liability, **6:**795
  as tragedy of the commons
    solution, **10:**1328
  See also intellectual property
private schools, **7:**935, 936, 938
privatization, **8:**1030-33
  British Airways, 126, **1:**125
  capitalism, **2:**182, 183
  deregulation, **3:**358, 362
  education industry, **3:**402-4,
    405-10
  energy industry, **3:**418
  subsidy and, **9:**1256
Procter & Gamble, **1:**37
Prodigy, **10:**1406
Producer Price Index, **2:**271
product development, **8:**1034-38
  advertising and, **1:**31
  brand names and, **1:**116-18
  genetic engineering and,
    4:555-59
  information technology,
    5:668-72
  innovation and, **5:**679-80
  research and development, **8:**111
  reverse engineering and, **8:**1122
productivity, **8:**1039-44
  agriculture, **1:**43, *44*, 47, 48
  assembly line, **1:**81, 82, **6:**829
  business cycles, **2:**149, 151
  division of labor, **3:**370-72,
    9:1204, **10:**1400
  economic growth and, **3:**388,
    391
  ergonomics and, **4:**454
  Industrial Revolution, **5:**658
  information technology and,
    5:669-70, 671-72
  just-in-time concept and, **6:**741,
    742
  labor unions and, **6:**763-64
  as Leading Economic Index
    component, **6:**778, 779
  management theory, **6:**824, 825

NAICS codes, **7:**928
  privatization and, **8:**1032
  profit and loss and, **8:**1051
  recreation and, **8:**1101
  robotics, **1:***110*
  service economy and, **9:**1178
  Southwest Airlines, **9:**1221
  tariff effects, **9:**1270
  telecommuting, **9:**1291
  unemployment effects, **10:**1342
productivity paradox, **8:**1039
product liability, **8:**1045-47
  "lemon laws," **2:**272
  Philip Morris, **7:***1001*, 1004
  risk management, **8:**1125, 1127
  tort actions, **6:**794, 796
product placement, **1:**27, 29, *30*
product standards, **10:**1322, 1323
Professional Golfers Association,
    9:1224
professional associations, **8:**1048-49
  five largest, **8:***1048*
  licensing, **10:**1375
  public relations, **8:**1067
  realtors, **8:**1090-91
  trade associations vs., **10:**1317
  See also chambers of commerce
professional licenses. *See* vocational
    licensing
professional sports. *See* sports
    industry
profit and loss, **8:**1050-53
  Amazon.com, **1:**50
  balance sheet, **1:**97
  breakeven point, **1:**119-20
  British Airways, **1:**124
  cartels and, **2:**187-88
  cash flow and, **2:**190
  competition and, **2:**244, 246
  corporate, **3:**301, 302, *305*
  corporate social responsibility vs.,
    3:301
  costs and, **3:**310
  customer service and, **3:**334
  division of labor and, **3:**372, 388
  e-commerce companies, **5:**714
  economic growth and, **3:**389
  economies of scale and, **3:**396-98
  education industry, **3:**404, 410
  Enron accounting and, **3:**422
  entrepreneurship, **3:**424
  Fortune 500 and, **4:**521
  futures market, **2:**226, **4:**530
  Hewlett-Packard divisions, **5:**620
  IBM losses, **5:**637
  income statement, **1:**26, **5:**647
  minimum wage and, **7:**880
  monopoly and, **7:**902-3, *904*
  overhead, **7:**974-75
  partnership, **7:**978
  price fixing and, **8:**1017, 1018,
    1133
  pricing and, **8:**1021, 1022
  research and development and,
    8:1111-12
  small business, **9:**1198
  supply and demand factors,
    8:1050-51
Wal-Mart, **10:**1387

profit sharing, **2:**239, **3:**299
  Ford Motor, **4:**513
  Lands' End, **6:**770
  Southwest Airlines, **9:***1220*,
    1221
  United Automobile Workers,
    10:1351
progressive tax, **5:**645-46, **9:**1272
promissory note, **1:**84, 86, **2:**163,
    3:343
property rights. *See* intellectual
    property; private property
protectionism, **8:**1054-57
  arguments for, **10:**1324-25
  balance of trade and, **1:**94-95
  capitalism and, **2:**178, 179
  competition vs., **2:**245, 246
  European Union and, **4:**460
  GATT and, **4:**540, 543, 545,
    10:1425
  Great Depression, **4:**563, **5:**581,
    583
  mercantilism and, **6:**850, 851,
    852
  tariffs, **1:**94-95, **6:**850-52,
    8:1016, **9:**1270
  as trade policy, **5:**706-7
Proudhon, Pierre-Joseph, **6:**838,
    8:1028
public assistance. *See* welfare
Public Citizen, Inc., **2:**274, **7:**926,
    927
public goods, **8:**1058-60
  microeconomics and, **7:**871-72
  recreation and, **8:**1100, *1101*
  Smith on, **9:**1204, **10:**1400
  tragedy of the commons and,
    10:1326
  types of, **8:***1059*
Public Interest Research Group,
    7:927, **9:**1258
public relations and marketing,
    business practice, **8:**1061-65,
    1066, 1068-69
  demand creation, **8:**1051
  demographics, **3:**355-57
  distribution channels, **3:**366-69
  goals of, **8:***1069*
  market research, **6:**835-36
  process phases, **8:***1066*
  Southwest Airlines, **9:**1221
Public Relations Consultants
    Association (Britain), **8:**1067
public relations industry, **8:**1066-69
  careers in, **8:**1067
  responsibilities, **8:***1064*
  tools of, **8:***1061*
Public Relations Society of America,
    8:1067
Public Safety Research Institute,
    7:927
public sector unionism, **6:**763,
    8:1070-73
  strikes, **9:**1254, 1268
  Taft–.Hartley Act and, **9:**1268
  teachers and, **7:**937-38
Public Utility Holding Company Act
    (1935), **8:**1105, *1106*

Public Works Administration,
    2:180, **6:**750, **7:***941*, 943
publishing industry, **8:**1074-79
  advertising, **1:**31-33
  Amazon.com, **1:**49-50, **8:**1077,
    1079
  AOL Time Warner, **1:**64, 65, 66
  Black Enterprise, **1:**114-15
  careers in, **8:**1077
  copyright, **2:**280-83, **8:**1112
  Disney and, **10:**1393
  e-business, **3:**382
  Farrar, Straus & Giroux,
    4:472-73
  Graham and, **4:**570-72
  Guinness Book of Records, **5:**593,
    594
  Hearst and, **5:**609-12, **8:**1075,
    1081
  international trade show, **2:***171*
  Johnson and, **6:**739-40
  Kinko's and, **6:**754
  market channels, **2:***171*
  Martha Stewart Omnimedia,
    9:*1238*, 1239, 1240
  Merrill and, **6:**859
  Pulitzer empire, **8:**1075, 1080-82
  Time Inc., **1:**66
  Wall Street Journal, **10:**1383-86
  Winfrey and, **10:**1410-12
Pulitzer, Joseph, **5:**609, **8:**1075,
    1080-82
Pulitzer Prizes, **8:**1075, 1080,
    1081-82
  categories, **8:**1082
  Farrar, Straus & Giroux winners,
    4:*473*
  for Graham autobiography,
    4:*571*, 572
  Wall Street Journal, **10:***1383*, 1385
Pullman, George, **3:**298, 299,
    9:1252
Pullman Company, **8:**1083-84
Pullman strike (1894), **9:**1252
Pure Food and Drug Act (1906),
    1:*121*, 122, **4:***448*, **5:***614*, 615
Putnam, Samuel, **6:**728

Q

Quesnay, François, **9:**1203
quotas
  employment, **1:**35
  import, **1:**70, 94, 95, **5:**706, 707,
    8:1054-55, 1057, **10:**1322,
    1323
  tariffs vs., **9:**1270
  university admissions, **1:**35-37
Qwest Communications
    International, **1:**90, **9:**1288

R

R&D. *See* research and development
Radclyffe, Charles, **10:**1378
radio, **5:**582, **7:**943, **9:**1282
  advertising, **1:**31, 32, *33*,
    2:265-66
  market research, **6:**833
  networks, **8:**1147
  Sarnoff and, **8:**1146-48

station ownership regulation, 2:266

transistor, 9:1217, *1218*

Radio Corporation of America. *See* RCA

Radisson, Pierre-Esprit, 5:622

Rail Passenger Service Act (1970), 10:1330

Railroad Average, 3:*376*, 377

railroad industry, 10:1329-30
  Brotherhood of Sleeping Car Porters, 8:1083-84
  Carnegie and, 2:184-85
  Chiquita and, 2:204
  deregulation, 8:1109
  Great Depression, 5:583
  Industrial Revolution, 5:653-54, *657*, 658
  Morgan financing, 7:906
  rate regulation, 8:1103-4, *1106*
  Rockefeller and, 8:1129
  Santa Fe trail and, 8:*1142*, 1144, 1145
  security industry and, 9:1176
  small-to-big business changeover, 9:*1197*
  Standard Oil and, 9:1231-32
  strikes, 9:1250-51, *1252*
  Swiss bank underwriting, 10:1346
  tourism and, 10:1311, 1312, 1313
  Vanderbilt and, 10:1362, 1363-64
  working conditions, 10:1418

Ramazinni, Bernardino, 4:454

Randolph, A. Philip, 8:1083-86

Random House, 8:1078

Rasheed, Abdul, 2:202

rational choice school, 9:1165

Ratner, Brett, 2:*193*

raw materials, 8:1087-89
  competition entry barrier, 7:900, *903*
  economic growth and, 3:*388*, 389
  energy industry, 3:414-19
  environmentalism and, 4:437, 439
  forest products industry, 4:617-18
  gross domestic product vs., 3:*388*
  population growth and, 6:817-18

Raytheon Corporation, 3:352, 353, 5:651

RBC. *See* Royal Bank of Canada

RBC Financial Group, 8:1131

RCA, 1:103, 4:549, 8:1146-48, 9:1218

RCA Laboratories, 8:1148

Reagan, Ronald, 3:300, 5:699, 6:751, 764, 10:1339, 1352
  air traffic controllers strike, 9:1254, 1268
  antitrust enforcement, 9:1187
  capitalism and, 2:*181*, 182-83
  defense industry and, 3:352
  deregulation, 3:358, 8:1109
  EPA and, 4:445

Greenspan and, 5:586

military spending, 4:478

monetarism, 4:527

Screen Actors Guild presidency, 9:*1169*, 1171

tax policy, 5:699

real estate industry, 8:1090-95
  capital gains, 2:175
  careers in, 8:1095
  contract law, 2:279
  corporate profits, 3:*305*
  debt and, 3:345, 346
  lending rules, 3:314, 316
  as market research source, 6:836
  mortgages, 7:913-15
  private property and, 8:1027-28
  professional associations, 8:*1048*
  Trump and, 10:1335-38
  valuation, 10:1360, 1361

real estate investment trusts, 8:1094-95

recession, 8:1096-98
  business cycles and, 2:152, 178
  Consumer Confidence Index, 2:261
  General Motors losses, 4:554
  government policy, 3:390
  income distribution, 5:644
  inflation slowed by, 5:659
  interest rates and, 3:316, 391
  inventory overhangs, 6:726-27, 731
  investment and, 6:729-30, 731
  Keynesian macroeconomics and, 6:750, 812
  labor market, 6:759
  mid-1970s, 7:947
  strikes and, 9:1250

Reconstruction Finance Corporation, 9:1200, 1201

recording industry. *See* music industry

Recording Industry Association of America, 2:284

recreation industry, 8:1099-1102
  arts and entertainment, 1:72-75
  careers in, 8:1102
  gambling, 4:534-36
  motorcycles, 5:598
  sports, 9:1223-27
  tourism, 10:1311-16
  Yamaha products, 10:1436

Reebok, 7:952

Regents of the University of California v. Bakke (1978), 1:36-37

Reginald Lewis International Law Center, 6:793

regulation of business and industry, 8:1103-9
  advertising, 1:32
  affirmative action and, 1:34-37
  agriculture, 1:47-48, 70
  airline ticket prices, 8:1024
  arbitration, 1:67-68
  AT&T, 1:88-89
  automobile safety, 7:927
  business cycles and, 2:151, 180
  business ethics and, 2:157-58
  business law and, 2:160-65

capitalism and, 2:179-83

chemical toxins, 9:1194, 1195

civil rights law, 1:56-60

competition and, 2:245, 246

Constitution and, 2:254, 255-57

consumer protection, 2:268, 272-75, 6:796

corporate social responsibility and, 3:300, 301

corporations and, 3:300, 301, 302

credit, 3:315-16, 318

credit card loans, 3:320-21

disability provisions, 1:56-60

e-business, 3:384

economic growth and, 3:389-90

energy industry, 3:416-17, 418

Enron collapse and, 3:423

environmentalism and, 4:439-51

equal employment opportunity and, 4:452-53

ergonomics and, 4:456

externalities, 4:465

Fair Labor Standards Act, 4:466-67

family leave, 4:469-71

Federal Trade Commission, 4:484-87

fishing industry, 4:508-10

food processing, 5:614-15

franchises, 4:523

futures market, 4:531

gaming industry, 4:536

genetically modified foods, 4:559

Great Depression, 3:359, 5:585, 8:1104-5, 1107

human resources compliance, 5:630-31

inflation and, 5:663, 8:1021

insurance companies, 5:683

intellectual property, 5:687-88

legal services, 6:781-84

liability, 6:797-99, 8:1046-47

licenses, 6:801-4

merger and acquisition, 6:853, 854

microeconomics and, 7:869, 871

minimum wage, 4:466, 7:877-82, 8:1013, 1014-15, 10:1417, 1418

mining, 7:885

monopolies, 7:902, 903-4

Nader campaign for, 7:917

natural monopolies, 8:1015-16, 1021

New Deal, 2:180, 7:941-42, 943

price controls, 8:1013-16, 1021

privatization vs., 8:1030-33

profit and loss and, 8:1051

rule of law and, 8:1138

securities market, 1:55, 9:1172-74

Smith's free market vs., 9:1204-5, 10:1400

smoking bans, 7:1003

sustainability and, 9:1266-67

telecommunications, 1:66, 2:246, 8:1105, 9:1286

time line, 8:*1106*

as tragedy of the commons solution, 10:1328

utilities, 8:1105-9, 10:1356, 1358-59

vocational licensing, 10:1374-76

working conditions, 7:960-63, 10:1417

See also antitrust; deregulation

Rehabilitation Act (1973), 1:34, 56, 2:*213*, 4:452-53

Rehwoldt, Sheri, *as contributor*, 2:215-16, 3:380-81, 6:739-40, 8:1140-41

Reichardt, Carl, 10:1046, *1407*

Reid, Harry, 2:255

Reinhart, Peter, *as contributor*, 1:54-55

REITs, 8:1094-95

Reliant Energy Company, 9:1224-25

RE/MAX (realtor), 8:1091

Remington, Frederick, 5:610

Remington Rand Corp., 2:250, 5:633

Renaissance Learning, 3:407

Renaissance Software, Inc., 5:648

REO auto company, 4:550

Republican Party, 7:954, 8:1130
  economic theory, 4:527
  environmentalism, 4:442, 448
  Wall Street Journal and, 10:*1383*, 1384

Research & Polling, Inc., 6:837

research and development, 8:1110-12
  Dow Chemical, 3:374, *375*
  Edison projects, 3:399-401
  expenditures (1960-2000), 8:*1110*
  General Electric, 4:548, 8:1111
  genetic engineering, 4:555-59
  IBM, 5:632-37, 8:1111
  information technology, 5:669, 670
  innovation and, 5:679-80
  intellectual property costs, 5:690
  by multinationals, 7:919
  patent rights, 8:1112
  product development, 8:1034, 1037
  productivity and, 8:1041
  public good and, 8:1059
  reverse engineering, 8:1121-23
  Xerox, 10:*1429*, 1430-32

reserve requirements, 7:*893*, 894, 895

Resettlement Administration, 7:*941*

Resor, Stanley, 1:32

resource allocation
  price controls and, 8:1016
  private property and, 8:1028
  productivity and, 8:1041
  profits and, 8:*1050*
  scarcity and, 9:1162

Resource Conservation and Recovery Act (1976), 4:*448*

restraint of trade
  rulings, 8:*1104*
  Sherman Antitrust Act, 9:1187-89
  See also antitrust; monopoly

resume, **5:**627, 629, 716, **6:**735, 736, **8:1113-14**, **10:**1302
retail and wholesale, **8:1115-20**
   advertising, **1:**27-30
   bar codes, **1:**103-5
   Better Business Bureau, **1:**112
   book superstores, **8:**1079
   brand names, **1:**116-18
   Consumer Price Index, **2:**269-71
   corporate profits, **3:***305*
   credit cards, **1:**52, 53, **3:**319
   credit history, **3:**324
   customer service, **3:**333-35
   distribution channels, **3:**366-69
   e-business, **3:**382-85
   entrepreneurship, **3:**424
   innovation, **5:**679
   inventory, **6:**725
   just-in-time industry and, **6:**744
   minimum wage, **7:**880, 881
   NAICS codes, **7:**928-29
   online sales, **1:**49-50
   pricing, **8:**1018, 1024, 1025
   retail, **8:**1115-18, 1119
   small business component, **9:**1196
   temporary workers, **10:**1301
   Wal-Mart, **3:**424, **10:**1387-90
   wholesale, **8:**1118-20
   See also consumerism
Reuters, **10:**1434
Reuther, Walter, **1:**40, **2:**222, **10:**1351
revenue tariffs, **5:**706
Reverend Billy (Bill Talen), **2:**267
reverse engineering, **5:**636, 649, **8:1121-23**
R. G. Dun & Company, **3:***336, 337*
R. H. Macy's, **3:**333, **8:**1115
Ricardo, David, **2:**178, **6:**851
Rice, Linda Johnson, **6:***739*, 740
Rice Broadcasting, **10:**1339
Riddle, John, *as contributor*, **5:**715-16, **7:**954-55, **8:**1048-49, **9:**1290-92
Ridge, Tom, **3:**403
Rifkin, Jeremy, **8:**1042
Rigas, John, **3:**297
right-to-work laws, **9:**1253
risk management, **8:1124-27**
   bonds vs. stocks, **9:**1242
   capital gains and, **2:**176
   credit history, **3:**326
   credit ratings, **3:**317, 328, 337
   debt and, **3:**344
   Enron, **3:**421
   futures market, **2:**197-98, 226, **4:**529, 530, 531
   insurance industry, **5:**681-83
   interest rate, **5:**696
   investment, **3:**294, **6:**728, 729
   labor market, **6:**759
   returns and, **9:**1159, 1241-43
   rule of law and, **8:**1139
   supply and demand factors, **8:**1050
   venture capital, **10:**1368
risk rating, **3:**317, 328

R. J. Reynolds, **7:**1004, **8:**1046
RJR Nabisco, **5:**637, **7:***1001*, 1002
Roberts, Julia, **6:***799*
Robinson, Harriet H., **6:**806
Robinson, James, **1:**52
Robinson, Smokey, **4:**568-69
Robinson, Solveig, *as contributor*, **8:**1074-79
Robinson-Patman Act (1936), **4:**485, **7:***900*, **9:**1197
robotics, **1:***110*, **8:***1040*
Roche, James M., **4:**553
Rockefeller, David, **7:**945
Rockefeller, John D., **2:**186, **5:**583, **8:1128-30**
   National Black Chamber of Commerce, **7:**933
   oil refining, **10:**1305
   profit and loss, **8:**1050, 1051, 1133
   public relations, **8:**1066
   Standard Oil, **7:**901, *902*, **8:**1133, 1134, **9:**1231-34
   vertical integration, **7:**972
Rockefeller, John D., Jr., **8:**1130, **9:***1232*
Rockefeller, Nelson Aldrich, **8:**1130
Rockefeller, William, **8:**1129, **9:***1231*
Rockefeller & Andrews, **9:**1231
Rockefeller, Andres & Flagler, **8:**1129
Rockefeller Center (N.Y.C.), **1:**92, **8:**1130
Rockefeller Foundation, **8:**1130
Rockefeller Institute, **4:**555, **8:**1130
Rockefeller University, **8:**1130
Rockwell International, **3:**353, **10:**1350
Rodriguez, Alex, **9:**1227
Rodriguez, Arturo, **1:**69
Roe v. Wade (1973), **2:**257
Rogers, Richard, **1:**77
Rollins, Hugh, **9:**1220
Roosevelt, Eleanor, **6:**740
Roosevelt, Franklin D., **3:**360, 365, **5:**698, **10:**1384
   bank closure by, **9:**1172
   capitalism and, **2:**179, 180, *181*
   environmental projects, **4:**439, *440*
   fair employment practices, **8:**1085
   farm program, **1:**47
   labor relations, **1:**39, **6:**763, **7:**939, **9:**1252, 1274
   minimum wage, **7:**878-79
   New Deal, **5:**585, **6:**750, **7:***941*, 943, 996, **9:**1210
   Perkins and, **7:**994, *995*, 996
   regulatory legislation, **8:**107, 1104, *1105*
   social security, **9:***1211*, 1212
Roosevelt, Theodore, **1:**67, **4:**439, *440*, **5:**615, **7:**907
Root, Elihu, **3:**350
Root, Elisha King, **5:**693
Ross, Diana, **4:**569
Ross, Steve, **1:**65

Rossotti, Charles O., **5:**700
Roth IRA, **9:**1159, *1160*
Rousseau, Jean-Jacques, **2:**199
Royal Bank of Canada, **8:1131-32**
Royal Dutch/Shell, **3:**416, **7:**719-20, **8:1133-36**, **10:**1307
Ruckelshaus, William D., **4:**445
rule of law, **8:1137-39**
   business law, **2:**160-65
   components of, **8:**1137-38
   Constitution as., **2:**253-57
   contract law, **2:**276-79
   copyright, **2:**280-84
   corporations and, **3:**302
   private property and, **8:**1026
   privatization and, **8:**1032
"rule of reason" (judicial), **8:**1104, **9:**1189
Rural Electrification Administration, **7:***941*
Russell, Bertrand, **6:**749
Russia
   IMF loan, **5:**703
   McDonald's, **6:**848
   nonprotected intellectual property, **6:**803
   oil production, **7:**970
   private property status, **8:**1026
   privatization, **8:**1032, 1033
   See also Soviet Union
Rustin, Bayard, **8:**1086

S

S&P 400 Index, Domini 400 Social Index vs., **3:***301*
S&P 500 Index, **1:**54, **2:**152, 225, **4:**521, **6:**779
   mutual index funds and, **7:**923
   Nasdaq Composite index vs., **7:**931
Safe Drinking Water Act (1974), **4:**448
SAG. *See* Screen Actors Guild
Saint-Simon, Henri de, **9:**1206, 1207
Salazar, Antonio, **4:**475, 476
sales tax, **9:**1272, 1273
   information technology, **9:**1282
   small business, **9:**1199
   state rates, **9:***1273*
Salinas de Gortari, Salinas, **7:***956*
Samuel, Marcus, **8:**1133, *1134*
Samuelson, Paul, **8:1140-41**
Sanitas Nut Food Company, **6:**745
Santa Clara County v. Southern Pacific Railroad (1886), **3:**302
Santa Fe Trail, **8:1142-45**
Sanyo, **7:**909
Sarah's Kitchen, **9:***1198*
Sarandon, Susan, **9:***1171*
Sarbanes, Paul, **9:***1173*
Sarbanes–Oxley Act (2002), **2:**157, 159
Sarnoff, David, **8:1146-48**
Sarnoff Corporation, **8:**1148
Saro-Wiwa, Ken, **7:**920, **8:**1135
Satterlee, Herbert, **4:**550
Saudi Arabian Oil Company, **10:**1307
Savery, Thomas, **5:**653

savings account, **6:**729, **9:**1157, 1158, 1159
savings and investment options, **9:1157-60**
   business cycles, **2:**149, 151, 152
   capital gains, **2:**175-76
   compound interest, **2:**247-48
   consumer confidence, **3:**315, 318, 364
   disposable income and, **3:**363-65
   diversification, **9:**1158, 1159, 1160, 1243
   economic growth and, **3:**363-64
   Fidelity Investments and, **4:**491-92
   initial public offering and, **5:**676-78
   Merrill Lynch and, **6:**858, 859-60
   mutual funds, **3:**293-94, 301, **7:**922-24
   personal finances and, **4:**499
   risk and returns, **9:**1158-59, 1241-43, 1246
   Schwab and, **9:**1166-68
   stocks and bonds, **3:**302, **9:**1241-45
   wealth from, **10:**1398
   See also pension and retirement plans
savings and loans, **8:**1094
Say, Jean-Baptiste, **6:**750
Say's Law, **6:**750
SBA. *See* Small Business Administration
SBC Communications, **1:**90, **3:**376, **9:**1288
scabs, **9:**1250
Scalia, Antonin, **1:**58
scarcity, **9:1161-63**
   intellectual property and, **5:**689
   microeconomics and, **7:**869-72
   opportunity cost and, **7:**964
   price controls and, **8:**1016
   valuation and, **10:**1360
Schlaet, Arnold, **10:**1305, *1307*
Schlappi, Michael, *as contributor*, **4:**555-59
Schlender, Brent, **7:**874
Schneider, Ralph, **3:***321*
Schotz, John, **6:**775, 776
Schug, Mark, *as contributor*, **3:**319-23, **7:**964-65
Schultz, Howard, **9:**1235, *1237*
Schultz, Theodore, **5:**625
Schultz v. Wheaton Glass Company (1970), **10:**1414-15
Schumacher, E. F., **4:**441, **9:**1264
Schuman, Robert, **4:**457
Schumpeter, Joseph A., **5:**690, **9:1164-65**
Schwab, Charles, **9:1166-68**
Schwab, Michael, **5:**601, 602
Schwartz, Robert, **2:**152
Schwarzenbach, Ernest B., **9:***1217*
Schweizerische Bangesellschart, **10:**1347
Scientific Data Systems, **10:**1430-32
Scott, Thomas A., **2:**184, 185
Scott Newman Foundation, **7:**945

Screen Actors Guild, **9:**1169-71
Scripps, Edward W., **8:**1075
Scripps Howard, **8:**1075
Sea Around Us, The (Carson), **9:**1194
search engine, **10:**1433-34
Sears, **3:**376, **4:**513, **5:**679, **7:**909, **10:**1389
    catalog sales, **2:**265
    credit card, **3:**319
    employment discrimination complaints, **4:**453
    Lands' End acquisition by, **6:**770, 772
seasonal unemployment, **10:**1343, 1344
seasonal workers, **10:**1303
Seattle Computer Products, **7:**874
secondary boycotts, **6:**768, **9:**1269
securities. *See* stocks and bonds
Securities Act (1933), **9:**1172
Securities and Exchange Commission, **1:**55, **3:**403-4, **4:**519, **7:**930, **8:**1105, **9:1172-74**
    accounting industry oversight, **2:**260
    commissioners, **9:**1173
    day trading and, **3:**342
    initial public offering and, **5:**677
    merger and acquisition filing, **6:**853
    New Deal and, **7:**943, **9:***941*
    securities prospectus approval by, **9:**1244
    United Brands' ethics charge, **2:**206
Securities Exchange Act (1934), **7:**943, **8:**1105, *1106*, **9:**1172-73
Securities Industry Association, **7:**930
Securities Investor Protection Corporation, **9:**1157, 1173
security industry, **9:1175-77**
    industrial espionage and, **5:**648-52
    strike breaking by, **9:**1250, 1251, 1252
Seitz, Peter, **6:**813
Selden, George, **4:**511-12
Self, James K., *as contributor*, **7:**956-59, **9:**1272-73, **10:**1322-25
self-employment
    freelancing, **4:**524-26
    social security coverage, **9:**1214
    See also entrepreneurship
self-interest, **3:**424, **5:**690
    economic growth and, **3:**389
    environmentalism and, **4:**441-42
    profits and, **8:**1050
    as Smith free-market basis, **2:**177, **7:**869, **9:**1202, 1203-4, **10:**1400
Selig, Bud, **9:**1227
Selig, William N., **5:**611
sellers and buyers. *See* supply and demand
Sen, Amartya, **6:**818

seniority system, **2:**237, 238, 239
September 11 (2001) terrorist attack
    airline subsidy and, **9:**1256
    bankruptcies and, **1:**101-2
    consumer spending and, **8:**1097, 1101
    defense industry and, **3:**350, 354
    Federal Reserve and, **4:**480
    government regulation and, **3:**362
    security industry and, **9:**1177
    tourism effects, **10:**1315
    Wall Street Journal and, **10:***1383*, 1386
Sequoia Capital, **10:**1433
Service Corps of Retired Executives, **9:**1198, 1201
service economy, **9:1178-83**
    bundling and, **1:**137-38
    corporate profits, **3:***305*
    cost and, **3:**307
    e-business and, **3:**382, 384
    economic growth and, **3:**392
    immigrant workers and, **5:**642
    income distribution and, **5:**644, *645*
    information technology and, **9:***1282*
    labor unions and, **1:**42
    pay equity, **7:**987, 989
    small business component, **9:**1196, 1197
    tourism and, **10:**1312-16
    wealth distribution and, **10:***1397*
Service Employees International Union, **1:**42
Seven Arts Productions, Ltd., **1:**65
Seven-Up, **7:**1002
severance pay, **9:**1229
sex discrimination, **1:**34, **2:**212-14, **10:**1413, 1414-15, 1418
sex tourism, **10:**1315
sexual harassment, **2:**213, **5:**630, **9:**1170, **1184-86**, **10:**1414, 1415, 1416
Shannon, Claude E., **5:***663*, 665
Shaw, Jane S., *as contributor*, **10:**1326-28
Shell Oil. *See* Royal Dutch/Shell
Shell Transport & Trading Company, **8:**1133, *1134*, *1136*
Sherman, John, **9:***1187*
Sherman Antitrust Act (1890), **2:***181*, **6:**762, **9:1187-90**, 1197
    AT&T and, **1:**88, 89
    General Motors and, **4:**553
    Microsoft and, **7:**874, 875
    passage of, **8:**1104, *1106*, *1128*, 1130
    price fixing illegality, **8:**1018, 1019, 1051
    provisions, **2:**245, **7:***900*, 903-4
    Standard Oil and, **7:***902*, 904, **8:**1130, **9:***1231*, 1234
Shewhart, Walter, **10:**1310
Shi Guangsheng, **10:***1427*
shipping industry, **7:**890-91, **10:**1329, 1418

shoe industry, **3:**355, **7:**950-53, 958
shopping malls, **2:**266, 267, **8:**1093, 1095, 1116
    number and retail sales (1990-2001), **8:***1116*
    outlet pricing, **8:**1025
shortages
    price controls and, **8:**1013, 1016
    supply and demand, **9:**1261-63
short-term capital gains, **2:**176
short-term loan. *See* commercial paper
Shuttlefly, **2:**216
Siegel, Jeremy, **9:**1159
Siegel, Zev, **9:**1235
Sierra Club, **4:**516, **7:**958
Sikorsky, Igor, **9:**1191-93
Sikorsky Aircraft Corporation, **9:**1193
Sikorsky Manufacturing Corporation, **9:**1192
Silent Spring (Carson), **2:**268, **3:**299-300, **4:**439, *440*, 443, 447, **9:**1194-95
Silicon Graphics, **2:***215*, 216
Silicon Valley
    Cisco Systems, **2:**207-9
    economic conditions, **4:**566-67
    entrepreneurship, **3:**424, 427
    Hewlett-Packard, **4:**501, **5:**619-21
    Intel, **5:**684
    Netscape Navigator, **5:**711
    venture capital, **10:**1369-70
    wealth and, **10:**1397
    Whitman and, **10:**1408
    Xerox PARC, **10:**1430
silver, **8:**1087
    coins, **7:**898
    futures market, **2:**198, 225
    mercantilism and, **1:**92, **6:**849, 850
    mining of, **7:**898
    production (1990-2000), **8:***1089*
Simon & Schuster, **8:**1078
Simon Property Group, Inc., **8:**1095
Sinclair, Upton, **2:**267
Singer, Isaac, **6:**828
Singer Sewing Machine Company, **4:**522, **7:**916
Single European Act (1986), **4:***457*, 459
Sisson, Mary, *as contributor*, **1:**64-66, 70-71, 76-77, 87-90, 112-13, 124-26, 131-35, 136-38, **2:**189-90, 236-41, 242-46, 249-52, 258-60, **4:**443-46, 524-26, 537-39, **5:**588-91, 603-8, 673-75, 684-86, 692-93, **6:**725-27, 772-77, **7:**883-87, 890-92, 916-21, 925-27, 976-79, **8:**1021-25, 1099-1102, 1121-23, **9:**1178-83, 1259-63, 1284-89, **10:**1368-73, 1374-76
sit-down strike, **1:**38, 40, **4:**550, 552, *553*, **9:**1253, **10:**1349
Six Sigma program, **4:**549

Sixteenth Amendment, **5:***697*, 698
Skilling, Jeffrey, **3:**422, *423*
SkillSoft, **3:**406
Slater, Samuel, **5:**657
Sloan, Alfred P., **4:**551, *552*
Sloan School, **6:**843
slogans, **1:**29, 32, **2:***218*
small business, **9:1196-99**, 1200-1201
    Americans with Disabilities Act impact, **1:**59-60
    Black Enterprise and, **1:**114, 115
    chambers of commerce, **2:**191-93
    credit history, **3:**326
    Economic Opportunity Act and, **3:**393
    entrepreneurship, **3:**425-27
    as Fair Labor Standards Act exemptions, **4:**467
    freelancing vs., **4:**524
    Lewis law firm and, **6:**792
    management, **6:**822
    minimum wage and, **7:**877, 881
    National Black Chamber of Commerce, **7:**933-34
    partnership, **7:**976
    public relations, **8:**1069
    retail sales, **8:**1117
    social security coverage, **9:**1214
    venture capital, **10:**1368-70
Small Business Administration, **1:**60, **6:**792, 836, **7:**934, **9:**1197-98, **1200-1201**, **10:**1370
Small Business Administration Act, **9:**1196
Small Business Development Centers, **9:**1201
Small Business Investment Company (SBIC) program, **9:**120, 1200, **10:**1370
Small Defense Plants Administration, **9:**1201
Smaller War Plants Corporation, **9:**1200-1201
"smart" devices, **5:***651*, **7:**898, **9:**1177
Smith, Adam, **9:1202-5**
    capitalism and, **2:**156, 177-78, *181*
    copyright and, **2:**281
    on division of labor, **3:**370-71, 388, 389, **9:**1204, **10:**1400
    economic growth and, **3:**388-89
    entrepreneurship and, **3:**424
    free market theory, **1:**92, **5:**705-6, **6:**851, **7:**901, **9:**1203-4, **10:**1396, 1400-1401
    "invisible hand" concept, **2:**156, **3:**358, 361, **5:**690
    key ideas of, **9:***1204*
    Malthusian theory vs., **6:**816, 817
    mercantilist theory vs., **6:***849*, 851
    as microeconomics founder, **7:**869

Smith, Adam (cont.)
  Veblen's consumer-influenced theory and, 10:1365
  Wealth of Nations, 10:1400-1401
Smith, Al, 7:994
Smith, Fred, 4:488, 489
Smith, Frederick (father), 4:488
Smith, Hamilton, 4:555
Smith, Lois, *as contributor*, 1:116-18, 3:329-32
Smith, William A., 9:1231, 10:1305
Smits, H. N. J., 9:1265
Socal. *See* Chevron
social class. *See* class
social cost, 10:1326
social democracy, 9:1208-9, 1210
socialism, 9:1206-10
  capitalism and, 2:178, 183, 9:1164, 1165
  energy industry, 3:418
  Marx and, 6:838
  private property and, 8:1028
  privatization and, 8:1033
  Schumpeter theory and, 9:1164, 1165
  strikes and, 9:1252
  utopian communities, 2:227, 9:1206, *1209*
Socialist Party, U.S., 8:1083, 9:1210
Social Science Research Council, 8:1140
Social Security Act (1935), 5:633, 7:942-43, 9:1211, 1212
  amendments, 9:1214, 1215
  Perkins and, 7:996, 997
Social Security Administration, 9:1199, 1214
social security and Medicare, 2:180, 9:1211-16
  Consumer Price Index, 2:271
  cost-of-living adjustment, 3:*311*, 5:662
  human resources department, 5:630
  IBM contract, 5:633
  identity theft and, 3:328
  payroll and, 7:990, 992-93
  wealth distribution and, 10:1396
Social Security Board, 9:1212, 1214
Sohio, 9:1234
sole proprietorship, 9:1198
Solow, Robert, 8:1039, 1110
"Some Aspects of the Pure Theory of Capital" (Samuelson), 8:1140
Sonny Bono Copyright Extension Act (1998), 2:165, 284
Sontag, Susan, 4:473
Sony Corporation, 7:889, 908-9, 9:1217-19
Sony Music, 8:1018, 9:1219
Sony Pictures China, 9:1219
Sony Pictures Classics, 9:1219
Sorenson, Charles, 1:82
Sotheby's, 8:1019, 1020
Southard, Jo Lynn, *as contributor*, 7:987-89
South Improvement Company, 9:1231-32

Southwest Airlines, 2:169, 3:334, 8:1127, 9:1220-22
Soviet Union (former)
  Afghanistan invasion, 2:231, 232, 3:354
  cold war and, 2:180-81, 230, 231
  collapse of, 2:*181*, 183, *228*, 232, 3:359, 4:563, 9:*1209*
  communism, 2:179-82, 227-31, 9:1207, 1208, 1210
  Goodwill Games and, 10:1340
  IMF and, 5:702
  information technology, 5:*663*, 665, 712
  perestroika, 2:*181*
  space race, 3:351
  See also Russia
soybean crop, 1:43, *44*, 45, 70
  futures market, 2:225
space program, 3:351, 353, 374, 4:550, 553
  shuttle disaster (1986), 10:1339
space tourism, 10:1315
special drawing rights (SDRs), 5:702
specialization. *See* division of labor
specialized small business investment companies (SSBICs), 9:1200
Spector, Robert, 3:335
speculation, 2:152, 5:678, 6:858, 8:*1143*
  currency, 4:462
  futures market, 2:197-98, 226, 4:529-31
Spencer, Herbert, 6:817
Spielberg, Steven, 10:1411
Spies, August, 5:601, 602
Spitzer, Eliot, 6:860, 8:1018
sports industry, 9:1223-27
  Americans with Disabilities Act ruling, 1:58
  careers in, 9:1224
  collective bargaining, 2:225
  consumer demographics, 3:355
  Disney hockey franchise, 10:1393
  Major League Baseball Players Association, 6:813-15
  Nike and, 7:950-53
  television broadcasts, 10:1339
  Turner and, 10:1339, *1340*
spreadsheet, 3:338-39, 340, 6:826
Springfield System, 6:828
Squibb. *See* Bristol-Myers Squibb
Squibb, Charles and Edward, 1:122
Squibb, Edward Robinson, 1:122
SRI funds, 3:301
SRI International, 8:1148
S. S. Kresge, 10:1387
stagflation, 2:182, 5:661, 6:751
Staggers Rail Act (1980), 8:1109
Stalin, Joseph, 2:179, 228, 229, 9:1207, *1209*
Stamp Act (1765), 6:851
Standard & Poor's 500. *See* S&P 500 Index
Standard Industrial Classification (SIC), 7:228, 928, 8:1115

standardization
  assembly line, 1:81-82
  benchmarking, 1:110-11
  British Airways, 1:125
  corporate accounting, 8:1052-53
  IBM personal computer, 2:251, 252
  interchangeable parts, 5:657, 658, 692-93
  ISO 9000, 1:110-11, 6:732-34, 10:1318
  manufacturing, 6:828
  McDonald's operation, 6:756-57, 847, 848
  trade association, 10:1318
standard of living, 9:1228-30
  cost of living, 3:311, 313
  economic growth and, 3:388, 392
  entrepreneurship and, 3:428
  foreign worker wages and, 4:565
  income distribution and, 5:645
  Industrial Revolution and, 5:653
  international trade and, 5:708
  liberal economic theory and, 10:1396-97, 1400
  personal finance and, 4:497-98, 500
  worker demands, 3:372
Standard Oil, 8:1104, 9:1231-34
  breakup of, 7:902, 904, 9:1188, 1234, 10:1305
  as monopoly, 7:901, *902*, 904
  Rockefeller and, 8:*1128*, 1129-30
  Shell competition, 8:1133, 1134
  Texaco and, 10:1305
  vertical integration, 7:972, 8:1129
Standard Oil Co. v. United States (1911), 7:902
standards. *See* standardization
Stanford University, 2:215, 3:424, 4:528, 5:619, 620, 9:1166, 10:1433
  Fiorina and, 4:501, *502*
  genetic engineering, 4:555
  Yahoo! search engine, 5:711, *712*
Stanley brothers, 10:1330
Stanley Home Products, 1:76
Stanley Steamers, 10:1330
Staples, 9:1200
Star (computer), 10:*1429*, 1431-32
Starbucks, 2:267, 9:1235-37
Star Enterprise, 10:1307
Star-Kist Tuna, 1:139-40
StarLink, 4:559
State Street v. Signature (1998), 7:986
statutory liability, 6:796-97
steam power, 5:653-58, 665, 668, 6:828, 9:1278, 1279, 10:1329, 1330
steamship industry, 10:1362-64
Stearns, Dick, 6:769
steel industry, 5:658
  Carnegie and, 2:184-86
  competition and, 2:246
  downsizing, 3:378, 6:832
  innovation and, 5:679, *680*
  labor unions, 1:40

Morgan and, 7:905, 906
  pricing and, 8:1013, 1016, 1050, 1056
  raw materials, 8:1088
  smelting plant, 6:*830*
  strikes, 9:1251-52
  subsidy, 9:*1262*, 1263
  tariffs, 1:95, 2:246, 4:460, 8:1056, *1057*, 9:*1262*
  U. S. Steel, 10:1353-55
Steel Trust, 9:1232
Steinbeck, John, 5:584
Steinem, Gloria, 8:1077
Stephenson, George and Robert, 5:654, *657*
Stern, Richard, 2:278-79
Stevenson, Adlai, 4:533
stewardship, 8:1027, 1028, 1029
Stewart, Martha, 1:118, 8:1100, 9:1238-40
Stewart, Meredith, 3:*422*
Stigler, George, 3:358, 359, 4:528
Stillman, Charles B., 7:936
Stock and Exchange Board. *See* New York Stock Exchange
Stockholm Conference on Human Environment (1971), 4:439, *440*
stock market crash (1929), 2:149, *151*, 180, *181*, 3:317, 364, 5:581, 583, 6:750, 858, 859, 7:947, 10:1384, *1385*
  Great Depression and, 8:1097, 1131-32
  SEC founding following, 9:1172
stock market crash (1987), 2:152, 6:792, 9:1174
  Federal Reserve and, 4:480
stock market crash (2000), 2:190
stock options, 2:241, 3:296, 9:1229
  for Starbucks employees, 9:1236
  technology boom, 10:1398
  for Wal-Mart employees, 10:1390
stocks and bonds, 9:1241-45
  accountant audits, 2:260
  American Stock Exchange, 1:54-55
  as assets, 1:84, 196
  bond issuance, 3:317
  bonds vs. stocks, 9:1242, 1245
  bull markets, 7:947-48
  business cycles and, 2:149, 151-52, 180, *181*, 3:364
  business ethics and, 2:153
  as capital, 2:*173*, 174
  capital gains, 2:175-76
  Chicago Board of Trade traders, 2:198
  compound interest return, 2:247
  corporate financing with, 3:302
  corporate governance and, 3:293-97, 303-4
  corporate scandal effects, 3:297
  day trading, 3:341-42, 9:1245
  debt claims, 3:344-45
  discount brokers, 9:1167, 1245
  dividends, 3:302, 304, 317
  Dow Jones Average, 3:376-77

e-business and, **3**:382
exchange rates and, **4**:462
federal regulation, **7**:941, 943,
    8:1105, **9**:1172-74
Federal Reserve and, **4**:480, 482
Fidelity Investments and,
    4:491-92
financial managers and, **4**:493-96
fraud arbitration, **1**:68
futures market, **2**:198, *225*
Great Depression and, **5**:581,
    582, 583
income statement, **5**:647
initial public offering, **5**:676-78
investment analysis, **6**:728
as investment option, **9**:1157-58,
    1159
as Leading Economic Index
    component, **6**:778, 779
margin buying, **5**:581-82
mergers and acquisitions and,
    6:853, 854-55
Merrill Lynch and, **6**:858-60
monetary policy and, **7**:894
Morgan and, **7**:906, *906*, 907
mutual funds, **7**:922-21
Nasdaq, **7**:930-32
New York Stock Exchange,
    7:947-49
risk management, **8**:1127
risks and returns, **9**:1158-59,
    1241, 1242-43, 1245
Schwab and, **9**:1166-68
socially responsible investing,
    3:301
as Southwest Airlines employee
    benefits, **9**:1221
stockholder reports, **4**:*493*
stocks vs. bonds, **9**:1158-59
valuation, **10**:1360
wealth generation from, **10**:1398
Stockton and Darlington Railway,
    5:654, *657*
Strachey, Lytton, **6**:749
straight-line depreciation, **1**:61-62
strategic planning, **9**:1246-48
Straus, Robert W., Jr., **4**:472, *473*
Strauss, Levi, **6**:*785*, *786*
strikes, **9**:1249-54
    AFL-CIO history, **1**:*38*, 39, 40
    banana workers, **2**:205
    California farm workers, **2**:196
    collective bargaining, **2**:221, 223
    colonial-era printers, **10**:1417
    corporate responsibility and,
        3:299
    Haymarket Square riot, **5**:601-2
    legal restraints, **6**:764, 767, 768,
        9:1268
    professional sports, **6**:814, *815*,
        9:1227
    Screen Actors Guild, **9**:1169,
        1171
    as socialist agenda, **9**:1210
    Teamster, **9**:1276
    textile mills, **10**:1417
    United Auto Workers,
        10:1349-50, *1352*
Stringfellow, **10**:1331-32

Stroh brewery, **7**:1002
structural unemployment, **10**:1343,
    1344
subsidy, **4**:477, **9:1255-58**
    agriculture, **1**:47, 70, **7**:941,
        9:1255, 1257, *1258*
    competition vs., **2**:245
    microeconomics and, **7**:871
    price controls and, **8**:1013, 1016
    sports facilities, **9**:1225-26
    steel industry, **8**:1056, **9**:*1262*,
        1263
    trade policy, **1**:95, **4**:543, **5**:706,
        8:1056, **10**:*1323*, 1324-25
Subway, **3**:427, **4**:*523*
sugar, **2**:217, 219, 225
    price supports, **1**:70
Sugar Act (1764), **6**:851
Sullivan, Colleen, *as contributor*,
    1:27-30, 114-15
Summers, Lawrence, **3**:359-60
Sunkist, Inc., **1**:31
Sun Microsystems, **4**:501, **5**:670
    browser, **2**:216
    inventory overhang, **6**:727
    Java programming language,
        5:711, *712*
    team-up strategy, **5**:680
Sun Yat-sen, **2**:229
supercenters, **8**:1116, **10**:1390
Superfund, **4**:444-45, *446*, *448*
supermarkets. *See* grocery industry
supply and demand, **9:1259-63**
    business cycles, **2**:149, 150
    capital gains and, **2**:*175*
    capitalism and, **2**:177
    commodities market, **2**:225-26
    comparative advantage, **2**:233-35
    competition and, **2**:242-46
    demand pull inflation theory,
        5:660-61
    elasticity, **9**:1263
    exchange rates, **4**:461
    externalities, **4**:463, 464, *465*
    free market and, **6**:816,
        9:1203-4, **10**:1400
    Great Depression and, **5**:582-83
    inventory and, **6**:725-26
    just-in-time inventory and,
        6:741-44
    Keynesian economics and, **6**:750
    labor market and, **6**:758-59
    labor unions and, **6**:765
    Leading Economic Index and,
        6:778
    microeconomics and, **7**:869-70
    monopolistic pricing and, **7**:903
    oil prices and, **7**:970
    population growth and, **6**:816
    price controls and, **8**:1013, 1014,
        1016
    price fixing and, **8**:1018
    pricing and, **7**:903, 970,
        8:1021-22, 1025, 1050, 1103
    profit and loss and, **8**:1050-51
    property rights and, **8**:1026
    Say's Law and, **6**:750
    scarcity and, **9**:1161-63
    technology and, **9**:1281

valuation, **10**:1360-61
    Veblen theory and, **10**:1365
supply chain. *See* business-to-
    business sales
supply-side economics, **6**:751
Supreme Liberty Life Insurance
    Company, **6**:739
surgery, **5**:605, 608
surplus
    federal, **4**:477, 478, 503
    supply and demand, **9**:1261
Survey Research Center, **2**:261-62,
    6:779
sustainable development, **3**:301,
    9:1264-67
    economic growth and, **3**:390
    energy industry and, **3**:418
    environmentalism and, **4**:442
    fishing industry and, **4**:510
    World Trade Organization and,
        4:545
Suzuki Motor Company, **4**:554,
    5:599
sweatshops, **4**:564, 565-66,
    10:1418, 1420
Sweeney, John J., **1**:38, 42
Swift Company, **1**:81
swine production, **1**:45, 46
    futures market, **2**:*225*
Swiss Banking Corporation,
    10:*1346*
Sylvan Learning, **3**:407
Sylvis, William H., **10**:1413
synergy, **1**:66, 123

T
Tabulating Machine Company,
    5:632, *633*
Taft, Robert, **9**:1268
Taft, William Howard, **10**:1418
Taft–Hartley Act (1947), **1**:*38*, 40,
    6:764, 767, 768, **7**:940,
    9:1268-69, **10**:1351
    anticommunist loyalty oath,
        9:1170
    provisions, **9**:1253, *1269*
takeover. *See* merger and acquisition
takings clause (Fourth
    Amendment), **2**:256
Talen, Bill (Reverend Billy), **2**:267
Tan, Bill, *as contributor*, **1**:78-80
Tandy, Vertner Woodson, **10**:1381
tangible assets, depreciation of,
    1:61-63
Tappan, Lewis, **3**:336, 337
Tarbell, Ida, **9**:*1231*, 1233, 1234
Target, **8**:1018, **10**:1387
target marketing, **6**:837
tariff, **9:1270-71**
    balance of payment, **1**:92
    balance of trade, **1**:94
    business cycles and, **2**:151
    as competition barrier, **2**:245,
        246
    countries with highest-lowest
        barriers, **8**:*1056*
    free trade vs., **2**:178, 179, 180,
        245
    GATT rounds, **4**:540, 543, 545,
        10:1425

Great Depression, **5**:581, 583
    as import limitation, **10**:1322
    intellectual property piracy, **6**:803
    Latin American banana exports,
        2:206
    mercantilism and, **6**:849, 850,
        851, 852
    NAFTA and, **7**:956
    as price control, **8**:1016
    protectionism, **1**:94-95,
        8:1054-57
    steel industry, **1**:*95*, **2**:246, **4**:460,
        8:1056, *1057*, **9**:*1262*
    as trade restriction, **5**:706, 707
    types of, **8**:1054
    See also protectionism
Tartikoff, Brandon, **6**:774
Tate, John, **7**:*949*
Tatum, Donn, **10**:1392
taxation, **9:1272-73**
    business cycles and, **2**:150, 151,
        152, 180
    as business liability, **1**:86, 97
    of capital gains, **2**:175-76,
        9:1158-59
    debt deductibility, **3**:317, 346
    earned income tax credit, **6**:759,
        7:881
    on entrepreneurs, **3**:428
    federal budget and, **4**:477, 479
    fiscal policy and, **4**:503
    Hamilton's views on, **5**:595, 596
    income distribution and, **5**:644,
        645-46
    information technology and,
        9:1282
    Internal Revenue Service,
        5:697-700
    international travel receipts,
        10:*1312*
    Keynesian economics and, **2**:180,
        3:390, **6**:750
    mercantilism and, **6**:851
    microeconomics and, **7**:872
    nonprofits' exemption, **7**:954,
        955
    on partnerships, **7**:978
    payroll functions, **7**:990, *991*,
        992-93
    per capita disposable income
        and, **9**:1228
    personal deductions, **4**:500
    price controls and, **8**:1016
    for public goods, **8**:1059, 1060
    real estate write-offs, **8**:1094-95
    recession and, **8**:1098
    savings and investments and,
        9:1158-60
    small business and, **9**:1199
    social security and Medicare,
        9:1211-16
    subsidy payments from,
        9:1255-58
    Swiss law on, **10**:1347
    wealth distribution and, **10**:1396,
        1397
    See also tariff
Taxpayer's Bill of Rights, **5**:697, 699

Taxpayers for Common Sense, 9:1258
Taylor, Frederick, 4:454, 6:823-24
Taylor, Hobart, Jr., 1:35
Taylor, Michael, 10:1326
Teacher's International Union of America, 7:936
team concept, 3:372, 6:741-43
Teamsters Union, 1:38, 40, 6:765, 9:1274-76
    corruption and, 6:764, 767
    farm workers and, 2:195
    strikes, 9:1254
Technicon, 3:386
technology, 9:1277-83
    agriculture, 1395
    arts and entertainment, 1:74-75
    assembly line, 1:81-82
    bar codes, 1:103-5
    bundling, 1:137
    capitalism and, 2:177
    certification, 10:1376
    child labor and, 2:201
    Clark and, 2:215-16
    comparative advantage and, 2:233
    competition and, 2:246
    credit card transaction, 3:321-22
    data management, 3:338-40
    day trading, 3:341-42
    defense industry, 3:350-53
    division of labor and, 3:370
    Dow Chemical, 3:373-75
    downsizing from, 3:378
    e-business, 3:383
    economies of scale and, 3:396
    Edison and, 3:399-401, 4:546-48
    education industry, 3:408-9
    energy industry, 3:418, 419
    entrepreneurship and, 3:424
    environmental laws and, 4:449-50
    ergonomics and, 4:454-56
    fishing industry, 4:508
    forest products industry, 4:516-17
    freelancing and, 4:526
    futures markets, 2:197, 198
    General Electric, 4:548, 549
    General Motors, 4:553-54
    genetic engineering, 4:555-59
    globalization and, 4:563-64, 566-67
    gross national product linked with, 8:1110-11
    health care, 5:605, 606
    Heinz, 5:614
    Hewlett-Packard, 5:619-21
    IBM, 5:632-37
    income gaps and, 4:561
    industrial espionage and, 5:648-52
    Industrial Revolution, 5:653-58
    innovation and, 2:246, 5:679, 680
    Intel, 5:684-85
    intellectual property and, 2:164-65
    labor market and, 6:759

licenses and, 6:802, 803, 804
Lowell Mills, 6:808
market research, 6:834
Microsoft, 7:874-76
mining industry, 7:86, 883
monopoly and, 3:361
Nasdaq stock, 7:931-32
New York Stock Exchange, 7:948-49
product development and, 8:1037
productivity and, 8:1039, 1040, 1041, 1044
raw materials, 8:1088
reverse engineering, 8:1121-23
security industry and, 9:1177
service economy and, 9:1181-82
Southwest Airlines, 9:1222
standards, 9:1281
stock trading and, 1:54, 9:1245
structural unemployment and, 10:1344
telecommunications, 9:1284, 1286-89, 10:1357
temporary workers and, 10:1301, 1302
tourism and, 10:1316
trade associations and, 10:1318-19
training programs in use of, 3:406-7
transportation, 10:1329, 1332
venture capital and, 10:1368, 1369
wealth distribution and, 10:1397-98
Wells Fargo, 10:1406-7
Xerox, 10:1429-32
See also information technology; *specific types*
Tecolote Research, 3:352
Teenage Research Unlimited, 3:355-56
Telecommunications Act (1996), 9:1287-88, 1289
telecommunications industry, 9:1284-89
    Americans with Disabilities Act compliance, 1:58-59
    AT&T, 1:87-90
    bundling, 1:137
    business travel effects, 10:1316
    careers in, 9:1289
    cash flow, 2:190
    cellular telephones, 5:663, 664
    Cisco Systems, 2:209
    corporate profits, 3:305
    deregulation, 2:246, 3:358, 359, 360-61, 8:1109
    e-mail, 3:411-13
    information technology and, 5:663, 664, 671, 9:1282
    as infrastructure, 5:673, 674
    monopoly vs. competition, 2:245, 246
    Morse and, 7:910, 911-12
    NAICS codes, 7:928, 929
    Nasdaq stock and, 7:931

as natural monopoly, 1:89, 2:245, 8:1103, 1109
regulation of, 1:66, 2:246, 8:1105, 9:1286
Sarnoff and, 9:1146-48
security industry and, 9:1176
Sony, 9:1217-19
utilities industry, 10:1356-57
telecommuting, 5:620, 670, 9:1290-92
    Kinko's services, 6:754
    principles of, 9:1291
    working conditions, 10:1420
telegraph, 5:657, 7:910, 911-12, 8:1146, 1147
    invention of, 9:1284-85
Telemarketing and Consumer Fraud and Abuse Prevention Act, 2:275
telephone service, 5:663, 664, 673, 7:912, 9:1282, 1284-89
    Americans with Disabilities Act and, 1:58-59
    antitrust and, 9:1188
    AT&T and, 1:87-90
    bundling and, 1:137, 8:1109
    competition, 2:246
    customer service, 3:334
    deregulation, 3:359, 360-61, 10:1359
    economies of scale and, 3:398
    Edison and, 3:400, 401
    as monopoly, 9:1285-86
    strike, 9:1252
    as utilities industry sector, 10:1356-57, 1358
    yellow pages advertising, 1:33
television, 9:1282
    advertising, 1:27, 31, 32, 33, 140, 2:266, 267
    AOL Time Warner, 1:65, 66
    color, 8:1148, 9:1217
    commercial-free, 1:29
    Henson Muppets and, 5:616-18
    interactive, 1:75
    market research and, 6:833
    Martha Stewart Omnimedia and, 9:1240
    news coverage, 8:1075
    product placement, 1:27, 29, 30
    programming needs, 1:75
    recording devices, 1:29
    Sarnoff and, 8:1146, 1147, 1148
    Screen Actors Guild and, 9:1171
    sports broadcasts, 9:1223, 1224, 1226, 10:1339
    station ownership regulation, 2:246
    Turner and, 10:1339-41
    Winfrey and, 8:1078, 10:1410, 1411-12
television sets
    price fixing, 8:1019
    Sony, 9:1217
    standard of living, 9:1229
Tellme Networks, Inc., 10:1372
temporary workers, 10:1301-4, 1420
    freelancers vs., 4:524
    outsourcing, 7:973

tender offers, 9:1173
Tengelmann, 8:1118
Tennessee Valley Authority, 7:941, 943, *943*, 9:1255-56
Terman, Frederick, 5:619
Terminal Railroad Association case (1912), 9:1189
Tesco, 8:1118
Tesla, Nikola, 4:547
Texaco, 2:157, 9:1234, 10:1305-7
Texas Instruments, 5:636
Texas Oil Company, 10:1305, *1307*
Texas Rangers (baseball), 9:1227
Texas Utilities Company, 3:377
textile industry
    cartel, 2:188
    cotton cloth, 5:654-58
    GATT failure with, 4:545
    Great Depression, 5:583
    Industrial Revolution, 5:654-58, 6:828, 9:1277, 1278
    job shortages, 6:832
    labor unions, 1:40
    Lowell Mills, 6:805-8
    NAFTA protests, 7:958
    strikes, 9:1250, 1252
    subsidies, 10:*1325*
    women mill workers, 10:1413
    working conditions, 10:1417
Thatcher, Margaret, 2:181, 182-83, 3:358, 4:459-60, 6:751, 8:*1031*, 1032
theme parks, 10:1392, 1393
Theory of Business Enterprise, The (Veblen), 10:1366
Theory of Economic Development, The (Schumpeter), 9:1164, *1165*
Theory of Moral Sentiments, The (Smith), 9:1202-3, 1205
Theory of the Leisure Class, The (Veblen), 3:358, 10:1365-67
Thiel, Peter, 7:898
Third Amendment, 2:256
"Third Way" social policy, 9:1209, 1210
Third World. *See* developing nations
Thirteenth Amendment, 2:210
Thomas, Clarence, 2:257
Thomson, J. Edgar, 2:184, 185
Thomson, William Curtis, 7:1000
Thomson-Houston Company, 4:547, 548
Thomson Learning, 3:406
Thoreau, Henry David, 4:439
Three Mile Island nuclear accident, 3:300-301, 4:439
ticketless travel, 9:*1220*, 1222
Ticket to Work and Work Incentives Improvement Act (1999), 9:1216
timber. *See* forest products industry
time-motion analysis, 4:454, 512, 6:825
Time Warner, 3:301, 402, 8:1075, 1077, 1079, 9:1240
    merger with America Online, 6:853, 854
    See also AOL Time Warner

Title VII. *See* Civil Rights Act (1964)
Tito, Dennis, **10**:1315
Tito, Josip, **2**:230
TiVo (DVR), **1**:29
TLC (The Lewis Company), **6**:792
TLC Beatrice, **6**:792
tobacco industry
  advertising, **1**:32, 139
    Philip Morris, **7**:1001-4
    product liability suits, **8**:1046
    public relations/marketing,
      8:1069
Tobacco Trust, **9**:1233
Tobin, Daniel J., **9**:1274, 1275
Toffler, Alvin, **5**:663, 665, **9**:1290
Tokyo Round, **4**:540, 543
Tokyo Stock Exchange, **6**:850, *858*
Tokyo Telecommunications
  Engineering Corporation,
  9:1217, *1218*
Tokyo Telecommunications
  Research Institute, **7**:908
Tokyo Tsushin Kogyo K.K. *See* Sony
  Corporation
toll-free phone number, **6**:770
Toman, Ed, **6**:846
Tomlinson, Ray, **3**:411, **5**:712
Torquay round, **4**:540
tort law, **2**:161-62, **6**:795-99,
  8:1045
totalitarianism, **9**:1207, *1209*
Total Quality Management, **6**:826,
  10:1308-10
  ISO 9000 standards, **6**:732-33
  Japanization and, **6**:830-31
  just-in-time inventory and,
    6:741, 742-43, 744
  Xerox, **10**:*1429*, 1432
Touchstone Pictures, **10**:1393
tourism industry, **10**:1311-16
  airlines and, **1**:124, 125, 126,
    8:1024, **9**:1221, **10**:1334-35
  American Express services, **1**:51,
    52, 53
  chambers of commerce and,
    2:*193*
  credit cards and, **3**:320
  exchange rate and, **4**:462
  recreation and, **8**:*1099*, 1100,
    1101
Townsend, William, **5**:*586*
Townsend Acts (1767), **6**:851
Townshend, Charles, **9**:1202
Toxic Substances Control Act
  (1976), **4**:*448*
Toyoda, Eiji, **6**:830
Toyota, **6**:741, 743, 830-31
Toyota Production System,
  6:830-31
Toys R Us, **3**:382
TQM. *See* Total Quality
  Management
trade associations, **10**:1317-19
  five largest, **8**:*1048*
trademark, **5**:630, **10**:1320-21
  amortization of, **1**:61, 63
  brand names as, **1**:117
  business law, **2**:160, 164
  Coca-Cola protection, **2**:218

copyright vs., **2**:283
franchise, **4**:522-23
as intangible asset, **1**:*84*, 85
license and, **6**:801
patent vs., **7**:980
product development, **8**:1037
property rights and, **8**:1029
Royal Dutch/Shell, **8**:1133, 1134
small business, **9**:1199
Wells Fargo, **10**:1405, 1407
Xerox, **10**:1429
Trade Name Registration Act,
  9:1198
trade policy, **9**:1270-71,
  10:1322-25
  capitalism and, **2**:178-81
  comparative advantage, **2**:233-35
  European Union, **4**:*457*, 458,
    459, 460
  exchange rates, **4**:461-62
  Hudson's Bay Company,
    5:622-24
  interstate commerce regulation,
    8:1103-4, 1105
  mercantilism, **5**:705, **6**:849-52
  protectionism, **8**:1054-57
  Smith economic theory, **9**:1203
  types of, **10**:*1323*
  unfair practices, **8**:1056
  World Trade Organization,
    10:1427-28
  See also free trade; international
    trade; tariff
Trade-Related Aspects of Intellectual
  Property Rights, **10**:1427
trade secret, **2**:164, **8**:1037, 1112
trade shows, **2**:*171*, **8**:1049,
  1068-69
trade union. *See* labor union
Traditional IRA, **9**:1159, *1160*
Traf-O-Data, **7**:873, *874*
tragedy of the commons, **4**:441,
  8:1027, **10**:1326-28
Trammell Crow Co., **8**:1095
Transco Energy Company, **3**:420
Transcontinental and Western Air,
  Inc., **4**:552
transistors, **2**:251, **5**:684, **7**:909,
  9:1217, *1218*
transnational company. *See*
  multinational corporation
Transportation Average, **3**:377
transportation industry, **10**:1329-32
  as advertising venue, **1**:32
  American Express, **1**:51
  British Airways, **1**:125-26
  civil rights law and, **1**:58, **2**:210
  deregulation, **3**:358, **8**:1109
  Dow Jones Average companies,
    3:377
  federal regulation, **8**:1105, *1106*,
    1107
  FedEx, **4**:488-90
  Industrial Revolution and,
    5:653-54
  as infrastructure, **5**:673, *675*
  Mitsubishi, **7**:890-91
  natural monopolies and, **8**:1103
  New Deal measures, **7**:941

petroleum products, **3**:415-16
pricing, **8**:1024
productivity, **8**:1040
Santa Fe Trail, **8**:1142-45
Sikorsky and, **9**:1192
Southwest Airlines, **9**:1220-22
standard of living and, **9**:1229-30
Standard Oil and, **9**:1231-32
Teamsters and, **9**:1274-76
technology and, **9**:1279
tourism and, **10**:1311-12, 1316
Vanderbilt and, **10**:1362-64
Wells Fargo and, **10**:1405
See also specific types of
  transportation
Trans Union Corporation (credit
  bureau), **3**:325
travelers' checks, **1**:51
travel industry. *See* tourism industry
Treasury bills (T-bills), **9**:1158, 1159
  returns, **9**:1242-43
Treasury bonds, **3**:*314*, 315, **6**:779,
  7:894, 906, **9**:1241, 1242
Treasury Department, U.S., **5**:697,
  8:1092
  Federal Reserve and, **4**:102
  Hamilton as first secretary of,
    5:595, 596
  Samuelson and, **8**:1141
Trevithick, Richard, **5**:657, **10**:1329
Tribune Company, **8**:1075
Trippe, Juan, **10**:1333-35
Trotsky, Leon, **2**:228, **9**:1207
Troyer, Andrea, *as contributor*,
  2:153-59, 276-79, **6**:794-800,
  801-4, 853-57, **8**:1045-47,
  9:1255-58
trucking industry
  deregulation, **3**:358, **8**:1109
  NAFTA protests, **7**:958
  productivity, **8**:1041
  risk management, **8**:*1127*
  Teamsters and, **9**:1274
  temporary workers, **10**:1301
  wholesale jobbers, **8**:1118-19
Truman, Harry, **5**:698-99, **7**:996,
  10:1384
  armed forces desegregation,
    8:1085
  social security, **9**:1214
  Taft–Hartley and, **9**:*1268*
Trump, Donald, **8**:193, **10**:1336-38
Trump Organization, **10**:1336
Trump Plaza Hotel and Casino
  (Atlantic City), **10**:1336
Trump Shuttle Airline, **10**:1336,
  1337
trust. *See* antitrust; monopoly
"truth in advertising" movement,
  1:32, 112, 113
Truth-in-Lending Act, **3**:320, 321,
  4:485
Tsai, Gerald, **4**:491
Tsunoda, Yuji, **9**:*1237*
Tucker Anthony Sutro, **8**:1132
Tull, Jethro, **5**:657
Turner, Ted, **1**:*65*, **10**:1339-41
Turner Broadcasting System, **1**:64,
  10:1339, 1341

Turner Classic Movies, **10**:1341
Turner Communications, **10**:1339
Turner Foundation, **10**:1341
Tuskegee Institute, **7**:933, **10**:1382
Tuttle, Connie, *as contributor*,
  1:38-42, 67-69, **2**:199-203,
  3:350-54, **9**:1249-54,
  1274-76
TWA, **1**:101, *102*, **4**:552
Twain, Mark, **5**:609
20th Century-Fox, **6**:772, 773
Tyco International, **2**:153, *158*
tying (bundling practice), **1**:137-38

U

UAW. *See* United Automobile
  Workers of America
Ubico, Jorge, **2**:204, 205
UBS AB. *See* Union Bank of
  Switzerland
UBS Asset Management, **10**:1346
UBS Warburg, **10**:1346
UFW. *See* United Farm Workers
Ulrich, Lars, **9**:*1283*
U-Matic, **9**:1218
UMW. *See* United Mine Workers
undocumented immigrants,
  5:639-41
unemployment, **10**:1342-45
  business cycles, **2**:149, 151, 152,
    178
  downsizing, **3**:378-79
  excess inventory and, **6**:726
  fiscal policy and, **4**:503
  freelancing and, **4**:525
  Great Depression, **4**:466, **5**:581,
    584, 585, **8**:1097
  income distribution and, **5**:644
  inflation and, **5**:661
  Keynesian model and, **3**:364,
    365, 390, **6**:750, 810
  labor market and, **6**:759
  as Leading Economic Index
    component, **6**:778, 779
  macroeconomics and, **6**:810-11,
    812
  measurement of, **10**:1345
  from merger or acquisition,
    6:853
  minimum wage and, **7**:881,
    8:1014, 1015
  monetary policy and, **7**:893
  New Deal measures, **7**:940,
    941-42, 996
  recession and, **8**:1096
  as social cost of economic
    growth, **3**:391-92
  stagflation and, **2**:182, **6**:751
  subsidy programs and,
    9:1255-56
  temporary workers and, **10**:1303
unemployment insurance, **2**:180,
  5:630, **7**:942, 995, 996,
  9:*1211*, 1212, **10**:1345
  small business tax, **9**:1199
  wealth distribution and, **10**:1396
Uniform Commercial Code, Article
  3, **2**:*162*, 163

Uniform Computer Information Transactions Act (1999), 2:279, 6:803-4
Uniform Offering Circular, 4:523
Uniform Partnership Act, 7:976
Unilever PLC, 1:106, 108
Union Bank of Switzerland, 10:1346-48
Union Carbide, 3:373, 374, 376, 4:441, 9:1264, 1266
Unión de Paises Exportadores de Banano, 2:06
Union Iron Works, 2:185
unionization. See labor union
Union of Swiss Banks, 10:1347
Union Pacific Railroad, 3:377, 8:1144, 10:1330
unions. See labor union
union shop, 9:1269
Union Trust Company, 10:1405-6
Unisys, 7:986
United Automobile Workers of America, 1:38, 40, 6:763, 766, 10:1349-52
  collective bargaining, 2:222, 10:1349, 1350
  General Motors and, 4:552, 553
  pattern bargaining, 6:763
United Brands, 2:204, 206
United Farm Workers, 1:69, 2:194, 195, 196
United Fruit, 2:204, 205, 206
United Kingdom. See Great Britain
United Mine Workers, 1:39, 40
United Nations
  child labor and, 2:201, 202-3
  Commission on Sustainable Development, 9:1266
  Conference on Trade and Employment, 10:1428
  Convention on Contracts for the International Sale of Goods, 2:279
  environmentalism and, 1:80, 4:439, 440
  fishing industry and, 4:506, 509, 510
  international contracts, 2:279
  International Monetary Fund, 5:701-3
  International Standard Industrial Classification System, 7:928
  Korean War, 2:229
  Monetary and Financial Conference, 10:1421
  multinational corporations and, 3:306
  Secretariat Building steel beams, 10:1354
  Supplementary Convention on the Abolition of Slavery, 2:203
  tourism and, 10:1313
  Turner philanthropic gift, 10:1339, 1341
United Negro College Fund, 4:539
United Parcel Service (UPS)
  MaxiCode, 1:105
  strike, 2:221, 9:1253, 1254, 1276
  temporary workers, 10:1301

United Press Association, 8:1075
United Press International, 8:1075
United States Airline Deregulation Act, 8:1106, 1109
United States Chamber of Commerce, 2:191-92, 8:1048
United States Football League, 10:1336
United States Hispanic National Chamber of Commerce, 2:193
United States Junior Chamber of Commerce, 2:192-93
United States Steel Corporation, 2:186, 5:673, 679, 9:1168, 1251-52, 10:1353-55
  collective bargaining, 1:39
  Morgan and, 7:905, 906
United States v. Addyston Pipe and Steel Co. (1898), 8:1019
United States v. Morrison (1994), 2:253-54
United States v. The Amistad (1841), 3:337
United States v. Topco Associates, Inc. (1972), 2:245
United Steelworkers of America, 1:40, 6:813
United Technologies Corporation, 9:1193
Universal Music, 8:1018
Universal Product Code, 1:103-4, 105
Universal Studios, 7:889
University of Chicago, 2:182, 3:358, 6:841
  economics Nobel laureates, 4:528
  Friedman and, 4:527, 528
  Graham and, 4:572
  Rockefeller philanthropy and, 8:1130
  Samuelson and, 8:1140, 1141
  Veblen and, 10:1365
University of Michigan
  Index of Consumer Sentiments, 2:261-62, 263
  Survey Research Center, 2:261-62, 6:779
University of Pennsylvania, 6:843, 7:994, 10:1336
University of Phoenix Online, 3:406
UNIX, 5:670, 710, 712
Unsafe at Any Speed (Nader), 2:268, 274, 4:552, 554, 7:925
UPC. See Universal Product Code
UPS. See United Parcel Service
upward sloping supply, 9:1261
upward sloping yield curve, 5:695
urban areas
  capitalism and, 2:178
  division of labor and, 3:371
  public goods and, 10:1400
  top tourist sites, 10:1314
  wealth distribution and, 10:1395-96
Uruguay Round, 4:540, 543, 545, 10:1428
USAA (insurance and financial services), 3:335

usage method (depreciation), 1:63
U.S. Freightways, 3:377
U.S. Rubber Company, 3:376
U.S. Steel. See United States Steel Corporation
utilitarianism, 2:153, 9:1202
utilities industry, 10:1356-59
  careers in, 10:1357
  corporate profits, 3:305
  deregulation, 2:246
  Dow Jones Average, 3:376, 377
  economies of scale, 3:397, 398
  as infrastructure, 5:673
  municipal ownership, 8:1031
  as natural monopoly, 2:245, 246, 7:900-901, 904, 8:1015-16, 1021, 1103, 1107-8
  New Deal measures, 7:941, 943
  price controls, 8:1016
  price discrimination, 7:903
  privatization, 8:1032
  state regulation, 8:1105, 1106, 1107-9
Utility Average, 3:377
utility patents, 7:980-83, 8:1112
utopianism, 2:227, 9:1206, 1209
Utyke, Dennis, 6:752

V
vacation industry. See tourism industry
Vail, Alfred, 7:911
Valentine, Don, 2:207
Valentine, Thomas W., 7:935
valuation, 10:1360-61
  formulas, 10:1360
  intellectual property, 5:689
  money as unit of, 7:897
  opportunity cost and, 7:964, 965
  price acceptance and, 8:1024-25, 1060
  private property, 8:1026, 1028
  scarcity and, 9:1162
  Smith economic theory and, 9:1203
  of trademark, 10:1321
  See also amortization and depreciation; assets and liabilities
Van Buren, Martin, 10:1417
Vanderbilt, Cornelius, 10:1362-64
Vanderbilt University, 10:1364
VanFossen, Phillip J., as contributor, 3:311-13
Vargas, Getúlio, 4:476
VCRs (videocassette recorders), 1:29, 74-75, 7:909
  Sony, 9:1218
Veblen, Thorstein, 3:358, 10:1365-67
Venable, Willis, 2:217
venture capital, 2:173, 3:346, 427, 6:792, 10:1368-73
  for Cisco Systems, 2:207
  Clark enterprises, 2:215, 216
  Lewis's minority firms, 6:792
  for small businesses, 9:1200
  for Yahoo!, 10:1433
venture capital firms, 10:1369-73
verbal contract, 2:277-78, 279

Verizon Communications, 1:90, 9:1288
Verlagsgruppe Georg von Holtzbrinck, 4:472
Verne, Jules, 9:1191
VERs. See voluntary export restraints
vertical integration, 2:185, 186, 9:1189
  outsourcing vs., 7:971
  petroleum industry, 7:972
  Rockefeller and, 8:1129
vertical marketing system, 3:369
  conventional channel vs., 3:368
Viacom, 8:1079
Videx, 1:123
Viner, Jacob, 4:528
Violence against Women Act (1994), 2:253-54
Visa cards, 1:52-53, 3:319, 321
vision statement, 9:1246
Vivendi, price fixing case, 8:1019-20
vocational licensing, 10:1374-76
Volcker, Paul, 4:483, 7:945
Volkswagen, 10:1377-79
voluntary export restraints, 10:1322-23
Volunteers in Service to America (VISTA), 3:395
voting rights, 1:39, 2:211, 10:1396
Voting Rights Act (1965), 1:56, 2:213
vouchers, school, 3:402, 404, 7:936, 938, 8:1033
VW. See Volkswagen

W
Wabash, St. Louis and Pacific Railway Company v. Illinois (1886), 8:1103
WACC equation, 4:494
wage gap. See pay equity
wage-price controls, 5:661-62, 8:1016
Wagner, Ray, 6:772
Wagner, Robert F., Sr., 7:939, 9:1212
Wagner Act (1935). See National Labor Relations Act
Wagner–Steagall Act (1936), 8:1105, 1106
Walcott, Derek, 4:473
Waldron, Randall, as contributor, 3:396-98, 8:1013-16
Walker, A'Lelia, 10:1381, 1382
Walker, Madame C. J., 10:1380-82
Walker Club, 10:1382
Walker Method, 10:1381-82
Wall Street Journal, 3:376, 377, 381, 8:1075, 10:1383-86
  corporate image ranking, 1:108
Wall Street Journal Europe, 10:1386
Wal-Mart, 10:1387-90
  blocking strategy, 5:679-80
  bond issuance, 9:1242
  competition, 8:1018
  credit card antitrust suit, 1:53
  entrepreneurial innovation, 3:424
  environmentalism and, 4:442

globalization, 4:564-65, 8:1118
innovation, 5:679
just-in-time inventory, 6:744,
 9:1280, 10:1389
stock issuance, 9:1241
technology use, 9:1280
vertical marketing system, 3:369
Walsh–Healey Act (1936), 10:1418
Walt Disney Company, 1:66, 2:267,
 6:856, 7:888-89, 10:1391-94
Walt Disney Studio Entertainment,
 5:619-21, 10:1393
Walt Disney World, 10:1392, 1393
Walton, Sam, 3:424, 6:744,
 10:1387-88
 Ten Rules for Building a Business,
 10:1388, 1390
Walton's Five and Dime, 10:1387
Warburg Dillon Read. See UBS
 Warburg
Wards Cove Packing Co. v. Antonio
 (1989), 2:212, 213
warehouse clubs, 8:1116
Warner, Abe, 1:64, 65
Warner, Harry, 1:64, 65
Warner, Jack, 1:64, 65
Warner, Kate, 9:1176
Warner, Sam, 1:64, 65
Warner Books, 1:64
Warner Bros., 1:64, 65
Warner Bros.-Seven Arts, 1:64, 65
Warner Communications. See AOL
 Time Warner
Warner Music, 8:1018
Washbush, John, as contributor,
 6:819-22, 823-27,
 10:1308-10
Washington, Booker T., 7:933, 934
Washington, Derrick, 2:214
Washington, George, 5:595, 596,
 597
Washington Post, 4:570-72, 8:1075
waste disposal
 environmentalism and, 4:438,
 442, 450
 EPA limits, 4:443, 444, 448, 450
 privatization and, 8:1033
 See also hazardous waste
water energy, 3:414, 415
 Lowell Mills, 6:807, 808
Watergate scandal, 4:571-72, 5:699
water pollution. See
 environmentalism
water wheel, 5:655, 656, 657,
 6:807, 808
Watford, Odessa, 3:404
Watkins, Sherron, 3:423
W. Atlee Burpee Company, 1:23
Watson, James, 4:555
Watson, Thomas J., 5:632-33, 634
Watson, Thomas J., Jr., 5:634
Watson, Tom, 9:1226-27
Watt, James, 5:653, 656, 657, 665
WB (television), 1:64, 66
wealth distribution, 10:1395-99
 business estimates by firm size,
 9:1199
 economic growth and, 3:392

Economic Opportunity Act,
 3:393-95
entrepreneurship and, 3:426
Forbes richest Americans list,
 6:739, 740
Great Depression, 5:581, 583
income distribution, 5:644, 645
intellectual property and, 5:687
Internet access and, 5:714
mercantilist theory of, 2:177,
 6:849, 850, 9:1203
monopoly and, 9:1234
private property and, 8:1028
redistribution of, 9:1209
Rockefeller and, 9:1233
service economy and, 9:1178
Smith's theory of, 9:1203, 1204,
 10:1400
Stewart and, 9:1234
taxation and, 9:1272
technology and, 9:1277, 1280-81
Trump and, 10:1336
Veblen leisure class theory and,
 10:1366
Walker and, 10:1380
Walton and, 10:1390
Winfrey and, 10:1412
Wealth of Nations, The (Smith),
 2:177-78, 181, 5:705-6, 6:849,
 851, 9:1202, 1203-4,
 10:1400-1401
 division of labor example,
 3:370-71
 economic growth concept, 3:388
 excerpt, 10:1401
 key ideas of, 10:1400
 microeconomics and, 7:869
Webber, J. Leroy, 1:121
Weber, Max, 6:820, 823
Web sites. See Internet
Webster, William, 5:700
Wedgwood, Josiah, 5:656
W. Edwards Deming Institute,
 10:1310
Weeks, Shelton, as contributor,
 2:173-74, 175-76, 4:493-96
weighted average cost of capital,
 4:494
Weinstein, Bob, 7:888-89
Weinstein, Harvey, 7:888-89
Weiss, Bernard, 4:555
Welch, Carolyn, 10:1402
Welch, Jack, 3:379, 420, 4:547,
 549, 10:1402-4
Weldon, Fay, 1:30
welfare
 Great Depression, 5:585
 Malthusian arguments against,
 6:817
 Medicaid, 9:1214
 reform, 9:1211, 1215-16
 social security vs., 9:1211
 state public assistance porgrams,
 9:1212
welfare capitalism, 2:180, 181,
 3:299
Welfare Reform Act (1996), 9:1211,
 1215-16
welfare state, 7:941, 9:1208

Welles, Orson, 5:611, 612
Wells, Frank, 10:1392, 1393, 1394
Wells, H. G., 9:1282
Wells, Henry, 1:51, 10:1405, 1406
Wells, Mary, 4:569
Wells & Co., 1:51
Wells Electronic Banking System,
 10:1406-7
Wells Fargo, 1:51, 10:1405-7
Wentworth, Don, as contributor,
 9:1161-63
Wessel, David, as contributor,
 8:1039-44
Western, John, as contributor,
 2:166-68, 7:971-73
Western, Linda, as contributor,
 10:1317-19
Western Electric Company, 1:87-88,
 89, 90, 6:825, 10:1310
Western Health Reform Institute,
 6:745
Western Union, 1:88, 3:399, 400,
 9:1284, 1285
Westinghouse, 3:371, 8:1147
Westinghouse, George, 4:547, 548
Wharton School, 6:843, 10:1330
wheat crop, 1:43, 44, 45
 futures market, 4:530
Wheeler, Harry C., 9:1252
Wheeler Lea Act (1938), 4:485
Whelan v. Jaslow (1986), 7:986
Whitacre, Mark, 1:71
Whitaker & Baxter, 8:1068
White, Ellen G., 6:745
Whitehead, A. N., 6:749
Whitehead, John, 7:945
Whitehead, Mary Beth, 2:278-79
"white knight" metaphor, 6:853,
 856
Whitman, Christie Todd, 4:444
Whitman, Meg, 10:1408-9
Whitney, Eli, 1:81, 5:655, 657, 658,
 693, 6:828
Whiton, Alexander, 4:511
Whittle, Christopher, 3:402, 403,
 404
Whittle Communications, 3:402
wholesale. See retail and wholesale
Wholesome Meat Act (1967), 2:268
wildcat strike, 9:1254, 1268
wilderness areas, 8:1059, 1100,
 1102
wildlife protection, 4:439, 443, 450,
 515-16
Wiley, Ralph, 3:373, 374
Wilkins, Roy, 6:739
Williams, Roy, 9:1275
Willson, Millicent, 5:611-12
Wilson, Charles E., 4:552
Wilson, Edmund, 4:473
Wilson, Jackie, 4:568
Wilson, Owen, 2:193
Wilson, Terrance, 1:71
Wilson, Woodrow, 4:485, 9:1252
wind energy, 3:414, 415, 419
Windows (operating system), 1:138,
 5:636, 689, 690, 7:874-75, 876
 free browser, 8:1025
 license, 6:802

Winfrey, Oprah, 1:115, 8:1078,
 9:1236, 10:1410-12
Winn-Dixie (supermarkets), 1:105
wireless technologies, 5:669, 670,
 671, 9:1219
Wobblies. See International Workers
 of the World
Wolfe, Tom, 4:473
women in the workforce,
 10:1413-16
 affirmative action, 1:34
 Ash's career, 1:76-77
 Asian Development Bank
 program, 1:78, 79
 benefits programs, 2:238
 building trades, 1:135
 civil rights law, 2:210, 212-13,
 236
 corporate social responsibility,
 3:300
 demographics, 3:355, 357
 equal employment opportunity,
 4:453
 Fair Labor Standards Act, 4:467
 family leave, 4:468-71
 Fiorina as first Fortune 500 CEO,
 4:501-2, 5:620-21
 first bond saleswoman, 6:858
 freelancers, 4:525-26
 Graham as Washington Post
 publisher, 4:570, 571-72
 income distribution, 5:645
 income median, 1:36
 information technology and,
 5:670
 labor unions and, 1:38, 39, 40,
 42, 2:221
 Lansing's career, 6:772, 773
 Lauder's career, 6:775-77
 legal services, 6:783
 management theory and, 6:827
 Mary Kay sales by, 1:77
 mill and sweatshop workers,
 6:806-8, 10:1417, 1418
 minimum wage and, 7:877, 878,
 879, 881, 882
 pay inequities, 2:236, 4:467,
 7:987-90, 10:1413, 1414-15
 Perkins's career, 7:994, 995
 professional associations, 8:1048
 Screen Actors Guild and, 9:1170
 sexual harassment and,
 9:1183-86, 1184-86
 Small Business Administration
 and, 9:1201
 Stewart's career, 9:1238-40
 teachers' union and, 7:935-36
 Walker's career, 10:1380-82
 wealth distribution, 10:1397
 Whitman's career, 10:1408-9
 Winfrey's career, 10:1410-12
Women's Business Centers, 9:1198,
 1201
women's rights, 7:935, 936, 987-90,
 9:1170
Wonder, Stevie, 4:569
wood. See forest products industry

Woodford, Chris, *as contributor*, **5**:663-67, 701-3, **9**:1264-67, **10**:1421-24, 1425-28
Woodruff, Paul, **2**:219
Woods, Mel, **6**:*856*
Woods, Tiger, **1**:115, **7**:952, **9**:1223, 1227
Woodward, Bob, **4**:572
Woolco, **10**:1387
Worker's Bill of Rights, **6**:767, 768
workforce. *See* labor market
working conditions, **10**:1417-20
   affirmative action and, **1**:34, 35, 36-37
   AFL-CIO and, **1**:39
   arbitration and, **1**:68
   assembly line and, **4**:513
   Ben & Jerry's employees, **1**:108
   building trades and, **1**:133
   business ethics, **2**:154, 155, 157, 158
   Chavez and, **2**:194-96
   child labor and, **2**:200-203
   civil rights laws, **2**:213-14
   collective bargaining for, **2**:221-24
   compensation and, **2**:236-41
   corporate responsibility and, **3**:298, 299-300, 301, 306
   disability provisions, **1**:56-60
   division of labor benefits, **3**:370-72, 388
   downsizing and, **3**:378-79
   economic growth and, **3**:389
   eight-hour day, **5**:601
   employer-provided health insurance, **5**:606
   equal opportunity and, **4**:452-53
   ergonomics, **4**:454-56, **10**:1419-20
   Fair Labor Standards Act, **4**:466, 467
   family leave, **4**:468-71

farm workers, **2**:194-96
fatal injuries (2000), **10**:*1419*, 1420
flexible schedules, **1**:60
Ford employees, **4**:513, **6**:829
Haymarket Square riot, **5**:601, 602
Heinz employees, **5**:614
Hewlett-Packard innovations, **5**:619-20
human resources department and, **5**:630
IBM employees, **5**:633
information technology and, **5**:671-72
Japanese workers, **6**:831
labor market and, **6**:759
labor unions and, **6**:766
legislation, **10**:1418
Levi Strauss employees, **6**:786
liberal economics and, **10**:1396
Lowell Mills, **6**:806, 807
management theory and, **6**:823, 825-26
manufacturing jobs, **6**:832
minimum wage, **7**:877-82, 879, 943
multinationals and, **7**:918, 919, 921
Nader safety campaign, **7**:927
Nike employees, **7**:918, 952-53
OSHA and, **7**:960
overtime, **4**:466, **5**:630
Perkins reforms, **7**:994-95
regulatory activity, **8**:*1106*, 1107
retirement plans, **4**:499
sexual harassment and, **9**:1185-86, **10**:1414-16
social reform, **2**:178
Southwest Airlines employees, **9**:1220-21
stress factors, **7**:962
strikes and, **9**:1249-51, 1252
telecommuting and, **9**:1290-92

tort liability and, **6**:796
trade policies and, **1**:94
   United Auto Workers, **10**:1349
   women workers, **10**:1413
Workingman's Party, **1**:38, **9**:1251
Workmen's Compensation Act, **7**:994-95
Works Progress Administration, **7**:*941*, 942, 943
work stoppages. *See* strikes
work-to-rules strategy, **6**:764
World Bank, **1**:78, **2**:180, *181*, **4**:563, 565, 567, **6**:751, **10**:1421-24, 1425
   information technology, **5**:671
   International Monetary Fund and, **5**:702, 703
   international trade, **5**:708-9
   privatization studies, **8**:1031
   recession and, **8**:1098
   "Rule of Law and Development," **8**:1139
   sustainable development, **9**:1267
World Bank Group, **10**:1422
World Business Council on Sustainable Development, **9**:1265, 1266, 1267
WorldCom, **1**:89, **3**:297, 306
   business ethics, **2**:153
World Gift Co., **1**:76-77
World Health Organization, **10**:1313
World Hunger Relief, Inc., **5**:*715*
World Tourism Organization, **10**:1313, 1315
World Trade Center, **10**:1386
World Trade Organization, **1**:95, **2**:*181*, 232, **4**:563, **5**:708, **10**:1425-28
   antiglobalization protests, **4**:566, **7**:967
   fair trade complaints, **10**:1325
   GATT as forerunner, **4**:540, 543, 563
   member nations, **2**:232, **10**:1426

World Wide Web. *See* Internet
Worthington Foods, **6**:*746*, 748
Wrangler (jeans company), **6**:786
Wright, Orville and Wilbur, **10**:1331, 1333
written contract, **2**:277-78
WTO. *See* World Trade Organization

X
Xerox Corporation, **1**:37, **9**:1292, **10**:1429-32
   downsizing, **3**:378
   research and development, **8**:1111
XKL (company), **2**:207
Xlibris, **8**:1078

Y
Yahoo!, **4**:492, **5**:711, *712*, **7**:876, **10**:1433-34
Yale University, **4**:488, **10**:1333, 1365, *1366*
Yamaha, Torakusu, **10**:1435
Yamaha Corporation, **10**:1435-36
Yamaha de Mexico, **10**:1436
Yamaha International Corporation, U.S., **10**:1436
Yang, Jerry, **5**:711, **10**:1433, *1434*
Yellow-Dog Contract, **7**:939-40
Yergin, Daniel, **3**:359
Yersai, Raj, **3**:384
yield curve, **5**:695-96
York Factory, **5**:623
Young, McGee, *as contributor*, **9**:1200-1201
Young, Stanley, **4**:472, 473

Z
zaibatsu system, **7**:891-92
Zell, Sam, **8**:1095
Zenith, **8**:1019
Zworykin, Vladimir, **8**:1148